Revelation, Reason, and Faith

REVELATION, REASON, AND FAITH

ESSAYS IN HONOR OF TRUMAN G. MADSEN

EDITED BY

DONALD W. PARRY, DANIEL C. PETERSON,
AND STEPHEN D. RICKS

Provo, Utah
Foundation for Ancient Research and Mormon Studies
Brigham Young University

Frontispiece by Mark A. Philbrick

Foundation for Ancient Research and Mormon Studies
Institute for the Study and Preservation of Ancient Religious Texts
Brigham Young University
P.O. Box 7113
University Station
Provo, Utah 84602

Library of Congress Cataloging-in-Publication Data

Revelation, reason, and faith : essays in honor of Truman G. Madsen /
edited by Donald W. Parry, Daniel C. Peterson, and Stephen D. Ricks.
    p. cm.
Includes bibliographical references and index.
  ISBN 0-934893-71-3 (alk. paper)
  1. Church of Jesus Christ of Latter-day Saints. I. Madsen, Truman G.
II. Parry, Donald W. III. Peterson, Daniel C. IV. Ricks, Stephen David.
BX8637 .R48 2002
  230--dc21

                                                    2002014081

CONTENTS

Introduction

Teacher, scholar, researcher, speaker, university administrator, church leader, religious ambassador, friend—in each of these regards Truman G. Madsen has shone brilliantly and memorably. This volume of essays is a tribute to Professor Madsen's unforgettable, inspirational contributions to the academic life at Brigham Young University, at the Jerusalem Center for Near Eastern Studies, and in other settings, and a sign of gratitude for his marvelous example as mentor and friend.

The themes of this volume of essays reflect Madsen's research and academic interests: Joseph Smith and the earliest history of the Church of Jesus Christ of Latter-day Saints, temples, Judaism and Mormonism, theology, and philosophy. The authors of these essays—representing various disciplines and faiths—reflect the range of the appeal of Madsen's academic work and the extent of his academic contacts.

We announced plans for the publication of this volume of essays in honor of Madsen at the banquet and meeting of the Foundation for Ancient Research and Mormon Studies (FARMS) on 5 November 1999. We solicited articles from among his wide-ranging acquaintances. The extent of the response was extremely gratifying. This volume is a result of those efforts.

The opinions expressed in these articles are those of the authors. They do not necessarily represent the opinions of the volume's editors, the Foundation for Ancient Research and Mormon Studies, the Institute for the Study and Preservation of Ancient Religious Texts, Brigham Young University, the Church of Jesus Christ of Latter-day Saints, or the authors' employers.

The production of this tribute to Truman Madsen would not have been possible without the sterling efforts of the editorial and production staff of FARMS: Shirley S. Ricks coordinated the work of Angela Clyde Barrionuevo, Alison V. P. Coutts, Julie A. Dozier, Naomi L. Gunnels, Tessa Hauglid, Ellen Henneman, Paula W. Hicken, Sunny Larson, Shannon Murdock, David Pendleton, Linda Sheffield, and Elizabeth Watkins. We also wish to thank Don E. Norton, who interviewed Madsen for his educational biography; Dillon K. Inouye for his tribute to him as a teacher; Daniel B. McKinlay for his bibliography of Madsen's works; and Paula W. Hicken for providing an index for the volume.

TRUMAN MADSEN,
ON HIS EDUCATION

In the beginning was "Grantsville," where our homes abutted Grandfather's (President Heber J. Grant's) bungalow high on the avenues in Salt Lake City. Here lived the families of seven of his ten daughters: a clustering community, close in every way. In the mix were well over thirty cousins.

These surroundings and the death of my mother, Grandfather's ninth daughter, when I was only two years old, meant three things. First, from birth and, as it were, by adoption, I, and my two brothers, were enveloped in this large, cultured, traveled, studious, bookish family. Second, we were tutored by grandparents and parents for whom religion compassed the universe. Truth is truth wherever found. So it is with the good and beautiful. Third, my father, who didn't remarry until we three boys were all married, devoted much of his time and life to his sons. Through him and our sensitive and caring aunts, my educated mother's influence was transmitted.

Grandfather Grant was anxious that his children have the best educational opportunities he could provide. For example, throughout the several years he was president of the European Mission, he arranged for his wife, Emily Wells Grant, to acquaint his daughters with the European heritage. They traveled in Britain and on the Continent, visiting the historic sites, opera houses, museums, castles, concert halls.

In due time my mother became the first woman to graduate from the University of Utah in mathematics and, I believe, with highest honors. She then attended Radcliffe College in Boston and studied modern literature. Until her marriage she was a teacher at a Salt Lake college. To my sorrow, I didn't inherit mother's propensity for advanced mathematics, though I did for literature.

My father introduced us to the great books. He had only a high school education, but he was a wide-ranging and voracious reader. At a crucial point in his teens, when he was trying to find a spiritual footing, he fasted and prayed—according, I suppose, to Moroni's formula—then opened the Book of Mormon at random. His eye fell on the verse "O then, is not this real? I say unto you, Yea, because it is light; and whatsoever is light, is good" (Alma 32:35). (I have only lately realized how many of my essays touch on the theme of light.) That, and similar experiences, put Jesus Christ at the center of his life and, as we grew up, of ours. His mission to California, his work as a director of Temple Square, and twenty-eight years of service on the general board of the Mutual Improvement Association pushed his roots deep into vital religion.

So our exposure to the scriptures and, as we matured, the classics was a nightly event. This was before television, the Web, and electronic games. Reading aloud in rotation was an education in itself. From our earliest years together we took turns, our father nudging us in our pacing and diction and pronunciation. He was a self-taught master of English. If we didn't know a word, he would ask us to look it up. "Consult the dictionary, and you will remember it."

My public education began with Wasatch School, then Ensign School, then Bryant Junior High School, then on to East High School, even though East was some distance away. Many of us commuted by bus. In the public schools, I think I was simply a "cafeteria" student, taking a little of this and a little of that and getting by. In retrospect, three things stand out.

First, my study of Latin, though superficial, helped me immensely with English. The first word I learned in Latin was from an almost deaf uncle who loved to read the Bible in early translations. The word was *misericordium,* which means "compassion." Everything I have since written on the roles of the Messiah embraces that core insight.

Second, my teachers had an individual concern for students. One took me aside and said, "I've seen the results of your IQ test. You're not carrying enough of a load; you're just taking easy stuff." She meant classes like gym, study hall, shorthand, and transcription.

Third, there was generated in me a perpetual fascination with music and the arts. This bloomed under Lisle Bradford, one of the most talented and disciplining choir directors in the West. I sang bass in her a cappella choir. In rehearsal and performance I never took my eyes off her. Artistic impulses were reinforced by two distinguished figures on the Madsen side of my family, Drs. Franklin and Florence Madsen, thanks to whom our home was heavy-laden with classical music recordings and piano rolls. Uncle Frank also taught me and my brothers some vocal lessons and the rudiments of conducting.

Whenever we had to speak in school, in church, or in public— such assignments were more frequent in those days—Dad was a conscientious coach. His younger brother, Julius, and he had been thespians, Julius directing and my father performing in the legendary "Mission Play" in a huge theater in San Gabriel, California. An astounding three thousand performances were given before the Depression closed the play. These Madsen brothers brought a dramatic flair to everything they did. For us, repetitive practice did not make perfect, but it did make clear. Dad would persist, "You can say that better." In the same mode, we were often encouraged to repeat back at the dinner table the gist of what we had learned each day in school. This enhanced my sensitivity to the spoken as well as the written word, a bent toward teaching, and a passion to communicate.

I early made it a rule, when teaching, to imagine the person or persons I was quoting sitting in the corner of the class. They would check every sentence, glare at even the slightest distortion, and approve and applaud only if I presented their case as they would. Only then would critical analysis or evaluation begin.

During my first two years at the University of Utah, I was groping for a major. To earn my way, I worked every school night as a waiter, from nine P.M. till one A.M. Bedtime was about two A.M. I would go to my classes blurry. Each morning I woke up saying to myself, "This weekend I'm going to quit the job. This is crazy." But then by evening, I'd be more alert and go back to work. Amidst my college sampling of subjects, there was one constant. I took every class offered by Lowell Bennion and T. Edgar Lyon at the University of Utah Institute of Religion. Bennion, a living social conscience, could fill the blackboard with ideas elicited from his thoughtful questions about scriptural texts and contexts. Lyon was a mine shaft of scrupulously accurate history, particularly church history. He taught me to shave away myths from facts.

The war slowed down the normal educational processes. My older brother joined the air force. Because I had slipped a disk in high school I was classified "4-F" and was therefore rejected in the draft. Instead, I joined the civilian-military in the Ninth Service Command at Fort Douglas. I drove every kind of truck in the motor pool, even eighteen-wheelers. Maneuvering in the driver's seat was bearable, amidst sciatic pain, but standing was torment. Finally, when all else failed, I had surgery.

Then came the mission. My older brother and I were called at the same time, had a joint farewell, and were assigned to the same mission. It was New England, which then included the Maritime provinces of Canada, under President S. Dilworth Young. He was a General Authority, a wise practicalist—he sent us out without purse or scrip—and also a man of poetic sensitivities and gifts. He extended my mission three months, pulled me into the mission office, and amidst the daily regimen, encouraged me toward creative writing. Cambridge was an academic crossroads, and we saw the comings and goings of LDS scholars at MIT, Harvard, and adjacent schools.

A few days after my return home, John A. Widtsoe, then of the Twelve and himself a Harvard man, spoke in my hearing. His easy familiarity with sacred writings, history, poetry, and the latest word in natural science impressed me. Shyly I approached him afterward and said, "Could I talk to you sometime about vocation?" I knew he'd been a university president.

He invited me to his home. Almost every room was shelved with books from floor to ceiling. He asked., "What are you interested in? What have you done?" Then, "You haven't focused on anything yet."

I nodded.

"That's the trouble with you young people. You take classes on impulse. You need to look ahead twenty years and ask yourself, 'What do I want to be twenty years from now?'"

After further probing, he said, "The future belongs to science." And then, "Think about Homer's field [Homer Durham taught political science]." Aside from his specific counsel, Elder Widtsoe recommended three searching questions that influenced my later decisions: "What am I good at, or what, in time, could I become good at? What do I like to do? What does the world need?" (Elder Widtsoe later told me that he had to relearn the fundamentals of his field—agrarian chemistry—three times. Little did I know then how radically the premises of philosophical analysis would shift in my lifetime.)

Back at the University of Utah, I toyed with political science as a major for a time. Several of my friends were eventually able to combine political studies with law, then enter civil service. That was the direction my brothers were going. I soon learned that political theory is itself enmeshed in philosophical frameworks. I would become enamored of the three Johns of American republicanism: John Milton, John Locke, John Stuart Mill.

In my senior year, the consensus of my professors was that I would do well in three areas: comparative literature, psychology, and philosophy. In the field of literature, it was S. B. Neff, a slow-spoken, pedantic, Oxford type who taught me Shakespeare. Louis Zucker, a classicist who brought Homer to life, was another mentor. Probably without realizing it, he planted in me the seed of a lifetime interest in Judaism. Brewster Ghiselin had done a benchmark book called *The Creative Process,* a collection of the methodologies of famous writers, scientists, and mathematicians. I learned from his class some implications of Paul Valéry's "one line given of God." Along the way, C. Lowell Lees, the theater man, tutored me in French and pushed me toward Professors Plummer and Garff in speech.

As for psychology, I experimented one summer with graduate courses in that field. The training, though brief, was helpful when, decades later, I joined in some projects with clinical psychologist Allen Bergin.

The three prominent philosophers at the University of Utah were Waldemar Read, a recognized authority on John Dewey and the pragmatists; O. C. Tanner, whose course in the philosophy of religion provided a comprehensive overview; and Sterling McMurrin, whose long suit was the history of ideas. In all my studies since, I have found no one who can match McMurrin for his approach to the free-will–determinism issue, his assessment of the philosophical implications of a finite God, or his account of theodicy. McMurrin also alerted me to the writings of historian-theologian B. H. Roberts. Years later when I was assigned to write a biography of Roberts, I was, in a measure, prepared.

Toward the end of my undergraduate days, one of my professors suggested I try for the Rhodes Scholarship in PPE—philosophy, politics, and economics. I reached the finals but did not attain the scholarship. After I completed the required spectrum of philosophy courses, I graduated.

For a master's degree I proposed working in the history of philosophy and writing a thesis on psychologist-philosopher William James. My prospectus was approved by Professor Read. Timid about line-by-line scrutiny, I went home, hid up for several months, and returned with the thesis complete. Shortly thereafter, McMurrin called me in and said with a smile, "You have written a thesis we can't turn down, but what do you think a committee is for?" The committee met, made suggestions, and gave me an oral examination. The degree was granted. My thesis title was "The Ethics of William James."

The more I studied philosophy, the more my concern was to specialize prior to generalizing. What emerged as the "stuffing" of my philosophical inquiries was biblical studies and the history of religion. So we return to my intrigue with Harvard. Hesitantly and prematurely I had earlier applied to Harvard's graduate program, but not in philosophy. Harvard had turned me down. So I assumed that door was closed.

I then considered and actually traveled to four colleges in California: University of Southern California, UCLA, Stanford, and UC Berkeley. When I walked into the library at USC, a brochure on the bulletin board headlined "The F. C. S. Schiller Essay Contest" announced an award for the best essay on William James's philosophy of life. I won the contest and then the Mudd Fellowship in philosophy at USC. I was assuming that would be where I would complete my Ph.D.

Again, I studied philosophy and religion side by side. The departments intertwined. Personalist Ralph Tyler Flewelling was one of the impressive figures. He was touted in Russia as a prime threat to dialectical materialism. Donald Rhoades gave an outstanding course in types of religious philosophy. Donald Rowlingson solidified my grasp of higher and lower criticism of the Bible. Here also I first heard a guest lecturer, Martin Buber, unaware that I would someday be associated with the Buber Institute in Jerusalem and immersed in Hasidism. Then, sitting in the library one day, I had a strange thought: "Now you can go to Harvard." I applied again, this time sending my USC graduate record, and was admitted.

The dominant philosophy at Harvard then was logical positivism, sometimes called logical empiricism and language analysis. W. V. Quine was the master logician, and British philosophers Gilbert Ryle and J. L. Austin were invited to hold special seminars. Three exceptions to the mold were Harry Austryn Wolfson, who taught Spinoza; Platonist Raphael Demos; and Henry Aiken, who was into new models of ethical discourse. John Wild, advocate of Aristotle and Thomism, was now championing existentialism and Heidegger.

My doctoral exams were in three required fields: history of philosophy, metaphysics and epistemology, and ethics. Then I opted away from the fourth area, which was set-theory and formal logic. At the cost of another year, I undertook doctoral exams in the history and philosophy of religion: Old Testament, New Testament, history of theology, Augustine, Calvin, Kierkegaard, D. C. Macintosh, and Paul Tillich. Kenneth Ch'en gave me private tutoring in Buddhism. The biblical text men were Robert Pfeiffer, Amos Wilder, and Krister Stendahl. I had by now married a budding Old Testament scholar, Ann, with whom eventually I studied Hebrew. She would deepen my roots, especially in Isaiah.

Tillich had come during my second year at Harvard. He was appointed University Professor, which meant he could teach anything he chose, and credit was given in any department in the university, including philosophy. His flagship courses were religion and culture and the history of Christian thought.

The professor who "Englished" Tillich's thick Germanic style was John Dillenberger, a Reformation theologian. He coordinated my work in the history and philosophy of religion. He later became head of the Graduate Theological Union at Berkeley, which was one reason why I was invited there as a commuting professor. The union is a consortium of ten different schools in the San Francisco area.

Now I needed a dissertation topic. Could I use the tools of analytic philosophy and language analysis? I proposed a critical dissertation on Paul Tillich's theory of religious symbols. Tillich made a radical disjunction between literal and symbolic usage, between sign and symbol. His position, which permeates his entire systematic theology, could be called pansymbolism: everything religious is symbolic. He shifts from issues of truth or falsehood to the question of whether symbols do or do not express "ultimate concern," his definition of religion. For Tillich, the entire world of interpretation since Philo, scriptures included, is grounded in one imperative: Don't take it literally.

My analysis attempted to show, in a word, that his distinction is an untenable dualism, that when he himself asks, "What does the symbol mean?" he either leaves the symbol hanging, resorts to negations, or reintroduces literal meanings and many of the very propositions his theory claims to exclude. Tillich gave full approval to those who resisted him only if they had a technical apparatus and arguments that were in a measure original. Under that edict I flourished. My degree was granted. All this was a dress rehearsal for work I have since done on texts of the restoration in terms of clarification and comparison.

This, in outline, is the background of my work in philosophy and theology, some textual studies, a preoccupation with Joseph Smith—what can be seen in and through his massive contribution—in the total sweep of Western religion, and my forays into church history, biography, and the thought and character of the main figures of the restoration movement.

When I left Harvard, many opportunities were unforeseen, not even dots on the horizon. My involvement with all of them has given me a sense of meaning in my earlier studies. These include:

1. The Institute of Mormon Studies, which enlarged research projects in and beyond the Mormon purview.

2. The Religious Studies Center and its monograph series, including several in comparative religion, such as *Reflections on Mormonism* and *The Temple in Antiquity*.

3. The Richard L. Evans Chair. This endowed chair sponsored me through more than five hundred trips to colleges and universities and institutions worldwide. It has brought one hundred fifty guest lecturers to seminars, workshops, and symposia at BYU. It also helped underwrite my guest professorships at Northeastern University in Boston, Haifa University in Israel, and the Graduate Theological Union in Berkeley.

4. The National Endowment for the Humanities. My White House appointment to this panel of thirteen scholars and thirteen citizens was for six years. We were entrusted with hundreds of millions of dollars to supplement projects in libraries, museums, research institutions, scholarships, and the like. We met every three months as final arbiters. These concentrated decisions taxed every strand of my training in the humanities.

5. The Jerusalem Center for Near Eastern Studies. To me, this building and curriculum have meant five years living in the Holy Land, forty-five directed study tours, and two years as director.

6. *The Encyclopedia of Mormonism*, a Macmillan project that I helped to edit. After favorable reviews, it is finding its way into libraries throughout the world.

7. The Dead Sea Scrolls Foundation, which is now bringing world recognition to BYU in the recovery and digitizing of ancient texts, including heretofore baffling Dead Sea Scroll fragments.

Years ago I aspired to write a book on the variety and unity of Mormon experience—to present a verifiability thesis and plead for the reopening of many windows to the totality of human experience. The Mormon heritage is nothing if it is not experiential. Overall, I see it as the one mighty hope of reunion among the world faiths and in world thought. Our century has been dominated—in philosophy, in much theology, and in the scientific and technological fields—by the experience of the absence of God. The future, for those who can join hands with the Latter-day Saints, is in the experience of the presence of God.

Over the years, as I've traveled the circuit of adult education, I've tried to encourage students at every stage of life. I have urged that we don't have an accurate measure of an individual's "intelligence" and that, even if we did, it is not, contrary to the popular impression, a fixed entity. It can be increased and honed. We all have different talents, and the good news is that everyone is, or can become, a bit of a genius at something.

I see our legacy, therefore, as an inescapable mandate: to be lifetime learners and, simultaneously, teachers. Said Joseph Smith, "We should gather all the good and true principles in the world and treasure them up, or we shall not come out true 'Mormons.'"[1] We must, in John Taylor's phrase, reach for "everything pertaining to learning of every kind."[2] Many lose heart about making any sort of contribution because they see people who are thirty or forty years down the road and conclude, "I could never do that." But to paraphrase William James, if you remain faithfully busy in your chosen field or avocation each available hour of the working day, you can with confidence count on waking up some morning one of the competent ones of your generation.

In the few areas in which I consider myself competent, I have tried to be diligent and studious and to learn from oncoming generations. I live in gratitude for students and associates who have excelled their mentor. All I have done, I think, will be done over again and better. Because of my multiple interests, I'm sure I have scattered energies when I could have been more focused. To bring them all to fruit, I need a longer life—much longer.

Notes

1. *Teachings of the Prophet Joseph Smith,* comp. Joseph Fielding Smith (Salt Lake City: Deseret Book, 1972), 316.

2. *Journal of Discourses,* 21:100.

Truman Madsen, Valued Teacher

Dillon K. Inouye

We are thankful to the Lord, we fortunate ones, for a good friend if we have one, an exemplar if we know one, a stern and sturdy scriptural giant if we seek one, a teacher "sent from God" if we are lucky enough to learn from one, and an all-around splendid exemplar of the Christian element of the broad human race. Truman is many things, of which the above suggestions are only the beginning.

Elder Marion D. Hanks,
on Truman Madsen's seventieth birthday

Introduction

No celebration of the professional life of Truman G. Madsen would be complete without an acknowledgment of his contributions as a teacher. Although it is difficult to take the measure of a man while he is still living, I believe that any assessment will show that few teachers in the history of the professorate have had a greater influence on students. He joins Karl G. Maeser, B. H. Roberts, Hugh Nibley, and others as a bellwether, for example, for faithful Mormon intellectuals. In addition, as much as any other teacher in the history of Brigham Young University, he has served as a bridge builder, assisting some to understand and others to respect the messages of the restored gospel.

Reading this personal tribute embarrassed Truman. When he saw it, he quoted President Gordon B. Hinckley's statement, "Adulation is poison." I see my tribute as appreciation, not adulation, and I attributed Truman's concerns about toxicity to his characteristic modesty.

Truman in the Classroom

I am one of thousands of students whom Truman taught during his university career. Many know him better and have worked more closely with him, but I may be more representative of his typical student. I first met Truman in 1961, when he was in his fourth year at Brigham Young University and I was a freshman in his Book of Mormon and introduction to philosophy courses. He taught in the old Joseph Smith Building, which was at the time the center of BYU campus.

Truman looked like a philosopher. He was taller than average, with deep-set eyes and a large head. His characteristic expression suggested thought and mental activity. Because of his angular features, charismatic presence, flair for the dramatic, and lean frame, one could see why one of his friends referred to him as "an emaciated Charlton Heston." So striking was his physical appearance that when he entered the room or merely paused before speaking, we found ourselves leaning forward in anticipation.

When Truman began to speak, we became aware of his mellifluous voice. It was pleasing and seemed to resound from his whole body. He was a master of vocal expression. Merely by inflection, he could present, promote, question, or forcefully drive home a point. His diction was measured, often cadenced, and was always precise. He had a gift for language and verbal expression.

In his Book of Mormon class, Truman introduced us afresh to Joseph Smith, the Book of Mormon, and the gospel of Jesus Christ. Although most of us had been taught the basic insights of

the restoration before coming to BYU, Truman had a way of placing gospel subjects in a new, and for us more interesting, light.
Like the diamond cutter who turns and facets his gems to reflect
maximum light, so, too, did Truman approach fundamental topics in ways that allowed the light of the restored gospel to be more
fully exposed and appreciated. When, for example, we read in
Alma 38:12, "bridle all your passions," Truman helped us to see in
the nuances of that phrase the difference that a restored knowledge of an embodied God could have on theology, religion, and
the joys of marriage, hearth, and home.

We appreciated Truman's pedagogical skills. Because he had
an unusual ability to understand what was happening inside his
students' heads, he knew what to do to make his lectures clear and
interesting. Because the subject matters he introduced were often
new to us, he took the time to lay the proper foundation of definitions—introducing the new in terms of the old, the unfamiliar
in terms of the familiar. He also used internal summaries and advanced organizers to telegraph the scope and sequence of his lessons. If we did not understand a point, we could interrupt at any
moment and ask questions. Even the most ill-conceived questions
received respectful answers. Sometimes, to help us get a feeling
for the personalities of those involved, Truman would enact his
impressions, or imitations, of them. I can still hear Truman's impression of his teacher Paul Tillich's guttural voice and German
accent in referring to God as the "ultimate ground of Being."

Although Truman's technical gifts were well deployed, we
learned that they were mere accompaniments to a deep mastery
of his subject matter and the testimony of the Spirit that made his
lessons vital and life changing. In meekness and with appreciation, Truman showed us some of the "crown jewels" of the Mormon heritage.

Although we profited from the doctrinal and theological discussions of our faith, we appreciated also Truman's willingness to
share personal stories that added interest to his presentations and

drove home important points. I learned about these in my introduction to the Book of Mormon and introduction to philosophy classes, somewhere between the Psalm of Nephi and Friederich Waisman's *On Verifiability*. Sharing these stories made Truman human. His sharing them with us made us feel as if we were his friends, if not his intimates.

The confidentiality of friends is precisely what Truman drew us into. He took us to his home, apologized for the spare furnishings, showed us the stereo system purchased in lieu of furniture, shared his prized recordings, engaged us in the discussion of inspiring topics, and served us Sister Madsen's refreshments. The confidentiality of friends was also the basis of his presentations to us. He spoke to us not as a pedant or know-it-all, but as a brother and friend who respected us as his friends. Although he himself thrived on the subtle and abstract nature of philosophical and theological arcana, he never spoke down to us. He made us each feel that we were colleagues capable of joining him on the academic mountain.

So engaging was his teaching that we often lost track of time and space. When the bell rang, we would be startled that the time had gone by so quickly. But in spite of the seeming shortness of the hour, our memories contained many of the insights, the lecture content, the stories, the anecdotes, and the feelings that we still remember decades later. Of all my memories, two reminiscences dominate: the love and respect that Truman had for Joseph Smith, and the way our hearts burned within us when he testified of the truthfulness of the restored gospel of Jesus Christ. When Truman spoke about these subjects, he had what Arthur Henry King called a "Scandinavian pellucidity." I thought that I could see a light emanating from his face, almost making his bones visible. The way we felt during those times is one reason that we have gone to hear him again and again during the intervening years.

Truman's Contribution as a Teacher

Truman's Impact on Me

Most teachers aspire to make a difference in the lives of their students; Truman has been more successful than most. My own life is representative. As I look back with the 20/20 vision of hindsight, it is clear that Truman's impact upon me has been immense, affecting the quality of all my days in the forty years since I first met him. The way in which I see the world bears his influence, not just in my own work in educational psychology, but also in my philosophical foundations.

Truman helped us know our religion. He introduced us to the theological and philosophical underpinnings of the Church of Jesus Christ of Latter-day Saints. Because of our respect for his competence and character, we were not afraid that our explorations would lead us out of the church or of religion. "If Truman with all his knowledge can still believe, then we, who will probably never know as much, need not fear," we thought.

Truman introduced us to the world of ideas. Our explorations of philosophy with him as our guide were exhilarating. His Socratic approach found a responsive chord in us. From him, we received our first inklings of the history of ideas and the types and problems of philosophy. Who was Plato's Socrates and what has been his influence on Western civilization? What were the contributions of Aristotle? How did St. Augustine platonize the theology of the Christian church? How did St. Thomas Aquinas aristotelianize it? How did William James distinguish the mystical from the ordinarily religious? How might we evaluate Cardinal Newman's claim that faith was a descant upon doubt? My first encounter with questions like these came in Truman's classes. John Welch, one of his students-become-colleague, wrote down a typical Madsen statement: "Kierkegaard gave us an either/or. Joseph Smith gave us a both/and."

Truman taught us lessons that we could expand beyond the classroom. When we wrote student papers, he taught us to look deeper than the easy answer and to think beyond the cut-and-dried. The themes he addressed in class were dynamic and growing. Because he did not prematurely bring closure to his discussion of topics, we found it easy to extend his lessons as we learned more. We learned to love the things he loved. Most of us have spent the rest of our lives learning more about them and sharing them with others.

Truman introduced us to other teachers and sources of help. He did this by freely and frequently expressing his admiration for other scholars in the field and related fields. He often spoke of modern philosophers like Paul Tillich (the subject of his Harvard dissertation), William James (the subject of his master's thesis at the University of Utah and of his F. C. S. Schiller Essay Contest prize at the University of Southern California), Maurice Merleau Ponty, and Willard Van Orman Quine. He also mentioned the work of contemporary Latter-day Saint scholars like Chauncey Riddle, Hugh Nibley, Wes Belnap, David Yarn, Daniel Ludlow, Richard Anderson, and Spencer Palmer. Although he did not always agree with his former teachers at the University of Utah and Harvard, his respect for them was clearly evident. These informal, offhand introductions gave us the names of those who could guide us in further expansions of the topics we first encountered in his classes.

Truman's Impact on Those He Mentored

In addition to the thousands—more accurately, hundreds of thousands—of students whom he taught in the classroom or who heard him speak, Truman has had a decisive influence on those students for whom he became a personal mentor or advisor. Some to whom he was a mentor have since become his colleagues in the Philosophy Department and Religious Studies Department. These students have long been Truman's protégés and colleagues by affection. To name only a few, both Terry and Susan Warner and Noel and Sydney Reynolds had wedding receptions at the Madsens' home. Dennis Rasmussen was one of the Madsens' missionary sons. S. Kent Brown now serves as one of Truman's colleagues in biblical studies.

Truman's Impact on BYU

Truman's teaching, recruitment, mentoring, and encouragement of students played a key role in the historical development of BYU. Today, competition among students to get into BYU is intense, and investments in faculty and the physical plant have allowed BYU to take its place among modern universities. It was different when the Madsens first came to BYU.

Truman began his teaching career at BYU in 1957 as an assistant professor in the Department of Religion, which then included philosophy. One marvels at the weekly schedule of the young faculty member. On weekdays, he would prepare and teach an average of three or four classes in religion and philosophy, conduct research, and write articles. On weekends and some weekday evenings, he would serve as bishop of the BYU 11th Ward, supervising ward activities and counseling members until late in the evening. (English professor Don Norton and I still remember the young bishop pulling up to the Joseph Smith Building in his overloaded Volkswagen, with members of his 11th Ward flock literally hanging out the windows.)

Often on Friday afternoons, when his classes were over, he would drive with colleagues like Stephen Covey, Lynn McKinlay, Robert Thomas, and Reed Bradford to stake centers in places like Reno, Oakland, Los Angeles, or Portland, where they would present Know Your Religion or Education Week programs. Richard Henstrom, who directed BYU's Know Your Religion programs for many years, told me that many parents who heard Truman and his colleagues at Know Your Religion firesides decided to send their children to BYU to be educated under "teachers like these." Quietly and without fanfare, the demand to be educated at BYU is growing, not only in the number of students who seek admission but also in their quality and serious intent. Brother Madsen, as a practitioner of excellence and one of the dedicated faculty who were willing to travel to the ends of the earth to help the Saints "know their religion," was a leader in the intramural and extramural building of the modern BYU.

Truman's Impact as an Emissary of the Church and BYU

One who thinks that Truman's outreach has been of prime importance is Hugh Nibley. In his letter to Truman on Truman's seventieth birthday, he asks,

> How do I know thee? Let me count the ways. That is easy, because there is only one—as an emissary of the gospel. Truman is less like anybody else than anybody else is. He defies classification. My favorite orator in these drab days: cool, precise, but punchier than a pile driver when he wants to be.
>
> Who else could have brought a dozen world-famous Jewish and gentile scholars to Provo, corralled them into a snowbound cabin and made them talk, without a knife, gun, or glowing cigarette? May I remind you that these guys were Number One, top-drawer in their fields.
>
> [Truman is] . . . a diplomat as shrewd as Talleyrand but obvious as a child, boldly giving away his secret plans and desires, which are simply to advance the Kingdom of God on earth with whatever will do it.
>
> Truman leaves his mark in the bemused minds of those intellectuals whom he does not hesitate to challenge. He has a casual approach, like an intellectual Jacob Hamblin (and Jacob was no slouch), sizing up suspicious and wary gentiles and bringing them around with a forceful and sometimes subtle persuasion. He defies criticism because he defies classification. He would be perfectly at home in a frontiersman's leather jacket or a cummerbund with banks of medals and orders—trivia to

him, but filling a purpose—the Kingdom, always the Kingdom.
I wonder if he ever thinks of anything else.

Truman has a way of turning up out of nowhere, suddenly
standing at one's elbow or gazing down from the stand. Like
the Three Nephites, the Wandering Jew, and President Hinckley,
he is meant to circulate among mankind, in all things, through
all things, and about all things.

It is an impertinence to try to pin down such a character;
it can't be done. But wherever you may find him, in celestial or-
bit or brief overnight abode, you can be sure that the work of
the Lord is going on. Long may he elude, delight, and inspire us.

Nibley's salutation—one Latter-day Saint treasure saluting another—was never intended for public circulation, but I have asked
for permission to print it here, because it serves to epitomize Truman's contributions as an emissary.

New England Mission

In 1962, when Truman was thirty-five, the sphere of his teaching contributions was broadened by a call to serve as the president
of the New England Mission of the church, headquartered in Cambridge, Massachusetts. While still raising their young family, the
Madsens adopted hundreds of missionary sons and daughters as
part of their circle of concern. Because Truman had received a
Harvard Ph.D. in philosophy and religion, many doors were
opened and invitations issued that would otherwise have been
withheld. The young mission president grew in his ability to articulate and compare the message of the restoration with other
faiths and philosophies.

More Distinctions

When the Madsens returned to BYU at the end of their mission, the students and faculty of BYU showed their appreciation
of Truman's teaching by formal awards. In 1966, students in the
Honors Program voted Truman Honors Professor of the Year. The

next year, in 1967, his faculty colleagues awarded him the Karl G. Maeser Distinguished Teaching Award, and in 1972, the Associated Students named him Professor of the Year. In 1972, he was appointed director of Judeo-Christian Studies in BYU's Religious Studies Center and director of the Institute of Mormon Studies.

The Richard L. Evans Chair

In 1972, Truman's role as a bridge builder was formalized when he became the first occupant of the Richard L. Evans Chair. Jointly sponsored by an independent foundation and the university, it was designed for "two-way exchange" in comparative religion. As other groups (such as the Kennedy Center, of which Truman was a fellow) became involved, it developed into an intercultural, interdisciplinary effort. The chair sponsored programs in colleges and civic organizations, underwriting symposia, interfaith conferences, seminars, and workshops. It brought more than a hundred distinguished scholars to campus for special lectures and discussion. For Truman, over two decades, the assignment meant hundreds of trips to educational institutions in almost every state of the United States and on the European continent. In addition, it meant forty-five travel-study trips to Israel, three years as "commuting professor" at the Graduate Theological Union in Berkeley, and one as guest professor at Haifa University. Truman, as teacher, was participant, moderator, contributor, and facilitator.

I personally witnessed Truman in action in his Evans Chair role when he came to Stanford University to speak in Stanford Memorial Chapel. There, he engaged our Dean of the Chapel, Robert Hamerton-Kelly, and other campus divines in a discussion of "images of God." As one might imagine, the discussion proceeded at a high level of sophistication, with each speaker in turn offering up a different image of God. When it was Truman's turn to speak, he acknowledged the several contributions of the panelists and then began to teach the Mormon doctrine of deity to those on the panel and those assembled *in their own theologico-philosophical tongue.* When he finished, I thought I could see on the faces of those assembled the respect they had for Professor Madsen, for his cogent comments, and for the Mormon religion he represented. Among those who applauded most warmly were students from the Stanford 1st and 3rd Wards, who saw in Brother Madsen's performance a vindication of their faith.

Multiply this example by more than a hundred universities across the world, and we begin to grasp the range of Truman's role as an emissary. In most cases, Truman traveled by himself to bear witness and spread understanding of the restoration. Although it is difficult to quantify the number of those who came to believe or respect the distinctions of Mormonism, the effect of Truman's teaching was perhaps epitomized by a Scandinavian scholar who was apprehensive that Truman would simply evangelize for his own faith. He insisted that Truman lecture to his class on philosophical and theological issues. Erlend Peterson, now vice-president of international relations for BYU, arranged the meeting in Oslo. Peterson recalls that Truman first outlined the philosophical beliefs of the Neoplatonists and traced their influence on historical Christianity. He then showed how the theological framework of the dominant wings of Christianity was more like the tenets of Neoplatonism than the sayings of Jesus. He concluded by testifying that unlike many modern Christian churches, his own church had returned to the categories of the New Testament. After Truman had spoken, his host said, "I see that Professor Madsen is a very dangerous man. He could almost persuade me to become a Mormon." (The professor, Guttorm Fløistad, has written an article in this Festschrift).

Director of the Jerusalem Center for Near Eastern Studies

In 1991, while still pursuing the mission of the Evans Chair, Truman was appointed director of the BYU Jerusalem Center. In this chapter of Truman's and Ann's life, they wrote their message in the hearts of Jewish and Arab citizens of the Holy Land, who in turn inscribed their affection in the hearts of the Madsens. In their directing role, the Madsens also served as hosts to many church members who visited the Jerusalem Center as students or as tourists.

Truman continued in his formal role as emissary until his retirement from BYU in 1994, at which time he became a professor emeritus. Upon "retirement" and in recognition of his lifetime contributions to the university as teacher, scholar, and citizen, Truman was invited to address those in attendance at the BYU spring commencement exercises, an honor accorded to only a handful of faculty in the history of the university.

Influencing a Multitude

Through the years, Truman's teaching created a demand among many who voted with their feet to hear him teach again and again. As the numbers of these students multiplied, so did the demand for his books, his articles, and tape recordings of his lectures. I saw this phenomenon firsthand when my wife, Jeanne, served as chair of the BYU Women's Conference sponsored by the university and the Relief Society. When planning for most speakers, rooms of conventional size were adequate. When planning for Truman, the Marriott Center was often used.

In preparing this tribute, I asked the BYU Office of Institutional Assessment to estimate the number of students that a typical BYU professor might expect to teach in a thirty-seven-year career. Their estimate was between 7,000 and 18,500 students, depending on class load and students per class. Truman taught a full quota of students in his classes in the religion and philosophy departments, but in addition, he taught—by my estimate—approximately 300,000 to 400,000 additional students. These were students who came to BYU Education Weeks, Know Your Religion series, panels, symposia, institutes, and invited addresses to members of the church and members of other faiths and cultures. Also included would be those students who did not hear him in person but became acquainted with his teaching through transcripts and audio recordings of his lectures.

This difference between an average of, say, 15,000 in a typical career and 400,000 in Truman's career tells us a lot about the influence of Truman's teaching. Not only did he teach many students, but he taught many different kinds of students, of all ages and backgrounds. Thousands of individuals from many different parts of the world elected to hear Truman again and again—often in the face of competitive attractions. This is one dimension in which Truman's teaching is unique, perhaps inimitable.

Still to be acknowledged, but more difficult to estimate, is his indirect influence on the families and associates of his students. Who knows how many people now speak of "eternal man," "the highest in us," and the many contributions of the Prophet Joseph Smith without attributing credit to Brother Madsen as the conduit through which the ideas were initially presented to them?

The Qualities of a Gospel Messenger

Herbert Walberg, in a synthesis in the *Handbook of Research on Teaching* published by the American Educational Research Association in 1986, summarized several decades of research on excellence in teaching by identifying eight dimensions of teaching which studies have found to be highly correlated with positive results. These traits include the teacher's clarity, flexibility, enthusiasm, task orientation, use of student ideas, indirectness, structuring, and sparing use of criticism.[1] Truman scores high on these traditional variables.

An Example of Truman's Teaching

On 13 March 2001, I invited Truman to speak as a guest lecturer in my experimental general education class. I wanted my students to have a taste of what I had enjoyed when Truman was my teacher. Because I wanted them also to be drawn, as my associates and I had been, into the confidentiality of friends, I asked Truman to speak autobiographically about themes from his book *The Highest in Us.* This book begins with an account of the conversion of Lorenzo Snow, and thus Truman made frequent references to him in this presentation. With the exception of the citation near the end from Emmeline B. Wells, Truman spoke from memory without notes during the entire ninety minutes.

The excerpts which follow exemplify what I have said about Truman's teaching. Although more autobiographical than most, these informal remarks typify much of Truman's classroom teaching. They show the narrative or storylike quality of Truman's discourse, which is so helpful for memory, visualization, and recall. They illustrate the order of his presentation of ideas, each idea proceeding in a natural and logical order, interspersed with parenthetical material that enlivens the discourse and intensifies interest. We see Truman progressively revealing new aspects of his subject matter to lift and inspire his audience, showing in the example of his own lived experience the power of the restored gospel to change a life and a career.

I find these excerpts to be precious because of what they reveal about a man who, at my request, was willing to open his heart. The excerpts which follow throw light on key turning points in Truman's life, turning points which are not illumined elsewhere in print. One can see in Truman's narrative how, line upon line and precept upon precept, Truman came to the insights in *The Highest in Us.* As you read what follows, please remember that Truman is speaking informally and that my transcript only imperfectly captures the real thing. Lost is all of the expressive information of Truman's voice, his face, and his body language.

Madsen on *The Highest in Us*

Why did you write a book on memory?

You will see. I was born into a family of three boys. I was number two. When my younger brother was born, my mother lasted about a month and then because of a condition that could have been reversed with a shot of penicillin, which wasn't available then, she passed away. I was then two and a half and have no memory—I put that in italics—*no memory* of her. My earliest memory was in the home of an aunt, a marvelous woman who tried to fill the breach. All my life I have wanted two things: to find a way through memory study to go back earlier and to come to understand what might have been a relationship prior to mortality. So if you've looked at some of the things I've written or said, you'll find a preoccupation with the premortal life.

The phrase you sang today from "O My Father": "I had learned to call thee Father through thy spirit from on high"—the way you saw it on the screen today, "spirit" has a small *s*. That may or may not be the way it was originally written. Eliza R. Snow, of course, had in mind *the* Spirit, with a capital *S*. But there's another sense in which she believed, as did her brother Lorenzo, that the spirit, the individual spirit locked within us, does carry, though under amnesia, the record of our former life, and that the Lord ordains that, as we honor the deepest of those impulses in response to the realities of this world, some of those memories are brought back to us. We have at least flashes or glimpses, and they are in me a most powerful motivational force.

Occasionally I have probed the life of Orson F. Whitney. This man, almost forgotten now, a member of the Twelve—some spoke of him as the Milton of Mormonism—wrote a classic poem called "Elias." I learned, while in Israel with President Hugh B. Brown, the following quick glimpse. He, Elder Hugh B. Brown, was walking down a street in Salt Lake. It's a steep hill, Third Avenue, close to what we used to call Memory Grove—interesting in the present context. As he walked, he saw another man walking toward him. He thought he recognized him, but he didn't know him. But there was a sense that he did. "When we were side by side," he told me, "it was almost as if I felt an electric shock. We both took a few steps, stopped, turned around and stared at each other, and then walked on without a word. I learned later that he was Orson F. Whitney, a member of the Council of the Twelve. I am now a member of the Council of the Twelve, and I am assured we knew each other before."

Well, it was Orson F. Whitney who wrote an article we call now "Spirit Memories." If you want to see the response of President Joseph F. Smith to his reflections, it's on page thirteen of *Gospel Doctrine.*

Why did you end up coming to Brigham Young University when you said that you never would?

You want to be careful about telling the Lord what you won't do. I can't explain now why we were set against it, but both Ann and I were sure that once I had a degree we would look for some place in the East. For example, I would have loved to teach at Amherst, Massachusetts, and have Ann study Emily Dickinson in a wonderful college town. But we were rigidly opposed to going to BYU. One night we both sat up in bed and said, "Guess what! We're supposed to go to BYU."

I've often said in retrospect that we don't ever get—at least I haven't—a life blueprint, a total blueprint of outcomes. In some ways we can be grateful for that. But all I have received, and I'm most grateful, is at certain turning points a nudge and then, in retrospect, looking back, have been able to say, "Oh, that makes sense. That makes sense. That's the way it's supposed to be."

People say, "Well, the Lord really isn't interested in such decisions as your vocation or even your marriage. That's your business. He'll back you up as long as you live the basic principles of the gospel and live a meaningful life. You shouldn't put the burden on him." But I give you my personal experience that that's a little too hasty and superficial. I think the Lord knows us better than we know ourselves. I think that he knows something about why we are here now and not some other time or place and that we ought to seek his guidance, even if it's very difficult at times to receive and recognize.

So we came here, and in the "looking-back" feeling, we have no regrets. None.

Why did you focus so much in your writing on the nature of man and then tie that, as you frequently do, to the ultimate nature of God?

In my book I write of an exchange that occurred in Worcester, Massachusetts, at Holy Cross University—a collision between the Mormon understanding of a personal God in whose image we are and the classical traditional view that God, to be God, must be described, if at all, in the ultimate categories of Greek philosophy. I still remember somebody standing up and reeling off the negative theology: "God is not anything like man. Beyond space, beyond time, beyond everything."

I remember saying, "You have just given me a catalogue of Plato-tudes. But let me ask questions about Christ. Was Christ a person?" Yes. "Was he somewhere between, say, five and seven feet tall?" Yes, he was. "Did he have a body?" Yes. "Will he always have a body?" Yes. "Is there any reason why we cannot honor and admire and even worship him in his present glorified condition as a person?" No. All right, then, back to the Father. "What about the Father?" Oh, no, no, no. And then they gave me the same list. I couldn't resist saying, "You've been saying that Mormons aren't really monotheists. They are polytheists. And I ask you the question: "Don't *you* have two Gods, totally different Gods? Haven't you created for me a hard problem in prayer and worship? How can I honor Christ and try to be Christlike when it will mean that I am becoming totally *un*like God, who is so much beyond?"

He said, "You don't understand the Trinity." I had studied Augustine at Harvard, and I admit I didn't understand. I passed the exam, but I don't think Augustine himself understood the

Trinity. Trinitarianism is a series of paradoxes and contradictions. The impact on Judaism, Christianity, and Islam of that view of the ultimate first cause in Aristotle or ultimate being in Plato was a very unfortunate wedding, and it took a boy—a fourteen-year-old boy—to say, "The emperor has no clothes!" Or, to reverse the metaphor, "The emperor has been smothered under the Greek clothing."

Lorenzo Snow had it given to him in power, as if a conduit had opened between him and heaven, that just as an earthly father and mother have children who inherit their very nature, so do we inherit ours from God. I tell you from much experience and travel that we are among the few who take that seriously. I studied under Paul Tillich. The ultimate position of Paul Tillich is that God is—as he put it with a capital *B* and a capital *I*—"Being-Itself" and that God is absolutely not a person, period. The boy Joseph learned otherwise, and so did Lorenzo Snow. They gave their lives to try to communicate that glorious principle. It doesn't seem glorious to others. It seems blasphemous, it seems inferior, it seems crude. Isn't that an interesting inversion?

We held in Jerusalem a council, as it were, of world-renowned theologians. We decided to call it "The Search for Human Nature." There were representatives of Roman Catholicism, Greek Orthodoxy, Protestantism, three different Jewish points of view, and a man who was an expert on oriental religions. At the end we had an opportunity to talk about the Latter-day Saint understanding.

Listening to the alternatives, I came to understand what a brilliant philosopher once said to me: "You Mormons have the gospel that's *really good news!*" He was saying that we have dropped, like a clod of mud, a series of hopelessly misleading premises. We don't have to work with them anymore. There is no such thing, for example, as an *ex nihilo* creation. There simply isn't. You cannot bring something out of nothing. We drop once and for all the dogma of original sin—that somehow Adam and Eve committed a horrible, totally defiling transgression that ruined the future of all the human family. "If only they had not done that, we could all be in Paradise." That's the view, and then it gets compounded in Calvin with the notion of utter and total depravity. This premise is introduced in order to justify perfect honor for God. You are a worm, but God will save you in spite of your worminess, and that is called grace.

Now, we understand grace profoundly in the church, but what we don't accept is the notion that there is nothing of worth in you. Your spirit self and the intelligence that's part of it are altogether good. And your present body is not totally depraved. If you misuse it and pervert it, you can eventually become what you shouldn't have become. But that will be against your basic nature. The Book of Mormon talks a good deal about "the natural man," but it is not talking about original sin. It's talking about something else, and I won't take time to elaborate now. My point is that the gospel is really good news. You are somebody in the eyes of God, and that is because you partake of his very nature.

Lorenzo Snow saw that. One day he was here in what was then the academy, BYU Academy. There was a mirror through which he could see the children who were playing, but they could not see back to him, and he noticed that they were working with clay and were forming round balls which he thought for the moment they might be using for playthings. Instead, they were making clay earths. Lorenzo Snow began to weep. "Why?" someone asked him. He said, "Those children do not know that in due time they may actually make worlds." That's how literal he was about the power that resides in our potential to become.

How, Truman, did you end up focusing on teaching as much as on writing?

In a successful academic career those should, of course, be combined. BYU, as an undergraduate institution, puts tremendous emphasis on teaching. I hope they continue to do so. We do not have the greatest graduate schools in the world, although some are measurably impressive.

I had a set of crises. I had to come home and have major back surgery just on the eve of undertaking my dissertation, and I had to take my final written exams when I had excruciating sciatic pain. My wife was expecting our second child. Her father was dying of cancer. I was in no sense secure in the feeling that I would finish at Harvard.

In that crisis hour, a concerned aunt, the one who took me in as a babe, called one of the Brethren [Elder Harold B. Lee] and said, "Please give Truman Madsen a blessing." He came, knocked on the door, and said, "I came to give you a blessing." He pulled me out of that struggle. One key phrase and answer to the question I asked was, "You will be a valued teacher." I have tried.

How have you dealt with other struggles and setbacks and tragedies?

We all have them. Again, I invoke Brother Lorenzo. He was present in the incredible and glorious outpourings of the Kirtland Temple. They thought, as I have written, that the Millennium had come. They had no disposition even for their former habits or sins. "This must be the Millennium."

The Prophet had to alert them, "Yes, it's beautiful, but it's all to prepare us. Get ready, brethren, because the opposite will come." And of course it did. He also said—which I find hard—"God will feel after you, and he will wrench your very heartstrings. And if you cannot stand it, you will not be worthy of the kingdom of God." With that as a premise, I've gone through our history and many of the lives of our great men and women. I can find a wrench—at least one—in every life I study. There have been a few in mine.

Ann bore three marvelous children, but we hoped for more. So, as a family, we had periodic fasting and praying for about twenty-five years. Occasionally, we would overhear Latter-day Saints, not wanting to be thoughtless, say, "I wonder why the

Madsens don't have any more children." Well, so did we. In the letters we wrote to each other, wherever we were in the world, there was a final salutation, which was "Keep the baby faith!" If we are at peace now about it—and we are, both of us—it is partly because we came to recognize that we were to reach out to others not born to us but who were nevertheless part of our larger family in the real world.

You all know Hugh Nibley. I was in the auditorium the night they presented as kind of a premiere the videotape on his life called "The Faith of an Observer." At the end of their interviewing him in Egypt, he, sitting on the hot desert sands and unaware that the camera was rolling, told this midrash about Abraham. On just such a day, he is looking out of his tent, a day which they describe as the very belching of hell, so hot that you can see thermals in every direction. Abraham is worried. Somebody may be out there in that torrid heat. So he sends his trusted servant, Eliezer, to go out and look in every direction to see if anybody is faltering. He comes back and says, "No one. I found no one." But the Jews have a saying that sometimes a servant cannot be trusted to do a hard task. So Abraham, though aged and infirm himself, goes out in the heat in every direction. He finds no one.

But when he returns to that tent three persons are standing there—angels, and in one case perhaps the Lord himself. They promise him what he has wanted all his life—a son. And a son he had. Jewish lore says that Sarah was not only beyond the child-bearing years, but one account says that she didn't even have a womb, so it was a total miracle for her to deliver a child. But the lovely legend is that when she did, every line in her face disappeared, and that from then on, when she was asked, "How old are you?" she replied, "The same age as my son. My life began when he was born."

If I had time, I would dwell on what all that meant for the later sacrifice required of Abraham and Sarah. But as it applies to me and to you, I believe that sooner or later the Lord feels after us to the very place and point that we are most resistant to him and asks us to give the last thing we want to give. Sometimes he takes it. Sometimes he simply says your willingness is enough.

This is also subjective, and I hope I am not betraying a confidence. I sat in the Jerusalem Center one night on New Year's Eve as Robert Cundick played "Jesu, Joy of Man's Desiring" on the organ. Elder James E. Faust, not then of the First Presidency, and Elder Jeffrey R. Holland, not then of the Twelve, were sitting in the comparative darkness looking out at the vista that is, if tradition is right, Mount Moriah. Elder Faust turned to Elder Holland and said, "Talk about Abraham." And, as if he was given a cue, Elder Holland launched eloquently, as only he can, into the point that Abraham came to that mount with his son. And his son was delivered from sacrifice by a ram in a thicket. But the Son of God ascended the same mount. And he *was* the ram, the Lamb. He was not delivered. He participated, gave, suffered, sacrificed.

Tests come in two ways: One is the ultimate extremity when, yes, the only way out is death—if you want to honor your covenants. But the other is to live your whole life as a genuine, put-on-the-altar sacrifice, your will swallowed up in his. That's Christlike.

Lorenzo Snow understood that. He used to say to the Saints, "It's going to be rough. But it won't be as rough—it will smooth things out—if you will totally live the commandments."

Why have you emphasized the temple so much in your teaching and writing?

Soon after my mission I was called to the Ensign Stake Temple Committee. As a result, I was on a monthly schedule of meetings, and I had to go to the temple every Friday night. Within a short time it began to sink in. I think I've read everything that's ever been written in terms of the basic arguments against temple ordinances or the Mormon practices. They fly off like so much water off a duck's back. I know the contrary is true.

Some of you heard me tell of being in California, and down comes President McKay to ask for the one million dollars that the local Saints were to raise in order to build the Los Angeles Temple. How I got in that meeting I don't know. I had no official calling. But at the end of their commitment he gave what I consider one of the finest, clearest talks ever on "why temples?"

That's the origin of the quotation I wrote down in shorthand and which I have memorized: "Brothers and sisters, I believe there are few"—I am quoting—"even [among] temple workers who understand the full meaning and power of the temple endowment. Seen for what it is, it is the step-by-step ascent into the eternal presence. If our young people could but glimpse it, it would be the most powerful spiritual motivation of their lives." That enhanced, for me, the temple odyssey.

One night I was so close to Brother Nibley in the seating of the Provo Temple that I could make out his profile. And it was obvious that he was totally absorbed in listening, wholeheadedly and wholeheartedly. Downstairs in the locker room I made bold to say, "Brother Nibley, what was going on in that mind of yours? You could do the temple ceremony in your sleep! You know it backwards and forwards. You have been studying world ritual for fifty years, and yet you were right on the edge of your chair."

He said, "Well, I always come to the temple with a theme in mind."

That was new to me, and I said, "Like what?"

"Well, tonight it was beauty. And I made several wonderful discoveries."

The next time, I went with that in mind, and yes, indeed, I found some wonderful things. I wish I had his whole list. But here is a man who has taught me that as far back as Egypt and earlier, there was at least a semblance of imitation of a complete and comprehensive ritual process that was, they understood, to lead us back to the very presence of God.

I have been asked, "Why isn't more said about Jesus in the temple?" It's like saying, "Why isn't Christ ever mentioned in the New Testament?" Jesus is everywhere in the temple. Every symbol, every statement ultimately ties back to him. The ultimate culmination is a tie to the Lord Jesus Christ, who is in the exact image of the Father. So I would say in one sentence that, for me, the temple has brought meaning and power and purification into my life by binding me to the power of Christ's atonement. That is where the atonement is written in our flesh.

I had the privilege of witnessing the conversion of a Congregational minister who, after his one-year waiting period, had the experience of the temple. Because of Protestant leanings and some unfortunate experiences with other kinds of ritual—fraternal ritual—he was not only *not* helped or inspired by the process, but he was turned off. He decided he would tell no one, and he could go on being a good Latter-day Saint. He just wouldn't be a temple-going Latter-day Saint.

One Sunday a discerning woman cornered him. "John," she said, "how do you feel about the temple?"

"Oh, all right, I guess."

"John, how do you really feel about the temple?"

"Well, I had some problems."

"I thought so. Come with me." She took him home and introduced him to her husband, who had had a similar experience but who now was totally dedicated to the process. (John had talked indirectly to others, including me, about his problem quietly; and he summed it up by saying, "I love you, but you didn't help me. You didn't help me. But he did.")

"Oh, what did he say?"

Now, it may not mean anything to those of you who have been and are yet to go, but what he said was basically this: "It is one thing, John, to have intellectual understanding, conceptual grasp, of principles. It is something else to have it written in your flesh. The temple writes it in your flesh." Somehow that broke the dam, and John became zealous to his last breath.

As Nibley says, "The temple is designed"—this is his summary phrase—"to reverse the blows of death." And that includes sin. Sin is always death-bringing, even if you only die a little. There are deaths *in* the body—as we somehow diminish light in the head, somehow diminish the sensitivity of our hearts, somehow even betray the creative and procreative powers we have. That's a form of death. The death *of* the body is the one we are all worried about, but we are worried falsely. That's not what we should focus on. It's avoiding the deaths that sin brings—that is what the temple reverses, cleanses, purifies, purges, heals. Why? Because it is the power of Jesus Christ, called "the power of godliness" (D&C 84:20, 21).

How did you get started with—some say your preoccupation, some say your obsession—with Joseph Smith? You just can't leave him alone. You go on reading about him, you go on studying—all his teachings, line by line, and then his life. Surely there are others to study.

Oh, yes, lots of others, but yes, since day one—what day was that? I am going to tell you—it has been Joseph Smith. Part of that again is very, very personal. When I was only a nineteen-year-old and a very young one, the bishop walked into my house and called my brother on a mission. He had just come out of the air corps after the Second World War (he was a couple of years older). He was on the verge of a business proposition that was to be consummated the next day. He said, "Bishop, as far as I am concerned, you couldn't have come on a worse night. The fact that you're here shows that I'm wrong, so the answer is yes, I'll go."

I remember walking to the back room of the house, saying to myself, "My own brother is going on a mission. That gives me only two years. I'd better get serious about the scriptures." (I had a mandate in my patriarchal blessing, "Master the scriptures." I've tried.) I felt totally inadequate.

The next week the bishop came back to our house and said, "We've been talking it over and we've prayed about it. We'd like to call you too, Truman, and we'll have a joint farewell."

"You what?"

"We will have a joint farewell for you and your brother."

Instead of demonstrating my brother's faith, I said, "Oh, bishop, not so soon, not so soon." I really fought it. Eventually I came around, and we did indeed have a joint farewell. We went to the then-MTC—it was the so-called mission home in Salt Lake City—and we went to serve in New England.

The mission president wisely never made us companions. That would not have been good chemistry. He knew it. I was still insecure and needed to make my own way. I had begged him to let me stay three extra months. He wrote me a letter and said, "Your brother is going to pick you up in May. He will be released. You will not. He will take you to the birthplace of Joseph Smith."

We, having tried to serve, stood near the thirty-eight-and-a-half-foot shaft. Sunset. Three hundred sixty degrees of greenery. And I still remember his looking up and saying, "I love you, Joseph Smith."

Now, we didn't know that he would come home, marry, have two little children, be summoned by the National Guard to serve in Korea, and, on his eighty-second mission, crash and not come home. I thank God I had the shared experience with him before his death. Part of my concern to honor and study the Prophet comes out of that one climactic afternoon.

Another part is hard to put into words, so I am going to use somebody else's. I wrote a book on B. H. Roberts, one of our best historians and doctrinal writers in the first hundred years, and certainly the most comprehensive. He was asked to give a tribute to a famous Latter-day Saint woman who was known all over the church as Aunt Em—Emmeline B. Wells. She was wife to Daniel H. Wells.

"Someday," she wrote, "and sometime, if I should live on"—she was then 82—"I may converse with you as I only do to a few choice souls. Not that I can give you new thoughts—you get those from the depths that are found in your own heart—but to exchange or interchange thoughts with one of superior intelligence is a luxury in this barren world of cold communication." She's not talking about IQ. She's talking about intelligence in the Lord's definition.

"When I recall"—now listen—"as I sometimes do, if I ever have time to think of the past, the spiritual converse of a few intimate friends of the Prophet Joseph, I marvel at how I have lived all these later years without now and then drinking at the fountain of that inspiration that seemed to fathom the depths of eternal wisdom and with a grace so modest, yet so sublime, that one sat, as it were, entranced, listening as one would to music of celestial beings. I wonder if you will comprehend me, but you who have studied the Prophet deeply must know that the men and women who sat with him partook more or less of that spirit of eternal truth. And it lingered with them while they lived [they are all gone now] and we only dream of them and fancy their influence lingers near and plod on among the other wanderers, and now and then we get a germ of finer thought from those we meet on life's journey. And in humility and obedience we surrender our own will to his who sees not as man sees."

I have a testimony that that is true. And I wasn't there. I'm a secondhand witness. Emmeline poured that testimony into her children. My own grandfather sat entranced day after day in the old Lion House in the presence of Eliza R. Snow, who, next to his mother, was the most profound influence in teaching him that Joseph Smith was the grandest man that ever lived, with the exception only of the Lord Jesus Christ.

Do you think the church—and the modern restoration movement—needs "intellectuals" in the world's definition, and do you consider yourself an "intellectual"?

I've been asked that in various ways—some courteous and some not. I am only one more ordinary man. Any ascription to me of unusual brain power or anything like it is not really true. To be honest with you, in English classes at the high school I attended, they did an IQ test, and I never found out the results. I didn't want to know. I was terrified to find out. The only clue I ever had that I might have been a little ahead is that my teacher finally said, "You're not taking a sufficient load in school, young man. You are not doing justice to your own potential."

The point is, whatever I can give you in the way of credentials, even the things that Dillon has said about merciful students who gave me awards, doesn't prove anything. I believe that when the Lord said, "The glory of God is intelligence, or, in other words, light and truth" (D&C 93:36), that is not synonymous with saying, "Or, in other words, a Ph.D. from Chicago or Harvard or Stanford." There is something about our individual spirit and its communion directly with *the* spirit of God that is the ultimate teaching process and the source of genuine learning and intelligence.

Yes, there are skills and talents, I have no doubt. And they are needed. And whatever your own discovery of your aptitudes may be, I pray that you will take that as a gift and magnify it.

My answer to this question about intellectuals is that the church needs all of us at our best and that we owe it to those who have gone before—who couldn't have such opportunities—we owe it to them to apply ourselves without stint in magnifying our gifts.

Ultimately, you will be reckoned as intelligent, here and in the life to come, to the degree that you have inherited and practically embraced in your cell structure the light and power of God. How do I know that? President Joseph Fielding Smith (he was at the time president of the Salt Lake Temple, and I think there is a connection) said his favorite verse was, "That which is of God is light; and he that receiveth light"—and that isn't just here [pointing to the head], it's the whole apperceptive mass—"he that receiveth light, and continueth in God, receiveth more light; and that light groweth brighter and brighter until the perfect day" (D&C 50:24).

Add section 84 ["For the word of the Lord is truth, and whatsoever is truth is light, and whatsoever is light is Spirit, even the

Spirit of Jesus Christ," D&C 84:45] and parallels in 88. "Intelligence cleaveth unto intelligence; . . . truth embraceth truth; . . . light cleaveth unto light" (D&C 88:40). It's just like two candles that get close enough together that they become one flame.

Lorenzo Snow was visited one day by a man named Reverend Prentice. It's on record. My grandfather kept a copy of this and sent it to every one of his children. He said that the reverend walked into what he considered was more or less a business office—the office of the First Presidency—where decisions were made and problems solved. Reverend Prentice didn't expect to see what he saw. What he saw, he said, was the holiest face, except one, he had ever seen in his life. And that was Lorenzo Snow. He tried to put into words something about the eyes, something about the grace and modesty, something about the peace of his personality, but he ended up saying, "There aren't words." His conclusion was, if the Church of Jesus Christ can produce even a few persons like that man, they will not need a lot of books or tracts or an extensive missionary program. The world will see. Holiness is another name for the effects of the Spirit of God on the total soul. Lorenzo Snow knew that.

I've been up on the Mount of Transfiguration several times. We don't know for sure if that is the exact mount, but there are lots of high mountains in the Galilee. It is significant that Jesus is transfigured. Apparently he was filled with light. "Glistering" is the way the gospel account puts it (see Luke 9:29). So were Peter, James, and John transfigured (see Matthew 17:5). You have parallel accounts of the Nephite multitude (see 3 Nephi 17:24; 19:13–14, 25).

At the end of the Gospel of Matthew, Jesus says, "All power is given unto me in heaven and in earth" (Matthew 28:18). But the Joseph Smith Translation says that Jesus uses this phrase when he comes down from the Mount of Transfiguration: "All power." Now listen, if that's true of Jesus, can anything like that be said of his disciples or even some such as us, a mere humble fellowship of ordinary people? Listen to these exact words. "He that is ordained of God and sent forth, the same is appointed to be the greatest, notwithstanding he is the least and the servant of all" (D&C 50:26).

I sometimes went as a stake president into bishops' offices and said, "Your chart's upside down: bishop, counselors, all these others at the top, and then, way down here, those other nameless, faceless people. Turn it up the other way. Bishop, you are the servant of all." That's the difference between the quest for power in Nietzsche's sense, power that tromps on the heads and doesn't care if the blood squirts. Power, or *Macht* in German—that's the kind of power that corrupts and the absolute of which corrupts absolutely. Christ's power is always persuasive and never coercive. He promises that power to his disciples, not the other kind.

"He that is ordained of God and sent forth, the same is appointed to be the greatest, notwithstanding he is the least and the servant of all. Wherefore, he is possessor of all things." Now listen: "The life and the light, the Spirit and the power, sent forth by the will of the Father through Jesus Christ, his Son" (D&C 50:26–27). But in the next verse, and here's the "but"—"but no man is possessor of all things except he be purified and cleansed from all sin" (D&C 50:28).

Now, to sum it up one other way—I've been in running correspondence with a fine minister who is doing a book against us. It's against Lorenzo Snow's couplet, which he considers the absolute heresy of the Church of Jesus Christ. He hasn't written it in bitterness. He's lived among us for twenty-seven years. For Christmas a year ago I sent him a seventeen-page document. What I did was to take every sentence in the New Testament in which Jesus characterizes himself and then find a matching sentence in which he characterizes his followers. "I am the light of the world" (John 8:12); "ye are the light of the world" (Matthew 5:14). "I am the salt of the earth" (paraphrase of Luke 14:36 JST); "Ye are the salt of the earth" (Matthew 5:13). "I am the true vine" (John 15:1); "ye are the branches" (John 15:5). "I have living water to give" (paraphrase of John 4:10–11); "he that believeth on me . . . out of his belly shall flow rivers of living water" (John 7:38). "I am the living bread which came down from heaven" (John 6:51); ye are to "feed my sheep" (John 21:16–17). On and on.

Conclusion: Everything you can say about Christ as to his attributes and powers, you can ultimately say about yourself in potentia. That's what he came to make real, not just possible. It was always possible. He came to make it actual. So, he says, to sum it up in Doctrine and Covenants 93, "I give unto you these sayings that you may understand and know how to worship, and know what you worship, that you may come unto the Father in my name, and in due time receive of his fulness. For if you keep my commandments you shall receive of his fulness, and be glorified in me as I am in the Father" (D&C 93:19–20).

Is there any conceivable insight that is more life-transforming than that? It was Lorenzo Snow's guiding star from his early days. For all of my limitations and weakness, it has also been my guiding star.

Note

1. Herbert J. Walberg, "Synthesis of Research on Teaching," in *Handbook of Research on Teaching,* ed. Merlin C. Whittrock (New York: Macmillan, 1986).

CHAPTER 1

WILLIAM JAMES ON RELIGION AND GOD: AN INTRODUCTION TO *THE VARIETIES OF RELIGIOUS EXPERIENCE*

M. Gerald Bradford

William James (1842–1910) was a remarkable individual. He combined profound intellectual talents and brilliant gifts—especially as a writer and a teacher—with a genuine humanity. His personality was irrepressible and fully present in his writings. Based primarily on his pioneering two-volume work *The Principles of Psychology* (1890)—which helped establish the discipline in this country and abroad and out of which grew his own distinctive philosophical view of the world; his companion study of religion, *The Varieties of Religious Experience* (1902); his celebrated *Pragmatism* (1907); and his other writings—James established himself as a world-renowned psychologist and philosopher.[1] We continue to learn more about James as a thinker and a person as more of his voluminous correspondence becomes available.[2] He remains the subject of a number of major biographies and important studies.[3]

While James was interested in a wide range of issues, we know that the subjects he dealt with in depth were of vital importance to him. Jamesian scholars are increasingly of the opinion that a survey of the entire sweep of his intellectual achievements reveals "that two subjects continued to engage his attention from beginning to end—religion and human nature."[4] In connection with these interests, he also worked out a distinctive view of God, what I call his "practical theism."[5]

As a Latter-day Saint, I find much of what James says about religion to be close to the mark. Moreover, I find many of his ideas about God to have certain affinities with how deity can be viewed from a Latter-day Saint perspective. I was first introduced to James years ago by Truman G. Madsen. Madsen, it turns out, is a long-time student of James.

For those interested in reflections on Latter-day Saint thought and teachings, particularly in comparison with the views of others, no one in this generation has had a greater impact or made a more lasting impression than Truman Madsen. His reputation in this regard rests largely on the influence of his book *Eternal Man*. First published in the mid-1960s as a series of articles and later in 1966 as a book, *Eternal Man* contains Madsen's musings on a number of issues or, as he terms them, "anxieties" about the human condition—issues ranging from ideas about human beginnings, problems of identity and self-awareness, and the mind-body problem to the issue of human freedom and the problem of evil and human suffering. Madsen's objective is straightforward: to show how these concerns can be framed differently and to pose possible alternative resolutions as a result of viewing such matters from the perspective of Latter-day Saint belief in the premortal existence of man, particularly as Madsen understands this belief (taking his cue largely from the teachings of the Prophet Joseph Smith). While his focus, of course, is on the eternal nature of man, Madsen also shows how distinctive Latter-day Saint views of deity can profoundly alter our thinking about such issues. It is interesting to contemplate how Madsen's understanding of James may have helped him think through these issues.

In 1951 at the University of Utah, Madsen wrote his master's thesis in philosophy on James; it is entitled "The Ethics of William

James." In his chapter "God and the Moral Life," Madsen deals at some length with James's views on God. Madsen points out that James rejects such ideas as "infinite," "transcendent," "principle," "absolute essence," "first cause," and "law" in reference to the concept of God and instead argues that we need to think of God as having, quoting James, "an environment, being in time and working out a history just like ourselves."[6] Madsen emphasizes that, for James, the most important thing about God is that we can be intimately related with him: "In whatever other respects the divine personality may differ from ours or may resemble it, the two are consanguineous at least in this—that both have purposes for which they care, and each can hear the other's call."[7] Madsen observes that, for James, it is in direct experiences with the divine, not in creedal expressions or theological abstractions, that we come to a proper understanding of God. Furthermore, Madsen correctly points out that while James's conclusions about God are always couched in tentative language, he seems sure of two things: (1) that God is real because he produces real effects in our lives, and (2) a correct understanding of God requires that we talk about him in qualified terms. God is both ideality and actuality. He is finitistic and attainable by acts of will as well as by psychological processes. Madsen concludes that, for James, God makes faith in the "seen world's goodness" possible, he lets loose in us the "strenuous mood," and he represents the "finally valid casuistic scale" upon which our right conduct must ultimately be founded and judged. God, in other words, is the final sanction of ethical conduct.

A year after he earned his Ph.D. in the history and philosophy of religion from Harvard, Madsen published an essay on James entitled "William James: Philosopher-Educator."[8] Then in 1976 he wrote and presented a paper on James entitled "The Lost Dimension of Psychology: William James Revisited" at the annual American Psychological Association meetings held in Washington, D.C.

In his classic study of religion, *The Varieties of Religious Experience*, James deals in depth with religion and God, along with a host of other subjects. This essay is an introduction to *Varieties*. My objective is threefold: following a brief outline of the work, I reconstruct the general theory about religion that James advances. Next, I try to clarify what he says about God. Finally, I address the issue of the religious availability of his practical theism. To those reading *Varieties* for the first time and to others already familiar with this work, my hope is that this summary of James's views will awaken in some and reinforce in others an appreciation of what we can learn from this important thinker.

The Varieties of Religious Experience

Varieties is, in large measure, a continuation of James's earlier psychological investigations.[9] It is also a work in the philosophy of religion. His goal is to describe religion in all its variety and to justify its worth.[10] He takes a very broad view of his subject and acknowledges that his interpretation of religion is not fully adequate to the task, given the abundance and variety of religious experiences. Nevertheless, he puts forth a general theory about religion to account for and unify the rich variety of documentary evidence he has collected and, on the basis of this, concludes with what he takes to be true and distinctive about religion. Unquestionably, what James says about God in *Varieties* contributes significantly to the overall development of his distinctive view of God.

James's genius is evident in his imaginative and insightful use of selections from the material he has collected and in his vivid and descriptive ongoing commentary, every bit as much as it is evident in the way he develops and articulates the theoretical aspects of the work. He collected accounts depicting a range of human experiences, not just religious experiences. He assembled, for example, expressions of loss and despair, panic, fear; feelings of nothingness, spiritual torment, skepticism, and doubt; instances of happiness; dramatic accounts of conversions—religious and otherwise; acts of heroism; occurrences of ecstatic surrender and aesthetic feelings; accounts of sacrifice and confession; expressions of prayer and worship; and descriptions of various forms of inspiration. He relied on the writings of firsthand participants and qualified observers and drew on accounts from adherents of both Western and Eastern traditions. He collected material from the lives of saints, writers, poets, philosophers, theologians, religious founders, mystics, artists, and ordinary people. And he included accounts from Jews, Catholics, Protestants, Muslims, Latter-day Saints, Hindus, Buddhists, Christian Scientists, Transcendentalists, Quakers, atheists, neurotics, and many others.

Varieties consists of twenty lectures. In his initial lecture, James roughly spells out what he intends to do and sketches his experiential approach to the study of religion. His focus is on the personal dimension of religion rather than on religious institutions and thought; he is interested in more developed and vivid expressions of firsthand religious life—religious feelings and impulses, states of mind, and experiences as recorded in individual works of piety and autobiography—by those for whom religion "exists not as a dull habit, but as an acute fever," those individuals he calls "religious geniuses" (p. 15).

James tells us he will rely on what can be observed psychologically, even biologically, in the life of the religious person and on what the person says about his own experiences. He employs an "empirical test," one that judges the significance of the religious life by its "fruits not its roots." Following his conviction that our perceptual-active level of experiencing the world is what is fundamental and is the basis for determining what is real, meaningful, and of value, his approach does not rely on deductive methods or on various theories about the origins of religion; rather, he explores and compares the full range of religious experience as it is immediately given and, as much as possible, in the context of lived experiences. He looks, in other words, to the future, to the consequences of such experiences in the lives of individuals. James asks, "when we think certain states of mind superior to others, is it ever because of what we know concerning their organic antecedents?" And he quickly answers, "No!" "It is always for two entirely different reasons. It is either because we take an immediate delight in them; or else it is because we believe them to bring us good consequential fruits for life" (p. 21). The significance of religious experiences can only be

> ascertained by spiritual judgments directly passed upon them, judgments based on our own immediate feeling primarily; and secondarily on what we can ascertain of their experiential relations to our moral needs and to the rest of what we hold as true.
>
> *Immediate luminousness,* in short, *philosophical reasonableness,* and *moral helpfulness* are the only available criteria. (p. 23, James's emphasis)

In his second lecture, James puts forth his working definition of "religion" and the object of religious experience, the "divine." For him, religious experiences are special instances of human experience of a much wider scope. They are best seen as expressions of our various moods and aims used to constitute a higher order of meaning. That which makes an experience religious is not so much in the psychophysical makeup of the individual as it is in the *object* that is experienced, as *experienced,* and in the nature of our *reactions* to the object. James stipulates that for the purposes of his lectures he means by "religion" those *"feelings, acts, and experiences of individual men in their solitude, so far as they apprehend themselves to stand in relation to whatever they may consider the divine"* (p. 34, James's emphasis). It is best, he says, to speak of religion as a person's "total reaction upon life." Here the individual goes behind the

> foreground of existence and reach[es] down to that curious sense of the whole residual cosmos as an everlasting presence,

intimate or alien, terrible or amusing, lovable or odious, which in some degree everyone possesses. This sense of the world's presence, appealing as it does to our peculiar individual temperament, makes us either strenuous or careless, devout or blasphemous, gloomy or exultant, about life at large; and our reaction . . . is the completest of all our answers to the question, "What is the character of this universe in which we dwell?" It expresses our individual sense of it in the most definite way. (pp. 36–37)

And since not all "total reactions" are religious, "there must be something solemn, serious, and tender about any attitude which we denominate religious. If glad, it must not grin or snicker; if sad, it must not scream or curse" (p. 39). The emphasis here is on *solemnity*.

Building on this meaning of religion, James stipulates that by the "divine" he means "not merely the primal and enveloping and real, for that meaning if taken without restriction might well prove too broad. The divine shall mean for us only such a primal reality as the individual feels impelled to respond to solemnly and gravely, and neither by a curse nor a jest" (p. 39). Then, by comparing and contrasting accounts of religious experience where the divinity of the object and the solemnity of the reaction are too well marked for doubt, we are most likely to find that "element or quality in them which we can meet nowhere else" (p. 44).

The "reality of the unseen" is the focus of the third lecture. One of the subjects James turns to time and again in *Varieties* is his distinction between ordinary consciousness and a wider, subliminal, or transmarginal consciousness—what, most of the time, he calls the subconscious and what Eugene Taylor calls "consciousness beyond the margin."[11] Our ordinary states of consciousness reveal to us the ordinary, everyday world. But James thinks there is sufficient evidence to enable us to speak of other states of consciousness, ones that make us aware of another, wider world, a reality or order that is unseen. Speaking of this wider consciousness, he suggests that for some of us, some of the time, it is as if we have a *"sense of reality, a feeling of objective presence, a perception of what we may call 'something there,'"* more deep and more general than any of our particular senses can reveal. On the basis of this we sometimes speak of religious individuals possessing the objects of their belief in the form of quasi-sensible realities, directly apprehended. James points out that these "feelings" of an unseen reality are as convincing to those who have them as any direct sensible experience can be. Moreover, for those who have them, and have them strongly, the probability is that they cannot help regarding them as genuine perceptions of truth, as revelations of a kind of reality that no adverse argument, however unanswerable, can dispel (see pp. 55, 59, 66, James's emphasis).[12] Based on this, he offers, at this early stage in his study, a preliminary observation, anticipating what he will say in his concluding lecture: "Were one asked to characterize the life of religion in the broadest and most general terms possible, one might say that it consists of the belief that there is an unseen order, and that our supreme good lies in harmoniously adjusting ourselves thereto. This belief and this adjustment are the religious attitude in the soul" (p. 51).

In the next four lectures, in the context of how individuals grapple with evil, suffering, and opposition in life, James compares and contrasts what he calls "healthy-minded individuals," those who are "once-born" in terms of how they deal with the world, and "sick souls," those "twice-born" individuals whose troubled dealings with the world result in their longing to be reborn. He appears to have two primary reasons for spending as much time as he does on healthy-mindedness and on what he calls the religion of healthy-mindedness, given that after this he never returns to the subject again. In the first place, while he holds that a healthy-minded approach to the world answers real psychological needs on the part of many of us most of the time, he nevertheless concludes that this perspective is an inferior form of religiosity and is also found wanting philosophically because of its inability to come to terms with the reality of evil and suffering. Second, his detailed treatment of the religion of healthy-mindedness and his sensitive handling of its strengths and weaknesses allows him, in rather dramatic fashion, to compare and contrast this with what, in the last analysis, he considers to be the more complete form of spirituality—namely, those religious traditions (particularly Buddhism and Christianity) that answer to the needs of the sick souls of this world.

For James, it is the religion of the sick soul that ranges over the wider scale of experiences, best develops the pessimistic elements of life, and best comes to terms with the reality of evil. This form of spirituality reveals more about the human condition than any other form of religious expression. In fact, the religion of the sick soul becomes normative for James for the balance of his study. James seems personally to have identified with this type of personality. His discussion of the divided self and unification, or conversion; of the qualities of saintliness, mysticism, prayer, and other religious characteristics; and finally of his development of a general theory about religion and his thinking about God are all done in terms of this distinctive form of religiosity.

In lectures 8, 9, and 10, James again turns to the sick soul, only this time in terms of the more abstract notion of the divided self and the various ways in which such individuals achieve a radical transformation of their lives. The focus is on those experiences some have, beginning with a heightened sense of how dissatisfied they are in identifying with their present, lower (meaning inferior), divided self. This very awareness, James argues, is evidence of an apprehension on their part of a higher (meaning better) self with which they can potentially identify. For some, this transformation process continues to the point where, in fact, they are able to identify with a new, higher self and thereby overcome their prior divided state. James calls these profound personality changes "conversion" experiences. In this context, James further develops his distinction between ordinary consciousness and a wider consciousness. This distinction and his use of the concept of the subconscious play a central role in his account of conversion experiences and in what he eventually concludes about the distinctiveness and truth of religion.

While focusing on conversion experiences associated with the religion of the sick soul and by emphasizing the more involuntary and sudden changes experienced by some of these individuals in contrast to the voluntary and gradual kinds of change that others undergo, James makes a number of observations: In these cases individuals often talk as if it is their higher self—that which is emerging, that which is being "born"—that takes the lead in the transformation process. It is this higher self that is influenced by the divine; moreover, the subconscious is the means by which divine influence is experienced. Also, these individuals, more often than not, admit that the unification they have achieved—their being born anew—did not come about by reliance on their own volition or resources; rather, it was realized as a result of a self-surrender on their part, by "letting go."

In lectures 11 through 15, James deals with "Saintliness," using this term very broadly as the name for those expressions of charity, devotion, trust, patience, and bravery found in varying degrees in most religious persons. These characteristics run the gamut from the highest instances of human heroism, achievement, and sacrifice to, unfortunately, what can result when such qualities are taken to extremes—for instance, fanaticism, bigotry, self-denial, or a morbid inability to deal with the world. These five lectures, as a group, constitute a preliminary conclusion in two respects: First, James appraises the value of religion in the lives of many individuals in terms of human nature and human social development over the course of history and concludes that the "best fruits of religious experience are the best things that history has to show. . . . The saintly group of qualities is indispensable to the world's welfare" (pp. 210, 299). These individuals represent not only the genuinely strenuous life but also a more authentic life. Second, he produces a "composite photograph" of spiritual emotions common to all "saints" and "present in all religions":

> 1. A feeling of being in a wider life than that of this world's selfish little interests; and a conviction, not merely intellectual, but as it were sensible, of the existence of an Ideal Power. . . .
>
> 2. A sense of the friendly continuity of the ideal power with our own life, and a willing self-surrender to its control.
>
> 3. An immense elation and freedom, as the outlines of the confining selfhood melt down.
>
> 4. A shifting of the emotional centre towards loving and harmonious affections, towards "yes, yes," and away from "no" where the claims of the non-ego are concerned. (pp. 219–20)

These beliefs and experiences, he says, have practical consequences in the lives of religious individuals, reflected in various forms of asceticism, strength of soul, purity, and charity.

Having reached this interim conclusion, James spells out the basis upon which he will determine whether what religion claims is true. In lectures 16, 17, and 18, he deals with the phenomenon of mysticism and the role philosophy can play in better understanding and justifying religion. His chief interest in mystical experiences is whether they might form a "warrant for the truth" of that form of religion in which the sick soul is rescued through a second birth. Returning to the theme of his initial lectures, where he criticizes other approaches to the study of religion, James argues that if philosophy could shed its penchant for metaphysical speculations, for coming to conclusions in such matters on the basis of a priori definitions and deductions—what he calls instances of "high-flying speculation"—and adopt instead a method of criticism and induction, or, in other words, transform itself into what he calls a "science of religion," then real progress could be made in understanding religion. It seems evident that James sees himself doing precisely this.

In lecture 19 he deals with other characteristics of religion, chiefly prayer. For James, the genuineness of religion is indissolubly bound up with the question of whether prayerful consciousness "is or is not deceitful." The conviction that something is genuinely transacted to consciousness is at the very core of living religion.

For the most part, James confines his theoretical reflections about religion and God to his conclusions (lecture 20) and his postscript.[13] Here he sums up his major contentions: there really are multiple states of consciousness, and, on the basis of this, there is clear evidence of a wider world, an unseen reality or order, from which the visible world draws its significance. For those of us who are religious, our supreme good lies in harmoniously adjusting ourselves to this unseen reality. Prayer or inner communion with this wider world is a means by which work really is done and by which spiritual energy flows into this visible world and produces real effects, psychological and material. Those who are the beneficiaries of these influences experience a new zest for life in the form of either lyrical enchantment or an appeal to earnestness and heroism and realize an assurance of safety, a temper of peace, and a preponderance of loving affection for others. James explains how his idea of the subconscious provides an answer to how such a "harmonious adjustment" is possible, puts forth his general theory about religion and his first hypothesis about God, and argues for the truth of both. Finally, he summarizes what else he thinks we can conclude about God.

James reveals something of his own perspective in *Varieties* and something about what he personally means by God in a letter to his friend, Henry W. Rankin, written 16 June 1901, just as he was finishing the delivery of his first ten lectures at Edinburgh.

> In these lectures the ground I am taking is this: The mother sea and fountain head of all religions lie in the mystical experiences

of the individual, taking the word mystical in a very wide sense. All theologies and all ecclesiasticisms are secondary growths superimposed; and the experiences make such flexible combinations with the intellectual prepossessions of their subject, that one may almost say that they have no proper *intellectual* deliverance of their own, but belong to a region deeper, & more vital and practical, than that which the intellect inhabits. For this they are also indestructible by intellectual arguments and criticisms. I attach the mystical or religious consciousness to the possession of an extended subliminal self with a thin partition through which messages make irruption. We are thus made convincingly aware of the presence of a sphere of life larger and more powerful than our usual consciousness, with which the latter is nevertheless continuous. The impressions and impulsions and emotions and excitements which we thence receive help us to live, they found invincible assurance of a world beyond the senses, they melt our hearts and communicate significance and value to everything and make us happy. They do this for the individual who has them, and other individuals follow him. Religion in this way is absolutely indestructible. Philosophy and theology give their conceptual interpretations of this experiential life. The farther margin of the subliminal field being unknown, it can be treated as by Transcendental Idealism, as an Absolute mind with a part of which we coalesce, or by Xian [Christian] theology, as a distinct deity acting on us. Something, not our immediate self, *does* act on our life! So I seem doubtless to my audience to be blowing hot & cold, explaining away Xianity [Christianity], yet defending the more general basis from which I say it proceeds.[14]

James's General Theory about Religion

In *Varieties*, James embarks on yet another course in his ongoing effort to learn more about human nature and the human condition—hence the subtitle of the book: *A Study in Human Nature*. Among other things, he meant the subtitle to emphasize his thesis that one major function of religion is to confront us with the question of our individual destinies. As he puts it,

> The pivot round which the religious life, as we have traced it, revolves, is the interest of the individual in his private personal destiny. . . . The gods [that are] believed in—whether by crude savages or by men disciplined intellectually—agree with each other in recognizing personal calls. Religious thought is carried on in terms of personality, this being, in the world of religion, the one fundamental fact. To-day quite as much as at any previous age, the religious individual tells you that the divine meets him on the basis of his personal concerns. (p. 387)

Religion forces us to look to the future and to consider the darker aspects of life, the vulnerabilities and mysteries of life. How we experience the world is never fully determined in advance. Rather, life presents itself as a vague, undetermined, incomplete world horizon. Elemental life really is mysterious and precarious; it is our familiarity with aspects of life that blunts our sensitivity to this. The more we can understand about life, the more we might be able to understand about the divine. For James, "however particular questions connected with our individual destinies may be answered, it is only by acknowledging them as genuine questions, and living in the sphere of thought which they open up, that we become profound. But to live thus is to be religious" (p. 394).

James begins articulating his general theory about religion by asking two different kinds of questions: First, what does religion in general reveal about our individual destinies? Does it reveal anything distinct enough to be considered a general message for humankind? Put another way, what role does religion play in diagnosing the human condition? Second, could such a common message or diagnosis be true? His answer to the first set of questions is that most religions seem to agree that many individuals experience themselves in a state of uneasiness—in other words, they are divided selves. Reduced to its simplest terms, the claim is that at least for some of us, something is wrong about us as we naturally stand. Furthermore, religion claims that there is a solution to this state of uneasiness—namely, that some of these divided selves can be made whole, can be reborn. As James puts it, *"we are saved from this wrongness* by making proper connexion with higher powers" (p. 400, James's emphasis).

What this means is that such individuals, insofar as they suffer from their wrongness and criticize it, are "to that extent consciously beyond it, and in at least possible touch with something higher, if anything higher exists" (p. 400). In other words, these individuals, in sensing their own helpless state, become at the same time aware of a better, "higher part" of themselves, even if initially they are not certain whether they can identify with this higher self. Furthermore, this crucial experience is such that these individuals apprehend this higher part of themselves as being intimately related to something other than themselves, "a more of the same quality." For James, some of these individuals eventually identify their "real self" with this germinal higher part of themselves and, what is equally important, *"become conscious that this higher part is coterminous and continuous with a more of the same quality, which is operative in the universe outside of him, and which he can keep in working touch with, and in a fashion get on board of and save himself when all his lower being has gone to pieces in the wreck"* (p. 400, James's emphasis).

All the important phenomena of religious life are summed up in these general terms, according to James. They allow for the divided self and the struggle for unification or conversion; they involve the change of personal center and the surrender of one's lower self, along with an appreciation of how the new self that is born is not the old self in a new guise; they express an apprehension of the exteriority of a helping power and account for our sense of union with it; and they fully justify our newfound feelings of happiness, security, and peace.

James admits that, up to this point, he has been dealing only with psychological phenomena. "They possess, it is true, enormous biological worth. Spiritual strength really increases in the subject when he has them, a new life opens for him, and they seem to him a place of conflux where the forces of two universes meet; and yet this may be nothing but his subjective way of feeling things, a mood of his own fancy, in spite of the effects produced" (p. 401).

The question is, what, if anything, is true about such experiences? When James turns to this question, he turns from consideration of the psychological and even biological makeup and function of religious experiences to the purported object of religious experience. In an important footnote at this juncture in his argument, he points out that he is using the term *truth* in this context to mean something *in addition to* the value for life that religion brings (see p. 401 n. 23). In other words, while an appeal to the psychological and biological consequences for life resulting from religious experiences is of vital importance, it is not sufficient to settle the question of the truth of such matters. Hence, James relies on what he calls his "reconciling hypothesis," one, he argues, that stands beyond the differences existing among competing religious claims and yet is, at the same time, sufficiently in accord with the facts not to be dismissed out of hand. He puts forth his hypothesis, speaking very broadly and intentionally using the vague term *the more* to make reference to what he earlier called "the wider world, the unseen reality or order, the divine." He is convinced his general theory can provide an explanation of religion that will explain matters, fit the facts, and yet not go beyond the evidence. The central questions are, "Is such a 'more' merely our own notion or does it really exist? If so, in what shape does it exist? Does it act, as well as exist? And in what form should we conceive of that 'union' with it of which religious geniuses are so convinced?" (p. 401).

These are the kinds of questions that all religions ask. Nearly all religious persons agree that "the more" exists. Some claim that it exists as a personal god or gods; some conceive of it as an ideal tendency embedded in the eternal structure of the world. Nearly all agree that it acts as well as exists and that something real is effected when we throw our life into its hands. It is when "union" with this unseen reality is described that speculative differences begin to surface. And it is on this important point that James thinks his general theory can be expressed and defended without having to introduce any "over-beliefs"—his label for thoughts and ideas about the divine.

What is needed, James maintains, is a "definite description" into which terms like *the more* and our *union* with it can be translated. He obviously wants to avoid using the language of a particular religious tradition and turns to more neutral terms borrowed from psychology. The key concept here is the subconscious. He notes it is a well-accredited psychological entity; it is exactly the mediating notion he needs. James's thesis implies that the phenomena of prayer, mystical consciousness, and conversion can all be understood as "invasions" from the subconscious, which itself stands under influences emanating from an unseen reality or order—a wider world. His reconciling hypothesis amounts to the following: "whatever it may be on its *farther* side, the 'more' with which in religious experience we feel ourselves connected is on its *hither* side the subconscious continuation of our conscious life" (p. 403, James's emphasis).

James thinks this explanation has the advantage of providing a means for recognizing the insights of science—namely, the acknowledgment of the subconscious as a psychological fact, something comparable religious explanations often lack. At the same time, it vindicates the religious person's conviction that in these experiences he is influenced by an external power. Invasions from the subconscious region are experienced by the religious person as encounters with that which is objective to him and suggests an external cause, if not control. Moreover, his hypothesis highlights the fact that since, in the religious life, such control is experienced as "higher" and since, on the basis of this explanation, it is primarily the higher faculties of our own hidden self—of our new emerging higher self—that are doing the controlling, we can conclude that "the sense of union with the power beyond us is a sense of something, not merely apparently, but literally true" (p. 403).

To open this particular door on the subject, James argues, is really all that such a general theory can do. If we were to step through the door and begin to talk in any detail about the nature and meaning of "the more," we would, in effect, leave the field of theory formation and verification behind. Short of this, James concludes that "Disregarding the over-beliefs, and confining ourselves to what is common and generic, we have in *the fact that the conscious person is continuous with a wider self through which saving experiences come,* a positive content of religious experience, which, it seems to me, *is literally and objectively true as far as it goes*" (p. 405, James's emphasis). As it turns out, James thinks the testimony of religious experience can support one additional hypothesis, this time explicitly about God. I will turn to this next.

James on God

The linchpin that holds James's general theory about religion together is his account of how some of us experience God. Earlier, in *The Will to Believe,* he raised the same issue—how can we portray our sense of being intimately related to God without lapsing into a view that implies we are somehow identified with God? At that time he argued, largely on conceptual grounds, that "anything more than God is impossible," meaning that any view of our union with God that interprets such in a strict ontological sense is impossible. In *Varieties,* James arrives essentially at the same conclusion, but now he establishes his point on experiential grounds—on the basis of how we experience that which we take to be the divine. He thinks, as a psychologist, that it is not possible to say more about the object of religious experience than that "whatever it may be on its *farther* side, the 'more' with which in religious experience we feel ourselves connected is on its *hither* side the subconscious continuation of our conscious life" (p. 403, James's emphasis). To claim anything more about the farther side of God is to rely on one's over-beliefs.

Speaking of over-beliefs, James points out how, for instance, mysticism, Vedantism, and transcendental idealism all put forth various monistic interpretations of how we are or become one with God, while other religious traditions defend alternative views. If we follow any one particular theological or philosophical view, we do so for a host of reasons, not the least of which is because we find such beliefs to be particularly compelling. Such over-beliefs, James says, are absolutely indispensable to one's religion. Because of this we should always treat them with deference and tolerance. "The most interesting and valuable things about a man are usually his over-beliefs" (p. 405).

At this point James puts forth another hypothesis—that God is real. This time he labels it as one of his own over-beliefs. He returns to his earlier contention that, on occasion, the further limits of our consciousness plunge us into a dimension of reality altogether different from the sensible and merely "understandable" world. Such experiences absolutely overthrow the pretension of our ordinary or rationalistic states of consciousness to be the sole and ultimate dictator of what we may believe. Indeed, he argues that these other states of consciousness may prove to be superior points of view, windows through which the mind looks out upon a more extensive and wider world, "other orders of truth" to which we can respond in faith. And to the extent that our ideal impulses have their origin in this wider world, we belong to this world as well, since we belong in the most intimate sense possible wherever our ideals belong (see p. 406).[15] Furthermore, whenever we relate with this wider world, whenever we communicate with it, something really happens: work is done on our personalities, we are reborn, and real consequences follow in terms of how we conduct our lives and how we relate to others and to the world.

Then, on the grounds that that which produces real effects within another reality must be deemed a reality itself, James concludes that this wider world—God, if you will—is real. One of the consequences that follow from this is that, as James puts it, "we and God have business with each other." In opening ourselves to God's influence, we fulfill our deepest destiny. The world takes a turn for the better or the worse depending on whether or not we fulfill or evade God's demands.

James then calls attention to another important consequence. While these real effects manifest themselves in the lives of individuals, their influence extends far beyond this. Religious individuals believe that they and the whole universe of beings to whom God is present are "secure in his parental hands." That is, God's existence is the guarantor of an ideal order that shall be permanently preserved. This world may be destroyed; but if it is part of an ideal order, the ideal will be brought to fruition so that where God is, tragedy is only provisional, only partial. Shipwreck and dissolution, in other words, are not the final end of things (see p. 407). For James, only when this broader perspective is taken, only when this added step of faith concerning God is taken, only when remote, objective results are predicted can religion be freed from being viewed as merely a cluster of immediate firsthand experiences and begin to be seen as an approach to the world that makes a real difference, one that makes real claims about the way things are. If we view God only as that which enters into the religious individual's experience of union with something higher than himself, then our view of deity is too small, too limited. To acknowledge God as the preserver of ideal values and as that which is incorporated into wider cosmic relations is really another way of saying that religion, functioning at its highest level, is not merely an illumination of facts already given elsewhere; it is not merely a passionate dimension of life that views things in a rosier light and has God as its object. It is all of these things, but it is much more! Religion, understood in this sense, postulates new facts. The world interpreted religiously is not the natural world taken over again. It is the world with something added—a world constituted differently, with different events, and requiring different conduct on our part. This view of religion is what we ordinarily mean by the term. This is the common man's practical view of religion. Only philosophers and theologians think that they can make nature divine without adding any concrete detail to it and merely by calling it an expression of absolute spirit.

James believes that this practical, "pragmatic" way of viewing religion is the deeper view. "It gives it body as well as soul, it makes it claim, as everything real must claim, some characteristic realm of fact as its very own" (p. 408). And while he is not certain what the other characteristics of God may turn out to be, he is confident that

> The whole drift of my education goes to persuade me that the world of our present consciousness is only one out of many worlds of consciousness that exist, and that those other worlds must contain experiences which have a meaning for our life also; and that although in the main their experiences and those of this world keep discrete, yet the two become continuous at certain points, and higher energies filter in. By being faithful in my poor measure to this over-belief, I seem to myself to keep more sane and true. . . . Assuredly, the real world is of a different temperament—more intricately built than physical science allows. So my objective and my subjective conscious both hold me to the over-belief which I express. Who knows whether the faithfulness of individuals here below to their own poor over-beliefs may not actually help God in turn to be more effectively faithful to his own greater tasks? (p. 408)

But James, having come to the conclusion that God is real, does not let the matter rest. In his postscript, he steps further through the door he opened earlier and, while telling us more about where he is coming from, reveals some of his own over-beliefs about God.

James is intuitively suspicious of those who speculate about God—particularly those who come to conclusions about God based on a priori definitions and deductions and who, on the basis of this, work out full-fledged and elaborate theologies. Therefore, it is not surprising to find that in proceeding down this path he is cautious and speaks in a tentative, measured way. What he is confident about is that lives can be changed for the better. Furthermore, he is convinced that in some instances these changes come about precisely because individuals experience an unseen reality, an Ideal Power, something other than themselves with which they can be intimately related and in which they "find their greatest peace." Initially, all James was willing to say about God is that he is real because he produces real effects in individuals' lives. Now he ventures to say more about God, but only on the basis of what can be inferred from how individuals experience the divine and the differences these experiences make in terms of how they relate to others and the world.

If all thinkers were divided into the two classes of naturalists and supernaturalists, James tells us he would place himself among the supernaturalists. And then among this group, he would classify himself as a "piecemeal" or "crass" supernaturalist, thereby differentiating himself from those he calls "refined" supernaturalists. The latter acknowledge the reality of the ideal but bar it from interfering causally in the real world. According to this view, the ideal is not a world of facts, but of meanings only. It is a point of view for judging facts. In this view, no divine aid comes as a result of prayer; furthermore, this position too easily lapses back into a naturalism. It takes the claims of the physical sciences at face value. It leaves the laws of life as naturalism finds them, with no hope of remedy. It confines itself to sentiments *about life* as a *whole*—sentiments which, while admirable and adoring, need not be so, as evidenced by numerous pessimistic points of view. In other words, refined supernaturalists require that, for all intents and purposes, we dispense with practical religion. When proponents of this view conclude that "perhaps the best thing we can say about God is that he is the Inevitable Inference," James observes that many individuals are more than willing to let such views of religion and deity simply evaporate. Would any martyrs "have sung in the flames for a mere inference, however inevitable it might be?" James asks. Religious personalities, like Saint Francis or Luther, James reminds us, "have usually been enemies of the intellect's pretension to meddle with religious things" (p. 396 n. 10). Indeed, for James, it is strange how, following the lead of refined supernaturalists, we define God as one who "can raise no particular weight whatever, who can help us with no private burden, and who is on the side of our enemies as much as he is on our own. Odd evolution from the God of David's psalms!" (p. 410 n. 1).[16]

This view of God comes about because refined supernaturalists demand that no concrete particular of experience should alter God's nature; that God be viewed as relating to the world only en bloc, not in particular; and, in James's happy phrase, that God be understood as doing "only a wholesale, not a retail business." The obvious question is, what would it mean for something to exist that makes no difference in our world? Our whole interest in the question of whether God exists lies in what difference this would make in our lives. To illustrate his point, James calls attention to the Buddhist idea that all facts are under judgment of higher laws. Buddhists and other average religious individuals, he says, do not interpret the word *judgment* in an academic way. For them, judgment carries "*execution* with it, is *in rebus* as well as *post rem,* and operates 'causally' as partial factor in the total fact" (p. 411, James's emphasis). For James, judgment and execution do indeed go hand in hand. The only way the largest number of legitimate religious requirements are going to be met will be in terms of a piecemeal supernaturalism. In taking this position, James clearly sees himself in the minority and feels like a man who must set his back against an open door to prevent it from being slammed shut.

In answer to the question of what particular differences result from the fact of God's existence, James calls attention first to what prayerful communion immediately suggests—something ideal, which in one sense is part of ourselves but in another sense is not ourselves, which actually exerts influence, raises our center of personal energy, and produces regenerative effects unattained in other ways. "At these places at least, I say, it would seem as though transmundane energies, God, if you will, produced immediate effects within the natural world to which the rest of our experience belongs" (p. 412).

Another difference is personal immortality. James readily admits, "Religion, in fact, for the great majority . . . *means* immortality, and nothing else" (p. 412, James's emphasis), but he leaves this topic aside, focusing, instead, on yet another difference—on whether or not God must be viewed as infinite. In raising this issue, James moves further in the direction of spelling out some of the implications of his practical theism. He acknowledges that it is not uncommon to speak of God as the "one and only" and to conceive of God as being infinite. Yet, he asks, where is the warrant for jumping to this conclusion? "Religious experience, as we have studied it, cannot be cited as unequivocally supporting the infinitist belief" (p. 413). The only thing that religious experience unequivocally testifies to is that "we can experience union with *something* larger than ourselves and in that union find our greatest peace" (p. 413, James's emphasis). It is only various philosophical, theological, and, in particular, mystical schools of thought that immediately infer that God must be infinite, the all-inclusive soul of the world.

The practical needs and experiences of most religious individuals, James argues, are sufficiently met by a limited, qualified view of God or, in other words, a practical theism—a belief that beyond each of us and in a fashion continuous with us a larger power or self exists that is friendly to us and our ideals. On the basis of how we experience ourselves in the world and what we know about religious experience, all that is required for many of us is that God be viewed as greater than ourselves, not necessarily as infinite and certainly not as absolute. "All that the facts require is that the power should be both other and larger than our conscious selves. Anything larger will do, if only it be large enough to trust for the next step. It need not be infinite, it need not be solitary" (p. 413).

But James goes even further and suggests that God might conceivably be only a larger and more godlike self, of which our present self would then be but a mutilated expression. In fact, the universe might conceivably be a collection of such larger selves, of different degrees of inclusiveness, with no absolute unity realized in it at all—in which case, James readily admits, we would have a sort of polytheism. He does not, on this occasion, defend this view, but only suggests that such a conclusion, such a "pluralistic hypothesis," is in keeping with the testimony of religious experience. In fact, most people, according to James, view God in this polytheistic sort of way. Those who believe in the absolute or require that God be viewed as infinite argue that unless there is one, all-inclusive God, our guarantee of security is left imperfect. Only in the infinite are all saved. And following this view, if there are different gods, each caring for a part, then some portion of us may not be covered with divine protection, and our religious consolation might fail to be complete. But this is precisely the claim that James is calling into question. His position is that the way we experience the world suggests that, indeed, portions of it may not be saved. Common sense has always been content with the notion of a partially saved world. At this point, he puts forth a variation on the position he took earlier in dealing with the reality of evil.

Just as it may prove, James argues, that some instances of evil are simply gratuitous, that portions of the universe may irretrievably be lost, and that because of this the problem of evil calls for a practical, not a speculative solution, so likewise with God: it may prove that, for most of us, God is best viewed as that which is other than infinite.

In his lecture on the "sick soul," James deals briefly with implications that follow from acknowledging the reality of evil and suffering. In the course of this, he outlines his distinctive approach to the issue. To begin with, James observes that whenever theism is erected into a systematic philosophical position, not only is God inevitably seen as the All-in-All, but the logic of the position requires its advocates to hold that evil, like everything else, has its foundation in God, with all the attendant problems of reconciling this requirement with the companion notion that God be viewed as absolutely good. For James, cast in these terms, the reality of evil becomes a speculative issue, one that seems to have no possible resolution. And since this irreconcilable dilemma came about in the first place because of the monistic assumptions upon which the position is founded, why not, James asks, cut loose from these presuppositions altogether and allow that the world has existed from its beginnings in pluralistic form, "as an aggregate or collection of higher and lower things and principles, rather than an absolutely unitary fact?" If one were to adopt this pluralistic point of view and still hold to the position that evil is real, he would necessarily face the possibility that some elements of the universe make no rational sense at all—that there are evils that are not instrumental to any higher goods, that cannot be rationally explained at all, and that must be treated as so "much irrelevance and accident—so much 'dirt,' as it were, and matter out of place." This is what James means when he speaks of "gratuitous" evil and of having to face the fact that such realities can only be dealt with practically and not speculatively or theoretically. According to James, this is precisely what the ordinary religious person does: he confronts evil on a piecemeal, one-step-at-a-time, practical basis; and this is also why, for most of us, God need not be viewed as the All-in-All but merely as that which is larger and more powerful than ourselves and our circumstances, that which is large enough to trust for the next step (see pp. 112–14).

Aspects of James's distinctive view of God are scattered throughout the entire range of his writings, and one would need to review all of them in order to get a full picture of his practical theism.[17] In *Varieties,* in addition to establishing to his satisfaction that God is real, James's view of God comes down to the following: When we speak of salvation, most of us seem to imply that this is a situation conditional upon the success with which each of us does our part—who knows whether our faithfulness to our own over-beliefs here below "may not actually help God in turn to be more effectively faithful to his own greater tasks?" Partial, conditional salvation is most familiar in the abstract. The difficulty comes in working out the details. The important point for James is that some seem willing to be among the unsaved remnant, if only they can be persuaded that their ideals and their cause will prevail, if only they have a chance of salvation.

We gain an added appreciation of how James came to these views on God by considering whether or not such a God can function as an appropriate object of religious worship. While James does not explicitly deal with this issue in these terms, his treatment of what he takes to be the distinctive characteristics of religious attitudes, plus his claim about the only conditions under which worshipful activities such as prayer can be said to be meaningful, contributes to the position he takes on the question of God.

The Religious Availability of James's Practical Theism

At one point in *Varieties,* James anticipates what could be called a "religious" objection to his practical theism. He acknowledges that many ordinary people, as well as theologians and philosophers, assume God to be "one and only" and infinite, and he admits that "hardly anyone thinks it worth while to consider, and still less to uphold," any other view of God (pp. 412–13).

H. P. Owen, for instance, summarizes the issue well in his study of ideas about deity: "Although the concept of a finite God can satisfy some it cannot satisfy other elements in religion. Thus while it permits us to regard God as Friend and Helper it has no room for the theistic (and in particular the Judeo-Christian) experience of him as a self-existent mystery on whom we are absolutely dependent and who merits our complete devotion."[18] And the British philosopher J. N. Findlay, in his celebrated attempt to disprove the existence of God, argues that reflection on the nature of religious attitudes leads "irresistibly" toward a view of God as that which is unsurpassable in every respect.[19] Only a being that far exceeds human levels of power, wisdom, love, and other respected qualities would be an appropriate object of the deference, awe, and devotion involved in religious worship. But Findlay goes even further. It would be "wholly anomalous to worship anything *limited* in any thinkable manner." This is because all limited superiorities are "tainted with an obvious relativity, and can be dwarfed in thought by still mightier superiorities, in which process of being dwarfed they lose their claim upon our worshipful attitudes." A worthy object of worship "can never be a thing that merely *happens* to exist, nor one on which all other objects merely *happen* to depend. . . . And not only must the existence of *other* things be unthinkable without him, but his own non-existence must be wholly unthinkable in any circumstances." The only possible adequate object of worship, following this view, "should have an *unsurpassable* supremacy along all avenues; . . . it should tower *infinitely* above all other objects."[20]

According to these authorities, a qualified or limited view of God is ruled out as religiously unavailable. James's idea of God, following this line of reasoning, may have certain theoretical strengths but is surely inadequate to the demands of religious worship. This conclusion rests, in large measure, on a particular understanding of attitudes of religious worship, and it is precisely on this issue that James takes exception to prevailing views. If, following James, we understand what is distinctive about religious attitudes differently, it ensues that a different view of God may well count as a worthy object of religious worship.

James and Findlay may agree that attitudes presume certain characteristics in their objects and that the presence or absence of these characteristics is a crucial determinant of the appropriateness of an attitude in any given instance. Still, their respective positions on God and religious attitudes could not be further apart. Comparing James and Findlay on these two subjects is worthwhile.

Findlay's thinking on these matters is particularly clear. His rendition of what constitutes appropriate attitudes of religious worship is straightforward. He builds on this and, as we have pointed out, argues that only a being that exists necessarily is fit to be worshiped. However, since modern-day thinking rejects the idea of necessary existence as senseless or impossible, we are forced, according to this authority, to conclude that the only appropriate object of religious worship does not exist.[21] For different reasons, as indicated below, James also objects to attributing necessary existence to God; but because he understands religious attitudes differently, it does not follow for him that God does not exist.

"We might say," Findlay observes, "that a religious attitude was one in which we tended to abase ourselves before some object, to defer to it wholly, to devote ourselves to it with unquestioning enthusiasm, to bend the knee before it, whether literally or metaphorically." Findlay takes this to be a "perfectly plain" and universally accepted idea of worship; what it emphasizes is the sense of awe and contrition the worshiper feels in the presence of that which towers over him. Such attitudes emphasize our sense of unworthiness in the presence of the "wholly other." The same religious attitude that presumes overwhelming superiority in its object of worship also reduces us, "who feel the attitudes, to comparative nothingness."[22] In other words, for Findlay, what is most characteristic of religious attitudes are feelings and expressions of self-effacement.

James likewise describes religious attitudes in reference to the object of worship. All our attitudes, he says, are due to the "objects" of our consciousness—the things we believe to exist, whether really or ideally, along with ourselves (see p. 51). And while James and Findlay describe such attitudes in reference to our sense of dependence upon God, which manifests itself in the forms of sacrifice and self-surrender, once we learn how James is using such terms, the divergence of their positions becomes clear. For James, the central characteristic of religious attitudes is not one of self-effacement but rather a higher emotion or type of happiness, one that results from the relationship that we experience with the divine and one that reflects our newfound sense of self.

For James, even the simplest healthy-minded type of religious consciousness evidences this complex sacrificial attitude in which a higher happiness holds a lower happiness in check, while at the other extreme are those whose sacrificial attitudes take on "monstrously ascetic forms." James grants that there are those sick souls who literally feed on the negative principle, on humiliation and privation, on thoughts of suffering and death. Their souls grow in happiness in proportion to the worsening of their outward state. But it is only at what James calls the "fanatical" end of the spectrum that we see instances of full-fledged self-abasement reflected in religious attitudes.

James acknowledges, along with Findlay, that what counts as religious attitudes has much to do with determining the kind of object that we worship. What he has learned from his study of religion and what Findlay seems not to appreciate is that the whole phenomenon is more complex than any single formula will allow or any single description will portray. There really is a *variety* of religious experiences, and the divine "can mean no single quality, it must mean a group of qualities, by being champion of which in alternation different men will find worthy missions." Each attitude, James says, is a

> syllable in human nature's total message, it takes the whole of us to spell the meaning out completely. So a "god of battles" must be allowed to be the god for one kind of person, a god of peace and heaven and home, the god for another. We must frankly recognize the fact that we live in partial systems, and that parts are not interchangeable in the spiritual life. . . . If we are sick souls, we require a religion of deliverance; but why think so much of deliverance, if we are healthy-minded? (pp. 384–85)

The important lesson James draws from this is needed as much today as it was in his day. Without question, some individuals seem to have broader experiences and higher vocations in the religious realm just as they do in the social world. What each of us must do is to stay within our own view of the world, whatever it may be, and tolerate others in their respective positions.

For James, a person's religious attitudes may range from moods of sadness to moods of gladness, from experiences of fear to expressions of joy. Nevertheless, he thinks it is possible to isolate what is distinctive about religious attitudes. This he does by distinguishing the religious life from the moral life. Both religion and morality, as forms of life, are concerned with the manner of our acceptance of the world. After all is said and done, we are, in the end, absolutely dependent on the world and must perform some sort of acts of sacrifice and surrender to it. The moral response is reflected in attitudes of manliness, stoic resignation, and philosophical objectivity. Such a person, James says, can contemplate whatever ideal aspects of existence his philosophy is able to present to him and can practice whatever duties—such as patience, resignation, and trust—that his ethical system requires. Such a person lives on the loftiest, largest plane. He is a high-hearted freeman and no pining slave. The moral acceptance of the world requires that the individual hold his ground, that he exert himself in withstanding evil and opposition.

But, James reminds us, in the face of illness, when the prospect of death looms large, or when we are beset with morbid fears arising from a sense of powerlessness or the failure of our purposes, this attitude inevitably breaks down. On such occasions, what the person craves "is to be consoled in his very powerlessness, to feel that the spirit of the universe recognizes and secures him, all decaying and failing as he is" (p. 45). And to have these cravings satisfied is an absolutely distinctive feature of the religious life. Where the moralistic stance relies on our efforts to exert ourselves, James says, the religious stance results from a higher kind of emotion in the presence of which we no longer feel as if we are on our own.

> There is a state of mind, known to religious men, but to no others, in which the will to assert ourselves and hold our own has been displaced by a willingness to close our mouths and be as nothing in the floods and waterspouts of God. In this state of mind, what we most dreaded has become the habitation of our safety, and the hour of our moral death has turned into our spiritual birthday. The time for tension in our soul is over, and that of happy relaxation, of calm deep breathing, of an eternal present, with no discordant future to be anxious about, has arrived. Fear is not held in abeyance as it is by mere morality, it is positively expunged and washed away. (p. 46)

What we need to appreciate, James says, is that while morality requires us to exert ourselves and hold our own in order to achieve our goals, religion, at least for some of us, somehow enables us to obtain similar ends not by holding on but by letting go. For some, at the very moment when all seems lost, they find they have been saved from their desperate straits. They experience a higher kind of emotion, in the presence of which no exertion of volition is required. Indeed, they experience a new life. They are reborn.

James does not know how this attitude is achieved; it is religion's secret. It is enough for him to conclude that because of this we can properly speak of religion as an infinitely passionate thing. Like love, wrath, hope, ambition, or jealousy, religion adds an enchantment to life, an enchantment that comes as a gift but is an absolute addition to the subject's life. It gives the recipient a new sphere of power; it redeems and vivifies his interior world when the outer world disowns him. "If religion is to mean anything definite," James concludes,

> it seems to me that we ought to take it as meaning this added dimension of emotion, this enthusiastic temper of espousal, in regions where morality strictly so called can at best but bow its head and acquiesce. It ought to mean nothing short of this new reach of freedom for us, with the struggle over, the keynote of the universe sounding in our ears, and everlasting possession spread before our eyes. (pp. 46–47)

This happy state of mind is what we find only in religion. It is distinguished from other forms of happiness by the characteristic of solemnity. "A solemn state of mind is never crude or simple—it seems to contain a certain measure of its own opposite in solution. A solemn joy preserves a sort of bitter in its sweetness; a solemn sorrow is one to which we intimately consent" (p. 47). James associates more commonplace expressions of happiness with the "reliefs" most of us feel when we experience life as a series of momentary respites, resulting from time and again being able to avoid confronting evil and suffering. But in its most distinctive embodiments, religious happiness is no mere feeling of escape (contrary to the teachings of Freud and others). The genuinely religious person does not escape from life but confronts evil and opposition outwardly, as a form of sacrifice, precisely because inwardly he knows them to be permanently overcome. For James, in those states of mind that fall short of religion, attitudes of self-surrender are submitted to as an imposition of necessity, and acts of sacrifice are undergone at the very best without complaint. But for the religious person, sacrifice and surrender are positively espoused, and even unnecessary sacrifices are made in order that happiness may increase. *"Religion thus makes easy and felicitous what in any case is necessary"* (p. 49, James's emphasis).

A major focus of James's interpretation of religious attitudes is the awareness individuals have of being intimately related to the divine; this awareness is expressed particularly in prayer, taken in the broadest sense to mean every kind of inward communion or conversation with the divine. "Prayer in this wide sense is the very soul and essence of religion" (p. 365). The genuineness of religion is thus indissolubly bound up with the question of whether prayerful consciousness is or is not deceitful.

> The conviction that something is genuinely transacted in this consciousness is the very core of living religion. As to what is transacted, great differences of opinion have prevailed. The unseen powers have been supposed, and are yet supposed, to do things which no enlightened man can nowadays believe in. It may well prove that the sphere of influence in prayer is subjective exclusively, and that what is immediately changed is only the mind of the praying person. But however our opinion of prayer's effects may come to be limited by criticism, *religion, in the vital sense in which these lectures study it, must stand or fall by the persuasion that effects of some sort genuinely do occur.* Through prayer, religion insists, things which cannot be realized in any other manner come about: energy which but for prayer would be bound is by prayer set free and operates in some part, be it objective or subjective, of the world of facts. (p. 367, emphasis added)

What are we to make of these two descriptions of religious attitudes? What implications follow from taking self-effacement as the central element in the complex of religious attitudes? Why Findlay emphasizes this feature seems clear enough: it follows from his insistence that the only possible object of religious worship is God viewed as a necessary being.[23] The trouble is, a literal rendering of the notion of complete self-abasement or total deference to God would result in there being no "self" to show devotion. Even a metaphorical rendering of the idea of being reduced to "comparative nothingness" suggests that selfhood is diminished; and, as David Mason puts it, "the notion of glorifying some object by abasing ourselves, while common enough, is not merely a kind of specious humility, but bad logic. It simply does not follow that we can add to another's value by detracting from our own."[24] What would it mean to suggest that God is glorified by my demeaning myself?

The real dilemma for Findlay is that he presumes it is meaningful to speak of ourselves as "nothing," to abase ourselves in reference to God, in the context of viewing God as a necessary being. By definition, such a God depends on nothing outside of himself: he has no needs, his existence and nature are unconditioned, and nothing we do can influence him. But if this is the case, what could it possibly mean to speak of self-effacement given that this notion, in turn, relies upon the presumption that what we do can influence God? When, on occasion, we speak of ourselves as "nothing before God," we could be acknowledging how far we have strayed from God as one who forgives and whose love is without limit. Speaking this way, to paraphrase Mason, need not be taken to mean that we literally view ourselves as worthless. Rather, it could be another way of saying that we realize that we have, in various ways, broken or violated our relationship with God, that we have endeavored to establish ourselves apart from God, knowing all the while that only by being in closer relationship with God are we enhanced. Using such language could be an awareness on our part, however dimly felt, that we can never stray completely from God and so can never totally obliterate our selfhood.[25]

This alternative way of using the language of self-effacement rests on a view of God as a being with whom we can be intimately related, one to whom it makes sense to pray and whose forgiveness is worth seeking. On this view, basic religious attitudes need not require that the object of worship be in all ways necessary—quite the contrary: the attitudes that form the heart of religious worship emerge out of experiencing God as a being with whom we are genuinely related. And this requires that the object of worship be qualified or limited in some sense. This is James's position.

Furthermore, for James, the proper object of religious worship is not merely an ideal, but a reality, one that produces real effects in the world and is, in turn, affected by how we respond. "Who knows whether the faithfulness of individuals here below to their own poor over-beliefs may not actually help God in turn to be more effectively faithful to his own greater task?" (p. 408). All that religious experience unequivocally testifies to, according to James, is that we can, on occasion, experience a relationship or union with something larger than ourselves and in that union find our greatest peace. All we need infer from this is that God be viewed as larger and other than our conscious selves—large enough to "trust for the next step," large enough to make possible "a chance of salvation."

However, following Findlay, if God towers "*infinitely* above all other objects" and if it is "wholly anomalous to worship anything *limited* in any thinkable manner,"[26] not only does it make no sense to speak of self-effacement, but we are forced to conclude that on this view there is "such an unbridgeable gap between the object and the worshiper that it is impossible for there to be a genuine relationship" between one who prays and the object of his prayers.[27] But if this is the case, then a whole range of concepts such as trust, love, gratitude, repentance, filial piety, and even fear becomes meaningless when spoken of in reference to God. Praise, petitions, thanksgivings, appeals for forgiveness—all such expressions are appropriately directed only toward a being who is neither completely ineffable nor completely transcendent to us.[28] Whatever the merits of Findlay's criticism of the necessary existence of God, he does not seem to appreciate how his criticism of this concept bears on his portrayal of religious attitudes. Those who adopt Findlay's position would appear to face two seemingly untenable alternatives: either disparage as idolaters all religious believers who worship anything less than a necessary being or dismiss those who do worship such a god as engaging in meaningless activity. In any event, it is hard to envision how Findlay's view of deity and his corresponding view of self-effacement as the central element in the complex of religious attitudes can be said to be religiously available.[29]

James, on the other hand, focuses instead on how the idea of God functions in the lives of common religious believers. On the basis of this, he defends the position that the real religious needs of such individuals, as evidenced by what they do in prayer and in other acts of worship and as reflected in the various attitudes they assume, are more than met by a belief that, beyond each of us and in a fashion continuous with us, there exists a larger power or self that is friendly to us and our ideals. On the basis of how we experience ourselves in the world and what we know about religious experience, all that is required—at least for many of us—is that God be viewed as greater than ourselves, not necessarily as infinite or as the absolute. "All that the facts require is that the power should be both other and larger than our conscious selves. Anything larger will do, if only large enough to trust for the next step. It need not be infinite, it need not be solitary" (p. 413).

In his lecture on philosophy, James deals briefly with classical philosophical theism.[30] He lists some of the metaphysical characteristics traditionally attributed to God—not only his necessary existence but also his aseity (independent origination), immateriality, simplicity, indivisibility, and so on—and asks what possible difference these characteristics can make to a person's religious life, whether or not they are true. These attributes, he says, are the result of a mere "shuffling and matching of pedantic dictionary-adjectives, aloof from morals, aloof from human needs, something that might be worked out from the mere word 'God' by one of those logical machines of wood and brass." Indeed, he dismisses talk of God in these terms as having "the trail of the serpent over them. . . . Instead of bread we have a stone; instead of a fish, a serpent" (p. 352). What keeps religion going, James says, is something other than abstract definitions and systems of concatenated adjectives, something different from faculties of theology and their professors. "All these things are after-effects, secondary accretions upon those phenomena of vital conversation with the unseen divine, of which I have shown you so many instances, renewing themselves *in saecula saeculorum* in the lives of humble private men" (p. 352).

James is more open to the so-called "moral" attributes of God, but only because he interprets them in his own distinctive way. God's holiness, he says, means that God can will only that which is good; his omnipotence means that he can secure the triumph of good over evil; his omniscience means that he can discern our true nature and character; his justice means that he will punish us for what he sees; his love means that he will pardon us as well; and his immutability means that we can count on him securely. These attributes have value, James points out, precisely because they enter into our lives. Still, he questions the utility of talking about God in these terms for the following reason: What dogmatic theology represents is an attempt to transcend the sphere of individual feelings and direct experiences of the divine and to establish religion on the footing of impartial reason. Such efforts attempt to make religion universal by coercive reasoning and, in the process, to transform it from a private faith into a public certainty. They attempt to rescue its affirmations and private revelations from obscurity and mystery and make them transparent and public. But in James's viewpoint, this will never work, precisely because

What religion reports . . . always purports to be a fact of experience: the divine is actually present, religion says, and between it and ourselves relations of give and take are actual. If definite perceptions of fact like this cannot stand upon their own feet, surely abstract reasoning cannot give them the support they are in need of. Conceptual processes can class facts, define them, interpret them; but they do not produce them, nor can they reproduce their individuality. There is always a *plus,* a *thisness,* which feeling alone can answer for. Philosophy in this sphere is thus a secondary function, unable to warrant faith's veracity. . . .

. . . I think we must conclude that the attempt to demonstrate by purely intellectual processes the truth of the deliverances of direct religious experience is absolutely hopeless. (pp. 358–59, emphasis added)

The book of Job laid out this whole issue ages ago, according to James. "An intellect perplexed and baffled, yet a trustful sense of presence—such is the situation of the man who is sincere with himself and with the facts, but who remains religious still" (p. 353).

To compare James and Findlay on the subject of religious worship reveals significant differences of opinion, even at the level of description. It also points out the fact that to hold, as Findlay does, that the essential characteristic of religious attitudes is an expression of self-effacement and to contend that this interpretation is universally acceptable is simply not the case. Among the possible interpretations of religious attitudes, many would not identify self-effacement as the essential element. Findlay's view on religious attitudes and God seems, by all accounts, far removed from the world of real religious concerns, while James's emphasis on a higher type of emotion and happiness—a revivified and redirected sense of self, and the view of God that they imply—seems to be fully available. James, in other words, makes a strong case for the claim that his view of deity can indeed function as an appropriate object of religious worship in the lives of many individuals.

For James, a look at the religious life as it is really lived, and not as it is portrayed theoretically by theologians and philosophers, reveals that these kinds of experiences amount to an expression of hope, a different way of being in the world, one that relies upon a genuine chance of salvation. "No fact in human nature," James concludes, "is more characteristic than its willingness to live on a chance" (p. 414). And no assessment of the human condition is more characteristic of James's position than this—the reality of a chance of salvation, which translates into a belief in the reality of God as that which is other than the absolute or infinite and "through which saving experiences come," is what makes the difference between a life in which the keynote is hope and one in which the keynote is resignation.

Summary Observations

Because James cast his net as wide as he did in assembling his examples of religious experiences from both Western and Eastern cultures; because of the imaginative selections he made of this material, coupled with the vivid descriptions he offered of these accounts; and because of the insightful theoretical claims he made about religion in general, God, and a host of other subjects, *Varieties* has proven to be a classic. As John E. Smith observes, many writers have come to the conclusion that "whatever views we may hold concerning religion or James's interpretation of the cases he cited, the sorts of experiences he described represent the essential facts to be dealt with."[31]

As I have summarized in this paper, James chose to focus on what he called the "religion of the sick soul"—those troubled and divided selves who long for deliverance and in many instances do achieve a rebirth. He coupled his empathetic portrayal of these individuals and their experiences with his conviction that there is an unseen reality, and he put forth his theory that those who achieve a second birth do so by identifying with their higher self—

by becoming conscious that they are coterminous with an unseen presence, a "more" of the same quality with which they can get on board and save themselves when their lower self has gone to pieces in the wreck. One of James's beliefs is that this "more" is God and that those of us who open ourselves to God's influence fulfill our deepest destiny. James is willing to grant that God is real since he produces real effects. Each of us, and the world itself, takes a turn for the better or the worse, depending on whether we fulfill or evade God's demands.

Other than this, James spoke about God in measured ways. The divine, he held, can mean no single thing; it takes the whole of us to spell the meaning out completely. He was willing to suggest what God may be like but only on the testimony of religious experience. According to him, God need not be infinite; all that we can know with confidence is that we can realize a union with *something* larger and other than ourselves and in that union find our greatest peace. God may even be a larger, godlike self, one of many. For most religious individuals, James thinks, all that is required is that God be viewed as friendly to us and our ideals, that we be persuaded that in God our cause will prevail, and that we have a chance of salvation.

Critics of views of deity such as James's argue that such a God is not a fit object of religious worship. That depends on a number of things, not the least of which is what is meant by attitudes of religious worship. James came to his position on what is distinctive about religion by contrasting it with morality. For James, the central characteristic of religious attitudes is not self-abasement in the face of God; it is not to view ourselves as nothing. It is, in fact, just the opposite. What is distinctive about religious attitudes is a higher emotion, an exaltation, a kind of happiness that is the result of the intimate relationship we experience with God and our resultant newfound sense of self. For James, everything hangs on our being genuinely related to God; but for this to be possible, we need to speak of God in qualified terms, as other than infinite or absolute. James's view of the attitudes of religious worship and his corresponding position on God seem, by most accounts, to be a real option for many religious individuals—one that enables them to be in the world in a different way, to live life in terms of hope and a chance for salvation.

Smith calls attention to two other factors that have contributed to the influence *Varieties* has had ever since it was first published. At the turn of the century, the climate of opinion in both philosophy and religious thought was dominated by various traditions of philosophical idealism, following the lead of Kant and Hegel. The emphasis was on religious *ideas* and *doctrines* and on the contention that religion could only be properly understood from within this perspective. Contrary to this reigning zeitgeist, James demonstrated that religion must first of all be understood in terms of the vivid experiences of individuals who are struggling with personal concerns and crises to which religious faith can and does provide an answer.

> James succeeded in conveying the sense that, whereas much previous philosophy of religion was largely a dialectic of ideas, his account of the attitudes manifested in the experiences of the once- and twice-born, the sick soul, the divided self, conversion, and saintliness was a revelation of living religion in its pristine form. . . . Thus, James for some time to come established "religious experience," both in name and substance, as the central focus for the philosophical interpretation of religion.[32]

Not only this, but Smith reminds us that James had another objective in writing *Varieties,* one that makes the work of even greater worth: he wanted to establish the importance of religion in modern life. James was fully aware of and respected the aims of science. He also knew he was addressing an audience whose religious instincts were being thwarted by scientific positivism as well as by religious orthodoxies.[33] What James refused to do was disconnect his understanding of religion from what he took to be the true intent of scientific inquiry. Both perspectives focus on facts; and for James, as we have shown, religion, properly understood, has facts of its own and makes a real difference in the world. Smith acknowledges this and correctly concludes that *Varieties* stands "as a necessary corrective to the fideistic tendency manifested in the religious thinking of recent decades, which has resulted in the encapsulation of religion within the walls of sheer faith, where it is divorced from any form of knowledge."[34] James never accepted such a bifurcation.

The year 2002 is the centennial of the publication of *Varieties.* It has stood the test of time.

Appendix A
Approaches to William James

The first, and for many still the most influential, biography of James was written sixty-five years ago by his friend and colleague at Harvard, Ralph B. Perry, *The Thought and Character of William James,* 2 vols. (Boston: Little, Brown, 1935). The first major biography of James after Perry's was Gay Wilson Allen's *William James: A Biography* (New York: Viking, 1967). James's most recent biographer is Linda Simon; see her *Genuine Reality: A Life of William James* (New York: Harcourt Brace, 1998).

A fruitful intellectual tension exists in Jamesian studies resulting from the fact that while many scholars come at his work primarily from the perspective of philosophy, usually focusing on his pragmatism, others approach him first and foremost from the vantage point of psychology. The best work on James from this latter perspective, in my opinion, is being done by Eugene Taylor. See his *William James on Exceptional Mental States: The 1896 Lowell Lectures* (New York: Scribner's, 1982). See also his and Robert H. Wozniak's *Pure Experience: The Response to William James* (Bristol, Eng.: Thoemmes, 1996). See also Taylor's *William*

James on Consciousness beyond the Margin (Princeton: Princeton University Press, 1996).

In the 1960s, on another front, several scholars began to emphasize those insights in *Principles* that presaged phenomenology—stream of consciousness, pure experience, and radical empiricism—and advanced a significantly different interpretation of James. Having discovered James's importance for Edmund Husserl and the emergence of phenomenology as a method of philosophical reflection, some initially located James within the phenomenological movement itself, calling him a "protophenomenologist." The prevailing consensus is that James is best seen as having worked out his own distinctive phenomenology of consciousness and experience contemporaneously with the emergence of phenomenology. This insight into James's thought has proven to be a real breakthrough in Jamesian studies.

Building on efforts to see James in this new light, Bruce Wilshire has written an important study of James's whole philosophy. See his introductory essay to his *William James: The Essential Writings* (Albany: State University of New York Press, 1984). According to Wilshire, many students of James have failed to appreciate that his thought represents a new vision of the philosophical enterprise, one which "overwhelms traditional distinctions and terms." James advanced a view of the world that is much more comprehensive than most have realized and one that has a center. "James undercuts and reverses the tradition of modern epistemology regnant in various forms since Descartes. . . . James repudiates all this. He claims this tradition rests on a blindness to everyday experience of the world as we actually live through it. The tradition plasters over this experience with distinctions that are not true." Wilshire then summarizes the center of James's vision, in terms of what it opposes, in the following way:

> First, James claims that we do not, in the life we actually live, experience the world as mental: and what the experience is experienced *as* is what the experience *is*.

Second, he claims that we do not experience discrete bits of things, but whole "fields" irreducible in their wholeness.

Third, our most fundamental experience and knowledge of the world is not in the form of clear and distinct ideas, but rather of ones which are vague to various degrees. (That ideas can be important and true but vague is an extraordinary thought.)

Fourth, knowledge of the world requires constant, active interpretation in terms of values or standards set within an ever-present and vague world-horizon, with temporality an essential dimension; thus that sensations are allegedly passively received is not a criterion of objectivity.

Fifth and finally, there is no internal or strictly subjective realm inhabited by sensations, feelings, and values which is set over against a realm of brute fact ascertained by the dispassionate methods of mathematical physics; hence there is no fundamental gulf dividing science from ethics or thought from life. (Wilshire, *William James,* xviii–xix)

James's alternative theory of knowledge requires that what can be said to be known must be built upon and do justice to pre-reflective, pretheoretical knowledge and experience. By this Wilshire means deliberate theorizing and knowledge by acquaintance. Furthermore, according to Wilshire, James's center of vision includes his distinctive views of the "self" and of spirituality, autonomy, and freedom, which, in turn, become the basis upon which he develops his own ethics, aesthetics, metaphysics, epistemology, philosophy of science, and philosophy of religion.

In another important work, *William James's Radical Reconstruction of Philosophy* (Albany: State University of New York Press, 1990), Charlene H. Seigfried also builds upon a similar understanding of James's center of vision and, in effect, reconstructs James's reconstruction of philosophy. Other recent full-length studies of James include William Joseph Gavin, *William James and the Reinstatement of the Vague* (Philadelphia: Temple University Press, 1992); George P. Graham, *William James and the Affirmation of God* (New York: Lang, 1992); Ellen K. Suckiel, *Heaven's*

Champion: William James's Philosophy of Religion (Notre Dame: University of Notre Dame Press, 1996); Richard M. Gale, *The Divided Self of William James* (Cambridge: Cambridge University Press, 1999); David C. Lamberth, *William James and the Metaphysics of Experience* (Cambridge: Cambridge University Press, 1999); and Eugene Fontinell, *Self, God, and Immortality: A Jamesian Investigation* (New York: Fordham University Press, 2000).

Appendix B
James's Writings on God

James's treatment of the subject of God, like his dealing with religion, is scattered throughout the entire range of his writings. A basic outline of his distinctive view of God is found initially in the introduction to the first book he ever published, an edited collection of his father's writings, *The Literary Remains of the Late Henry James* (Boston: Houghton Mifflin, 1884), included in *Essays in Religion and Morality,* number 11 in The Works of William James (Cambridge: Harvard University Press, 1982), 3–63; next in the following six articles: "The Will to Believe," "Is Life Worth Living?" "The Sentiment of Rationality," "Reflex Action and Theism," "The Dilemma of Determinism," and "The Moral Philosopher and the Moral Life," collected in *The Will to Believe,* first published in 1897, number 6 in The Works of William James (Cambridge: Harvard University Press, 1979); followed by what he says about God mainly in the postscript to *Varieties;* then in lectures I, III, and VIII, and appendix I, "Philosophical Concepts and Practical Results," in *Pragmatism;* and finally in several of his Hibbert Lectures, especially I, III, IV, V, and VIII, in *A Pluralistic Universe,* first published in 1909, number 4 in The Works of William James (Cambridge: Harvard University Press, 1977).

Notes

I am indebted to a number of colleagues who took the time to read and comment on earlier drafts of this paper. I want to thank, in particular, James E. Faulconer, Daniel C. Peterson, and Louis C. Midgley.

1. Beginning in 1975 the American Council of Learned Societies teamed up with Harvard University Press to produce a definitive, critical edition of James's writings. Known as The Works of William James, the series is edited by Frederick Burkhardt, Fredson Bowers, and Ignas K. Skrupskelis. *The Principles of Psychology,* in three volumes, is number 8 in the series (Cambridge: Harvard University Press, 1981), *The Varieties of Religious Experience* is number 13 (1985), and *Pragmatism: A New Name for Some Old Ways of Thinking* is number 1 (1975). These are three of seventeen titles (nineteen volumes) in the series, the last of which was published in 1988. Such an ambitious effort is rare in scholarly publishing and reflects the importance and esteem accorded to James's work in the fields of psychology and philosophy. In this paper, all references, as well as all page citations to James's writings, will be to editions in this series.

2. In 1992 the University Press of Virginia began publishing a definitive collection of James's letters. Nine volumes of a projected twelve-volume series entitled The Correspondence of William James have appeared to date. The first three volumes include the correspondence between William and his brother, the celebrated novelist Henry James, and cover the period 1861 to 1910. Volume 4 includes James's correspondence beginning in 1856. Volume 9 includes letters up to 1901. The entire series is edited by Ignas K. Skrupskelis and Elizabeth M. Berkeley.

3. See appendix A, "Approaches to William James."

4. John E. Smith illustrates this point in his introduction to the 1985 edition of *Varieties,* xiii.

5. I borrowed the term from James himself. In *Varieties,* in the lecture on the sick soul in the context of talking about the reality of evil, James says, "philosophic theism [by which he means the concept of the Absolute] has always shown a tendency to become pantheistic and monistic, and to consider the world as one unit of absolute fact; and this has been at variance with popular or *practical theism,* which latter has ever been more or less frankly pluralistic, not to say polytheistic, and

shown itself perfectly well satisfied with a universe composed of many original principles, provided we be only allowed to believe that the divine principle remains supreme, and that the others are subordinate." James, *Varieties,* 112, emphasis added. See appendix B, "James's Writings on God."

6. James, *A Pluralistic Universe,* 144.

7. James, *The Will to Believe,* 98.

8. Truman G. Madsen, "William James: Philosopher-Educator," *BYU Studies* 4/1 (1961): 81–105.

9. In 1897 James was asked to give the Gifford Lectures on Natural Religion at Edinburgh University. Finally, in the summer of 1901 he delivered the first ten lectures and in the summer of 1902 gave the remaining ten lectures. His lectures in 1902 had been prepared in advance and the first edition of *Varieties* was published in England on the day he gave his final lecture, 9 June 1902. Between 1902 and 1985, when the definitive critical edition of *Varieties* was published, the original publisher and other publishers issued fifty-six impressions of the work (not counting foreign language translations).

Varieties contains much that comes from James's earlier studies in psychopathology. These were extensive and formed the basis of a set of Lowell Lectures he delivered in Boston in 1896, entitled "Exceptional Mental States." The title indicates James's position: he sees no sharp distinction between healthy- and morbid-minded individuals. Eugene Taylor has reconstructed these lectures and demonstrated that they provide a link between *The Principles of Psychology* and *Varieties.* Taylor shows that James *did not,* as has been widely assumed, turn from science toward religion and "mysticism" after 1890. While it is true that James became increasingly disenchanted with positivistic trends and the kind of scientific psychology being developed in America, one that "restricted itself more and more to the laboratory and to the filtering of reality through a clouded lens of statistical analysis," at the same time, rather than turn his back on the subject, he sought to broaden the discipline by including within it the study of psychic phenomena, the subconscious, and religious experience. According to Taylor, James "hoped less to make such explorations scientifically respectable than to use them as a means for transforming the ever-narrowing definition of science itself." Eugene

Taylor, *William James on Exceptional Mental States: The 1896 Lowell Lectures* (New York: Scribner, 1982), 2.

10. James's approach in *Varieties* is a reflection of his general philosophical view of the world and portrays his ongoing attempt to better understand our mode of being in the world. It is based on his concept of pragmatism and on an incipient metaphysics he worked out earlier in *Principles* and subsequently called "radical empiricism." It reflects his conviction that our everyday experiences of the world as we actually live through them are fundamental and ultimately the basis for determining what is real, meaningful, and of value. Not surprisingly, James thought this was the way most of us assess the validity of our own religious experiences.

James's pragmatism, viewed outside the context of his notion of our experience of the world, will inevitably result in a distortion of what he means. His ideas of "thoughts verifying themselves" or being true because they "satisfy" some ends are invariably dismissed, on the basis of modern epistemology, as "subjective." For James, truth pertains to mind, but mind can only be understood in terms of its (our) prereflective, pretheoretical experiences of the world. This is the basis of James's rejection not only of traditional rationalism and empiricism, but also of his rejection of traditional realism and idealism—these traditions all understand "mind" as somehow independent of the experienced world, as a means or agency for knowing the world. But for James, "mind" always needs to be spoken of in terms of embodied beings—beings who are in the world and act upon the world. And as a consequence, the world is knowable only to the extent that it falls within our purposeful, ideal, and often spontaneous goals or aims.

The three key elements in James's radical empiricism are implicit in his pragmatism: (1) his postulate that all philosophical discussion of what is needs to be restricted to experientially derived terms, (2) his statement of fact that the relations between things are just as much matters of direct experience as are the things themselves, and (3) his generalization that experience exhibits its own continuous structure and there is therefore no need to postulate any transcendental connectives.

11. Eugene Taylor, *William James on Consciousness beyond the Margin* (Princeton: Princeton University Press, 1996); see appendix A.

12. Amplifying this line of thought, James contends: "If we look on man's whole mental life as it exists, on the life of men that lies in them apart from their learning and science, and that they inwardly and privately follow, we have to confess that the part of it of which rationalism [his emphasis here is on reason and logic] can give an account is relatively superficial. It is the part that has the *prestige* undoubtedly, for it has the loquacity, it can challenge you for proofs, and chop logic, and put you down with words. But it will fail to convince or convert you all the same, if your dumb intuitions are opposed to its conclusions. If you have intuitions at all, they come from a deeper level of your nature than the loquacious level which rationalism inhabits. Your whole subconscious life, your impulses, your faiths, your needs, your divinations, have prepared the premises, of which your consciousness now feels the weight of the result; and something in you absolutely *knows* that that result must be truer than any logic-chopping rationalistic talk, however clever, that may contradict it. . . . The truth is that in the metaphysical and religious sphere, articulate reasons are cogent for us only when our inarticulate feelings of reality have already been impressed in favor of the same conclusion. Then, indeed, our intuitions and our reason work together. . . . The immediate assurance is the deep thing in us, the argument is but a surface exhibition. Instinct leads, intelligence does but follow. If a person feels the presence of a living God . . . your critical arguments, be they never so superior, will vainly set themselves to change his faith." James, *Varieties*, 66–67.

13. Initially, James planned to devote the second half of the Gifford Lectures to a philosophical interpretation of material he collected on religious experience. The first half was to be a phenomenological description of case material. But as he collected more and more documentation, he significantly revised his original plan for the lecture series: the amount of space devoted to his own philosophical conclusions was correspondingly limited to his concluding lecture and postscript. See the note by his son Henry James, ed., *The Letters of William James* (Boston: Atlantic Monthly, 1920), 2:169–70, and James, *Varieties*, preface, 5.

11. *Correspondence of William James*, 9:501–2, James's emphasis. In another letter to a friend, Frances Morse, written 12 April 1900, James describes his objectives in writing the Gifford Lectures this way: "The

problem I have set myself is a hard one: 1st to defend (against all the prejudices of my 'class,') 'experience' against 'philosophy' as being the real backbone of the world's religious life—I mean prayer, guidance and all that sort of thing immediately and privately felt, as against high and noble general views of our destiny and the world's meaning; and second, to make the hearer or reader believe what I myself invincibly do believe, that altho all the special manifestations of religion may have been absurd (I mean its creed and theories) yet the life of it as a while is mankind's most important function. A task well nigh impossible, I fear, and in which I shall fail; but to attempt it is *my* religious act." Ibid., 185–86, James's emphasis.

15. See also *Principles,* in which James emphasizes that the sense of our own existence, of our own being in the world, is the ground of certainty for our beliefs, that "whatever things have intimate and continuous connection with my life are things of whose reality I cannot doubt." James, *The Principles of Psychology,* 2:926.

16. This oblique reference to the biblical view of God, on James's part, is the subject of a recent article on James's view of God by BYU philosopher David Paulsen. See his essay "The God of Abraham, Isaac and (William) James," *Journal of Speculative Philosophy* 13 (1999): 114–46. Paulsen argues that James's limited or qualified view of deity has much more in common with one rather straightforward and plausible biblical view of God than with what he calls the "God of the philosophers." Furthermore, Paulsen argues that James's view of God anticipates a notion of deity that is emerging from contemporary trends of thought in certain evangelical Christian circles, positions sometimes referred to as "free-will theism" or "the openness of God movement." Paulsen has written extensively on the idea of divine embodiment, first in "Must God Be Incorporeal?" *Faith and Philosophy* 6/1 (January 1989): 76–87; then in "Early Christian Belief in a Corporeal Deity: Origen and Augustine as Reluctant Witnesses," *Harvard Theological Review* 83/2 (1990): 105–15; in "Reply to Kim Paffenroth's Comment," *Harvard Theological Review* 86/2 (1993): 235–39; and most recently, with Carl Griffin, in "Augustine and the Corporeality of God," *Harvard Theological Review* 95/1 (2002): 97–118. See also Paulsen's treatment of this subject in reference to Latter-day Saint views of God in "The Doctrine of Divine Embodiment:

Restoration, Judeo-Christian, and Philosophical Perspectives," *BYU Studies* 35/4 (1995–96): 7–94.

17. See appendix B. Several scholars have observed the importance of the subject of God in James's writings; see, for instance, John E. Smith, *The Spirit of American Philosophy* (New York: Galaxy, 1963); Edward C. Moore, *William James* (New York: Washington Square, 1965); and Robert J. Roth, "The Religious Philosophy of William James," *Thought* 41 (1966): 251. Still, as Roth notes, "the task of reconciling the scientific and religious currents of his time was something that preoccupied James throughout his scholarly life. Treatments of him have not sufficiently taken into account the fact that the problem of God is central to his thought." I agree. There are at least three major reasons for this: First, James himself never systematically treated the subject. Second, many approach James's thought about God from the perspective of modern philosophy—particularly that of his own work on pragmatism—and thereby often fail to fully understand what he means by certain key concepts in accordance with his distinctive psychological and metaphysical view of the world. And last, it seems obvious that James's unorthodox, if not heretical, views on God contribute to a relative lack of attention to this aspect of his thought.

18. H. P. Owen, *Concepts of Deity* (New York: Herder and Herder, 1971), 59.

19. J. N. Findlay, "Can God's Existence Be Disproved?" in *New Essays in Philosophical Theology,* ed. Antony Flew and Alasdair MacIntyre (New York: Macmillan, 1966), 47–56.

20. Ibid., 51–52, Findlay's emphasis.

21. "Modern views make it self-evidently absurd (if they don't make it ungrammatical) to speak of such a Being and attribute existence to him. It was indeed an ill day for Anselm when he hit upon his famous proof. For on that day he not only laid bare something that is of the essence of an adequate religious object, but also something that entails its necessary non-existence." Ibid., 55.

22. Ibid., 49, 51.

23. James would readily classify Findlay as one who has a penchant for metaphysical speculation, for coming to conclusions in such matters strictly on the basis of a priori definitions and deductions.

24. In a detailed and helpful study of religious worship, David Mason deals with Findlay's views on the subject, among those of others, and offers insightful criticism of his thinking on religious attitudes. I follow a number of Mason's leads here. See David R. Mason, "An Examination of 'Worship' as a Key for Re-examining the God Problem," *Journal of Religion* 55 (1975): 76–94, esp. 83.

25. See ibid.

26. Findlay, "Can God's Existence Be Disproved?" 51, Findlay's emphasis.

27. Mason, "An Examination of 'Worship,'" 83–84.

28. Mason follows Charles Hartshorne and others in arguing that rather than forming the idea of worship around the notion of self-effacement, a better option, one "more in accord with the most profound religious sensibilities; one which is also capable of sustaining a rigorous secular examination," would be to understand worship in terms of "the idea which lies at the base of biblical religion . . . the important religious and secular idea of love." But then, on the basis of this, Mason, like James, insists that we speak of God in qualified ways. According to Mason, properly conceived basic religious attitudes do not and cannot require that the object of worship be in all ways necessary. "The attitude which forms the heart of worship is love and this, as we have seen, requires that the beloved be, in some sense, contingent." Ibid., 84, 88.

29. Mason is forced to conclude that Findlay's position on the religious attitude "is riddled with inconsistencies, is self-defeating, does not glorify God, and so is of very doubtful adequacy." Ibid., 83.

30. It is important to point out that most of the time when James is dealing with classical theism, his focus is on the notion of the absolute as articulated by various forms of philosophical idealism. He was clearly a critic of this way of thinking—this sterile abstraction, he held, purports to explain everything but in fact changes nothing. *Varieties*, at least, offers little evidence that James was fully acquainted with the way God, viewed as absolute, functions in various established religious traditions. Nevertheless, not surprisingly, there are times when he reveals that he is sensitive to what some religious people may mean when they speak of God as absolute. This comes through, for instance, when James notes that, for many, God is the name for "whatever is most primal and enveloping

and deeply true" and when he expresses the belief of most religious persons in the following way: "God's existence is the guarantee of an ideal order that shall be permanently preserved. This world may indeed, as science assures us, some day burn up or freeze; but if it is part of his order, the old ideals are sure to be brought elsewhere to fruition, so that where God is, tragedy is only provisional and partial, and shipwreck and dissolution are not the absolutely final things." James, *Varieties,* 407.

31. Smith, introduction to *Varieties,* xi.

32. Ibid., xii–xiii.

33. Carol Zaleski, in her helpful critique of James's efforts in *Varieties,* observes that it was "James who kept the door open when the reigning positivisms and skepticisms were slamming it shut in the face of those who sought a scientific blessing for their faith; it was James who kept the door open when the established orthodox traditions were, by dint of their own apologetic and imaginative failures, slamming it shut in the face of countless unchurched aspirants." See Carol Zaleski, "Speaking of William James to the Cultured among His Despisers," in *The Struggle for Life: A Companion to William James's* The Varieties of Religious Experience, ed. Donald Capps and Janet L. Jacobs (West Lafayette, Ind.: Society for the Scientific Study of Religion, 1995), 59.

34. Smith, introduction to *Varieties,* li.

CHAPTER 2

JESUS RESEARCH AND THE APPEARANCE OF PSYCHOBIOGRAPHY

James H. Charlesworth

It is a pleasure to honor Truman G. Madsen, with whom I have enjoyed fruitful conversations in Provo, Jerusalem, and elsewhere. As I assess the present state of Jesus Research—or the Third Quest of the Historical Jesus—a new method of research appears surprising. It is the appearance of psychobiography. Before we can discuss this new aspect of Jesus Research, we need to review the study of the historical Jesus from circa 1835 to the present. Of course, the limitations of this essay demand brevity. Perhaps such focus will advance one of the reasons for this essay: to encourage others to become involved in the study of the historical Jesus from various scientific and theological perspectives.

The incomparably great Albert Schweitzer once referred to the "chaos of modern lives of Jesus."[1] He was referring to the books on Jesus that appeared after his *magnum opus* on the historical Jesus. Schweitzer was not a prophet; he was merely prescient. As one sees the veritable flood of books on Jesus, one may be forgiven for thinking that the field is in more chaos today than when Schweitzer wrote. Some among the weak-minded think the study of the historical Jesus is a dead end. Others parade their ignorance in thinking that Papias (whose work is lost) and Irenaeus (who was a defender of the faith) were reporting objectively that at least two gospels were composed by eyewitnesses of Jesus.[2]

In the field of Jesus Research, as well as in archaeology, we confront the minimalists and the maximalists. In this short review essay, I shall attempt to point out how and why these extremists have followed the blind and fallen into a pit. I also wish to point out that behind the apparent chaos is an unparalleled consensus on methodology and on some major aspects of Jesus' life and thought. The difference between a book by a scholar and one by a non-scholar is the amount of attention given to methodological issues and the degree to which a scientific, unbiased method is followed in asking historical, literary, and theological questions. All scholars who are focusing their research on the historical Jesus acknowledge that the historical-critical method needs to be employed. Too few scholars recognize and attempt to supplement their Jesus Research by including insights obtained from sociology, anthropology, archaeology, rhetoric, and perhaps psychobiography.

The field of Jesus Research is vast. No one has read all the publications. It may be impossible now even to claim to have read all the important publications since they are so numerous, scattered in so many different fields, and written in over twenty languages. Fortunately, we have a useful bibliographical guide to most publications up until 1996: Craig A. Evans's *Life of Jesus Research*.[3]

My inaugural at Princeton Theological Seminary in 1984 was focused on "Jesus Research." I stressed that from A.D. 30 (the date of the crucifixion) to 1835 (the date of the appearance of the first critical examination of the life of Jesus, David F. Strauss's *Das Leben Jesu*), the approach to Jesus was devotional.[4] That is to say, Christians had approached Jesus by worshiping him as the Christ, the Son of God. In the early centuries, scholars claimed, and thence it was presupposed, that eyewitnesses composed the gospels: Matthew and John were apostles, Mark was the assistant of Peter, and Luke was the companion of Paul.

The years from 1835 until 1906 were filled with excitement in the historical search for Jesus. Strauss initially, and others intermittently, dreamed of giving persons in the pew a reliable biography of the one they followed. Many, including Strauss, were finally led to question whether an informed and enlightened person could still remain a Christian.

Some scholars claimed Mark was the most reliable biographer of Jesus; others defended John. Some arguments may have been by scholars, but they were hardly scholarly. Some New Testament experts even claimed that Judas was the Beloved Disciple of the Gospel of John. The distinguished Frenchman Ernst Renan opined that Jesus' painful last moments in Gethsemane may have been due to his regret over the women he should have loved in Galilee. The famous church historian Adolph Harnack claimed that Jesus taught the fatherhood of God, the brotherhood of humankind, and the ethic of love. Readers were not hearing the voice of the Galilean rabbi; they were in touch with French romanticism and German idealism. The attentive reader pondered why Jesus was so misunderstood by his followers and why he was crucified. This period (1835–1906) has come to be known as the "Old Quest for the Historical Jesus."

In the first edition of his study on the historical Jesus, published in 1906, Schweitzer showed that all who had written during the nineteenth century were simply offering a view of Jesus that they could admire or understand. His work, *The Quest of the Historical Jesus*,[5] is not only a classic, but it is perhaps the most influential study of Jesus ever published. Virtually every scholar who has been working independently has come to agree with Schweitzer that Jesus was deeply influenced by Jewish apocalypticism.[6]

George Tyrrell, an Irish modernist and Roman Catholic, insightfully emphasized a statement that is too often associated with Schweitzer (although it was clearly influenced by him). In his review of Harnack's *What Is Christianity?* Tyrrell stated that those who had written a putative historical work on Jesus had merely peered down the well of history and seen the reflection of their own faces.[7]

Thus the historical search for Jesus died in many seminaries and universities—especially in the influential and leading German institutions. The formative judges—like Rudolf Bultmann, Karl Barth, and Paul Tillich—announced that it was not only impossible to achieve, but that it was also irrelevant for Christian faith.[8] A slogan seemed to be heard: all the Christian needs to know is that one who is saved is saved by "faith alone." This cliché not only misrepresents the complex theologies of Luther and Paul,[9] but it also masquerades as a mandate to be lazy and forgo historical research. Sadly, these perspectives, now clearly disproved by biblical scholars and theologians, can be heard as ghostly echoes in lectures and sermons.

From 1919 (the date of Barth's commentary on Romans) and the 1920s (the beginnings of Bultmann's school) until 1953, the theology of Bultmann and Barth flourished, but they and their followers tended to denigrate historicism. Although many New Testament scholars, especially the Frenchman Pierre Benoit and the Norwegian Nils A. Dahl, stressed the importance of historical research on Jesus before 1950,[10] it is widely recognized that Ernst Käsemann opened up "the New Quest for the Historical Jesus" in 1953.[11] He did so boldly—before Bultmann and at a celebratory gathering of his students. Käsemann demonstrated that there is history in the New Testament. Arguing that Christian theology was grounded not in ideas or existentialism, Käsemann was able to convince many New Testament experts that Christianity was founded on real history and that there was some continuity between Jesus' words and the kerygma.

This New Quest slowly sank from view, perhaps because it was heavily laden with theological interests and with a lingering fascination with existentialism. Lack of dedication to sociology and archaeology and too much interest in Christology marred an objective historiographical search for an understanding of Jesus before age thirty. About 1980 something new appeared in scholarship,[12] which I have called "Jesus Research." Regardless of their own theology or beliefs, many scholars around the world found it interesting and important to ask historical questions. First-century buildings and pavements found unexpectedly in Jerusalem raised questions about what kind of people walked there two thousand years ago.

Jewish and Christian historians pondered what can be known concerning the founder of the Qumran Community (the anonymous Righteous Teacher), Hillel (the "Pharisee" who was a close antecedent of Jesus), Gamaliel, and Johanan ben Zakkai (the one who chaired the first rabbinic "academy" at Jamnia). They also found themselves asking similar questions about Jesus of Nazareth. This new approach was distinct from the previous ones that had dominated the field: it was not tied to a theologically motivated "search" for Jesus. Jesus Research was often stimulated by studies of the Dead Sea Scrolls, early rabbinics, Josephus, and other early Jewish writings—especially the Old Testament Apocrypha and Pseudepigrapha. This study was actual "research"; that is, archaeology, anthropology, and sociology became important in the study of the historical Jesus. Sometime in the late 1980s, Jesus Research was infiltrated—some might say contaminated—by authors, some of whom are scholars, who basically took up the Old Quest, seeking to find a Jesus whom they could follow or worship. The most attractive of their books may be Marcus Borg's *Jesus, A New Vision*.[13] It is understandable why some scholars call the new period of the study of the historical Jesus the "Third Quest" or "Third Search."[14]

Some experts may find a distinction between the study of Jesus before and after 1980 (or later) to be misleading. Granted, such distinguished scholars as Guignebert, Goguel, Loisy, Strauss, and Bauer would disclaim that their studies were motivated by theological agendas. It is also not fair to brand Bultmann as one whose christological concerns simply dictated his historical research. It is surely debatable to what degree Borg, John Dominic Crossan, and others like Luke Johnson are true historians whose work is not in any way shaped by christological perspectives. What I wish to stress is that more concern for objective research on Jesus is apparent today than it was before approximately 1980.

More illustrations are necessary to clarify that the paradigm shift is not only apparent but real and that the new wave of research is not different only because of more primary data like the Dead Sea Scrolls and other archaeological discoveries that antedate A.D. 70. Once David Flusser's book *Jesus* could end by reporting Jesus' death. Now his study requires an epilogue in which he can show how the ideas of the historical Jesus evolve into the faith of Christians. Once Father Marie-Joseph Lagrange, the founder of the École Biblique et Archéologique Française in Jerusalem, had to keep one eye looking out for possible Vatican censorship. Now Roman Catholic scholars are free to explore historical issues: Raymond E. Brown[15] and John Meier can query the historicity of the virgin birth (and yet confess it liturgically), and in the École Biblique, Jerome Murphy-O'Connor can publish a life of Paul that is in no way designed to please the papacy.[16]

Of course, vast differences exist in contemporary Jesus study. At the outset one can try to bifurcate scholars into those who, like E. P. Sanders, want history and not confessionalism and those who, like Borg, mix history and Christology; but, finally, all such neat categories, like liberal versus conservative, distort rather than represent. Books in the field of Jesus Research—like those by Flusser, James H. Charlesworth, Meier, Richard A. Horsley,[17] and Sanders—appear alongside other publications on Jesus that resist categorizing, such as those by Ben Witherington, Crossan, Nicholas T. Wright,[18] and Paula Fredriksen.[19]

Once one scholar, Schweitzer, could summarize the study of the historical Jesus during the nineteenth century. The review of the study of the historical Jesus during the twentieth century is a monstrous task. Three experts now seek to assess what has been happening. Walter P. Weaver, Pendergrass Professor of New Testament Emeritus, at Florida Southern College, completed the first book in 1999; it is entitled *The Historical Jesus in the Twentieth Century.*[20] He covered the study of the historical Jesus from 1900 to 1950. Ernst Baasland, a New Testament scholar who has become a bishop of the Lutheran Church in Norway, will cover the period from 1951 to 1980, and Charlesworth will assess the period from 1981 to 2000. The publisher of the trilogy is Trinity Press International.

For those who cannot spend months working through the erudite and exhaustive volumes on Jesus by Meier entitled *A Marginal Jew,*[21] a small book entitled *Jesus Two Thousand Years Later* may be attractive. This latter book contains essays that are written for nonscholars.[22] Five well-known scholars—Weaver, Crossan, Sanders, Amy-Jill Levine, and Charlesworth—present their ideas in this recent volume in the Faith and Scholarship Colloquies that are held each year at Florida Southern College.

What Can Be Known about Jesus' Actions?

A remarkable consensus has appeared among many of the leading scholars regarding Jesus' actions. Here are some Jesus traditions that seem to be, if not virtually *bruta facta,* at least highly probable conclusions:

- Jesus grew up in Nazareth.
- He was baptized by John the Baptizer.
- He was obsessed with doing God's will.
- He was "intoxicated" with another dimension and identified himself as a prophet.[23]
- He chose twelve men to be his disciples.

- He was very close to Mary Magdalene.
- He performed healing miracles.
- He taught in synagogues (at the beginning only, perhaps), small dwellings, and on the fringes of villages (not cities).
- In shocking contrast to the actions of many Pharisees and the Essenes, he associated with the outcast, physically sick or impaired, and social misfits.
- He went to Jerusalem to celebrate Passover and worship within the temple cult.
- He frequented the temple, worshiped there, and taught in the porticoes.
- When he was in Jerusalem, he attacked some corruptions in the temple cult.
- His meals were often religious events, and his last meal with his disciples was at Passover time in Jerusalem.
- He seems to have been betrayed by Judas and was certainly denied by Peter.
- He was forcefully taken by some Jews, most likely some related to the cult.
- He was crucified by Roman soldiers outside the western walls of Jerusalem.[24]
- He died before the beginning of the Sabbath on Friday afternoon.

During thirty years of lecturing on Jesus and the Twelve, and pointing out that Peter is always first and Judas last, I strove to convince my students that Jesus' followers created the concept of Twelve. Since it is undeniable that Judas is in the list and is often referred to as one of the Twelve, I now conclude that Jesus chose twelve. I am pleased to observe that Sanders and Meier—leading experts in Jesus Research—independently came to the same conclusion: that Jesus certainly had some political agenda.[25] In *Who Was Jesus?* Hendrikus Boers points to the evidence that Jesus' followers "were armed in Gethsemane," and thus it is "difficult to deny that he himself may have been involved in armed resistance against Rome."[26] I find it absurd that leading scholars stress, on different occasions, two mutually exclusive ideas—sometimes claiming that Jesus had a political agenda and at other times arguing that he was not interested in or linked with politics. We should rather consistently stress that politics and religion in first-century Judaism cannot be distinguished or separated.[27] The absurd inconsistency in scholarly publications should have been broken by Borg's superb book *Conflict, Holiness, and Politics in the Teachings of Jesus*[28] and by a collection edited by Ernst Bammel and Charles F. D. Moule entitled *Jesus and the Politics of His Day*.[29]

Debates certainly continue regarding Jesus' actions. In no way was Jesus a marginal Jew[30] or a peasant.[31] He was devoutly Jewish; and he was far too sophisticated, learned, and involved with urban life to be a "peasant." Sometimes these discussions appear without the demeanor of scholarly dialogue.

Central to the previous reflections are methodological searches for authenticating Jesus' activities. Fortunately, Bruce Chilton and Evans have edited a book that will be essential in any future search for Jesus' actions. In *Authenticating the Activities of Jesus*, nineteen established New Testament experts share their own methods and conclusions.[32] The purpose of the collection is "to clarify what procedures should be undertaken to distinguish tradition and meaning that stem from Jesus from that which stems from later tradents and evangelists"[33] A third of the book is on methods and assumptions and two-thirds on authenticating the activities of Jesus. Seventeen essays appear in this volume; eleven are new, and six have been revised. J. D. G. Dunn and most scholars who contributed to this volume (and its companion) are convinced that the goal of Jesus Research or the Third Quest will be—or is—most likely successful. Martin Hengel and Evans present papers to show that Jesus did have a messianic mission. Personally, I am convinced that while Jesus never declared himself to be the Messiah (the Christ), he may have had a messianic self-understanding.[34]

In *Authenticating the Activities of Jesus,* William Klassen brilliantly raises again a perplexing question—what did Judas betray?—and disagrees with Charlesworth, Borg, Ruth Tucker, Crossan, and others. Klassen rightly points out that the New Testament verb used to describe Judas' act is *paradidomi.* It means "to hand over," or "transmit," and not "betray" (which is *prodidomi,* a verb that does not appear in the New Testament; compare the obviously incorrect reading in Mark 14:10 that is found in only Codex Bezae). Thus, Klassen is convinced that "Judas acted in obedience to Christ's will and that in his act of handing over could have been obedient to God's will."[35] Klassen is correct to point out that Judas is a much more positive character than Christian traditions allow; he was certainly one of the Twelve, and he may have been the treasurer of Jesus' group (see John 12:6; 13:29). The tendencies of the later strata of the Gospels do certainly increase the vilification of Judas, but narrative exegesis and the rhetorical thrust of the Gospels clarify that Judas left Jesus' group, joined his enemies, and initiated a process that eventually led to Jesus' crucifixion. We have no way of knowing Judas's motives or Jesus' final evaluation of him.[36]

It is important, of course, to seek to know what can be reliably ascertained about the reasons for Jesus' horrible death in A.D. 30.[37] Jesus ascends to Jerusalem from Galilee in order to celebrate Passover. Pontius Pilate brings thousands of his soldiers from Caesarea Maritima to the Holy City. Pilgrims flood in from everywhere: from as far away as Parthia in the East and Rome in the West. The city becomes electric with messianic and eschatological fever, as the Jews begin to celebrate—actually relive—how God acted on their behalf and saved them from the pharaohs. In his well-written *Jesus: A Revolutionary Biography,* Crossan captures the social setting. Caiaphas and Pilate "would no doubt have agreed before such a festival that fast and immediate action was to be taken against any disturbance and that some examples by crucifixion might be especially useful at the start."[38] For Caiaphas and Pilate, who must preserve order amidst potential crises and perhaps against the wishes of most in the Sanhedrin, Jesus was dangerous because of his ability to arouse unruly crowds (the most unstable of social institutions).

What Can Be Known about Jesus' Teaching

While it is important to know something reliably about Jesus the man, it is equally central—and perhaps more important for many scholars—to examine what can be known regarding his teachings. A major turning point in the study of Jesus by a Jew is seen in the brilliant and challenging trilogy written by Geza Vermes of Oxford: *Jesus the Jew: A Historian's Reading of the Gospels* (1973), *Jesus and the World of Judaism* (1983), and *The Religion of Jesus the Jew* (1993). Another pioneer in Jesus Research is the late David Flusser, an incredibly erudite and creative professor of the Hebrew University in Jerusalem. In the major revision of his book *Jesus,* he focuses attention on Jesus' concept of love.[39] In contrast to the Jewish authors who reject Jesus because of his apparently absurd command to love our enemies (see Matthew 5:44), Flusser has crafted a sensitive and scholarly book that is one of the best discussions of Jesus' understanding of love. Flusser sees a markedly "new sensitivity" among Jesus' contemporary Jews; Jesus knew that love must include all and be like God's mercy (see Matthew 5:4; Luke 6:36). From years of discussing Jesus with Flusser, I have come to perceive Jesus' teachings more clearly. Jesus taught that love defined by boundaries may be only a self-serving affection. As we reflect on our own lives, and as we grow older, it becomes obvious that we cannot know who our friends or our enemies may be—and that such a bifurcation of humanity distorts reality. Moreover, if we do not strive to love our enemies, how are we to live in a world without enemies?

One of Flusser's students has written a solid assessment of Jesus' parables. Brad Young's *The Parables* focuses on the attempt to understand Jesus in light of what can be known of Jesus' own time.[40] Young rightly points out that "Christian" interpretation, even by the early Greek scholars, often missed Jesus' message because they removed him from his Jewish environment. There should be no doubt that the parables originate with Jesus, though edited by the Evangelists, and Charles W. Hedrick rightly sees Jesus' creativity in them.[41]

Most scholars concur that Jesus' central message is the dawning of God's rule (the Kingdom of God—for Matthew, "the Kingdom of Heaven"). Thus, among the most certain aspects of Jesus' teachings are the following:

- His central proclamation was the dawning of God's rule.
- His custom was to speak pictorially, using parables.
- He knew Greek and Hebrew, but his usual speech was in Aramaic.
- He seems to have taught his disciples a special way to pray (the Lord's Prayer).
- In line with ideas implicit in the world of other early Jews, Jesus taught his followers that they should love their enemies.
- He often argued with the Pharisees because his theology was close to theirs.
- He was influenced by some Essene thought (as reflected in the Dead Sea Scrolls) but would have been highly critical of their predestinarian beliefs and exclusivism.[42]
- He apparently perceived his mission and that of his followers to be focused on Israel alone (compare "go nowhere among the Gentiles" in Matthew 10:5).
- He argued against the Jerusalem-based, elevated concept of purity and most likely attacked the money changers in the Temple.

Of course, every part of this list—and also the previous one—can be and has been debated. What I present is only a consensus I observe in experts who have been independently involved in Jesus Research.

More should be reported about Jesus' teachings. I am personally convinced, and most experts in Jesus Research would concur, that his teaching was eschatological and apocalyptic. This issue is unfortunately no longer a major consensus among authors, but it is clearly a consensus among scholars who have studied early Judaism and the earliest stratum of Jesus traditions. Klassen is certainly correct to stress that members of the Jesus Seminar try "to free" Jesus from the "shackles of Jewish apocalypticism" so that they may "tailor Jesus to their own likes" and so "find him more palatable."[43]

Such massive disagreement in published books leads us to ponder how one can access Jesus' message. I agree with Wright and disagree with Sanders that Jesus called sinners to repent (compare John 7:53–8:11, which has as strong a case for representing Jesus as any other section of the New Testament, even though it is not original to John).[44] Other lists, often strikingly similar to mine, are provided by Wright and Sanders. I agree with Evans in adding to their lists "that Jesus was viewed by the public as a prophet, that the Romans crucified him as 'king of the Jews,' and that following Easter his followers regarded him as Israel's Messiah."[45] Thus the pendulum has swung from the declarative "we cannot know anything about Jesus" to the interrogative "how much can we reliably know about the historical Jesus?" Perhaps the central issue once again concerns methodology. How do we know we are hearing Jesus' own voice and not merely distorted echoes passed on by those who never knew him?

Chilton and Evans have also edited a work entitled *Authenticating the Words of Jesus*. Again the purpose is to seek behind redactions some reliable traditions that derive ultimately from Jesus. The book includes seventeen essays; almost all are by leading experts who write in English. Essays on methodology are presented by Evans, Chilton, Bruce J. Malina (whose essay is superb), and Tom Holmén.[46] Two essays are directed to the Lord's Prayer.

Only one essay is devoted to "the Son of Man," and in it Chilton makes some important contributions. He fails to realize, however, that today most experts on the Pseudepigrapha conclude that the author of *1 Enoch* 37–71 tends to identify the Messiah with the Son of Man[47] and that this tradition antedates Jesus' own authentic words.[48] If this document, the so-called *Parables of Enoch,* is prior to or contemporaneous with Jesus, then "Christian" theology is much closer to some forms of Judaism than we expected, and we may have an invaluable source for grasping the self-understanding of Jesus. Yet, I do want to prescind from a creative suggestion by J. C. O'Neill in his *Who Did Jesus Think He Was?* O'Neill is convinced that Jesus' claims in the Gospel of John do not derive from Jesus but from Jewish documents that antedate Jesus.[49]

Only one essay in *Authenticating the Words of Jesus* is directly on the parables.[50] In one of the best essays in these two volumes on authenticity, Klassen demonstrates how the command to love our enemies is both authentic to Jesus and also rooted in the Greek theater and in the new morality appearing in early Jewish theology (as Flusser's book also demonstrates).[51] It is a pity that the index to Chilton and Evans's book is limited only to biblical literature.

Both of the volumes by Chilton and Evans appear in a series inaugurated and edited by Bruce M. Metzger: New Testament Tools and Studies. Each is obviously intended as a reference work for scholars. The essays are mostly in English, but one is in German. The discussions often demand knowledge of Hebrew and Greek philology. It is a pity that all the authors are (or seem to be) Christians; that is, some superb work on Jesus is being published by Jews and others that defy the traditional labels. More research should have been grounded on sociology and archaeology (a dimension of Jesus Research that will be corrected by the proceedings of the millennium celebration held in Jerusalem in August 2000).[52] While these reference volumes are handsome, they are also extremely expensive. Each costs $160. One can imagine that some scholars who must study them may not be able to afford them.

What are the tendencies of these essays? There is a move to distance research from the popular and often journalistic publications of the Jesus Seminar which, inter alia, has sought objective proofs and announces, with distorted methodology, that Jesus must be divorced from Jewish apocalypticism. Many readers will agree with Wright that the Jesus Seminar employs a misleading methodology, with five gospels but "no Gospel." Yet, some good is coming out of the Jesus Seminar, and Robert W. Funk's initiative and desire to take the historical Jesus seriously is commendable.[53]

Funk's essays show a willingness to consider Jesus' messianic self-understanding. He demonstrates an awareness that Jesus was thoroughly Jewish and that the New Testament Gospels incorrectly tend to shift the blame for his death onto "the Jews." He also tends to avoid positivism (which claims something like objective, unedited data regarding Jesus) and to keep clear of the distorting claim that all conclusions are merely tenuous speculations by scholars.

We are now in a new day in the study of the historical Jesus; our world is different. One difference is placarded by some words written by Hermann Gunkel, the great German biblical scholar who wrote during the first half of the twentieth century. It is riveting to hear Gunkel's words: "To us, for whom war has become the solution for the problems of today, this book (the Old Testament) can become a source of strength. Our people also will remain invincible if we know both: the heroism of the sword and the heroism of faith."[54] I am convinced that world leaders today have learned that war is not "the solution for the problems of today," but no one would be so foolish as to suggest that there is peace on our fragile globe.

Scholars should be grateful to Chilton and Evans for the two books highlighted in this review essay—*Authenticating the Activities of Jesus* and *Authenticating the Words of Jesus.* This adds to the attractiveness of their other works, especially their earlier edited collection of essays in *Studying the Historical Jesus: Evaluation of the State of Current Research,*[55] as well as those in *Jesus in Context: Temple, Purity, and Restoration.*[56] Reading the contributions to these books leaves one with an impression of diversity but not chaos.

Jesus Research and the Appearance of Psychobiography

The two volumes in New Testament Tools and Studies are helpful, but they could have been much better. It is not easy to separate the story of Jesus into his deeds and his words. Sometimes Jesus' message is most articulate in his actions. This point is made when one looks at the books that study Jesus from the sociological and psychological point of view—perspectives noticeably absent in the NTTS collection.

Shirley J. Case introduced the sociological approach to Jesus before World War II. He died in 1947 before he could complete his second book on Jesus.[57] Gerd Theissen, in a brilliant monograph, began the new wave of studying Jesus in light of sociology. His book appeared in 1978 under the title *Sociology of Early Palestinian Christianity.*[58] Horsley added a major contribution to this field in 1989. His book is focused on Theissen's *Sociology and the Jesus Movement.*[59] While no recent book has been dedicated to a sociological biography of Jesus, and I am not familiar with a possible neologism such as "sociobiography," much valuable information regarding the social world of Jesus is amassed in *The Jesus Movement: A Social History of Its First Century.*[60] Still waiting to be written are major monographs on sociology and Jesus, for example, taking into account Gustave Le Bon and other sociologists' insights into the "crowd" and the importance of the crowd in Jesus' story.[61]

In contrast to a sociological study of Jesus, a psychological assessment of Jesus has assumed some prominence after being relatively dormant for over fifty years. While no one should attempt to psychoanalyze Jesus—as if one could put him on a couch and cross-examine him—it is essential to complete what is known from other methodological approaches by adding what one trained in psychology may see or query.[62] Jesus Research (or the Third Quest) has been converging with psychobiography and psychohistory. Two superb attempts at a psychobiography of Jesus have appeared; they deserve highlighting, if only briefly.

John W. Miller has written *Jesus at Thirty: A Psychological and Historical Portrait.*[63] Miller, who was formerly director of Psychiatric Rehabilitation Services at a hospital and taught religion at the college level, is convinced that the proper method to use in writing a psychological biography of Jesus is a refined method adapted from Freud, Fromm, Erikson, and Levinson. Especially important for Miller is Freud's insight into the oedipal complex. Miller attempts to demonstrate that Jesus was estranged from his family, lost his father at an early age, and became a surrogate father and husband. During his baptism by John the Baptizer, Jesus had a powerful pneumatic experience and broke with his mother at age thirty. Jesus, however, resisted the temptation to be the Messiah, did not marry (because his father was not around to find him a woman), and found peace in recognizing that he had found a heavenly Father.

Critics will easily point out that Miller places too much emphasis on Luke's portrayal of Jesus: that he was the firstborn and began his ministry at thirty (which Miller admits may actually be between ages 28 and 33).[64] They will find his analysis unconvincing because he misses the tendencies of the Evangelists *(Redaktionsgeschichte)*. Miller does miss the advancements made since Jeremias on "Abba"[65] and incorrectly claims that only women were with Jesus at the cross (see John 19:26–27).[66] Yet scholars may learn from Miller's book; he does show that one can obtain some insight into Jesus' early years by looking at what is reported about him after he joins John the Baptizer. He does bring into shocking focus the apparently reliable evidence that Jesus was estranged from his mother and siblings (but not his father).

New and even more challenging is Donald Capps's *Jesus: A Psychological Biography.*[67] Capps, a professor at Princeton Theological Seminary and a leading specialist on the psychology of religion, carefully assesses what advances have been achieved by those dedicated to Jesus Research. He chooses to focus on Jesus' role as healer. Capps certainly demonstrates that Jesus scholars have inadvertently drawn conclusions about Jesus that impinge on the field of psychology. He shows also that psychological theories are not only legitimate but essential in the historical reassessment of Jesus the man.

More sensitive than Miller to the way the Evangelists' communities and the Evangelists themselves shaped and edited the Jesus traditions, Capps rightly claims that Jesus, as most scholars contend, performed healing miracles. Capps explores Jesus' role as exorcist-healer and makes some fascinating suggestions.[68] His discoveries are often fresh, and they provide a stimulus to more explorations.

Capps's book is also controversial. For example, Capps is convinced that Jesus' birth was illegitimate,[69] that Joseph failed to adopt him, and that "Jesus was a melancholic male who turned to an alternative religious formulation—based on belief in Abba—to address and overcome his melancholia."[70] What may be most impressive about the studies by Miller and Capps is that they are not pathologies as were many of the early attempts to study Jesus in light of Freud and psychology. Miller and Capps present a portrait of Jesus as one who overcame major psychological problems and emerged as *a healthy male.*

Conclusion

Johnson, in his *The Real Jesus,* rightly stresses the fundamental truth of the story in the Gospels. Story is essential for humans.

We are able to obtain meaning only when we put facts—or lists of apparent facts—into a framework or story. Johnson thus wisely points out that "the most critical thing about a person is precisely what most eludes the methods of critical historiography, namely, the *meaning* of a character."[71] Indeed, I agree with Johnson that our "problem is not the lack of data, but the inaccessibility of meaning" in the vast primary data. "Meaning derives from the interpretation of the facts rather than the facts themselves. And such interpretation depends on story."[72] Have not the psychologists of religion helped us see that psychobiography is important in comprehending the story of Jesus?

We need to comprehend that history is accessible only through tradition and comprehensible only through interpretation.[73] Thus we need to ask the following question: "Is the New Testament witness so powerful to so many because the story is not only historical but also real?" Is not the story of Jesus fundamentally founded on some real, uninterpreted events in history?[74] Thus I must disagree with Johnson, who is too focused on exposing the problems with the Jesus Seminar, when he advises that "Christian faith (then and now) is based on religious claims concerning the present power of Jesus."[75] That statement can be used out of the context in which Johnson has carefully crafted it; if so, it can lead to Docetism, ahistorical mysticism, and idealism. I am convinced we should add to Johnson's assessment that these "religious claims" must be grounded not only in what is putatively the "real Jesus" but also in the secular history of Rome and of Judaism. We professors must not teach something that would make our students sound foolish in the halls of the Hebrew University in Jerusalem.[76]

Why is Jesus Research necessary? Jesus Research should begin with purely historical and scientific methods and honest questions. It must be "disinterested" in the sense that one should not lead the evidence to obtain a desired conclusion. When scientific research is completed—if only temporarily—then there is more to do, at least for the Jew and the Christian (including the Latter-day Saints). We need to be alert and to explore how sacred traditions and faith are informed by the ramifications of the scientific study of antiquity, especially Jesus in the first half of the first century A.D.

Christians need to avoid some major pitfalls. On the one hand, we must not err and seek to ground Christian faith on some mirage of objective scientific knowledge. To remove from Christian faith the scandalous and the gnawing uncertainty of a personal and total commitment drains authentic spirituality of faith. On the other hand, authentic Christian faith is more than a Kierke-gaardian leap of faith. If one is to follow Jesus, then some reliable knowledge about how he lived and what he thought is imperative. If Christianity is to survive or blossom in the ever increasingly secular world, it must be more aware of its origins in first-century Jewish culture. It must also be grounded and enriched by absorbing the truths authentically embodied in Jesus' life and message.[77] And as Madsen points out, after living in Jerusalem, one must avoid the fallacy of thinking that "the main vehicle" for understanding Jesus is his words. We should also comprehend that his meaning comes to life when we experience and imagine his environment and circumstance.[78]

Schweitzer, who perceived Jesus to be incomparably great, saw chaos in the works on the life of Jesus that postdated his own *magnum opus*. On the one hand, Schweitzer and his generation were correct to point out that we cannot psychoanalyze Jesus—as if we could use Freudian methods to examine Jesus who lies before us on a couch. On the other hand, it is also unwise to follow Bultmann and his school and refuse to consider Jesus' self-consciousness because his earliest followers and the earliest sources had no objective interest in his personal development. As I pointed out in *Jesus within Judaism*, every person has some self-understanding; hence, the historian and not only the theologian is entitled to ask about Jesus' self-understanding. Now, with the new methods developed from psychologists of religion, we can explore the psychobiographical possibilities as we imagine Jesus, the man, in his earthly context. Perhaps the following are only minor questions: What was Jesus' relationship with his father, Joseph, and his mother, Mary?[79] What was his relationship with John the Baptizer and Mary Magdalene? Did he have an elevated ego, and did he claim that he was the Messiah? Surely, historical research leads us to ask questions that have been charted by the psychologists of religion.

In the twenty-first century we may, at first glance, see an even greater chaos among Jesus scholars than Schweitzer envisioned. With patience and more pellucid perception we may comprehend a challenging consensus that helps us see through the mists of history more clearly. Certainly, there is at least a consensus regarding the big questions: Who was Jesus? Who did he think he was? What was his purpose? How did he think he was related to God?

Belief in Jesus Christ is rooted in faith in a Jew named Jesus and dedicated to a faithful and honest—and above all a scientific and disinterested—inquiry into the What *(Was)* and the How *(Wie)* that give meaning to the dilemma of a public crucifixion and confer sense on the That *(Das)*.

Can any of these questions be adequately assessed without any concern for psychobiography? And should those who work on Jesus' psychobiography not be better trained in the archaeology and history of first-century Palestinian culture? I am convinced most experts on the historical Jesus would today say "yes" to both questions.

Addendum

After this essay had been completed, another book appeared that belongs within the category of a psychobiography of Jesus. It is Andries van Aarde's *Fatherless in Galilee: Jesus as Child of God*

(Harrisburg, Pa.: Trinity Press International, 2001). The author is a professor of New Testament at the University of Pretoria in South Africa.

Andres van Aarde—informed by Erickson's *Young Man Luther* (which seems to have stimulated those engaged in a psychobiography of Jesus), by specialists in Jesus Research (especially Crossan, Horsley, Meier, and Sanders), and also by the challenging claims made by Schaberg—is convinced that Jesus' loss of his father is fundamental in understanding Jesus' message and life. Aarde is convinced that Jesus, who became fatherless, called on God to act paternally on behalf of his children, Israel. Jesus not only destroyed conventional patriarchal values in early Judaism, he "focused his ministry on 'fatherless' children and 'patriarchless' women."[80]

Aarde's *Fatherless in Galilee* prompts some brief reflections on the differences between the psychological study of Jesus at the beginning of the twentieth century and the recent psychobiographies of Jesus. Four differences make the two periods of work paradigmatically different. First, in Schweitzer's day, psychopathologists simply applied Freudian psychology to ancient sources in an attempt to prove some mental disorder in Jesus' mind; that is, the sources for studying Jesus were the paranoid persons in their own clinics. Second, these authors, in contrast to those who write psychobiographies of Jesus, were untrained in New Testament research and remained uncritical of the sources about Jesus. Third, the authors of the pyschobiographies, in contrast to the former attempts, take seriously the historical context of Jesus and learn from some of the leaders in Jesus Research. Fourth, as Schweitzer pointed out in his *Psychiatric Study of Jesus,* the psychopathologists depicted a hallucinating Jesus. Thus, the psychopathologists projected onto the first century and Jesus a portrait of a liberalized, indeed paranoid, Jesus that existed only in their own "modern" conceptual world. In summation, the psychopathological approaches to Jesus were unscientific psychological creations, but the current psychobiographers are informed by and contribute to historical research. They help us explore what the intention of the human Jesus was in his own context.

Notes

1. Walter P. Weaver, *The Historical Jesus in the Twentieth Century, 1900–1950* (Harrisburg, Pa.: Trinity Press International, 1999), xi.

2. This perspective appears in the uninformed, uncritical, and journalistic book by Lee Strobel entitled *The Case for Christ: A Journalist's Personal Investigation of the Evidence for Jesus* (Grand Rapids, Mich.: Zondervan, 1998). I am encouraged that Strobel moved from atheism or skepticism to Christianity by his own search for Jesus, but his search is far from objective and critical, despite the promises of the attractive anecdote that begins the book (pp. 9–15). I would expect all scholarly work to lead to a better perception of truth.

3. Craig A. Evans, *Life of Jesus Research* (Leiden: Brill, 1996).

4. Of course, Albert Schweitzer was correct to point out that Reimarus was the inaugurator of the Old Quest.

5. Albert Schweitzer, *The Quest of the Historical Jesus: A Critical Study of Its Progress from Reimarus to Wrede,* trans. William Montgomery, 2nd ed. (London: Black, 1911).

6. One needs to be careful not to confuse the German second edition with the English second edition (which was based on the German first edition).

7. George Tyrrell had focused his thoughts on the liberal Protestant Adolph Harnack: "The Christ that Harnack sees, looking back through nineteen centuries of Catholic darkness, is only the reflection of a liberal Protestant face, seen at the bottom of a deep well." Of course, Tyrrell's own fiery spirit and some tension between Catholics and Protestants are not well hidden in this outburst. See Tyrrell, *Christianity at the Crossroads* (1909; reprint, London: Allen and Unwin, 1963), 49. I am grateful to Weaver for his discussions in *The Historical Jesus* on Tyrrell's pellucid insight.

8. One of the best examinations of the denigration of historicism by Barth and Bultmann is by Hugh Anderson in *Jesus and Christian*

Origins: A Commentary on Modern Viewpoints (Oxford: Oxford University Press, 1964), 16–55.

9. For a recent discussion that attempts to show that Paul possibly knew about Jesus' life and teachings and not only about his passion and resurrection, see David Wenham, "The Story of Jesus Known to Paul," in *Jesus of Nazareth: Lord and Christ—Essays on the Historical Jesus and New Testament Christology,* ed. Joel B. Green and Max Turner (Grand Rapids, Mich.: Eerdmans, 1994), 297–311.

10. Pierre Benoit, "Réflexions sur la 'Formgeschichtliche Methode,'" in *Exégèse et théologie* (Paris: Cerf, 1961), 1:25–61. See the recent collection of Nils A. Dahl's essays in *Jesus the Christ: The Historical Origins of Christological Doctrine,* ed. Donald H. Juel (Minneapolis: Fortress, 1991).

11. Ernst Käsemann, "The Problem of the Historical Jesus," in *Essays on New Testament Themes,* trans. W. J. Montague (London: SCM, 1964).

12. W. Barnes Tatum rightly sees the shift from a theologically loaded "quest" to a new approach to the historical Jesus. He calls it "post-quest" and places the date at 1985 because of the appearance of Sanders's *Jesus in Judaism* and the first session of the Jesus Seminar in that year. Neither initiated the new movement, but both were part of it. See Tatum, *In Quest of Jesus,* rev. ed. (Nashville: Abingdon, 1999), 102–3. Tatum's 1985 date cannot have been in his first edition (1982), yet that book signifies that something new in the study of the historical Jesus had begun.

13. Marcus J. Borg, *Jesus, a New Vision: The Spirit, Culture, and the Life of Discipleship* (San Francisco: Harper & Row, 1987). See Borg, *Jesus in Contemporary Scholarship* (Valley Forge, Pa.: Trinity Press International, 1994); Borg, ed., *Jesus at 2000* (Boulder, Colo.: Westview, 1997); as well as Borg and Nicholas T. Wright, *The Meaning of Jesus: Two Visions* (San Francisco: HarperSanFrancisco, 1999).

14. Ben Witherington III, *The Jesus Quest: The Third Search for the Jew of Nazareth* (Downers Grove, Ill.: InterVarsity Press, 1995).

15. Raymond E. Brown, *The Birth of the Messiah: A Commentary on the Infancy Narratives in the Gospels of Matthew and Luke,* rev. ed. (New York: Doubleday, 1993).

16. Jerome Murphy-O'Connor, *Paul: A Critical Life* (Oxford: Oxford University Press, 1997).

17. See especially Richard A. Horsley, *Jesus and the Spiral of Violence: Popular Jewish Resistance in Roman Palestine* (San Francisco: Harper & Row, 1987).

18. Nicholas T. Wright, *Jesus and the Victory of God* (London: SPCK, 1996); Wright, *Who Was Jesus?* (Grand Rapids, Mich.: Eerdmans, 1992).

19. Paula Fredriksen, *From Jesus to Christ: The Origins of the New Testament Images of Jesus* (New Haven: Yale University Press, 1988); and Fredriksen, *Jesus of Nazareth, King of the Jews: A Jewish Life and the Emergence of Christianity* (New York: Knopf, 1999).

20. Weaver, *The Historical Jesus,* 449 pages.

21. John P. Meier, *A Marginal Jew: Rethinking the Historical Jesus,* 3 vols. (New York: Doubleday, 1991–2001).

22. James H. Charlesworth and Walter P. Weaver, eds., *Jesus Two Thousand Years Later* (Harrisburg, Pa.: Trinity Press International, 2000).

23. I agree with Borg, *Jesus, the New Vision,* that Jesus "was dominated throughout by intercourse with the other world" (p. 42) and that he identified "himself with the prophets" (p. 48).

24. It is certain that Romans were responsible for Jesus' crucifixion. See John D. Crossan, *Who Killed Jesus? Exposing the Roots of Anti-Semitism in the Gospel Story of the Death of Jesus* (San Francisco: HarperSanFrancisco, 1995).

25. E. P. Sanders, *Jesus and Judaism* (Philadelphia: Fortress, 1985), 61–119; John P. Meier, "The Circle of the Twelve: Did It Exist during Jesus' Public Ministry?" *Journal of Biblical Literature* 116/4 (1997): 635–72.

26. Hendrikus Boers, *Who Was Jesus?* (San Francisco: Harper & Row, 1989), 93.

27. See the important insights found in Doron Mendels's *The Rise and Fall of Jewish Nationalism* (New York: Doubleday, 1992).

28. Marcus Borg, *Conflict, Holiness, and Politics in the Teachings of Jesus* (New York: Mellen, 1984).

29. Ernst Bammel and Charles F. D. Moule, eds., *Jesus and the Politics of His Day* (Cambridge: Cambridge University Press, 1984).

30. The title of Meier's book, *A Marginal Jew,* is not representative of Meier's erudite insights. When Meier uses the term *marginal,* he means

that Jesus' life would not have been featured on CNN and that he was not a typical Jew.

31. John D. Crossan does argue that Jesus was a peasant. See especially Crossan, *The Historical Jesus: The Life of a Mediterranean Jewish Peasant* (San Francisco: HarperSanFrancisco, 1991).

32. Bruce Chilton and Craig A. Evans, eds., *Authenticating the Activities of Jesus,* New Testament Tools and Studies 28.2 (Leiden: Brill, 1999).

33. Ibid., ix.

34. I agree with Peter Stuhlmacher that any attempt to build bridges of understanding between Christians and Jews must be honest. For example, Christians should not think they are being admirably objective by claiming that Jesus must not be allowed to make messianic claims. Stuhlmacher, *Jesus of Nazareth—Christ of Faith,* trans. Siegfried S. Schatzmann (Peabody, Mass.: Hendrickson, 1993), 5.

35. William Klassen, "The Authenticity of Judas' Participation in the Arrest of Jesus," in *Authenticating the Activities of Jesus,* 407.

36. John Spong is convinced that Judas was a name (and story) invented by "Christians." See Spong, *Liberating the Gospels: Reading the Bible with Jewish Eyes* (San Francisco: HarperSanFrancisco, 1997), 257–76.

37. In addition to the other works already cited, see Raymond E. Brown, *The Death of the Messiah: From Gethsemane to the Grave* (New York: Doubleday, 1994); and Ellis Rivkin, *What Crucified Jesus?* (Nashville: Abingdon, 1984).

38. John D. Crossan, *Jesus: A Revolutionary Biography* (San Francisco: HarperSanFrancisco, 1995), 152.

39. David Flusser, with R. Steven Notley, *Jesus,* 2nd ed. (Jerusalem: Magnes, 1998).

40. Brad H. Young, *The Parables: Jewish Tradition and Christian Interpretation* (Peabody, Mass.: Hendrickson, 1998).

41. Charles W. Hedrick, *Parables as Poetic Fictions: The Creative Voice of Jesus* (Peabody, Mass.: Hendrickson, 1994).

42. See the contributions in James H. Charlesworth, ed., *Jesus and the Dead Sea Scrolls* (New York: Doubleday, 1992).

43. William Klassen, "The Authenticity of the Command: 'Love Your Enemies,'" in *Authenticating the Words of Jesus,* ed. Bruce Chilton and Craig A. Evans, New Testament Tools and Studies 28.1 (Leiden: Brill, 1999), 386 n. 4 and 386.

44. See Nicholas T. Wright, *Jesus and the Victory of God* (London: SPCK, 1996); Sanders, *Jesus and Judaism;* and Sanders, *The Historical Figure of Jesus* (New York: Penguin, 1993).

45. Craig A. Evans, "Authenticating the Activities of Jesus," in *Authenticating the Activities of Jesus*, 5.

46. Those who are interested in methods for ascertaining authentic Jesus tradition should also consult Craig A. Evans's *Jesus and His Contemporaries: Comparative Studies* (Leiden: Brill, 1995), 1–49.

47. See especially James C. VanderKam, "Righteous One, Messiah, Chosen One, the Son of Man in 1 Enoch 37–71," in *The Messiah: Developments in Earliest Judaism and Christianity,* ed. James H. Charlesworth (Minneapolis: Fortress, 1992), 176–85.

48. See, e.g., George W. E. Nickelsburg, "Enoch, Books of," in *Encyclopedia of the Dead Sea Scrolls,* ed. Lawrence H. Schiffman and James C. VanderKam (New York: Oxford University Press, 2000), 1:250; Paolo Sacchi, *L'apocalittica giudaica e la sua storia* (Brescia: Paideia editrice, 1990), 154–69; and Siegbert Uhlig, *Das Äthiopische Henochbuch* (Gütersloh: Mohn, 1984).

49. John C. O'Neill, *Who Did Jesus Think He Was?* (Leiden: Brill, 1995), 6, 164–87. I do not agree that the Gospel of John was put together by "only collectors and dramatists" (p. 185).

50. Klassen, "The Authenticity of the Command."

51. For the latest on Jesus' morality, see Anthony E. Harvey, *Strenuous Commands: The Ethic of Jesus* (Philadelphia: Trinity Press International, 1990).

52. It is focused on *Jesus and Archaeology,* and all the leading archaeological experts participated. The proceedings will be published by Eerdmans in 2003. A very helpful, but dated, guide to Jesus and archaeology is John J. Rousseau and Rami Arav, *Jesus and His World: An Archaeological and Cultural Dictionary* (Minneapolis: Fortress, 1994). Also, see the equally dated book by James H. Charlesworth entitled *Jesus within Judaism: New Light from Exciting Archaeological Discoveries* (New York: Doubleday, 1988).

53. Robert W. Funk, *Honest to Jesus: Jesus for a New Millennium* (San Francisco: HarperSanFrancisco, 1996); Funk (and the Jesus Seminar), *The Acts of Jesus* (San Francisco: HarperSanFrancisco, 1996); Robert W. Funk, Roy W. Hoover, and the Jesus Seminar, *The Five Gospels: The*

Search for the Authentic Words of Jesus (New York: Macmillan, 1993). It is interesting to observe that the two volumes by Funk and the Jesus Seminar and the two volumes edited by Chilton and Evans are divided into Jesus' acts and Jesus' words. I am dubious that a comparison of the four books would be fruitful: they are not responding to each other, and too many other important related works would be ignored.

54. Hermann Gunkel, *Israelitisches Heldentum und Kriegsfrömmigkeit im Alten Testament* (Göttingen: Vandenhoeck & Ruprecht, 1916), 2–3, translated in Klassen, "The Authenticity of the Command," 392.

55. Bruce Chilton and Craig A. Evans, eds., *Studying the Historical Jesus: Evaluation of the State of Current Research* (Leiden: Brill, 1994).

56. Bruce Chilton and Craig A. Evans, *Jesus in Context: Temple, Purity, and Restoration* (Leiden: Brill, 1997).

57. Early portions of it are at Florida Southern College. I am grateful to Weaver for the opportunity to study these pages.

58. Gerd Theissen, *Sociology of Early Palestinian Christianity,* trans. John Bowden (Philadelphia: Fortress, 1978). Also, for superb reading to obtain a feeling for life in ancient Palestine during the time of Jesus, see Theissen, *The Shadow of the Galilean: The Quest of the Historical Jesus in Narrative Form,* trans. John Bowden (Philadelphia: Fortress, 1987).

59. Richard A. Horsley, *Sociology and the Jesus Movement* (New York: Crossroad, 1989).

60. Ekkehard W. Stegemann and Wolfgang Stegemann, *The Jesus Movement: A Social History of Its First Century* (Minneapolis: Fortress, 1999).

61. See, e.g., Gustave Le Bon, *The Crowd: A Study of the Popular Mind* (New York: Viking, 1960). See also Elias Canetti, *Crowds and Power,* trans. Carol Stewart (New York: Seabury, 1978); and R. Fenn, "Crowds, Time, and the Essence of Society," in *Secularization, Rationalism, and Sectarianism: Essays in Honour of Bryan R. Wilson,* ed. Eileen Barker, James A. Beckford, and Karel Dobbelaere (New York: Oxford University Press, 1993).

62. Contemporary visions of Mary are well known, but visions of Christ are habitually kept secret and unexamined. For a recent attempt to take these "Christic visions" seriously and to study them in light of earlier books by Sparrow and Huyssens (and in light of P. Feyerabend's work in the philosophy of science), see Phillip H. Wiebe, *Visions of Jesus: Direct*

Encounters from the New Testament to Today (New York: Oxford University Press, 1997).

63. John W. Miller, *Jesus at Thirty: A Psychological and Historical Portrait* (Minneapolis: Fortress, 1997).

64. Ibid., 80.

65. See the contributions in James H. Charlesworth, "A Caveat on Textual Transmission and the Meaning of *Abba:* A Study of the Lord's Prayer," in *The Lord's Prayer and Other Prayer Texts from the Greco-Roman Era,* ed. James H. Charlesworth, Mark Harding, and Mark C. Kiley (Valley Forge, Pa.: Trinity Press International, 1994), 1–14.

66. Miller, *Jesus at Thirty,* 72.

67. Donald Capps, *Jesus: A Psychological Biography* (St. Louis, Mo.: Chalice Press, 2000).

68. There is no doubt that Jesus did perform amazing healings; his opponents admitted as much when they said he was able to perform such healings because he was possessed. For a recent study of Jesus' healings, see Stevan L. Davies, *Jesus the Healer: Possession, Trance, and the Origins of Christianity* (New York: Continuum, 1995).

69. This position was developed by Jane Schaberg in *The Illegitimacy of Jesus: A Feminist Theological Interpretation of the Infancy Narratives* (New York: Crossroad, 1990).

70. Capps, *Jesus,* 260.

71. Luke T. Johnson, *The Real Jesus: The Misguided Quest for the Historical Jesus and the Truth of the Traditional Gospels* (San Francisco: HarperSanFrancisco, 1996), 133.

72. Ibid.

73. I am here indebted to conversations with Ernst Käsemann.

74. See my further reflections in "The Historical Jesus: Sources and a Sketch," in *Jesus Two Thousand Years Later,* 84–128.

75. Johnson, *The Real Jesus,* 133.

76. I am most grateful to Truman G. Madsen for the opportunity to teach in the Jerusalem Center for Near Eastern Studies. Madsen begins one of his publications as follows: "Daily for the past two years I have looked out from the Jerusalem Center on the Mount of Olives to the vista of the ancient city of Jerusalem." Indeed, I have seen the view—at sunset it can be spiritually invigorating. See Madsen, "The Temple and

the Atonement," in *Temples of the Ancient World,* ed. Donald W. Parry (Salt Lake City: Deseret Book and FARMS, 1994), 63–79.

77. I have tried to avoid referring to non-English publications, but one work is extremely important to note. Criteria for authenticating Jesus' traditions behind the Jesus traditions are assessed in Gerd Theissen and D. Winter's *Die Kriterienfrage in der Jesusforschung* (Freiburg: Universitätsverlag Freiburg Schweiz, 1997). Also, see Gerd Theissen and Annette Merz, *The Historical Jesus: A Comprehensive Guide,* trans. John Bowden (Minneapolis: Fortress, 1998).

78. Truman G. Madsen, "The Olive Press: A Symbol of Christ," in *The Allegory of the Olive Tree,* ed. Stephen D. Ricks and John W. Welch (Salt Lake City: Deseret Book and FARMS, 1994), 1–10.

79. Truman G. Madsen rightly points out that in the early traditions recorded in the New Testament, a kinship was perceived between Messiah and Father and thus between Jesus and God. See Madsen, "'Putting on the Names': A Jewish-Christian Legacy," in *By Study and Also by Faith: Essays in Honor of Hugh W. Nibley,* ed. John M. Lundquist and Stephen D. Ricks (Salt Lake City: Deseret Book and FARMS, 1990), 1:458–81, see esp. 467.

80. Andries G. van Aarde, *Fatherless in Galilee: Jesus as Child of God* (Harrisburg, Pa.: Trinity Press International, 2001), 205.

CHAPTER 3

ROOM TO TALK:
REASON'S NEED FOR FAITH

James E. Faulconer

Truman G. Madsen's slim volume *Eternal Man*[1] had a profound effect on me, and when I ask others who were students in the late sixties or early seventies about it, I find that it was equally important for them. The book was not academically profound, but then it had no pretensions to be. As Madsen says in the introduction, its chapters were intended "as a kind of 'midrash.' . . . The goal has been to clarify rather than to verify, with little room for argument, except an implicit appeal to introspection" (p. viii).

The result of that goal was that one can find much to challenge in the book: Must we understand the doctrine of premortally existent intelligences to imply that we have existed eternally as individuals? Does Madsen not create straw persons in his descriptions of orthodox Christian and other beliefs? For example, is it true that religious existentialism, such as that of Søren Kierkegaard, is "utter pessimism" (p. 29)? And does Madsen not reify being when he argues against the dualism of traditional theology by dismissing its concerns for nothing and for being (see pp. 31–32, 44)? Does he not dismiss too easily some of the traditional problems of theology and the philosophy of religion, such as how it is possible to speak meaningfully of a being who transcends our mortal finitude (see p. 35)? How does defining freedom as self-determination remove all the problems of freedom and determinism (see p. 66 n. 9)? It would not be difficult to add to the list.

But adding to the list would be beside the point. It would mean refusing to recognize the book for what it claims to be and is: a primer to aid us in our introspection about the intellectual strengths of our belief in the premortal existence of spirits. If, as such a primer, the book raises these questions and more, it fulfills its function, inducing us to think about its topic. Perhaps it will someday even goad one of us to provide the promised "tome which is not pressed [as Madsen's was] for abbreviation" (p. viii)—a tome that one wishes Madsen himself could find the time to offer, all the while recognizing that his life continues to be busy enough to make that difficult.

However, for many like myself, *Eternal Man* was important not so much because of the problems with which it dealt or the positions that it took on the questions of the eternality of individuals, divine omnipotence, the materiality of the Divine, human freedom, and so on, but because of what it did. More than teaching a particular doctrine or suggesting any particular solution to a philosophical or theological problem, the book gave its readers permission to think about these kinds of problems, to read the books listed in its many footnotes, and to explore books like them. *Eternal Man* said, "It is good to think about and deal with these issues." It gave those of us in college and graduate school in the late 1960s an alternative to the two most common positions taken with regard to such things: "One position assumes that they [the ideas about premortal existence] are so remote and incomplete that a 'practical man' avoids thinking about them. The other assumes that by mere reference to pre[mortal] existence one can 'explain' all events and eventualities" (p. 14). By writing *Eternal Man*, Truman Madsen said to me—and, I believe, to many others—"Take seriously the admonition from the Prophet Joseph Smith that introduces chapter two: 'When things that are of the greatest importance are passed over by weak-minded men without even a thought, I want to see truth in all its bearings and hug it to my bosom'" (p. 23). Reading *Eternal Man* made me want not to be one of the "weak-minded." The book gave me an intellectual goal and told me that my new goal was not only commensurable with my faith, but an expression of it.

In reminding us that Joseph Smith described the gospel as requiring "careful and ponderous and solemn thoughts" (p. ix), Madsen said, "A related kind of authority is needed in this realm. It is what, in the vernacular is called 'room to talk'" (p. ix). By suggesting the possibility of taking our faith seriously while also understanding the writings of scholars, and of thinking about both without being ashamed of or frightened by one or the other, Madsen opened such a room, and many entered.

Given today's hypersensitivities of various kinds, such room to talk is as difficult to come by as it ever was. Some, recognizing that current trends of thinking are not consonant with the gospel (as if they ever were), think that we should shut our eyes and ears to such things and that, especially, we should not speak of them to the young for fear of corrupting them. Others think that it is enough merely to repeat conventional wisdom about the gospel or even, perhaps, merely to repeat the truths of the gospel. For them, repetition without investigation is enough to answer all questions. A few others, convinced that this or that seemingly newfangled notion is, at last, the answer to our problems and questions, would either ignore the gospel or twist it into a shape that better fits their new-found intellectual faith. But all these kinds of problems respond to the difficulties of the intellect with one kind of dogmatism or another. They shut the door on any room to talk.

In this paper, I address the relation of faith to reason. I doubt that I will add new insights to the discussion of that hoary subject.

Rather than do so, I intend to say a few things that I hope will, in imitation of *Eternal Man,* use the topic to open, and leave open, room to talk. I argue that faith and reason are commensurable. I have heard persons whose ideas I respect suggest otherwise. Nevertheless, I think my conclusion is one with which most members of the Church of Jesus Christ of Latter-day Saints would agree.[2] In making this argument, though I argue for what I believe to be true, I leave open the possibility that I am wrong. One reason that philosophers offer arguments is to make it possible for others, by following the steps of their reasoning, to show them where they went wrong.

Besides arguing for the commensurability of faith and reason, I will go further. I suggest that faith is fundamental to reason, though I do no more than sketch an argument for that suggestion.[3] The full argument for that claim would take at least another paper and probably a book. Neither of the positions that I outline is novel, and in some circles they may even be ordinary. But the marvel of the ordinary and wonder at that marvel is sometimes itself not so ordinary. In fact, I think it has become so *in*ordinate in our day that we often need to be reminded of quite ordinary things. So I offer here some musings and reflections on the relation of faith to reason, with an argument or two, in the same spirit as that found in *Eternal Man*—namely, as points for reflection and thought more than as a philosophical treatise.

In particular, I want to suggest that faith is fundamental to reason, but let me begin my reflections on that claim with a story, for my reflections have their genesis in an experience that occurred about seven years ago. I think the story illustrates that rationality cannot be reduced to sets of propositions or beliefs related to each other by implication. Instead (and I argue that this is true of every kind of rationality), rationality must begin with something outside of such sets and relations, as I think my experience will suggest.

My oldest daughter had been an officer for one of the Utah chapters of the Future Homemakers of America, and the state organization held its end-of-the-school-year banquet in Salt Lake City. I was going through all the usual hoopla politely but condescendingly. I was there to do my duty as a father, although I would have much preferred to be elsewhere. Chicken dinner for 750 accompanied by speeches and awards for a large group of fourteen-through seventeen-year-olds was not my idea of a great way to spend my Saturday afternoon. Sitting next to me at the table for parents was a couple about my age, both of whom were obviously enjoying what I was merely tolerating, from the food to the entertainment. When I asked where they were from, he replied, "Wayne County."

"Where in Wayne County?"

"Just Wayne County."

"How far away is that?"

"About a four-hour drive."

It quickly began to be more difficult for me to condescend. Their four-hour trip made my forty-five-minute one look like a walk across the street, but I was the one who was slightly irritated about having to make the trip. On the other hand, had I stopped to reflect (although I did not), I could have explained their enjoyment of the occasion geographically: such things might look good in comparison to the pleasures of Wayne County. Our conversation continued:

"About what time will you get back tonight?"

"About 11:00."

"Well, at least tomorrow is Sunday. Maybe you can sleep in."

Stupid me. I had assumed that all people have five-day-a-week jobs, Monday through Friday, and that they work from eight to five.

"Well, it's lambing season and one or the other of us has to get up every hour to check the sheep. We trade off, so we can sleep about two hours at a time."

Condescension turned to humiliation: this man and woman loved their daughter more than I loved mine. Though, unlike me, they actually had to sacrifice to be at the banquet, they were pleased to be there, enjoying what happened not because they were so intellectually blighted that they thought that seventeen-year-olds actually have much of importance to say and certainly not because they liked the food on the menu or found the pleasures of Wayne County so abysmal. They were there because they loved their daughter and took pleasure from seeing her enjoy herself and be honored. I love my daughter, too, but what I saw as an inconvenient and mildly irritating responsibility that is consequent on loving that daughter, they saw as part of that love. That experience *persuaded* me in a moment that they were right and I was wrong. Their lives were right in a way that mine was not, and I came to that understanding by seeing a small part of their lives.

The couple next to me did not think—almost certainly would not have thought—to offer me what philosophers recognize as rational arguments, and they almost certainly did not have the training to do so in a way that I would acknowledge as philosophical. In spite of that, their behavior did allow me to come to a conclusion: the conclusion that one should enjoy such events. They did not intend to do so. I had no impression that they were trying to teach me anything—certainly not that I was wrong. Nevertheless, being in their presence did persuade me. They *were* something like evidence; they did not offer it. I would have had to have been unreasonable to deny the conclusion that their behavior persuaded me to accept. What was the nature of the experience I had in comprehending what their lives revealed? How did that experience make it possible for me to be persuaded, to come to a rational conclusion, immediately and without a chain of reasoning (deductive or inductive) from assumptions to conclusion?

How did seeing them and talking with them make possible a rational belief that I was wrong (the *conviction* that I was wrong, if I can use the word in both of its senses) without any chain of reasoning? What I saw in them was neither an axiomatic truth nor a truth deduced from axioms. It was not a "bare empirical fact" (granting, for the argument, that there are such dubious things). It was not an objective truth.[4] But neither was it merely a subjective opinion. My judgment of myself was rational. Some evidence that it was a rational belief rather than a merely subjective one is that others, hearing the story, know its conclusion before I tell it; they are able to adduce the same conclusion from the story that I did from the experience. The behavior of the couple from Wayne County was like evidence for a rational conclusion, but it did not require that I begin with a belief and then come to a conclusion based on that belief in order to be persuaded.

Before trying to give an account of why the kind of knowledge I acquired that afternoon was rational, let me be clear about what I am saying: Seeing the couple next to me and listening to them talk about their daughter was sufficient to persuade me (in a sense of the term that I will leave open) of the inferiority of my love for my daughter compared to their love for theirs. That is not to say that I could not have been wrong about that belief. It is only to say that the belief to which I came was rational. It had sufficient grounds and could not be explained solely in terms of my previous beliefs. It was not just subjective. This is also not to say that persuasion cannot take other forms. It is only to suggest that this event raises important questions about rationality, particular questions that may help us think about rationality as a whole. Careful readers may worry that I neglect important distinctions in this paper: they might argue that rationality cannot be reduced to a response to relevant information, that giving reasons for a belief is not the same as being evidence for a belief, and so forth.[5] Nevertheless, recognizing the legitimacy of that worry, I will proceed. I am not arguing that response to relevant information and rationality are the same, and I do not think my argument requires that they be the same. Instead, I am looking at a particular kind of case—the case in which I find myself persuaded of something based on something that our ordinary metatalk about reason seems to exclude or at least to render problematic, as in the example of the couple from Wayne County. That kind of case is sufficient for the purposes of this paper—namely, to raise questions about our understanding of reason that will allow me to argue that reason and faith are commensurable and to sketch an argument that reason requires faith.

I will suggest that faith and reason are commensurable by arguing that reason always requires something outside the chain of reasons (such as my experience of that couple). In addition, as mentioned, I will sketch what I think may be an argument that the relation of reason to what is outside itself is a matter of faith. If that is the case, then at least one way in which faith and reason are commensurable is that the latter requires the former.

Before I make my case, however, let me briefly take up another way in which faith and reason are commensurable: not only does reason need faith, but faith needs reason. If, as it is often defined, faith is understood to be belief or even knowledge in the absence of compelling reasons, then it is obviously true by definition that faith and reason are mutually exclusive. When we talk about faith, if we are not careful, we almost always slip into our semiphilosophical or theological mode and, when we do, we are likely to say something in which faith is defined in this way.[6] Although this response is common, I think it is seriously mistaken. Alvin Plantinga has argued—brilliantly, I believe—that we should reject that definition: compelling experience may be sufficient, even in the absence of compelling beliefs.[7] Faith is best thought of, not as belief in the absence of reasons, but as fidelity to something that one has been given, such as an experience or covenant, or trust in someone, such as God. That is how it seems most often to be used in the scriptures.

Besides appealing to Plantinga's argument, I have additional grounds (some of them related to Plantinga's) for rejecting the common separation of faith from reason. For one thing, to think in that way confuses faith with opinion (although even opinion has its reasons and evidences—often, but not always, poor ones). If we confuse faith and opinion, we should not be surprised when arguments showing the insufficiency of opinion and the necessity of moving from opinion to knowledge grounded in reason also work as arguments against faith. But it is a mistake to define faith as belief without reasons.

Paul is explicit about faith being a matter of evidence: "Now faith is the substance [ὑπόστασις—*hypostasis,* meaning 'reality' or 'realization'] of things hoped for, the evidence [ἔλεγχος—*elenchus,* meaning 'proof' or 'argument for']⁸ of things not seen" (Hebrews 11:1). Nephi and Lehi, the sons of Helaman, convert hundreds to faith by offering them great evidence (see Helaman 5:50). Several years later, Nephi tells the people that their unbelief is unreasonable, a rejection of convincing evidence (see Helaman 8:24). Faith has reasons and requires them; at least part of what is wrong in the supposed confrontation between faith and reason is that a poor definition of faith is used. However, since I will assume that most of the audience of this essay consists of practicing, faithful Latter-day Saints, this argument needs little development. They already know, at least in their hearts, that there is more to faith than belief without reason; that faith is essentially trust and fidelity rather than belief, though beliefs will result from trust and fidelity; and that, when they do, they will have their reasonable ground. Thus my primary focus will be on the nature of reason and its relation to faith.

Aristotle says that to be human is to be rational.⁹ Along with most people, I am willing to accept that assumption without further proof, but the assumption cannot mean that to be human is to offer and listen to arguments. Aristotle's claim is not that human beings are all philosophical in the conventional sense of the term. At best, Aristotle is making the weaker claim that all human beings are capable of using reason. But what does that mean?

In its essence, the problem of reason is simple: does reason have a reason? And if it does, how do we think that reason? How do we establish certain knowledge when reason reaches its end? With some important qualifications, René Descartes—one of the most important fathers of modernism to whom we owe much of our contemporary, ordinary understanding of reason (our "common sense")—assumes that reason has no reason: it begins from principles that are intuitively known to be true without reference to anything else and proceeds logically from step to step, establishing knowledge as certain when it reaches its end.[10] In contemporary philosophical jargon, he is a foundationalist: according to Descartes, there are self-certifying, rational foundations to reason.

It is true that Descartes must know that there is a God in order to know that there really is a world that can be the object of his ratiocination, but, although the existence of the world and our knowledge of that existence require God, reason does not. If it did, Descartes believes, we would never get to a knowledge of God's existence or even of our own, for it requires reason to know either. Thus, Descartes's methodological doubt can get us to the conclusions he reaches only because, for him, reason is self-grounding and complete. It is the only thing without reason; it is its own reason. Despite the fact that much twentieth-century philosophy on both sides of the Atlantic has devoted itself to a critique of the Enlightenment notion of reason, and even with the introduction of such things as probability theory, studies of induction, and new theories of logic, I think that many people—certainly most nonphilosophers—continue to think of reason in terms that are ultimately Cartesian: reason is self-grounding and, in principle, eventually capable of giving a complete description of the world.

But I see only two possible consequences of the claim that reason is self-grounding and complete: radical skepticism or totalitarianism. David Hume shows us the first of these: if we accept Descartes's foundationalist position and reject the proof for God's existence (as we most certainly can when we confine our thinking to what can be demonstrated by reason unaided), then we are reduced to the tautologies of pure logic and to reporting the fact of immediately present experience (which may not be able to be plural without losing its immediacy). Even memory of very recent events cannot be trusted.[11]

On the other hand, if we find a rational way around Hume's argument, a way of speaking about the world rationally (or if, as many have done, we ignore Hume's argument), then we accept Descartes's assumption that reason is ultimately adequate to the world: it is, in principle, possible to make a list of the true propositions that give a complete description of the world at any given point in time and to relate those propositions to one another by logical implication alone. Emmanuel Levinas argues that such an understanding of reason is not just mistaken but eventually amounts to totalitarianism—even political totalitarianism—and, in the end, the horror of Auschwitz.[12]

As extreme as that claim is, I find it plausible, although I can here do no more than give a précis of an argument for it. As moderns, we assume that reason makes us masters of this world. To use Francis Bacon's phrase, "knowledge is power" (knowledge rather than virtue, as it was for Plato and other ancients). Given the modern view, the world, including other persons and ourselves, is a set of objects subject to rational investigation. If Bacon is right that knowledge is power, then the search for absolute knowledge (knowledge without limits) is the same as the search for absolute power (power without limits). In our century, that search for power in the form of knowledge, loosed from its traditional mooring in the search for the Good (as it must be loosed if we accept Bacon's identification of knowledge and power), has cost millions of lives and caused unspeakable horror and suffering.[13]

However, even if we reject Levinas's claim as exaggerated, the modern understanding of reason contains an irony: the attempt to fulfill our desire to give a complete description—to say "the last word"—can only result in continuing babble and never in the last, controlling word for which the search for power hungers. In *Metaphysics,*[14] Aristotle argues that without something outside the chain of explanations, there can be no actual explanation.[15] I think that is an argument whose power is often overlooked. Aristotle calls this something the *archē* (ἀρχή), the "origin." It is tempting to think that the *archē* is either the first in the series of efficient or other causes or to think of it as the first instance in a chain of rational explanations. However, to understand it in either of these ways is a mistake, for these two ways of understanding the *archē* are of a piece. Each reduces the *archē* to something with the same philosophical and perhaps ontological status as any other moment in the chain of explanation or account, the only difference being that, mysteriously, it is the first of those moments. Understood that way, Aristotle's argument makes no sense.

However, as we see in Thomas Aquinas's use of Aristotle's argument in the proofs for God's existence,[16] that is a misunderstanding of the argument. As I think Aquinas's use shows, Aristotle's point is that there must be something outside of or beyond or prior to any chain of reasons that grounds the chain in question, or there will be no real reasonings.[17] There must be what Jacques Derrida calls the *supplement,* although the name itself indicates that one speaks from within a chain of reasons rather than from any external point of view.[18] One speaks of what is beyond reason from within reason because there is no alternative.[19]

Expanded, Aristotle's point is this: potentially every chain of reasons—every reasoning or explanation—is infinitely long. No matter where I stop, in principle someone could ask, "And what explains that?" Nevertheless, our chains of reasoning do *not* go on to infinity. Something stops them; something makes any particular stopping point of an adequate chain of reasoning the appropriate place to stop. That which constitutes the adequate stopping point of a chain of reasons, however, is itself not part of that chain. The reason for the explanation is outside the chain. (It could be, and often is, something as straightforward as a state of affairs, "the way things are.") Thus, the real origin or first cause of any chain of reasons is not the point at which we stop saying, "A because of B because of C," but something that is not itself part of the chain, something that we do not account for in our chain of reasons or causal account. It is the ground or origin, the *archē,* that gave rise to the chain (and can, therefore, also give rise to a chain with only one link, the conclusion). That which gives rise to a chain of reasons is something that cannot itself be explained; it is an "uncaused cause," to use the traditional terminology, and cannot be included in the chain of reasons.[20]

Of course, as I pointed out earlier, in principle it *is* always possible to give an account of whatever we can point to, and, on reflection, we can always point to the origin of a chain of reasons. However, when we do so, we remove it from its status outside the chain of reasons. It ceases to be the origin of the chain and becomes one of the things in the chain—namely, its first element. But that means that something new has taken its place as the origin of the chain of reasons as the supplement—in other words, as the ground of explanations and reasons that is not itself part of the chain of reasons. Thus, if we take the Cartesian understanding of reason seriously, if we assume that the origin of reason is not supplemental to reason, that there is nothing outside the process of reason because reason is self-grounding, then we will have no way to stop giving reasons in any particular case.[21] Without a supplement, an *archē,* every chain of reasons will go on to infinity and so will not do as a chain of reasons. An explanation that cannot come to an end is no explanation at all. If explanation requires a last word rather than a supplement, then the desire for the last word is implicitly the desire for garrulousness, not understanding.

This observation that the use of reason depends on something external to that use is a matter of common sense. As always, philosophers argue for what ordinary people know without having to argue it. (From the reports one sees in the news, which are not always to be trusted, one suspects that those in charge of deciding what kinds of social science research projects to fund with government money are all philosophers.) In addition, many more philosophers have known this than have not. Medieval Christians certainly knew that explanations require something beyond them and their processes. The various sorts of empiricists also knew it, as did the Romantics. Marxism maintains that reason has a supplement and, like Christianity, reminds us that ignoring that fact is seldom done in innocence. Plantinga gives us perhaps the best explanation in analytic philosophy of this truth that we all already know.[22] Deconstruction begins with the assumption of this need for something more and then tries to show places in texts and philosophies at which that dependence on what is beyond reason shines through the text. Feminism allies itself with Marxism, although sometimes only implicitly, in recognizing both that reason is not self-grounding and that the claim that it is, is not innocent. Every ordinary member of the church knows that something more than reason is needed. But in spite of the fact that "everyone" knows, at least implicitly, that reason requires a supplement, I think it is also true that few people recognize that fact when they think about reason or faith and that fewer still recognize its implications or the questions it raises.

Having argued that reason requires a supplement, let me now turn to that supplement: what can we say about its character, if anything? and what is its relation to reason? For our purposes, these are the same as the question of how we can reasonably talk about what falls outside reason, so I will treat them as one question. On the face of it, we seem to be faced with a dilemma:

> In order to speak reasonably about something, it seems that it must be within reason.
> The supplement of reason is outside reason.
> So, we cannot speak reasonably about it.

That conclusion at least raises doubts as to the tenability of the second premise, the premise for which I have argued. The argument seems self-contradictory.

To deal with this problem, we need to begin by considering ways in which I think we cannot talk about the supplement of reason. When we hear people talk about faith and reason in church talks or classes or serious conversations about serious matters, they often use the language of Romanticism: there are things to be known and things to be felt; things to be explained rationally and things that defy rational explanation but are known by means of some other faculty. We sometimes use the word that the Romantics gave us for that other faculty, *intuition;* sometimes, instead, we speak of feeling; sometimes we associate the promptings of the Holy Ghost with the Romantic faculty for knowing. Those who take this approach see the problem of reason as we usually understand it, and they try to solve that problem by supplementing reason's realm with another—that of feeling—a realm that goes beyond our ability to conceive and that gives unity to the whole of experience.

However, there are philosophical problems with Romanticism.[23] Having created two realms of knowledge, those who think in this way find that they have doubled their problems. The problem with reason is that it cannot answer the question of how we can know things like the supplement of reason. It is not clear how creating an additional realm of knowledge—the realm of feeling—solves the problems of the first, the realm of reason. In fact, it is unclear how having two realms of knowledge and two faculties for knowing solves the problems that follow from relying on reason alone. If I know by intuition or feeling in one realm, why can I not know that way in the realm of reason? If I cannot know by intuition in the realm of reason, how am I able to know that way in the other realm? Additionally, if reason and intuition are separate realms, why doesn't one of the two realms end up encompassing the other? And if one does not encompass the other, how can I speak of knowledge in both realms? What do the two have in common that allows me to speak of knowledge in both without there being some way of bringing them together, something in common to them? If reason and intuition are distinct ways of knowing, what holds them together so that I, an individual, can make sense of each? With Romanticism, not only are human minds caught in the clutches of Enlightenment, foundationalist reason, we are also hopelessly and essentially schizophrenic.

My final objection to the Romantic solution to the problem of reason is that, by moving everything that could not be understood by Cartesian reason, such as religion and art, to the realm of feeling, Romanticism deprecates those things. Without intending to, certainly, Romantics make *any* talk of knowing the objects of religion metaphorical at best, thereby robbing important parts of our lives, such as religious and aesthetic experience, of their ability to give us genuine knowledge.[24] Their approach to knowledge creates a dilemma: I cannot know the truth about the most important things rationally, and I cannot know what the other way of knowing them is unless I have already experienced it.

Given these problems with Romanticism, though religious people and artists often use the language of Romanticism to talk about the relation of their concerns to reason and to explain their experiences and knowledge, Romanticism will not do. Whatever the relation between reason and its supplement, that relation must be understood from within reason or it will fall into the abyss of irrationalism or, at best, be subordinated to the whim of subjective sentiment (which is where Romanticism ends up, in spite of itself, by cutting itself off from reason). Whatever the relation of reason and its ground, we must understand reason in a way that will allow us to do so without dropping beauty, art, religion, love, feeling, the good, and so on into the abyss of the irrational or nonrational.

It will perhaps be surprising to some that I think Kierkegaard understood that point quite well. In his work, because he understood that we can understand the relation of reason to its supplement only from within reason, he used pseudonyms and irony in his philosophical texts (at the same time that he was writing quite straightforward religious sermons). He wanted to pay appropriate due to reason without falling into the trap of making it independent of faith. As I understand Kierkegaard's best-known treatise on faith, *Fear and Trembling*, Abraham is faced with a paradox when he is asked to sacrifice his son Isaac. He must obey God, who commands him to kill his son, but he knows that it is unholy to kill another person. Revelation contradicts ethical obligation. It is not uncommon to understand this paradox as a contradiction between reason and revelation: revelation and reason are incommensurable and revelation trumps reason.

However, instead, I think that the paradox of Abraham is not that revelation must contradict reason, but that Abraham cannot make himself understood to foundationalist philosophers and those of Kierkegaard's countrymen who think they have gone beyond Descartes's methodological doubt to Hegel's rational certainty. Abraham cannot speak, says Johannes de Silentio,[25] and yet he does speak. What Abraham says, however, is "absurd"—meaning that it cannot be heard by the foundationalist philosopher, *not* that it has no meaning. I take it that Kierkegaard is relying on the root meaning of the word *absurd*, "what cannot be said, what is voiceless," and so, also, "what cannot be heard."

The ab-surdity[26] to which the story of Abraham points is the voicelessness of what lies outside the strict economy of Cartesian doubt and certainty. As a result, the ab-surdity that Silentio discovers is *only* meaningless or irrational if we insist that meaning and rationality are products of "the system" only, of Cartesian rationality only. To be sure, what is outside the system is paradoxical—in other words, strange and marvelous rather than self-contradictory (again, I take Kierkegaard to be relying on the root meaning of the word *paradox:* "what is other than our expectations")[27]—but it is not unreasonable or contrary to reason, except from the point of view of a reason that has been artificially and narrowly defined. As I understand Kierkegaard, Abraham cannot be understood *if, and only if,* one rejects the origin of his knowledge, which modern philosophers (in other words, philosophers from Descartes through at least Hegel) and those who accept their views reject.

To use Aristotle's word again, what is outside reason is, in fact, the *archē* of reason, its origin. However, it is an *archē* that we can hear only from within reason (since we take account of things always from within reason), so we tend to hear it as if it were also within reason. It is as if we are listening to someone calling from outside the house, but we assume that they are inside—or, perhaps more accurately, it is like hearing someone quietly whisper something to us and believing that we are hearing ourselves think.

Within reason, its *archē* can be said and, in fact, is always said. Reason can and does give an account of itself. However, the account is always ironic, in a way that I will try to explain. There is no straightforward, non-question-begging, rational account of reason. One can be deaf to reason's supplemental *archē*. One can refuse it recognition. One can refuse to hear what is said by means of, rather than merely within, reason. For the foundation or origin of reason does not show itself unambiguously—clearly and distinctly or, in other words, theoretically. It cannot give itself clearly and distinctly, or it would be one more thing *within* the realm of reason, rather than its supplement. But the fact that something cannot be said clearly and distinctly does not mean that it cannot be said well, or that it cannot be heard, or that it cannot be understood without difficulty.

The profundity of the origin of reason is not necessarily the profundity of complexity and obscurity. Martin Heidegger (who himself sometimes, but not always, confused profundity with complexity) writes in *The Principle of Reason* of "the second tonality" of the principle of sufficient reason. This tonality does not deny that everything has an explanation but alerts us to the fact of the *archē*, of what can always be heard from beyond reason as well as always ignored.[28] Kierkegaard helps us see the necessity of such an *archē* by showing the impossibility of giving a merely theoretical explanation of Abraham—along with the impossibility of simply writing Abraham off as a madman, as one who acts without, or outside of, reason. Narratives and deconstructions of texts can help us catch a glimpse of the *archē*, the unavoidable but always indirectly seen "supplement" of reason. So can carefully listening to the "tones" of propositions in otherwise logical discourse, hearing what those propositions also say. But nothing can *guarantee* that we will hear what comes to us from the *archē*, from that which reason must call its supplement but which is really its origin. One must learn to read and hear with Kierkegaardian irony, which is not to say one thing and to mean another but to know that one always says more than is apparent on the surface, and it is to take account of that "more than." To read and hear ironically is, thus, always to say something about one's extrarational foundations, though one speaks of them, finally, only implicitly.

Since we must assume that we speak ironically whenever we speak reasonably, we must also be suspicious of taking up irony as a posture. In the first place, if Kierkegaard, Heidegger, the Medievals, and other important thinkers—such as Nephi, the son of Lehi—are right, then ordinary language, even the "clear and distinct" and often not-so-ordinary language of rational philosophy, is already ironic.[29] I need not add anything to it for it to be ironic.

In the second place, only the character of the speaker can give a guarantee that what he or she says is said with the proper irony, and no speaker can guarantee his or her own character except by being of good character.

Thus, the answer to the question of how we are to understand the *archē* of reason from within reason is related to that of Plato: we understand the origin of reason as we understand the sun, not by looking at it directly with philosophical and theoretical eyes, but by the light it sheds on the things in the world, by the fact that we can see at all, by the fact that reason is possible. We see reasonably—or, in other words, we see by the origin of reason—without ever seeing the supplemental origin directly.[30] Nevertheless, the *archē*, like the sun, is never far from us; it is everywhere to be seen and never to be pointed out directly, even though when we point at anything we point by means of it.

But why is that *archē* to be thought of in terms of faith rather than, as for Marxists, in terms of material history or, as for feminists, in terms of the history of oppression? That question is the hardest one I brook, but I think I can say something about it. I can at least make what I think is a reasonable suggestion.

The first, quick answer is deceptively simple: for something to be the ground for a knowledge claim, I must trust it and be faithful to it. However, as I said, the simplicity of this answer is deceptive. Hidden in it are a host of questions and philosophical problems, such as what it means to be faithful to an experience.

With an eye toward beginning to say something about the profundity of that simplicity, let me explore one way of talking about the relation of reason to its supplemental, archaic origin. It takes very little to notice that reason and explanation often involve our obligation to others. One can, of course, point out that not all reason begins with obligation. It is not difficult to think of cases of reasoning that have not been initiated by an obligation. That response, however, can perhaps be overcome by arguing that other uses of reason are parasitic on reason as a response to obligation. Or it may be overcome by arguing that the word *obligation* must be understood more broadly. In any case, for now, grant the Levinasian thesis that reason begins in obligation to another.[31] Why reason except to explain? Why explain if there is no one to whom we owe an explanation? In a solipsistic universe, reason and explanation make no sense (if only because language makes no sense). The solipsist who argues for his solipsism contradicts that solipsism in making his argument. If this is true, then what is outside of reason, making it possible, is essentially not a thing or principle, but another person. The principle of noncontradiction is necessary to all reasoning, but its necessity comes not from itself but from the demand that I give an acceptable explanation to another.[32] In Levinas's terms, the principles of reason have their origin in the apologetic character of reason, which is the very basis for my existence as a unique individual.[33] He says, "[The singularity of my existence] is at the very level of its reason; it is apology, that is, personal discourse, from me to the others."[34] With an argument that I can only allude to here, Levinas argues that the other person is, ultimately, God.[35]

Although she does not deal directly with Levinas, Marlène Zarader helps us understand Levinas's recourse to God by pointing out that, in the Jewish tradition (she points explicitly to the medieval commentator Nachmanides), language, and therefore reason, is, in its essence, a response to God.[36] The Bible understands language to be a matter of experience, the experience of hearing a call and responding. When God speaks, he does not reveal himself in the hurricane or the fire, but in a voice that addresses us (recall 1 Kings 19:11–13). Zarader takes prophetic speech to be paradigmatic of all speech and says: "The prophet speaks to the people and can be understood by them because his speaking remains ordained by a call that preceded it."[37]

To Levinas's argument that obligation to God and fidelity to him is the *archē* of reason, I would add at least one thing, also at least partly a matter of faith. However, adding this additional point will return at least some of what I suggested could be taken away when I suggested that nonobligational reason may be parasitic on obligational reason. In addition, what I say will question whether God is the only origin, or supplement, of reason.

I am interested in what has sometimes been called Heidegger's paganism, a description used to denote the fact that Heidegger does not consider the world simply as something created *ex nihilo*, but as something that has its own existence and, therefore, its own power to appear to us and to demand our attention, a power that cannot be completely attributed to God's creative act. For Heidegger, the power of the world to reveal itself not only cannot be reduced to divine fiat,[38] but it also cannot be reduced either to our subjective wills or to the objects of rational research.[39] The world itself has the power to ground our conclusions.

Levinas's understanding of matters is more in line with traditional theology and its supposition of the creation of the world from nothing.[40] The consequence of such an understanding is that the world itself and things in the world do not have their own existence, so they do not have their own power to show themselves to us, to reveal something. If the world is created *ex nihilo*, then revelation comes from God *in toto*, and, ultimately, he is the only supplement of reason. However, Latter-day Saint belief rejects the notion of *ex nihilo* creation and so implicitly includes the idea that the things of the world have power of their own to reveal themselves. Though all things are dependent on God for their existence in the world and thus all things point to his existence (Alma 30:44), each thing also has an aspect of independent existence and thus the power to show itself. The appearing of the world is not reducible to will, neither to that of the Divine nor to that of human beings. Heidegger's so-called pagan understanding of the world as existing, in some sense, in itself is more useful to Latter-day Saint thinkers than is Levinas's, though the latter does much to help us understand reason as response.

Heidegger also speaks of our relation to and understanding of the world in terms of two registers or orders of thinking.[41] Though Heidegger uses the word *reason* for only one of those registers, I think that is a mistake; there is no reason not to speak of each as reason. One of the registers of thought is what we usually think of when we think of reason, a thinking determined by logic. That is a register that we cannot do without. If thinking is to be at all useful, it must include logic.

Nevertheless, the logical register of thought requires another, the register of faithfulness, memory, and recognition. In other words, it requires the relation to a supplement that makes it possible and meaningful. Without the relation to a supplement, the first register remains free-floating and, therefore, pointless. But unlike Levinas, Heidegger believes that it is as possible to be faithful to the things in the world that come to us, to be called by the things we encounter and to hearken to that call, as it is to be called by another person and to hearken to her. For Heidegger, faithfulness to the world is as possible as is faithfulness to another person, and I believe that Heidegger has much for Latter-day Saints to think about in this regard.

Reason in the primary sense is the welcoming, remembering, recognizing response to a call from someone or something, a response that makes possible reason in the narrower sense.[42] As Otto Pöggeler points out, for Heidegger the essence of thought is not questioning, though the thinker must question. The essence of thought is not questioning because questioning relies on already finding oneself called by something and submitting oneself to it.[43] One cannot question unless one is already in a world that reveals itself and makes demands. In other words, the essence of thinking—of reason—is response, and very like the response of religious faith, even when it is a response to something other than God.[44]

As Zarader explains, this idea that reason is a matter of response is not new. In fact, in discussions of how knowledge is understood in the Bible, it is almost a commonplace that Hebrew thought takes knowledge to be a matter of hearing, acquaintance, and obedience, while Greek thought (which gave us philosophy and thus the primary way in which we think about thinking and reason) takes it to be a matter of sight, possession, and control. Too simply put (but perhaps good enough for our purposes here), for the biblical prophet, to know the truth is to be called and to obey that which calls one. For the Greek philosopher, to know the truth is to see something and to grasp what one sees.[45] We ask someone, for example, "Did you get it? Did you grasp it?" However, as David Banon says, for biblical writers the basic structure of knowledge is not that of "'possession,' but that of 'fidelity.'"[46] Heidegger's view has much in common with the biblical view, though he not only seems to have been unaware of that fact but took pains to insist that faith and "thinking" (his term for philosophy from this broader perspective) were separate matters.[47]

Given the similarity between Heidegger's understanding of knowledge and the biblical understanding, it may seem strange when Levinas worries that Heidegger's paganism opens the door to idolatry. Nevertheless, it is well that he should worry. In the first place, idolatry succeeds best when it imitates the truth.[48] In the second place, Heidegger's biography shows why we should worry.[49] But the door that opens to idolatry also opens to God. Because false worship is an imitation of true, what leads to one can also lead to the other.[50] Although Levinas is unwilling to allow the irony of Heidegger's understanding of the world, we ought to welcome it. Even knowing the dangers that Heidegger's understanding courts (and nothing essential can avoid danger), we ought to welcome Heidegger's "pagan" understanding of the world as a world that gives itself to us and demands our response, our reason.

There are several reasons why the risk involved is ultimately worth running. The first is that to call Heidegger a pagan, as Levinas does, is really only to say that he accepts the world itself as a thing of value and does not assume that its only value comes from the fact that it was created by God. In other words, he is a pagan because he implicitly rejects the idea of *ex nihilo* creation. Latter-day Saints should not find that particularly troubling. The second, more substantial, reason for accepting this risk is that faith requires it. Without risk, there is no faith. Of course, that is not to say that we ought to seek out risks or that the riskier a faith claim the more likely it is to be true. It is only to say that risk-free knowledge is not the kind of knowledge we can have of these matters.

Thus, using Heidegger's thought as a corrective to Levinas's, I am willing to say that not only are other persons—ultimately the divine Person—the *archē* or supplement that makes reason possible, but so is the appearing of the world.[51] Contrary to the philosophical as well as the theological tradition, the *archē* is not singular. The unity of the *archē* is in us, in our lives, acts, and everyday understanding, rather than in our wills and theoretical speculations, for the latter are but a representation or manifestation of the former. That is why, on a daily basis as well as ultimately, practice must take precedence over theology and speculation. The ultimate unity and, therefore, the ultimate rationality of our lives is to be found in our acts (including what we say and think) rather than only in our reflections and theories. The impetus and unity of our lives is practical rather than merely cognitive.

Thus my understanding of the relation of faith and reason is simple: We find ourselves in the world, surrounded by things and people, both of which lay claim on us, call us, making demands that we respond, that we account for ourselves, that we act. Of course, we know from latter-day revelation that we initially found ourselves before God, to whom we responded. He is, after all, our Creator, even if that creation did not happen *ex nihilo*. He called us into existence and continues to call us: "Hear, O Israel."[52] However, once we were in relation with him, we also found ourselves in the presence of others and of things, both of whom call to us, demanding our response by posing problems and questions, whether explicitly or not. If we take those calls seriously, being sufficiently faithful to those making demands on us, whether people or things, that we make an adequate response to their calls, we act rationally. In its multiplicity, the call is sufficient as an origin of reason. It is basic; it cannot be reduced to one of my beliefs. It stands outside of beliefs as their origin, initiating chains of reasons.

Because we exist, we account for ourselves before God, in relation to others, and in the world. We cannot avoid giving those accounts; we cannot avoid reason. Reason begins in an act of faith (trust and fidelity), in faithful response to those beings who surround us and precede us, whose very existence calls to us, making demands on us that interrupt our being: first God, then persons, then things. But not only does reason require faith; faith also requires reason. Although their relation is asymmetrical, with more area covered by faith than reason, either without the other is lame or blind or both. Faith makes space for us to talk and to reason with God, with each other, and with the world. By creating the space for reason, faith makes it possible for us to live responsibly, responsively. That space for response created by faith and carried out with reason, the room to talk, is the room into which Truman Madsen invited so many of us to enter, an invitation for which we thank him with these essays.

Notes

1. Truman G. Madsen, *Eternal Man* (Salt Lake City: Deseret Book, 1966).

2. Of course, arguing for a conclusion with which most already agree may be a problem: we often overlook the deficiencies in the arguments of those with whom we agree.

3. A sketch can create room for discussion by suggesting a topic and outlining an approach to that topic that is worth considering, while allowing the details and even the decision about the ultimate value of the approach to be worked out in further discussion.

4. The phrase *objective truth* gets used in many ways. In common usage it means little more than something like "real truth." However, the strict, philosophical sense of *object* is "that which stands at the other end

of a perceptual or mental directedness or of a possible directedness." On this understanding, there are objects that are not physical objects (such as mathematical and other ideas), and there can be things that are not objects (such as things to which no one is presently directing any awareness). In the strict sense, to be objective is to consider things simply as standing at the other end of a perceptual or epistemic directedness and, therefore, to ignore other possible relations to that which one considers. I here use the phrase *objective truth* in this more strict sense: the truth as it pertains to objects of that sort.

5. My thanks to Mark Wrathall for helping me see the importance of this problem.

6. Although most people would not think of themselves as philosophers or theologians or even think of themselves as ever engaging in philosophy or theology, most still use the methods and concepts given to them by philosophy to talk about various matters, including the nature of reason. It is natural to use that kind of thinking when we talk about certain subjects. The problem is that, when we do so, we almost always unconsciously use the ideas, concepts, and methods of reasoning that we have inherited, without reflection, in our common language and culture. Since these are "natural" to us as part of our "common sense," it is not surprising that we use them to discuss philosophical and theological problems, whether or not we recognize that we are doing so. However, since these ideas and concepts are also unexamined, we often make mistakes when we use them, including the mistake of introducing ideas that are incompatible with other ideas that we hold. (This natural and understandable reversion to common sense is my understanding of the phrase that speaks of mingling the philosophies of men—in other words, their common sense—with scripture.)

7. For the details of Plantinga's views, see Alvin Plantinga, "Reason and Belief in God," in *The Analytic Theist: An Alvin Plantinga Reader,* ed. James F. Sennett (Grand Rapids, Mich.: Eerdmans, 1998), 102–61; Plantinga, *Warrant: The Current Debate* (New York: Oxford, 1993); and Plantinga, *Warrant and Proper Function* (New York: Oxford, 1993). Plantinga argues for a number of conclusions regarding reason. For my purposes, the only one that is relevant is that it is possible to have grounds for belief that are not themselves beliefs.

Also, notice that the word *reason* is ambiguous. Sometimes it means only "a sufficient basis or ground for beliefs." At other times it means "a belief upon which it is possible to ground other beliefs." At still at other times it means "the process of moving from grounds (of either sort) to conclusions." Plantinga shows that it is possible to have reasons in the first sense that are not reasons in the second two senses. In keeping with ordinary usage, throughout this essay I will use the word *reason* for each of its meanings, assuming that the context will make clear which meaning I intend. (For an additional take on a Plantingian view, see Merold Westphal, "Whose Philosophy? Which Religion? Reflections on Reason as Faith," in *Transcendence in Philosophy and Religion,* ed. James E. Faulconer (Bloomington: Indiana University Press, 2002). Because this book has not yet been published, references to its pages will be preceded by "MS" for *manuscript,* referring to the page in the manuscript where the citation can be found.

8. I am grateful to James Siebach for first pointing this out to me, as well as for making me think about its importance to our understanding of the relation between faith and reason.

9. *Nichomachean Ethics* 1097b24–1098a3.

10. For perhaps the best place to see Descartes's discussion of reason, see his *Discourse on Method.* Of course, Descartes's view is not created out of whole cloth. It has everything to do with the tradition from which he comes, and it remained the dominant way of understanding science— knowledge—for a long time. See Barry Gower, *Scientific Method: An Historical and Philosophical Introduction* (London: Routledge, 1997), 1–108, for a good overview of both the importance of this view of science and how it changed.

11. See David Hume, *A Treatise of Human Nature.* I believe that Hume gives this argument, not because he is a radical skeptic, but because he is radically skeptical about rationalism. I take his argument to be a *reductio ad absurdem* of the rationalist position. But that does not change the point I am making here.

12. See, for example, Emmanuel Levinas, *Totality and Infinity,* trans. Alphonso Lingis (Pittsburgh, Pa.: Duquesne University, 1969), 21–25; and Levinas, *Otherwise Than Being: Or, Beyond Essence,* trans. Alphonso Lingis (The Hague, Netherlands: Nijhoff, 1981), 4–5, 118–19, 159–60,

and 177. Though perhaps shocking, this conclusion is shared by other contemporary European thinkers. See, for example, Jean-François Lyotard, *Heidegger and "the Jews,"* trans. Andreas Michel and Mark S. Roberts (Minneapolis: University of Minnesota Press, 1990).

13. This is not to deny that previous eras have also been guilty of horrors and holocausts. It is only to point out the connection between modern philosophy and the modern versions of such horror.

14. Aristotle, *Metaphysics* 994a1–20.

15. Of course, not all rationality consists in creating chains of reasons. However, that is irrelevant to this argument. Aristotle's point, that chains of reasons require a ground, applies equally to any other form of rationality. So the point I make here with regard to chains of reasons applies equally well to other forms of reasoning. For the purposes of this paper, I do not believe that the difference between chains of reasons and chains of explanation is important.

16. Thomas Aquinas, *Summa Theologiae: Latin Text and English Translation* (New York: McGraw Hill, 1964–76), Q.2, A.3.

17. I have sometimes also argued, though not in print, that the belief in the *archē* is at the root of the problem of the common understanding of reason. Here I may seem to contradict that claim. I think that my claim that the *archē* is behind the standard view of reason is true, although there is not space enough here to lay out the difference in the two conceptions of *archē*, both philosophically derived from Aristotle, that are at work. Suffice it to say that the problematic view of the *archē* is a view that takes it to be the first in the causal or logical chain, a reified originary point for explanation—precisely the position I here argue against.

18. For an interesting and relevant discussion of Derrida's work, see Kevin Hart, *The Trespass of the Sign: Deconstruction, Theology, and Philosophy* (Cambridge: Cambridge University Press, 1989).

19. The claim that there is no alternative may seem too strong, but it will do for the purposes of this paper. However, I am willing to take quite seriously the idea that there is a kind of speaking that is an alternative to the narrow, Cartesian understanding of reason, though not an alternative that is really external to reason—something Martin Heidegger sometimes called *poetry*. See my later discussion of Kierkegaard and irony for a first suggestion of how we might understand this alternative; see pp. 101–4.

20. As used here, "uncaused cause" is not the contradiction that it appears to be. It is a way of pointing to that which initiates the chain of reasoning—in other words, brings it about or causes it—but is not itself part of that chain and so is not named as a cause in the chain. Much use of this phrase and of this argument confuses reasoning and explanation, in which there must always be an "an uncaused cause," with what is, where it is not obvious that there must be such a cause. Such thinking moves from epistemology to ontology without the resources for doing so. Being outside the chain of reasons, the "uncaused cause" is not a cause in the same sense as any of the items in the chain. That is the substance of Aristotle's point.

21. Descartes tells us that first principles are things that we see to be true without further reflection. It is possible to read that this declaration itself recognizes the need for a supplement. In fact, his recourse to the proofs of God's existence (see *Meditations*) can be read as just such a recognition. (For a reading of Descartes along these lines, see Levinas's interpretation of Descartes in *Totality and Infinity*, 210–11 and 48–52.) Nevertheless, the standard way of reading Descartes, and so of understanding reason, has been much as I describe it in the body of the text, and that standard reading is what I find fault with.

Note, too, that I equivocate here on *reason* and *explanation*, but recall note 15. Every explanation is an exercise of reason and prototypical for what it means to exercise reason. I do not think that the equivocation damages my argument.

22. See the works referenced in note 7.

23. Though I am not a Romantic, the position for which I argue has a number of parallels with philosophical Romanticism. That should not be surprising since both are attempts to respond to the problem posed by Kant's metaphysics: how are we to think transcendence in an immanent world? Given these parallels, my objection here is not so much an objection to philosophical Romanticism as it is an objection to the popular form it often takes. That is what I am describing here. An objection to philosophical Romanticism would require a separate paper. However, to avoid clumsiness, I will refer to popular Romanticism as Romanticism, without the qualifier.

24. See Hans-Georg Gadamer, *Truth and Method*, 2nd rev. ed., trans. Joel Weinsheimer and Donald G. Marshall (New York: Continuum, 1993), for an important exposition of both the history of this mistake and an alternative to it.

25. Cited in Søren Kierkegaard, *Fear and Trembling: Repetition*, ed. and trans. Howard V. Hong and Edna H. Hong (Princeton: Princeton University, 1983), 115–20. Notice that the name of Kierkegaard's pseudonymous author, Johannes de Silentio, suggests that it is really the author rather than Abraham who is unable to speak.

26. I hyphenate the word to remind us that I am using it in the special sense just explained.

27. *Oxford English Dictionary*, s.v. "paradox," and Henry G. Liddell, Robert Scott, and Henry S. Jones, eds., *A Greek-English Lexicon*, 6th ed. (Oxford: Clarendon, 1968), s.v. "παραδοξία."

28. Martin Heidegger, *The Principle of Reason*, trans. Reginald Lilly (Bloomington: Indiana University Press, 1991), 39–40.

29. Nephi tells us of the importance of plain language but quotes extensively from Isaiah (compare 2 Nephi 25:4 and 26:33). His idea of plain language is not the same as ours, and he makes the point ironically, though seemingly unconscious of his irony.

30. Wrathall has reminded me that Plato says the philosopher does eventually see the sun straight on (*Republic* 516b). That is true, but the allegory of the cave does not have the philosopher see the sun in this world, and I part company with Plato at exactly the point where he proposes another world in which to see it. In other words, Plato is wrong about that.

31. See, for example, Levinas, *Totality and Infinity*, 201.

32. It is important to realize that this demand is not necessarily either explicit or conscious. The point is not that a person says, "I demand this of you," but that the person's existence before me requires me to do and say things, regardless of what the person says. The demands of a person's existence before us may even contradict his or her spoken demands, as they often do when our young children demand things of us—things that we know we ought not to give them, things that their being-before-us not only does not demand, but demands that we refuse.

33. Besides the quotation that follows, see Levinas, *Totality and Infinity,* 252–53; see also 40, 219, 240–46, 284, 293, and 301.

34. Ibid., 253. I have spoken of the origin that is outside of any chain of reasons. Levinas speaks of the idea that overflows the one who thinks it (e.g., ibid., 20–21). These are two ways of making the same point.

35. See, for example, ibid., 77–79. Whether Levinas speaks of God is a complicated matter. As Westphal points out, Levinas says, "It is our relations with men . . . that give to theological concepts the sole signification they admit of. . . . Everything that cannot be reduced to an interhuman relation represents not the superior form but the forever primitive form of religion" (ibid., 79; cited in Westphal, "Whose Philosophy? Which Religion?" MS 19). Levinas also speaks of the necessity of atheism (*Totality and Infinity,* 77), but (quite surprisingly) in the same place he speaks of atheism as necessary to a relation with God. His point is that a true relation with God requires that we separate ourselves from the god of superstitious worship. See also Paul Ricoeur on this theme: "Reason, Atheism, and Faith," in Alisdair C. MacIntyre and Paul Ricoeur, *The Religious Significance of Atheism* (New York: Columbia University Press, 1969), 58–98. Although I have doubts about the clarity of the dichotomy between proper worship and superstition, I think it is clear that Levinas does believe that what we could call his "fundamental ethics," the relation to others that grounds reason, points us toward God.

36. Marlène Zarader, *La dette impensée: Heidegger et l'héritage hébraïque* (Paris: Editions du Seuil, 1990), 62.

37. Ibid. This paragraph summarizes the discussion on pages 61–64. In criticizing Heidegger, Zarader argues that, as the Bible has been read in the Jewish tradition, it offers an alternative to our usual understanding of language and philosophy—an alternative that has many things in common with the alternative we find in Heidegger's work but that does not insist on only the Greek origins of that alternative and that escapes some of the problems that Heidegger's thinking encounters.

38. Interestingly, Heidegger argues that to mistake God for being is to forget that God must be a being and so cannot be being itself. See, for example, Martin Heidegger, "Letter on Humanism," trans. Frank M. Capruzzi and J. Glenn Gray, in Martin Heidegger, *Basic Writings: From Being and Time (1927) to The Task of Thinking (1964),* ed. David F.

Krell, 2nd rev. and expanded ed. (San Francisco: HarperSanFrancisco, 1993), 251–53, esp. 253; and Heidegger, "Phenomenology and Theology," in *The Piety of Thinking*, trans. James G. Hart and John C. Maraldo (Bloomington: Indiana University Press, 1976), 5–21.

Works such as Jean-Luc Marion's *God without Being*, trans. Thomas A. Carlson (Chicago: University of Chicago, 1991), look for a way around that argument, but I find it compelling: God cannot be being itself and still be a god; he must be a being. See Michel Henry, *Incarnation: Une philosophie de la chair* (Paris: Seul, 2000), esp. 7–32, for another argument that for Christianity God is necessarily a being, in fact, a being of flesh. Of course, Marion does not argue that God is being itself, but he wishes to avoid the conclusion that God is a being within being. Putting God outside of being also makes him no longer *a* god. Perhaps, however, Marion would argue that this is his point and the point of monotheism: God is not *a* god; he is *the* God. But that is a discussion for another paper.

39. One reason that the world and its power to reveal itself cannot be reduced to the objects of rational research is that the object of rational or scientific research is not the thing that we encounter but a conceptual relative of that thing, a relative created by adumbrating a set of conditions and assumptions that define the ways in which we will take up and examine the thing in question. In other words, the scientific object is not the thing itself but an object created by the methods of science and the background assumptions of those methods. As a result, strictly speaking, the object of research is a product of the subject, not an independent thing that demands our attention. This does not, as many may worry, imply that Heidegger is arguing that scientific conclusions are merely subjective. Quite the contrary. His point is that the very possibility of doing science requires that we deal with things as objects and that objects are, by definition, one end of an intentional ray that has a subject at the other end and a particular context that makes it possible as the object that it is (in the case of science, its methods and background assumptions). For more on this point, see Martin Heidegger, "The Age of the World Picture," in *The Question Concerning Technology and Other Essays*, trans. William Lovitt (New York: Harper Colophon, 1977), 115–54. See also Edwin A. Burtt, *The Metaphysical Foundations of Modern Physical*

Science (1932; reprint, Atlantic Highlands, N.J.: Humanities, 1980), esp. 298–99.

40. It is important to point out that Levinas explicitly gives another meaning to the term *ex nihilo* than that which we find in the theological tradition. He says that creation *ex nihilo* means that the created being is completely different from and separate from the Creator, that he or she is not reducible to a part or affect of the Creator. See Levinas, *Totality and Infinity*, 63. Given this understanding, there *might be* a sense in which a Latter-day Saint could subscribe to the idea of creation *ex nihilo*. Nevertheless, because the term is almost always used in accordance with the standard meaning, I use that standard meaning even when talking about Levinas.

41. See Martin Heidegger, *What Is Called Thinking?* (New York: Harper & Row, 1968), for one of the central locations of this discussion. See also Heidegger, *The Principle of Reason*, 39–40.

42. Of course, to designate one as primary and the other as secondary, or narrower, is not to demean the second. The primary tonality of reason is the relation to the *archē* that makes the secondary possible, but the primary without the secondary is incomplete.

43. Otto Pöggeler, *Der Denkweg Martin Heideggers* (Pfullingen: Neske, 1963), 268–80. See also Jacques Derrida's discussion of this in *De l'Espirit: Heidegger et la question* (Paris: Galilee, 1987), e.g., 36–37, 69–70, 132, 145–47. Both Pöggeler and Derrida refer specifically to Martin Heidegger, *Unterwegs zur Sprache* (Pfullingen: Neske, 1961), 174. (I am grateful to Marlène Zarader for pointing out this shared reference. See *Dette impensée*, 223 n. 36.)

44. Zarader gives an excellent overview of Heidegger's understanding of thought. See *Dette impensée*, esp. 92–100 and 112–23.

45. Fuller discussions of this notion are available in any number of places. For a detailed linguistic discussion of the Old Testament understanding and its relation to the Greek and New Testament understandings, see Gerhard Kittel, ed., *Theological Dictionary of the New Testament*, trans. Geoffrey W. Bromily (Grand Rapids, Mich.: Eerdmans, 1964–76), s.v. γινώσκω, γνῶσις, ἐπιγινώσκω, ἐπίγνωσις, καταγινώσκω, ἀκατάγνωστος, προγινώσκω, πρόγνωσις, συγγνώμη, γνώμη, γνωρίζω, γνωστός (Rudolf Bultmann). For broader discussions, see Thorleif

Boman, *Hebrew Thought Compared with Greek* (New York: Norton, 1960); my "Hebrew versus Greek Thinking," in *Scripture Study: Tools and Suggestions* (Provo, Utah: FARMS, 1999), 135–53, which relies heavily on Boman; or David Banon, *La lecture infinie: Les voies de l'interprétation midrachique* (Paris: Seuil, 1987).

46. Banon, *Lecture infinie,* 173. As does Banon's, many discussions of this difference note that in Genesis 4:1, "And Adam knew Eve his wife," the use of the Hebrew word for knowledge *(da'at)* as a term for sexual relations is not a euphemism. From an Old Testament point of view, knowledge is a matter of intimacy rather than possession.

47. Zarader, *Dette impensée,* convincingly demonstrates both the similarity of Heidegger's thought to biblical thought and his denial of that similarity. Of course, the traditional interpretation of the Old Testament would have it, as Levinas does, that knowledge as it is understood in the Old Testament comes ultimately from the demands of God and would not leave room for the demands of things. It remains a fact, however, that Heidegger's understanding of knowledge has a great deal in common with that in the Bible; and I suspect that Latter-day Saints in general will have no trouble with the idea that things have some kind of existence above and beyond the existence that God gives them, although no thing exists completely independent of God.

48. Jean-Luc Marion's *L'idol et la distance* (Paris: Grasset, 1977) says a great deal about why this is the case.

49. In a part of his life that remains wrapped in difficulty as well as confusion, Heidegger joined the Nazi party in the early 1930s and supported the Nazi takeover of the universities, although they later refused to acknowledge his support. Heidegger's relation to Nazism remains, most unfortunately, ambiguous at best. There are a good many books on the issue, from those that smack of yellow journalism to the apologetic. For those looking for a readable discussion of Heidegger's thought that includes a discussion of his Nazism, see either George Steiner, *Martin Heidegger* (Chicago: University of Chicago, 1989); or Richard F. H. Polt, *Heidegger: An Introduction* (Ithaca, N.Y.: Cornell University, 1999).

50. This has always been the case. See the aforementioned piece by Ricoeur, "Atheism." See also Marion's discussion of the relation between worship and idolatry in both *L'idol et la distance* and *God without Being.*

Although I do not believe in the absolutely transcendent god whom Marion discusses, much of his discussion, particularly that of the difference between an idol and an icon, is illuminating. It can help us think about our own God-talk even if, in the end, we find Marion's analysis insufficient.

51. Although I now would side with Heidegger's position more strongly than I did at that time, for more on this "conflict" between Levinas and Heidegger, see my essay, "The Uncanny Interruption of Ethics: Gift, Interruption, or . . . ," *The Graduate Faculty Philosophy Journal* 20/2 and 21/1 (1998): 233–47.

52. This call to Israel is frequent in the Old Testament—sufficiently frequent that we may think of it as the essence of the Lord's demand of Israel. For example, see Deuteronomy 5:1; 6:3–4; 9:1; 20:3; Psalms 50:7; 81:8; Isaiah 44:1; 48:1; Jeremiah 2:4; 10:1; 42:15; Ezekiel 18:25; Hosea 4:1; 5:1; Amos 3:1; 5:1; and Micah 3:1, 9. It is also the way in which the Savior introduces the first great commandment in Mark 12:29, quoting not only the commandment to love God, but the command to hear. Neither Judaism nor Christianity can conceive of religion without doing so in terms of response to God's call.

CHAPTER 4

THE MIND'S ROAD TO FULFILLMENT, SELF-REALIZATION, AND EXPERIENTIAL KNOWLEDGE: SOME TAGOREAN VIEWS

Guttorm Fløistad

To participate in a conversation with Truman Madsen or to attend one of his lectures is a remarkable event. He never leaves you untouched. Through his calm speech and behavior, he takes you to deeper layers of human existence.

How he accomplishes this is hard to explain. One reason is certainly to be found in his profound knowledge of the history of philosophy and religion. Decisive, however, is the fact that, in a unique way, he practices the basic law of rhetoric: He always stands for what he is saying. His words never leave his being—which becomes our being.

Truman Madsen reminds me of another wise man, Rabindranath Tagore (1861–1941).

The mind's road to fulfillment is a central theme in Tagore's writings, in his philosophical essays as well as in his novels and poetry. Sometimes, as in the beginning of the novel *Sadhaná*, he speaks, like the Buddha, of a liberation of the mind.

Most classical philosophies and great religions likewise deal with the mind's road to fulfillment as a central theme. Baruch Spinoza, sometimes called the Hindu—and also the Buddhist—of the West, speaks of a liberation of the intellect, culminating in man's intellectual love of God.[1] Dante Alighieri's *Divina Commedia*

(1318), being an apology for Christianity, describes man's passage from hell, via purgatory, to paradise. Bonaventura attempts to blend the philosophy of Plato and Aristotle with Christianity under the title *The Mind's Road to God* (1251).

Everyone with some knowledge of Western philosophy and literature will know the fate of this topic in the course of the last three centuries. The mind's road to God has to many—perhaps to most—people become an empty phrase, but especially to philosophers. No trace of it remains in philosophical discourses. In the 1880s Nietzsche declared the death of God: "We are ourselves the murderer"—saying, in effect, that we had lost our sense of direction. We no longer knew what was upward and what was downward.[2] In the 1920s, Franz Kafka, a contemporary with Tagore, wrote a short story about the hunter Gracchus, who after his death sailed toward heaven. However, he was soon distracted by the view of his home or whatever—and lost the direction. Since then, he has been sailing on earthly waters, not knowing where heaven is. Jean-Paul Sartre, in his *Being and Nothingness*—the existentialist version of classical metaphysics—underlines man's search for a godlike being. In the middle of the twentieth century, however, this was "a useless passion" *(une passion inutile).*[3]

The mind's road to fulfillment and, hence, the proper meaning of self-realization were therefore threatened. But Tagore, blending philosophical and religious wisdom from both the East and the West, was in a position of strength. He was fully aware of the ongoing dissolution of religious and philosophical values in the West and its long-term effect on Indian society. At the same time, he was firmly rooted in the ancient traditions of India, fortified by his broad knowledge of philosophy and religious tradition in general. The history of mankind, Tagore warns, had reached a level where the whole man, the ethical man—perhaps without knowing it—had given himself away to the limited objectives of political man and businessman, which are often devoid of an ethical commitment. It was time to take heed.[4] To understand such a warning is no easy matter. Strictly speaking, if we are to believe Tagore, the mind's reminder to itself of the ultimate goal of human existence, the urge toward fulfillment, is the proper meaning of self-realization.

In itself this model is commonplace in religious and metaphysical thinking. In the West this paradigm ranges from Plato's ideal world inherent in the mind to Martin Heidegger's concept of the mind's calling on itself. It is a call to a more genuine being than the mass culture allows.[5] The question here is: What chances are there to succeed in our present-day culture of media and consumption? In which directions should we sail? Tagore, trained and deeply involved in that kind of thinking, was in a far better position to provide an answer than we, at least most of us, are about a hundred years later.

Individual Uniqueness

Self-realization as a search for fulfillment is a personal matter. Even though the goal for which we are striving is common to us all, the way for each to achieve it is personal and unique. It depends on one's own history and personal experiences.

The idea of a personal and unique individuality appears to be the opposite of what characterizes any mass culture. The course of economic development and its outlet in the culture of media and consumption seem to gradually destroy individual and even cultural diversity and cause us to be identical. This process is described by philosophers almost the world over—most vividly, perhaps, by Heidegger in his *Being and Time*. We are *no one* in particular, he concludes.[6] Social and cultural ties—which bind people together in friendship, families, institutions, local communities, and companies—suffer accordingly. These relationships certainly involve an enormous amount of common knowledge, most of which is historical and silent. But the ties that really bind people together and enable them to identify with the group are basically personal, and personal relationships always have an emotional component. Personal and emotional ties account for the mutual sense of belonging to and caring for one another. The homogeneous culture of entertainment, consumption, and money tends to empty those basic relationships.

The Individual's Representation of the Infinite

How can one be rescued as an individual from this process of devaluation? Tagore's answer reflects his personal philosophical and religious position: We are unique in the way in which we represent the *Infinite*. We are part of the universe and thereby carry the unity of all things; this unity is without limits and is thus Infinite.[7]

He offers some help in understanding this concept by saying that the mind may involve and represent the Infinite, or the universe as a whole, in varying degrees. The extent to which the mind actually represents the Infinite depends, presumably, on the kind of knowledge it is able to exercise. Thus we are unique to different degrees. However, this way of thinking, though well known from the history of philosophy, may not be particularly illuminative to most people in the twenty-first century. Our minds are usually immersed in a restless reality. The Tagorean notion of the Infinite remains presumably the same. Anyone who engages in the restless society becomes in the long run restless himself—and will not be in a position to grasp the meaning of the *unique* and *personal Infinite*.

Explaining what the Infinite is not is fairly straightforward. Knowledge of the Infinite is not the same as knowing an infinite number of things or the many laws governing their interrelationships. Thus natural sciences cannot contribute to our understanding of the Infinite. In this respect, it is no wonder that Tagore held science in low esteem. No scientific discovery, however valuable in other respects, can ever contribute to our search for fulfillment, to our proper self-realization. Tagore would undoubtedly hold that knowledge of human beings involves, beyond a scientific comprehension of them, an understanding of their unique participation in the Infinite as a whole.

To Tagore, the Infinite is obviously what we would call an *experiential* notion—that is to say, in order to understand it, we have to share the experience of its meaning. And this experience is both general *and* unique. The fact that others may have the same experience is no argument against its uniqueness. Hegel nicely illustrates this in his story of a couple sitting in a public garden. The couple is deeply in love, and they experience their loving relationship as highly personal and unique. Yet some yards away sits another couple experiencing the same loving feelings.[8]

In this context it is fairly obvious what experiential knowledge means and that this knowledge has a strong emotional component that significantly contributes to the experience each of the participants undergoes in being a part of the whole. One is even tempted to say that a loving relationship, in its own way, is a model of something infinite. It is equally obvious that, in a loving relationship, it is too late to speak of "you" and "me." We are somehow united.

Such a model of unification goes beyond the usual dichotomies known from science and the major trends in philosophy (for example, Descartes): that is, the dichotomies between man and world, between subject and object, between mind and body, and between language and reality. But does a loving and unifying relationship, as a model, apply to these dichotomies as well? An answer to this question should lead us to a wider, and perhaps even deeper, understanding of Unity and the Infinite. The overall purpose is a practical one: What chances do we have, in a restless society, of experiencing the Infinite, of perceiving something divine? I shall limit myself to a brief exposition of a few selected topics, taken partly from Western philosophies in the same tradition as

Tagore. Tagore himself attaches major importance to the role of aesthetics and the role of women as mothers.

The Mind's Interaction with the Environment

A first step is to observe that a human being is continually interacting with the environment. The interaction is with nature, the social environment, and history. Through these interactions we build our own history, our life history. Being the result of a series of interactions, a person's life history, or inner world, is never entirely private. Each person's history is unique, being the result of a variety of relations in a variety of contexts in different places at different times. One person's history, however, does share common experiences and values with another's. Our experiences often overlap through personal encounters, education, and work.

We are all part of an enculturation process. That is how we become part of a community and acquire communal values. Experiences that in the outward sense may appear the same do not make us homogeneous or identical; every new experience is shaped by the previous ones and acquires—or may acquire—a meaning more or less different from the meaning attached to the same experiences as undergone by others. That is how a common experience becomes personalized and creates individual commitment.

The point is that the things, events, or persons with whom we relate become part of our own being. That is why Spinoza can say that the mind is nothing but a complex idea[9] and Heidegger can say that the world is part and parcel of man's being.[10] In other words, if we relate ourselves to what is continually changing and restless, this is what we ourselves become. What remains the same or only slowly changes has the opposite effect.

The Principle of Self-Realization

The *moral* character of our relations, or relational existence, is best explained in terms of the principle of self-realization and self-preservation. To many of the great philosophers of the past—

including thinkers as different as Augustine, Spinoza, and Heidegger—this principle is a basic feature of human existence. Some consequences of this principle are clear enough. Whatever our relations are with nature, other human beings, or history, they are of a moral character. In varying degrees, they serve our endeavor to unfold our capacities and take care of ourselves, as well as bind together the larger community. Ethical norms and rules usually apply to our conduct with others and, thus, to the community of humankind. Ethics is a theory of how you and I ought to behave together to the advantage of both and, ultimately, to the advantage of humanity at large. The principle of universality is basic to ethics.

The principle of self-realization and self-preservation does not run counter to the interest of other people, to communal life. It serves it. All the great philosophers of the past have dealt with the question of what self-realization really means, and most of them have arrived at the view that, if you are to succeed in your own life, you should at the same time care for others. A strong community and a community feeling enable you to concentrate your physical and mental powers on your own self-development and, at the same time, on assisting the development of others. Pure selfishness creates conflicts and negative moods and detracts from both your self-development and community building. The most instructive way of phrasing this view that I have found appears in a 1970 book, *Individuality and the New Society,* edited by the American philosopher Abraham Kaplan. The book is addressed to the new generation of his day. At the end of his introduction, he asks: "What does it mean for you to develop yourself?" He answers: "It is the predicament, the opportunity, and the glory of every man that he becomes an individual only as he reaches out to the rest of mankind."[11]

This traditional view of self-realization may not be easy to understand in those cultures that, like the West, give priority to individual freedom and rights. Over the last five hundred years or so, this idea has been combined with the concept of technological progress and economic growth. The ultimate result is the development of the modern welfare society, which, according to John Kenneth Galbraith, represents "the culture of contentment" (the title of one of his books).

Today the long-term costs of an emphasis on individuality are discovered and experienced by more and more people, including many outside the West. Individual freedom and rights, together with the welfare state, foster selfishness, removing individuals from each other and from nature and, worse yet, destroying community values and ultimately themselves. Left to itself, individual freedom is self-destructive. Witness the growing number of lonely people and the tens of thousands of young people and children, both in Western and Eastern societies, who harm themselves even to the point of committing suicide in the belief that no one cares for them anymore. Selfishness invades even families and friendships. The most basic needs of a human being are not freedom and rights but the sense of belonging to a community and experiencing mutual caring and love. That is what gives direction to our freedom. Freedom requires some degree of social security. And according to ancient wisdom, both in the West and the East, social security originates in belonging to a group and having someone who cares for you.

The Dialectical Approach

The dialectical approach to man's self-realization may be further illuminating. The principle goes back to Plato, especially to his dialogue *Parmenides,* and even further back to Chinese and Indian philosophy. In this discussion, I shall focus on Hegel. While looking for a principle in terms of which he could explain historical change, he found an analog in the relationship between man and woman as a prototype of a dialectical relationship. Perhaps he was inspired by the principle of yin and yang in Taoism. At any rate, the relationship between the sexes makes it easy to explain the dialectical principle as a basic principle of change and of growth. The principle rests on his observations, first, that life is a constant, interrelated pattern of opposites (man and woman, light and darkness, heat and cold, and so on) and second, that a human being is limited in itself and is in no way self-sufficient in the sense that God is said to be. Therefore, any human being is in need of something beyond itself and is therefore necessarily related to something outside itself. By its very nature, an individual transcends itself.

A love relationship is an instructive case. In a love relationship, so Hegel's analysis goes, one gives oneself away to another person. To make this statement, one certainly does not need philosophy. The additional observation is, however, telling: one gives oneself away in order to enrich one's own being and to become more complete and, consequently, part of a community. Thus a love relationship is a fulfillment.[12]

Hegel's use of this model to explain historical change—and he applies it more or less justifiably to all cultures—is not the topic here. Let me just remark that the dialectical principle may be regarded as valid in all our relationships. We are continually giving ourselves away to another person, to a group of people, to ideas and tasks, to nature, and to God. This is how we create history. Inherent in this endeavor is always the hope of some fulfillment. If the environment blocks this endeavor over a period of time, mental suffering is likely to occur.

Women in India

In connection with this model of the human need for community as a part of self-fulfillment is the role of family and of the wife and mother in particular. Tagore's view on the role of women in family life and consequently in society as a whole is more radical than that of most writers on the theme. He identifies the mother as the central person in the transmission of values in the family. She exercises love and care and is much more important than the father.[13] Tagore goes even further in his view on the prolongation of life. Woman, he says, is what nature needs for its renewal; man is, in this respect, barely needed.[14] In the opening words of Tagore's novel *The Home and the World,* Bimala describes her mother in the following way: "Her face carried the sign of something holy and divine, of depth and peace."[15] Whenever a woman "moves around serving her household," Tagore says, "light and music come out of her body."[16]

Descriptions such as these certainly have a poetical flavor. Anyone, however, who has some knowledge of the great philosophies of the past knows that these very words are used to designate experiences of a unity of all things, also called God or Substance, the infinite Beauty of all things, and the Mystic. The terms *holy* and *divine*, as used by Tagore, speak for themselves. The relation of the Holy to the concept of wholeness should also be noticed. As to his references to light and music, the philosophy of Plato and Plotinus is sometimes called "light metaphysics"—the light coming from God. Music, according to Eastern traditions, is what most contributes to the perfection of man. And the perfect being is one who basically communicates *humility,* one who is the servant of life itself. That is where a woman's expression of peace and depth comes from. To be the servant of life is one's highest achievement. Humility is receptiveness, and it calls for personal relations and commitment.[17]

As is obvious from this perspective, a woman's experience of life goes far beyond her pursuit of household things. Presumably by virtue of her very nature, she is able to transcend every item in her doings. Everything, like herself, is subordinated to a higher purpose, to be at the service of life itself. Women are, in a peculiar way, like the unity of all things, both immanent and transcendent.

Compared with women as the servants of life, men's primarily action-oriented behavior in the pursuit of technological progress, efficiency, and profit is fairly modest. Business leaders have even reduced themselves to the level of being servants of their shareholders. From a certain point of view, as women would know, most men in our present-day restless society appear to be slaves of a system. Yet many of them either neglect women or demand them to follow. The overall view of what life is about is, in a way, being forgotten.

Tagore's high esteem for woman has several sources. His primary source was his loving relationship with his wife, who died too young. She gave him the model of a perfect human being: she was able to exercise love in all her relationships without expecting reward—a property usually attributed to God. His other sources were the old Hindu scriptures, the Vedas and the Upanishads. Unlike the view of woman presented in official Hindu teaching and in textbooks published in the West, the old Vedas and Upanishads teach a different story. In these traditions, subordinated to men though they may be, women are the great teachers. Their way of teaching is through love, caring, and affection, the most effective language of all. Women are therefore "divine treasures for family life" and, consequently, for society at large. Woman is God incarnate. That is why she transmits peace, depth, and eternity. Tagore emphasizes the importance of being familiar with history. This traditional Indian view of women is an important part of that history.

This view of women as mothers, however, is hardly prevalent in Western societies. Rather, women have been held in very low esteem. According to Mary Wollstonecraft, they are the real slaves, as compared with the freemen and citizens. Almost throughout European history, women have been denied access to education and politics. Simone de Beauvoir, a major figure in the feminist movement, even regarded motherhood as a burden. A woman became almost a slave to her children, born and unborn, whereas men kept their freedom. The only solution for women, according to de Beauvoir, was to adopt the rationality of men.[18]

Simone de Beauvoir has many followers. She has, over the years, also accumulated a number of opponents. The well-known American writer Adrienne Rich published in 1976 the book *Of Woman Born.*[19] In contrast to de Beauvoir, she advocated a new and more positive evaluation of woman's body, motherhood, and self-knowledge. Perhaps the most profound analysis of women's nature is given by the Jungian psychoanalyst Clarissa P. Estés in her book *Women Who Run with the Wolves,*[20] in many ways a remarkable work. But this is not the topic here. Let me just remark that the author appears to be inspired not only by Jung's depth psychology, but just as much by the Taoist concept of yin and yang. Passages in the book also point to the Tagorean view of women.

Aesthetic Experience

Tagore's metaphor of women's service as music hints at the role he feels that aesthetic experience plays in human self-realization. Our experience of unity is of many kinds and has many levels. Something in human nature makes us transcend ourselves in search of a wider and richer reality than we have within ourselves. Communication, cooperation, rituals, customs, friendship, and love are all indicators of this search—all provide evidence that we are more than merely ourselves. We are all carrying experiences of a unity within us, from infancy and onward. It is too late for us to be on our own. We are somehow reaching out for higher levels of experience and awareness. Presumably, this applies also to those who are reaching out for riches. From the perspective of motherhood and values and interpersonal encounters, these material cravings seem rather pointless. They are surface happenings. The collection of things, Tagore says, is not self-realization.[21] Most of us are looking for more lasting experiences. To undergo these experiences is one thing; to explain them is another. The history of philosophy and of art is full of those experiences and of more or less successful descriptions of them.

Tagore also deals with *aesthetic* experience.[22] In listening to music and drama and looking at paintings, we should not forget that we are moving into a realm of experience that can hardly be understood properly unless one is familiar with that kind of experience beforehand. This is because aesthetic experiences and emotions are, first and foremost, a kind of knowledge, not of specific material objects or of the natural laws governing their relation, but of something of a different sort. Ordinary experience, according to Tagore, is directed outward; the self remains in the background. In aesthetic experiences, the objects move into the background—they do not disappear; rather, one's awareness of them is deepened. Objects, of whatever kind, become part of a wider reality, just as we are ourselves. Aesthetic experiences offer us a glimpse of that wider reality in which awareness goes beyond sense perception and intellectual cognition. In such an experience the "I" and the world of things are intimately related—even united. Tagore does not pretend that we understand reality as it is. But, he contends, we find the most illuminating experience of it in artistic creation. In such acts of creation, reality comes before our conscience unveiled, and we are somehow united with the world.[23]

At the same time, Tagore thinks that truth and beauty are closely interwoven; they are, in fact, identical.[24] Truth in this context has nothing to do with correspondence between statements and reality. This is a very restricted notion of truth. In the present context, truth applies to man's self-realization. Coming from classical philosophy in the West, this concept is familiar ground. Tao, dharma, Itinerarium Mentis, liberation of the mind—they all belong to the same category of thought. Truth is true self-realization, the unfolding of the inner self. Self-realization is self-creation. For example, an artist creates a piece of art, while others create something corresponding to their nature. Things in nature have their unfolding, their true becoming.

Truth and beauty thus have a *moral* dimension. A true self-realization is an understanding of what we *ought* to be and do. We are carrying an imperative within us. This imperative may certainly be covered up and may be forgotten in a display of selfishness. But we all know when we succeed in becoming ourselves. Ethics and aesthetics—moral good and beauty—are two faces of the same coin, and both are intimately related to unity. True self-realization is the attainment of higher stages of experience and awareness of unity. In this pursuit, we have all succeeded at some time and in some manner.

Kinds of Knowledge

The progression of an individual's self-realization runs through different stages of awareness or knowledge. The number of stages varies, ranging from three (according to Tagore and Spinoza), to six (delineated by Bonaventura), up to eight (as in Buddhism). Three stages appear to be basic to all these systems; if more stages are counted, they seem to be specific applications or expansions of the three basic ones.

The *first* kind of knowledge is a display of self-interest. It guides the pursuit of our daily business. Spinoza calls it knowledge by imagination and by opinion and hearsay. Self-interest is a knowledge based on the external appearance of things and, for the most part, is related to our interests. We are interpreting things not with a view to knowing what they are in themselves but with a view to satisfying our needs.[25] This way of looking at things is certainly useful and may even be necessary in order to find our way through the wilderness of daily life. But self-interest hardly contains much commitment to communal values and certainly often leads to conflicts of interest. In the worst cases of selfishness combined with a strong dependency on external things, it may even lead to the basic illnesses of mankind. Tagore calls these illnesses expressions of greed. Spinoza lists five types of greed that lead to the destruction of the human mind and body by turning man into a slave. They include strong ambition, craving for luxury, lust for property, drug addiction, and uncontrolled sexual desire. These widespread illnesses distort the balance and harmony both within man and between man and nature in society.[26]

The *second* kind of knowledge—knowledge of reason or of natural laws common to man and nature—may help to restore the balance. Tagore's view on natural science is mentioned above; he does not hold it in high esteem, simply because science and its explanation of nature in terms of universal laws do not allow for personal relationships. He nevertheless regards science as necessary. He even admits that modern science "is Europe's great gift to humanity for all times to come." He further holds that "we, in India, must claim it from her hands, and gratefully accept it in order to be saved from the curse of futility by lagging behind. We shall fail to reap the harvest of the present age if we delay."[27] However, Tagore draws attention to a danger for the Indian national culture resulting from an educational system dominated by science and technology.[28] There is a risk, he says, that one will educate oneself away from the national culture, from all ideas of further liberation of the mind, and, worst of all, from the capacity to enter into personal and emotional relationships. Thus we would educate ourselves away from harmony and unity and from values. Tagore sees a danger in the scientific and technological language: It is useful, but without due caution it may come to dictate our thoughts and emotions.[29]

Self-realization proper is only possible using the *third* kind of knowledge, which is admittedly difficult to describe despite the fact that most of the classical philosophers, Aristotle and Spinoza included, employ it. However, a few (external) characteristics are easily given: This kind of knowledge is concerned with wholeness or unity. A situation is a whole of a limited kind. The ultimate whole or unity is God, or reality as a whole. In this aspect, we may call it the intellectual love of God. Similar to the relation between man and woman, in experiencing the intellectual love of God we are united with reality as such. The third kind of knowledge therefore goes beyond the distinction between subject and object. Intuitive knowledge of this kind does not allow for a distinction between knowledge and ethics (and, in fact, the title of Spinoza's work on the theory of knowledge is often called *Ethica*). The intellectual love of God is both a cognitive and an emotional-moral concept. The highest kind of knowledge is a loving, caring, and joyful knowledge—for reality in general and for human life in particular. At the same time, it is fulfillment and peace—as exemplified in Bimala's mother.

Tagore describes the highest kind of knowledge in similar ways. He sums it up in relation to the Sanskrit word *saccidànanda,* which says that Reality is essentially One. Our understanding of it has, however, three phases *(sac-cid-ànanda):* The first refers to the fact that things *are:* they belong to each other "through the relationship of common existence."[30] Second, we are related to all things in our knowledge of them—that is, a knowledge of the common property of being. The third phase, *ànanda,* shows that we are united with reality in a loving and joyful relationship. The ultimate purpose of life, or our self-realization, lies in an increasing "unification" with all reality.[31] Such purpose reveals itself in an "expression of sympathy," of love and care for life itself.

Strangely, if you want to perfect yourself in the process of self-realization, you will only succeed by subordinating yourself to others, as in a love relationship. In the end, perfection requires subordinating yourself to the entire reality. In the unification with others, you experience freedom. No wonder, then, that the great religions and moral systems of the world point to *humility* as the basic moral virtue. Only as a servant of life can you really succeed and be free and in charge of yourself. Humility makes you powerful. Says Tagore: "We come nearer the great when we are great in humility."[32] Fortunately, a few genuine servants, both men and women, exist in our restless societies. In their own way, they are the true teachers.

Notes

1. Spinoza, *Ethica* 5.15. References to this work give part and proposition number rather than page number. The edition used is Baruch (Benedictus) Spinoza, *Éthique: Démontrée suivant l'ordre géométrique et divisée en cinq parties*, ed. and trans. Charles Appuhn, 2 vols. (Paris: Garnier, 1953). The original work dates to 1677.

2. Friedrich Nietzsche, *Die fröhliche Wissenschaft*, ed. Wilhelm Weischedel, vol. 2 in Werke in drei Bänden, ed. Karl Schlechta (Munich: Hanser, 1954–56), 7–274, no. 125. The work originally appeared in 1882.

3. Jean-Paul Sartre, *Being and Nothingness: An Essay on Phenomenological Ontology*, trans. Hazel E. Barnes (London: Methuen, 1957), 615. The work's original edition came out in 1943.

4. Rabindranath Tagore, *The English Writings of Rabindranath Tagore*, ed. Sisir Kumar Das (New Delhi: Sakitya Akademi, 1997), 2:424. All references to Tagore are to this edition.

5. Martin Heidegger, *Being and Time*, trans. John MacQuarrie and Edward Robinson (London: SCM, 1962), 312. This work was first published in 1927.

6. Ibid., 165.

7. Tagore, *English Writings*, 2:316.

8. Cf. ibid., 356.

9. Spinoza, *Ethica* 2.14.

10. Heidegger, *Being and Time*, 92.

11. Abraham Kaplan, "Perspectives on the Theme," in *Individuality and the New Society*, ed. Abraham Kaplan (Seattle: University of Washington Press, 1970), 20.

12. G. W. F. Hegel, *Grundlinien der Philosophie des Rechts* (Frankfurt am Main: Suhrkamp, 1971), 1:244.

13. Tagore, *English Writings*, 3:676–79.

14. Ibid.

15. Rabindranath Tagore, *The Home and the World* (New York: Macmillan, 1920), 1.

16. Ibid.

17. Tagore, *English Writings*, 1:403, no. 57.

18. Simone de Beauvoir, *Le deuxième sexe*, 2 vols. (Paris: Gallimard, 1949).

19. Adrienne Rich, *Of Woman Born: Motherhood as Experience and Institution* (London: Virago, 1976).

20. Clarissa P. Estés, *Women Who Run with the Wolves: Myths and Stories of the Wild Woman Archetype* (New York: Ballantine Books, 1992).

21. Tagore, *English Writings*, 2:294.

22. Ibid., 334.

23. Ibid., 356 and 359.

24. Ibid., 357.

25. Spinoza, *Ethica* 2.40.

26. Ibid., 2.4.

27. Tagore, *English Writings*, 2:565.

28. Ibid.

29. Ibid.

30. Ibid., 512.

31. Ibid.

32. Ibid., 1:403, no. 57.

Chapter 5

The Utility of Faith Reconsidered

Louis Midgley

> Still others argue that religions, though illusory and false, are yet fruitful; and that the results that follow depend not on their being true, but only on their being firmly believed.
>
> Truman G. Madsen[1]

When I began my undergraduate work at the University of Utah in 1948, I met a remarkable group of impressive, somewhat older students, one of whom was Truman G. Madsen. We became friends. At about the time I met Madsen, Sterling McMurrin (1914–99),[2] a fashionable, genteel, cultural-Mormon teacher, was introducing him to various strands of contemporary Protestant theology; I underwent the same indoctrination by McMurrin in 1953. Madsen and I were singularly intrigued by what we found in the writings of Paul Tillich (1886–1965), then a celebrated Protestant theologian. Madsen eventually wrote his dissertation on Tillich at Harvard University. Later, when Madsen returned to Cambridge, Massachusetts, as president of the New England Mission, I was finishing my own dissertation on Tillich at Brown University in Providence, Rhode Island.

Quite unlike McMurrin, who was fond of some features of Tillich's theology, both Madsen and I rejected his system, which we saw as the latest in a long line of efforts to substitute Being-Itself for the living God revealed in the scriptures. Tillich carried to their logical conclusion the most radical implications inherent in the decisions that theologians of the third or fourth centuries A.D. (if not earlier) had made to employ categories borrowed from pagan Greek philosophy in an effort to explicate their understanding of divine things. For our rejection of Tillich's theology and for other reasons, we probably both disappointed McMurrin—at least, I am confident that I did. Yet I learned much from him. In his elegantly delivered lectures, he drew attention to various writers and books as he sketched his version of the history of philosophy and theology. I read the literature he and others mentioned and eventually began fashioning my own account.

I wish to honor my friend Truman Madsen with the following essay, in which I set forth some of the discoveries that resulted from my efforts to recover several interesting and crucial strands of intellectual history. Specifically, I focus on the debate over the practical (moral or political) role of faith (often vaguely called "religion"), beginning with Plato (427–347 B.C.) and recurring in works of various writers up through Alexis de Tocqueville (1805–59). Indeed, this issue continues to confront philosophers today, despite the efforts of those like Karl Marx (1818–83) to end the discussion.

Natural Theology

Can we live well either with or without religion? Even when religion has been seen as a *pharmakon* (drug, narcotic, or opiate), its practical utility has been recognized, though not necessarily celebrated. The struggle over the question of the utility of faith goes back to the beginnings of philosophy. The issue always seems to have been whether human beings can lead more meaningful and productive lives with the help of religion or in its absence, or whether it really makes a difference either way. There has never been much in the way of a consensus.

My first encounter with the notion that the truth of religion lies in its utility as the ground of moral discipline and restraint, or as a kind of social cement, was in a little book entitled *Dialogues Concerning Natural Religion*.[3] Reading this book by David Hume (1711–76)—the great Scottish historian, philosopher, and essayist—was for me a truly liberating experience. What Hume, following the common eighteenth-century usage, often calls *natural religion* was previously known as *natural theology*.[4] This expression typically identifies an understanding of divine things (set forth in arguments for the reality of God) that is presumably accessible to pure reason (what Hume calls *natural reason*) apart from any privileged divine revelations such as those recorded in the Bible or other sacred writings considered by various religions as scripture. This occurs when Augustine (A.D. 354–430) borrows from the Academic philosopher Marcus Terentius Varro (116–27 B.C.)[5] a threefold classification system of theology in which the *civil* (or political) and the *fabulous* (or mythical, consisting of "lying fables" fashioned or manipulated by priests and poets)[6] are opposed to *natural* (or physical) theology.[7] Augustine seems to have adopted Varro's classification in an effort to dispose of the then-dominant Roman civic cult and its related unseemly mythical embellishments and aberrations. Since it tends in some degree to form good citizens by promoting political virtues believed necessary for living well in communities, Augustine accepts civil theology, whatever its flaws, as having advantages over the myths or fables of poets. But, he contends, natural theology—that is, the work of philosophers eager to comprehend the nature of divine things—yields a true, though perhaps not an entirely full, conception of the nature of the divine and is therefore superior to both civil and fabulous theologies. Augustine thus accords greater weight in his thought to the efforts of philosophers—especially Plato and his followers—to discover through reason the truth about divine things.[8]

But this does not explain why Augustine adopts Varro's classification of theology. Varro's *Antiquities*,[9] from which the scheme originates, is also the primary source for Augustine's attack on Roman religion in the first part of *The City of God*.[10] In using Varro's words to testify against the civil theology of the Romans, Augustine first heaps praise on Varro,[11] then indicates that Varro wrote forty-one books of antiquities. These he divides into "human and divine things."[12] Then Augustine provides a kind of table of contents for this famous, but unfortunately now lost, volume.[13] He agrees with Varro that the truth about divine things is to be found in an understanding of their "nature," using both the Latin *natura* and the Greek *physis*. Augustine then notes that Varro explains "that he had written first concerning human things, and afterwards of divine things, because these divine things were instituted by men:—'As the painter is before the painted tablet, the mason before the edifice, so states are before those things which are instituted by states.'"[14]

But is it not the case that the creator must necessarily precede the creation? Then should not that which is divine naturally precede that which is human? Augustine thus asks why Varro, in parts of his *Antiquities*, "seems to pass over no portion of the nature of the gods[.] Why, then, does he say, 'If we had been writing on the whole nature of the gods, we would first have finished the divine things before we touched the human'?"[15] Augustine argues that Varro writes first of human things because he is writing only on the cult of the Romans—that is, on their gods as portrayed in myths and fables for political purposes—and not on the nature of divine things. If he had been addressing the nature of divine things, they would have preceded human things. Augustine then insists that this was Varro's way of indicating that the Roman cult was a mere human creation and not truly divine, for if he had dealt with the nature of divine things, then "its due place would have been before human things in the order of writing."[16]

> For in what he wrote on human things, he [Varro] followed the
> history of affairs; but in what he wrote concerning those things

which they [the Romans] call divine, what else did he follow but mere conjectures about vain things? This, doubtless, is what, in a subtle manner, he wished to signify; not only writing concerning divine things after the human, but even giving a reason why he did so; for if he suppressed this, some, perchance, would have defended his doing so in one way, and some in another.[17]

Augustine concludes his examination of the significance of the structure of Varro's *Antiquities* with the claim that by "writing the books concerning divine things," Varro "did not write concerning the truth which belongs to nature, but the falseness which belongs to error."[18] This conclusion allows Augustine to employ Varro as a witness against the Roman cult. According to Augustine, Varro was much like Seneca, whom he describes as not willing to publicly "impugn" the civil theology of the Romans. Instead, like other wise men, he feigned respect for the Roman cult for the sake of the city. Seneca,

> whom philosophy had made, as it were, free, nevertheless, be-
> cause he was an illustrious senator of the Roman people, wor-
> shipped what he censured, did what he condemned, adored what
> he reproached, because, forsooth, philosophy had taught him
> something great—namely, not to be superstitious in the world,
> but, on account of the laws of cities and the customs of men, to
> be an actor, not on the stage, but in the temples—conduct the
> more to be condemned, that those things which he was deceit-
> fully acting he so acted that the people thought he was acting
> sincerely.[19]

Augustine's adoption of Varro's famed threefold classification of theology enables him, in addition to invoking Varro against the Roman cult, to call upon him as a witness that the truth about divine things is in the quest for knowledge of the nature of things—that is, in natural theology. He explains in detail how Varro provided what would now be called naturalistic explanations of the deeper meanings presumably embodied by the gods of the Romans. The vulgar beliefs concerning the gods are clumsy approximations of, for example, "the patterns of things, which Plato called ideas."[20] When seen as allegories, their deeper truth begins to shine through. In fact, this description seems strikingly like Augustine's own way of reading the Bible; it was while studying the books of certain Platonists that Augustine came to see that what he had always reproached Christians for believing could be understood as allegorical.[21] Be that as it may, Augustine attributes to the learned and wise Varro the idea that "the one true God" is the one "who is wholly everywhere, included in no space, bound by no chains, mutable in no part of His being, filling heaven and earth with omnipresent power, not with a needy nature," and so forth.[22] What Augustine attributes to Varro looks much like Augustine's own natural theology—that is, his account of the true nature of God as discerned through reason.

It should also be remembered that the idea of a distinction between the natural and supernatural, which the modern mind tends to take as a given, has a beginning and an extraordinary history. Long before such a distinction existed, those seeking wisdom by unaided human reason sought to discover what they thought was the nature *(physis)*, essence, form, idea, or substance of things, especially the nature of the highest, most fundamental, or First Things. According to Aristotle (384–322 B.C.), the first philosophers were known as "physical investigators," or those who discoursed on nature, as distinguished from those who talked about the gods or divine things. The Greek word *physis,* from which we get words like *physics* or *physical,* originally meant growth, or that into which a thing can grow if given the right conditions, and hence also the type or character of a thing that distinguishes it from other things. But the word also identified things that are not made but simply are—the highest or First Things, in which everything that either grows or is made is ultimately grounded and upon which such things ultimately depend; in other words, it meant something like "nature" in the sense of *ousia* (essence) and not merely rocks, dirt, trees, or other existing stuff. When the term is understood this way, nothing is higher than nature—not even divine things, unless they are identified with or subsumed under nature. The traditional first part of philosophy, the inquiry into *physis,* allowed nothing beyond or above nature, however it was understood. The modern distinction between a natural and supernatural realm was simply not possible. Instead, the struggle to know the form, essence, or substance behind the multiplicity of things was simply an effort to identify *physis.*

As far back as Aristotle, was there not something analogous to the natural-supernatural distinction? Put another way, does not the term *metaphysics*—an old, vague, and yet respected word— imply something like a supernatural realm, something above, beneath, beyond, or behind *physis?* Although it originally did not, it certainly does here and now. Our word *metaphysics* comes from the Greek *ta meta ta physika* ("the things after the physics"). This was the name purportedly given by Andronicus of Rhodes to Aristotle's First Philosophy, which he placed after the corpus of Aristotle's book called *Physics.* In other words, the phrase referred solely to the location of certain texts in an edition of Aristotle's works. In Latin, this term eventually became *metaphysica* when Boethius, in the sixth century, made one word out of the phrase. Averroës (A.D. 1126–98) and others later popularized the word. But even then it was simply the name for the first part of philosophy— specifically, for their understanding of Aristotle's effort to identify the nature of things, including the First Things, which presumably ground and explain everything else. Again following Aristotle, this was the science of something called Being—not in the sense of this or that being or thing that exists, but Being as such. When Christians began to explicate their understanding of divine things in the categories of pagan philosophy, eventually God was seen as Being-itself—the ground of everything that is, the power of being in everything that exists, the First Thing that created everything out of nothing, and so forth. This endeavor was, as I have shown, occasionally called natural theology.

Christians struggling to account for what God does for human beings came to contrast their own nature (or *physis*)—what they can possibly grow into apart from God—with *charis*, that which is a gift, that which is bestowed. The word *charismatic*, meaning one with a special divine endowment or gift, still identifies one who receives something that goes beyond a natural endowment, achievement, or expectation. This may help to explain why "the first use of the word 'supernatural' occurs in Greek and actually post-dates Augustine by some one hundred and fifty years."[23] Earlier, an older and more easily understandable distinction between nature and grace can be seen in various efforts to account for the fall and redemption; this distinction then comes to play a role in some early accounts of the atonement.

According to one authority, what is now called "naturalistic humanism" (that is, what skeptical contemporary philosophers say about divine things) "has developed in opposition to supernaturalism, and especially to theism."[24] This is certainly the linguistic horizon on which these things are now seen and debated. However, the modern distinction between the natural and supernatural is not found in the Bible or in early Christian theology, though later interpretations may sometimes read it back into these earlier texts and periods since it has become the uncritically accepted lens through which people here and now tend to see the world. The fact is that the naturalistic humanists of our day are in some crucial ways thinking in terms of natural theology as that expression was originally understood. The difference is that modern atheists tend to discount the utility of religious beliefs in molding dispositions and providing a social cement, whereas premodern atheists tended to be cautious and hence respectful of faith, even though they believed it to be unfounded.

Hume's Mitigated Skepticism

Natural theology subsequently came to identify attempts of theologians and philosophers to reach conclusions about the nature of deity by unaided human reason. In his *Dialogues,* modeled on *De rerum deorum,* the famous dialogue of Marcus Tullius Cicero (106–43 B.C.), Hume assesses the coherence of what had, following Augustine's appropriation of Varro's terminology, come to be known as natural theology. In examining this literature, Hume seems to argue that the traditional proofs for the reality of God, first set forth in book 10 of Plato's *Laws,* are highly problematic, if not incoherent. Hume then draws attention to the significance of faith that appears when the limits of natural reason are fully acknowledged. He also identifies a kind of melancholy that the recognition of these limits may provoke since the questions addressed are of profound importance and since he notes at times a resistance among nonbelievers to trusting prior to rational proof of the reality of God. Hume ends his *Dialogues* by having Philo, his mitigated skeptic, insist that "the most natural sentiment which a well-disposed mind will feel on this occasion"—that is, when the limits of natural reason and hence the misfortunes that attend the rational proofs for God have been confronted—

> is a longing desire and expectation that Heaven would be pleased to dissipate, at least alleviate, this profound ignorance, by affording some more particular revelation to mankind, and making discoveries of the nature, attributes, and operations of the divine object of our Faith. A person, seasoned with a just sense of the imperfections of natural reason, will fly to revealed truth with the greatest avidity: while the haughty dogmatist, persuaded that he can erect a complete system of theology by the mere help of philosophy, disdains any farther aid, and rejects this adventitious instructor.[25]

These enigmatic remarks—coming at the very end of the *Dialogues* and voiced by Philo, who seems to express best what can be ascertained of Hume's own opinions—have often been ignored or brushed aside as merely an ironic rhetorical flourish. I wonder if those who do so have taken Hume seriously. Be that as it may, what Hume argues through his Philo is that "to be a philosophical sceptic is, in a man of letters, the first and most essential step towards being a sound, believing Christian."[26] This could be true even if Hume was not himself a believer. If what is meant by "philosophical sceptic" is one who is wary of the possibility that unaided human reason (what Hume called "natural reason") can ascertain the truth about divine things, then I must be counted as such a one. And it was from reading Hume's *Dialogues* that natural theology lost for me any of its vaunted charms—hence the liberating experience of which I spoke.

In his *Enquiry Concerning Human Understanding,* Hume also argues that a proper appreciation of the limits of natural reason

> may serve to confound those dangerous friends or disguised enemies to the *Christian Religion,* who have undertaken to defend it by the principles of human reason. Our most holy religion is founded on *Faith,* not on reason; and it is a sure method of exposing it to put it to such a trial as it is, by no means, fitted to endure.[27]

Hume closed his *Enquiry* with the observation that the theology one finds in what he called "divinity or school metaphysics" ought to be tossed into "the flames: For it can contain nothing but sophistry and illusion."[28] He insisted instead that for those inclined to the Christian religion, the "best and most solid foundation is *faith and divine revelation*."[29]

The Ancient Form of Argument for the Utility of Religion

It is not at all clear that Hume himself had even a semblance of such a faith. He could, however, discern its proper role in the lives of the faithful and was hence concerned with the question of the utility of faith for those who are believers and also for civil society. At the end of the *Dialogues,* his Cleanthes makes the claim that "religion, however corrupted, is still better than no religion at all. The doctrine of a future state is so strong and necessary a security to morals, that we never ought to abandon or neglect it."[30] This opinion and its place in the *Dialogues* are somewhat similar to the opinion with which Cicero seems to have concluded his famous dialogue on religious beliefs. It will be recalled that Cicero, in *De rerum deorum,* has his interlocutors, after having spent the night pounding away at the absurdities of various vulgar opinions about divine things, begin the next day by going forth to at least appear to defend and serve the cult for the sake of the city.

But the argument for the utility of religion—that its truth is to be found merely in its utility—has a long history, best told from its beginning by going back to Plato. The arguments set forth for God in book 10 of the *Laws* are clearly part of practical—that is, moral and political—philosophy as that intellectual endeavor was originally understood. The virtues, or human excellences, necessary to sustain good regimes necessarily depend upon education, or correct indoctrination. A good regime thus needs the proper habituation of its youths, and this depends on rewards and punishments designed to sustain and reinforce obedience to the laws that generate virtuous habits. But, given the power of *thumos* ("desire")—especially among youths but also among childlike adults, which is to say most human beings most of the time— more is needed than merely proximate rewards and punishments: duty and obedience to laws need the backing of belief in ultimate or divine rewards and punishments, or obedience to law languishes. Fostering the necessary virtues upon which good regimes rest thus requires belief that the laws and their sanctions ultimately have a divine source and sanction.[31]

Beginning in book 5 of Plato's *Laws,* the ideal regime is described as small (with a population of no more than 5,040 landholders or citizens), with one religion, one language, no foreigners, subsistence agriculture, and therefore no commerce and none of the resulting luxury. Such a regime would support substantial equality and social solidarity.[32] These conditions were thought to be necessary for a well-constituted regime as a means of avoiding, among other evils, *stasis* (civil strife),[33] which was always believed to be the primary threat to the existence of stable republics. Likewise, those who believe in "active gods," and not in the static notions of the divine fashioned by those involved in the quest for knowledge of the nature of things, are potentially profoundly disruptive for a stable regime. Stability could be disordered by a *mantic* (prophet) going around announcing that the actual laws of the given city, and hence also the acts of the citizenry, are an abomination in the sight of God. So strict controls should also be placed on that source of disruption.

But is a belief in an ultimate distributive and retributive justice standing behind the network of rules set down by the lawgiver(s) really necessary to ground and support the virtues required in a civilized regime? Note that Plato's *Laws* begins with the opinion that it is just to claim that the laws have a divine source (*Laws* 624a), though immediate disagreement about the god to whom credit is due and about the content of the laws ensues. Plato also refers to the legendary Minos, the one who is reputed to have visited with Zeus in his cave and received oracles in preparation for setting down the laws for the Cretans (*Laws* 624b). But Plato's drama immediately moves to the Athenian stranger (Socrates in Crete?) and his two wise old companions; as they ascend from human to divine things—that is, as they climb from the sea coast to the cave and temple of Zeus—they begin to legislate for a city that exists only in their speech. So the drama seems to tell us that laws are human conventions after all, merely the work of wise old men, though the laws are to be given every appearance of being divine for the good of the city.

Could it be that the reticence of premodern philosophers to attack the absurdities of political and poetic theology was grounded in a sense of the necessity of such beliefs as ordering devices for communities? Of course, this is not to discount entirely their fear of persecution for public manifestations of impiety. But at least in some instances philosophers were cautious about revealing their heresies precisely because they seemed to believe that only the wise, and not the vulgar, were genuinely capable of the necessary restraint once the fear of divine rewards and punishments was removed. In this regard, it should be recalled that Augustine, in his anxiety to discredit pagan political theology, draws on Varro's earlier treatment of pagan ideology. Describing Varro as the most wise and learned of the pagans, Augustine shows how he wrote esoterically, hiding his heresies from the vulgar, while signaling to the wise that the gods were useful, perhaps even necessary, human inventions.

Now in a Modern Setting

But leaving Plato's fascinating and instructive treatment of these and related matters aside, it is apparent that something like the issue of the utility of religion is again raised in David Hume's *Dialogues*. "For if finite and temporary rewards and punishments have so great an effect, as we daily find," Hume has his Cleanthes ask, "how much greater must be expected from such as are infinite and eternal?"[34] But then Hume's Philo asks why, "if vulgar superstition be so salutary to society," is it the case "that all history abounds so much with accounts of its pernicious consequences on public affairs?"[35] Thus it appears that, from Hume's perspective, the utility of belief in God is at least debatable. Concerning religion, Hume's Philo observes further that

> factions, civil wars, persecutions, subversions of government, oppression, slavery; these are the dismal consequences which always attend its prevalence over the minds of men. If the religious spirit be ever mentioned in any historical narration, we are sure to meet afterwards with a detail of the miseries which attend it.[36]

Hume thus seems to argue that religious differences and the resulting quarrels may well be one of the leading sources of faction, civil war, and other attendant evils that disturb and even destroy civil society. But, it must be noted, in these observations Hume has in mind actual regimes and not merely one fashioned in speech, which is what Plato generated in the *Laws* when he confronted these same issues. Hume insists that evils such as "factions, civil wars, persecutions, subversions of governments," and so forth can often be traced back to religious differences and the often bitter and divisive quarrels they generate.

In 1950 I purchased a copy of David Hume's *Essays: Moral, Political and Literary* in a bookstore in Wellington, New Zealand.[37] As I examined those essays, I was stunned to discover language here and there—and crucial ideas—that James Madison and Alexander Hamilton (both writing under the pseudonym Publius) had clearly borrowed from Hume in fashioning their 1787 explanation of the principles behind the proposed Constitution of the United States.

For example, Publius argued that the "mischiefs of faction"[38] were the mortal disease that had vitiated the small republics of antiquity. And by "mischief" James Madison did not have in mind something merely playful, but a disease that he considered ultimately fatal to a regime if not treated and cured. His whole endeavor was to explain how the founders had managed to fashion such a cure, not by doing away with the freedom that makes factions flourish, but by finding ways of controlling their pernicious effects. Publius plowed new ground in republican theory by recommending a large commercial republic that could not only tolerate but actually benefit from diverse religious opinions and yet contain and control the mischiefs of partisanship and faction. In doing this, Publius broke with the traditional small-republic theory by drawing on and modifying ideas set forth earlier by David Hume. This connection is now well known, but in 1950, when I first encountered Hume's *Essays,* I assumed that I had been inattentive to the sources of Madison's argument in the *Federalist* concerning the mischiefs of faction and their potential remedy in an extended republic. I did not then realize that no one had, to that point at least, noticed that Madison and Hamilton had borrowed crucial ideas from Hume's *Essays* when they wrote the *Federalist* in 1787.[39]

Instead of insisting on religion as the primary source of republican virtues and then stressing the absolute need for such virtues, Publius treated the religious spirit, much like Hume, as one of the primary sources of the mischiefs that threatens republican regimes. Following Hume, Publius argued that in constituting a republic one ought to begin with the assumption that the virtues will not restrain evil—or, in Hume's terms, one must assume that every man is a knave, which assumption is false in fact but still true in theory.[40] Hence the following observation by Madison:

> All civilized Societies would be divided into different Sects, Factions, & interests, as they happened to consist of rich & poor, debtors & creditors, the landed, the manufacturing, the commercial interests, the inhabitants of this district or that district, the followers of this . . . religious Sect or that religious Sect. In all cases where a majority are united by a common interest or passion, the rights of the minority are in danger. What motives are to restrain them?[41]

Could we not rely on the moral sentiments or the conscience of the faithful? Not according to Madison, echoing Hume: "Conscience, the only remaining tie, is known to be inadequate in individuals: In large numbers, little is to be expected from it. Besides, Religion itself may become a motive to persecution & oppression.—These observations are verified by the Histories of every Country."[42]

When Madison took up the task of defending the plan for the proposed American republic, he was confronted by a citizenry already deeply divided on religious matters, one that already lacked both the foundation and much of the content of what had previously been understood as the necessary republican virtues. In addition, republican or civil liberty not only permitted but encouraged and facilitated sectarian religious differences. Indeed, one of the primary objects of a well-constituted republic, from the perspective of Madison, was the protection of individual conscience and especially the right of choice on religious matters. Whatever else might be said about the passion for building Zion—a zeal that has marked a portion of the American character—those efforts, though rightfully protected by republican principles, are not directly part of the republican program. In the American republic, at least as it was proposed by Madison, the work of the religious spirit should remain outside the official sphere of the regime. Ultimately, he saw the quarrels of religious sectarians as a source of competing and potentially fatal factious quarrels.[43]

Madison argued in *Federalist* 51 that

> in a free government, the security for civil rights must be the same as for religious rights. It consists in the one case in the multiplicity of interests, and in the other, in the multiplicity of sects. . . . The degree of security in both cases will depend on the number of interests and sects; and this may be presumed to depend on the extent of country and number of people comprehended under the same government.[44]

This is, of course, the basic argument offered by Madison for an extended, compound republic as was set out in the proposed Constitution. Hence, in *Federalist* 10, Madison declared that "a religious sect, may degenerate into a political faction in a part of the . . . Confederacy; but the variety of sects dispersed over the entire face of it, must secure the national Councils against any danger from that source."[45] Just as enlarging the sphere of republican government would tend to increase the likelihood of a variety of sects, it would also make it less likely that any one sect could constitute a majority faction or that some alliance of sects might be formed and thereby tyrannize competing opinions. In this same way, a large commercial republic would reduce the likelihood of any other faction forming a tyrannical majority.

Instead of seeing the religious spirit as a necessarily salutary source of virtues, modern republican theorists have sometimes pictured it as yet another in a long list of potential vehicles available for gratifying ambition, manipulating others, exercising unrighteous dominion, or expressing or justifying aggression and violence, and not as a way of finding favor in the sight of God and cooperating for the common good. In these defiled manifestations, the religious spirit is perverse and mean; it is not calculated to enlarge the soul and bring peace and prosperity. Contrary to this view, Hume had his Cleanthes insist:

> The proper office of religion is to regulate the heart of men, humanize their conduct, infuse the spirit of temperance, order, and obedience; and, as its operation is silent, and only enforces the motives of morality and justice, it is in danger of being overlooked, and confounded with these other motives. When it distinguishes itself, and acts as a separate principle over men, it has departed from its proper sphere, and has become only a cover to faction and ambition.[46]

Hume's Philo also argued that religions may often work precisely "in direct opposition to morality; . . . the raising up a new and frivolous species of merit, the preposterous distribution which it makes of praise and blame, must have the most pernicious consequences, and weaken extremely men's attachment to the natural motives of justice and humanity."[47] In these remarks we see one element of the popular argument for "political atheism" as that concept was presented, for example, by Francis Bacon (1561–1626).

Hume raised the issue of whether religion has political utility in one other context. In the *Enquiry*, Hume creates a hypothetical case in which "a friend who loves skeptical paradoxes"—an

Epicurean, many of whose "principles" Hume insists he cannot approve—is brought to face the charge that a school of philosophy, by "denying a divine existence, and consequently a providence and a future state, seem[s] to loosen in a great measure, the ties of morality, and may be supposed, for that reason, pernicious to the peace of civil society."[48] This argument then confronts "questions of public good, and the interest of the commonwealth."[49] The Epicurean then defends his views from the charge that they undermine the public good in what Hume calls a "harangue."[50] Hume subsequently offers against Epicurean atheism a minimal, bland version of the argument that allows for at least the possibility of a provident deity. The Epicurean responds with the claim that the political interests of society have no connection at all with what are merely abstruse philosophical disputes.

The Epicurean, by arguing that "religious doctrines and reasonings *can* have no influence on life, because they *ought* to have no influence" has overlooked, according to Hume, the fact that the citizenry may reason differently and might actually "suppose that the Deity would inflict punishments on vice, and bestow rewards on virtue."[51] Hume then points out that the practical or moral issue does not depend on speculation about whether the Epicurean is right but on what people actually believe about such matters.

> Whether this reasoning of theirs be just or not, is no matter. Its influence on their life and conduct must still be the same. And, those, who attempt to disabuse them of such prejudices, may, for aught I know, be good reasoners, but I cannot allow them to be good citizens and politicians; since they free men from one restraint upon their passions, and make the infringement of the laws of society, in one respect, more easy and secure.[52]

At this point in his argument, Hume seems to grant that something can be said for restraining atheism for practical, moral, or political reasons. The difficulty that then must be confronted lies in finding a way to impose the necessary salutary restraints on atheism and yet allow the necessary freedom to science and other useful pursuits that seem to him to be altogether desirable. Hume seems willing to recommend taking whatever risk that allowing atheism might require. He does so in order to guarantee that science is not hobbled by what seems to be a legitimate concern over the moral restraints necessary for public order that religion tends to provide.

And in an American Setting—Tocqueville on the Utility of Religion

In his justly famous *Democracy in America*,[53] Alexis de Tocqueville (1805–59) linked political theory, understood as a branch of practical or moral speculation, to arguments about the utility of religion. In addition, he set forth arguments that religion is necessary to properly civilize and morally restrain citizens in times of equality, thereby helping to make democracy safe for the world.

In 1831, when only twenty-six years old, Tocqueville traveled with his friend Gustave de Beaumont for nine months in the United States. This journey was ostensibly to study the American prison system. Tocqueville, however, had much more than this in mind.[54] He spent much of his time gathering information for what eventually became the book *Democracy in America*. His writing is, by and large, immediately intelligible yet also subtle, puzzling, and many-layered. I will examine some of what Tocqueville said in his famous book about religion both in America and, more generally, in the democracy of the times.[55]

Tocqueville identifies the guiding principle or "spirit" animating democratic man—the peculiar and predominating element that controls all the rest of his nature—as the love of equality, not as a fondness for freedom, which is always subordinate and easily jettisoned. He strives to demonstrate that this "principal passion," equality, becomes a kind of "delirium" (pp. 480–81), for its charms are simply overpowering. He also shows how this passion affects religious faith, concluding that when equality begins to reign, everyone seeks the grounds for belief within oneself. He labels this disposition "individualism" (p. 482), an expression borrowed and popularized to describe the ethos preferred by those for whom equality is the dominant passion. The result of individualism, which is the recent "democratic" and somewhat moderate manifestation of selfishness (see pp. 482–84), is an assortment of "isolated individuals" who "no longer feel bound by a common interest" to the fate of those around them (p. 484). Instead, they are "reduced to being occupied only with" themselves (p. 485). They thus lack public-spiritedness, or virtue, or a willingness to sacrifice their own immediate interests for the common good (see p. 484). But they sometimes "enjoy their newly acquired independence only with a sort of secret restiveness" (p. 485).

Tocqueville then moderates his rather bleak portrait of individualism by showing that free institutions may induce care for others and thereby generate a spirit of mutual helpfulness. Such sentiment, supported by what he called "self-interest well understood" (p. 500), provides the necessary grounds for virtuous acts. Tocqueville thus strives to show that selfishness—a narrow, unrestrained pursuit of self-interest—in general destroys public virtue but that its American version is not virulent or especially dangerous, for it induces sentiments that yield mutual helpfulness. But even that doctrine is flawed and cannot by itself sustain the citizens of a democratic regime. Such salutary behavior somehow rests more on the doctrine of self-interest well understood. But in a democratic regime, the proper understanding of self-interest is itself simply not self-sustaining; it needs the support of education that teaches self-sacrifice for a larger and remote private good as well as for the common good. And Americans rightly call in the aid of every device to induce this self-sacrifice because, as Tocqueville explains, "the century of blind devotions and instinctive virtues is already fleeing far from us, and I see a time approaching when freedom, public peace, and social order itself will not be able to do without enlightenment" (p. 503).

Having thus demonstrated the value of some form of "enlightenment" to moderate the dangerous tendencies of selfish individualism, Tocqueville then introduces his argument: "If the doctrine of self-interest well understood had only this world in view, it would be far from sufficient; for there are a great number of sacrifices that can find recompense only in the other world; and whatever effort of mind that one makes to prove the utility of virtue, it will always be hard to make a man who does not wish to die live well" (p. 504). Thus the issue is whether "self-interest well understood can be easily reconciled with religious beliefs" (p. 504).

Those Tocqueville labels "philosophers" are the ones who claim that self-interest, if well understood, is compatible with religious beliefs. The "founders of almost all religions" have "only moved the goal back; instead of placing the prize for the sacrifices they impose in this world, they have put it in the other" (p. 504). It is not, therefore, the fear of divine retribution so much as it is the longing for rewards that leads to self-sacrifice. "The philosophers who teach this doctrine say to men that to be happy in life one ought to watch over one's passions and carefully repress their excesses; that one can acquire a lasting happiness only in refusing a thousand passing enjoyments, and finally that one must constantly triumph over oneself to serve oneself better" (p. 504).[56] This represents the core of what "self-interest well understood" means for Tocqueville, who discounts the differences between the moral teachings of those he calls "philosophers" and those he refers to as "the founders of almost all religions" (p. 504). This tactic facilitates his subordination of religion to philosophy or his appropriation for political purposes of the teachings concerning divine things, for his philosophers teach a mercenary morality in which the goal is happiness understood as the gratification of appetites. The goal

for Tocqueville is thus the gratification of lasting rather than passing or momentary pleasures. It does not include the kind of demands found in the teaching of prophets or the founders of religion. Whatever their deeper differences from the philosophers
may be, asserts Tocqueville, they "have held to nearly the same
language" (p. 504).

Tocqueville also contrasts the moral teachings of those who
stress self-interest and whose morality thus seems mercenary with
the teachings of the founders of religions. He notes that Christians
claim "that one must prefer others to oneself to gain Heaven," thus
appealing to self-interest,

> but Christianity tells us as well that one ought to do good to
> those like oneself out of love of God. This is a magnificent ex-
> pression; man penetrates the Divine thought by his intelli-
> gence; he sees that the goal of God is order; he freely associates
> himself with that great design; and all the while sacrificing his
> particular interests to the admirable order of all things, he ex-
> pects no other recompense than the pleasure of contemplating
> it. (pp. 504–5)

But Tocqueville also knows of the opinion that believers who "practice virtue out of a spirit of religion act only in view of recompense." Those who say such things are, from Tocqueville's perspective, simply deceiving themselves (p. 504). "I therefore do not
believe," he claims, "that the sole motive of religious men is interest; but I think that interest is the principal means religions themselves make use of to guide men, and I do not doubt that it is only
from this side that they take hold of the crowd and become popular" (p. 505).

Those influenced by preachers and hence charmed by a popular teaching will easily practice their religion out of a sense of self-
interest. They will also perform their duty out of self-interest, and
they will place in this world the interest they have in doing it (see
p. 505). But this amounts to a fundamental modification of Chris-

tianity or at least a shift in its moral horizon. The point of Christian teaching is certainly not merely to habitually and effortlessly sacrifice "the pleasure of the moment" for the lasting interests of one's life (p. 505). The sacrifices are to be made for God and not merely as some more effective way of grasping pleasures in this life.

Fortunately for democratic man, "American preachers constantly come back to earth and only with great trouble can they take their eyes off it. To touch their listeners better, they make them see daily how religious beliefs favor freedom and public order, and it is often difficult to know when listening to them if the principal object of religion is to procure eternal felicity in the other world or well-being in this one" (pp. 505–6).[57] Preachers in America soon learn, he claims, that they must cater to the passions of the herd or go unattended (see pp. 419–21). It is thus in their own self-interest to bow somewhat before the passion for comfort, physical well-being, entertainment, material possessions, and sensual gratifications. Preachers hope to make the mad search for such things somewhat restrained and more or less legal. They even become as spies who have scouted the territory beforehand and present themselves as better fitted to lead others safely to the promised land of lasting pleasures and happiness in this life (and, almost as an afterthought, perhaps in the next one as well). They help induce some measure of virtue by reconciling self-interest to religious beliefs and by allowing the one to come to the aid of the other.[58]

But even for Tocqueville's American preachers, the love of comfort still remains the dominant passion, though moderated somewhat by religious sentiments. The love of comfort leads not so much to great crimes and terrible excess as to indulgences and small iniquities. This process continues in American society today, with the passion for wealth leading to white-collar crime or to homes that rival hotels. Tocqueville insists that "these objects are small, but the soul clings to them: it considers them every day and from very close; in the end they hide the rest of the world from it, and they sometimes come to place themselves between it and God" (p. 509). In so doing, they expose an underground of deeper longings, which, when suppressed, break out in forms of "religious follies"—such as "bizarre sects"—which portend the possibility of an "enormous reaction" to the excessive "search for material goods alone" (p. 510) generated by the freedom available to democratic man. These manifestations of the religious spirit, however, are generally seen as aberrations, Tocqueville claims, and are mocked by most Americans.

Tocqueville then describes how greed generated by prosperity turns eventually against self-interest well understood and weakens the virtue necessary for a moderate, safe, and decent democracy. He argues that "men who live in centuries of equality have a continuous need for association in order to procure for themselves almost all the goods they covet" (p. 515). But being filled with "excessive taste" for the good things of this world and quite unmindful of one another, they are ready to hand themselves over "to the first master who presents himself. The passion for well-being is then turned against itself and, without perceiving it, drives away the object of its covetousness" (p. 515). This is the dangerous stage in which democratic man, confronted with rumors of public passion that disturb the trivial pleasures of private lives, comes to fear an approaching moral anarchy and hence is ready to jettison liberty. Tocqueville thus paints a dark picture of a world in which virtue has fled and with it liberty and the search for even higher human things.

What can possibly save democratic man from such a fate? The answer is that, if anything can do it, it is religion, for religious beliefs at times turn the attention of citizens toward divine things, toward beliefs that restrain the greed that otherwise leads to tyranny (see pp. 517–21). Tocqueville returns once again to the themes he introduced earlier, but now he invents an edifying picture of a people turning on the Sabbath to hear preachers who instruct them of "the innumerable evils caused by pride and covetousness. [They are] told of the necessity of regulating [their] desires, of the delicate enjoyments attached to virtue alone, and of the true happiness that accompanies it" (p. 517). Here, once again, are the salutary moral teachings of philosophers placed in the mouths of preachers, who provide the moral education necessary to limit the excesses of selfishness lurking just beneath the surface of individualism.

When offering this analysis, Tocqueville remarks:

> In another place in this work I sought causes to which one must attribute the maintenance of Americans' political institutions, and religion appeared to me one of the principal ones. Now that I am occupied with individuals, I find it again and I perceive that it is not less useful to each citizen than to the entire state. (p. 518)

Then he argues that "Americans show by their practice that they feel every necessity of making democracy more moral by means of religion. What they think in this regard about themselves is a truth with which every democratic nation ought to be instilled" (p. 518) among all peoples in ages of equality. But how can it accomplish such wonders?

Tocqueville assumes that the founder, the one who possesses the lawgiver's art, should know what is best for the particular society which he has founded and should arrange things with a noble end in view. At this point Tocqueville assumes for himself the role of lawgiver; he opines on what is necessary for the good of democratic peoples. In an aristocratic age, the lawgiver would have no need to be concerned about religion but would instead want to "stimulate the sentiment of needs among such a people" and thereby make them focus on "well-being" (p. 518). He would strive to send them in search of affluence. But in a democratic age the wise legislator must "have other cares. Give democratic peoples enlightenment and freedom and leave them alone. With no trouble they will succeed in taking all the goods from this world . . . , and render life more comfortable, easier, milder every day; their social state naturally pushes them in this direction" (p. 518). This is the "honest and legitimate search for well-being," but as a person is so engaged, "it is to be feared that he will finally lose the use of his most sublime faculties, and that by wishing to improve every-thing around him, he will finally degrade himself. The peril is there, not elsewhere" (pp. 518–19). Whatever its strengths, democracy has a crucial defect: it threatens the highest possibilities in humankind by turning attention away from noble deeds and self-sacrifice to gratification of immediate, petty wants.

Switching from the concern for the democratic man to a concern for the human race as such, Tocqueville sees some hope. "Legislators of democracies [that is, founders] and all honest and enlightened men" have a solemn duty to "apply themselves relent-lessly to raising up souls and keeping them turned toward Heaven" (p. 519). This mastering of the legislator's art, he implies, might be the means for the higher perfection of the soul of citizens. And exactly what might constitute such a cultivation of the soul? Initially, Tocqueville describes the goal of the legislator as generating "a taste for the infinite, a sentiment of greatness, and a love of im-material pleasures" (p. 519). Then he indicates that efforts must be made by the legislator to counter certain "harmful theories that tend to make it believed that everything perishes with the body" (p. 519). Tocqueville's label for these "harmful theories" is "materialism." Those who profess such views must be considered "the natural enemies of this people" (p. 519).

Since democracy springs from a passion for physical well-being and earthly pleasures, it is easy for this materialism to take root and become excessive, thereby undercutting and destroying the salutary effects of self-interest well understood. It does so by turning the search for comforts and pleasures into a kind of mad-ness. Since Tocqueville speaks from the point of view of the wise legislator representing the interests of the honest and enlightened and attempts to locate a palliative for the sickness that must eventually infect democracy, he could easily turn to a set of beliefs, in which he did not himself believe, to work their wonders on democratic man.

What set of beliefs might counter the threat posed by the materialist malady? Whatever it is, according to Tocqueville, it has something to do with the work of "Socrates and his school" (p. 520) and would be a practical means of treating the malady by directly contradicting the core materialist belief. Instead of holding that nothing but matter exists, that "everything perishes with the body," Tocqueville's wise legislator would teach that the soul is immortal. Such a dogmatic belief would presumably prevent democratic man from experiencing the liberation of the passions and the wanton indulgence of the appetites that overcame Tocqueville in his father's library when he was sixteen.

The incident is at once more trivial and more profound than it seems. Tocqueville had at a young age lost his Catholic faith, though he seems to have gone along with appearances and never seems to have made public his religious skepticism. He also seems, however, to have found it impossible to discuss his lack of faith with his wife, an English lady who had been brought up as an Anglican but had become a Roman Catholic prior to their marriage. Tocqueville took part in the salon life of Paris, where he enjoyed clever conversations and witty exchanges with those of cultivated and refined talents. He exchanged letters with one such cultured woman, an interesting Russian lady by the name of Sophie Swetchine. One letter to her contains the deepest secrets of his life, including a confession of his loss of faith in Roman Catholicism when he was sixteen as a result of encountering the skeptical literature of the Enlightenment.[59]

But Tocqueville was not the village atheist. He seems to have regretted and not celebrated his loss of faith and was fully aware of how that loss had unloosed his own passions. Thereafter he pondered the possible effects of such an event on others, especially on those in France who were then involved in the struggle to fashion a stable democratic regime out of the ruins of an old aristocratic order. The prospects genuinely alarmed him. He was convinced that citizens in a democratic regime—even more than those of an aristocratic one—needed the moral discipline of an uncritically accepted Christian faith. In the introduction to *Democracy in America,* he insists that those who are committed to liberty but are not themselves believers need to realize that freedom cannot be had without morality and that morality cannot last without faith. In addition, he offers a warning to democracies against certain powerful elements at work in the new order, speaking "in the name of progress, striving to make man into matter," and thereby "want[ing] to find the useful without occupying themselves with the just, to find science far from beliefs, and well-being separated from virtue" (p. 11; cf. p. 42). Thoughtful and faithful citizens have a duty to moderate democracy—to purify it and control its thirst for well-being, to restrain its wanton passions. They should strive to somehow render it safe for the world. A striking feature of *Democracy in America* is the attention given by Tocqueville to the role of faith and the situation of churches in providing the necessary moral foundation for democracy.

Tocqueville discovered numerous versions of Christian faith in America, which at the time of his visit was swarming with competing preachers and sects. He saw the proliferation of sects in America as flowing from both freedom and equality. He notes in *Democracy in America* that the passion for equality in the citizenry places authority in the individual, and therefore each isolated social atom turns to the maelstrom of public opinion for the ground of belief. The judge of both human and divine things becomes the individual, but the individual tends to be at the mercy of public opinion (see p. 407). He theorizes that the opinion of the majority assumes the role of supplying individuals with ready-made opinions, thereby relieving them of the necessity of fashioning their own. Philosophical, moral, religious, and political theories are mostly determined by fashions and thus rest on the shifting sands of public opinion. Even religion in America is less a matter of divine special revelation than it is an expression of uncritically accepted public opinion. And Tocqueville warns that "in centuries of equality, one can foresee that faith in common opinion will become a sort of religion whose prophet will be the majority" (p. 410).

For Tocqueville, the opinions on which a regime necessarily depends "are born in different manners and can change form and object; but one cannot make it so that there are no dogmatic beliefs, that is, opinions men receive on trust without discussing them" (p. 407). Without such beliefs "there is no common action, and without common action men still exist, but a social body does not" (p. 407). Tocqueville thus held that dogmatic beliefs are both necessary and desirable. By accepting some opinions without discussion, one takes on a salutary bondage of the mind, which is necessary in both the moral realm and the life of the mind. These observations, according to Tocqueville, apply to the philosopher as well as humankind in general (see p. 408). Even in religious life, citizens look within the confines of public opinion for the final authority and not to the heavens. Tocqueville thus observes:

> Men who live in times of equality are therefore only with difficulty led to place the intellectual authority to which they submit outside of and above humanity. It is in themselves or in those like themselves that they ordinarily seek the sources of truth. That would be enough to prove that a new religion cannot be established in these centuries, and that all attempts to cause one to be born would be not only impious, but ridiculous and unreasonable. One can foresee that democratic peoples will not readily believe in divine missions, that they will willingly laugh

at new prophets, and that they will want to find the principal arbiter of their beliefs within the limits of humanity, not beyond it. (p. 408)

This observation may help us to understand the immense hostility faced by Joseph Smith and his followers. The reason behind this mocking attitude is that Americans, as well as others enthralled by debased notions of equality, "will want to find the principal arbiter of their beliefs within the limits of humanity, and not beyond it" (p. 408). According to Tocqueville, citizens in democratic times will strive to find the authority for everything in themselves; hence, they will tend to spurn efforts to call them to the service of some authority beyond themselves. And, in addition, under such notions of equality the majority or those who presume to speak for it ultimately determine or are believed to determine the content and moral message of religious beliefs, including even those that presumably come down from the heavens through special divine revelations.

It appears that Tocqueville, while very curious about churches and religious matters in America, was entirely unaware of Joseph Smith, who in 1831 was just beginning to found a community resting on belief in a divine mission. Tocqueville's understanding of the dynamics of American religiosity helps one better comprehend why the faith Joseph Smith advanced seems in crucial ways unlike the brands common in his world and why it was greeted with hostility. It also might help one identify and appreciate some of the distinctive American elements that have both frayed and molded Mormon culture and against which the prophetic voice continues to speak.

Though not favoring a religious establishment (that is, a state church), Tocqueville prescribes a kind of bland civic religion in which an essential dogma would be the immortality of the soul. In his opinion, all the various American sects of the time offered sufficiently similar moral teachings to fit this requirement. In

order for such a teaching to be effective in countering materialism, selfishness, and instant gratification run wild, he cautions
that "one must maintain Christianity within the new democracies
at all cost[s]" (p. 521). But then the question remains: "What means,
therefore, remain to authority to bring men back toward spiritual-
ist opinions or to keep them in religion that evokes them?" (p. 521).
Tocqueville grants that his recommendation is likely to do him
harm in the eyes of politicians, but "the only efficacious means
governments can use to put the dogma of the immortality of the
soul in honor is to act every day as if they themselves believed it."
He adds that "it is only in conforming scrupulously to religious
morality in great affairs that they can flatter themselves they are
teaching citizens to know it, love it, and respect it in small ones"
(p. 521).

These are the broad outlines of Tocqueville's argument for
the political "utility of religion."

> Most religions are only general, simple, and practical means
> of teaching men the immortality of the soul. That is the great-
> est advantage that a democratic people derives from beliefs,
> and it is what renders them more necessary to such a people
> than to all others.
>
> Therefore when any religion whatsoever has cast deep
> roots within a democracy, guard against shaking it; but rather
> preserve it carefully as the most precious inheritance from aris-
> tocratic centuries; do not seek to tear men from their old reli-
> gious opinions to substitute new ones, for fear that, in the pas-
> sage from one faith to another, the soul finding itself for a
> moment empty of belief, the love of material enjoyments will
> come to spread through it and fill it entirely. (p. 519; cf. p. 448)

There is little in any of this to suggest that the opinions advanced
by philosophers or by legislators are, or need to be, simply true.

> There are religions that are very false and very absurd; never-
> theless one can say that every religion that remains within the
> circle I have just indicated and that does not claim to leave it ...

imposes a salutary yoke on the intellect; and one must recognize that if it does not save men in the other world, it is at least very useful to their happiness and their greatness in this one. (p. 418)

What has this got to do with "Socrates and his school"? Why would Tocqueville introduce Socrates (that is, Plato) at the crucial point in his argument? He grants that "it is not certain that Socrates and his school had decided opinions about what would happen to man in the other life" (p. 520). But what Tocqueville calls "Platonic philosophy" included—publicly, at least—a doctrine of immortality, and this gave that philosophy the "sublime spark that distinguishes it." Plato's dialogues contain accounts, Tocqueville recognizes, that counter anticipations of modern materialism. Those dialogues include noble or sublime, though not necessarily true, *mythoi* or even poetic *theologia*—noble lies, whose teachings seem best fitted by wise legislators to counter materialism (see p. 520). Are we to assume this to be the proper course for enlightened men or the wise legislator?

Those who have accepted the Prophet Joseph Smith and his restoration message continue to insist—rightly, I believe—that the gospel to which they are committed is nothing if not simply true. And they prosper thereby. But what of those few who now seem inclined to toy with the idea that the truth of the Latter-day Saints' faith is to be found merely in its ability to deal with pressing social problems? One must ask if the salutary moral impact of a faith could survive the reduction of that faith to a useful mythology. Religious beliefs, when treated as merely useful, may, of course, impel a few to reach beyond greed, selfishness, and the quest for simple physical comforts to higher and more noble and lasting things. But it is not likely that much in the way of genuine self-sacrifice can survive such a transformation.

Tocqueville strove to indicate how religious beliefs restrain the dominant passions unleashed in democratic ages. "In men, the angel teaches the brute the art of satisfying itself" (p. 521). But it is also true that whatever tends to elevate, enlarge, and expand the soul in turn enables it to better succeed, even in those undertakings that are not the soul's primary concern. In order to master the world by controlling their own souls, human beings must learn to suppress the abundance of petty, passing desires in order to satisfy the great longing that looks toward heaven. Through these observations Tocqueville introduces once again, though now with a somewhat different vocabulary, the practical link between self-interest and religion. In order to serve his own best interests, particularly the passion for comfort and wealth, the democratic citizen must learn to frustrate or dampen some of his immediate interests and appetites. "The principal business of religions" (p. 422), and something that "religious industry" does rather well, "is to purify, regulate, and restrain the too ardent and too exclusive taste for well-being that men in times of equality feel" (p. 422). "Religions supply the general habit of behaving with a view to the future. In this they are no less useful to happiness in this life than to felicity in the other. It is one of their greatest political aspects" (p. 522; cf. pp. 42–43). Without the habit of sacrificing immediate advantage for greater future gratifications— which sounds much like self-interest properly understood—even the democratic passion for physical comforts cannot persist. Therefore, "philosophers and those who govern ought constantly to apply themselves to moving back the object of human actions in the eyes of men; it is their great business" (p. 523).

It would be a mistake, according to Tocqueville, for preachers to direct all attention to the future life. Why? Simply because the "taste for well-being forms the salient and indelible feature of democratic ages"; hence, any attempt to "destroy this mother passion" would eventually cause religion to destroy itself (p. 422). After describing "the principal business of religions" as the moderation of the "taste for well-being," Tocqueville immediately adds: "I believe that they would be wrong to try to subdue it entirely and to destroy it. They will not succeed in turning men away from love of wealth; but they can still persuade them to enrich themselves only by honest means" (p. 422). Preachers can succeed in their business only by restricting their encouragement in the honest pursuit of prosperity. Tocqueville's struggle to make a large place for religion in a democratic society can be understood as something like the endeavor of certain philosophers to show a certain deference to the opinions on which society rests, and hence especially to religious opinions, for practical or political reasons.

One cannot, it seems, separate passages on religion in *Democracy in America* from the larger context of Tocqueville's analysis and preserve the integrity of his arguments. His own uneasiness with those skeptics who mock the traditional beliefs echoes something that reaches perhaps as far back as Plato and consequently to philosophy in its original form. Even the uneasiness Plato expressed in the *Laws* about believers in divine beings who intervene in human affairs—who like atheists, were said to be dangerous to a well-ordered regime—is reflected in Tocqueville's consternation over the possibility of a genuinely vital new faith in democratic times. Such efforts, whatever their impact on believers, are profoundly unsettling for the larger community and may thus be seen in some crucial ways as disturbing the democratic ethos. They begin to dissolve the social cement of dogmatic beliefs—the sentiments and opinions on which society rests. They may even eventually begin to challenge the moral substance of society, whatever its traditional content. From Tocqueville's perspective, it is enough for the democratic citizen to assume that he has control of his own beliefs and is the master of his world—even though he is obviously in a kind of "salutary bondage" to dogmatic beliefs—simply because he accepts the most important opinions on trust in the ever-shifting sands of public opinion.

Preachers, Tocqueville insisted, must not confront the passions of the citizen directly, but only indirectly and mildly; they must appear to show that religious beliefs and demands are fully compatible with self-interest well understood and so allow a rather full scope for the somewhat modified egoism characteristic of and essential to the democratic ethos. What this means is that there can be no genuinely effective restraints on the passions and appetites of democratic man because whatever restraints might actually flow from religion are themselves subject to the same debasements as the human soul of itself.

Tocqueville, it should be noted, did not turn to public education to stimulate the desire for independence and give democratic citizens a deeper understanding of the nature and dangers of their own society. He obviously did not have such a confident view of the powers of general enlightenment, of a self-generating, self-sustaining, publicly held wisdom, of an education shorn of moral roots. He turned instead to other agencies for practical (or political) education to provide the necessary restraints that might help prevent the gross debasement of humankind, which itself could yield a new and even more terrible soft tyranny.

Marvin Zetterbaum has shown that Tocqueville was more concerned about the "utility of religion" than about its truth—that for him the truth of religion is its utility.[60] Zetterbaum rightly complains about Tocqueville's ploy. Among other reasons, it is unsound because it is an effort to employ religion as a socially useful myth and, as such, is bound to fail precisely because the social usefulness of such myths depends upon their being believed. It is unlikely that myths (meaning, in this context, dogmatic religious beliefs) held to be merely salutary or socially useful, but not in some fundamental sense simply true, will have the power needed to effect the social control that Tocqueville deemed necessary. Zetterbaum also correctly laments that advancing

> salutary myths cannot but weaken genuine religious belief rather than strengthening it, for by propagating them men are emboldened to consider religion from a functional point of

view. But there is no assurance that genuine religion is necessarily salutary, and in case of conflict, society will surely sacrifice the genuine for the salutary. Moreover, the effectiveness of spiritualistic myths is dependent on whether their nature remains hidden; they are not likely to retain their usefulness if they are known to be myths.[61]

Zetterbaum thus raises the decisive issue, especially from the point of view of genuine believers, regarding the position that the truth of religion is to be found merely in its utility as a social cement. Without the color of public authority, moral restraints work their magic, as Zetterbaum recognized, only when they are freely chosen—that is, genuinely believed. When they have their roots in religious dogmas, they move and restrain only to the extent that they are genuinely believed. It is at exactly this point that Zetterbaum notices a problematic element, if not a fatal weakness, in Tocqueville's argument: A salutary myth is only effective if it is not known as merely salutary. As soon as it is known to be contrived by purely human artifice, even if it is the work of some human lawgiver, it loses much, if not all, of its moral authority and power.[62]

Others want to quarrel with Tocqueville because they see his concept of freely chosen restraints grounding public virtue as stripping citizens of liberty. This complaint reflects a strange form of liberal dogmatism, not to mention moral blindness, but it is common even among Latter-day Saints, where confusion over moral agency is transformed into liberal slogans about the evils of something called blind obedience or into complaints about the supposed shackles of faith. Does a fondness for freedom of choice demand that one reject the consequences of freely accepted moral restraints? Does it demand that one reject the willingness to sacrifice immediate self-interest for something eventually good for all, which Tocqueville saw as one of the most salient political consequences of religion? At least from the perspective of believers, such a willingness to sacrifice immediate interests is the means for liberating them from bondage to base and demonic things. Tocqueville was willing to make political use of such consequences. He would even strive to simulate the effects of sacrifice for the common good by contriving religion, if that were the only alternative to moral chaos in democratic times.

Those who doubt that any good whatsoever can flow from religious faith—those deeply into what can be called "political atheism"—might also find Tocqueville's argument disconcerting. To believers, arguments that transform God and divine things into mere useful social conveniences must appear ultimately as a form of blasphemy. That is not to say that believers deny that useful consequences flow from belief; in fact, they insist on it. Tocqueville's point is that it makes no difference to society whether a religion is simply true, for such is only of concern to individuals and especially to the faithful—only the individual has any stake in the primary consequences of religious faith as opposed to its secondary consequences (see p. 278). Cannot both those who believe and those who sense something of the utility of religion— the indirect or secondary influence of faith—understand and even appreciate the significance of belief for the immediate practical (or moral) life of a people (see pp. 290–91)?

Tocqueville is aware that churchmen can be aligned on the wrong side of issues affecting liberty, and he is certainly no naive apologist for churches, their material interests, or their agents. He also holds that those who take up the standard of liberty might end up advocating policies inimical to liberty. Both possibilities present dangers in a democratic society. When certain necessary "dogmatic beliefs"—or opinions uncritically accepted—are challenged, according to Tocqueville, the principle of liberty is easy prey for an ardent and debased notion of equality with which it is quite inconsistent. It is precisely the liberals who spoil liberty— not from low motives, but rather with a naive confidence that leads easily to tyranny in the sacred name of liberty. It is exactly when a public agency claims the right to control or manipulate morality or when it ignorantly presumes to do so that liberty is crushed and replaced with a terrible, though perhaps bland, tyranny. Tocqueville fears such an eventuality; it is to provide a protection against it that he recommends that wise legislators (or just and good men) make possible the necessary moderation of democratic tastes and passions by means of religion.

It is precisely Tocqueville's argument that the principle of equality, when coupled with a lack of moral restraints on appetites and passions, eventually turns democratic citizens into grains of dust—all equally powerless, equally unimportant, and equally fearful, and hence ready to abandon liberty at a moment's notice when the call comes offering comfort, ease, and plenty. It is religion that demands sacrifice and thereby provides the necessary moral discipline; it is the spokesmen for religion who may, even in a weak way, insist on the postponement of gratifications, who lead people to look to the heavens or at least the distant future for the final rewards for sacrifices and who thereby perfect the virtues needed by democratic man at times when commercial passions are joined to the lust for a debased notion of equality.

Between Tocqueville and those who see religion as the general designation for all that degrades humankind, or merely as a skillfully administered narcotic crafted and employed solely for base purposes or with debasing consequences, is a gulf. This gulf is precisely the one that separates the active hostility or detached neutrality of the dogmatic political atheism found among secular fundamentalists, who now dominate much intellectual life, from the more cautious and less active variety found among the ancients. That older view permitted and even insisted upon a prominent place for religion, especially in the moral realm and particularly in the life of republics. It is in his view of the utility of religion where those elements in Tocqueville's thought appear that make him something less than a simple child of modernity—he is less so than the American founders he admired and much less so than those who simply ignore, disregard, downplay, or despise religion. He was within the general horizon of modernity, especially on certain issues, but certainly not within the form of modernity that makes war on all religion as a dangerous illusion or patronizes it as a delusion and therefore the symptom, if not the source, of the societal diseases that afflict humanity.

Tocqueville appears to have taken pains to avoid confronting, at least in public, the question of whether any religious teachings are simply true—that is, whether they have ultimate rather than merely proximate consequences. In public, he addressed the question of the practical or moral role of beliefs—their social utility, or what Tocqueville called their secondary rather than primary consequences—which he thought was the proper kind of question to be addressed by one concerned with a secondary question like the life and death of society. One need not be a believer to have an appreciation for the secondary consequences of faith or for the practical impact of religious devotion. One does get hints about Tocqueville's position on such issues when he gently mocks the prospects for a faith founded on a modern mantic or makes remarks about the majority of "believers" basing their faith on opinions rather than on revealed doctrine (see p. 410).

An Epilogue

Because of the ubiquity of the word *religion*, it has become necessary to employ it as the label for, among other things, the exploration of opinions about divine things. Since such a quest was once part of the quest for a knowledge of the nature of things, the possible answers appear to be something very much like purpose or "function"—the reason "for which" a thing exists. The word *theology*, which from the linguistic horizon of antiquity is the more proper designation, comes eventually to be joined and even somewhat replaced by the later and still more obscure term *religion*. I have noted how this conjunction can be seen in David

Hume's willingness to alternate between *religion* and *theology.* Where religion bears the stamp of human manufacture—acting as a mere soothing *pharmakon,* if not an entirely demonic element—the question of its function still remains paramount. When something called religion is denounced as a justification for the evils of this world, a consolation, or an opiate, it is nevertheless treated as having some prominent albeit malevolent social function. Even in that case the paramount question concerns the utility of religion rather than its truth as such. Some of the apologists for religion have differed from its most radical critics more on how they assess the details of its political or practical utility than on whether that was the appropriate standard by which it should be judged. Where do Latter-day Saints stand on such issues? Are we merely cultural Mormons, or are we genuinely faithful? For me this is a question well worth asking.

A few among us seem tempted to suggest that what they like to call "the religion of the Latter-day Saints," like all social institutions, must be judged not on whether the revelation is really true but according to its usefulness in dealing with the problems of humanity. To continue to be concerned about the truth of the prophetic claims is, they suggest, to remain in bondage to an embarrassing polemical past. They thereby turn away from such questions as whether Jesus was resurrected or whether there was a Lehi colony and insist instead that it is the usefulness of the faith as a social cement and consolation for the evils of this world that should really be of concern to the Saints.

But what is really needed is not guile but genuine faith, as even Hume realized when he made reference to "those dangerous friends or disguised enemies to the *Christian Religion,* who have undertaken to defend it by the principles of human reason."[63] He further suggests that Christianity "cannot be believed by any reasonable person without" a miracle taking place to bring about such faith, and this explains why he was critical of what he calls "the principles of those pretended Christians" who picture the faith "not as the word or testimony of God himself, but as the pro-duction of a mere human writer and historian."[64]

In our setting, some of these writers then find nothing prob-lematic about turning to naturalistic categories to explain the faith of the Saints (in their sense, the Mormon myth) and then to as-sess its mere usefulness. The power of this so-called myth—though it does not appeal, they sometimes maintain, to the rational fac-ulties—may somehow help to organize the moral disposition as well as tap the creative power of those whose lives it somehow comes to control. Here we see at work among a few of the Saints the subtle inroads of the argument that the truth of religion is its utility. These writers claim that, in the final analysis, the faith of the Saints must be judged on its capacity to mold character and so forth. In this way they ignore the content of the faith in which it is taught that we are judged by God and not the other way around. Be that as it may, in this way they strive to justify a thoroughly naturalistic assessment of what they call the Mormon myth. But, as I believe I have demonstrated, treating the ground and con-tents of faith as merely salutary must ultimately be seen by believ-ers as a form of blasphemy, even though they necessarily insist on the usefulness of their faith. And when the content of faith is seen as merely salutary—a kind of noble lie or a soothing, controlling, or even necessary *pharmakon*—even its obvious usefulness is thereby radically compromised. For the myth to work its won-ders, it cannot be considered merely salutary but must be seen simply as true. So the utility argument surrenders much of its util-ity, and hence its attractiveness, when it becomes the locus of loy-alty and is thereby known for what it is.

Notes

I wish to thank Brian D. Birch, Ted Vaggalis, Todd Compton, and others who read earlier drafts of this essay. I have striven as best I could to consider each suggestion. And, in addition to honoring my good friend Truman Madsen with this essay, I also present it to my former students, especially to those who over the years have read with me David Hume's *Essays* and other writings, Alexis de Tocqueville's *Democracy in America,* and the *Federalist.*

1. Truman G. Madsen, "Joseph Smith and the Ways of Knowing," in *Seminar on the Prophet Joseph Smith, Brigham Young University, February 18, 1961* (Provo, Utah: Department of Extension Publications, 1964), 41.

2. McMurrin began his professional career in 1938 as a Latter-day Saint seminary teacher in rural Utah and Idaho, and then in 1940 he was employed as an institute teacher in Arizona. During this time he worked in the summers on his Ph.D. at the University of Southern California. After receiving his degree in 1946, he taught at USC before moving to the University of Utah in 1948, where he had once studied.

3. See the essays on religion conveniently made available in J. C. A. Gaskin's edition of Hume's *Dialogues and Natural History of Religion: Principal Writings on Religion, Including* Dialogues Concerning Natural Religion *and* The Natural History of Religion (Oxford: Oxford University Press, 1993), 29–133; or David Hume, *Writings on Religion,* ed. Antony Flew (La Salle, Ill.: Open Court, 1992), 182–292. I still have the little paperback edition of Hume's *Dialogues* (New York: Hafner, 1953) that I originally read, which is brimming with my primitive markings and marginalia. This tattered thing is like an old friend.

4. See *Dialogues* (Gaskin ed.), 32, 129, or *Writings,* 188, 291, where Hume employed the expression *natural theology.*

5. See Augustine, *The City of God,* trans. Marcus Dods (New York: Random House, 2000), 4.1, 9, 22, 31; 6.2–12; 7.5–6, 9, 28–30. When quoting from *The City of God,* I use this translation.

6. Augustine used both the Latin and Greek words for each type of theology.

7. On the Greek word *physis,* see pp. 145–46.

8. See Augustine, *City of God,* book 8, which should be compared to his comments, in his *Confessions,* on the role of certain books of the Platonists in his conversion.

9. Varro, *Antiquitates rerum humanarum et divinarum (Antiquities of Human and Divine Things).* This work, like most of Varro's writings, is known mostly in fragments, some of which are preserved in Augustine's writings. The primary source for understanding Varro's position is

Cicero's dialogue entitled *Academica* (second version), book 1, in which Varro, a fellow Academic, is cast as engaging in a hypothetical conversation with Cicero.

10. See Augustine, *City of God,* books 1–10.

11. Ibid., 4.1; 6.2.

12. Ibid., 6.3.

13. Ibid.

14. Ibid., 6.4.

15. Ibid.

16. Ibid.

17. Ibid.

18. Ibid.

19. Ibid., 6.10.

20. Ibid., 7.28.

21. See Augustine's *Confessions,* trans. R. S. Pine-Coffin (London: Penguin Books, 1961), 7.20, where he describes how reading some books of the Platonists, presumably those by Plotinus (A.D. 204/5–270) and Porphyry (ca. A.D. 234–301), had shown him to think of the divine as incorporeal; Augustine originally censured the Bible for teaching and Christians for believing that God was corporeal. Cf. *Confessions* 8.2. Study of the Platonists also opened to Augustine ways of overcoming the offending language in the Bible by interpreting it allegorically, that is, by reading it as containing in its vulgar, unrefined language a deeper understanding of divine things and hence a partially hidden natural theology that those with a philosophic disposition could uncover.

22. Augustine, *City of God* 7.30.

23. Frederick Van Fleternen, "Nature," in *Augustine through the Ages: An Encyclopedia,* ed. Allan D. Fitzgerald (Grand Rapids, Mich.: Eerdmans, 1999), 585–87 at 586.

24. Kai Nielsen, *Naturalism and Religion* (Amherst, N.Y.: Prometheus Books, 2001), 267.

25. Hume, *Dialogues* (Gaskin ed.), 129–30; *Writings,* 291–92.

26. Hume, *Dialogues* (Gaskin ed.), 130; *Writings,* 292.

27. David Hume, *An Enquiry Concerning Human Understanding,* in *Essential Works of David Hume,* ed. Ralph Cohen (New York: Bantam Books, 1965), 141; *Writings,* 87, emphasis in original.

28. Hume, *Enquiry,* 167.

29. Ibid., emphasis in original.

30. Hume, *Dialogues,* 121.

31. Hence also the demand—for example, in book 10 of Plato's *Laws*—for severe punishments for atheists, who are pictured as mortal enemies of the ideal regime, since they challenge the opinions about an ultimate justice and divine retribution upon which such regimes are founded. See Plato's *Laws*—especially 909e, where the death penalty is mentioned—in *The Laws of Plato,* trans. Thomas L. Pangle (New York: Basic Books, 1980).

32. See Plato, *Laws* 726a–747a.

33. The Greek word *stasis,* carrying the primitive meaning of something like "set," "position," or "stance," is sometimes translated "faction," but it can also be translated as "quarrel" or even "civil war." Allan Bloom preferred "faction" to the other alternatives. See his translation of *The Republic of Plato* (New York: Basic Books, 1968). The passages are found at 351d–352a, 440b, 440e, 444b, 459e, 464e, 465a–b, 470b–d, 471a, 488b, 520c–d, 545d, 547a–b, 554d, 556e, 560a, 566a, 586e, 603d. On the other hand, Thomas L. Pangle prefers "civil war." See his translation, *The Laws of Plato,* passages 628b–c, 630b, 636b, 678e, 679d, 690d, 708b–c, 713e, 715b, 729a, 744d, 757a, 757d, 832c, 856b, 869c, 945e. In the words *stasiodes* or *stasiotikos* a move in meaning is made from "quarrel" or "faction" or "party" to something like "sedition."

34. Hume, *Dialogues,* 121–22.

35. Ibid., 122. There is a long tradition, for polemical purposes, of blurring the distinction between religion and superstition. Translators differ on whether the Latin *religio* should be translated as "superstition" or "religion" in *De rerum natura (On the Nature of Things),* the famous Epicurean didactic poem of Lucretius (ca. 99–55 B.C.). Though shy and retiring, Epicureans, it should be noted, were the closest to being overt atheists among the ancients. The reason for such caution might be that political atheism was feared precisely because regimes were thought to rest on myths about the laws that linked them in various ways to the gods, often through lawgivers or legislators. Modern political atheism, as is made clear by Karl Marx, rests on a conscious choice to make war

on all belief in the divine as the first step in liberating humankind from every form of bondage.

36. Hume, *Dialogues,* 122.

37. The quaint little edition of Hume's *Essays* that I first read and still own was published in London by Grant Richards in 1908. But see the nicely edited version of Hume's *Essays: Moral, Political, and Literary,* ed. Eugene F. Miller, rev. ed. (Indianapolis: LibertyClassics, 1987).

38. This phrase is found in the famous tenth number of *The Federalist.* See *The Federalist,* ed. Jacob E. Coke (Middletown, Conn.: Wesleyan University Press, 1961), 58, 61.

39. Douglass Adair was the first to notice Madison's dependence upon ideas set forth by Hume in his *Essays.* The probable source for the novel idea that a large or extended republic, rather than a small one, would provide a cure for the mischiefs of faction was the essay entitled "Idea of a Perfect Commonwealth," *Essays,* 512–29. In speculating about the possibility of France or Great Britain—what were then clearly mixed regimes— ever being "modelled into a commonwealth," or pure republic, Hume explains that "such a form of government can only take place in a city or small territory." Then he adds the following pertinent observation: "Though it is more difficult to form a republican government in an extensive country than in a city; there is more facility, when once it is formed, of preserving it steady and uniform, without tumult and faction." Hume, *Essays,* 527. Democracies are turbulent. "For however the people may be separated or divided into small parties, either in their votes or elections; their near habitation in a city will always make the force of popular tides and currents very sensible. Aristocracies are better adapted for peace and order, and accordingly were most admired by ancient writers; but they are jealous and oppressive. In a large government, which is modelled with masterly skill, there is compass and room enough to refine the democracy. . . . At the same time, the parts are so distant and remote, that it is very difficult, either by intrigue, prejudice, or passion, to hurry them into any measures against the public interest." Hume, *Essays,* 528. Adair pointed to this essay as the source for Publius' justification for the way the founders had sought a cure for the "mischiefs of faction" by extending and compounding the proposed republic. See

Adair's "'That Politics May Be Reduced to a Science': David Hume, James Madison, and the Tenth Federalist," in his *Fame and the Founding Fathers: Essays by Douglass Adair*, ed. Trevor Colbourn (New York: Norton, 1974), 93–106.

40. "Political writers have established it as a maxim, that, in contriving any system of government, and fixing the several checks and controuls of the constitution, every man ought to be supposed a *knave*, and to have no other end, in all his actions, than private interest. By this interest we must govern him, and, by means of it, make him, notwithstanding his insatiable avarice and ambition, co-operate to [the] public good. Without this, say they, we shall in vain boast of the advantages of any constitution, and shall find, in the end, that we have no security for our liberties or possessions, except the good-will of our rulers; that is, we shall have no security at all." Hume, "On the Independency of Parliament," *Essays*, 42.

41. James Madison, *Notes on the Debates in the Federal Convention of 1787*, ed. Adrienna Koch (New York: Norton, 1969), 76. Madison's remarks were drawn from his memorandum made in April 1787 on the "Vices of the Political System of the United States," prior to the Philadelphia Convention. See *The Papers of James Madison*, ed. Robert A. Rutland et al. (Chicago: University of Chicago Press, 1975), 9:355.

42. Madison, *Notes on the Debates*, 76; see *Papers of James Madison*, 355–56.

43. There are those whose loyalty to the republic defended by Madison may at times be compromised by an even deeper, premodern-style passion for a community joined in the same beliefs, with interests united and directed by a common faith, where, as much as is possible, there will be no disputations over doctrine that divide the community into warring factions. Madison strove to allow such religious communities to exist in peace in his extended commercial republic by providing security for their rights against the tyranny of a majority faction, which otherwise would employ the power of the regime to vex its competitors. The language found in D&C 101:76–80, I believe, should be read with these considerations in mind.

44. *Federalist*, 351–52.

45. Ibid., 64–65.

46. Hume, *Dialogues,* 122.

47. Ibid., 124.

48. Hume, *Enquiry, Section XI,* in *Essential Works of David Hume,* 142–43.

49. Ibid., 144.

50. Ibid.

51. Ibid., 153, emphasis in original.

52. Ibid., 153–54.

53. The first volume of *Democracy in America* appeared in France in 1835, while the second appeared in 1840. These two volumes were then translated into English by Tocqueville's friend Henry Reeve and then later by George Lawrence. A much improved translation by Harvey C. Mansfield and Delba Winthrop is now available. Hereafter, citations will refer to this latter edition of *Democracy in America* (Chicago: University of Chicago Press, 2000) and will appear parenthetically in the text.

54. For some indication of his interests and the information he gathered, see the diaries, notes, and literary sketches he made on his visit, conveniently available in Alexis de Tocqueville, *Journey to America,* trans. George Lawrence, ed. J. P. Mayer (Garden City, N.Y.: Doubleday, 1971).

55. Tocqueville fits well the model of the noble gentleman. Coming from the French aristocracy, he was refined, restless, temperamental, and uneasy about his accomplishments. He was also above lusting for the gratification of base appetites. He appears to have thought that the proper work for a man of his sensibilities and cultivated capacities was to do something for the welfare of humankind. An aristocratic pathos led him to strive for great deeds. His literary endeavors might be seen as political acts intended to advance what he considered a noble cause. He seems to have sought appropriate ways of manifesting his own nobility and thereby also gaining justifiable fame.

56. Mansfield and Winthrop provide a note at this point in their translation identifying René Descartes, Thomas Hobbes, John Locke, Charles-Louis Montesquieu, David Hume, and Adam Smith as having advanced just this theory.

57. The "greater part of American ministers" are, according to Tocqueville's notes, entrepreneurs "of a religious industry." Tocqueville, *Journey to America,* 189.

58. Tocqueville helps us understand why the Saints have a tendency to move away from the radical demands placed on them and even further from a genuine effort to build Zion as they become charmed by the American ethos and converted to taking care of what they see as their self-interest, often understood as the gratification of their appetites.

59. See André Jardin, *Tocqueville: A Biography,* trans. Lydia Davis with Robert Hemenway (New York: Farrar, Straus and Giroux, 1988), 61–66.

60. See Marvin Zetterbaum, *Tocqueville and the Problem of Democracy* (Palo Alto: Stanford University Press, 1967), 116–17.

61. Ibid., 122.

62. Ibid., 19, 118–23.

63. Hume, *Enquiry,* 141.

64. Ibid., 141–42.

CHAPTER 6

THE SPIRITUALITY OF LOVE: KIERKEGAARD ON FAITH'S TRANSFORMING POWER

C. Terry Warner

As the quiet lake is fed deep down by the flow of hidden springs, which no eye sees, so a human being's love is grounded, still more deeply, in God's love. If there were no spring at the bottom, if God were not love, then there would be neither a little lake nor a man's love. As the still waters begin obscurely in the deep spring, so a man's love mysteriously begins in God's love.[1]

When I was Truman Madsen's philosophy student back in the early 1960s, debates were not uncommon on campus between teachers of note, usually from BYU or the University of Utah. One of the issues raised in one of these debates—I cannot remember whether the setting was large and public or small and informal—was this: Do we need to love God before we can love our fellowmen, or must we love our fellows first? Or is it even possible to love the one without loving the other? At the time it seemed a significant issue. A few persuasive people in the Latter-day Saint community, like legions in the culture beyond, were bent on secularizing religious doctrine (the term used then was *humanizing*) and argued that our horizontal relationships with others underpin our vertical relationship with God. And, perhaps backed into a position more extreme than they otherwise might have chosen, those who felt uncomfortable with this kind of revisionism found themselves arguing that the God-relation must come first; everything else depended on it. God had commanded both kinds of love, vertical and horizontal; none of the parties to the debate challenged that. But was one of these relationships somehow more basic than the other? More to the point, who should come first in our life—God or others?

On this and a number of other issues, I made little advance until I read Søren Kierkegaard.[2] This Danish contemporary of Joseph Smith must be considered one of the few bona fide geniuses in the Western philosophical tradition who have lent their intellects without reserve to the service of God and their fellowmen. At least in my way of reading him, he sought in virtually every waking moment of his productive life to make the message of the scriptures and its personal and social implications effective for himself and in the lives of his readers, and, unlike many other religious voices, he never sought to soften his message to make it inoffensive to human reason. Though he said himself that he held no authority,[3] and he did not, the voluminous writings of his short lifetime—he lived to age forty-two and published about twenty-seven books—repeatedly illuminate the scriptures in ways that are, to my mind, harmonious with Joseph Smith's teachings to a remarkable extent and are often helpful for understanding them. And like the words we have from the Prophet himself, Kierkegaard's ideas incisively expose the weaknesses of the philosophical, theological, and psychological tradition he inherited. Many of these ideas, often distorted by having been torn from their religious context, play crucial roles in the work of some of the central figures of twentieth-century thought—Heidegger, Jaspers, and Sartre being among the most noteworthy.[4] His position on the question about whether love of God or love of other human beings comes first is one of his numerous psychological teachings that are both firmly rooted in his faith and insufficiently appreciated by the powerful intellects who have drawn on his work for their own purposes.

Kierkegaard's position on love of others and love of God (which for him is tantamount to faith) is rooted in his unusual idea of what it means to be a self. According to this idea, the self is not an entity of any kind but an active relating to others—not a "thing" but an activity. Each individual determines the kind of self he will be, Kierkegaard says, by the way he relates to others. In this paper I first sketch this relational idea of the self and then show how, according to Kierkegaard, the self is deepened when its fundamental relationship is with God, and deepened to the greatest extent when that relationship is with Christ. After that I demonstrate how this conception of the self leads inevitably to his views about love of fellowmen. We will discover that, for Kierkegaard, faith must be first in our personal priorities; yet he insists that, properly understood, faith and love are equally basic and indeed are one and the same thing.

Much of what I present diverges from how Kierkegaard has been commonly understood. Indeed, widespread acceptance of misconceptions of what he thought about selfhood, faith, and love have, at least until recently, kept the world in ignorance of what I believe to be his most important ideas. I discuss some of these traditional misconceptions and then try to clear them up, partly with insights drawn from recent scholars as eager as I am to rectify past misinterpretations and partly with observations of my own.[5]

This paper assumes no prior familiarity with Kierkegaard on the reader's part. It tries to illuminate the issue at hand by connecting ideas broadly developed in various parts of Kierkegaard's writings, rather than by a close textual analysis that would be accessible only to scholars.

Kierkegaard's Conception of Selfhood

Kierkegaard's most direct and famous formulation of what it means to be a human self opens the brilliant little book, *The Sickness unto Death*.[6] Though this formulation has proven a frustration to many readers, I shall try to express its basic idea without relying too heavily on Kierkegaard's technical terminology. He says, in effect, that a human being becomes a self just insofar as he becomes reflectively thoughtful about his existence. He calls this reflective thoughtfulness "inwardness." (Some social psychologists call it, or at least part of it, being aware and critical of oneself and, by this means, able to control one's conduct.) We individually achieve this inwardness or self-consciousness by adopting categories for organizing experience and standards for guiding our conduct that are supplied by another or others. We become the selves we are by making others' ways of being our own and regulating our thoughts and actions accordingly.

Thus we are guided by and measure ourselves against the largely unquestioned, sovereign expectations of our society of origin. In Kierkegaard's way of speaking, we are "before" such beings;[7] we might say we "live before them," or "under their eye." We define ourselves in terms of the criterion of selfhood they have given us and direct ourselves toward ends that we learn from them. Moreover—and this is a crucial point—each of us is a self of greater or lesser depth depending on the nature of the being or beings we take as our criterion; we will be as shallow as cattle, Kierkegaard quips, if we have taken cattle as our criterion of selfhood. "Everything is qualitatively whatever it is measured by."[8] This means that, though as physical organisms we may stand separate from and exist independently of each other, as selves or spirits we do not. We are none of us complete in ourselves. We are instead relational, mediated beings profoundly connected to those we measure ourselves by.

Kierkegaard introduces this point in *Sickness unto Death* with these words (be warned that many have found this formulation incomprehensible): the self emerges only insofar as it "relates to itself, and in relating to itself relates to something else."[9] We can capture part of what this means as follows: The self exists in being conscious of itself and achieves this consciousness of self by being conscious of another; prior to attaining this consciousness, one is not yet a self. Thus consciousness of another plays a *constitutive* role in the establishment of the self. For that reason, Kierkegaard calls this other before which the individual lives "the power that established" that individual's self.[10]

So which being or beings an individual lives before and takes as his measure makes the most profound difference in the nature of his selfhood. If he lives before society, he inevitably uses the way the crowd or mass of men behaves to justify his own behavior and thus evades responsibility for himself. In Merold Westphal's clarifying formulation, if the power before which he lives is society, then it is not only society's voice *to* which he responds; it is also society's voice *with* which he responds.[11] The measures of legitimacy and worth by which the others in society aspire, admire, envy, distinguish, judge, and rank themselves become his own measures. Hence, by means of this undeliberated and unnoticed process of adopting the socially prevailing ways of being as his own, Kierkegaard says, he evades responsibility for the person he thereby becomes and effectively assimilates himself into the crowd, the mass of humanity. He pawns himself out to the world, "as exchangeable as a coin of the realm."[12]

Furthermore, because "getting ahead" and distinguishing himself according to the prevailing standards is honored by his people, he is enjoined by them to take command of himself, set his goals, and make something of himself. But again, says Kierkegaard, to the extent that he does this he paradoxically loses hold of himself. In his efforts to preside over his own well-being in self-sufficiency and make something worthwhile of himself, as society teaches him to do, he flees responsibility for himself. He takes himself to be listening to his own voice and asserting his own identity and freedom when in fact he is not speaking for himself as an individual truly responsible for himself. Instead, he is doing and saying the sorts of things that have been given him by birth and by upbringing to do and say. No matter how decisively he tries to take charge of himself, so long as he lives before society, he cannot find a voice of his own in which to declare who and how he shall be.

At some point, perhaps as early as emergence from childhood, a person may make God his establishing power. Living before God uniquely enables him, as an individual, to "come to himself." In this context, the counterpart of the point I made about the identity of the secular person's voice and the voice of society is this: If a person lives before God rather than before society, then the voice *to which* he responds is the voice of God, and the voice *with which* he responds is his own. In one way it is God's voice, to be sure, for by yielding to him the person becomes God's instrument. But at the same time, he also becomes truly himself. For only in this way does he gain his identity as a being free to act independently of concerns about measuring up, fears of others' opinions, and petty likes and dislikes that would drive him if his entire compass of concern were limited to his comparative and competitive relationships with other human beings. In Timothy Jackson's words, "True omnipotence and omnibenevolence [when acknowledged and accepted in faith] generate freedom in creatures, not necessity or servile dependency."[13] True omnipotence and omnibenevolence offer liberation from the idea that we can and ought to preside autonomously over ourselves. Again, and paradoxically, we act freely only insofar as, before God, we give up trying to be in charge of ourselves—for the alternative, which is resistance to God, amounts to nothing more than self-deceived submission to the silent control of the crowd.

The Condescension of Christ

Ponder for a moment the situation in which the members of society each live before society. Here, each individual seeks to qualify by measures generally accepted by all and passes on to others (most especially his or her children) the measures by which they, too, are to become acceptable. Into this setting of worldly concerns comes the God-man, Jesus Christ. He comes to offer us, who are members of human society, liberation from the deception, inauthenticity, and despair of our worldly ways. Though patently capable of exceeding *any* of us in *any* of the measures by which we assess and rank one another, "He the almighty who can do all things" gives these measures no allegiance whatsoever, but "in love sacrifices all things."[14] He consorts with those whom we have labeled deficient—the diseased, the blue-collared, the uncool, and the uncouth—and in so doing he presents himself as a living reproach to everything from which we have drawn our sense of identity, importance, and legitimacy. He does this not only by what he says, but by how he *is*—"with the silent and veracious eloquence of deeds."[15] He, the loftiest of all, offers himself to us in a manner that we inevitably label the lowliest of all, and this lays bare the emptiness, the impotence, the selfishness, and the blindness of all our strategies to manage and make something of ourselves.[16]

How do we react when we encounter this Being who is at once the loftiest and the lowliest of all? In one of two ways, and we decide which. We may respond by accepting and seeking to emulate his example, which means sacrificing our self-importance and renouncing the sense of ourselves we have obtained from society. Or we may refuse to make this sacrifice and renunciation, in which case his example will strike us as offensive. He will then stand as a reproach to our worldly achievements and status and consolations. In either case, he confronts us as an *occasion* for offense, and we choose whether we will take offense or not.

I have already mentioned one of the reasons so many of us readily find him offensive. We have drawn from the world a false identity and placed our hopes in protecting and promoting it. Christ extends to us an invitation that requires us to leave behind this false identity or role,[17] as if he were at one and the same time calling us near and pushing us away—calling the self we can become by following him, and pushing away the self we are now choosing to be. It is as if Christ were saying (in the words of Virgil, which Kierkegaard quotes in the epigram to *Training in Christianity*), "Away, away, O unhallowed ones."[18]

Besides serving as a reproach to our worldly ways, Christ is an occasion for offense for at least two other reasons. One is that he comes offering us forgiveness for the sins that we, in our self-absorption and competitiveness, have committed against one another and against him.[19] Obviously, to receive this gift of forgiveness, we must acknowledge being in the wrong before him.[20] Accepting an offer of liberation from bondage requires recognizing that bondage and forswearing whatever we are doing to keep ourselves in bondage. To paraphrase Paul, when the commandment comes, our naive self-absorption turns into sin (see Romans 7:9)—sin that we must repent of and forsake.

A third reason why he comes among us as an occasion for offense is this: His invitation to walk with him in lowliness asks us to become, with him, a reproach to the pride and selfishness of our fellows and to be willing to suffer their wrath and persecution, just as he has done. Thus it comes about that, humanly speaking, the invitation can feel both like a condemnation from him and a requirement to undergo the condemnation of the world. "The reward for his love is to be hated."[21] Though from the divine point of view, what the invitation offers is salvation itself—we discover this if we accept the invitation—most of us find it offensive.

Kierkegaard does not try to hide his amazement at the love expressed in the God-man's redemptive rescue mission, which an angel speaking to Nephi called "the condescension of God" (1 Nephi 11:16). Such love! exclaims Kierkegaard, that subjects itself to rejection and scorn and suffering at the hands of the beloved in order to bring that very beloved a chance for liberation and peace![22] In the period of the later authorship when he produced the works from which I am mainly drawing the ideas of this paper, Kierkegaard meditated often in the Church of Our Lady, which was only five minutes' walk from where he lived much of that time. In that church Thorvaldsen's recently installed *Christus* stood before Kierkegaard's contemplative gaze, with the scars clearly visible in his hands, feet, and side, and with the invitation to "come unto me" (Matthew 11:28) inscribed below.

How Love Springs from Faith

I have outlined Kierkegaard's reverent studies of Christ's invitation because it is by response to that invitation that we can become lovers of our neighbor. If we accept the invitation, which means following and emulating him in our own daily walk, we obtain the freedom from self-absorption and develop the depth of soul that love requires. In *Works of Love,* Kierkegaard takes great pains to explain why this must be so. In "You Shall Love Your *Neighbour*,"[23] one of the discourses in that book, he analyzes the way in which what we humanly call love untouched by faith (whether erotic love or love between friends) is attracted to the qualities of the beloved and is therefore based on our preferences. This makes merely human love self-serving. To see this, imagine that you know a certain individual who possesses characteristics toward which you are drawn; she might, for example, be lively, appreciative, or affectionate, and she might reciprocate your interest in her, which fills deep needs in you. Having the companion you prefer and obtaining fulfillment of your need for what she brings into your life—these are your motivations for what you call your love for her. For Kierkegaard, such a romantic or friendly relation cannot count as genuine love, partly because of its inevitable inconstancy. It is subject to shifts both in your preferences and in the qualities of the person you believe you love. "Love is not love which alters when it alteration finds."[24]

Human attraction based upon preference cannot count as love for another reason. It fails to relate to the other person as an individual. It relates to her instead as a member of a class, any and all of whose members possess the desired qualities. This makes of her something fungible—replaceable by any other member of the class without loss. Despite the preferential lover's convictions to the contrary, he freely chooses to relate to an abstraction and therefore relates perversely; he masses the so-called beloved together with all others possessing her same qualities, whereas if he loved her he would love her truly for herself alone, as an individual.

In these and other ways, what many ordinarily and erroneously call "love" is based on, or is a consequence of, the qualities of its object, the so-called beloved. By contrast, what truly deserves to be called love is *an expression of the condition of the lover.* Imagine, says Kierkegaard, two artists. One travels the world over to find a human subject worthy of his artistic gifts but has yet to discover a single one not made unworthy of his portrayal by some fault or other. The second, modest about his talent, has yet to find a face so faulty as to make him unable to discern in it something beautiful to be portrayed. "Would this not indicate that precisely this [latter individual] was the artist, one who by bringing a certain something with him found then and there what the much-travelled artist did not find anywhere in the world, perhaps because he did not bring a certain something with him!"[25] The fastidiousness that some call love vigilantly picks up on every evidence of what we misguidedly call "lovability" and "unlovability," whereas genuine love directs itself to whoever happens to be nearby (as Kierkegaard points out, neighbor means "near-dweller"),[26] loving each individual, one at a time, for himself or herself alone. In this we find the sort of irony Kierkegaard perceived everywhere in human life: We can love a single individual, Kierkegaard says, only insofar as we can love every individual, and we can love every individual only insofar as we can love *any* individual! That love is a quality of the lover means that the lover can, like Christ himself, love whoever happens to live next door, not just a preferred few.

At this point, we want to know what is the "certain something" that the lover possesses and the self-absorbed person lacks? It is faith. A faithful relationship to God endows us with the capacity to relate to others independently of our preferences. If we lack this faith, we are bound to serve ourselves in all our horizontal relationships; they cannot qualify as love simply because *we*, being self-serving, cannot qualify as lovers. The "certain something" that makes a person a lover of her neighbor is made possible by Christ's invitation and made actual by our faithful acceptance of that invitation.

In becoming aware of the invitation, we acquire a new breadth of freedom, and in accepting the invitation—in responding with faith—we exercise that freedom. Further examination of Kierkegaard's conception of the self shows us how this happens. For Kierkegaard, the self is not merely an active relating to others; it is a *free* relating. *We* determine how we will relate to others. Hence, the way we perceive and relate ourselves to the events, circumstances, and people around us is our act. In Kierkegaard's terminology, we "appropriate" all of these; that is, we impart to them the meaning they will have for us and thus the influence they will have upon us. We choose how they will affect us. Thus *how* we appropriate them—the interpretation or meaning we impart to them—is our individual truth and the only truth with which we can possibly have anything to do;[27] we "appropriate in freedom everything that comes to [us]."[28] (Kierkegaard calls our individually appropriated truth "subjective," not to diminish it but to highlight our responsibility for it. Indeed, he does not think any such thing as an "objective" truth is possible—that is, a truth that is not the free appropriation and expression of some existing individual.)[29] Our experiences of and responses to our neighbor are free appropriations—either self-serving or pure, depending on whether our primary relation is to God and, if that God is understood to be Christ, depending on whether we are giving ourselves over to emulate him.

Thus he deepens us inwardly by opening up a way of life we could not otherwise even conceive and simultaneously endows us with freedom to accept or reject that way of life. In other words, as our selfhood deepens through encountering him, our possibilities for appropriation expand—including the possibility of perceiving others with love, without regard for ourselves.

Faith and Love Are One

What has been presented thus far might seem to establish decisively that faith is fundamental and love is its derivative. But this does not follow from what we have learned of Kierkegaard's views, and he takes pains to explain why. Even though faith must be primary in our minds and hearts, it cannot be separated from love. When we choose Christ above all others, we simultaneously and by the same act choose to love. It is precisely in the free act of willingly giving up everything necessary in order to love that we find ourselves lifted out of our egoism and opened to the deepest needs of other people. The "certain something" that then flowers in us and makes us capable of loving our neighbor *comes with* our transformation, through faith, from self-absorption and worldliness. Our focus shifts from a preferred few because, reckless now of our own advantage in comparison to others, we no longer base our responses on distinctions among them. Opening upward opens us outward as well; appropriating the invitation in faith changes us into beings who appropriate our opportunities to love others. "Love to God and love to neighbor are like two doors that open simultaneously, so that it is impossible to open one without opening the other, and impossible to shut one without also shutting the other."[30] In relation to God, what we are speaking of goes by the name of faith, while in relation to neighbors it goes by the name of love. It is the manner of existing before God in which the person freely chooses to respond to others in love. And love is the manner of existing among others in which the person freely chooses to respond faithfully to Christ. We cannot maintain a merely dyadic relation of faith with God any more than we can maintain a merely dyadic relation of love with our neighbor. "Worldly wisdom thinks that love is a relationship between man and man . . . [but it] is a relationship between man-God-man, that is, that God is the middle term."[31]

We now have the answer to the question raised by this paper. In the order of *being,* so to speak, love and faith are one; neither is more basic than the other because they are two manifestations, one vertical and one horizontal, of the same condition of a human soul. But in the order of *human intention,* faith must come first, for all the reasons we surveyed above. Taking an aspirin and thinning my blood are the same act, but I do not know how to thin my blood by trying to do so directly. What I *can* do directly is take the aspirin and thereby thin my blood indirectly. In this same way, emulating Christ and loving my neighbor are the same act. And though I do not know how to "make myself" love my neighbor by trying to do it directly, I can do it indirectly by emulating Christ in faith.

Having Once Received the Invitation, We Can Never Go Back

I have set forth some of Kierkegaard's reasons for saying that, without faith, relationships must be self-serving, and in doing so have drawn upon Kierkegaard's most sustained and concentrated writing on love, *Works of Love.* But the thrust of Kierkegaard's writings on faith show the situation to be much more complicated than he describes it in that book (I confess to being puzzled by this), and I want to say something about this complication in order to strengthen the case for the priority, in our intentions, of faith.

Our faithless relationships with others may not be merely selfish, as *Works of Love* suggests; they may be perverse, corrupt, and sinful. This happens when our relation to God is resistant—

when, upon encountering his invitation, we find it offensive and refuse it. If in response to that invitation we do not confess our fault and seek to emulate him, then *whatever* we do instead will express the offense we are taking, even if it mimics with consummate skill the professions of belief and the discipline of true disciples. Our former activities that we may have naively found delightful now take on a certain bizarre utility: we throw ourselves into them mutinously,[32] attributing to them an appeal strong enough (as we suppose) to justify or excuse us in rejecting or discounting him. From this point onward, we no longer simply look out for Number One, keep company with those who enjoy the things we enjoy, perform our civic duties, or even champion Christ as the greatest teacher, intellect, or leader.[33] Instead, we now do these things in order to distract ourselves from the invitation, or to heighten its offensiveness so we can feel justified in marginalizing, deferring, or rejecting it. We value the things of the world according to their usefulness in enabling our flight from Christ. Never in this condition do we find simple delight in these things, as does the person Kierkegaard calls the "Knight of Faith." The faithless self-worrier is a utilitarian of a particularly dismal and despairing sort, using the gifts of life not to benefit himself or others but to help him evade the task of his existence before God.

In this way the person for whom faith is a possibility—the person to whom the invitation is extended—has left neutral ground, and, therefore, his failure to make emulating Christ his highest priority will color whatever else he does with tinges of defiance.[34] He will carry out his service to others as a form of mutiny in order to insist he is doing something more important or urgent than giving himself to God. Thus his concern to vindicate himself will compromise the purity of his intentions; it will express the lack of that "certain something" which makes social acts loving. Only if faith comes first—only if he lets himself be utterly vanquished by Christ—can he escape these perversions of his loving intentions. Not to choose Christ completely once we have encountered him is to choose instead the wretchedness of defiance and endless rationalization, and deep, often unrecognized despair.

How Kierkegaard's Emphasis on Faith Has Been Often Misunderstood

For most of the century and a half since his death, Kierkegaard has been conventionally and widely portrayed as holding to a decidedly *nonrelational,* or individualistic, theory of the self. Each person, he is supposed to have believed, stands independent of every other, isolated within his appropriated, subjective interpretation of things and free of all outside influences whatsoever. It is easy to see that, for a being so radically autonomous, relationships with others cannot be essential to his selfhood. They will not connect him with others, subject to subject, because such a connection would compromise his independence. Only to God does this *sort* of being relate in a unique sort of relation that mysteriously does not compromise his autonomy. For this supposed individualism, Kierkegaard has been both admired—called the true founder of existentialism, for example—and criticized. He has been criticized because the individualism that has been ascribed to him precludes emotionally rich and committed human relationships. It might allow for a certain austere, bloodless dutifulness, such as Kant's "good will," but not for love.

Admittedly, Kierkegaard makes many statements that, when not interpreted in the context of his overall authorship, seem to support or even require this individualistic interpretation. For example, "to subjective reflection, truth becomes appropriation, inwardness, subjectivity, and the point is to immerse oneself, existing, in subjectivity."[35] Even a number of Kierkegaard's discussions of faith seem to support the individualistic interpretation. For example, in *Training in Christianity* he says outright that "love of God is hatred of the world."[36] It should not surprise us that many of Kierkegaard's readers have supposed his ideal of selfhood to be an individual insulated from others by his exclusive relation to God.

But in the last quarter of the twentieth century a new wave of scholars began to reconsider this interpretation and to discover that when the total thrust of Kierkegaard's work is duly appreciated, a solid basis for a social program and loving relationships emerges after all. Indeed, many of these scholars have recognized what I am emphasizing in this paper, that for Kierkegaard the self is individual, independent, and free only *because of* its essentially relational character—only because it comes into existence by acknowledging, responding to, and learning from God and neighbors.[37] Some writers have resisted this interpretive trend, so that Kierkegaard scholarship is currently divided on the issue I am raising in this paper. I will briefly mention a few of the traditional criticisms and, partly with the help of some of the more recent authors, show where I think it goes wrong. My rejoinders will give me a chance to amplify what has already been said about Kierkegaard's conception of how faith makes love possible.

In what has become perhaps the most widely known attack upon Kierkegaard, Martin Buber insists that Kierkegaard condemns all association with other people. He condemns it, says Buber, because any such association would compromise the relation to God.[38] It is true that Kierkegaard says we compromise our relation to God if we mass ourselves together with "the crowd" and its ways and thus evade our responsibility to become whole, self-transparent individuals. Contra Buber, however, Kierkegaard does not mean by this that *all* our relations with others compromise our faith; only when we lose ourselves in this crowd or mass of men does this happen.

What Buber misses in Kierkegaard is inseparable from Kierkegaard's relational theory of the self and the doctrine of individual freedom it contains. By our free responses, we tie ourselves in one way or another to other people; we either love them or use them to help us flee our existential responsibility. For just this reason, as Stephen Crites has written, "the mass man is a social pathology not inherent in sociality as such."[39] In other words, mass man is others seen through the eyes of one evading his existential responsibility; the pathology is in the individual, not in any assemblage of people. Therefore Buber is wrong to say that the choice Kierkegaard offers us is between either (1) relating to God or (2) relating to the crowd. The choice Kierkegaard lays out is between (1) relating to God in faith and to others individually, as loved neighbors, and (2) relating resistantly to God and evasively to others as a crowd. It is ironic that Buber misreads Kierkegaard so fundamentally, for, as his great book *I and Thou* makes abundantly clear,[40] Buber himself distinguishes the two ways of being identified by Kierkegaard, only one of which is a relation to God and to others. The nonrelational "I-It" mode is our ego-centered observing of external things, including other living beings, as objects, whereas in the "I-Thou" mode we establish a profound, heedful relation to all other beings. Buber fails to see that Kierkegaard had already drawn a similar distinction and thus had anticipated him by a century.[41]

Though it will take us briefly from the subject of faith's relation to love, it is worth noting that even those earlier commentators who attend explicitly to Kierkegaard's doctrine of freedom tend to get it wrong. The highly influential Louis Mackey argues that, for Kierkegaard, individual freedom is absolute and cannot be affected in any way by any earthly externals, such as the actions or needs of others. The "matter, content, locus, opportunity, or exigence for action," according to Mackey, the individual "must generate out of his own freedom."[42] But by his doctrine of radical freedom Kierkegaard did not mean that externals, such as the needs of others, cannot affect us; he meant that *we decide,* through our free appropriation, *how* they will affect us. For Kierkegaard, our freedom implies the possibility of being influenced in any of several ways, and at least one of these is sensitive and responsive to others' situations. Freedom as he conceives it makes it possible for us to be bound more closely to others; it does not, as Mackey thinks, separate us from them.

A variant of Buber's criticism, articulated by Mark C. Taylor, holds that, for Kierkegaard, being a Christian is a matter of inwardness in relation to God that is so intense and absolute that any social ties would compromise it.[43] Like other critics I am citing here, Taylor generates his position by attending to isolated, if plentiful, passages from Kierkegaard, such as, "intercourse with God is, in the deepest sense, absolutely non-social."[44] But the thrust of Kierkegaard's authorship does not support Taylor's position. For example—and I'll cite just one of many considerations here—Kierkegaard insists that if the God-relation remains a matter of "hidden inwardness," isolated from public view, it falls fatally short of true faith. For true faith must be manifest in works, including neighborly works, and these works must spring from a willingness to sacrifice and to suffer whatever might be necessary in order to emulate Christ. Merold Westphal makes this point decisively.[45] He shows that for Kierkegaard, who addresses these issues primarily in his later writings, we do not enter the realm of genuine faith in God until we have taken Christ as our prototype and thereby patterned our lives on his. This means making sacrifices and risking persecution, as did the apostles of old, in order to bear witness of the truth and minister to others. In *Training in Christianity,* Kierkegaard writes of people wanting to abolish the dangerous rigor of Christ's invitation to emulate him. They try to abolish it by seeking "falsely to transform the Christian life into hidden inwardness." This keeps the sacrifices strictly private, so that the social advantages of piety might not be lost. "In this way," Kierkegaard continues, "established Christendom becomes a collection of what one might call honorary Christians, in the same sense as one speaks of honorary doctors who get their degree without having to take an examination."[46] Inwardness is essentially selfish if it does not witness, serve, and sacrifice in order to invite others to come to Christ and thereby risk rejection.

Another influential misunderstanding of Kierkegaard originates in the work of the Marxist Theodor Adorno. In the late 1930s he famously complained about Kierkegaard's insistence that love cannot be based on distinctions among people. If taken seriously, this idea, he said, "actually leaves the world to the devil" by making us blind to the temporal conditions of others and unable to help them improve their lot in this world.[47] The net effect of this Christian concentration on changing people's inner being results in indifference to their temporal miseries. This is a reactionary doctrine, Adorno says, a "stubborn maintenance of the 'givenness' of the social order [which] is socially conformist and ready to lend its arm to oppression and misanthropy."[48]

To this objection we point again to Kierkegaard's conception of the freedom of the relational self. Jamie Ferreira points out that what Kierkegaard says of those who love—that they themselves have determined how they see others—goes also for all the individuals around them. They too choose how the circumstances affect them. Hence, people who are disadvantaged can be just as resentful, calloused, and self-serving as the advantaged ones and will be stuck in this mode unless they, too, first learn to love.[49] That is why love requires first of all that we impart to others the best gift, which is to help them become merciful and loving themselves. "[It is said:] 'The poor, the wretched may die—therefore it is very important that help be given.' No, answers the eternal; the most important is that mercifulness be practiced or that help be the help of mercifulness. . . . That a man dies is, eternally understood, no misfortune, but that mercifulness has not been practised is."[50] Love gives others mercy by mercifully teaching them mercy and expecting mercy of them. (Just how this can be done

I will describe momentarily.) The message for Adorno is that mercy of this kind prepares them both to help themselves materially and to receive material help in the right sort of way. Writes James Collins perceptively in one of the early books on Kierkegaard in English, "the preparatory work must be done in the soul of the individual, where all decisive battles are fought and permanent foundations laid."[51] Simply dispensing aid to others without putting their deeper welfare first would be subordinating their need to our own interest and making ourselves seem more important than we are. For even if we set no price on the service we offer, we will do so only to ensure that our "generosity" "expresses the value [we] attach to [ourselves]."[52] Expecting no growth on the part of the recipients, but valuing instead only the gift we are giving, is pure self-indulgence, and, like all indulgence, it tends to provoke the recipients to resentment and supplies them with an excuse for *their* failure to be merciful. Better to render them service that is animated by that "certain something" which, because it is truly merciful and loving, aims to help them also attain that "certain something."[53]

I recognize that someone assessing Kierkegaard from a worldly perspective will scarcely be able to take such talk as this seriously. But the faithful will find it persuasive. For, having themselves been vanquished by the truth, who is Christ, they have come to regard it as all-important. And this truth includes the realization that the most important thing for their neighbor is for him also to allow himself to be vanquished by that truth.[54] They attach no importance to themselves as sources of succor but focus instead on helping the needy one acknowledge his guilt before God and thus join them in being vanquished by the truth. "The lover hides himself" so that "through the help of love the [heretofore] unloving person becomes clearly aware of how irresponsibly he has acted so that he deeply feels his wrong doing."[55] To have the truth become the most important thing in one's own eyes is nothing more nor less than wanting the truth to become the most important thing in one's neighbor's eyes and to rejoice, not in oneself, but in the neighbor's rejoicing and in God, who gives the increase.

So, then, how do we influence another to acknowledge his guilt and succumb to God? How does love, as Kierkegaard conceives it, make any sort of positive difference in the world? How does it bring benefit to people in need? When we emulate Christ, we in effect relay his invitation to the people around us; indeed, as Kierkegaard wants us to remember, the invitation came to us in the first place with "an endorsement designating where it should be forwarded."[56] In many instances we extend the invitation—we forward it—without deliberately intending to do so, but simply by walking among our fellows in the way he did: harmlessly and in lowliness of heart. Our ways, like his, invite them to reconsider their ways—not as measured against our ways, but against his. He is their measure. "For the lover humbles himself before the good, whose needy servant he is, and, as he himself admits, in frailty; and the vanquished one humbles himself not before the lover but before the good."[57] In witnessing our love for the good, which is Christ, others are introduced to it through us and are thus properly disturbed in their idolatry and complacency.

This brings us to the final traditional criticism we will consider. If our allegiance is wholly to God, then in his service we are sooner or later likely to run roughshod over the legitimate interests of our fellowmen. The example often cited is the one Kierkegaard himself used in his magnificent study of faith, *Fear and Trembling*.[58] I speak of Abraham, the father of faith, who in obedience to God willingly took all the steps necessary to sacrifice his son. Giving up this son, from whom Abraham believed his most prized promises from God would flow, qualifies Abraham as supremely faithful; without hesitation he yielded what, up to that time, he might well have thought of as his own best interest. But from Isaac's point of view, this apparently faithful act seems at the very best to be insensitive and at the worst abusive. Says Robert M. Adams laconically, "'sacrificing' a person is apt to be harmful to the person sacrificed."[59]

Does the Abraham example not demonstrate that Kierkegaardian faith and Kierkegaardian love cannot coexist? Was not his willingness to sacrifice his son self-absorbed, calloused, and abusive? From a worldly or ethical point of view, yes. But not from the point of view of faith. For, just as Abraham trusted God in regard to his own promise, so he trusted God in regard to Isaac's welfare. It misreads this book to grant Abraham a faithful point of view with regard to his own interests and require of him a worldly point of view with regard to Isaac's.

And besides, what was the alternative? To give Isaac the experience and memory of a father who resisted God in order to preserve his own social propriety and respectability? Instead of teaching Isaac about faithfulness, it would have provided him an example of something else, something misleadingly called faith, which has the convenient utility of being compatible with self-service. Abraham had no choice, in faith, but to act faithfully in the assurance that "for God everything is possible"[60] for all his household, including himself, and for his posterity after him.[61]

Summary

Throughout *Sickness unto Death* are found variations on the principle that we become who we are when finally we are able to rest "transparently" in God.[62] Woven into the pages of *Training in Christianity* are variations on the principle that we attain this rest by coming to and emulating Christ. Prominent in *Works of Love* are variations on the principle that the joy of this condition is what we who love want most to share and that we share it best simply by being faithful, since this introduces others in the most inviting way possible to the object of our devotion. And featured in *Training in Christianity, For Self-Examination,* and *Judge for Yourself!*

are variations on the principle that emulating Christ means works on behalf of others, works of witnessing, service, and sacrifice.[63] The Knight of Faith does not withdraw into contemplation. Instead, his love of God, which is the "certain something," shines like the truth in every particular act he does on behalf of his neighbor—shines with an existential or living irresistibility that is not unlike Christ's invitation and that invites his neighbor to reflect, in the light of that truth, upon himself and his responsibility.

In contemplating this kind of love, I might repeat the language with which I tried to express Kierkegaard's amazement in contemplating Christ's love. Such love in us! that we would risk rejection and suffering in order to serve our neighbor, inviting him to consider and be vanquished by the truth that has vanquished us. Nevertheless—or, perhaps, therefore—we accept cheerfully our trials and losses. As Mormon taught and as Joseph Smith wrote when he translated Mormon's sermon in the synagogue, with faith comes the meekness and lowliness of heart—the freedom from envy, selfishness, pettiness, pride, and anger—that enables our acts of service to be free of hypocrisy (see Moroni 7:43–45).

Any relation to the neighbor that falls short of this recklessness simply cannot accompany a straightforward relation to God, for it misconceives God. It supposes him to be a "respecter of persons" willing to collaborate in one's project of serving oneself above others and calling it love. It makes him discriminatory and judgmental. "What you do unto men you do unto God," Kierkegaard writes.[64] And it shrivels the unloving one into a fastidious judge for whom all others become unloving and unworthy. The passage I just quoted continues: "and therefore what you do unto men God does unto you."

On the other hand, those who in faith give up their anxious self-management and recklessly turn themselves over to emulating Christ, no matter what the cost, reap the reward of these principles: What they do unto men they do unto God in the very same act;

they make him the source of the incomprehensible love that animates them. And, simultaneously, God does likewise unto them; he makes them a source of that love for others. The invitation is the ultimate expression of God's love for us. The acceptance of the invitation awakens in us the same kind of love. "Christianly understood, to love human beings is to love God and to love God is to love human beings."[65] Though love of God is sought first, it is not achieved first and then followed by love of neighbor; we will look in vain for a process or discipline to carry us from faith to love. Love of God *is* love of neighbor.

Notes

1. Søren Kierkegaard, *Works of Love: Some Christian Reflections in the Form of Discourses,* trans. Howard Hong and Edna Hong (New York: Harper and Row, 1964), 27.

2. Søren Kierkegaard was born 5 May 1813 in Copenhagen, Denmark. He died 11 November 1855 at Frederik's Hospital, also in Copenhagen.

3. At the end of "On My Work as an Author," Kierkegaard writes: "Without authority, to call attention to religion, to Christianity, is the category for my whole activity as an author, integrally regarded. That I was 'without authority' I have from the first moment asserted clearly and repeated as a stereotyped phrase." Søren Kierkegaard, *The Point of View,* trans. Walter Lowrie (London: Oxford, 1939), 155.

4. See Roger Poole, "The Unknown Kierkegaard: Twentieth-Century Receptions," in *The Cambridge Companion to Kierkegaard,* ed. Alastair Hannay and Gordon D. Marino (Cambridge: Cambridge University Press, 1998), 51–54.

5. Jorgen Bukdahl's *Søren Kierkegaard and the Common Man,* trans. Bruce H. Kirmmse (Grand Rapids, Mich.: Eerdmans, 2001), originally published in 1961, was one of the earlier efforts to present Kierkegaard as deeply preoccupied with the relationship of Christian faith and social relationships, particularly in the everyday lives of common people.

6. Søren Kierkegaard, *The Sickness unto Death: A Christian Psychological Exposition for Edification and Awakening,* trans. Alastair Hannay (London: Penguin, 1989).

7. For Kierkegaard's seminal discussion of this matter, see *Sickness unto Death*, 109–15.

8. Ibid., 111.

9. Ibid., 43.

10. Ibid., 44.

11. See Merold Westphal, "Kierkegaard," in *A Companion to Continental Philosophy*, ed. Simon Critchley (Oxford: Blackwell, 1998), 131, and "Kierkegaard and Hegel," in *The Cambridge Companion to Kierkegaard*, 108–9.

12. Kierkegaard, *Sickness unto Death*, 64. "One kind of despair allows itself to be, so to speak, cheated of its self by 'the others.' By seeing the multitude of people around it, by being busied with all sorts of worldly affairs, by being wise to the ways of the world, such a person forgets himself, in a divine sense forgets his own name, dares not believe in himself, finds being himself too risky, finds it much easier and safer to be like the others, to become a copy, a number, along with the crowd" (ibid., 63–64).

13. Timothy Jackson, "Arminian Edification: Kierkegaard on Grace and Free Will," in *The Cambridge Companion to Kierkegaard*, 238.

14. Søren Kierkegaard, *Training in Christianity*, trans. Walter Lowrie (Princeton: Princeton University Press, 1957), 80.

15. Ibid., 13.

16. Ibid., 105–6.

17. Kierkegaard, *Works of Love*, 95.

18. In *Training in Christianity*, "Away, away, O unhallowed ones" appears in the original Latin, "procul o procul este profani." For the English translation cited here, see the Hong translation of this book, entitled *Practice in Christianity*, trans. and ed. Howard Hong and Edna Hong (Princeton: Princeton University Press, 1991), 5.

19. The offense occasioned by the forgiveness of sins is treated by Kierkegaard in *Sickness unto Death*, subsection B of section B of part 2, entitled "The Sin of Despairing of the Forgiveness of Sins" (pp. 146–58). The broader context of the discussion is given in the whole of section B, "The Continuation of Sin" (pp. 138–65). Hannay's translation does not designate subsections.

20. Søren Kierkegaard, *Either/Or: Part II*, trans. and ed. Howard Hong and Edna Hong (Princeton: Princeton University Press, 1987), 346–54.

21. Kierkegaard, *Works of Love*, 119.

22. See Kierkegaard, *Training in Christianity*, 171 (cf. 1 Nephi 11:16).

23. Kierkegaard, *Works of Love*, 58–72.

24. Shakespeare, Sonnet 116.

25. Kierkegaard, *Works of Love*, 156–57.

26. Ibid., 37.

27. Cf. ibid., 351: "Christianly understood you have absolutely nothing to do with what others do to you; it does not concern you."

28. Kierkegaard, *Either/Or Part II*, 250.

29. See Søren Kierkegaard, *Philosophical Fragments/Johannes Climacus*, trans. and ed. Howard Hong and Edna Hong (Princeton: Princeton University Press, 1985), 166–72.

30. *Søren Kierkegaard's Journals and Papers*, trans. and ed. Howard Hong and Edna Hong (Bloomington: Indiana University Press, 1967), quoted in Michael J. Matthis, "Kierkegaard and the Problem of the Social Other," *Philosophy Today* 38 (1994): 419.

31. Kierkegaard, *Works of Love*, 112–13.

32. See Kierkegaard, *Training in Christianity*, 86–95.

33. Ibid., 26–39.

34. See Kierkegaard, *Sickness unto Death*, 111–15.

35. Søren Kierkegaard, *Concluding Unscientific Postscript to Philosophical Fragments, Vol. 1*, trans. and ed. Howard Hong and Edna Hong (Princeton: Princeton University Press, 1992), 192.

36. Kierkegaard, *Training in Christianity*, 218.

37. Good examples of this trend are found in George B. Connell and C. Stephen Evans, eds., *Foundations of Kierkegaard's Vision of Community: Religion, Ethics, and Politics in Kierkegaard* (Atlantic Highlands, N.J.: Humanities Press, 1992); and George Pattison and Steven Shakespeare, eds., *Kierkegaard: The Self in Society* (New York: St. Martin's, 1998). Other examples include Edward F. Mooney's book *Selves in Discord and Resolve: Kierkegaard's Moral-Religious Psychology from* Either/Or *to* Sickness unto Death (New York: Routledge, 1996); and Arnold B. Come's volume *Kierkegaard as Theologian: Recovering My Self* (Montreal: McGill-Queen's University Press, 1997).

38. Martin Buber, *Between Man and Man*, trans. Ronald G. Smith (New York: Macmillan, 1965), 40–82.

39. Stephen Crites, "*The Sickness unto Death:* A Social Interpretation," in *Foundations of Kierkegaard's Vision of Community,* 150.

40. Martin Buber, *I and Thou,* trans. Walter Kaufmann (New York: Scribner's Sons, 1970), and "The Question to the Single One," in *Between Man and Man.*

41. Brian T. Possner develops this point in "Chary about Having to Do with 'The Others': The Possibility of Community in Kierkegaard's Thought," *International Philosophical Quarterly* 39 (1999): 413–27. Kierkegaard's distinction differs from Buber's in this: for Kierkegaard, the "objective" attitude toward others can be replaced with compassion for others by having faith, whereas for Buber that "I-It" attitude is always with us, balancing, competing with, and sometimes undermining the open "I-You" attitude.

42. Louis Mackey, "The Loss of the World in Kierkegaard's Ethics," *Review of Metaphysics* 15 (1962): 613.

43. Mark C. Taylor, *Kierkegaard's Pseudonymous Authorship: A Study of Time and the Self* (Princeton: Princeton University Press, 1975); Taylor's critique is fully discussed in Gregory R. Beabout and Brad Frazier, "A Challenge to the 'Solitary Self' Interpretation of Kierkegaard," *History of Philosophy Quarterly* 17/1 (2000): 76–98.

44. Quoted in Beabout and Frazier, "A Challenge to the 'Solitary Self' Interpretation," 76.

45. Merold Westphal, "Kierkegaard's Teleological Suspension of Religiousness B," in *Foundations of Kierkegaard's Vision of Community,* 110–29.

46. Kierkegaard, *Training in Christianity,* 246, quoted in ibid., 124.

47. M. Jamie Ferreira, "Other-Worldliness in Kierkegaard's *Works of Love,*" *Philosophical Investigations* 22/1 (1999): 66.

48. Ibid.

49. Ibid., 76–79.

50. Kierkegaard, *Works of Love,* 302; see the essay in which this appears: "Mercifulness, a Work of Love," in *Works of Love,* 292–305.

51. James Collins, *The Mind of Kierkegaard* (Chicago: Regnery, 1953), quoted in Anthony Imbrosciano, "Kierkegaard's 'Individual,'" *International Philosophical Quarterly* 33/4 (1993): 446.

52. Kierkegaard, *Training in Christianity,* 11.

53. Although I have no room to elaborate on it here, I should mention Kierkegaard's conviction that the highest relation between persons, short of the love described in this paper, is what, in respectful reference to Socrates, he calls "maieutic." By this he means the humble service that one person renders by assisting another person to bring forth the best that is in him—just as Socrates "taught" by assisting the "learner" to recognize the understanding he already possessed. See Kierkegaard, *Philosophical Fragments,* 10–11. Moreover, Kierkegaard strove to make all his writing maieutic in just this sense and therefore to make it loving according to his own well-wrought conception of love. See Kierkegaard, *The Point of View,* 5–9. In fact, Kierkegaard's concern that his writing be maieutically effective can be taken, quite apart from the arguments he offered, as a demonstration of his conviction that the quality of our social relations is a vital correlative of the quality of our soul.

54. Kierkegaard, *Works of Love,* 306–16.

55. Ibid., 314, 312.

56. Ibid., 159.

57. Ibid., 313.

58. Søren Kierkegaard, *Fear and Trembling: A Dialectical Lyric,* trans. Walter Lowrie (Princeton: Princeton University Press, 1952).

59. Robert M. Adams, "The Knight of Faith," *Faith and Philosophy* 7/4 (1990): 389.

60. Kierkegaard, *Sickness unto Death,* 68.

61. Frequently, the criticism we have just considered has been reinforced by interpretations of Kierkegaard's own life. His scandalous breaking of his engagement with his beloved Regina has been called a protection of his vocation as a single-minded author in God's service and held up as a manifestation of his conviction that nothing should be allowed to encroach upon a life of faithful service to God. See Alastair Hannay, *Kierkegaard* (London: Routledge, 1982), 73–84. See also Robert Bretall, *A Kierkegaard Anthology* (New York: The Modern Library, 1946), 116. Kierkegaard is charged with sacrificing Regina without regard for her hopes and desires, just as Abraham is charged with being willing to sacrifice Isaac without regard for his welfare.

I cannot adequately respond to this charge here. The considerations, including biographical details and implications of the biographically relevant parables in the "Problem III" section of *Fear and Trembling*, are too complex and subtle to be reviewed in a few paragraphs or even a few pages. So I must content myself with expressing my belief that, when all these considerations are thoroughly reviewed in light of an informed understanding of Kierkegaard's idea of the self and its freedom and a careful rereading of all he wrote about the breakup, the following conclusion will win out.

Fundamentally, Kierkegaard did not end his engagement with Regina primarily to protect his faith and his authorship from the ravages of the institution of marriage. He did not believe that genuine faith could be compromised by earthly commitments. In fact, he believed the opposite—that faith flourishes in loving relationships and indeed is precisely the means by which such relationships can be loving rather than selfish. He broke with Regina because he doubted that his faith was strong enough to assure her the selfless love that marriage required and that she deserved. While composing *Fear and Trembling*, Kierkegaard writes in a journal entry dated 17 May 1843: "If I had faith, I should have remained with Regina," quoted in Bretall, *A Kierkegaard Anthology*, 126. Kierkegaard broke with Regina primarily out of concern for her and not primarily out of concern for himself and his calling in life.

Admittedly, other factors played a role in his decision, so I do not claim that he acted with a perfect single-mindedness or even with confidence. In fact, he later regretted his decision. My contention is that the thrust of his intent at the time was not simplistic self-regard but rather concern for the person he loved as much as he was capable of loving.

62. Kierkgaard, *Sickness unto Death*, 44.

63. Westphal cites these works to make this point in "The Teleological Suspension of Religiousness B," 114. See Søren Kierkegaard, *For Self-Examination; Judge for Yourself!* trans. and ed. Howard Hong and Edna Hong (Princeton: Princeton University Press, 1990).

64. Kierkegaard, *Works of Love*, 352.

65. Ibid., 351–52.

Chapter 7

"Jesus, the Very Thought of Thee": Understanding the Christ of the Restoration and the Reformation

Gary P. Gillum

Introduction

Lutherans pray much like members of the Church of Jesus Christ of Latter-day Saints do. When my mother and father taught me how to pray as a child, they clearly championed a Father in Heaven who not only would listen to my prayers, in the name of Jesus, but who was a person not unlike my earthly father—only more divine. Years later, this childhood-ingrained concept was challenged during my theological studies as I learned about the inscrutable theology of the Godhead as set forth by the ecumenical creeds and statements of church councils. But answers to two watershed prayers during these painful years reaffirmed to me that my Heavenly Father had not forsaken me,[1] and they encouraged me to continue my search for truth.

Continue I did, but I began to resent being trained to be an ecclesiastical politician or an esoteric mini-theologian when I simply wanted to be a pastor of my own flock.[2] Far too many of the theologians and professors teaching me were so concerned about examining the details and looking beyond the theological mark that they could not see the big picture. They missed the general message of salvation, even though they were proficient in higher criticism and historical and literary analysis. I found that I could not deal with obscurantism or any -ism like it. And my spiritual sensitivities rebelled at the authority some ministers arrogated to themselves.

My pain was very much like that of Serapion, the fourth-century monk who became a victim of the Anthropomorphite-Origenist controversy[3] (which grappled with the nature of the Godhead without the benefit of revelation).

> A certain Serapion, a man so old and accomplished in so many virtues, . . . when he realized that the anthropomorphic image of the Godhead which he had always pictured to himself while praying had been banished from his heart . . . suddenly broke into the bitterest tears and heavy sobbing and, throwing himself to the ground with a loud groan, cried out: "Woe is me, wretch that I am! They have taken my God from me, and I have no one to lay hold of, nor do I know whom I should adore or address."[4]

As I became increasingly uncomfortable with these nonbiblical interpretations concerning my Heavenly Father, which as a pastor I would later have to preach to congregations as truth, I also began to question the nature and person of Christ. Like many other seekers throughout history, I naively and desperately sought the truth in practice, as well as in belief, when it came to my spiritual life. So I read Martin Luther's works for further wisdom, while getting insights from my favorite "watchdog" theologians like C. S. Lewis and Dietrich Bonhoeffer. Ultimately, I lost patience and took the same risk Joseph Smith did: I asked of God.[5]

A few years after my conversion to the Church of Jesus Christ, I had become increasingly intrigued by Joseph Smith's comment that he considered Luther's translation of the Bible to be better than the King James Version in some particulars.[6] I even wondered if Joseph would have found it necessary to inquire about the true church if a Lutheran congregation had been available to him, for even after thirty years in the Church of Jesus Christ, I realize that the most important teaching of all, the atonement of Jesus Christ—to which everything else is an appendage[7]—is nearly identical in the doctrines of the Lutheran Church and the Church of Jesus Christ. I vividly recall the only question a concerned and loving Pastor Heine asked me when he learned that I had joined "the Mormons": "Gary, do you still believe that Jesus Christ died for your sins and rose again?" When I happily responded in the affirmative, he replied, "That is good enough for me!" Would that all ministers had been so trusting of me.[8]

In any case, Martin Luther and Joseph Smith were my spiritual heroes. I now found myself thinking about them together, wondering what their conversations were like and how they might see us today. Lest it seem too far-fetched and speculative, I have transformed this "spirit-world" conversation into this essay and have attempted to use the facts to show how Martin Luther and Joseph Smith had the same yearnings to discover the nature of God and how both were successful in heightening our understanding of true Christianity and the nature of Jesus Christ. I will reveal much more about Martin Luther than Joseph Smith, simply because the Latter-day Saints already understand much about Joseph Smith. Moreover, I will discuss more similarities than differences, with the hope that we will all become more charitable and tolerant toward our brothers and sisters of different faiths.

Christology

Who is Jesus Christ, and what is our proper relationship to him and our Heavenly Father? To more fully understand the true nature of Jesus Christ, it is important to comprehend the true nature of the Godhead, especially of our Heavenly Father. Owing mostly to my background as both a Lutheran and a Latter-day Saint, I believe that few religious leaders in the past have depicted the true nature of the Godhead more accurately than did Martin Luther and Joseph Smith.

Christology is the term commonly used to identify the theological study of the human and divine natures and roles of Jesus Christ. It developed soon after the deaths of the apostles in the first century A.D. when conflicting teachings arose among early church scholars and leaders who felt that they possessed the true understanding of Christ. Christology became both a response to heresies concerning the person and work of the Messiah, as well as a systematic theology that all orthodox Christians could accept as containing true teachings concerning their Redeemer. Eventually these teachings were discussed in councils and set forth in creeds at Nicea (A.D. 325), Constantinople (A.D. 381), and Chalcedon (A.D. 451). These creeds insisted on a full communion of Christ's divine and human natures, as opposed to those teachings that he was either divine or human, or partly the one and partly the other.[9] In the minds of many Christians today, "Christology, the doctrine concerning God's revelation in Christ and the salvation wrought through Christ, constitutes the core of Christian theology and belongs to the centre of the church's proclamation."[10] Others insist that "the christological task is to get Jesus into language."[11] This makes the understanding of Christ a semantic problem. But most of us do not need the words: we *feel* the who and what of Christ.

The Church of Jesus Christ, quite fortunately and miraculously, has a distinctive understanding of God derived from its commitment that Jesus Christ reveals both what God is and what humans can become. Latter-day Saint belief that divinity is fully mature humanity allows the church to avoid the most intractable logical problems confronting Christology.[12] Yet our Christian brothers and sisters ignore thoughts about the deification of human beings. Second Peter 1:4 and Psalm 82:6 speak of deification, and the ante-Nicene fathers also had much to say about it. Most of the following quotations are found in *The Ante-Nicene Fathers* (hereafter *ANF*):[13]

- "It must be that thou, at the outset, shouldest hold the rank of a man, and then afterwards partake of the glory of God." Irenaeus, *Against Heresies* 4.39.2 (ca. 180, *ANF* 1:523).
- "They see that from Him there began the union of the divine with the human nature, in order that the human, by communion with the divine, might rise to be divine, not in Jesus alone, but in all those who not only believe, but enter upon the life which Jesus taught." Origen, *Against Celsus* 3.28 (ca. 248, *ANF* 4:475).
- "We have learned that those only are deified who have lived near to God in holiness and virtue." Justin Martyr, *First Apology* 21 (ca. 160, *ANF* 1:170).
- "How shall man pass into God, unless God has [first] passed into man?" Irenaeus, *Against Heresies* 4.33.4 (ca. 180, *ANF* 1:507).
- "Our Lord Jesus Christ, who did, through His transcendent love, become what we are, so that He might bring us to be even what He is Himself." Irenaeus, *Against Heresies* preface to book 5 (ca. 180, *ANF* 1:526).
- "Being baptized, we are illuminated; illuminated, we become sons; being made sons, we are made perfect; being made perfect, we are made immortal. 'I,' says He, 'have said that ye are gods, and all sons of the Highest.'" Clement of Alexandria, *The Instructor* 1.6 (ca. 195, *ANF* 2:215).
- "The Gnostic [man of God] is consequently divine, and already holy, God-bearing, and God-borne." Clement of Alexandria, *Stromata* 7.13 (ca. 192, *ANF* 2:547).
- "It is He alone who can make gods." Tertullian, *Against Hermogenes* 5 (ca. 200, *ANF* 3:480).
- "What man is, Christ was willing to be, that man also may be what Christ is. . . . What Christ is, we Christians shall be, if we imitate Christ." Cyprian, *The Treatises of Cyprian* 6.11, 15 (ca. 250, *ANF* 5:468, 469).

- Origen: "There is a well of living water in each of us, and it is 'a kind of heavenly perception and latent image of God.'"[14]

Why do many of our Protestant and Catholic brothers and sisters think contrary to these teachings? To believe in the deification of man would, in their eyes, lessen the inscrutability, majesty, and mystery of God the Father and make obsolete the doctrine of the Trinity as set forth in the Nicene and Athanasian Creeds.[15] In short, mainstream Christianity holds fast to tradition every bit as much as orthodox Jews do as portrayed by Tevye and his friends in *Fiddler on the Roof.*

Martin Luther

Martin Luther was a product of these councils and creeds and especially of the theology of Augustine, which stressed original sin and total depravity. But Augustine was also the founder of Luther's order, the Augustinians. Thus, Luther was mostly in harmony with the classical Christology of the ancient church and of the early church fathers, championing what Holsten Fagerberg, in his study of the Lutheran confessions, characterizes as "an assumption Christology."[16] Like many theologians before him, Luther could not conceive of the possibility that man could be raised to the level of godhood, so ingrained in him were Augustine's teachings about the utter depravity of man. It was much easier for the Savior to assume humanity and become like us. Accordingly, a simple theology of man and God being in the same image deteriorated into a doctrine wherein God and Christ are entirely different from man.

As Luther matured, he became increasingly confused and nervous about the true nature of God and sought answers through his extensive theological training and from his teachers and mentors. He even began to discount the doctrine of transubstantiation,[17] using words similar to our own Latter-day Saint scholars when they discuss the apostasy: "What is our response," he said, "when

Aristotle, and the doctrines of men, are made the arbiters of these very sublime and divine things?"[18] Gradually, Luther weaned himself from some of the "doctrines of men" and submitted to the words of the New Testament. He began to understand the potential divinity of all human life and the reality of a loving and gracious Father in Heaven, instead of viewing him as a judge ready to consign humanity to hell for their depravity.

> If you have a true faith that Christ is your Saviour, then at once you have a gracious God, for faith leads you in and opens up God's heart and will, that you should see pure grace and overflowing love. This it is to behold God in faith that you should look upon his *fatherly,* friendly heart, in which there is no anger nor ungraciousness. He who sees God as angry does not see him rightly but looks only on a curtain, as if a dark cloud had been drawn across his face.[19]

Is Luther's God the God of the creeds and councils? I do not think so. *Fatherly* is not an adjective a believer assigns to a philosophical construct who has no body, parts, or passions. Once Luther had come to a more correct understanding of his relationship to his Heavenly Father, it was much easier for him to come closer to a loving association with Jesus Christ. This quotation from his best-known work, *The Freedom of a Christian* (1520), is a prime example: "Christ has made it possible for us, provided we believe in him, to be not only his brethren, co-heirs, and fellow-kings, but also his fellow-priests. Therefore we may boldly come into the presence of God in the spirit of faith (Heb. 10:19, 22)."[20] This statement is very clear, but we can ponder why Luther did not follow his own advice to come into the presence of God in faith. What were his prayers like? Would he have thought it presumptuous to ask God himself about truth? Or were his prayers strictly liturgical, meditative, or worshipful?

Throughout his writings, Luther insists that God comes to us, not we to him. Thus, it seems likely that his answers came passively from his scripture reading, considerable education, meditation, and reason, and actively from pressures from German princes, Roman prelates, and faithful followers who insisted on immediate answers. Luther had looked forward to a "quiet life of scholarship and study." Instead, he was "plunged . . . into an ecclesiastical and political whirlpool."[21] Unlike a naive and unlearned Joseph Smith, Luther seemed to pay no attention to James 1:5, possibly because he dismissed the book of James as "an epistle of straw."[22] I am intrigued as I wonder what Luther would have said of Joseph's faith-in-action use of the "epistle of straw" to invoke the restoration.

Although Luther did not believe that God's word could be revealed directly to him (except through the scriptures), he nevertheless received what I am tempted to call a secondary revelation. He characterizes it in slightly different words, however. Compare this thought of Luther to Moroni 10:4–5:

> Not through thought, wisdom, and will does the faith of Christ arise in us, but through an incomprehensible and hidden operation of the Spirit, which is given by faith in Christ only at the hearing of the Word and without any other work of ours. . . . No one is taught through much reading and thinking. There is a much higher school where one learns God's Word. One must go into the wilderness.[23]

His German translation of the Bible and his many fine sermons and writings, as well as the words he wrote to many hymns, are witness to what I consider to have been the divine inspiration and guidance he received. Here is an example from one of his hymns:

> Thus spoke the Son, "Hold thou to me,
>   From now on thou wilt make it.
> I gave my very life for thee
>   And for thee I will stake it.
> For I am thine and thou art mine,
> And where I am our lives entwine,
>   The Old Fiend cannot shake it."[24]

These words speak of a closeness to and a love for Christ that is encouraged among all Christians. As if to continue the conversation from the hymn, Luther also writes:

> Now continue and rise beyond Christ's heart to God's heart and you will see that Christ would not have shown this love for you if God in his eternal love had not wanted this, for Christ's love for you is due to his obedience to God. Thus you will find the divine and kind paternal heart, and, as Christ says, you will be drawn to the Father through him. Then you will understand the words of Christ, "For God so loved the world that he gave his only Son, etc." (John 3:16). We know God aright when we grasp him not in his might or wisdom . . . but in his kindness and love.[25]

Luther not only knew his Savior, but he knew that "those who thus make Christ's life and name a part of their own lives are true Christians."[26] In "A Brief Instruction on What to Look For and Expect in the Gospels," he adds more specific counsel: "Now when you have Christ as the foundation and chief blessing of your salvation, then the other part follows: that you take him as your example, giving yourself in service to your neighbor just as you see that Christ has given himself for you."[27]

The same sentiment is repeated in other sermons and writings. In "Freedom of a Christian," he writes: "We conclude, therefore, that a Christian lives not in himself, but in Christ and in his neighbor. Otherwise he is not a Christian. He lives in Christ through faith, in his neighbor through love. By faith he is caught up beyond himself into God. By love he descends beneath himself into his neighbor."[28] Luther adds further testimony by reaffirming two truths with which we as Latter-day Saints are familiar: "The inner man, who by faith is created in the image of God, is both joyful and happy because of Christ in whom so many benefits are conferred upon him; and therefore it is his one occupation to serve God joyfully and without thought of gain, in love that is not constrained."[29] Finally, "Death is swallowed up not only in the victory of Christ but also by *our* victory, because through faith his victory has become ours and in that faith we also are conquerors."[30]

What Martin Luther Did Not Reform

Why did Luther not go further? People in the fifteenth through eighteenth centuries were still reticent to call upon Deity for answers to their more important questions. The authority of tradition in the Roman Catholic Church still held sway in people's minds when it came to matters of the Godhead. Luther would certainly have been burned at the stake for questioning such matters. It is for that reason that his Ninety-five Theses dealt with secondary spiritual matters like indulgences. Had he lived in our own day, his theses would probably have contained more about the nature of the Godhead and of man, of heaven and hell. Luther was not only meek, in the beginning, but cautious. And he was only looking for reform from *within* the Catholic Church. In his own words: "I have sought nothing beyond reforming the Church in conformity with the Holy Scriptures."[31] A further elaboration reveals Luther's heart and soul more than anything else he has written. This is Luther's response to the papal bull of excommunication, *Exsurge Domine,* found in his *Grund und Ursach aller Artickel,* published in Wittenberg by Melchior Lotter in 1521.[32] The Diet of Worms, which resulted in Luther's excommunication, took place on 6 January 1521.

> I have not pushed myself forward at all. If I could follow my own inclinations, I would always prefer to crawl back into my little corner. But my opponents have drawn me out again and again by craft and violence in order to acquire credit and honour by attacking me. Now that their game is falling through, my ambition is supposed to be the cause of everything. But, in the second place, even if they were right and I had really set myself up as a teacher, could God not have called and raised me up for this purpose? Do we not read that he usually raised up only *one* prophet from among his people, and never from the upper classes, but generally humble, despised individuals, even

common herdsmen. . . . I do not say that I am a prophet. I simply say that they will have to be afraid of this as long as they scorn me and heed themselves. . . . If I am not a prophet I am at least sure of this, that the Word of God is with me, and not with them, for I have the Scriptures on my side while they have only their own teachings. . . . But do I not preach a new doctrine? No. I simply say that Christianity has ceased to exist among those who should have preserved it—the bishops and scholars. . . . I do not repudiate the Church Fathers. But like all men, they, too, have erred at times. Consequently I believe them only in so far as they can prove their teachings from the Scriptures, which have never erred.[33]

What is remarkable about these words is that Joseph Smith could have said the same thing. And today, in a new millennium, some Lutherans continue to call Martin Luther a prophet!

Heavenly Father was aware of the spiritual unpreparedness of the people in Luther's day. He knew they were not ready for the earth-shaking revelations and pronouncements that Joseph Smith would bring forth in the early nineteenth century. According to Roland Bainton, one of Luther's biographers, "Luther for himself had had absolutely no experience of any contemporary revelation, and in times of despondency the advice to rely upon the spirit was for him a counsel of despair, since within he could find only utter blackness."[34] I believe that he would have obeyed a heavenly manifestation had one taken place. As it was, Luther's forays into truth were dangerous enough; witness the wars and politics that accompanied the Reformation and Counter-Reformation.

Fortunately, Luther left the door to the future slightly ajar: "Nor can a Christian believer be forced beyond the sacred Scriptures, . . . unless some new and proved revelation should be added; for we are forbidden by divine law to believe except what is proved either through the divine Scriptures or through manifest revelation."[35] Several questions immediately entered my mind as I read this interesting remark: How would this "new" revelation be proven? What would Luther accept as truth? How *else* could such a revelation be made manifest unless through God himself? And, if so, to whom on earth would it be manifested?

Hidden within Luther's writings and sermons are additional evidences that he was thinking of the more important matters and had opened some doors for someone else to enter and explore at a later time. In the words of A. Burt Horsley, "If we regard the Restoration as the fulfillment of a spiritual awakening process, the dawn of which appeared in the hour of the Reformation, then the Reformation becomes even more significant. It was not *disconnected* from the Restoration, but rather the preliminary phase of it."[36]

We also know that Luther's early theology was at odds with the councils and creeds, especially the doctrine of the Trinity. Toward the end of Luther's life, fellow reformer and successor Philip Melanchthon set him straight, as it were, and the changes in Luther's theology at the end of his life were reflected in the Schmalkald Articles. These articles were his theological will and testament and reflected traditional Christianity instead of what other theologians had earlier considered "confused." Luther scholar William R. Russell, building on a discussion by Edmund Schlink, describes what happened:

> Luther's theological priorities as expressed in [the Schmalkald Articles] would clearly seem to reveal at the outset a commitment to the classical creedal and theological traditions of the church catholic. However, interpreters of Luther have not always agreed about the genuineness of this commitment.
>
> Some scholars have concluded that Luther understood the Trinity in a way that was not really in keeping with the classical Christian tradition. Adolf von Harnack, for example, saw "no bridge" from Luther's interpretation of justification by faith to the Trinity and in the end, Luther's interpretation of the Trinity was an "unspeakable confusion," with modalistic tendencies. Karl Thieme argued with von Harnack but then discovered a "naive Ditheism" and "Tritheism" in Luther's writings—or at

least Thieme expressed a concern that the reformer's doctrine inferred such polytheism.[37]

Interestingly, these same arguments have been directed toward the Latter-day Saint theology of the Godhead.

Other researchers have concluded that Luther was not fully convinced of the veracity of the statements of faith in the creeds. Albrecht Ritschl, for instance, asserted that "Luther (and Melanchthon too, for that matter) adhered to the doctrine of the Trinity as a matter of strategic convenience, because it was required by the Justinian Code of the empire."[38] This code was promulgated by the Emperor Justinian in A.D. 529[39] and made trinitarian orthodoxy mandatory in the empire. Still in effect in Luther's time a millennium later, it was therefore a "political" theology that bound Luther to stay away from the higher theological issues. If Joseph Smith were to be known as nothing else, he should be known as the man who broke the bonds of the Justinian Code—thirteen centuries later—by restoring the correct teachings concerning the Godhead and our true relationship to Christ and Heavenly Father.

Finally, from the very beginning of the Reformation, Luther claimed in number thirty-seven of his Ninety-five Theses: "Any true Christian whatsoever, living or dead, participates in all the benefits of Christ and the Church."[40] If any statement is more obviously a harbinger of the restoration of temple work for the dead, I do not know what it is. Reading these words in this seminal work made me wonder what other prerestoration doctrines could be found within the amazing theology of Luther. If anything impresses me about his writings, it is not that Luther was wrong but that he was on the right track and simply did not go far enough. He desperately wanted to, and I am sure that Heavenly Father felt that Luther was a willing servant: it simply was not time yet. It appears that he had chosen and foreordained Luther to be the forerunner of plain and precious truths, not the restorer.[41]

Joseph Smith

If Augustine tampered with Paul, and Luther with both Augustine and Paul, then reformers like John Calvin, Huldrych Zwingli, John Wesley, and others who sprouted up after Luther were influenced by Luther, Augustine, and Paul, instead of going directly to the source. Joseph Smith brought an end to the tampering, borrowing, and political theologizing that such men created by the light of their own understanding. Joseph was no educated theologian like the men above. He was a child: naive, meek, teachable, open-minded, uneducated, and curious. He wanted direct and truthful answers no man could give him, so with his childlike faith he took the words of the apostle James at their face value and asked God directly. Like Martin Luther, he was sensitive enough to the Spirit to recognize that there needed to be a change. But, unlike Luther, being among a more tolerant political and cultural climate made it possible for Joseph to receive additional truths—even though he later suffered a martyr's death, like Jan Hus, for preaching doctrines that seemed heretical and blasphemous to some Americans in the 1830s and 1840s. For theologians to learn from a mere boy that "The Father has a body of flesh and bones as tangible as man's" (D&C 130:22) was to these learned men the height of falsehood, impertinence, ignorance, and blasphemy.

Fortunately, Joseph Smith's teachings were built on a foundation that did not differ from mainstream Christianity. To Joseph, Jesus Christ was still our Savior and Redeemer, our Mediator between God and man, our Advocate with the Father, the Judge of all mankind, and the Life and Light of the world. Thanks to the grace and goodness of God, the marvel of the atonement has always been taught—even throughout the dark centuries of the great apostasy. But Joseph restored the understanding of our *true* relationship to Christ and Heavenly Father by showing that we are divine sons and daughters who are sinners because we have broken the divine law and cannot embrace it fully again without the Savior's atonement.[42]

As a part of the restoration, Joseph Smith sought to restore additional principles of knowledge about the Savior. Foremost, he taught that the Jehovah of the Old Testament is none other than Jesus Christ. In a letter delivered from Kirtland to the brethren scattered from Zion (22 January 1834), Joseph Smith wrote: "Whenever the Lord revealed Himself to men in ancient days, and commanded them to offer sacrifice to Him, it was done that they might look forward in faith to the time of His coming, and rely upon the power of that atonement for a remission of their sins."[43]

If Martin Luther had studied the Old Testament and the book of Hebrews more carefully, he might have realized this for himself, but he had as little use for the book of Hebrews as he had for that of James, Jude, and Revelation.[44] Additionally, he would have learned that the term *Elohim* included Jehovah as Creator, who helped God the Father create the world. In the words of Origen, one of the early church fathers: "The *immediate* Creator, and, as it were, very Maker of the world was the Word, the Son of God; while the Father of the Word, by commanding His own Son—the Word—to create the world, is *primarily* Creator."[45]

Additionally, Joseph Smith learned that Jesus Christ presides as the God of this world (see D&C 39:1–4) and the father of those who are spiritually reborn (see D&C 25:1; 11:28–30). He is our Father because he "descended in suffering below that which man can suffer; or, in other words, he suffered greater sufferings, and was exposed to more powerful contradictions than any man can be."[46] "None were ever perfect but Jesus, and why was he perfect? Because he was the Son of God, and had the fulness of the Spirit, and greater power than any man."[47] These statements and many others show forth the glory and majesty of the truth of the restoration of the gospel. When I studied Martin Luther's arguments,

I felt (and still feel) words of powerful reason and sensitivity. But when I read the inspired words of Joseph Smith, I feel authority and divine empowerment through God. Every Latter-day Saint should become familiar with the sublime teachings of Joseph Smith through his first vision (see Joseph Smith—History 1), his *Lectures on Faith* (especially lecture 5), his King Follett discourse (given on 7 April 1844),[48] and his sermon given at a meeting in the grove east of the Nauvoo Temple on 16 June 1844.[49] These are the most well-known explications of Joseph's Christology and doctrine of the Godhead.

Conclusion

Like Martin Luther, Joseph Smith, and Serapion, we all have the right to "lay hold of" our Heavenly Father and to receive revelation from the original source. Many of us are grateful that we have had searching prayers like Luther's, for the words of his Small Catechism show that he relied on the Spirit: "I believe that I cannot by my own reason or strength believe in Jesus Christ, my Lord, or come to Him; but the Holy Ghost has called me by the Gospel, enlightened me with His gifts, sanctified and kept me in true faith."[50] But we are even more thankful that our answers were like Joseph's: "When the light rested upon me I saw two Personages, whose brightness and glory defy all description, standing above me in the air. One of them spake unto me, calling me by name and said, pointing to the other—*This is My Beloved Son. Hear Him!*" (Joseph Smith—History 1:17, emphasis in original). This clear and irrevocable response demonstrates that the Lord himself will not only change humanity's understanding of the Godhead but restore a correct understanding of the gospel of Jesus Christ. Luther may have preached the "priesthood of all believers" and Christian liberty, but Joseph Smith taught that revelation through the Holy Ghost was possible for all believers. History shows that neither Joseph Smith nor Martin Luther sought to begin a new church. In the beginning, all either wanted was enough truth to make him free, salvation from his sins, and knowledge of the real God.

Notes

1. Winfield, Kansas, at St. John's College, October 1962, and Kendallville, Indiana, at St. John Lutheran Church, July 1968. The former preceded my January 1963 auto accident and near-death experience. The latter led to my conversion to the Church of Jesus Christ of Latter-day Saints.

2. For example, John, a fellow college classmate, was forced to cease his studies for the ministry because he could not master New Testament Greek, but he would have made a very fine minister. Four years later, a professor told my parents that, while I was not very bright, I would nevertheless make a good minister. Where were the priorities?

3. Anthropomorphites believe that God the Father has a physical body like a man. Origen was an Alexandrian theologian who lived from A.D. 185 to 254. His most controversial beliefs were his concepts of the premortal existence of humans and the temporary character of the body. See Henry R. Saften, "Origenism," in *The New International Dictionary of the Christian Church,* ed. James D. Douglas (Grand Rapids, Mich.: Zondervan, 1978), 734.

4. Tim Vivian, trans., "Coptic Palladinana I: The Life of Pambo," *Coptic Church Review* 20/3 (1999): 78.

5. My conversion story is recounted in volume 2 of Hartman Rector Jr. and Connie Rector, eds., *No More Strangers* (Salt Lake City: Bookcraft, 1973), 145–58.

6. Joseph Smith, *History of the Church of Jesus Christ of Latter-day Saints,* 2nd ed. (Salt Lake City: Deseret Book, 1950), 6:307, 364.

7. See *Teachings of the Prophet Joseph Smith,* comp. Joseph Fielding Smith (Salt Lake City: Deseret Book, 1972), 121.

8. Other ministers have roundly and intolerantly condemned me, threatened me with excommunication, or literally knocked the breath out of me with a well-placed fist in my stomach.

9. See Raymond E. Brown, "Christology," in *The New Jerome Biblical Commentary,* ed. Raymond E. Brown, Joseph A. Fitzmyer, and Roland E.

Murphy (Englewood Cliffs, N.J.: Prentice-Hall, 1990), and John Hick, "An Inspiration Christology for a Religiously Plural World," in *Encountering Jesus: A Debate on Christology,* ed. Stephen T. Davis (Atlanta: Knox, 1988), 5–22, cited in Gary P. Gillum, "Christology," in *The Encyclopedia of Mormonism,* 1:272.

10. Martin Hengel, *Studies in Early Christology* (Edinburgh: Clark, 1995), vii.

11. William P. Loewe, *The College Student's Introduction to Christology* (Collegeville, Minn.: Liturgical Press, 1996), 202.

12. Blake T. Ostler, "A Mormon Christology," 1; manuscript in my possession.

13. *The Ante-Nicene Fathers,* ed. Alexander Roberts and James Donaldson (1885; reprint, Peabody, Mass.: Hendrickson, 1994); see David W. Bercot, ed., *A Dictionary of Early Christian Beliefs* (Peabody, Mass: Hendrickson, 1998), 199–201.

14. *Homélies sur la Genèse,* trans. Louis Doutreleau, in *Sources chrétiennes* 7 (Paris: Éditions du Cerf, 1976), 287–91, quoted in Patricia C. Miller, "Dreams in Patristic Literature: Divine Sense or Pagan Nonsense?" *Studia Patristica* 18/2 (1989): 187.

15. Latter-day Saints, after all, believe in the Father, the Son, and the Holy Ghost, and hence in a trinity in that sense. The mainstream Christian Trinity, however, is defined as the Father, Son, and Holy Ghost being one substance in three persons.

16. Holsten Fagerberg, *A New Look at the Lutheran Confessions (1529–1537),* trans. Gene J. Lund (St. Louis: Concordia, 1972), 117.

17. Transubstantiation is the doctrine that the bread and wine of the Eucharist are changed into the body and blood of Christ.

18. Martin Luther, "Against Transubstantiation," in *Readings in Christian Thought,* ed. Hugh T. Kerr (Nashville: Abingdon, 1966), 149.

19. Quoted in Roland H. Bainton, *Here I Stand: A Life of Martin Luther* (New York: Abingdon, 1950), 65, emphasis added.

20. Martin Luther, "Freedom and Service," in Kerr, *Readings in Christian Thought,* 151.

21. Kerr, *Readings in Christian Thought,* 140.

22. Bainton, *Here I Stand,* 331.

23. Ibid., 224.

24. Ibid., 66. This hymn verse may be sung to the melody of Luther's "A Mighty Fortress Is Our God." However, the original German words lend themselves more easily to the meter of the tune.

25. Martin Luther, "A Meditation on Christ's Passion," in *Martin Luther's Basic Theological Writings,* ed. Timothy F. Lull (Minneapolis: Fortress, 1989), 171.

26. Ibid., 172.

27. Martin Luther, "A Brief Instruction on What to Look For and Expect in the Gospels," in *Martin Luther's Basic Theological Writings,* 107.

28. Martin Luther, "Freedom of a Christian," in *Martin Luther: Selections from His Writings,* ed. John Dillenberger (Garden City, N.Y.: Doubleday, 1961), 80; also in Luther, "Freedom and Service," 154.

29. Luther, "Freedom and Service," 152–53.

30. Luther, "Freedom of a Christian," 66, emphasis added.

31. Quoted in Ernest G. Schwiebert, *Luther and His Times: The Reformation from a New Perspective* (St. Louis: Concordia, 1950), 509.

32. Original manuscripts of these forty-one articles written against the Roman Catholic Church are found in the vault of the Harold B. Lee Library at Brigham Young University.

33. Quoted in John M. Todd, *Martin Luther* (Westminster, Md.: Newman, 1965), 188.

34. Bainton, *Here I Stand,* 261.

35. Rheinhold Seeberg, *Text-Book of the History of Doctrines,* trans. Charles E. Hay (Grand Rapids, Mich.: Baker Book House, 1952), 2:290. Latin text from *D. Martin Luthers Werke,* Kritische Gesamtausgabe (Weimar: Böhlaus, 1966), 2:279: "Nec potest fidelis Christianus cogi ultra sacram scripturam, que est proprie ius divinum, misi accesserit nova et probata revelatio: immo ex iure divino prohibemur credere nisi quod sit probatum vel per scripturam divinam vel per manifestam revelationem" (Hora secunda continuata est disputatio eadem 5. die Iulii [in Leipzig], 1519).

36. A. Burt Horsley, "Martin Luther," in *Martin Luther: Two Essays by De Lamar Jensen and A. Burt Horsley* (Provo, Utah: BYU Department of History, 1984), 26–27, emphasis added.

37. William R. Russell, *Luther's Theological Testament: The Schmalkald Articles* (Minneapolis: Fortress, 1995), 61. Russell refers to the discussion

by Edmund Schlink, *Theology of the Lutheran Confessions* (Philadelphia: Fortress, 1961), 62 n. 16.

38. Russell, *Luther's Theological Testament,* 61; see Schlink, *Theology of the Lutheran Confessions,* 62 n. 16.

39. Robert G. Clouse, "Justinian Code," in *The New International Dictionary of the Christian Church,* 558.

40. Quoted in *Martin Luther: Selections from His Writings,* 494.

41. One of the greatest evidences of Luther's closeness to the truth is the inspiration he provided for Johann Sebastian Bach and his eternal music of the celestial spheres, always composed "to the Glory of God."

42. "Through the atonement of Christ and the resurrection and obedience in the Gospel, we shall again be conformed to the image of [God's] Son, Jesus Christ. Then we shall have attained to the image, glory, and character of God." *The Words of Joseph Smith,* comp. and ed. Andrew F. Ehat and Lyndon W. Cook (Provo, Utah: BYU Religious Studies Center, 1980), 231, punctuation altered for readability. Joseph Smith even recognizes the difference between *anthropomorphism* and *theomorphism* in the following thought from his *Lectures on Faith* (Salt Lake City: Deseret Book, 1985), lecture 5:2 (p. 59): "The Son, who was in the bosom of the Father, [is] a personage of tabernacle, made or fashioned like unto man, or being in the form and likeness of man, or *rather man was formed after his likeness and in his image*" (emphasis added). Obviously, this modern revelation confirms that the Anthropomorphist-Origenist controversy was misdirected; see note 4, above.

43. *History of the Church,* 2:17.

44. Bainton, *Here I Stand,* 332.

45. Origen, *Against Celsus* 6.60 (*ANF* 4:601, emphasis added).

46. Smith, *Lectures on Faith,* 59.

47. *Words of Joseph Smith,* 72.

48. *Teachings of the Prophet Joseph Smith,* 342–62; see Joseph Smith, "Sermon Delivered April 7, 1844," in *American Sermons: The Pilgrims to Martin Luther King Jr.,* selected by Michael Warner (New York: Library of America, 1999), 584–99.

49. *Teachings of the Prophet Joseph Smith,* 369–76.

50. Third Article on Sanctification, in *Dr. Martin Luther's Small Catechism* (St. Louis: Concordia, 1943), 11.

CHAPTER 8

SIN, SUFFERING, AND SOUL-MAKING: JOSEPH SMITH ON THE PROBLEM OF EVIL

David L. Paulsen and Blake Thomas Ostler

Nothing tests our trust in God or challenges the rationality of our belief in him more severely than human suffering and wickedness. Both are pervasive in our common experience. At the moment, the mention of the World Trade Center and Afghanistan evokes images of unspeakable human cruelty or grief, and Auschwitz and Belsen still haunt our memories. Truman Madsen has powerfully portrayed the unfathomable depth of human pain and anguish in his descriptions of persons seeking to maintain their faith in the face of seemingly horrendous evils:

As a beginning, let us walk into a hospital:

Here. This newborn infant with the lovely face. She could not have worthier parents. But she was born in total paralysis and is blind. The doctors do not know if she will survive. And if she does . . .

This bed is empty. Its occupant, a quivering psychotic with a wild stare, is upstairs undergoing shock treatment. He collapsed when his wife and two children were maimed in a fire, one beyond recognition.

Over here is a surgeon who had a rare brain disease and asked his closest friend to operate. The operation failed; and he has been, for nearly three years, a human vegetable. His friend has since committed suicide.

Somewhere tonight the families of these souls are crying themselves to sleep.

Now, if your arm will hold out, write as many zeros after a "1" as will portray similar reenactments of these scenes that are, or have been, or may be, on this planet. And that will be one thread in the tapestry of human misery.[1]

This, then, is the challenge: our moral sensibilities are so outraged by such evils that we may begin to question whether our world is really the product of an all-powerful, all-knowing, and morally perfect Creator. We are at a loss to see how a perfect God could have any morally sufficient reason for permitting such evils to occur. Of course, our perplexity is not merely conceptual, nor does it involve only the suffering of others. Few of us escape deep anguish, for it is no respecter of persons and arises out of our experiences of incurable or debilitating diseases, mental illness, broken homes, abuse, rape, wayward loved ones, tragic accidents, untimely death—the list goes on. Many of us are constrained to cry out from the depths of our souls: "Why, God? Why?" And many of us have prayed, often on behalf of a loved one, "Please, God, please help," and then wondered why all that we seem to hear is a deafening silence. All of us have struggled, or likely will struggle, in a very personal way with the problem of evil.

We say *the* problem of evil, but actually there are several.[2] We will consider here just three: the logical problem, the soteriological problem, and the existential problem. The logical problem of evil is the apparent contradiction between the world's evil and an all-powerful and all-loving Creator. The soteriological problem of evil is the apparent inconsistency between an all-loving Heavenly Father and particular Christian doctrines as to the means and scope of salvation. The existential problem of evil is the personal challenge of living trustingly and faithfully in the face of what seems to be overwhelming evil.

As Truman Madsen has long and well pointed out to us, Joseph Smith provided revealed insights that help us comprehend and cope with human sin and suffering. In this essay we draw on Truman's interpretive presentations of these insights in addressing these problems of evil. Truman first explored the bearing of Joseph Smith's revelations on the problem of evil in *Eternal Man*[3] and *Four Essays on Love*,[4] a project to which, as evidenced by the references to his work in this essay, he often returned.

The Logical Problem of Evil

Soaked as it is with human suffering and moral evil, how is it *possible* that the world is the work of an almighty, perfectly loving Creator? So stated, the logical problem of evil poses a puzzle of deep complexity. But the conundrum evoked by our reflection on this question appears to be more than just a paradox: we seem to stare contradiction right in the face. The ancient philosopher Epicurus framed the contradiction in the form of a logical dilemma: Either God is unwilling to prevent evil, or he is unable. If he is unwilling, then he cannot be perfectly good; if he is unable, then he cannot be all-powerful. Whence, then, evil? And eighteenth-century skeptic David Hume expressed the contradiction in much the same way:

> Why is there any misery at all in the world? Not by chance, surely. From some cause then. Is it from the intention of the deity? But he is perfectly benevolent. Is it contrary to his intention? But he is almighty. Nothing can shake the solidity of this reasoning. So short, so clear, so decisive.[5]

Hume's succinct statement has since provided the framework within which the logical problem of evil is discussed. However, we believe Hume's way of formulating the problem is far too narrow and therefore unjust to both challenger and defender of belief in God—especially to the Christian defender. We do not believe that for the challenger intent on disproving God's existence, the problem has been stated in its starkest terms. For in addition to affirming that God is (1) perfectly good and (2) all-powerful, traditional Christian theologians commonly affirm two additional propositions that exacerbate the problem: (3) God created all things absolutely—that is, out of nothing; and (4) God has absolute foreknowledge of all the outcomes of his creative choices. While apologists for belief in God have labored long to reconcile the world's evil with God's goodness and power, they have often overlooked the much more difficult task of reconciling evil, not only with his goodness and power, but with his absolute creation and absolute foreknowledge as well. Twentieth-century English philosopher Antony Flew takes these additional premises into account by arguing that any such reconciliation is impossible. It is perfectly proper in the face of apparently pointless evil, he says, to look first for some *saving* explanation that will show that, in spite of appearances, a loving God really exists. But Flew claims that believers have assigned God attributes that block a saving explanation altogether:

> We cannot say that [God] would like to help but cannot: God is omnipotent. We cannot say that he would help if he only knew: God is omniscient. We cannot say that he is not responsible for the wickedness of others: God creates those others. Indeed an omnipotent, omniscient God must be an accessory before (and during) the fact to every human misdeed; as well as being responsible for every non-moral defect in the universe.[6]

We can formulate Flew's version of the logical problem of evil as follows:

1. God exists; is morally perfect, omnipotent, and omniscient; and created all things absolutely.

2. Evils occur.

3. A morally perfect being prevents all the evils it can.

4. An omnipotent, omniscient, absolute creator can prevent all evils.

5. Hence, all evils are prevented. (1, 3, and 4)
6. Therefore, evils occur, and all evils are prevented. (2 and 5)

By means of this argument, Flew attempts to reduce traditional assumptions about the nature of God to a logical contradiction. Or, to state the argument less formally, if God creates all things (including finite agents) absolutely (that is, out of nothing), knowing beforehand all the actual future consequences of his creative choices, then he is an accessory before the fact and ultimately responsible for every moral and nonmoral defect in the universe. And if, as some believers allege, some human agents will suffer endlessly in hell, God is also at least jointly responsible for these horrendous outcomes. But if so, how can he possibly be perfectly loving? Given the traditional understanding of God, whatever our consistency-saving strategies, in the end (we believe) we must candidly confess that they are not very convincing.

On the other hand, this exclusive focus on reconciling evil with *just* a set of divine attributes is unfair to those of us who are Christian. For it fails to acknowledge the incarnation of God the Son in the person of Jesus of Nazareth and his triumph over suffering, sin, and death through his atonement and resurrection. Any Christian account of the problem of evil that fails to consider this—Christ's mission to overcome the evil we experience—will be but a pale abstraction of what it could and should be. We propose, then, to consider the problem of evil from this broader perspective, confronting it in terms not only of its starkest statement, but also of its strongest possible solution: a worldview centered in the redemptive work of Jesus Christ.

Christ revealed insights to Joseph Smith that *do* address the problems of evil in their broadest terms. These revelations suggest what we call a soul-making theodicy[7] centered within a distinctively Christian soteriology (or doctrine of salvation) but framed within a theology that rejects both absolute creation and, consequently, the philosophical definition of divine omnipotence, which affirms that there are no (or no nonlogical) limits to what God can do. These revelations also disclose the Lord's loving response to the question of the fate of the unevangelized: the redemption of the dead. The worldview framed by these revelations dissolves the logical and soteriological problems of evil while infusing with meaning and hope our personal struggles with suffering, sin, and death. To show that this is so is our purpose in this essay. As background for both understanding and appreciating the value of these revealed insights on the problems of evil, it will be useful to sketch some of the traditional Christian attempts to deal with the issues.

The Deterministic Tradition

The problem of evil is especially acute for those traditions which maintain that all things that occur are the effect of God's all-determining causal activity. Such prominent theological luminaries as Calvin,[8] Luther,[9] Augustine (on the dominant interpretation),[10] and Thomas Aquinas (on the majority interpretation)[11] all held that God predestines and causally determines all events that occur from the moment of creation. Truman Madsen explains,

> Augustine begins with a premise that God is all-powerful. To him that means all things, all else beside God, including space, time and the souls of men, were created by God from nothing. The puzzle arises as to why a being of unlimited power should have chosen to create such a universe as this: of pain, torment, and (on some views) endless damnation. Specifically, evil and the devil were among the realities God chose to create. Why, being good, could He—would He—do such a thing?[12]

Indeed, it can be further stated that since according to these views, God creates the universe out of nothing and determines every event that will occur in each moment of the world's existence,[13] he thus intends and causes all murders, rapes, abuses, diseases, cancers, earthquakes, death, pain, and so forth. These traditions make God at least the ultimate author, if not the proximate cause, of all evils.

In reply to these objections, defenders have argued that even though such events appear to be evil, God has a morally sufficient reason for causing each of them. A perfectly good being should not prevent all evils, for some evils may be instrumental in bringing about a greater good—a state of affairs whose value more than offsets the disvalue of the evil that gives rise to it. For example, a doctor may morally inflict the pain of a shot or even the amputation of a limb if the benefits will outweigh the cost. Thus a morally perfect being does not necessarily prevent all evil; rather, he maximizes the good, permitting those evils that bring about a greater good. So premise 3 of Flew's argument must be amended to take account of this insight. So revised, it might read as follows:

3'. A morally perfect being prevents all the evils it can without thereby preventing some greater good or causing some greater evil.

But the objector may persist: If God must allow evil to maximize the good, how can he be omnipotent? Surely, if God were omnipotent he could bring about all good without having to use evil as an instrument. Only if his power were limited in some way would he be so constrained.

To this, defenders of the traditional view might reply: To affirm that God is omnipotent does not mean that he can do absolutely anything. Rather, God can do anything that is logically possible—that is, he can do anything that has a self-consistent description. But not even an omnipotent being can create a perfectly round square or a four-sided triangle. So premise 4 of Flew's argument must also be modified. What the proponent of the traditional view really affirms is not 4, but rather

4'. An omnipotent, omniscient creator can do anything that is logically possible.

Given these amendments to premises 3 and 4 of Flew's argument, it would now read:

1. God exists; is morally perfect, omnipotent, and omniscient; and created all things absolutely.

2. Evils occur.

3'. A morally perfect being prevents all the evils it can without thereby preventing some greater good or causing some greater evil.

4'. An omnipotent, omniscient creator can do anything that is logically possible.

5. Hence, all evils are prevented.

But with premises 3 and 4 replaced with 3' and 4', 5 no longer follows as a matter of logic. What does follow is:

5'. Whatever evils occur are logically necessary to bring about a greater good or to prevent a greater evil.

Hence, 5' and 2 are no longer mutually contradictory.

True, our objector might answer, but one can easily resurrect the contradiction by plausibly revising premise 2 as follows:

2'. Evils occur that are not logically necessary to bring about a greater good or to prevent a greater evil.

When we replace premise 2 in the argument with premise 2', we can deduce:

6'. Therefore, evils occur that are not logically necessary to bring about a greater good or to prevent a greater evil; and all evils are logically necessary to bring about some greater good or to prevent a greater evil. (2' and 5')

So 6' is again a contradiction. The issue then becomes: Is premise 2' true? Do evils occur that are not logically necessary to bring about a greater good or to prevent a greater evil, given that God is all-controlling and determining?

In answering this question, it is important to clarify what is meant when one asserts that some state of affairs, *x*, is *logically* necessary for some different state of affairs, *y*. First, it does *not* suffice to show that x is *necessary* for y by showing that x is a *cause* of y since there may be alternative ways to bring about y. The claim that "x is logically necessary for y" entails that the state of affairs consisting of y without x is impossible. And this means not just biologically, physically, causally, or even ontologically impossible—an all-determining, absolute Creator who can do anything that is logically possible is not constrained by even the most basic structures of the world. He could have made those structures other than they are. Rather, the claim that "x is logically necessary for y" entails that the state of affairs consisting of "y and not x" is *logically* impossible—that is, it is self-contradictory.

Is it really the case that every evil that occurs in the world is such that, without it, God's achieving his good ends is self-contradictory? On pain of inconsistency, defenders of the view of God and creation presently under fire must answer affirmatively, but how this can be the case is totally incomprehensible. Can it really be believed in the integrity of one's heart that the dehumanizing abuse of a little girl is logically necessary for some greater good? If so, what greater good? And why *logically* necessary? Those who accept such a divinely deterministic view assert that, in some way incomprehensible to human reason, *every* instance of evil—the Holocaust, the attack on the World Trade Center, the brutal repression of women by the Taliban, the horrific acts of serial killers—is *logically* necessary for some greater good. However, in the end they must take refuge in sheer mystery, for one cannot even begin to fathom how this can be the case. Even if it were possible that such horrendous evils are logically necessitated by God's good purposes, such a claim fails to foster trust in God. As Peter Appleby claims: "If [God's] goodness is radically different from human goodness, there is little reason for calling it goodness at all, and still less for praising and glorifying it, as faith is wont to do. The child who is totally ignorant of his parents' values has no reason for admiring them, and still less for trying to emulate them."[14] If the purpose of a revealed religion is to assist mortals in comprehending their relationship to God and the meaning of their experience in the world that surrounds them, then the least satisfying theology is one that takes refuge in the claim that God's ways are totally beyond human understanding.

The Free-Will Defense

Some headway toward resolving the logical problem of evil is made when one gives up the notion that God is all-determining and all-controlling and affirms rather that God has endowed his human creatures with "free will," or a power of self-determination. Proponents of this position often claim that the intrinsic and instrumental value of human free will more than offsets any disvalue arising out of its misuse. This attempt to exculpate God from responsibility for the world's evils by tracing them instead to the bad choices of human beings is typically called "the free-will defense."[15] Some philosophers have claimed that the free-will defense, especially as that defense has been formulated by Alvin Plantinga,[16] solves the logical problem of evil. Let us look briefly at Plantinga's presentation of this defense.

It must be noted that Plantinga does not attempt to provide a theodicy, or a believable explanation of God's allowing evil to exist. More modestly, he argues only that the proposition that evil exists cannot be shown to contradict the proposition that God exists. He formulates his own version of free-will defense in response to J. L. Mackie's argument that it is logically possible for an omnipotent being to create a world containing free creatures who never choose wrongly. If there is no logical impossibility in a person's choosing the good on one occasion, Mackie argues, then there is no logical impossibility in a person's choosing the good on every occasion. Indeed, Mackie points out, Christians themselves believe that Jesus, though tempted and free to sin, remained spotless throughout life. Thus it is a logically possible state of affairs that all persons choose rightly on all occasions. So, Mackie continues, if God can, as traditional theists maintain, bring about any logically possible state of affairs, then he can bring about the state of affairs of all persons always freely choosing the good. Moreover, if God is perfectly good, that is certainly what God would have done.[17] Thus the fact that our world is permeated with evil logically precludes its being God's creation.

Now, it must be recognized that Mackie's argument is sound and seemingly decisive against those in the deterministic tradition who maintain that human freedom is compatible with causal determinism, like Augustine, Calvin, and possibly Aquinas.[18] Plantinga bases his defense on a stronger version of freedom known as "contra-causal" freedom—a mode of freedom not compatible with causal determinism. Thus Plantinga's defense assumes that human beings are endowed with contra-causal freedom and their actions are not controllable by God. It is not, therefore, logically consistent that God could create such persons and also *bring it about* that they *freely* choose the good, for that would amount to God causing their actions. The fact, then, that it is logically possible for a person to always freely choose the right does not entail that God could create such a person absolutely. It is logically impossible for God to *cause* someone to always *freely* (that is, without being caused to) choose the right.[19] Plantinga tries to stretch his free-will defense even further so that it also covers what is typically referred to as "natural evil." Natural evil is the human and animal pain and suffering that seemingly arise out of the operations of the laws of nature, such as disease, earthquakes, tornadoes, and volcanic eruptions. Plantinga urges that it is logically possible that even these evils are the outcome of the malevolent free choices of nonhuman spiritual agents. Hence, it is logically possible that all evil is consistent with the existence of God. And if so, Plantinga claims, the logical problem of evil is resolved.

However, we are far from convinced that Plantinga has adequately resolved the logical problem of evil. For example, merely showing that the claim that God exists is consistent with the observation that evils occur is not enough if the notion of God employed in the defense is divorced from the full conception of God accepted by believers. As already pointed out, in addition to affirming that God is (1) all-powerful and (2) perfectly good, traditional Christian theologians also affirm that God (3) created all things out of nothing and (4) has absolute foreknowledge of all the outcomes of his creative choices.[20]

Given this view of God, even if God endows his human creatures with contra-causal freedom, he still remains an accessory before the fact and is ultimately at least jointly responsible for everything that happens in the world, including the evil choices of those creatures. Additionally, God is responsible for every evil inasmuch as he knowingly chose to bring them all into existence when he created the world *ex nihilo*. Furthermore, God could have made a better world. For instance, he might have created a world with persons who are morally more sensitive than we are, or brighter and better able to prevent abuses and natural disasters. These qualities would certainly not reduce our free will.

In addition, it seems that a deep metaphysical dilemma exists in Plantinga's free-will defense. Plantinga essentially re-created Luis de Molina's notion of God's "middle knowledge," whereby God's knowledge includes not merely knowledge of what *will* in fact happen but also what *would* happen if creatures were placed in any specific circumstances.[21] According to Plantinga (and de Molina), before the creation out of nothing, God surveyed all the possible worlds that were within his power to create and he "saw" the *individual essences* of every person who could be created in those worlds. He also knew the truth value of all the propositions describing what those persons would do if created, including their free actions. (These propositions are known as "counterfactuals of freedom.") To his horror, argues Plantinga, it is just possible that God discovered that every individual essence would suffer from *transworld depravity*, because each individual would commit some evil action(s) in every world God could possibly create. Thus not even God could have created, for example, Zeno without instantiating (bringing about) in his creation of possible worlds those distinguishing properties essential to him, defining him uniquely as Zeno in every possible world. According to Plantinga, it is possible that the property of transworld depravity could be a part of every creaturely essence.

The problems in Plantinga's defense arise from the ontology of persons it assumes, for this ontology is not consistent with creation *ex nihilo*. Plantinga assumes that contingent realities (those that are not logically necessary) condition God's power even prior to the creation. However, for Plantinga, these contingencies are not actual intelligences or spirits who have existed from all eternity and were not created by God; rather, they are merely "individual essences" of *possible* persons who come to exist only if God chooses to create them. But we must ask how there could be any such limitations on God prior to his creative act. What could determine what a free creature will do? Certainly not God, for then the person would not be free. Nor could the circumstances in which the possible person is created determine his actions; if it were otherwise, the person would not be free in a contra-causal sense. Neither could the possible person herself determine what she would do because the merely possible does not exist and therefore cannot determine anything.[22] How could there be any truth value for propositions about a merely potential person whom God chose not to create? The notion that there is a foreknown truth about what possible free persons would do seems unintelligible.

Further, Plantinga's defense has a difficult time showing how natural evils are consistent with the existence of God. Plantinga argues that it is logically possible that so-called natural evils could actually be brought about by evil spirits who have free will. And indeed, it *is* logically possible—that is, if creation of such spirits with such powers is consistent with God's goodness in the first place. However, Plantinga has not shown (or even attempted to show) that God could have a morally sufficient reason for granting evil spirits such powers, especially when he knows beforehand that they will exercise them to bring about horrendous evils. The attempt to pass off the blame for natural evils to evil spirits does not relieve God of ultimate responsibility for natural evils. As Stephen T. Davis observes in his attempt to elucidate and defend Plantinga's free-will defense:

> Obviously, whether one speaks of the devil or not, it is *God* who is ultimately responsible for natural evil. He created the world in which natural evil occurs and, although God has the power to prevent natural evil (whether proximately caused by the devil or not), does not do so.[23]

Likewise, the story that evil spirits cause natural evils would not exonerate God from responsibility because God is responsible for creating these spirits in the first place. In order to grant evil spirits their own free will, God need not provide them with special powers enabling them to manipulate natural causes. For, on Plantinga's view, he also created us free but did not endow us with such powers. If God created these evil spirits out of nothing, knowing beforehand all the actual consequences of his creative choices, then he remains an accessory before the fact and ultimately responsible for every evil such agents bring about. The claim that it is possible that a world including evil spirits with such immense power granted to them is the best world an absolute creator can produce seems dubious indeed. It seems that rather than providing a defense, Plantinga succeeds only in creating an analytic scenario of God's culpability for natural evils.

Finally, Plantinga's defense, even if logically coherent, is wildly implausible. Few have seriously suggested that evil spirits actually cause earthquakes, cancer, and other such occurrences. Of course, Plantinga does not purport to provide a defense that is true or even plausible. He is only trying to show that the proposition that

God exists is not logically incompatible with the proposition that evil exists. While his careful analysis has significantly contributed to our understanding of the strictly logical problem of evil, it is wholly inadequate to resolve the problem of evil that actually confronts believers. A response concerned only with logic does little to vindicate trust in God in a world racked with horrendous evils. Plantinga assumes that faith is not challenged as long as God's existence is not shown to be logically incompatible with the existence of evil. But this assumption is false. His consistency defense is simply not satisfying to persons seeking to find meaning in the face of what seems to be overwhelming evil.

John Hick's Theodicy

Unlike a defense that merely attempts to show that God and evil are not necessarily incompatible, a theodicy is an attempt to actually reconcile God's goodness with the evils that occur in the world, thus affording the sufferer hope and comfort in the midst of trials. Contemporary philosopher of religion John Hick has developed a complete theodicy in his fine book *Evil and the God of Love*, which is widely recognized as a watershed work on the problem of evil.

Hick constructs a "soul-making" theodicy that resembles Joseph Smith's revelations in many respects. Setting out this theodicy, comparing and contrasting it with Joseph's revelations, and then assessing its strengths and weaknesses will enable a better understanding and appreciation of the bearing of Joseph's insights on a solution to the logical problem of evil.

Hick rejects the Augustinian position that Adam and Eve were originally created as perfect beings and then inexplicably chose evil. Instead, he constructs an "Irenaean theodicy" that harks back to Irenaeus, bishop of Lyon (ca. A.D. 220). Both Hick and Joseph Smith affirm that God's fundamental purpose in creating mortals and this world environment was twofold: first, to enable them, as morally and spiritually immature agents created in God's image, to develop into God's likeness through a process of deification, or *apotheosis*,[24] and second, to enable them to enter into an authentic (that is, free and uncompelled) relationship of love and fellowship with him. Hick argues that persons could not be created in this relationship as beings who were already spiritually perfect, for such a relationship would not be authentic: it would be coerced and contrived by God unilaterally. Rather, a genuine relationship must be freely chosen. To achieve these ends, it was necessary for God to endow human beings with the power of self-determination (or, as Hick calls it, incompatibilist freedom) and to preserve that freedom by placing them at an epistemic distance from himself. God effects this distancing, Hick suggests, by having humankind emerge out of a naturalistic evolutionary process as a race of largely self-centered, spiritually immature creatures. We begin our existence, according to Hick, as creatures who can at length be made into the image of God.

Like John Hick, Joseph Smith maintains that human beings begin as spiritually immature individuals in a state of innocence but that they are capable of spiritual growth through life experiences.[25] He also asserts that an epistemic distance is essential to spiritual growth; however, in Joseph Smith's view this distance is achieved through God's veiling of each individual's memory of him in the premortal existence so that all could exercise faith. Furthermore, like Hick, the Prophet also maintains that God gave mortals freedom to act for themselves and not merely to be acted upon (see 2 Nephi 2:26–27). The world is divided into "both things to act and things to be acted upon" (2 Nephi 2:14). Additionally, God gave mortals agency "to act for" themselves by placing them in an environment of "opposition in all things" so that they might know the sweet by tasting the bitter, know joy by experiencing misery, and know good because they must face evil (see 2 Nephi 2:16, 23). Hick says God also endowed us with a rudimentary awareness of him and some tendency toward moral self-transcendence. The

Prophet identifies this awareness or predisposition as the Light of Christ, or the Spirit, that "giveth light to every man that cometh into the world" (D&C 84:46). Soul-making—that is, spiritual development into the likeness of God—occurs as mortal beings overcome self-centeredness by making moral choices within an environment fraught with hardship, pain, suffering, and genuine risk.

To this point, the worldviews of John Hick and Joseph Smith are strikingly similar. However, they diverge on the mode of God's creation. Joseph denies creation *ex nihilo,* whereas Hick affirms it. Thus Hick affirms all four theological postulates—perfect goodness, absolute power, absolute foreknowledge, and absolute creation—which confront him head-on with Flew's divine complicity argument. To his credit, Hick expressly acknowledges the logical consequences of his position: God is ultimately responsible for *all* the evil that occurs in the world. Hick explains why this is so:

> One whose action, A, is the primary and necessary precondition for a certain occurrence, O, all other direct conditions for O being contingent upon A, may be said to be responsible for O, if he performs A in awareness of its relation to O and if he is also aware that, given A, the subordinate conditions will be fulfilled.... [God's] decision to create the existing universe was the primary and necessary precondition for the occurrence of evil, all other conditions being contingent upon this, and He took His decision in awareness of all that would flow from it.[26]

While acknowledging, given his theological assumptions, that God is ultimately responsible for all the evils that occur in the world, Hick believes that he can still consistently maintain that God is perfectly loving. Unlike those who affirm divine causation of all events, Hick need not show that *every* evil is logically necessary for a greater good. Rather, Hick need only show that evil is an inevitable consequence of the type of world necessary for God's purpose of bringing humankind to his likeness and into loving fellowship with him. To explain how God's love is possible, Hick affirms a doctrine of universal salvation. In Hick's view, all human beings will finally achieve an authentic relationship with God in a postmortal life, the value of which will far outweigh any finite evil suffered here. He explains:

> We must thus affirm in faith that there will in the final accounting be no personal life that is unperfected and no suffering that has not eventually become a phase in the fulfillment of God's good purpose. Only so, I suggest, is it possible to believe both in the perfect goodness of God and in His unlimited capacity to perform His will. For if there are finally wasted lives and finally unredeemed sufferings, either God is not perfect in love or He is not sovereign in rule over His creation.[27]

Though we find Hick's reasoning compelling and appealing, its scriptural warrant is questionable, and it gives rise to conceptual difficulties of its own. We will consider just four.

1. Though, in Hick's view, God endows humankind with a strong power of self-determination, it does not follow from his view that choices are made in a vacuum. They are always choices of particular persons with a particular nature. Recall that Hick describes mortal beings' primordial nature as being largely self-centered, with a rudimentary awareness of God and some tendency toward morality or self-transcendence. Since in Hick's account God creates these primordial tendencies in human nature, there is no reason why God could not have made human beings significantly more virtuous than they are. Why not, for example, give them some significant reduction in their sometimes overwhelming tendencies toward selfishness that lead to violence, rape, stealing, and other such behaviors? Why could God not have increased their natural aversion to violence? Why could he not have made them more morally sensitive or more intelligent and compassionate so as to see the consequences of their actions on others? Such

creative choices on God's part might have narrowed the options over which mortals' own choices might range, but such limitations are entirely compatible with a strong notion of self-determinative freedom and with God's soul-making objectives. Hick's absolute creator could have made a much better world than this without forfeiting the goals of bringing its human inhabitants freely into his image and fellowship. Indeed, such changes would decrease the evil, suffering, and struggle involved with realizing these goals.

2. On the other hand, it could not possibly be certain (as Hick claims) that God will *inevitably* lure every finite creature into a loving relationship with himself, given that mortal beings in Hick's view must have incompatibilist freedom to enter into such a relationship. One cannot be certain that there will not be, as C. S. Lewis suggests, "rebels to the end," with "doors of hell . . . locked on the *inside*."[28] This possibility cannot be precluded. Hick suggests that although, theoretically, God cannot guarantee that everyone will finally be saved, as a practical matter universal salvation may be affirmed because

> God has formed the free human person with a nature that can find its perfect fulfillment and happiness only in active enjoyment of the infinite goodness of the Creator. He is not, then, trying to force or entice His creatures against the grain of their nature, but to render them free to follow their own deepest desire, which can lead them only to Himself. For He has made them for Himself, and their hearts are restless until they find their rest in Him.[29]

But now Hick is waffling, for it appears that humans are not free after all: in his view, their natures compel them to God. Hick's position is inconsistent. To account for moral evil, he asserts that God gives mortals incompatibilist freedom and genuine independence to choose for themselves. But given Hick's affirmation of absolute creation and absolute foreknowledge, God's perfect goodness is possible only if not one soul is lost. To salvage God's goodness, Hick is forced to accept some mode of determinism that undermines his free-will defense.

3. Hick suggests a reason why God cannot simply create morally virtuous creatures. Virtue that God grants from the beginning is less valuable than virtue that is hard-won through real-life experience and the overcoming of temptations. A value-judgment underlies Hick's argument that God is justified in creating humankind less than perfectly virtuous, because "One who has attained to goodness by meeting and eventually mastering temptations, and thus by rightly making responsible choices in concrete situations, is good in a richer and more valuable sense than would be one created *ab initio* [from the beginning] in a state either of innocence or of virtue."[30] However, Hick's justification for creating a less than perfectly virtuous human nature is not consistent with the notion of God's perfect goodness which he seeks to defend. If tried moral virtue is somehow of greater value than untried moral virtue (and we agree with Hick that it is), then mortals who progress in moral virtue by rightly making virtuous decisions in concrete situations and in the face of genuine temptation possess a virtue greater than the absolute God who possesses such virtue necessarily. In other words, according to Hick's conception of deity, God did not overcome the obstacles and temptations required to attain the richest and most valuable type of virtue. Indeed, if Frederick R. Tennant is correct that the very notion of "good" has meaning only in the context of genuine temptation and trials, then calling God "good" is contradictory.[31] To maintain consistency, Hick needs to concede either that untried virtue can be as valuable as virtue tried in the crucible of human experience or, as Joseph Smith suggested, that God underwent such a crucible as a means of attaining his virtue.[32]

4. Both John Hick and Joseph Smith agree that the ultimate purpose for creating this mortal world is to bring human beings to God's likeness through the crucible of its refining fire; for over-

coming temptation and the experience of suffering assist in per-
fecting them.[33] Mortals are works in progress aimed ultimately
toward deification. According to one tradition, especially strong
in the Christian East, persons will be made divine. As Irenaeus
himself stated: "Our Lord Jesus Christ . . . did, through His transcendent love, become what we are, that He might bring us to be
even what He is Himself."[34] Irenaeus did not hesitate to say that
the goal was that humankind may be gods: "We have not been
made gods from the beginning, but at first merely men, then at
length gods."[35] The goal of deification is a very great good indeed,
for there is no imaginable greater good. The tradition that it was
possible to achieve such a goal was dominant in the early church.
As A. N. Williams explains:

> What is human destiny? To become God. That, at least, was the
> belief of the earliest Christians. Such an understanding is evi-
> dent in the letters of St. Paul (Rom. 8:11; 1 Cor. 15:49; and 2 Cor.
> 8:9) and the first Christians found it in the pages of the Hebrew
> Bible (Ps. 82:6, quoted in John 10:34). Above all, the nascent
> theological tradition pointed to 2 Peter 1:4: "Thus has he given
> us, through these things, his precious and very great promises,
> so that through them you may escape from corruption that is
> in the world because of him, and may become participants in
> divine nature." As the tradition reflected on these texts, deifica-
> tion became the dominant model of salvation and sanctification
> in the patristic period, from Ignatius of Antioch to John Da-
> mascene, in the West (in the writings of Tertullian and Augus-
> tine) as well as in the East. [36]

Yet neither Hick nor the earliest theologians of the tradition
can consistently assert that mortal beings shall be as God is, or
that they shall truly be gods. The problem is the doctrine of absolute creation from nothing. Given this doctrine, there is an infinite ontological gulf between God's mode of existence and ours.
God necessarily exists; he cannot *not* exist. However, persons are
created and have merely contingent existence. Not even God, in
such a view, can create persons with the potential to be what they

are, for by definition not even God can create an uncreated being. Hick realizes this and asserts merely that they shall be a "finite likeness" of God. But what is a created "finite likeness" of the infinite Uncreated Creator? The very idea expresses a vast and infinite difference that can never be bridged. In the end, the notion that humans may be as God must be seen as a conceptual contradiction within a tradition that maintains creation out of nothing. That, of course, is why so many in the tradition reject Joseph Smith's revelation that as God is, mortals may become.

Though we find John Hick's theodicy grounded in his doctrine of universal salvation most appealing, it, nonetheless, as outlined above, engenders a complex of conceptual difficulties. This brings us to consideration of Joseph Smith's revelations and their bearing on a solution to the problems of evil.

Joseph Smith's Way Out

Joseph Smith's way out of the logical problem of evil is to avoid going in. He remains outside this by rejecting the fundamental premises that give rise to the problem in the first place, including, prominently, the premise of creation out of nothing. Truman Madsen describes Joseph Smith's view of God this way: "He is not the *total* cause of anything. . . . God is forever surrounded by us, by co-eternal intelligences, and by the self-existent elements and principles of reality. . . . In His relationship to us, 'all things are possible' that are possible. But some things are impossible."[37] In contrast to the absolute creator of traditional theology, Joseph Smith affirmed that God is related to and hence conditioned by an eternal environment that, because it is not totally his creation, is not absolutely subject to divine fiat. The importance of this fundamental departure from traditional theology can hardly be overstated. The Prophet taught that God is a dynamic being involved in progression and process of time who intervenes to bring order out of chaos. God did not bring into being the ultimate constituents of the cosmos nor the space-time matrix that defines it. Hence, unlike the Necessary Being of classical theology who alone could not *not* exist and on whom all else is dependent for existence, the God of Latter-day Saint doctrine confronts realities that exist of metaphysical necessity independently of his own creative activity. Such realities include inherently self-directing beings (Joseph Smith called them "intelligences" or "premortal spirits"), primordial elements (matter or possibly mass-energy), the lawlike structures of reality, and eternal moral principles grounded in the intrinsic value of selves and the eternal requirements for their growth. With respect to creation, Joseph stated:

> You ask the learned doctors why they say the world was made out of nothing; and they will answer, "Doesn't the Bible say He *created* the world?" And they infer, from the word create, that it must have been out of nothing. Now, the word create came from the [Hebrew] word *baurau* which does not mean to create out of nothing; it means ... to organize the world out of chaos—chaotic matter. . . . Elements had an existence from the time [God] had. The pure principles of element are principles which can never be destroyed; they may be organized and re-organized, but not destroyed. They had no beginning, and can have no end.[38]

Joseph Smith also taught that persons were not created. Thus God did not survey all the possible persons he could create and then pick and choose those he wanted. Rather, he found himself in the midst of intelligences. His task was not to create beings out of nothing but to provide a plan for their growth if they were willing to confront the risk inherent in such an undertaking. As Joseph Smith explained: "We say that God himself is a self-existent being. . . . [But] who told you that man did not exist in like manner upon the same principles? Man does exist upon the same principles. . . . The mind or the intelligence which man possesses is co-equal [co-eternal] with God himself."[39]

The first principles of humankind are self-existent with God. God himself, finding that he was in the midst of spirits and glory, because he was more intelligent, saw proper to institute laws whereby the rest could have the privilege of advancing like himself. The relationship mortal beings have with God places them in a situation to advance in knowledge. He has power to institute laws to instruct the weaker intelligences that they may be exalted with himself, so that they may have one glory upon another and all that knowledge, power, and intelligence that are requisite in order to save them in the world of spirits.[40]

Indeed, these intelligences had freedom and will. Truman Madsen explains what this means in terms of God's ability to influence events in the universe:

> Actually, as soon as it is recognized, as in modern revelation it is, that there is more than one eternal will in the universe— indeed, an infinity of such wills or autonomous intelligences— we have cut the thread that supposes God can "do anything." In all-important ways even He, the greatest of all, can only do with us what we will permit Him to do.[41]

Of critical importance in Joseph Smith's view is the realization that human beings were not thrust into this existence without their consent. Truman Madsen also spells out this aspect of Joseph's worldview,

> Again, you assume that God alone accounts for your being here. . . . Instead, you and the child of your bosom counseled intimately with God the Father. Freely, fully, and with courage . . . you elected and prepared for this estate. The contrasts of the flesh, its risks, its terrific trials were known to you.[42]

According to Joseph Smith, God had a plan to facilitate growth by allowing individuals to exercise their agency in the presence of genuine danger, where they would not be coerced to choose righteousness or form relationships with God. There was no guarantee that they would return to God's fellowship and gain the goal of eternal life, or godlike existence, if they rejected God in this life. In Joseph's view, Satan also had a plan to coerce all persons to choose God and thus take all the risk out of mortality. Prior to this earthly existence, all were given a concrete choice regarding whether to confront this existence with its inherent risk as a means to grow into God's likeness, or to not confront the risk and be "damned," or stopped, in our progression toward incommensurate joy in the godlike existence of eternal life. All who confront the evils and temptations of this life chose to take on this experience. However, mortal beings were also promised a Savior who could redeem them from evil choices if they freely chose to enter into a relationship with him.[43]

Joseph also taught that each individual agreed that it would be necessary for all recollection of the premortal life to be blocked from consciousness during this mortal life in order to enable each to come freely to God in faith. However, God has created a way to recognize, know, and remember him that will not interfere with agency and exercise of faith. According to Joseph Smith, God enabled human hearts to remember and respond to him at the level of subjective feelings and stirrings in the soul (see D&C 8:2; 9:8). Thus only those who have humble and receptive hearts open to God's loving overtures will be aware of his existence and constant presence. People can choose to shut him out completely if they harden their hearts (see Alma 12:9–13). Consequently, remembering and entering into a relationship with God is a function of choosing to be open to his love.

God's purposes in creating the world, then, were to provide an environment in which mortal beings could learn by experience to grow from grace to grace, enter into a loving relationship with God, and gain the possibility of becoming as God is. Some laws God has instituted exist to facilitate such growth, but, as Joseph Smith taught, there are also "laws of eternal and self-existent principles"[44]—normative structures of some sort, we take it, that constitute things as they eternally are. What are some possible instances of such uncreated laws or principles? The risen Lord taught that "Intelligence, or the light of truth, was not created or made, neither indeed can be. All truth is independent in that sphere in which God has placed it, to act for itself, as all intelligence also; otherwise there is no existence" (D&C 93:29–30). We take this to mean that humans are eternal and inherently free to act for themselves independently of God. This implies as well that human beings are not necessarily equal in intelligence (see Abraham 3:18–21).

These eternal principles have illuminating implications. First, persons are eternally self-determining. If not free to act for themselves, they would lose their essential identity as individuals, for it is through the exercise of agency that individuals express their uniqueness and individuality. Second, the level of one's growth and intelligence is not a product of God's creative choice, but a primordial fact of the universe. Mortal souls cannot complain that God did not make them more virtuous and intelligent, for such factors are essentially up to them; God can only give assistance when it is sought.

Third, eternal principles define the ways in which matter may be organized. While it is more or less clear that there would be only chaos without God's organizing power (see Abraham 4), it is less clear which laws are instituted by God and which are eternal. Nevertheless, it seems that Joseph Smith maintained that matter has inherent tendencies that are eternal. In other words, God could not create matter out of nothing, he could not create matter that is not already extant in space-time, and he could not create the laws that define how matter acts once it is organized. Rather, the natural tendencies of organized matter are based on eternal principles. For example, not even God could organize an atom of oxygen and two atoms of hydrogen without the properties of water emerging from this organization. If God organizes oxygen and hydrogen into a water molecule, it has a natural tendency to freeze at 32 degrees Fahrenheit. Because these natural tendencies of organized matter exist independently of God's creative fiat, the possibility of indiscriminate natural evils is endemic to any creation God could bring about. Indeed, if God creates water, the possibility that persons may drown is also present.

The Book of Mormon prophet Lehi made reference to what we believe are some further eternal principles in his enlightening explanation of evil recorded in 2 Nephi 2 of the Book of Mormon. (In fact, Lehi provides a rather complete theodicy in this chapter.) According to Lehi, "Adam fell that man might be; and men are, that they might have joy" (2 Nephi 2:25). However, to attain this joy, Lehi taught,

> it must needs be, that there is an opposition in all things. If not so, . . . righteousness could not be brought to pass, neither wickedness, neither holiness nor misery, neither good nor bad. . . .
>
> And [so] to bring about his eternal purposes in the end of man, after he had created our first parents . . . , it must needs be that there was an opposition; even the forbidden fruit in opposition to the tree of life; the one being sweet and the other bitter.
>
> Wherefore, the Lord God gave unto man that he should act for himself. Wherefore, man could not act for himself save it should be that he was enticed by the one or the other. . . .
>
> [If Adam and Eve had not fallen] they would have remained in a state of innocence, having no joy, for they knew no misery; doing no good, for they knew no sin. (2 Nephi 2:11, 15–16, 23)

According to Lehi, God's purpose in creation was to provide a way for mortal beings to grow through experiencing opposition and thus to know joy. However, there are apparently states of affairs that even God, though almighty, cannot bring about. Even God could not bring one to joy without moral righteousness, to moral righteousness without moral freedom, or to moral freedom without an opposition in all things.[45] With moral freedom as an essential variable in the divine equation for spiritual growth, two consequences stand out: human beings must face the possibility of genuine moral evil, and they need a Redeemer.

In Joseph Smith's view, obtaining a mortal body is a great good that allows humankind to grow toward God's likeness. If all that one accomplishes in this life is to obtain a body, that in itself fulfills a primary purpose of God's plan.[46] Joseph Smith elaborated:

> Spirits are eternal. At the first organization in heaven we were all present and saw the Savior chosen and appointed, and the plan of salvation made and we sanctioned it. We came to this earth that we might have a body and present it pure before God in the Celestial Kingdom. The great principle of happiness consists in having a body.[47]

This life is not all that there is. Indeed, this life is only a moment in comparison to the eternity for which men and women are here preparing. If there had been no Savior, all would have been lost, and human suffering would be truly unredeemed and meaningless. However, because the Savior has overcome both spiritual and physical death, mortals can be brought back into God's presence and overcome death (see 2 Nephi 9). All will enjoy that degree of joy and divine glory that they are willing to abide, and those willing to keep all God's commandments will be granted the supreme joy of eternal fellowship with him as gods and goddesses (see D&C 76:51–58; 88:20–32).

Given Joseph's theological premises, we must modify the traditional definition of omnipotence. B. H. Roberts plausibly suggests that God's omnipotence be understood as the power to bring about any state of affairs consistent with the natures of eternal existences.[48] If omnipotence is so understood, we can, unlike those who affirm that God has unlimited power, consistently adopt an "instrumentalist" view of evil wherein pain, suffering, and opposition may become the means of moral and spiritual development. God is omnipotent, but he cannot prevent evil without preventing the possibility of greater goods or ends—the value of which more than offsets the disvalue of the evil. In Joseph Smith's theology, we see that these ultimate goods include soul-making, joy, and eternal (godlike) life in a relationship of intimate unity with the Father, Son, and Holy Ghost.

Armed with Joseph Smith's doctrine of entities coeternal with God and our revised definition of omnipotence, let us consider again the logical problem of evil and Antony Flew's argument charging God with complicity in all the world's evils. From Joseph Smith's theological platform, it does not follow that God is the total or even the ultimate explanation of all else. Thus his worldview does not imply that God is an accessory before the fact to all the world's evils. Nor does it follow that God is responsible for every moral and nonmoral defect that occurs in the world. Within the framework of eternal entities and structures that God did not create and cannot destroy, "the [logical] problem of evil . . . [and] a host of traditional paradoxes dissolve."[49]

First, God is neither the total cause of existence nor the author of all events that occur. Agents who are free to act for themselves have a power of self-determination that cannot be caused by God without violating free will. They possess this power of agency eternally. Thus God does not and cannot control the free action of agents—not, at least, without obliterating their identity as individuals. Indeed, perfect love could never sanction destroying a person's agency and, consequently, dissolving that person's identity. Therefore, the problem of an all-determining deity is avoided. Given Joseph Smith's view of eternally free intelligences and the gift of agency as a necessary condition to their growth to his likeness, the possibility of moral evils is a necessary feature of any world that could accomplish God's purposes for mortal beings.

Second, Joseph Smith's view is not plagued by genuinely evil events arising from the natural order such as diseases, earthquakes, and cancer. These events are features of any natural order that can exist as a cosmos rather than a chaos. God's choice was to create an ordered state of affairs out of a chaotic state of affairs consistent with the natural laws that actually obtain. Because only an ordered state of affairs can function in the process of soul-making, the choice to create this world and the ordered cosmos is an expression of his love for humankind. We hasten to add that Joseph Smith's view of natural law arose out of the idea that all aspects of reality, including the most minute particles, exercise some degree of intelligent activity of their own and respond to God in faith. Indeed, the ordering of the universe occurs because all elements "obey" God's word through their faithful response to him.[50] Thus God's power to bring about miracles increases according to the faithful response of realities cooperating with him in the process of this ongoing creation. God cannot work such miracles where faith is not present. Further, God is enabled by his divine knowledge to use eternal laws to overcome the effects of natural laws. For example, it is possible to lift tons of steel into the air by virtue of a jet engine and airfoil without revoking the law of gravity. In a similar manner, God utilizes his knowledge of eternal principles to work what appear to human beings to be miracles, or violation of the natural order. Thus because God has superior knowledge, he can utilize eternal principles to overcome the effects of some natural evils. He may do this in a manner analogous to the way humans created a vaccine for smallpox and eradicated the disease.

Moreover, in light of Joseph Smith's ontology of persons, it is not necessary to explain why God did not create better, more virtuous, or more morally sensitive individuals to people the earth. God never had the option of creating persons from nothing with just the characteristics he wanted. Rather, those persons who actually exist have always existed in their most essential form. His choice was to express his love for them by providing a way whereby they could experience consummate joy by becoming like him in a relationship of intimate unity and love. To do that, it is necessary to pass through this mortal life with all its attendant dangers.

Finally, Joseph Smith does not make God the exception to Hick's value judgment that freely developed virtue is better than any virtue creatable *ab initio.* For, according to Joseph, God also once experienced a mortality in which, presumably, he confronted genuine temptation and confronted real challenges.

Joseph Smith's revealed worldview not only dissolves the logical problem of evil, but it also throws light upon the experience of evil as mortal beings actually encounter it. We do not believe that we can explain why God allows each particular evil, nor that any theodicy has an obligation to do so. There remain genuine evils—both moral and natural—that cannot be explained away and whose character indicates that they are also real for God. In Joseph's thought, God too is confronted by the entailments of evil. God does not stand aloof; rather, he fully engages himself in winning human beings with his love and enhancing their capacities to feel joy in relationship with him. God shares humanity's struggle, sorrows over human failures, rejoices in mortal triumphs, and suffers when individuals suffer. God waits on our faith in him so that he may be enabled to eradicate more evil. An earnestness in human experience exists because the possibility of genuine triumph entails the possibility of genuine defeat. God truly feels a loss when humans choose evil over good, yet the possibility of victory justifies the harsh conditions of mortality. All mortal beings freely and knowingly chose to undertake mortal life. They are truly co-laborers with God in the work of eradicating evil, for God has not created evil nor the physical conditions from which it inevitably arises, nor would he allow evil could he end it without thereby making the victory impossible. Truman Madsen concludes,

> Thus, it is not a "decree" that stress and pain are part of growth and enlightenment. The universe and the selves within it simply operate that way. It is enough to know that God the Father and His Son Jesus Christ, though not the source of tragedy, yet have the power to enable us to climb above it, into everlasting joy.[51]

The Soteriological Problem of Evil

Earlier, when we introduced the logical problem of evil, we argued that most discussions of the problem were too narrow and especially unfair to the Christian believer in that they failed to take into account the problem's strongest solution—the incarnation of God the Son in the person of Jesus of Nazareth and his triumph over sin, suffering, and death through his atonement and resurrection. But ironically, the strongest solution to the problem of evil, when understood in traditional terms, becomes itself another problem.

There are two types of soteriological problems of evil.[52] The first type arises out of the New Testament teaching that salvation comes *only* through Christ. We call this the "exclusion problem." The second problem, which we call the "foreknowledge problem," arises because God created persons knowing that they would be consigned to hell.

The exclusion problem arises because some are said to be excluded from salvation for reasons beyond their power to alter. This would mean that God has unfairly curtailed their chances of entering into a loving relationship with him. For instance, John reports that Jesus claimed this very thing: "I am the way, the truth, and the life: no man cometh unto the Father, but by me" (John 14:6). Similarly, Peter affirms, "Neither is there salvation in any other: for there is none other name under heaven given among men, whereby we must be saved" (Acts 4:12). Yet, many people have lived and died without ever hearing of Jesus Christ or having a fair chance to understand and accept salvation through him. Thomas Morris, professor of philosophy at Notre Dame, in his book *The Logic of God Incarnate* calls the exclusion "a scandal" and explains it this way:

> The scandal . . . arises with a simple set of questions asked of the Christian theologian who claims that it is only through the life and death of God incarnated in Jesus Christ that all can be saved and reconciled to God: How can the many humans who

lived and died before the time of Christ be saved through him? They surely cannot be held accountable for responding appropriately to something of which they could not have knowledge. Furthermore, what about all the people who have lived since the time of Christ in cultures with different religious traditions, untouched by the Christian gospel? How can they be excluded fairly from a salvation not ever really available to them? How could a just God set up a particular condition of salvation, the highest end of human life possible, which was and is inaccessible to most people? Is not the love of God better understood as universal, rather than as limited to a mediation through the one particular individual, Jesus of Nazareth? Is it not a moral as well as a religious scandal to claim otherwise?[53]

Claremont professor of philosophy Stephen Davis expresses a similar perplexity. In a recent issue of *Modern Theology* he puts the problem this way:

> Suppose there was a woman named Oohku who lived from 370–320 B.C. in the interior of Borneo. Obviously, she never heard of Jesus Christ or the Judeo-Christian God; she was never baptized, nor did she ever make any institutional or psychological commitment to Christ or to the Christian church. She couldn't have done these things; she was simply born in the wrong place and at the wrong time. Is it right for God to condemn this woman to eternal hell just because she was never able to come to God through Christ? Of course not[;] . . . God is just and loving.[54]

The problem that Morris and Davis state can be expressed in terms of an inconsistent triad—a set of three premises, all of which are apparently true, yet the conjunction of any two of which seemingly entails the denial of the third:

1. God is perfectly loving and just and desires that all his children be saved.

2. Salvation comes only in and through one's acceptance of Christ.

3.   Millions of God's children have lived and died without ever hearing of Christ or having a chance to receive salvation through him.

Premise 3 is indisputable, forcing us to repudiate either 1 or 2, both of which seem clearly warranted on biblical authority. So how do we resolve the problem? One proposed answer is universalism, or the view, as John Hick believes, that God will finally save all his children. Universalists reject premise 2, but this seems inconsistent with biblical revelation. On the other hand, exclusivists affirm premise 2, concluding that Oohku and millions of others like her must be lost. But this leaves them unable to square their view with premise 1, for they must deny that God is just and loving in the way he deals with his children. Thus neither view is satisfactory.

However, Joseph Smith added another premise in his theology that renders the other three compatible:

4.   Those who live and die without having had a chance to respond positively to the gospel of Jesus Christ will have that chance postmortally.

Thank God for Joseph Smith! Not only was he God's conduit in the resolution of one more thorny problem of evil, but he was the instrument through whom God restored the knowledge and priesthood powers that make the redemption of the dead possible.

The soteriological problem of foreknowledge is similar to the exclusion problem, but it focuses on God's complicity in creating agents whom he knows will be damned and languish in hell. Why did God not create only those persons whom he could foresee would be blessed and not those whom he could see would be damned? The notion that God creates persons whom he knows will cause great evils and suffer eternally is inconsistent with perfect love. A related problem is: Why did God not foresee and refrain from creating those of the damned who would be moral monsters, who would create much more evil than good in this life? The responses to these problems are similar to those offered for the exclusion problem. Some adopt universalism and deny that any persons will ultimately be damned, but universalism struggles to resolve the second version of the foreknowledge problem, for certainly there are persons who are moral monsters (Hitler comes to mind). Others admit that some persons are damned but deny that hell is a place of eternal suffering and punishment. Indeed, perhaps the damned do freely choose hell because they would be unhappy in God's presence. It would simply be a better result for them to be placed in hell rather than in heaven. However, this reasoning fails to resolve the second version of the foreknowledge problem. God's creation of the embodiment of evil in the person of the devil, foreknowing that he would rebel and wreak havoc on this earth, is simply inexplicable within traditional theology. If God created the devil, knowing in advance of his rebellion and his intention to entice everyone he could into the depths of horrendous evils, then God is, again, ultimately responsible for these evils—indeed, he is the initial perpetrator of and accomplice in these evils. Stephen Davis responds to the question of why God didn't avoid creating those agents whom he foresaw would be moral monsters:

> Again I must say here that I do not know. It is similar to . . . particularly heinous events in world history: Christians need not feel that they can explain why God allowed them to occur. Ultimately it comes down to trust. Some people trust in God and some do not; the ones who do trust in God choose not to question him inordinately.[55]

But surely this refusal to countenance honest questions is unacceptable. Davis says that we will just have to trust in God, but the view that God created devils, knowing that they would perpetrate all the evil that they could in the world, certainly seems to be a breach of trust. To give the devil special powers to bring about devastating "natural" events, as Alvin Plantinga countenances, is simply unwise and inexcusably negligent. As an analogy, if a friend had knowingly recommended a child molester to watch our children and was aware of those tendencies that would lead to abuse, we would be entirely justified in distrusting that friend's judgment. Moreover, if that friend knew that the person hired to watch our children had a plan to molest them, then the friend would be culpable as an accomplice in the crime—and wouldn't be a friend! The view that God created Satan to tempt others to perpetrate evils on mortal beings leads to the same conclusion: God is an accomplice in Satan's evil.

Traditional theology apparently lacks adequate answers to assist one in maintaining both intellectual integrity and trust in God. It is inconsistent for the traditional theologian to maintain that God creates any persons, foreknowing that they will bring about more evil than good or will not be redeemed. Perhaps the traditional theologian could respond that after this life, the persons who caused so much evil will repent and bring about good that outweighs the evil for which they were responsible. Yet such a view of personal growth and repentance after this life is at odds with the traditional view that such persons are "damned" and consigned to hell. Only a view that sees humans as continually progressing toward God's likeness, even after this life, can offer such a response in the first place.

Of course, Joseph Smith significantly mitigated the foreknowledge problem by rejecting the crucial assumption that God created persons out of nothing. According to him, God started his creation of humankind with actual intelligences, each having a definite personal identity. Thus the opportunity to experience this world with all its trials and evils, its blessings and beauties, is an expression not only of the fact that these premortal intelligences trusted God but of the fact that God also trusted them. Moreover, in Joseph Smith's view, there is no need to answer the embarrassing question of why God created the devil if he knew beforehand all the vile evils that being would originate. Lucifer is as eternal as the other intelligences and just as inherently free to rebel if he so chooses. However, Joseph Smith's revelations suggest that God instrumentally uses Lucifer's rebellion as a means to move his plan forward, for Lucifer's negative labor provides an opposition in all things. Thus God deals with genuine evil using genuine power: he prepares a way that evil can be negated or turned to good within the scope of his plan, if mortals will cooperate with him in the enterprise. Conversely, because Lucifer has only as much power as mortals freely give him, Lucifer's evil is merely an extension of human evil. God, then, is responsible neither for the existence of evil nor for its effects on mortal beings. Instead, he is the means by which these effects may be mitigated and eventually vanquished.

The Existential Problem of Evil

Truman Madsen suggested that in terms of evil, "The problem you and I face is not simply the problem of exonerating God, but of coping with actual evils."[56] The existential problem of evil arises because the evils in the world challenge our ability to trust God. The challenge arises from a simple fact: the world can appear as if it were not made by a loving Father but by blind chance or by a wicked, malevolent being. The depth of the problem was stated perhaps most forcefully by Dostoyevsky in his novel *The Brothers Karamozov*. The fictional character Ivan Karamozov sets the problem in bold relief:

> This poor five-year-old girl was subjected to every possible torture by those educated parents. They beat her, birched her, kicked her, without themselves knowing why, till her body was covered with bruises; at last they reached the height of refinement: they shut her up all night, in the cold and frost, in the privy. . . . they smeared her face with excrement and made her eat it, and it was her mother, her mother who made her! And that mother could sleep at night, hearing the groans of the

poor child locked up in that vile place. . . . I'm not talking about the sufferings of grown-up people, for they have eaten the apple and to hell with them.[57]

In light of such horrendous evils, Ivan then tempts his brother Alyosha with this piercing question:

> Imagine that it is you yourself who are erecting the edifice of human destiny with the aim of making men happy in the end, of giving them peace and contentment at last, but that to do that it is absolutely necessary, and indeed quite inevitable, to torture only one tiny creature, the little girl. . . . would you consent to be the architect on those conditions?[58]

Ivan rebels. He cannot accept any way of reconciling such innocent suffering with a theory of "higher harmony." He rejects the idea that the ends justify the means—especially for a being who has absolute control not only over the purposes to be achieved but the infinite array of means to achieve them. In the end, the means appear to Ivan to be wholly unjust and immoral, regardless of the glory at the end. Ivan's protest is based on the simple fact that he cannot understand how there could possibly be any morally sufficient reason for permitting such evils. His rebellion is not a rejection of God's existence but of God's goodness. His outrage is that his trust has been breached by what others say is a God of love. His point is but a cry in the dark: "How can I trust God if he allows the most unthinkable evils to destroy innocents like the little girl?"[59]

We believe that Joseph Smith has a valuable contribution to make in responding to the existential problem of evil—the challenge of living trustingly and faithfully in the face of what seems to be overwhelming evil.[60] Joseph left us much by the way of revelation that speaks to this problem of evil, but perhaps his own life speaks more powerfully than words.[61]

In 1831 Joseph Smith resided in Hiram, Ohio, at the John Johnson farm. His wife Emma had lost twins in childbirth. In part to salve the pain of the loss, Joseph took in twin babies, Julia and Joseph, who were born to a church member whose wife had died in childbirth in Kirtland. On the evening of 24 March 1832, the twins were infected with measles, and Emma took Julia, while Joseph fell asleep on a trundle bed just inside the door of the farmhouse with baby Joseph. While Joseph slept, a mob broke down the door to the house. The men beat and choked Joseph Smith until he lost consciousness, and then they dragged him and Sidney Rigdon to a nearby field, where they were beaten and tarred and feathered. The pain of the beating was severe; the pain of removing the tar was excruciating. The morning following the assault, though he was still in pain and exhausted from being up all night after the beating, he preached a sermon at the John Johnson farm to a crowd that included many of those who had beaten him the night before. He baptized three people that day. However, baby Joseph, exposed to the cold of winter during that night, died within a few days as a result. Four of Joseph Smith's eleven children[62] died at birth, and a fifth died at fourteen months. In the face of such overwhelming loss, the Prophet taught: "All your losses will be made up to you in the resurrection, provided you continue faithful. By the vision of the Almighty I have seen it."[63]

Joseph's assurance was not a matter of speculation and argument but of prophetic vision. He knew that in the resurrection those who have lost children will have the opportunity to raise them—that is how the loss will be fully made up.[64] Further, little children who die in infancy are assured exaltation (see D&C 137:10). Their death is not an ultimate loss, for God in his perfect love has provided a way to overcome the loss. Their exaltation in great joy with God is guaranteed. These are words of comfort and love.

Joseph Smith's view of God's plan of salvation is a source of trust in God's perfect love.[65] The knowledge that all mortal beings consented to confront life's challenges as an opportunity to obtain the crown of eternal life in endless fellowship with God removes a sense of betrayal when life presents challenges that appear to be overwhelming. If the challenges were not real, the victory could not be won. Rather than Ivan's question, Joseph Smith envisions a God who asks us something like William James's famous proposition in his book *Pragmatism:*

> Suppose that the world's author put the case to you before creation, saying: "I am going to make a world not certain to be saved, a world the perfection of which shall be conditional merely, the condition being that each several agent does its own 'level best.' I offer the chance of taking part in such a world. Its safety, you see, is unwarranted. It is a real adventure, with real danger, yet it may win through. It is a social scheme of cooperative work genuinely to be done. Will you join the procession? Will you trust yourself and trust the other agents enough to face the risk?"[66]

Thus one's willingness to take on the challenge of mortal life was the ultimate expression of trust—trust in God, trust in others who would face the challenges as well, and trust in oneself to see it through. The question each individual faces is whether he or she will keep the trust and win the victory.

Perhaps another experience from the Prophet's life will illustrate his deep grasp of the meaning of evil in human experience. Even Joseph, who walked so closely with God, on occasion experienced the troubling sense of God's absence. In the dark days of 1838, a vast number of Latter-day Saint families had been driven from their homes by mobs. Fathers were tied to trees and bull-whipped. Thirty-four people, including women and children, had been massacred at a settlement known as Haun's Mill. Shortly thereafter, the Latter-day Saint settlement at Far West, Missouri, was besieged and sacked by state militia. Soldiers repeatedly raped some of the women. Joseph Smith was betrayed by a friend and turned over to "military" mobsters to be killed. He was taken to a small dungeon, ironically called Liberty Jail. During their four months of imprisonment there, Joseph and his companions were abused, beaten, given human flesh, poisoned, and left in unspeakably filthy conditions where the stench of human waste was ever present.

Joseph agonized over the tales of abuse of his beloved family and friends who had been turned out in the cold of winter while the homes they had built were pillaged and burned by mobs. Joseph felt abandoned by God. The world was upside down—the Saints were homeless and destitute, while the mobs enjoyed the spoils. In a prayer he questioned from the depths of his soul:

> O God, where art thou? And where is the pavilion that covereth thy hiding place?
>
> How long shall thy hand be stayed, and thine eye, yea thy pure eye, behold from the eternal heavens the wrongs of thy people and of thy servants, and thine ear be penetrated with their cries? (D&C 121:1–2)

In response to Joseph's prayer of desperation, God heard and spoke:

> My son, peace be unto thy soul; thine adversity and thine afflictions shall be but a small moment; And then, if thou endure it well, God shall exalt thee on high. . . .
>
> . . . Know thou, my son, that all these things shall give thee experience, and shall be for thy good. The Son of Man hath descended below them all. Art thou greater than he? (D&C 121:7–8; 122:7–8)

Confronted with what seemed to be overwhelming evil, Joseph found meaning in his suffering, maintained hope, trusted God, and kept the faith. And God spoke peace. Truman Madsen summed up Joseph Smith's triumphant message:

> The mortal experience will enable us to fly if we will let it, help it, use it with faith in the Christ who "descended below all." . . . There is meaning and purpose in all things we suffer; that "all

these things" can be for our good, however empty and barren they now appear. The elements of truth in the classical theories have been caught up in a greater whole. The Lord is not playing games with us. The outcome will far exceed the price; the "chastening" will be visioned as our blessing, the fiber of soul-quality will leave no regrets, only an infinite and eternal gratitude, and the partnership we forged with Him before we entered this refining fire will loom as marvelous to us as does the face of a loving mother in the eyes of the child who has just emerged from his fever . . . healed, alive, and prepared for life, eternal life, life like God's.[67]

The bottom line for Joseph is that the God we mortal beings worship participates in our struggles, suffers when we suffer, grieves for our failures, and rejoices in our triumphs. We cannot complain that God does not know, does not understand, has never been there, for both the Father and Son joined us in the mud and blood of human experience. God is our fellow laborer; he did not create the agents of evil, he did not contrive the natural world to overwhelm us with crushing evils, nor would he allow genuine evils if he could simply eliminate them by divine fiat. The ultimate purpose in human life is revealed through the experience of moral struggle and instances of suffering, to which we are challenged to respond in love. As Madsen said regarding Joseph Smith, "The blows, the searing trials that fell repeatedly on his mind, spirit, and body came trip-hammer hard. Yet his life, thoroughly documented by friend and enemy, shows that the sevenfold furnace need not destroy man. It may ennoble him and perfect him."[68] We mortals could have remained in a world where such challenges were not presented, but we chose life because through it we can come to the incomparable joy of fellowship and eternal life with our God and thereby grow into his likeness.

Notes

This essay is an expansion of a shorter piece by David L. Paulsen, entitled "Joseph Smith and the Problem of Evil," which was given as a forum address at Brigham Young University on 21 September 1999 and was published in *BYU Studies* 39/1 (2000): 53–65.

1. Truman Madsen, *Eternal Man* (Salt Lake City: Deseret Book, 1966), 53–54.

2. Presently, "the evidential problem of evil" is being much discussed. Under this rubric, the question is not whether God and evil are logically compatible, but whether, given the extent and kinds of evil we experience, it is reasonable to believe that God exists. Though we do not here explicitly address the issue under this name, our presentation of a Latter-day Saint theodicy bears significantly on a proper answer to the question. For an excellent anthology containing some of the best recent discussions of the issue, see Daniel Howard-Snyder, ed., *The Evidential Argument from Evil* (Bloomington: Indiana University Press, 1996).

3. Madsen, *Eternal Man;* see esp. chap. 5, "Evil and Suffering," 53–61.

4. Truman Madsen, *Four Essays on Love* (Provo, Utah: Communications Workshop, 1971); see esp. "Human Anguish and Divine Love," 55–71.

5. David Hume, *Dialogues concerning Natural Religion,* ed. Nelson Pike (Indianapolis: Bobbs-Merrill, 1970), 91.

6. Antony Flew, "Theology and Falsification," in *New Essays in Philosophical Theology,* ed. Antony Flew and Alasdair Macintyre (New York: Macmillan, 1955), 107.

7. Or what Truman calls an "instrumentalist" theory of evil. Refer to his lecture *The Problem of Evil,* recorded at Brigham Young University, Provo, Utah, 17 October 1966.

8. John Calvin's views are set forth in *Institutes of Christian Religion,* ed. John T. McNeil, trans. Ford L. Battles (Philadelphia: Westminster, 1960), 3.13.6.

9. J. I. Packer and O. R. Johnson, *Martin Luther on the Bondage of the Will* (Westwood, N.J.: Revell, 1957), 784–86.

10. Christopher Kirwan, *Augustine* (London: Routledge, 1989), 119–24.

11. Michael Miller, "Transcendence and Divine Causality," *American Catholic Philosophical Quarterly* 73/4 (1999): 537–45; Brian Shanley, "Divine Causation and Human Freedom in Aquinas," *American Catholic Philosophical Quarterly* 72/1 (1998): 99–122.

12. Madsen, *Four Essays on Love,* 56–57.

13. Many in the deterministic tradition maintain that a distinction can be made between God's intending and God's merely permitting evils. However, given divine determinism, the distinction simply will not hold. See David R. Griffin, *Evil Revisited* (New York: New York State Press, 1991), 13–14.

14. Peter Appleby, "Finitist Theology and the Problem of Evil," *Sunstone,* November/December 1981, 53.

15. In his works, Truman Madsen examines and rejects four theories of evil that attempt to reconcile the existence of God with the existence of evil. These include what he labels the punitive, illusory, perspective, and privative theories of evil. A fifth, which he believes is at the center of Joseph Smith's view, is the instrumental theory of evil. We will not explicitly address these here, but for his commentary, see Truman Madsen, *The Radiant Life* (Salt Lake City: Bookcraft, 1994), 59–62.

16. Alvin Plantinga, currently a professor of philosophy at the University of Notre Dame, is widely recognized as one of the premier contemporary Christian thinkers and as the author of *God, Freedom and Evil* (Grand Rapids, Mich.: Eerdmans, 1974).

17. J. L. Mackie, "Evil and Omnipotence," *Mind* (April 1955): 200–212.

18. See James F. Sennett, "The Free Will Defense and Determinism," *Faith and Philosophy* 8/3 (July 1991): 340–53.

19. Plantinga, *God, Freedom and Evil,* 45–53.

20. Traditional theologians are divided over whether God's foreknowledge consists in "simple foreknowledge," meaning knowledge of what will in fact occur in the future, or in "middle knowledge," which includes all things that could occur in addition to what will occur.

21. For excellent recent expositions of the notion of middle knowledge, see Luis de Molina, *On Divine Foreknowledge* (part 4 of *Concordia*), trans. Alfred J. Freddoso (Ithaca, N.Y.: Cornell University Press, 1988); and Thomas P. Flint, *Divine Providence: The Molinist Account* (Ithaca, N.Y.: Cornell University Press, 1998). Plantinga's more sophisticated

treatment of the free-will defense and middle knowledge is presented in *The Nature of Necessity* (Oxford: Clarendon, 1974).

22. The issue as to what or who brings about the truth of counterfactuals of freedom is an ongoing debate in the philosophy of religion. Thomas Flint argues that the truth value of counterfactuals of freedom assumes that *actually existing* persons have a type of "counterfactual power over the past," or ability to bring about the truth value of counterfactuals before they even exist, through backward causation. See Flint's "A New Anti-Anti-Molinist Argument," *Religious Studies* 35 (1999): 299–305. However, he does not show how the truth value of counterfactuals could be brought about by possible persons who are never created and therefore never exist! Flint is responding to William Hasker, "A New Anti-Molinist Argument," *Religious Studies* 35 (1999): 291–97; and William Hasker, "Middle Knowledge: A Refutation Revisited," *Faith and Philosophy* 12/2 (April 1995): 223–36. The literature on the argument is legion. See William Hasker, "Anti-Molinism Undefeated!" *Faith and Philosophy* 17/1 (January 2000): 126–31; William L. Craig, "On Hasker's Defense of Anti-Molinism," *Faith and Philosophy* 15/2 (April 1998): 236–40; Edward Wierenga, *The Nature of God: An Inquiry into the Divine Attributes* (Ithaca, N.Y.: Cornell University Press, 1988), 150–60; Thomas Flint, "Hasker's *God, Time and Knowledge*," *Philosophical Studies* 60 (1990): 103–15; William L. Craig, "Hasker on Divine Knowledge," *Philosophical Studies* 67 (1992): 89–110; Timothy O'Connor, "The Impossibility of Middle Knowledge," *Philosophical Studies* 66 (1992): 136–66; Robert Adams, "An Anti-Molinist Argument," *Philosophical Perspectives* 5 (1991): 343–53. For a more complete discussion of the issues surrounding the viability of middle knowledge, see Blake T. Ostler, *Exploring Mormon Thought: The Attributes of God* (Salt Lake City: Kofford Books, 2001), 163–80.

23. "Davis Response," in *Encountering Evil: Live Options in Theodicy*, ed. Stephen T. Davis (Atlanta: Knox, 1981), 97.

24. In expounding B. H. Roberts's treatment of the problem of evil, Truman Madsen suggested that suffering is necessary to obtain through experiences such attributes as love, gratitude, and joy. Thus the world environment containing evil is a positive thing in the sense that it satisfies some prerequisite for obtaining at least one divine attribute: love.

See Truman Madsen, "The Meaning of Christ—The Truth, the Way, the Life: An Analysis of B. H. Roberts' Unpublished Masterwork," *BYU Studies* 15/3 (1975): 284; and B. H. Roberts, *The Truth, the Way, the Life,* 2nd ed. (Provo, Utah: BYU Studies, 1996), 609–12.

25. See 2 Nephi 2:23, where Adam and Eve, as initially created, are described as being in a state of innocence.

26. John Hick, *Evil and the God of Love* (New York: Harper & Row, 1966), 326.

27. Ibid., 376.

28. C. S. Lewis, *The Problem of Pain* (New York: Macmillan, 1967), 115, emphasis in original.

29. Hick, *Evil,* 380–81.

30. Ibid., 291.

31. Frederick R. Tennant, *Philosophical Theology* (Cambridge: University Press, 1935), 2:188–89.

32. For a fuller presentation of this objection, see David L. Paulsen, "Divine Determinateness and the Free Will Defence," *Analysis* 41/3 (June 1981): 150–53.

33. Madsen suggests that Christ endured suffering as a part of his growing process, "But Christ went through what he had to in order to generate in his own center self compassion for us." *The Highest in Us* (Salt Lake City: Bookcraft, 1978), 30.

34. Irenaeus, *Adverses Haereses* book 5, preface.

35. Ibid., 4.38.4.

36. A. N. Williams, "Deification in the *Summa Theologiae:* A Structural Interpretation of the *Prima Pars,*" *Thomist* 61/2 (1997): 219.

37. Madsen, *Eternal Man,* 56–57.

38. Joseph Smith, *Teachings of the Prophet Joseph Smith,* comp. Joseph Fielding Smith (Salt Lake City: Deseret Book, 1976), 350–52. The view that matter is eternal and that God created by organizing chaotic matter is also taught in the Book of Abraham 3–4.

39. *Teachings of the Prophet Joseph Smith,* 352–53.

40. See ibid., 354.

41. Madsen, *Four Essays on Love,* 57.

42. Madsen, *Eternal Man,* 58.

43. These points are discussed in Joseph Smith's revelations found in D&C 29:35–43; Moses 4:1–4; 5:9–11; and Abraham 3:23–28.

44. *Teachings of the Prophet Joseph Smith*, 181.

45. Madsen further suggests that the law of opposition—the "have to suffer"—is eternal. See "The Meaning of Christ," 279–80.

46. *The Words of Joseph Smith*, comp. and ed. Andrew F. Ehat and Lyndon W. Cook (Provo, Utah: BYU Religious Studies Center, 1980), 62 (19 January 1841; McIntire Minute Book): "Joseph said that before the foundation of the Earth in the Grand Counsel that the Spirits of all Men ware subject to opression & the express purpose of God in Giveing it a tabernicle was to arm it against the power of Darkness" (spelling as in original).

47. *Words of Joseph Smith*, 60 (5 January 1841), extracts from William Clayton's Private Book.

48. B. H. Roberts, *The Seventy's Course in Theology*, vol. 2 (Dallas: Taylor, 1976), fourth-year lesson, 12, 70. More technically, we can say that an agent A has maximal power (in effect, the greatest power coherently possible) at a time t if A is able to bring about any state of affairs SA such that (a) SA does not entail that A does not bring about SA at t; and (b) SA is compossible with all events that precede t in time in the actual world up to t.

49. Truman Madsen, *Joseph Smith among the Prophets* (Salt Lake City: Deseret Book, 1965), 11.

50. Joseph Smith, *Lectures on Faith* (Grantsville, Utah: Archive, 2000), lecture 1, 22, states: "It was by faith that the worlds were framed—God spake, chaos heard, and worlds came into order, by reason of the faith there was in Him."

51. Madsen, *Eternal Man*, 18.

52. Madsen identifies another kind of soteriological problem of evil that we will not discuss here. In this view, if God created all evil, then the atonement wrought by his Son to overcome its effects is a drastic and cruel solution. But Joseph Smith's teachings, specifically those explained above, provide a rationale for the atonement by demonstrating that the eternal law of justice requires it. See Roberts, *The Truth, the Way, the Life*, 605.

53. Thomas V. Morris, *The Logic of God Incarnate* (Ithaca, N.Y.: Cornell University Press, 1986), 174–75.

54. Stephen T. Davis, "Universalism, Hell, and the Fate of the Ignorant," *Modern Theology* 6/2 (January 1990): 176.

55. Stephen T. Davis, "Free Will and Evil," in *Encountering Evil*, 82.

56. Madsen, *Problem of Evil.*

57. Fyodor Dostoyevsky, *The Brothers Karamozov*, trans. David Magarshack (England: Penguin, 1982), 283.

58. Ibid., 287.

59. See Brian K. Cameron, "A Critique of Marilyn McCord Adams' 'Christian Solution' to the Existential Problem of Evil," *American Catholic Philosophical Quarterly* 73/3 (1999): 419–23.

60. In a hypothetical dialogue between Joseph Smith and a mother of an infant born blind and paralyzed, Truman Madsen paints a dramatic picture of Joseph's response to the existential problem of evil. See *Eternal Man*, 53–61.

61. Madsen writes that Joseph Smith said "adversity had become second nature, but had only 'wafted me that much closer to Deity.'" *Joseph Smith among the Prophets*, 21–22.

62. Emma gave birth to nine children, and Emma and Joseph adopted the Murdock twins when their own twins died.

63. *Teachings of the Prophet Joseph Smith*, 296.

64. *Words of Joseph Smith*, 347, 354.

65. Truman Madsen speaks to this point extensively in the chapter of *The Radiant Life* entitled "Human Anguish and Divine Love."

66. William James, *Pragmatism* (New York: Longmans, Green, 1948), 290–91.

67. Madsen, *The Radiant Life*, 68.

68. Madsen, *Joseph Smith among the Prophets*, 23.

CHAPTER 9

ON THE MOTIF OF THE WEEPING GOD IN MOSES 7

Daniel C. Peterson

And it came to pass that the God of heaven looked upon the residue of the people, and he wept; and Enoch bore record of it, saying: How is it that the heavens weep, and shed forth their tears as the rain upon the mountains?

And Enoch said unto the Lord: How is it that thou canst weep, seeing thou art holy, and from all eternity to all eternity? (Moses 7:28–29)

The Divine Lament in Moses 7

In one of the most striking passages in scripture, the prophet Enoch sees God cry. He is astonished. The sight is simply too human, too much of a contrast with God's unimaginable power, for Enoch not to be amazed.

Were it possible that man could number the particles of the earth, yea, millions of earths like this, it would not be a beginning to the number of thy creations; and thy curtains are stretched out still; . . . how is it thou canst weep? (Moses 7:30–31)

God responds to Enoch's perplexity by describing his own internal, emotional conflict:

> Behold these thy brethren; they are the workmanship of mine own hands, . . .
>
> And unto thy brethren have I said, and also given commandment, that they should love one another, and that they should choose me, their Father; but behold, they are without affection, and they hate their own blood;
>
> And the fire of mine indignation is kindled against them; and in my hot displeasure will I send in the floods upon them, for my fierce anger is kindled against them.[1]
>
> . . . misery shall be their doom; and the whole heavens shall weep over them, even all the workmanship of mine hands; wherefore should not the heavens weep, seeing these shall suffer? (Moses 7:32–34, 37)

Clearly, although justice calls for God to punish his children, he is unhappy about what he must do. It causes him genuine pain.

This is a striking portrayal and one quite inconsistent with the notions of God's "impassibility" developed in high Christian theology, according to which God should have no such emotions.[2] The Unmoved Mover does not weep. Indeed, he cannot be affected in any way by anything that humans or his other creatures do since he is "pure act" (never effect) and "pure form" (never matter).[3] Furthermore, conflicting emotions within God are inconceivable on the common theological theory that God is utterly "simple," or indivisible—that he is, in the familiar phrase, "without body, parts, or passions."

"Th[is] doctrine," in the words of a standard reference work, "was a regular tenet of philosophical theology among the Greeks, and its foundation in Christian sources is probably due to direct Greek influences."[4] The concept of emotionless, impassible deity was, of course, quite foreign to those familiar with the Olympian gods of ancient Greece, who were not only embodied but whose lives were filled with impulsiveness, irrational anger, lust, and violence. It had little to do with them, for they were not the gods described and worshiped by philosophers like Plato, Aristotle, and

Plotinus. Similarly, it has never been easily reconcilable with the data of the Bible, where God explicitly speaks of his own jealousy (as at Exodus 20:5) and his yearning (as at Hosea 11:8) and where his wrath is on clear and frequent display.

> Hebrew religion . . . freely ascribed emotions to God.
>
> In Christianity there is an acute tension between the Greek and the Hebrew conceptions. On the one side there is the immutability, perfection, and all-sufficiency of God which would seem to exclude all passion, and this has been the basis of the traditional emphasis among theologians. But on the other side there is the central Christian conviction that God in His essence is love, that His nature is revealed in the Incarnate Christ and not least in His Passion, and that He "sympathizes" with His Creatures.[5]

Nonetheless, philosophical theology has mingled with a particular way of reading scripture to produce in many Christians a view of God the Father that, even if it seemingly allows certain emotions to him, nonetheless denies others, and so contrasts sharply with their view of God the Son. As the Lutheran biblical theologian Terence E. Fretheim puts it,

> The God of the [Old Testament] is commonly pictured . . . as primarily a God of judgment and wrath, an "eye for an eye, tooth for a tooth" kind of God, who is often vindictive and punitive, seldom gracious and compassionate. God is often depicted in terms of a kind of fatherhood that smacks of a certain remoteness and coldness and sternness, even ruthlessness, a picture that is believed to need decisive correction in the light of the coming of Jesus Christ. This . . . is at least in part due to scholarly neglect of those [Old Testament] images which portray God in nonmonarchical terms, not least those which depict God as one who suffers, as one who has entered deeply into the human situation and made it his own.[6]

This view of the God of the Old Testament is indeed in striking contrast to the picture given of Jesus in the New Testament.

As Fretheim says,

> The picture of Jesus presented often stands at odds with the commonly accepted picture of God. Attributes such as love, compassion, and mercy, accompanied by acts of healing, forgiving, and redeeming, tend to become narrowly associated with Jesus, while the less palatable attributes and actions of holiness, wrath, power, and justice are ascribed only to God. . . . People often seem to have a view which suggests that Jesus is friend and God is enemy. An understanding of the atonement gets twisted so that Jesus is seen as the one who came to save us from God.[7]

For, if ever there was "one who . . . entered deeply into the human situation and made it his own," it was the man known to hundreds of millions of Christians now and throughout history as the divine Savior of the world. There is great depth of love and caring and, indeed, of sorrowful pain in Jesus' lament over Jerusalem as it is recorded in Matthew:

> O Jerusalem, Jerusalem, thou that killest the prophets, and stonest them which are sent unto thee, how often would I have gathered thy children together, even as a hen gathereth her chickens under her wings, and ye would not!
>
> Behold, your house is left unto you desolate. (Matthew 23:37–38)[8]

Since, however, it is so difficult to blend the oil and water of a cold divine impassibility and Jesus' unmistakable compassion, Christian theoreticians have not infrequently claimed that such passages as John 11:35 ("Jesus wept") must refer to Christ's human nature rather than to his divine nature.[9] (This "two-natures" Christology is especially associated with the Council of Chalcedon, which was convened in A.D. 451.)

If Latter-day Saints held to mainstream Christian philosophical assumptions, they would find it just as difficult to explain how Jesus could ever have taken upon himself the weaknesses and pains of mortality "that he [might] know according to the flesh how to succor his people according to their infirmities" (Alma 7:12; cf. D&C 62:1; 88:6). For it would seem that the impassible God of traditional philosophical theology would be incapable of true incarnation, to say nothing of learning how to "succor" incarnate, mortal beings enmeshed in time and temptation. Fortunately, virtually from its beginning, latter-day revelation has allowed Mormons to bypass this traditional conundrum.

Jeremiah, the Weeping Prophet

In recent years, both biblical and philosophical theologians have rebelled against a view of the God of the Old Testament that represents him as cold, violent, distant, angry, and uncaring. "The number of adherents to the doctrine of divine impassibility has continuously decreased during the present century," observes Marcel Sarot, who regrets the trend. "Slowly but surely the concept of an immutable and impassible God has given way to the concept of a sensitive, emotional, passionate God. . . . By now most of the theologians who explicitly state their views on divine impassibility hold that this doctrine is to a greater or lesser degree false."[10] He goes on to cite Ronald Goetz, who notes that "the rejection of the ancient doctrine of divine impassibility has become a theological commonplace."[11]

In many instances, the rebellion against divine impassibility has occurred in the name of various theologies of liberation. The concept of God as a remote, unfeeling monarch—with whom his suffering Son or, in some Catholic images, his Son's virgin Mother, representing the empathetic feminine, must intercede—has served, in these views, to legitimate oppressive social structures that have victimized the poor and excluded women from power. Walter Brueggemann speaks for this influential movement in Catholic and Protestant circles when he asserts that "Western preoccupation with dominance and power is no doubt linked to and derived from our imperial 'image of God.'"[12]

Whatever motivates these modern thinkers, however, their willingness to entertain notions of a God who actively loves his children and is emotionally involved in what happens to them has freed them to take seriously the scriptural evidence for this notion. It has always been there, but centuries of philosophical and other kinds of misconceptions have, until the last few decades, largely managed to blunt its force. (As Sarot points out with regard to the greatest of all medieval Christian philosophical theologians, "When Aquinas tries to account for the usage of the Bible, which seems to ascribe emotions to God, he explains this language either as metaphorical or as denoting divine will-acts which are unaccompanied by emotions.")[13]

While advocates of the new approach have sought and found support for their position throughout the Bible (including, relevantly to my purposes in this essay, a persuasive demonstration of how the sad story of Hosea illustrates "the mingled sorrow and anger of God the lover"),[14] a major focus of such recent biblical scholarship has been the book of Jeremiah. This portion of the Bible is replete with images and divine statements that depict God as deeply caring and concerned about his children, worried even by the punishment that he himself is obliged to assign to them. Jeremiah 31:20 is typical of the kind of language that the prophet cites as divine speech: "Is Ephraim my dear son? is he a pleasant child? for since I spake against him, I do earnestly remember him still: therefore my bowels are troubled for him; I will surely have mercy upon him, saith the Lord."

But there is much more to be said about Jeremiah than this. Lehi's great contemporary has traditionally been regarded as "the weeping prophet." The epithet is not without justification, for, as the late Abraham Joshua Heschel, an illustrious rabbi and scholar, observes, "God's pain and disappointment ring throughout the book of Jeremiah."[15] There is, in fact, a whole lot of crying going on in Jeremiah; from the first to the last of the prophet's writings, we hear "a voice of grief, a voice of weeping."[16] "Let mine eyes run down with tears night and day," says Jeremiah 14:17, "and let them not cease." Jeremiah 9:18 even calls for professional mourners: "And let them make haste, and take up a wailing for us, that our eyes may run down with tears, and our eyelids gush out with waters."

But it is not only the prophet and his mortal contemporaries who have reason to cry. Because of the behavior of Judah, which will shortly lead to the destruction of Jerusalem and to the Babylonian captivity, God himself feels "shunned, pained, and offended."[17] In fact, he actually seems puzzled by their behavior:

> O generation, see ye the word of the Lord. Have I been a wilderness unto Israel? a land of darkness? wherefore say my people, We are lords; we will come no more unto thee?
>
> Can a maid forget her ornaments, or a bride her attire? yet my people have forgotten me days without number. (Jeremiah 2:31–32)

Although God will soon severely punish Judah, his mood as represented in Jeremiah is one of mingled "compassion and . . . anger," and "as great as God's wrath is His anguish."[18] "It is," says Heschel, who was a pioneer in the new theological approach (and one who cannot be faulted either for Christian apologetic or for currently fashionable political motives), "as if there were an inner wrestling in God."[19] Heschel can even speak of the divine "melancholy" of "God's sorrow."[20]

Yet Heschel stops short of the view of God implicit in Moses 7. He will not allow that God can weep, and he insists that it is the prophet who is lamenting on God's behalf, rather than God himself. "A sense of delicacy prevented the prophet from spelling out the meaning of the word: Mourn My people for Me as well." There is, he says, "a divine pathos that can be reflected, but not pronounced: God is mourning Himself."[21]

Fretheim, perhaps, comes closer to the view embodied in the Latter-day Saint Enoch text. "The suffering of prophet and God are so interconnected," he says of Jeremiah, "that it is difficult to sort out who is speaking in many texts. Nor should one try to make too sharp a distinction."[22] Nevertheless, he, too, pulls up short. "These texts should be interpreted in terms of the prophet's embodiment of God's mourning. . . . The prophet is an enfleshment of the emotions of God over what is about to occur."[23] He asserts further, "It is difficult to avoid the conclusion that the prophet's laments are a mirror of the laments of God. . . . The lamenting Jeremiah mirrors before the people the lamenting God."[24]

Just like Enoch, modern commentators on Jeremiah, virtually unanimously, have found astonishing the notion that God himself would weep. But what is surprising, even given an anthropomorphic view of God, becomes absolutely impossible when antianthropomorphism is assumed, as it often is, to be unquestionably correct.[25]

A New/Old Perspective on the Book of Jeremiah

In 1992, J. J. M. Roberts of Princeton Theological Seminary published in a South African journal of biblical studies an important article entitled "The Motif of the Weeping God in Jeremiah and Its Background in the Lament Tradition of the Ancient Near East."[26] Roberts concentrates in his study on Jeremiah 4, 8, and 14, all of which contain lamentation texts. In them and in the relevant surrounding chapters, he identifies three different voices. The first is that of the people themselves, which may be recognized without difficulty by its use of the first-person plural. A good example of this occurs in Jeremiah 14:7–9:

> O Lord, though our iniquities testify against us, do thou it for thy name's sake: for our backslidings are many; we have sinned against thee.
>
> O the hope of Israel, the saviour thereof in time of trouble, why shouldest thou be as a stranger in the land, and as a wayfaring man that turneth aside to tarry for a night?
>
> Why shouldest thou be as a man astonied, as a mighty man that cannot save? yet thou, O Lord, are in the midst of us, and we are called by thy name; leave us not.

Second, "There is also a feminine voice of the city or state personified as a woman and seen as the mother of her people."[27] We might illustrate this, as Roberts does, by using Jeremiah 10:19–21:

> Woe is me for my hurt! my wound is grievous: but I said, Truly this is a grief, and I must bear it.
>
> My tabernacle is spoiled, and all my cords are broken: my children are gone forth of me, and they are not: there is none to stretch forth my tent any more, and to set up my curtains.
>
> For the pastors are become brutish, and have not sought the Lord: therefore they shall not prosper, and all their flocks shall be scattered.[28]

Finally, there is a third voice in the laments, one that is generally identified as that of the prophet Jeremiah himself and the one that has led to his being characterized as "the weeping prophet." Jeremiah 9:1, in which, within a larger lament, the speaker cries out with passion, is probably the most important verse in this regard: "Oh that my head were waters, and mine eyes a fountain of tears, that I might weep day and night for the slain of the daughter of my people!"[29] Other passages that are commonly invoked to sustain the image of Jeremiah as a "weeping prophet" include 14:17–18 and 4:19–21, although, strictly speaking, the latter does not actually feature the language of weeping.

A passage that undeniably represents God as sorrowful and "conflicted," though not as weeping, is Jeremiah 12:7–8, which forms part of a substantially longer lamentation:

> I have forsaken mine house, I have left mine heritage; I have given the dearly beloved of my soul [yəḏiḏût napšî] into the hand of her enemies.
>
> Mine heritage is unto me as a lion in the forest; it crieth out against me: therefore have I hated it.

These verses combine unmistakably the fact of God's abandonment of and harsh judgment on his people with the sensation of his deep love for them. The expression "the dearly beloved of my soul" demonstrates quite clearly that the God speaking here is no distant, uninvolved, unemotional monarch. As Roberts observes of the passage, "God is passionately devoted to his people, but their hostility toward him has driven him to punish them."[30]

The same emotions are clearly recognizable in Jeremiah 4:19–22, in which, argues Roberts, it is God and not Jeremiah who is the speaker:

> My bowels, my bowels! I am pained at my very heart; my heart maketh a noise in me; I cannot hold my peace, because thou hast heard, O my soul, the sound of the trumpet, the alarm of war.
>
> Destruction upon destruction is cried; for the whole land is spoiled: suddenly are my tents spoiled, and my curtains in a moment.
>
> How long shall I see the standard, and hear the sound of the trumpet?
>
> For my people is foolish, they have not known me; they are sottish children, and they have none understanding: they are wise to do evil, but to do good they have no knowledge.[31]

This "inner wrestling" within God is, obviously, very similar to the depiction of God's conflicting emotions in Moses 7. Yet the parallel is even closer than that, for it is probable that the person lamenting in Jeremiah 9:1 and 14:17–18 is not Jeremiah, nor, indeed, any other mortal being. Roberts declares that "the figure portrayed as weeping in these passages is better understood as the figure of God. . . . This striking anthropomorphic imagery powerfully conveys Yahweh's passionate involvement in the fate of his people whom he loves though he must nonetheless hand them over to harsh punishment."[32] As Roberts further observes, "The assumption that the speaker of these passages should be identified with Jeremiah has hardly been challenged in the scholarly literature, even though that identification of the speaker is less than certain." He finds this surprising, in view of "the recent popularity of the theological concept of God as a God who suffers with his people,"[33] but he suggests a plausible reason: "Though most commentators give no reasoned argument for rejecting God as the weeping figure, the comments that are made suggest that the anthropomorphisms involved in such a portrait of God are simply too striking for most commentators to entertain seriously."[34] Yet it is just such a portrait that the book of Jeremiah offers us.

The ancient rabbis, not yet under the domination of Greek-inspired philosophical theology, were much more willing to entertain the possibility of genuine emotion, even weeping, in God, though they still found it difficult to imagine. Thus, for example, the fifth-century Babylonian Talmud reports:

> For three persons does the Holy One, blessed be He, weep every single day: for him who has the opportunity to study the Torah but does not engage in it, for him who does not have the opportunity to engage in study of the Torah but does so, and for a community leader who lords it over the community.[35]

More to the point, the Talmudic tractate *Hagigah* 5b seems to suggest that it is God—and not the prophet Jeremiah—who, as described in Jeremiah 13:17, weeps.[36] So, likewise, does the third-to-tenth-century compilation of lore relating to the school of the prophet Elijah known as the *Eliyyahu Rabbah:*

> He strikes both hands together, clasps them over His heart, then folds His arms as He weeps over the righteous sometimes secretly, sometimes openly. Why does He weep over them secretly? Because it is unseemly for a lion to weep before a fox, unseemly for a Sage to weep before his disciple, unseemly for a king to weep before the least of his servants, unseemly for a householder to weep before a hired man, as is said, *So that ye will not hear it, My soul shall weep in secret for your pride* (Jer. 13:17).[37]

The *Eliyyahu Rabbah* exhorts Jews to "come and see how plentiful always are the mercies of the Holy One in behalf of Israel, for (off and on) all their days they had been idol worshipers, but no sooner did they resolve upon repentance, slight as it was, than He wept for them." It warns "the peoples speaking the earth's seventy languages"—that is, the nations of the Gentiles—that they "should not gloat" over the divine sorrow, "saying as God weeps: What benefit to the Holy One in that He gave Israel the Torah, etc." And, although it expresses uneasiness at the very thought of comparing God to any other being, the *Eliyyahu Rabbah* goes on to comment that, "in comparison with other beings, no one feels such compassion for Israel as does the Holy One, who from the beginning intended His world for them."[38]

Finally, proem 24 of the *Midrash Rabbah* on Lamentations, a work dating to perhaps the fourth century A.D., represents God as weeping in a passage that is strikingly reminiscent of the scene depicted in Moses 7. Looking upon the destruction of the temple by the Babylonians, God begins to cry.

> At that time Metatron [who is Enoch] came, fell upon his face, and spake before the Holy One, blessed be He: "Sovereign of the Universe, let me weep, but do Thou not weep." He replied to him, "If thou lettest Me not weep now, I will repair to a place which thou hast not permission to enter, and will weep there," as it is said, *But if ye will not hear it, My soul shall weep in secret for pride* (Jer. XIII, 17).[39]

Thus, while the concept of a weeping God may seem strange to the conventional theology of mainstream Christendom, it was well known, if still somewhat disconcerting, to ancient Judaism. Understood in this light, Jeremiah 8:18–9:3 becomes a dialogue between God and his people, but also—and even more intriguingly—a poignant dialogue within God himself.[40]

> When I would comfort myself against sorrow, my heart is faint in me.
> Behold the voice of the cry of the daughter of my people because of them that dwell in a far country: Is not the Lord in Zion? is not her king in her? (Jeremiah 8:18–19)

The Israelites wonder if Jehovah has abandoned his beloved city, Jerusalem, here described in feminine language. But he interrupts their cry with an angry question: "Why have they provoked me to anger with their graven images, and with strange vanities?" (Jeremiah 8:19). He has not forsaken his people; *they* have forsaken *him*. Then we hear the remainder of the Israelites' cry, a plaintive expression of missed opportunity, of grace offered but neglected until too late: "The harvest is past, the summer is ended, and we are not saved" (Jeremiah 8:20).

However, although God must punish his children, he is deeply sorrowful about the fact; and, in a passage reminiscent of the famous "suffering servant" poem of Isaiah 53—and, indeed, perhaps foreshadowing the atonement of Jesus Christ—he declares that he suffers with and because of his people:

> For the hurt of the daughter of my people am I hurt; I am black; astonishment hath taken hold on me.
>
> Is there no balm in Gilead; is there no physician there? why then is not the health of the daughter of my people recovered?
>
> Oh that my head were waters, and mine eyes a fountain of tears, that I might weep day and night for the slain of the daughter of my people! (Jeremiah 8:21–9:1)

But mercy cannot rob justice (see Alma 42:25). In indirect answer to the question posed by "the cry of the daughter of my people," the Lord indicates that, while he has not actually left Jerusalem, he would rather like to do so.

> Oh that I had in the wilderness a lodging place of wayfaring men; that I might leave my people, and go from them! for they be all adulterers, an assembly of treacherous men.
>
> And they bend their tongues like their bow for lies: but they are not valiant for the truth upon the earth; for they proceed from evil to evil, and they know not me, saith the Lord. (Jeremiah 9:2–3)

Perhaps he would like to go away from them precisely because their sinfulness allows him no option but to chastise them. And the just punishment of the wayward Israelites, his children, causes God anguish.

> For the mountains will I take up a weeping and wailing, and for the habitations of the wilderness a lamentation, because they are burned up, so that none can pass through them; neither can men hear the voice of the cattle; both the fowl of the heavens and the beast are fled; they are gone. (Jeremiah 9:10)[41]

Notes from Mesopotamian Lament Literature

The motif of a deity's abandonment of his or her people, despite that deity's passionate love for them, has a venerable history in the ancient Near East—and, indeed, Roberts contends that Jeremiah's laments are modeled upon much earlier precedents.[42] This motif can be traced with particular clarity in the literature of ancient Sumer, in Mesopotamia. Early in the second millennium before Christ, the Sumerian empire entered a disastrous phase of its history. With the Amorites attacking from the Syro-Arabian desert, the Elamites attacking from the east, and dangerous intrigues within the empire itself, the Third Dynasty of Ur collapsed. It was a terrible and traumatic event. Roughly a generation later, about 1900 B.C., when the Sumerians had made a partial recovery (they were never to recover fully), two poetic laments were composed, entitled "Lamentation over the Destruction of Ur" and "Lamentation over the Destruction of Sumer and Ur." Within the next century or so, three more "Lamentations" appeared, treating, respectively, the destruction of the cities of Nippur, Erech, and Eridu.[43]

These five poetic laments follow a standard pattern in their explanation of the traumatic events they narrate: The decision to destroy the city is normally made by Enlil and the other chief gods in their divine council. The god and goddess of the affected city try to persuade the council to alter its edict but are unsuccessful. Finally, although they weep bitterly over the fate of their beloved city, the god and goddess are finally obliged to abandon it themselves, leaving it to its decreed destruction.[44]

The "Lamentation over the Destruction of Ur" serves as a good model of the genre. It begins with a long list of the various gods and goddesses who have abandoned their temples.[45] (Much the same thing occurs in the "Lamentation over the Destruction of Sumer and Ur," where "one of the stanzas mentions briefly virtually every important Sumerian city that had been destroyed by the enemy, as well as the name of its weeping divine queen.")[46] Thereupon, the city of Ur is summoned to take up lamentation, in response to which the god himself weeps:

> O city, a bitter lament set up as thy lament;
> Thy lament which is bitter—O city, set up thy lament. . . .
> Thy lament which is bitter—how long will it grieve thy weeping lord?
> Thy lament which is bitter—how long will grieve the weeping Nanna?[47]

In the third section of the "Lamentation," the goddess of the city speaks:

> After they had pronounced the utter destruction of my city;
> After they had pronounced the utter destruction of Ur,
> After they had directed that its people be killed—
> On that day verily I abandoned not my city;
> My land verily I forsake not.
> To Anu the water of my eye verily I poured;
> To Enlil I in person verily made supplication.
> "Let not my city be destroyed," verily I said unto them;
> "Let not Ur be destroyed," verily I said unto them;
> "Let not its people perish," verily I said unto them.
> Verily Anu changed not this word;
> Verily Enlil with its "It is good; so be it" soothed not my heart.
> For the second time, when the council had . . . ed
> (And) the Anunnaki . . . had seated themselves,
> The legs verily I . . . ed, the arms verily I stretched out,
> To Anu the water of my eye verily I poured;

To Enlil I in person verily made supplication.
"Let not my city be destroyed," verily I said unto them;
"Let not Ur be destroyed," verily I said unto them;
"Let not its people perish," verily I said unto them.
Verily Anu changed not this work;
Verily Enlil with its "It is good; so be it" soothed not my
heart.
The utter destruction of my city verily they directed,
The utter destruction of Ur verily they directed;
That its people be killed, as its fate verily they decreed.[48]

Her appeal having fallen on deaf ears, the goddess is herself obliged to withdraw from her own doomed city:

Its lady like a flying bird departed from her city;
Ningal like a flying bird departed from her city. . . .
Its lady cries: "Alas for my city," cries: "Alas for my house";
Ningal cries: "Alas for my city," cries: "Alas for my house. . . ."
Mother Ningal in her city like an enemy stood aside.
The woman loudly utters the wail for her attacked house;
The princess in Ur, her attacked shrine, bitterly cries. . . .
Her eyes are flooded with tears; bitterly she weeps.[49]

Finally, via a spokesman, her people complain against her:

O my queen, verily thou art one who has departed from
the house; thou art one who has departed from the city.
How long, pray, wilt thou stand aside in the city like an
enemy?
O Mother Ningal, (how long) wilt thou hurl challenges in
the city like an enemy?
Although thou art a queen beloved of her city, thy city . . .
thou hast abandoned;
[Although] thou art [a queen beloved of her people], thy
people . . . thou hast abandoned.[50]

A similar scene is sketched in the "Lamentation over the Destruction of Sumer and Ur," in which Zababa, a war god, and Baʾu,[51] a mother goddess, are obliged to leave their city and temples behind.

Zababa took an unfamiliar path away from his beloved
dwelling,

Mother Baʾu was lamenting bitterly in her Urukug,

"Alas, the destroyed city, my destroyed temple!" bitterly she
cries.[52]

Another relevant passage depicts the reluctant departure of
Nanna, the Sumerian moon god and the firstborn of Enlil, from
the city of Ur when his appeal to save that city has been turned
down.[53] His wife, Ningal, also departs the city:

"My son, the Noble Son . . . , why do you concern yourself
with crying?

O Nanna, the Noble Son . . . , why do you concern yourself
with crying?

The judgment of the assembly cannot be turned back,

The word of An and Enlil knows no overturning. . . .

O my Nanna, do not exert yourself (in vain), leave your city!"

Then, (upon hearing this), His Majesty, the Noble Son, became distraught,

Lord Ašimbabbar, the Noble Son, grieved,

Nanna, who loves his city, left his city,

Suʾen took an unfamiliar path away from his beloved Ur.

Ningal . . . in order to go to an alien place,

Quickly clothed herself (and) left the city.

(All) the Anunna stepped outside of Ur.[54]

In the "Lamentation over the Destruction of Ur," it will be recalled, Ningal protests that she had not willingly abandoned her city
to the Elamites and the Su-people and forsaken her temple. Rather, she says, she had pled with the great gods An and Enlil. When
that was not successful, she appealed to the council of the gods. But
the decree remained unaltered, her city was destroyed, and, in the
end, "Ningal, herself, had to flee the city."[55] In yet other texts, the
goddesses Ninisinna and Inanna, respectively the divine queens
of Isin and Erech, are forced to leave their cities because of the
cruel edict of An, their "father," or Enlil, "the lord of all the lands."[56]

In the "Lamentation over the Destruction of Eridu," we read of the desertion of the city by its god, Enki, and by Damgalnunna, a Sumerian mother goddess:

> Its lord stayed outside his city as (if it were) an alien city. He wept bitter tears.
>
> Father Enki stayed outside his city as (if it were) an alien city. He wept bitter tears.
>
> For the sake of his harmed city, he wept bitter tears.
>
> Its lady, like a flying bird, left her city.
>
> The Mother of the Lofty Temple, the pure one, Damgalnunna, left her city....
>
> Its lady, the faithful cow, the compassionate one, the pure one, Damgalnunna,
>
> Claws at her breast, claws at her eyes. She utters a frenzied cry.
>
> She held dagger and sword in her two hands—they clash together.
>
> She tears out her hair like rushes, uttering a bitter lament....
>
> Enki, king of the Abzu,
>
> Felt distressed, felt anxious. At the words of his beloved,
>
> He wailed to himself. He lay down and fasted.[57]

Still another interesting passage represents Nammu, the Sumerian goddess who was the mother of all mortal life, as lamenting the desertion of the city of Eridu by her son Enki and by Damgalnunna.[58] For all her sadness, however, it is noteworthy that Nammu herself deserts the city as well:

> Nammu, the mother of Enki, went out from the city.
>
> Her hands have become heavy through wailing. She cries bitter tears.
>
> She beats her chest like a holy drum. She cries bitter tears.
>
> "Enki keeps away from Eridu!"
>
> "Damgalnunna keeps away from Eridu! Oh my city!" she says.
>
> "The ruined city! My destroyed house!"[59]

Herbert Mason's verse rendition of the famous epic of Gilgamesh, while not translating a Sumerian city lament, is also of interest in this context:

> Ishtar cried out like a woman at the height
> Of labor: O how could I have wanted
> To do this to my people! . . .
> Old gods are terrible to look at when
> They weep, all bloated like spoiled fish.
> One wonders if they ever understand
> That they have caused their grief.[60]

Certain differences between the Sumerian laments and the book of Jeremiah are immediately apparent. For one thing, the Yahweh or Jehovah of Israel is not merely the city deity of Jerusalem. Rather, he is the supreme God and the head of the divine council.[61] (Elohim, as the Father, is largely—though not quite entirely—invisible in the Hebrew Bible.) No higher god overrules him. Thus, the judgment on Jerusalem and Judah is rendered by Jehovah himself, and, as recorded in Jeremiah, the conflict between divine wrath and divine compassion, which is objectified as a conflict between distinct gods in the polytheistic Sumerian texts, occurs within a single deity.

By the same token, in a text that mentions only one deity—and he a god—there cannot be any "weeping goddess" to serve as a parallel to the Sumerian Baʾu, Damgalnunna, Nammu, and Ningal. So is there no parallel at all to the goddess? Quite the contrary. Roberts is surely correct in arguing that "the weeping city goddess" shows up in Jeremiah in the guise of "the personified city as the mother of her people."[62]

Implications for the Book of Moses

It will be recalled that Roberts distinguishes three voices within the laments of the book of Jeremiah and contends that these reflect very ancient Near Eastern literary motifs. The first voice is that of the people themselves. Second is "a feminine voice of the city or state personified as a woman and seen as the mother of her people."[63] Roberts connects this feminine voice with the "weeping goddesses" of the Sumerian laments. Finally, there is a third voice, which Roberts identifies as that of God himself, weeping for the sins of his people and the punishment they will necessarily undergo at his hand. It will, perhaps, be profitable to treat these three "voices" briefly and in reverse order.

To begin with the third, the portrayal of a God agonizing over what might be termed "internal conflicts" has only recently begun to be recognized as genuinely biblical. Roberts claims, furthermore, that the motif of a "weeping God" has gone unrecognized by biblical scholars but that it is authentically biblical and authentically ancient. The Book of Moses, which was received by the Prophet Joseph Smith between June 1830 and February 1831, offers a spectacular instance of a suffering and weeping God, far clearer than anything in the Bible.

As to the second, feminine voice, no mother goddess is mentioned in the Book of Moses, nor is there a city that laments with a feminine voice. But this is hardly surprising, for Enoch's prophecy applies to the whole earth, so that there is no single city—certainly not his own, which was proverbially righteous—and no single state that we would expect to break out in lamentation for the universal catastrophe, the flood, that is about to occur. However, a feminine voice is heard to lament in Moses 7:48–49:

> And it came to pass that Enoch looked upon the earth; and he heard a voice from the bowels thereof, saying: Wo, wo is me, the mother of men; I am pained, I am weary, because of the wickedness of my children. When shall I rest, and be cleansed from the filthiness which is gone forth out of me? When will my Creator sanctify me, that I may rest, and righteousness for a season abide upon my face?
>
> And when Enoch heard the earth mourn, he wept, and cried unto the Lord, saying: O Lord, wilt thou not have compassion upon the earth?

Note that the earth identifies itself, or herself, as "the mother of men." The notion that the earth is feminine is a very old one, reflected in the fact that, in both Semitic and Indo-European languages, *earth* is generally a feminine word.[64] Hesiod's *Works and Days*, an early Greek poem whose links to ancient Near Eastern mythology are increasingly recognized, will serve to illustrate the point: The poet speaks of Zeus as "the father of men and gods" and of "Earth, the mother of all."[65] In the Book of Moses, since God has already identified himself as their Father, earth's identification of herself as "the mother of men" would seem to make her, at least metaphorically, the consort of God.[66]

Significantly, the personification of the earth as a vocal lamenter or accuser of human wickedness is an authentic feature of the indisputably ancient *Ethiopic Apocalypse of Enoch*. In that pre-Christian text, the earth brings an accusation against the wicked and oppressive "giants" otherwise known from Genesis 6:4, mention of whom also brackets the earth's lament in Moses 7.[67]

In consideration of the first voice, as a weeping, human, mortal speaker, Enoch himself may be the counterpart of "the voice of the people" recognized by Roberts among the lamentations preserved in Jeremiah.

> And it came to pass that the Lord spake unto Enoch, and told Enoch all the doings of the children of men; wherefore Enoch knew, and looked upon their wickedness, and their misery, and wept and stretched forth his arms, and his heart swelled wide as eternity; and his bowels yearned; and all eternity shook. . . .
>
> . . . He had bitterness of soul, and wept over his brethren, and said unto the heavens: I will refuse to be comforted. . . .
>
> And again Enoch wept and cried unto the Lord, saying: When shall the earth rest? (Moses 7:41, 44, 58)

It is instructive to compare and contrast the Sumerian laments with what we find in Moses 7. In the Sumerian materials, the people of the destroyed towns lament to their god or goddess his or her neglect, which has caused their suffering. By contrast, in Moses 7, a representative of the people of the earth laments the grief that the earth itself (or herself) feels for the sinfulness of its/her inhabitants. In the Sumerian laments, a mother goddess grieves the loss of her city, temples, and people. In Moses 7, in contrast, the earth mourns the sinfulness of those who inhabit her. Finally, in the Sumerian laments, the god of the destroyed city weeps for the city's destruction and the exile or death of its inhabitants, which has occurred by decree of other, superior, gods, whereas in Moses 7, God weeps for the wickedness of the people, which will bring destruction down upon them by his own decree.

A pattern seems to emerge from comparing and contrasting the two. In the Sumerian laments, all grieve for the suffering and destruction itself, rather than for what led to it. All attempt to shift the blame. All concentrate on their own losses. The situation is quite different, however, in Moses 7. In that text, all mourn the consequences of sin. All recognize where guilt and responsibility lie, and all concentrate on the sufferings of others. In other words, while Moses 7 seems to employ venerable ancient forms, it improves upon them by elevating them from the human to the divine level and in other ways giving them considerably greater spiritual depth.[68]

Conclusions

Modern revelation received through Joseph Smith clearly teaches of a God who is "passible," who has emotions. The God of the Book of Moses, who identifies his "work" and his "glory" as being "to bring to pass the immortality and eternal life of man" (Moses 1:39), is not a God who dwells far away, transcendent in lordly and dispassionate isolation. Likewise, in Zenos's allegory of the olive tree, that marvelous document from the Book of Mormon, "the Lord of the vineyard," God, weeps over his vineyard

(Jacob 5:41). And, indeed, modern revelation tells us that "the heavens wept over" Lucifer when he fell (D&C 76:26).

Although the literal truth of such depictions has long been rejected by orthodox Jewish and Christian theology, these portrayals offer a plausible picture of a personal God. As several contemporary philosophical theologians have argued,

> God is a loving person, and love requires emotional passibility. To love someone is to care about him, and to care about him is to care about what happens to him, and to care about what happens to him is to be affected by what happens to him; it is to be happy when things go well for him and to be distressed when things go badly for him. If a purported lover was emotionally unaffected by the good and bad fortune of his beloved, by her joys and griefs, it would show that he was no true lover, and if God, the greatest conceivable lover, is emotionally unaffected by our ecstasies and our agonies then it only shows that he is no lover at all. But God is love. Therefore God must be thought of as emotionally passible.[69]

Any expansion of the circle of one's love and concern is, concomitantly, an expansion of its circumference and of one's vulnerability. (The greater the volume of a bubble or balloon, the more space it encloses, the larger its surface area, and the greater its exposure.) Thus, in a very real and important sense, God, who loves more perfectly and more deeply than we can understand, is by that very fact rendered subject to pain.

The portrayal of God in Moses 7 has implications for us as well. It means that we should take very seriously the certainty that our sins grieve our Father and cause him pain. It may, perhaps, shed some light on the mechanism and process of Christ's atonement. Furthermore, it seems to indicate that there will never be a time, on earth or in eternity, when we will be utterly beyond pain, disappointment, and suffering. This may be disquieting to some, but the alternative is infinitely less attractive. For the alternative to emotional vulnerability, it seems clear, is emotional deadness; the only path to emotional impassibility is a path that kills love and caring. But the Buddhist ethic of severing oneself from "attachments," because they cause suffering, is not the Christian one. It is instructive that the Savior's command to be "perfect, even as your Father which is in heaven," comes in the context of, and concludes, a discussion of love (Matthew 5:48; cf. 3 Nephi 12:48).

The picture of a weeping deity offered by Moses 7, now belatedly recognized in the Bible, is much more attractive ethically—and much more available for prayer and invocation—than the cold and distant divinity of scholastic theology or the stern, loveless disciplinarian of many traditional readings of the Old and New Testaments. (Alfred North Whitehead once wrote that Aristotle's metaphysical speculations on the nature of his Prime Mover "did not lead him very far towards the production of a God available for religious purposes.")[70] But it does undeniably involve God in what Roberts calls "very anthropomorphic imagery . . . very striking anthropomorphic imagery."[71]

Thus, while some biblical scholars are now working their way through to a view of God that is, in its acceptance of divine emotionality, similar to the view revealed to Joseph Smith during the winter of 1830, they now face new problems: Whereas Latter-day Saints have long believed in a God endowed with both emotions and a body, those outside that religious tradition who advocate a suffering God will have to come to grips with the problem of anthropomorphism. And the problem may go beyond mere "imagery." Sarot, for example, refers to the dilemma that, he says, faced St. Thomas Aquinas: "The denial of emotion in God seems to go against the witness of Scripture, whereas the affirmation of emotion in God seems to be incompatible with the divine incorporeality."[72] Accordingly, observes Sarot, Thomas opted for a denial of divine emotion.

Professor Sarot agrees, contending that the concept of bodiless emotion is meaningless. For this reason, he says, advocates of divine emotion must accept an embodied deity—or else, if they are unwilling to do so, they must forgo divine emotion: "without corporeality, no emotion."[73] Since, for him and, presumably, for those he is addressing, Sarot's disjunction constitutes a devastating *reductio ad absurdum,* the choice is obvious beyond dispute: Because God obviously has no body, he just as obviously cannot have emotions.[74]

The prominent Catholic philosopher Alfred J. Freddoso argues along similar lines, reacting against a very interesting recent book that argues for divine mutability and a genuinely open future for both God and humankind. "A metaphysical conception of the divine nature," he contends,

> helps us divide the Scriptural descriptions of God into the literal and the metaphorical. The authors of *The Openness of God*[75] object to the division made on the basis of the traditional conception of God; in particular, they claim that many Scriptural descriptions of God are unjustifiably classified as metaphorical by appeal to the negative attributes (immutability, eternality, impassibility, simplicity) constitutive of the classical notion of divine transcendence. However, it is not at all clear on what basis the authors are making their own division into the literal and the metaphorical. Why, for instance, do they cling to the idea that God is immaterial and thereby relegate a whole host of Scriptural descriptions of God to the realm of the metaphorical, given that immateriality is just another one of those "Hellenistic" divine attributes that has little appeal for the modern mind? The authors insist, after all, that God has genuine emotions, and many of us who reject Cartesian dualism think that in the case of human beings certain bodily changes are essential to the having of emotions properly so-called. What makes the authors think that this is not true in the case of God as well? One might even perversely suggest that the "whole

emotional content" of the parable of the Prodigal Son is "profoundly altered" if we imagine that the father, because he has no body, is unable literally to embrace his son or to share the fatted calf with him.[76]

And Yale's Nicholas Wolterstorff, an eminent Calvinist philosophical theologian, takes essentially the same position. God cannot have emotions, he argues, "for a person can have an emotion only if that person is capable of being physiologically upset. And God, having no physiology, is not so capable." Thus, Wolterstorff concludes, "The tradition was right: God is apathetic. He does not grieve, neither in sympathy nor, as it were, on his own."[77]

The new dilemma, for mainstream Jewish and Christian theologians, is this: The Bible seems clearly to teach of a God who has emotions. Traditional theology insists that God is unembodied. But God must be embodied to have emotions. The question is whether Christians will, in the final analysis, opt for their traditional theology or for the Bible.

Notes

This paper was conceived and begun, and its first draft substantially completed, during a two-month seminar sponsored by the National Endowment for the Humanities (NEH) and led by Professor John Gager at Princeton University in the summer of 1994. I am grateful to Professor Gager and the Endowment for the financial support that allowed me to work on this and other projects at that time. Of course, neither he nor the NEH are to be blamed for the arguments contained herein. (The actual formal project of the seminar, which brought together about a dozen classicists, biblical scholars, and anthropologists and one Mormon Islamicist, was to attempt to define the term *magic* and to distinguish it clearly from *religion*. We were, by the way, unable to do so.) I offer this essay as a tribute to Truman Madsen, whose "Know Your Religion" lectures at a chapel in West Covina, California, in the late 1960s were a pivotal spiritual and intellectual event for me. The notion of a compassionate God discussed here is, I believe, congruent with one of his often-articulated themes.

On related issues, see Andrew Skinner's paper, "Joseph Smith Vindicated Again: Enoch, Moses 7:48, and Apocryphal Sources," in this volume, 365–81.

1. The contrast of God's angry action and his sorrowful pity is perhaps reflected in the distinction between, on the one hand, "the fire of [his] indignation . . . kindled against them," his "hot displeasure," and, on the other, the instrument of his punishment ("floods," corresponding to his tears and those of "the whole heavens . . . even all the workmanship of mine hands"), which will, presumably, extinguish his fiery wrath.

2. For a recent account, with abundant references, of one important strand of the scholastic theological position that insists that God is "immutable" and "impassible," see Marcel Sarot, "God, Emotion, and Corporeality: A Thomist Perspective," *Thomist* 58/1 (January 1994): 61–92, but esp. 76–82. The term *impassibility* derives from the Latin *passio* ("enduring" or "suffering").

3. According to Aristotelian cosmology (and according to the Neoplatonic views that, in this regard, depend upon it), the universe is a continuum ranging from pure form at the top (pure actuality, which acts but is never acted upon) to *hyle*, or "prime matter," at the bottom (which is acted upon but itself acts upon nothing and thus is "pure receptivity" or "pure potentiality"—not to be confused with the matter of everyday experience). The vast majority of beings in this scheme—which had enormous influence upon philosophical theology in Judaism, Christianity, and Islam—fall into the intermediate realm: They are compounds of form and matter, of actuality and potentiality, both acting and acted upon.

4. Frank L. Cross and Elizabeth A. Livingstone, *The Oxford Dictionary of the Christian Church*, 3rd ed. (Oxford: Oxford University Press, 1997), 823, s.v. "impassibility of God."

5. Ibid.

6. Terence E. Fretheim, *The Suffering of God: An Old Testament Perspective* (Philadelphia: Fortress, 1984), xv.

7. Ibid., 2. Many Christian gnostics, of course, actually did regard the God of the Old Testament as a foreign and hostile deity, from whom Jesus came to save us.

8. One could certainly read this passage as implying Jesus' identification of himself with the God of the Old Testament.

9. The Book of Mormon also represents the resurrected Christ as weeping, at 3 Nephi 17:21–22. Notice, incidentally, that here, too, the "multitude" found his weeping worthy of special remark. It is, I suspect, in this kind of reaction, analogous to Enoch's astonishment, that the psychological seed of later denials of divine emotion is to be found.

10. Sarot, "God, Emotion, and Corporeality," 61–62.

11. Ronald Goetz, "The Suffering God: The Rise of a New Orthodoxy," *Christian Century,* 16 April 1986, 385.

12. Walter Brueggemann, editor's foreword to Fretheim, *The Suffering of God,* xiii. It is not clear to me that Brueggemann is right since it does not seem obvious that "the West" has been any more preoccupied with "dominance and power" than any other region of high civilization in human history. I cite him merely to show the direction in which advanced theological opinion is moving.

13. Sarot, "God, Emotion, and Corporeality," 82.

14. Fretheim, *The Suffering of God,* 156.

15. Abraham J. Heschel, *The Prophets* (New York: Harper & Row, 1962), 1:109–10.

16. Ibid., 113.

17. Ibid., 112.

18. Ibid., 110.

19. Ibid., 112.

20. Ibid., 110, 111.

21. Ibid., 111.

22. Fretheim, *The Suffering of God,* 160.

23. Ibid.; cf. 157, 161. Compare the summary of Heschel's position offered by J. J. M. Roberts, "The Motif of the Weeping God in Jeremiah and Its Background in the Lament Tradition of the Ancient Near East," *Old Testament Essays: Journal of the Old Testament Society of South Africa* 5 (1992): 364.

24. Fretheim, *The Suffering of God,* 158.

25. For an example of this, see Sarot, "God, Emotion, and Corporeality," 61–92, on which more will be said below. Sarot actually believes that, if one can demonstrate that divine emotion implies divine corporeality, divine emotion is self-evidently impossible.

26. Roberts, "The Motif of the Weeping God," 361–74.

27. Ibid., 362.

28. This passage, incidentally, is prefaced by two verses (Jeremiah 10:17–18) beginning with a Hebrew feminine singular imperative: "Gather up thy wares out of the land, O inhabitant of the fortress."

29. Readers of Roberts's article should know that, following the versification of the Hebrew Bible, he refers to Jeremiah 9:1 KJV as 8:23 and accordingly alters the numbering of the other verses in chapter 9. I have changed the versification to correspond to the KJV. Jeremiah is identified as the speaker in this passage by—among many others—Guy P. Couturier in *The Jerome Biblical Commentary,* ed. Raymond E. Brown, Joseph A. Fitzmyer, and Roland E. Murphy (Englewood Cliffs, N.J.: Prentice-Hall, 1968), 1:311 [19:31–32]; M. McNamara, in *A New Catholic Commentary on Holy Scripture,* ed. Reginald C. Fuller, Leonard Johnston, and Conleth Kearns, rev. and updated (Nashville: Nelson, 1975), 609; Thomas W. Overholt, in *Harper's Bible Commentary,* ed. James L. Mays (San Francisco: Harper & Row, 1988), 615; and Donald Wiseman, in *The International Bible Commentary,* ed. F. F. Bruce et al. (Grand Rapids, Mich.: Zondervan, 1986), 771–72.

30. Roberts, "The Motif of the Weeping God," 364.

31. For the argument that this is God speaking, rather than Jeremiah, which seems rather obvious to me in view of verse 22, see ibid., 368–70.

32. Roberts, "The Motif of the Weeping God," 361. His argument is essentially found on pp. 363–64; the remainder of the article, to p. 372, consists of a discussion of ancient Near Eastern parallels that make his reading, in his opinion, more plausible. I shall not reproduce more of his argument than is relevant to my own somewhat different purposes.

33. Ibid., 363.

34. Ibid., 364.

35. Jacob Neusner, trans., *The Talmud of Babylonia: An American Translation, Volume XII, Hagigah* (Atlanta: Scholars Press, 1993), 19.

36. Ibid., 18.

37. *Eliyyahu Rabbah* 154, in William G. (Gershon Zev) Braude and Israel J. Kapstein, trans., *Tanna děbe Eliyyahu: The Lore of the School of Elijah* (Philadelphia: Jewish Publication Society of America, 1981), 375.

38. *Eliyyahu Rabbah* 154, in ibid., 375–76; cf. *Eliyyahu Rabbah* 115, in ibid., 292.

39. English translation from A. Cohen, trans., *Midrash Rabbah: Lamentations* (London: Soncino, 1939), 41.

40. On the identity of the speaker in these verses, see the argument advanced at Roberts, "The Motif of the Weeping God," 370–71.

41. The intervening verses, Jeremiah 9:4–9, catalog an array of sins committed by the Israelites against one another that will justify their punishment. One cannot fail to be reminded of Moses 7:33–34: "And unto thy brethren have I said, and also given commandment, that they should love one another, and that they should choose me, their Father; but behold, they are without affection, and they hate their own blood; And the fire of mine indignation is kindled against them."

42. Roberts, "The Motif of the Weeping God," 364–68.

43. For a good discussion of these documents, see Samuel N. Kramer, "The Weeping Goddess: Sumerian Prototypes of the *Mater Dolorosa*," *Biblical Archaeologist* 46/2 (1983): 69–80. Kramer dates the laments on 71; cf. Piotr Michalowski, *The Lamentation over the Destruction of Sumer and Ur* (Winona Lake, Ind.: Eisenbrauns, 1989), 6. Kramer's translation of the "Lamentation over the Destruction of Ur" is to be found in James B. Pritchard, ed., *Ancient Near Eastern Texts Relating to the Old Testament,* 3rd ed. with supplement (Princeton: Princeton University Press, 1969), 455–63. A critical text and translation, with commentary, of the "Lamentation over the Destruction of Eridu" appears in M. W. Green, "The Eridu Lament," *Journal of Cuneiform Studies* 30/3 (1978): 127–67.

44. Roberts, "The Motif of the Weeping God," 365.

45. Kramer, "Destruction of Ur," 455–56.

46. Kramer, "The Weeping Goddess," 72.

47. Kramer, "Destruction of Ur," 456. Nanna ("Full Moon") is, as his name indicates, a moon god.

48. Ibid., 458. The ellipses appear in Kramer's translation, as printed in Pritchard; I have omitted Kramer's italics.

49. Ibid., 459–61.

50. Ibid., 462. The parentheses and brackets appear in Kramer's translation.

51. The name Baʾu appears to be cognate with the Hebrew *bōhû* ("space"; KJV "void") of Genesis 1:2. One is tempted to speculate, in the interests of one of the subtheses of this paper, that she might therefore have earth-goddess associations. But the point is not essential.

52. Michalowski, *Destruction of Sumer and Ur,* 42–43 (lines 116–18). The Sumerian text and an English translation are given on facing pages.

53. Nanna is also known as Ash-im-babbar ("New Light") and as Su'en ("Crescent Moon").

54. Michalowski, *Destruction of Sumer and Ur,* 58–61 (lines 362a–65, 370–77).

55. Kramer, "The Weeping Goddess," 71.

56. For useful summaries, see ibid., 71–75.

57. Green, "The Eridu Lament," 132–33 (kirigu 1, lines 11–15), 136–37 (kirigu 5, lines 3–6), 140–41 (kirigu 7, lines 5–7).

58. Nammu is sometimes described as the mother of An and Ki, the archetypal Sumerian deities of heaven and earth.

59. Mark E. Cohen, *The Canonical Lamentations of Ancient Mesopotamia* (Potomac, Md.: Capital Decisions, 1988), 1:85 (original Sumerian text at 1:76–77); cf. the comments of Kramer, "The Weeping Goddess," 73, regarding the mourning of Ninisinna and Inanna.

60. Herbert Mason, trans., *Gilgamesh: A Verse Narrative* (New York: New American Library, 1970), 78.

61. I deal with this divine council in biblical thought in Daniel C. Peterson, "'Ye Are Gods': Psalm 82 and John 10 as Witnesses to the Divine Nature of Humankind," in *The Disciple as Scholar: Essays on Scripture and the Ancient World in Honor of Richard Lloyd Anderson,* ed. Stephen D. Ricks, Donald W. Parry, and Andrew H. Hedges (Provo, Utah: FARMS, 2000), 471–594. See also Daniel C. Peterson and Stephen D. Ricks, "The Throne Theophany/Prophetic Call of Muḥammad," in *The Disciple as Scholar,* 323–37; Daniel C. Peterson, "Nephi and His Asherah: A Note on 1 Nephi 11:8–23," in *Mormons, Scripture, and the Ancient World: Studies in Honor of John L. Sorenson,* ed. Davis Bitton (Provo, Utah: FARMS, 1998), 191–243.

62. Roberts, "The Motif of the Weeping God," 368. Notice, however, that feminine and masculine can be neatly combined within God in such passages as Isaiah 42:13–15: "The Lord shall go forth as a mighty man, he shall stir up jealousy like a man of war: he shall cry, yea, roar; he shall prevail against his enemies. I have long time holden my peace; I have been still, and refrained myself: now will I cry like a travailing woman; I will destroy and devour at once. I will make waste mountains and hills, and dry up all their herbs; and I will make the rivers islands,

and I will dry up the pools." Even so, the change in person (from third-person to first-person singular) may be significant.

63. Roberts, "The Motif of the Weeping God," 362.

64. Thus, for example, Hebrew *eretz*, Arabic ʿard, Greek *ge*, Latin *terra*, and German *Erde*.

65. Hesiod, *The Works and Days* 59 and 563, trans. Hugh B. Evelyn-White, LCL (Cambridge: Harvard University Press, 1914), 6–7, 44–45.

66. Widespread ancient conceptions in which rain represents the fructifying seed of the sky god, falling upon the earth mother, may not be irrelevant here.

67. *1 Enoch* 7:6, readily accessible in translation at James H. Charlesworth, ed., *The Old Testament Pseudepigrapha* (Garden City, N.Y.: Doubleday, 1983), 1:16. For the "giants" in Moses, see *1 Enoch* 7:15 and 8:18.

68. I thank Elizabeth W. Watkins for her analysis included in the preceding two paragraphs.

69. The argument, which he himself rejects, is summarized by Richard E. Creel, *Divine Impassibility: An Essay in Philosophical Theology* (Cambridge: Cambridge University Press, 1986): 113–14, emphasis deleted. Contemporary supporters of the doctrine of divine impassibility include Friedrich von Hügel, *Essays and Addresses on the Philosophy of Religion*, 2nd ser. (London: Dent and Sons, 1926), chap. 7; John K. Mozley, *The Impassibility of God: A Survey of Christian Thought* (Cambridge, England: University Press, 1926); and E. L. Mascall, *Whatever Happened to the Human Mind? Essays in Christian Orthodoxy* (London: SPCK, 1980), 64–96. At the Council of Calcedon (A.D. 451), the divine and human natures of Christ were distinguished on the basis that they were respectively impassible and passible.

70. Alfred North Whitehead, *Science and the Modern World: Lowell Lectures, 1925* (New York: Macmillan, 1962), 249.

71. Roberts, "The Motif of the Weeping God," 371.

72. Sarot, "God, Emotion, and Corporeality," 77.

73. Ibid., 82. See his entire article, 61–92, for a very serious argument against unembodied passibility. The position that emotions necessarily demand and entail corporeality is a venerable one, occurring in ancient and medieval philosophy as well as in modern philosophical theology. See, for example, Aristotle, *De Anima* 1.1.403a–b; also Averroës, *Middle*

Commentary on Aristotle's De Anima, trans. Alfred L. Ivry (Provo, Utah: BYU Press, 2002), 6–8 (paragraphs 12–16).

74. Alfred J. Freddoso's comment is instructive: "Having pondered at length the philosophical doctrines of God fashioned by these two brilliant and holy men [St. Augustine of Hippo and St. Thomas Aquinas], I find it difficult to entertain the idea that we moderns will be better positioned philosophically to make progress in our understanding of the divine nature once we set aside their principal metaphysical claims. . . . Again, having tasted of the spiritual riches contained in the extensive Biblical commentaries of St. Augustine and St. Thomas, I find it difficult to believe that we moderns will be better positioned theologically to make progress in our understanding of the Scriptural portrayal of God once we recognize that these commentaries and others like them are tainted with philosophical elements contrary to the Christian Faith." Alfred J. Freddoso, "The 'Openness' of God: A Reply to William Hasker," *Christian Scholar's Review* 28/1 (1998): 124. Intriguingly, though, Thomas himself seems to have rejected "Thomistic" doctrine at the end of his life. Here is the account given by the eminent Catholic philosopher Jacques Maritain, in his *St. Thomas Aquinas,* trans. Joseph W. Evans and Peter O'Reilly (Cleveland: World, 1958), 54: "One day, December 6, 1273, while he was celebrating Mass in the chapel of Saint Nicholas, a great change came over him. From that moment he ceased writing and dictating." When his companion, Reginald of Piperno, complained that there remained much work to be done, Thomas replied, "I can do no more." But the other man pressed the matter. "Reginald," Thomas answered yet again, "I can do no more; such things have been revealed to me that all that I have written seems to me as so much straw." On 7 March 1274 he died, at the age of forty-nine.

75. Clark H. Pinnock et al., *The Openness of God: A Biblical Challenge to the Traditional Understanding of God* (Downers Grove, Ill.: InterVarsity, 1994).

76. Freddoso, "The 'Openness' of God," 132, emphasis deleted.

77. Nicholas Wolterstorff, "Suffering Love," in *Philosophy and the Christian Faith,* ed. Thomas V. Morris (Notre Dame, Ind.: University of Notre Dame Press, 1988), 214.

CHAPTER 10

ANCIENT VIEWS OF CREATION AND THE DOCTRINE OF CREATION *EX NIHILO*

Stephen D. Ricks

Joseph Smith—prophet, seer, and revelator; translator of the Book of Mormon and the Book of Abraham; revealer of the Doctrine and Covenants; organizer and founder of the Church of Jesus Christ of Latter-day Saints; temple builder and city founder; mayor, lieutenant-general, and presidential candidate; husband and father—was nothing if not also a restorer of ancient doctrines. Joseph once claimed that many people opposed him because the doctrines he had restored set the teachings of traditional Christianity on their heads.[1] Some of Joseph Smith's unique doctrinal contributions deal with God's and Christ's nature and being, man's origin and destiny, the temple, and the sacred and eternal nature of marriage. To these should be added his powerful rejection of creation *ex nihilo* ("from nothing")—according to which doctrine God alone is eternal and uncreated while matter is not—and his affirmation of creation from preexisting matter. Abraham 3:24 in the Pearl of Great Price confirms the Latter-day Saint belief in creation from preexisting matter: "And there stood one among them that was like unto God, and he said unto those who were with him: We will go down, for there is space there, and we will take *of these materials,* and we will make an earth whereon these may dwell." In the King Follett Discourse, Joseph observed:

You ask the learned doctors why they say the world was made out of nothing, and they will answer, "Doesn't the Bible say He *created* the world?" And they infer, from the word create, that it must have been made out of nothing. Now, the word create came from the word *baurau,* which does not mean to create out of nothing; it means . . . to organize the world out of chaos—chaotic matter, which is element, and in which dwells all the glory. Element had an existence from the time He had. The pure principles of element are principles which can never be destroyed; they may be organized and re-organized, but not destroyed. They had no beginning and can have no end.[2]

Strikingly, recent scholarship has validated the Latter-day Saint rejection of the doctrine of *ex nihilo* creation. Scholars have noted that the doctrine of *ex nihilo* creation developed during the late second century to explain the resurrection of the body in response to Greek philosophy's belief in creation from preexisting matter. In addition, the concept is not clearly stated in the Bible nor is it found in the sacred literature of ancient Egypt and Mesopotamia or in the writings of early formative Judaism, which later introduced the doctrine. Indeed, many theologians, as well as philosophers of science, also deny creation *ex nihilo.*

Creation in the Sacred Literature of the Ancient Near East

Ancient Egypt

In ancient Egyptian literature, "natural and artificial images of creation exist side by side." In these accounts, creation was said to occur through birth from or fashioning by divine beings, or even by divine speech, but such reports are not described as creation *ex nihilo* "in the sense that the Christian apologists would later develop in the second century."[3]

In Utterance 80 of the Coffin Texts, Shu describes his own birth from Atum:

> He has fashioned me with his nose,
> I have gone forth from his nostrils;
> I put myself on his neck
> And he kisses me with my sister Māᶜet.
> He rises daily when he issues from his egg
> Which the god who went up shining fashioned.
> (CT 80 I 35–36)[4]

In Papyrus Leiden 350, chapter 200, we learn that:

> The sun himself is joined together in his body.
> He is the elder in Heliopolis.
> He is called Ta Tenen,
> Amun who came forth from Nun.
> His image is the upper part,
> His other becoming was among the Ogdoad.
> The prime one before the primeval Nonad, begetter of the
> sun.
> He completed himself as Atum, one flesh with him.[5]

The Egyptians did not have a concept of matter as did the later Greeks, but "presented in mythic terms the forces behind the formation of heaven and earth and traced their development in stages: 1) the waters of Nun 2) the fiery sun 3) air 4) the earth and heaven."[6] As a consequence, creation *ex nihilo* is never clearly outlined in ancient Egypt's mythic literature nor is it likely that it could have been conceived of by the Egyptians.

Mesopotamia

"The dogma of a *creatio ex nihilo*," observes Alexander Heidel, "was not shared by the Babylonians and Assyrians."[7] Nor was it to be found among the Sumerians. The Sumerian *Praise of the Pickax* provides a view of creation from preexisting matter and through a separation of heaven from the earth:

> The lord brought into being the beginnings splendidly,
> The lord, whose decisions cannot be changed,
> Enlil, to make the seed of the kalam (=Sumer) sprout from
> the earth/the netherworld,

To separate heaven from earth he hastened,
To separate earth from heaven he hastened.

. . .

He bound the pillar (of Heaven and Earth) in Duranki.
He worked with the pickax: the light of the sun came out.
He fixed (its) task: the work of hoeing.
He fixed the pickax and the basket (to be carried) in the
arms.[8]

The most significant creation account in Mesopotamian literature is the *Enuma Elish,* a text regularly recited at the Sumerian
zagmuk or Akkadian *akītu* festival, the most important event in
the Mesopotamian religious calendar. This festival constituted
"the confluence of every current of religious thought, the expression of every shade of religious feeling" among the ancient Mesopotamian peoples.[9] The festival served to reestablish the proper
pattern of nature—with order prevailing over chaos—and to re-
affirm the gods, the king, and his subjects in their respective roles
in the cosmic order. Traces of the *akītu* festival are found as early
as the third millennium B.C. in the yearly rites of the Sumerian
city-states of Ur and Erech, but no extensive evidence exists for its
celebration until the period of the late Assyrian and Late Babylonian kingdoms (750–612 B.C. and 650–539 B.C., respectively).
Among the documents recovered from this late period are priestly
commentaries—"order of service" manuals prepared to guide the
priest in the proper performance of the lengthy and complex rituals of the festival, which lasted through the first twelve days of
Nisan, the first month of the Babylonian calendar. On the fourth
of Nisan, in the temple of Marduk (the temple serving as a symbol
of the ordered universe in the ancient Near East), the priest was
instructed to read the *Enuma Elish,* the Babylonian creation story
that recounted the creation of the world from sweet and salt waters. The *Enuma Elish* is not simply speculative but seeks to establish Babylon's god, Marduk, as the chief of the Mesopotamian

pantheon and to confirm the preeminence of the temple of Marduk over all other sanctuaries in the ancient world.[10]

According to the *Enuma Elish*, the gods Apsu (sweet-water ocean) and Tiamat (saltwater ocean) grow weary of humans continually making noise and of the lively activity of the gods—Anshar and Kishar, Lahmu and Lahamu, Anu (god of heaven), and Ea (god of the waters, wisdom, and the arts) and Damkina—and decide to take action against them:

> They disturbed Tiamat *as they surged back and forth,*
> Yea, they troubled the mood of Tiamat
> By their *hilarity* in the Abode of Heaven.
> Apsu could not lessen their clamor
> And Tiamat was speechless at their *(ways).*
> (Tablet I:22–26)[11]

Apsu is provoked to wrath, but the gods who have chosen Ea as their leader succeed in slaying Apsu and building a palace/temple (Akkadian *ekallu*) over his corpse. Damkina and Ea, having moved into their palace/temple, became parents to Marduk, who turns out to be greater than any of his predecessors:

> Ea and Damkina, his wife, dwelled (there) [in the Apsu] splendor.
> In the chamber of fates, the abode of destinies,
> A god was engendered, most able and wisest of gods.
> In the heart of Apsu was Marduk created. . . .
> She who bore him was Damkina, his mother.
> (Tablet I:78–84)[12]

Roused to anger on account of Marduk's noisy behavior and desiring to avenge Apsu's slaughter, Tiamat commissions Kingu to destroy the other gods. First Anu and then Enki are asked to lead the army of the gods, but both decline. Finally, Marduk is asked and he agrees to do it if he is given power to determine destinies:

> They became very languid as their spirits rose.
> For Marduk, their avenger, they fixed the decrees.

> They erected for him a princely throne.
> Facing his fathers, he sat down, presiding.
> (Tablet III:137–38; IV:1–2)[13]

The gods in council agree to Marduk's demand. So assured, Marduk meets both Kingu and Tiamat in battle, where he defeats and slays them both. Marduk divides the corpse of Tiamat in two and creates the upper and lower parts of the cosmos from the pieces:

> Then the lord paused to view her dead body,
> That he might divide the monster and do artful works.
> He split her like a shellfish into two parts:
> Half of her he set up and ceiled it as sky,
> Pulled down the bar and posted guards.
> (Tablet IV:135–39)[14]

Marduk declares that Babylon is to be the new home for the gods and orders Ea to create man from the blood of the slain Kingu. The gods construct Babylon and a temple for Marduk and honor him with fifty epithets such as Marukka, Namtillaku, Namru, Ziku, and Tuku.[15]

Creation in the Sacred Writings of Ancient Israel, Formative Judaism, and Christianity

Ancient Israel and Formative Judaism

The late Professor Roland K. Harrison once noted that, although the notion of creation *ex nihilo* was "too abstract for the [Hebrew] mind to entertain" and was not so stated in the first chapter of Genesis, "it is certainly implicit in the narrative."[16] The genial professor's observations notwithstanding, I find no clear evidence from the Old Testament of such a belief in ancient Israel. While traditional Christian biblical scholars have generally understood the meaning of the Hebrew verb *bārāʾ* to imply creation from nothing, Shalom Paul asserts that "the verb *brʾ* used in the very first sentence of the creation story does not imply, as most traditional commentators believed, *creatio ex nihilo* but a concept that . . . denotes, as it does throughout the Bible, a divine activity effortlessly effected."[17] Indeed, the very phrasing of the first verses of Genesis argues against the idea of creation *ex nihilo*. If the first clause in Genesis, *bərēšîṯ bārāʾ*, is understood as an adverbial phrase, the notion of creation from nothing implied in Genesis 1:1–3 disappears: "When God set about to create heaven and earth—the world being then a formless waste, with darkness over the seas and only an awesome wind sweeping over the water—God said, 'Let there be light.'"[18] After an extensive discussion of these verses and against his own orthodox Jewish background, which accepts the doctrine of *ex nihilo* creation, Ephraim A. Speiser feels obliged to observe in an indirect way: "To be sure the present interpretation precludes the view that the creation accounts in Genesis say nothing about coexistent matter," which amounts to a roundabout denial of *ex nihilo* creation.[19] Even a modern Catholic theologian can no longer assert that "the first Genesis account expressly teaches that God created all things out of nothing. The notion of 'nothing' was unimaginable to the unphilosophical author."[20] Job 38:3–11 NIV gives an important building analogy that supports the idea of creation from preexisting matter:

> Brace yourself like a man; I will question you, and you shall answer me.
>
> Where were you when I laid the earth's foundation? Tell me, if you understand.
>
> Who marked off its dimensions? Surely you know! Who stretched a measuring line across it?
>
> On what were its footings set, or who laid its cornerstone
>
> while the morning stars sang together and all the angels shouted for joy?
>
> Who shut up the sea behind doors when it burst forth from the womb,
>
> when I made the clouds its garment and wrapped it in thick darkness,

> when I fixed limits for it and set its doors and bars in place,
> when I said, "This far you may come and no farther; here
> is where your proud waves halt"?

This passage in Job argues against creation *ex nihilo* and in favor of creation from matter—from sea and cloud. It uses the analogy of building—marking the dimensions, stretching a measuring line, setting footings, laying the cornerstones—and reveals an ambivalence toward the sea and a concern that the waters be controlled, concepts that are also found in texts from ancient Egypt and Mesopotamia.

Jewish texts in the Second Temple period also lack straightforward references to the doctrine of *ex nihilo* creation. An apparent reference to this teaching appears in the text of 2 Maccabees 7:28: "I ask you, son, look to heaven and earth and, seeing all things in them, be aware that God made them from non-being, and the race of men began in this manner."[21] But in the phrase *God made them from non-being,* this non-being "does not express absolute non-existence, only the prior non-existence of the heavens and earth. They were made to exist after not existing."[22] In Wisdom of Solomon 11:17, the author speaks of God's "all-powerful hand which created the world out of formless matter *(amorfos hyle)*."[23] In his commentary on the Wisdom of Solomon, Joseph Reider asserts that the phrase *amorfos hyle* "is entirely foreign to Jewish thought and conception."[24] Despite Reider's claim that the Jews believed in creation out of nothing, while the Greeks believed in creation out of formless matter which was eternal, this was not, strictly speaking, true, since according to Jonathan Goldstein, "no known pre-rabbinic Jewish text can be proved to assert the doctrine of creation *ex nihilo.*"[25] The Jewish scholar David Winston, in his study of this verse in the Wisdom of Solomon, comes to much the same conclusion: an unambiguous teaching of creation from nothing is missing in Second Temple Jewish literature, but "even in rabbinic literature such a doctrine appeared at best only in a polemical context, and . . . the more common view was probably the doctrine of creation out of primordial matter."[26]

The earliest reference to *ex nihilo* creation was expressed by Rabban Gamaliel II (first and second centuries A.D.) in a debate with a "certain" Greek philosopher:

> A certain philosopher asked R. Gamaliel, saying to him: "Your God was indeed a great artist, but surely He found good materials which assisted Him?" "What are they?" said he to him. "*Tohu, bohu,* darkness, water, wind *(ruaḥ),* and the deep," replied he. "Woe to that man," [R. Gamaliel] exclaimed.[27]

This relatively early evidence of creation from nothing may easily be viewed as Gamaliel's heated, polemical response to this philosopher, who followed the Greek philosophical tradition in believing in creation from preexisting matter. But even as late as the third century, Rabbi Yohanan maintained that God created the world by taking two coils (Hebrew *pəqî'ôṭ*) of fire and snow (that is, preexisting material) and joining them together.[28]

Creation in the New Testament

Paul Copan, in an energetic but ultimately failed effort to defend the notion of *ex nihilo* creation, marshals a number of verses in the New Testament that seem to support the doctrine. He presents an entire litany of passages from the Epistles of Paul and the Revelation of John: "from him . . . are all things" (Romans 11:36 NIV, NRSV); "through [Christ] are all things" (1 Corinthians 8:6 NRSV); "God who created all things" (Ephesians 3:9 NRSV); "by him all things were created" (Colossians 1:16 NIV); God is "the Alpha and the Omega" (Revelation 1:8 NRSV); and "you created all things, and by your will they existed and were created" (Revelation 4:11 NRSV).[29] These verses, intended to support the doctrine of creation *ex nihilo,* instead could be used to support the view that God existed prior to the formation of the world and was its creator or organizer, to indicate that God is sovereign over the world, and (strikingly for Latter-day Saints) to suggest that Christ was the God of the Old Testament. These verses further imply that resurrection can be effected by God without resort to creation from nothing.

But Copan's primary focus is on Hebrews 11:3, which states, "By faith we understand that the universe was formed at God's command, so that what is seen was not made out of what was visible" (Greek *eis to mē ek phainomenōn to blepomenon gegonenai*) (NIV).[30] But this passage may be interpreted in two ways, neither of which supports the notion of creation *ex nihilo*. The first denies that the cosmos originated from anything observable but does not affirm creation from nothing.[31] This may be a response to Philo's view of the visible universe (Greek *phainomenon*). According to another interpretation, the second part of this verse can also be rendered "so that the visible came about from the unmanifest." This not only resonated with the Platonist view because the matter from which the world was created "lacked all qualities,"[32] but also squared with rabbinic notions, which consistently affirmed belief in creation from unformed preexisting matter.

Second Peter 3:5 reflects ancient traditions of the Near East: "But they deliberately forget that long ago by God's word the heavens existed and the earth was formed out of water and with water" (NIV). This verse from 2 Peter reveals a continuity with the ancient traditions of Mesopotamia of creation from waters.

Early Christianity

Toward the end of the second century A.D., as if out of the blue, the doctrine of creation *ex nihilo* appeared. It was a position taken by the Christian apologists Tatian and Theophilus in the latter part of the second century and developed by many ecclesiastical writers thereafter, from Irenaeus to Augustine. The doctrine of creation *ex nihilo* can best be understood as an effort to defend the Christians' belief in the bodily resurrection of the dead, a notion that was inconceivable to Greek thought.[33] In Greek thought, matter was perpetually subject to change and could not become part of an eternal body. Humans had either to submit to the necessity of their own corruption or to try to escape from matter as immaterial souls. For Platonists, a hope of bodily resurrection was not only a deluded expectation of the impossible, but was also wrong-headed in that it sought to retain the body, the least inviting aspect of the human condition.[34]

Tatian, a native of Syria, was born of pagan parents. After much wandering and seeking, he became a Christian in Rome, believing that Christianity was "the only true philosophy."[35] While in Rome, Tatian frequented the school of Justin Martyr. However, despite their close personal and professional connections, their lives and writings reveal stark differences. While Justin attempted to find correspondences between Christianity and Greek philosophy and regularly walked about clothed in a philosopher's garb,[36] Tatian harshly rejected Greek thought. In his *Address to the Greeks (Oratio ad Graecos)*, Tatian underscores the basic premise of the doctrine of *ex nihilo* creation—that only God is eternal, while matter is not: "Our God does not have an origin in time: he alone is without beginning, while he himself is the beginning of all."[37] Tatian develops this thought by observing that "neither is matter without cause as is God, nor is it equal in power to God because it is without cause. It was generated and it was not generated by anyone else. . . . Therefore, we believe that there will be a resurrection of bodies after the consummation of everything."[38] And on the subject of the resurrection, Tatian observes that God would completely restore the individual's body to its original state.[39]

Theophilus of Antioch was born of pagan parents near the Euphrates in Syria and received a Greek education. He became a convert to Christianity as an adult, after serious study and reflection: "Do not be skeptical but believe; for I myself also used to disbelieve that this (the resurrection of the dead) would take place; but now, having taken these things into consideration, I believe."[40]

Theophilus's writings reveal his powerful opposition to Greek thought on creation: "Even the human artisan when he receives material from someone, makes whatever he wants from it. The power of God is seen in this, that he made what he wanted from the non-existent" (Greek *ex ouk ontōn*).[41] In contrast to earlier examples (such as 2 Maccabees 7:28), this use of *ex ouk ontōn* does not mean eternity of matter but expresses the notion of creation *ex nihilo*.[42] Theophilus rebuts the Greek concept of creation (possibly Plato in *Timaeus* 28c), according to which both God and matter are uncreated and coeternal, and he vigorously defends the idea of *ex nihilo* creation with the observation that, if both God and matter were uncreated, eternal, and immutable, God's absolute sovereignty would be compromised.[43]

Irenaeus was perhaps the greatest and most influential Christian writer of the later second century, less because he was an original thinker than because he was a vigorous systematizer and relentless defender of Christianity. Irenaeus was born in Asia Minor, possibly Smyrna, in the middle of the second century. For unknown reasons he was sent from Asia Minor to Gaul, where he became bishop of Lyon (Lugdunum). In his tractate *Against Heresies (Adversus haereses)*, written in Greek, Irenaeus summarizes the argument for *ex nihilo* creation with the observation: "We will not err in saying this about the substance of matter, that God brought it forth."[44]

Tertullian, like Augustine a native of North Africa, was the first of the church fathers to write in Latin and the writer to set the theological tone in Western Christianity about *ex nihilo* creation. In his dispute with Hermogenes, Tertullian framed his defense of *ex nihilo* creation in a *reductio ad absurdum* argument: if the good does not derive from matter[45] and since (in Hermogenes' view) matter is evil and not from God, and since (again, according to Hermogenes' view) nothing could derive from God's substance, then the good—and all other things—must derive from nothing at all.

While Tertullian set the tone and provided the conceptual and theological framework for Latin Christianity, Augustine was its "seal": Augustine's concepts were definitive for Catholic Christianity for centuries to follow. His views on creation were no exception. But whereas *ex nihilo* creation was introduced as an explanation for the bodily resurrection of the dead, Augustine defended it as a means of arguing against the Manichaean account of creation. In one anti-Manichaean tract, Augustine observed that God must have made the region of light from nothing at all in order to free him from any limitations or corruptibility.[46] Manichaean dualism and belief in creation from preexisting matter undermined God's omnipotence; an omnipotent God must therefore have created matter from nothing: "They thus believe that the creator of the world is not omnipotent; he could not have made the world unless some nature not created by him, like matter, had not helped him."[47] Finally, Augustine's assertion that a supremely good God created all things from nothing undercut the Manichaean claim that a necessary or efficacious principle existed.[48] The Manichaean challenge to Christianity disappeared within decades; however, the impact of Augustine on the subsequent course of Western Christian history was enduring.

Conclusion

With Augustine the wheel had turned. Thereafter the path was set for Western Christianity. The doctrine of *ex nihilo* creation received its classic expression in a declaration from the Fourth Lateran Council, which stated: "We firmly believe and simply confess that there is only one true God, . . . creator of all things invisible and visible, spiritual and corporeal; who by his almighty power at the beginning of time created from nothing *(de nihilo condidit)* both spiritual and corporeal creatures."[49] It remained thus even through the Reformation until the twentieth century, when a study of the ancient sources revealed a relatively late date for the appearance of the doctrine. However, it is still fiercely maintained by fundamentalist Protestants (who continue to rigorously exclude Latter-day Saints from Christianity because Latter-day Saints affirm a belief in the existence of matter before the creation), whose zeal for the doctrine, one suspects, may often be in inverse proportion to their understanding of it. However, an army of scholars and theologians—both Christian and Jewish[50]—either reject the doctrine of *ex nihilo* creation or are tentative and hesitant about it. Typical of these views is the observation by a philosopher of science, Ian Barbour, who straightforwardly declares that "Creation 'out of nothing' is not a biblical concept."[51] Further, Barbour observes that the Bible actually states that God created the world from preexistent matter:

> Genesis portrays the creation of order from chaos, and . . . the *ex nihilo* doctrine was formulated later by the church fathers to defend theism against an ultimate dualism or a monistic pantheism. We still need to defend theism against alternative philosophies, but we can do so without reference to an absolute beginning.[52]

Though the doctrine of creation from nothing still has its defenders, these are rearguard actions by theological enthusiasts, members of great theological "yawning" associations, and participants in meetings of societies of Christian philosophy. Latter-day Saints affirm creation, the bodily resurrection of the dead, and the sovereignty of God. Their crucial—and, in modern times, virtually unique—contribution to the conversation is an affirmation of the eternity of the matter out of which the world was formed, a contribution that the ancient sources also make.

Notes

1. See Heber C. Kimball, in *Journal of Discourses,* 3:262, and "Recollections of Oliver B. Huntington," *Young Woman's Journal* 4/7 (1893): 321.

2. Joseph Smith, *History of the Church* (Salt Lake City: Deseret Book, 1973), 6:308–9, also found in *Teachings of the Prophet Joseph Smith,* ed. Joseph Fielding Smith (Salt Lake City: Deseret Book, 1974), 350–52.

3. J. Noel Hubler, "*Creatio ex nihilo:* Matter, Creation, and the Body in Classical and Christian Philosophy through Aquinas" (Ph.D. dissertation, University of Pennsylvania, 1995), 14–15.

4. Translation from Raymond O. Faulkner, *The Ancient Egyptian Coffin Texts* (Warminster, England: Aris & Phillips, 1978), 1:84.

5. Translation from Hubler, "*Creatio ex Nihilo,*" 13–14; cf. transliteration (206) and original text (209).

6. Hubler, "*Creatio ex Nihilo,*" 14.

7. Alexander Heidel, *The Babylonian Genesis* (Chicago: University of Chicago Press, 1951), 37 n. 73.

8. Cited in Richard J. Clifford, *Creation Accounts in the Ancient Near East and in the Bible* (Washington, D.C.: Catholic Biblical Association of America, 1994), 31.

9. Henri Frankfort, *Kingship and the Gods* (Chicago: University of Chicago Press, 1978), 313.

10. See Stephen D. Ricks, "Liturgy and Cosmogony: The Ritual Use of Creation Texts in the Ancient Near East," in *Temples of the Ancient World,* ed. Donald W. Parry (Salt Lake City: Deseret Book and FARMS, 1994), 118–19, for a discussion of the Mesopotamian New Year festival.

11. This translation of the *Enuma Elish* is taken from Ephraim A. Speiser, "The Creation Epic," in *Ancient Near Eastern Texts Relating to the Old Testament,* ed. James B. Pritchard, 3rd ed. (Princeton: Princeton University Press, 1969), 61.

12. Ibid., 62.

13. Ibid., 66.

14. Ibid., 67.

15. See ibid., 69–72 (Tablets VI–VII).

16. Roland K. Harrison, "Creation," in *Zondervan Pictorial Encyclopedia of the Bible,* ed. M. C. Tenney (Grand Rapids, Mich.: Zondervan, 1975), 1:1023.

17. Shalom Paul, "Creation and Cosmogony in the Bible," in *Encyclopedia Judaica* (Jerusalem: Keter, 1972), 5:1059. Samuel G. F. Brandon, *Creation Legends in the Ancient Near East* (London: Hodder & Stoughton, 1963), 150 n. 2, makes a similar observation: "It cannot be inferred from this fact that the Priestly writer conceived of a creation *ex nihilo,* thus anticipating the later Christian formulation of this dogma; as we have seen, in the Priestly account the *tehom* preexists the first divine act of creation"; Wilhelm Foerster, *"ktizo,"* in *Theological Dictionary of the New Testament* (Grand Rapids, Mich.: Eerdmans, 1985); Paul Humbert, "Emploi et portée du verbe bara (créer) dans l'Ancien Testament," *Theologische Zeitschrift* 3 (1947): 401–22; Jutta Körner, "Die Bedeutung der Wurzel bara³ im Alten Testament," *Orientalische Literaturzeitung* 64/11–12 (1969): 533–40; Manuel Miguens, "BR³ and Creation in the Old Testament," *Liber Annuus Studii Biblici Franciscani* 24 (1974): 38–69.

18. Ephraim A. Speiser, *Genesis* (Garden City, N.Y.: Doubleday, 1964), 1:3.

19. Ibid., 13.

20. Robert Butterworth, *The Theology of Creation* (South Bend, Ind.: University of Notre Dame Press, 1969), 37.

21. Translation mine. Greek text in Solomon Zeitlin, ed., *The Second Book of Maccabees,* trans. Sidney Tedesche (New York: Harper and Brothers, 1954), 166; see Hubler, *"Creatio ex Nihilo,"* 90; Jonathan A. Goldstein, *2 Maccabees* (Garden City, N.Y.: Doubleday, 1983), 291.

22. Hubler, *"Creatio ex Nihilo,"* 90; see Gerhard May, *Creatio ex Nihilo: The Doctrine of "Creation Out of Nothing" in Early Christian Thought,* trans. A. S. Worrall (Edinburgh: Clark, 1996), 6–8; Georg Schuttmayr, "'Schöpfung aus dem Nichts' in 2 Makk 7,28?" *Biblische Zeitschrift,* n.s., 17 (1973): 203–22; David Winston, "The Book of Wisdom's Theory of Cosmogony," *History of Religions* 11/2 (1971): 186–87 nn. 4–5.

23. David Winston, *The Wisdom of Solomon* (Garden City, N.Y.: Doubleday, 1979), 233.

24. Joseph Reider, *The Book of Wisdom* (New York: Harper & Brothers, 1957), 145. Attestations of the phrase *formless matter,* in various permu-

tations, are found in Aristotle, *Physica* 191a, 10; Philo, *De specialibus legibus* 1.328–29; Plato, *Timaeus* 50D; Posidonius F 92.

25. Jonathan A. Goldstein, "Creation Ex Nihilo: Recantations and Restatements," *Journal of Jewish Studies* 38/2 (1987): 187.

26. Winston, "Book of Wisdom's Theory," 186.

27. *Midrash Rabbah* Genesis 1:9, trans. H. Freedman (London: Soncino, 1983), 1:8.

28. *Pirqe de Rabbi Eliezer* 3, discussed in fuller detail by Alexander Altmann, "A Note on the Rabbinic Doctrine of Creation," *Journal of Jewish Studies* 7/3–4 (1956): 196.

29. Paul Copan, "Is Creation Ex Nihilo a Post-biblical Invention? An Examination of Gerhard May's Proposal," *Trinity Journal*, n.s., 17 (1996): 77–93. Copan's essay is an extended review of the English translation of May's *Creatio ex Nihilo*, although, unfortunately, the author strays down other byways.

30. Several others have held that the writer of Hebrews 11:3 believed in creation *ex nihilo*, including F. F. Bruce, *The Epistle to the Hebrews* (Grand Rapids, Mich.: Eerdmans, 1964), 281; A. G. Widdess, "A Note on Hebrews XI.3," *Journal of Theological Studies*, n.s., 10 (1959): 327–29; Ronald Williamson, *Philo and the Epistle to the Hebrews* (Leiden: Brill, 1970), 312–13, 377–85.

31. William L. Lane, *Hebrews 9–13* (Dallas: Word Books, 1991), 332; Arnold Ehrhardt, "Creatio ex Nihilo," *Studia Theologica* 4 (1951–52): 27–33; also found in P. E. Hughes, "The Doctrine of Creation in Hebrew 11:3," *Biblical Theology Bulletin* 2 (1972): 64–77. In addition, two Jewish pseudepigraphic works, *2 Enoch* and *Joseph and Asenath*, appear to support the concept of *ex nihilo* creation. According to *2 Enoch* 25:1–2: "I commanded . . . [that] visible things should come down from invisible," and *Joseph and Asenath* 12:1: "Lord God of the ages, . . . who brought the invisible (things) out into the light," although the word *invisible* most likely refers to previously unformed matter rather than to creation *ex nihilo*.

32. Hubler, *"Creatio ex Nihilo,"* 108.

33. Jonathan Goldstein, "The Origins of the Doctrine of Creation Ex Nihilo," *Journal of Jewish Studies* 35/2 (1984): 127–35, was the first to observe a link between the doctrine of creation *ex nihilo* in formative

Judaism and the resurrection. In response to the critique of David Winston, "Creation Ex Nihilo Revisited: A Reply to Jonathan Goldstein," *Journal of Jewish Studies* 37/1 (1986): 88–91, Goldstein, "Creation Ex Nihilo: Recantations and Restatements," 187–94, reiterated his view that the development of the doctrine of creation *ex nihilo* was formulated to deal with the problem of resurrection but was at loose ends in explaining it. Goldstein took this position to explain the "two-body paradox," according to which one human could directly or indirectly consume the flesh of another, thereby rendering the resurrection of the other's body impossible. May, *Creatio ex Nihilo*, xii, specified the second century as the time when the doctrine of *ex nihilo* creation first appeared among Christians of that era to assert the sovereignty, omnipotence, unity, and freedom of God and as a response to the gnostic crisis. However, the late second-century apologists were responding to Greek philosophical concerns, not gnostic claims, and God's unity, freedom, and omnipotence were views shared with the Middle Platonists; see Hubler, *"Creatio ex Nihilo,"* 103–7.

34. Ibid., 102–3.

35. Johannes Quasten, *Patrology* (Utrecht-Antwerp: Spectrum, 1975), 1:220.

36. Justin Martyr, *Apology* 1.59; 2.8; *Cohortatio ad Graecos* 32.

37. Tatian, *Oratio ad Graecos* 4, in Patrologia graeca, ed. J.-P. Migne (Paris: Garnier, 1857–86), 6:813 (hereafter PG).

38. Tatian, *Oratio ad Graecos* 5–6, in PG 6:817.

39. Tatian, *Oratio ad Graecos* 6, in PG 6:820.

40. Theophilus, *Ad Autolycum* 1.14, in PG 6:1045.

41. Theophilus, *Ad Autolycum* 2.4, in PG 6:1055.

42. Hubler, *"Creatio ex Nihilo,"* but contrast with N. Joseph Torchia, *Creatio ex nihilo and the Theology of St. Augustine: The Anti-Manichaean Polemic and Beyond* (New York: Lang, 1999), 11, who hesitatingly suggests that both passages speak favorably of *ex nihilo* creation.

43. Theophilus, *Ad Autolycum* 2.4, in PG 6:1055; on creation in Theophilus, see Otto Gross, *Weltentstehungslehre des Theophilus von Antiochia* (Jena, Germany: Pohle, 1895).

44. Irenaeus, *Adversus haereses* 2.28.7, in PG 7:1:809.

45. Tertullian, *Adversus Hermogenem* 15.1–2, in Patrologia latina, ed. J.-P. Migne (Paris: Garnier, 1844–64), 2:234–35 (hereafter PL).

46. Augustine, *Contra epistulam Manichaei quam vocant fundamenti* 24.26, in PL 42:190–91.

47. Augustine, *De fide et Symbolo* 2.2, in PL 40:182.

48. N. Joseph Torchia, "The Implications of the Doctrine of *Creatio ex nihilo* in St. Augustine's Theology," in *Studia Patristica: Papers Presented at the Twelfth International Conference on Patristic Studies Held in Oxford, 1995,* ed. Elizabeth A. Livingstone (Louvain: Peeters, 1997), 33:270. See also Augustine, *Contra Faustum manichaeum* 21.5, in PL 42:391–92; *De moribus Ecclesiae catholicae et de moribus Manichaeorum* 2.4, 6, in PL 32:1102–3, 1105–7.

49. "Constitutions," Fourth Lateran Council, in *Decrees of the Ecumenical Councils,* ed. Norman P. Tanner (London: Sheed & Ward, 1990), 1:230.

50. The various Jewish scholars cited in this essay—Goldstein, Paul, and Winston—reject on historical grounds the concept of *ex nihilo* creation. In addition, others, including Barry S. Kogan, "Judaism and Scientific Cosmology: Redesigning the Design Argument," in *Creation and the End of Days: Judaism and Scientific Cosmology,* ed. Norbert Samuelson (Lanham, Md.: University Press of America, 1986), 97–156, and Norbert Samuelson, *Judaism and the Doctrine of Creation* (Cambridge: Cambridge University Press, 1994), also reject the doctrine of creation *ex nihilo*.

51. Ian Barbour, *Issues in Science and Religion* (New York: Harper & Row, 1971), 384.

52. Ian Barbour, *Religion in an Age of Science* (San Francisco: Harper & Row, 1990), 144.

CHAPTER 11

GENESIS 15 IN LIGHT OF THE RESTORATION

David Rolph Seely

For Truman G. Madsen, with admiration for his learning and love of the restoration and the ability to articulate it well, with acknowledgment for all that he has taught me through the spoken and the written word, and most of all, with appreciation for his friendship throughout the years.

The biblical narrative in Genesis 11:10–25:18 dramatically presents the events of Abraham's life and the covenant the Lord made with him. The covenant of Abraham provides the foundation for the whole story of the Bible, and the stories in the Genesis narratives serve two purposes: first, to teach the children of Abraham the promises of the covenant, and second, to show them how they can attain the blessings of the Abrahamic covenant by following the model of righteousness that their ancestors Abraham and Sarah displayed. Isaiah, speaking centuries after Abraham, explains: "Hearken to me, ye that follow after righteousness, ye that seek the Lord: look unto the rock whence ye are hewn, and to the hole of the pit whence ye are digged. Look unto Abraham your father, and unto Sarah that bare you" (Isaiah 51:1–2).

The narrative of Abraham has a certain rhythm. The covenant is first mentioned at the beginning of the story in conjunction with the Lord's command for Abraham to leave his native land and go to a new land. The Lord says, "And I will make of thee a great nation, and I will bless thee, and make thy name great; and thou shalt be a blessing: and I will bless them that bless thee, and curse him that curseth thee: and in thee shall all families of the earth be blessed" (Genesis 12:2–3). Inherent in this blessing, as clarified by the account in the Book of Abraham, are the promises of posterity, land, and priesthood (Abraham 2:9–11).

Throughout Abraham's life the Lord tested and tried him, and Abraham had to prove himself and solve numerous crises. Jewish tradition describes the Abrahamic narrative as the ten tests or trials of Abraham.[1] As Abraham passed each test, the Lord repeated and further clarified the covenant. Thus, the first test in the biblical narrative is the commandment for Abraham to leave the land of his birth to go to a new land.[2] In conjunction with Abraham's obedience, the Lord gives the covenant in Genesis 12:1–3. The next crisis involves the division of the land between Abraham and Lot (Genesis 13:5–13); the covenant is reaffirmed with emphasis on the promise of land (Genesis 13:14–17). Later, the Lord reaffirms the covenant in conjunction with the commandment of circumcision (Genesis 17:4–8), and finally, after the last and supreme test of the sacrifice of Abraham's son Isaac, the Lord swears an oath, "By myself have I sworn, saith the Lord, for because thou hast done this thing, and hast not withheld thy son, thine only son . . ." (Genesis 22:16). He then reiterates the promises of the Abrahamic covenant: "That in blessing I will bless thee, and in multiplying I will multiply thy seed as the stars of the heaven, and as the sand which is upon the sea shore; and thy seed shall possess the gate of his enemies; and in thy seed shall all the nations of the earth be blessed" (Genesis 22:17–18).

A pivotal chapter in this narrative is Genesis 15. In this chapter Abraham speaks to the Lord for the first time recorded in the Old Testament and asks the Lord how the divine promises of posterity and land are to come about. The Lord answers each of Abraham's questions and gives him concrete visual images or signs to mark their fulfillment. In Jewish tradition this chapter is referred to as the Covenant between the Pieces (Hebrew *ha-bərît bein ha-bətarîm*), referring to the strange and mysterious ritual in which Abraham slaughters five animals and lays the pieces end to end and the Lord passes between the pieces (Genesis 15:14–20 JST).

A substantial amount of critical scholarship, easily accessible through excellent commentaries, has been written about this chapter in Genesis, particularly regarding the mysterious ritual of the pieces.[3] And yet scholars have paid little attention to the wealth of knowledge about this chapter restored by modern revelation, in particular that contained in the Joseph Smith Translation (hereafter JST). In this short study, rather than attempting a comprehensive commentary on Genesis 15, I will simply review the chapter in its biblical context and in light of the restoration—noting those important things we can learn from the JST, the restoration scriptures (the Book of Mormon, Pearl of Great Price, and Doctrine and Covenants), and the teachings of the Prophet Joseph Smith. For the sake of simplicity, I will use the name Abraham throughout, except in the citations of the Genesis 15 text, which uses Abram.

Genesis 15 in Its Literary and Historical Context

The context of chapter 15 is important. The preceding chapters portray Abraham as proving his worthiness in a variety of ways. In chapter 12, when he is asked to leave his native land, Abraham silently obeys. When the servants of Lot and Abraham quarrel (chapter 13), it is Abraham, as the peacemaker, who comes forward and allows Lot to have his choice of the land. Chapter 14 details the capture of Lot and his subsequent rescue by Abraham, as the warrior. On his way home, Abraham stops to meet with Melchizedek, king of Salem and priest of the most high God, to receive a blessing at his hand. Abraham recognizes Melchizedek's priesthood authority and pays his tithes to him (cf. Alma 13:15). On this occasion, according to the Prophet Joseph Smith, Melchizedek taught Abraham about the priesthood and the coming of the Savior. The Prophet taught, "Abraham says to Melchizedek, I believe all that thou hast taught me concerning the priesthood and the coming of the Son of Man; so Melchizedek ordained Abraham [D&C 84:14] and sent him away. Abraham rejoiced, saying, Now I have a priesthood."[4] Latter-day Saints are fortunate to have important JST additions to the biblical text in Genesis 14 (Genesis 14:25–40 JST), which restore much knowledge about Melchizedek and the blessing he pronounced upon Abraham.[5]

Genesis 15 begins with dramatic statements that the Lord will be a shield to Abraham, will be a great reward to him, and will fulfill the blessings of Melchizedek (Genesis 15:2 JST). In response, Abraham, who up to this point in the biblical narrative has silently and dutifully obeyed the commandments of the Lord, speaks to the Lord for the first time in the record. The conversation is poignant—Abraham has been promised posterity, and yet he has no seed; he has been promised land, and yet he has no land; and he has been promised an "everlasting inheritance," and yet he is getting older and closer to dying. Important JST additions to chapter 15 (Genesis 15:2, 9–12 JST) indicate that Abraham's conversation with the Lord can best be understood in light of the blessing pronounced upon Abraham in Genesis 14:36–40 JST:

> And this Melchizedek, having thus established righteousness, was called the king of heaven by his people, or, in other

words, the King of peace. And he lifted up his voice, and he blessed Abram, being the high priest, and the keeper of the storehouse of God; Him whom God had appointed to receive tithes for the poor. Wherefore, Abram paid unto him tithes of all that he had, of all the riches which he possessed, which God had given him more than that which he had need. And it came to pass, that God blessed Abram, and gave unto him riches, and honor, and lands for an everlasting possession; according to the covenant which he had made, and according to the blessing wherewith Melchizedek had blessed him.

The Structure of Genesis 15 JST

Genesis 15 JST can be divided into five units: first, the Lord's declaration of blessings (vv. 1–2), followed by three nearly parallel units dealing with Abraham's three questions about the promised blessings: the promises that Abraham will have seed (vv. 3–8), that the land will be an everlasting inheritance (vv. 9–12), and that Abraham's posterity will inherit the land (vv. 13–20). Each of these three central units is tripartite, consisting of Abraham's question, the Lord's promise, and the Lord's giving to Abraham a dramatic visual sign by which he can understand and remember the promise. Verse 12 records Abraham's response to the Lord's promised blessings. The concluding unit (vv. 21–22) is a summary of the chapter in which the Lord once again covenants with Abraham. The Masoretic text preserved in the KJV does not have verses 9–12 JST about the everlasting covenant and thus deals only with the questions about seed and the inheritance of the land by Abraham's posterity.

The following table displays the contents of Genesis 15 JST in a convenient format.

The Structure of Genesis 15 JST

	Abraham's Question	Lord's Promise	Visual Sign	Abraham's Response
1. The Lord comes to Abraham in a vision and promises him blessings (1–2)				
2. Blessing of seed (3–8)	"Lord God, what wilt thou give me, seeing I go childless?" (3–4)	Lord promises Abraham seed: "he that shall come forth out of thine own bowels shall be thine heir" (5–6)	Abraham's seed to be as the stars in the heavens (7–8)	
3. Blessing of an everlasting inheritance (9–12)	"Lord God, how wilt thou give me this land for an everlasting inheritance?" (9)	Lord promises Abraham land for an everlasting inheritance: "Though thou wast dead, yet am I not able to give it thee? And if thou shalt die,	Abraham sees a vision of the days of the Son of Man (12a)	Abraham "was glad, and his soul found rest, and he believed in the Lord; and the Lord counted it unto him for righteousness" (12b)

4. Blessing of the land (13–20)	"Lord, whereby shall I know that I shall inherit it?" (14a)	Lord promises Abraham land: "I, the Lord, brought thee out of Ur, of the Chaldees, to give thee this land to inherit it" (13) yet thou shalt possess it, for the day cometh, that the Son of Man shall live; but how can he live if he be not dead? he must first be quickened" (10–11)	Covenant between the Pieces (14b–20)
5. The Lord makes a covenant with Abraham: "Unto thy seed have I given this land" (21–22)			

Genesis 15 JST and Commentary[6]

1. The Lord Comes to Abraham and Promises Him Blessings (1–2)

> *1 And it came to pass, that after these things, the word of the Lord came unto Abram in a vision, saying;*
>
> *2 Fear not, Abram; I will be thy shield; I will be thy exceeding great reward. And according to the blessings of my servant, I will give unto thee.*

The phrase *after these things* alludes to the events of Genesis 14, the rescue of Lot and the meeting with Melchizedek. Most commentators note that the imagery of the shield (Hebrew *māgēn*) is a purposeful military metaphor based on the crisis of the rescue of Lot and an allusion to Genesis 14:20 in which Melchizedek says, "blessed be the most high God, which hath delivered (Hebrew *miggēn*) thine enemies into thy hand." Likewise, the mention of the *exceeding great reward* may be a reference to Abraham's refusal to take monetary compensation for his military action (Genesis 14:22–24). In this context, the phrase may be a reassurance to Abraham that he will nevertheless be blessed temporally.

The sentence *and according to the blessings of my servant, I will give unto thee* is not found in the KJV. This important addition clearly places the promises in Genesis 15 JST in the context of the blessings that Melchizedek pronounced and that were alluded to in Genesis 14 JST: "And Melchizedek lifted up his voice and blessed Abram. . . . And it came to pass, that God blessed Abram, and gave unto him riches, and honor, and lands for an everlasting possession; according to the covenant which he had made, and according to the blessing wherewith Melchizedek had blessed him" (Genesis 14:25, 40 JST).

2. The Blessing of Seed (3–8)

Abraham's first question:

> *3 And Abram said, Lord God, what wilt thou give me, seeing I go childless, and Eliezer of Damascus was made the steward of my house?*

4 And Abram said, Behold, to me thou hast given no seed;
and lo, one born in my house is mine heir.

This is the first time that Abraham speaks to the Lord in the biblical text. In this passage Abraham approaches the Lord on a subject that must have been troubling him for some time. In light of the promise that he was to have seed, how was he to arrange his inheritance since he had no seed? Abraham has apparently already arranged for the inheritance of his household and made his steward Eliezer his heir.

The Lord promises Abraham seed:

5 And behold, the word of the Lord came unto him again,
saying,
6 This shall not be thine heir; but he that shall come forth out
of thine own bowels shall be thine heir.

The Lord promises Abraham literal seed. While Abraham 2:10 clearly indicates that anyone who receives the gospel will be counted as the seed of Abraham, it is equally clear that Abraham would have literal seed who would be blessed with the right of the priesthood (Abraham 2:11).

The promise of seed is a prominent part of the Abrahamic covenant. Indeed, the whole of the Abrahamic narrative is framed by genealogies: the genealogy at the beginning recounts the ten generations from Shem to Abraham (Genesis 11:10–32), and the genealogies at the end record Abraham's posterity through Keturah (Genesis 25:1–4) and Hagar (Genesis 25:12–18). The narrative in Genesis 25:19 through chapter 50, and through the rest of the Old Testament, traces Abraham's posterity through Isaac and Jacob. The seed of Abraham that will bless all nations is the Messiah, through Abraham's descendant David (2 Samuel 7), as foreshadowed by the story of the sacrifice of Isaac (Genesis 22). The coming of this descendant of Abraham and David—the Messiah—is the central focus of the New Testament (Matthew 1:1; Acts 3:25–26).

In Genesis 16, immediately following the promise of seed in chapter 15, Abraham and Sarah arrange another way to get literal seed from Abraham—through Sarah's handmaiden Hagar. In response, the Lord reaffirms his promise that Abraham and Sarah would have literal seed (Genesis 18:10).

First visual sign:

> 7 And he brought him forth abroad, and he said, Look now toward heaven, and tell the stars, if thou be able to number them. 8 And he said unto him, So shall thy seed be.

Three metaphors from nature are used as visual signs for the number of Abraham's seed in Genesis: the dust of the earth (Genesis 13:16), the stars in the heaven (Genesis 15:5), and the sand on the seashore (Genesis 22:17; Abraham 3:14). The image of the heavens is of particular interest in that Abraham, according to Abraham 3 and Josephus, was an avid and accomplished astronomer.[7]

Certainly these images refer to the earthly posterity of Abraham. At the same time, the vast number of posterity and the cosmic magnitude of the heavens, earth, and sea surely also point toward the promise of eternal increase given to those who become celestial beings (D&C 131:4; 132:16–17). It is interesting that these same three images are reflected in titles of God in the Abrahamic narratives: "the most high God, the possessor of heaven and earth" (Genesis 14:22); "I am the Lord thy God; I dwell in heaven; the earth is my footstool; I stretch my hand over the sea" (Abraham 2:7).

3. The Blessing of an Everlasting Inheritance (9–12)

Abraham's second question:

> 9 And Abram said, Lord God, how wilt thou give me this land for an everlasting inheritance?

The phrase *everlasting inheritance* is certainly an allusion to the Lord's promise in Genesis 14:40 JST: "And it came to pass, that God blessed Abram, and gave unto him riches, and honor, and lands for an everlasting possession; according to the covenant which he had made, and according to the blessing wherewith Melchizedek had blessed him."

The Lord's promise of an everlasting inheritance:

> *10 And the Lord said, Though thou wast dead, yet am I not able to give it thee?*
>
> *11 And if thou shalt die, yet thou shalt possess it, for the day cometh, that the Son of Man shall live; but how can he live if he be not dead? he must first be quickened.*

By the way the Lord answers Abraham's question it is plain that Abraham wants to know how he can inherit the land in an "everlasting" way, even though it is certain that he is going to die. Further, while the land of Canaan is the most prominent symbol of the covenant throughout the Old Testament, it is clear that the seed of Abraham will be given other lands as well. For example, the prophecy in the blessing Jacob gave to Joseph says that Joseph will be a bough "whose branches run over the wall" (Genesis 49:22), a promise fulfilled to the descendants of Lehi in the Americas (1 Nephi 2:20; Jacob 2:25; 3 Nephi 15:12, 13; 20:14, 22; 21:22; Ether 13:2–8). The promise of land to Abraham and his posterity thus extends beyond the geographical boundaries of the land of Canaan. Modern revelation teaches us that the geographical boundaries of the promised land will expand to include the entire earth, for the whole earth will become the celestial kingdom (D&C 88:19–20).

The Lord explains to Abraham that *everlasting inheritance* means that an inheritance in the promised land is not confined to mortality but extends to eternity. Through modern revelation we learn that, as covenanted in Genesis 15 JST, the seed of Abraham will find an everlasting inheritance in the promised land, and Abraham and his righteous, celestial seed will inherit the earth forever (D&C 38:20; 45:58; 56:20).

The Book of Abraham also teaches that the promise to Abraham's seed of the land as an everlasting possession was conditional, based upon their righteousness. The Lord says, "I will give unto thy seed after thee for an everlasting possession, when they hearken to my voice" (Abraham 2:6). While the covenant of the land to the seed of Abraham was unconditional in the eternal sense—that the righteous would eventually inherit the celestial kingdom—in the temporal sense the agreement was conditional upon obedience to the obligations of the covenant.

Second visual sign:

> 12a And it came to pass, that Abram looked forth and saw the days of the Son of Man,

While the details of the vision are not given, this visual sign of *the days of the Son of Man* is undoubtedly the most important vision in the chapter. Whereas Melchizedek had taught Abraham about the coming of the Son of Man,[8] Abraham now sees the vision for himself. His vision was probably similar to that seen by Enoch (Moses 7:47–59) and Nephi (1 Nephi 10–11) and must have included the vision of the death and resurrection of the Savior (Helaman 8:17; John 8:56).

The title *Son of Man* is a very ancient one, used already by Adam and Enoch in the Book of Moses (Moses 6:57; 7:47). In the context of Genesis 15 JST, it is worth noting that the Son of Man would also be a son of Abraham—the patriarch's descendant by whom one of the most important promises of the Abrahamic covenant would be fulfilled: "in thee shall all families of the earth be blessed" (Genesis 12:3). The first verse in the Gospel of Matthew traces the genealogy of Jesus back to Abraham (Matthew 1:1). Throughout the scriptures, Jesus Christ is to be understood as Abraham's promised literal seed, whose atonement would bless all the peoples of the earth. In a sermon to the Jews in Jerusalem, Peter explained, "Ye are the children of the prophets, and of the covenant which God made with our fathers, saying unto Abraham, And in thy seed shall all the kindreds of the earth be blessed. Unto you first God, having raised up his Son Jesus, sent him to bless you" (Acts 3:25–26). The Book of Abraham clarifies that just as the Savior, the seed of Abraham, would bless the families of the earth, so too the numerous seed of Abraham will bless the world through the gospel (Abraham 2:9–11).

Abraham's response:

> 12b . . . and was glad, and his soul found rest, and he believed in the Lord; and the Lord counted it unto him for righteousness.

The Hebrew word for *believed* (Hebrew hiphil for *'MN) means "to think, be convinced that, believe, put trust in, rely upon, believe in, or have faith."[9] Abraham has throughout his relationship manifested his faith and trust in the Lord through his obedience. Here, for the first time, he openly expresses his faith in the promises of the Lord—presumably those of his posterity, the land as an everlasting inheritance, and the coming of the Son of Man—two of which he would not see fulfilled in his lifetime.

The Lord acknowledges this statement of faith in the phrase *the Lord counted it unto him for righteousness*. The term *righteousness* (Hebrew ṣəḏāqāh) is important in the Bible: God is often described as "righteous" (Deuteronomy 32:4 [KJV, "just"]; Psalm 7:9), Noah was saved because he was "righteous" (Genesis 6:9; 7:1), and it is an important word in the story of Melchizedek in Genesis 14. The name Melchizedek ("King of Righteousness") includes the word *righteousness*. In Genesis 14 JST, righteousness is a particular attribute of Melchizedek: "Now Melchizedek was a man of faith, who wrought righteousness" (Genesis 14:26 JST); and "this Melchizedek, having thus established righteousness, was called the king of heaven" (Genesis 14:36 JST). The people of Melchizedek also demonstrated this trait in the way they sought for the city of Enoch: "and his people wrought righteousness, and obtained heaven" (Genesis 14:34 JST).

In this passage, Genesis 15:6 (15:12 JST), we see Abraham, known for his great works, being praised for his faith. Similarly, the Son of God gave the priesthood to the faithful people of Melchizedek "unto as many as believed on his name" (Genesis 14:29 JST). The New Testament quotes Genesis 15:6 several times in discussing the role of faith and works in justification. Both Paul and James quote the passage, although with very different emphases.

The apostle Paul quotes Genesis 15:6 in his letters to the Romans and the Galatians. In both accounts, Paul teaches that the verse is essential for a proper understanding of the process by which man finds justification through grace (Romans 4:3, 9, 22; Galatians 3:6). Paul's emphasis on the importance of faith is preserved in the JST, "For if Abraham were justified by the law of works, he hath to glory in himself; but not of God. For what saith the Scripture? Abraham believed God, and it was counted unto him for righteousness. Now to him who is justified by the law of works, is the reward reckoned, not of grace, but of debt" (Romans 4:2–4 JST). Many Christians read these passages in Romans as an argument that man is saved by grace and not works.

James, on the other hand, quotes Genesis 15:6 to explain that while Abraham's belief in God was imputed to him for righteousness, Abraham was justified by his works (James 2:20–24). James concludes from the story of Abraham that "by works a man is justified, and not by faith only" (James 2:24).

Interestingly enough, the passages in both Romans (4:2–5) and James (2:14–21) have significant JST changes that point out the importance of faith and works. The discussion in Romans 4 about Abraham's faith and righteousness can perhaps best be summarized by Paul's statement near the end of the chapter: "Therefore ye are justified of faith and works, through grace, to the end the promise might be sure to all the seed; not to them only who are of the law, but to them also who are of the faith of Abraham; who is the father of us all" (Romans 4:16 JST). The JST of the James passage concludes, "Was not Abraham our father justified by works, when he had offered Isaac his son upon the altar? Seest thou how works wrought with his faith, and by works was faith made perfect?" (James 2:20–21 JST).

4. The Blessing of Land (13–20)

The Lord promises Abraham land:

> 13 And the Lord said unto him, I, the Lord, brought thee out
> of Ur, of the Chaldees, to give thee this land to inherit it.

In this section, unlike the two preceding sections, Abraham's question follows the Lord's promise. The phrase *I, the Lord, brought thee out* (Hebrew hiphil of *YṢ*) *of Ur, of the Chaldees* has many echoes in scripture. It is reminiscent of God's initial command to Abraham, "Get thee out of thy country" (Genesis 12:1). Most important, it is the language used of the exodus: "I am the Lord thy God, which have brought thee out (also Hebrew hiphil of *YṢ*) of the land of Egypt" (Exodus 20:2; cf. Deuteronomy 5:6), which event is prophesied in Genesis 15:17 JST.

The idea of the phrase *this land to inherit it* is important because the theology of the land in the Old Testament rests on the fact that the Lord owns the land. He told Israel, "The land shall not be sold for ever: for the land is mine; for ye are strangers and sojourners with me" (Leviticus 25:23). The descendants of Abraham are thus heirs to the land, but the land belongs to the Lord.

Abraham's third question:

> 14a And Abram said, Lord, whereby shall I know that I shall
> inherit it? yet he believed God.

Abraham expresses his confidence in the Lord and at the same time asks how he will know that the promise of land will be fulfilled. Land is a central issue in the story of Abraham. One of Abraham's critical tests was to leave his native land in Ur and go to a promised land, where he would dwell the rest of his life. Ironically, Abraham would live his life as a stranger and a sojourner in this promised land; the only land that he would own would be a small cave that he purchased for the burial of his family (Genesis 23:3–20).

Third visual sign:

> 14b . . . And the Lord said unto him, Take me a heifer of three
> years old, and a she goat of three years old, and a ram of three
> years old, and a turtle-dove, and a young pigeon.
>
> 15 And he took unto him all these, and he divided them in
> the midst, and he laid each piece one against the other; but the
> birds divided he not.
>
> 16 And when the fowls came down upon the carcasses, Abram
> drove them away. And when the sun was going down, a deep sleep
> fell upon Abram; and, lo, a great horror of darkness fell upon him.
>
> 17 And the Lord spake, and he said unto Abram, Know of a
> surety that thy seed shall be a stranger in a land which shall not
> be theirs, and shall serve strangers; and they shall be afflicted, and
> serve them four hundred years; and also that nation whom they
> shall serve will I judge; and afterwards shall they come out with
> great substance.
>
> 18 And thou shalt die, and go to thy fathers in peace; thou
> shalt be buried in a good old age.
>
> 19 But in the fourth generation they shall come hither again;
> for the iniquity of the Amorites is not yet full.
>
> 20 And it came to pass, that when the sun went down, and it
> was dark, behold, a smoking furnace, and a burning lamp which
> passed between those pieces which Abram had divided.

Known as the Covenant between the Pieces, the mysterious
ritual described in this passage is unprecedented in scripture.
Clearly this is intended to be a covenant ritual; covenants are often
accompanied by the slaughter and sacrifice of animals. In Hebrew
the idiom meaning "to make a covenant" is rendered to "cut a covenant," as in the conclusion of the episode: "in that same day the
Lord made a covenant (kārat bərît) with Abram" (Genesis 15:21
JST). The drama is heightened by the setting: "the sun was going
down, a deep sleep fell upon Abram; and, lo, a great horror of
darkness fell upon him" (Genesis 15:16 JST). While the first visual
sign of the stars in the heaven appears to have taken place at night

(Genesis 15:7 JST), the time of day is not specified for the beginning of this particular ritual (Genesis 15:14 JST),[10] but by verse 16 (JST) *the sun was going down.* The meaning of the symbols present in the ritual are explained in neither the biblical text nor the JST; hence, this passage has many different interpretations.

In short, the Lord commands Abraham to take five animals: *a heifer of three years old, a she goat, a ram, a turtle-dove, and a young pigeon,* which he slaughters and cuts up. Abraham cuts the three big animals in two and arranges the pieces opposite each other; he doesn't cut up the birds. When the sun goes down, *a deep sleep [comes] upon Abraham.* The Lord then speaks to Abraham and explains the future of his seed in relationship to the promised land. For four hundred years they will serve an unnamed master as *a stranger in a land which shall not be theirs*—almost certainly a reference to Israel's sojourn in Egypt (Exodus 1–2). Afterwards they will come out *with great substance*—a promise fulfilled in Exodus 3:21–22; 12:36. *In the fourth generation* Abraham's posterity will come and inherit the promised land because by then the iniquity of the Amorites will be full. The Lord promises Abraham a long life and a peaceful death. Then, dramatically, when the sun goes down and it becomes dark, the Lord, represented by a *smoking furnace* and a *burning lamp,* passes between the pieces that Abraham has divided.

Scholars have turned to other biblical and extrabiblical evidence to find useful parallels that aid in the interpretation of this ritual. Three of the most common interpretations include the ritual as a covenant ratification sacrifice, as a symbolic representation of the history of Israel, and as a visual enactment of an oath of self-imprecation.[11]

1. *Covenant ratification sacrifice.* This view is championed by Gerhard F. Hasel, who has examined extrabiblical texts describing sacrifice and concluded that examples of political treaties (one of the most common forms of ancient covenants) from Mari

and Alalakh in the eighteenth century B.C. were accompanied and ratified by ceremonies that involved the killing of animals. He notes that the language of sacrifice in other Near Eastern cultures from the period of Abraham describes the ratification of a treaty or covenant similarly, "to kill (cut) an ass" (Akkadian *hayaram qatalum*), similar to Hebrew "to cut a covenant" (Genesis 15:21 JST). Hasel summarizes this view, "The killing and sectioning of the animals by Abram is the sacrificial *preparatio* for the subsequent divine *ratificatio* of the covenant by Yahweh who in passing between the pieces irrevocably pledges the fulfillment of his covenant promise to the patriarch."[12]

2. *Symbolic representation of the history of Israel.* Gordon J. Wenham interprets this ritual as a dramatization of the history of Abraham's posterity until they inherit the promised land,[13] "a solemn and visual reaffirmation of the covenant."[14] Drawing on the recent anthropological work of Mary Douglas, he notes that ancient Israel saw "a close relationship between the animal world and the human world."[15] He thus equates the five sacrificial animals taken by Abraham to correspond with "clean men," or ancient Israel, and the birds of prey, or the "unclean animals," with the Gentiles. Abraham driving away the birds of prey, according to this view, symbolizes Abraham's protection of his posterity. This action is perhaps both a reference to Abraham's past military foray against the Mesopotamian kings in Genesis 14 and to the future divine protection of his posterity from destruction by the Egyptians, from whom the Lord would eventually deliver his people. Perhaps it also represents the future inhabitants of the land of Canaan. The furnace of fire and the torch passing through the pieces represent the promise that the Lord would walk among Abraham's posterity (Leviticus 26:12). So just as Abraham's life would prefigure the future of his people, so this ceremony would prefigure the relationship of God with Abraham's posterity.

3. *Covenant oath ceremony of self-imprecation.* Many biblical commentators understand this ritual in light of a similar oath

ceremony in Jeremiah 34:18–19, in which the leading citizens in Jerusalem make a covenant and pass between the parts of a calf.[16] During the reign of Zedekiah the people of Jerusalem had sworn an oath to release their slaves. This oath is described in Jeremiah 34:18: "they cut the calf in twain, and passed between the parts thereof." Oaths in the Bible often include implied curses upon the individual swearing the oath should they fail to comply with the terms of the oath. A common oath formula included a phrase, "the Lord do so to me, and more also" (Ruth 1:17) if the individual did or did not do a certain thing (cf. 1 Samuel 3:17; 14:44; 2 Samuel 3:35).[17] Thus the Lord decrees destruction on those in Jerusalem who have not kept their oath, "The men who have violated my covenant . . . I will treat like the calf they cut in two and then walked between its pieces" (Jeremiah 34:18 NIV). Scholars suppose those who passed between the pieces of the calf proclaimed something like, "May God do to me [i.e., what had been done to the animal] and more also, if I do not faithfully keep the terms of the covenant."

In ancient Near Eastern parallels to such a ritual, a vassal swears allegiance to a sovereign power in a political treaty using a similar oath. One example from the first millennium B.C., a period much later than Abraham, is found in the Aramaic inscription Sefire I. Bir-Ga'yah, king of KTK, makes a treaty with Matiʿel king of Arpad, in which possible infractions by Matiʿel are expressed: "[Just as] this calf is cut in two, so may Matiʿel be cut in two, and may his nobles be cut in two!"[18]

Further evidence for such oaths of self-imprecation is found in the Book of Mormon. During Moroni's call to his people to defend their liberties, his people promise to defend their liberty "rending their garments in token, or as a covenant, that they would not forsake the Lord their God," and if they did, "the Lord should rend them even as they had rent their garments" (Alma 46:21). In the same episode the people "cast their garments at the feet of Moroni" with the self-imprecation "if we shall fall into transgression;

yea, he may cast us at the feet of our enemies, even as we have cast our garments at thy feet to be trodden under foot, if we shall fall into transgression" (Alma 46:22).

If indeed this ritual is one of self-imprecation, here is a unique and unprecedented scene of the Lord God of Israel taking the role of the vassal and swearing a most solemn oath in which he takes upon himself the sanctions of the pieces of the animals and confirms the promise of the land to Abraham.[19]

> *18 And thou shalt die, and go to thy fathers in peace; thou shalt be buried in a good old age.*

Clearly one of the issues on Abraham's mind throughout this chapter is that he is getting old and close to dying. He has already contemplated the possibility of Eliezer as his heir (Genesis 15:3 JST), has asked the Lord how he will have an everlasting inheritance, though he will die (Genesis 15:9–10 JST), and has questioned his role in the future history of his people. The promise that Abraham shall go to his fathers in peace (Hebrew *šālôm*) may be a play on Genesis 14:17 JST, where Melchizedek is the king of Salem (Hebrew *šālēm*), and 14:33 JST "he [Melchizedek] obtained peace in Salem, and was called the Prince of peace." All this is significant in light of Abraham's statement of his quest in the Book of Abraham, "having been myself a follower of righteousness, desiring also to be one who possessed great knowledge, and to be a greater follower of righteousness, and to possess a greater knowledge, and to be a father of many nations, a prince of peace" (Abraham 1:2). Thus in Genesis 15 JST Abraham is compared in righteousness and peace to Melchizedek.

> *19 But in the fourth generation they shall come hither again; for the iniquity of the Amorites is not yet full.*

Four generations is most likely to be understood as a restatement of the four hundred years in Genesis 15:17. Strictly speaking, the length of a *generation* in the Bible is the length of the time between the birth of parents and the birth of their children—a period of 15–25 years. But in order to make this statement compatible with the four hundred years in Genesis 15:17 JST, perhaps the term *generation* signifies the lifetime of a person (70–140 years).[20]

The concept that Israel needs to wait until the *iniquity of the Amorites* is full is clarified in the Book of Mormon: "but behold, this people had rejected every word of God, and they were ripe in iniquity and the fulness of the wrath of God was upon them" (1 Nephi 17:35).

The Book of Abraham teaches that the promise of the land to Abraham's posterity was conditional, "I will give unto thy seed after thee for an everlasting possession, when they hearken to my voice" (Abraham 2:6). When the iniquity of the descendants of Abraham was full, God would allow them to be destroyed and scattered from their promised land as well (1 Nephi 17:43; cf. Alma 10:19; Ether 2:9–10).

> 20 . . . behold, a smoking furnace, and a burning lamp which passed between those pieces which Abram had divided.

Almost all commentators agree that the *smoking furnace* and the *burning lamp* are symbols that represent the presence of the Lord. It may be a case of hendiadys,[21] where both symbols are meant to refer to the same entity. Similar language is used of the presence of the Lord on Sinai, "fire" and "smoke of a furnace" (Exodus 19:18; 20:18), and in the "pillar of a cloud" and "pillar of fire" in the wilderness (Exodus 13:21). If indeed this is a covenant self-imprecation ceremony, the *smoking furnace* and the *burning lamp* represent the Lord swearing to a solemn and touching oath regarding the land. If this is a historical representation, then it illustrates the Lord's promise of his presence in the midst of his people, as dramatized later by the pillar of cloud and fire in the exodus and by the symbolism of the presence of God in the tabernacle and the temple.

5. The Lord Makes a Covenant with Abraham (21–22)

> *21 And in that same day the Lord made a covenant with Abram, saying, Unto thy seed have I given this land, from the river of Egypt unto the great river Euphrates;*
>
> *22 The Kenites, and the Kenazites, and the Kadmonites, and Hittites, and the Perizzites, and the Rephaims, and the Amorites, and the Canaanites, and the Girgashites, and the Jebusites.*

As I mentioned earlier, the language *the Lord made a covenant* is literally "cut a covenant," emphasizing the connection between sacrifice and covenant making. From the beginning Adam and Eve offered sacrifice in similitude of the Lamb of God.

In history the closest Israel ever came to conquering these ideal borders *from the river of Egypt unto the great river Euphrates* was in the time of David and Solomon (2 Samuel 8:3; 1 Kings 4:21).

This is the longest of the seventeen lists in the Bible of the peoples who inhabited the promised land before the conquest.[22] The Book of Abraham refers to the promised land as "the land of Canaan" (Abraham 2:15–18). The Book of Mormon never mentions the Canaanites but refers to "the children of this land" (1 Nephi 17:33).

Conclusion

A careful reading of Genesis 15 in light of modern revelation, in particular the Joseph Smith Translation, teaches us much. First and foremost, chapter 15 reveals a dynamic relationship between God and Abraham—a relationship in which Abraham can discuss the feelings and concerns of his heart with God, who hears and answers him.

The promises of the Abrahamic covenant pronounced in chapter 15—posterity, eternal inheritance, and land—are clarified by a study of the account of the blessing of Melchizedek restored in Genesis 14:25–40 JST. The whole of Genesis 15 is enriched by an understanding that Abraham seeks to model himself after Melchizedek.

Throughout the Abrahamic narratives, the Lord commands and promises, and Abraham faithfully obeys. But in chapter 15 the roles are somewhat reversed. Here it is Abraham who questions the Lord and his promises, and it is the Lord who confirms them in a dramatic fashion by passing through the pieces of the sacrifice. Throughout these narratives Abraham repeatedly proves his righteousness through his acts, but in chapter 15 he proves his righteousness through his faith. In chapter 15 Abraham provides for his posterity the model of faith by believing in those promises that are not readily believable: that he will have literal seed from his body, although he and his wife are getting old; that he will be resurrected through the sacrifice of the Son of Man and will possess the land as an everlasting inheritance; and that in the future his posterity would come out of bondage to possess the land. The righteousness of Abraham in chapter 15 lies in his trust, confidence, and faith in the Lord's promises, and the Lord's promises are sealed with a solemn oath when he passes between the pieces.

Notes

1. Rabbinic tradition preserves several different lists of these trials. The Mishnah records, "With ten trials was Abraham, our father, proved, and he stood [firm] in them all; to make known how great was the love of Abraham, our father (peace be upon him)." J. Israelstam, trans., *Aboth* 5.3, in *The Babylonian Talmud: Seder Nezekin,* ed. Isidore Epstein (London: Soncino, 1935), 59–60. A convenient summary and review of the rabbinic material can be found in the *Babylonian Talmud,* ibid., 59.

2. Interestingly enough, according to one rabbinic tradition, Abraham's first test occurred when he was cast into a furnace in Ur and came out unscathed, having been saved by the archangel Michael. See *Midrash Rabbah* Genesis 64:13 (London: Soncino, 1983), 369; and *Aboth* 5:3, in *The Babylonian Talmud: Seder Nezekin,* 59. See also John A. Tvedtnes, Brian M. Hauglid, and John Gee, eds., *Traditions about the Early Life of Abraham* (Provo, Utah: FARMS, 2001). Rabbinic tradition preserves different lists of the tests. According to I ARN [Aboth de Rabbi Natan], they include: "Two trials at the time he was bidden to leave Haran, two with

his two sons, two with his two wives, one in the wars of the Kings, one at the covenant 'between the pieces' (Gen. XV), one in Ur of the Chaldees." Another tradition in "II ARN [Aboth de Rabbi Natan] Ch. XXXVI speaks of ten trials, but names only nine: (i) at Ur; (ii) *Get thee out of thy land* . . . (Gen. XII, 1); (iii) The famine when he left Haran (ibid. v. 10); (iv) Sarah at Pharaoh's palace; (v) Sarah at Abimelech's; (vi) Circumcision; (vii) The covenant '*between the pieces*'; (viii) With Isaac; (ix) With Ishmael." Ibid., 59 n. 6. The Book of Abraham preserves the story of Abraham being delivered by an angel from sacrifice on an altar where he was offered for sacrifice with the consent of his own father Terah (Abraham 1:1–17; Facsimile 1).

3. Recent and excellent commentaries on Genesis include Walter Brueggeman, *Genesis* (Atlanta: Knox, 1982); Victor P. Hamilton, *The Book of Genesis: Chapters 1–17* (Grand Rapids, Mich.: Eerdmans, 1990); J. Gerald Janzen, *Abraham and All the Families of the Earth: A Commentary on the Book of Genesis 12–50* (Grand Rapids, Mich.: Eerdmans, 1993); Nahum M. Sarna, *The JPS Torah Commentary: Genesis* (Philadelphia: Jewish Publication Society, 1989); and Gordon J. Wenham, *Genesis 1–15* (Waco, Tex.: Word Books, 1987).

4. Joseph Smith, *History of the Church of Jesus Christ of Latter-day Saints,* 2nd ed. (Salt Lake City: Deseret Book, 1950), 5:555.

5. Unfortunately, because the biblical events recounted in the narrative in the Book of Abraham end with Abraham in Egypt (Genesis 12:10–13 = Abraham 2:21–25), the Book of Abraham has no information about Genesis 14 or 15.

6. Because the Latter-day Saint edition of the King James Version of the Bible does not reproduce the entire text, Genesis 15 JST is quoted from *The Holy Scriptures: Inspired Version* (Independence, Mo.: Herald Publishing House, 1974), 34–35.

7. Josephus says of Abraham, "Berosus mentions our father Abraham, without naming him, in these terms: 'In the tenth generation after the flood there lived among the Chaldeans a just man and great and versed in celestial lore.'" Josephus, *Jewish Antiquities* 1.158, in *Josephus,* trans. H. St. J. Thackeray, LCL (Cambridge: Harvard University Press, 1978), 79.

8. See the Joseph Smith statement in *History of the Church,* 5:555, note 4 above.

9. William L. Holladay, *A Concise Hebrew and Aramaic Lexicon of the Old Testament* (Leiden: Brill, 1971), 20.

10. This might suggest that the events in chapter 15 of Genesis occurred over a period of two days.

11. The various interpretations are discussed by Gerhard F. Hasel, "The Meaning of the Animal Rite in Gen. 15," *Journal for the Study of the Old Testament* 19 (February 1981): 61–78.

12. Ibid., 70.

13. Gordon J. Wenham, "The Symbolism of the Animal Rite in Genesis 15: A Response to G. F. Hasel," *Journal for the Study of the Old Testament* 22 (February 1982): 134–37. Wenham explains his interpretation further in his commentary on Genesis in *Genesis 1–15,* 330–35.

14. "It is not a dramatised curse that would come into play should the covenant be broken, but a solemn and visual reaffirmation of the covenant that is essentially a promise." Wenham, "Response," 136.

15. Ibid., 134.

16. It should be noted that some scholars do not believe that the ritual in Jeremiah 34:18–19 is a useful parallel to the ritual in Genesis 15, due to the differences in setting and details between the two narratives; see Hasel, "The Meaning of the Animal Rite," 62–63. Those scholars who dislike the interpretation of the ritual in Genesis 15 as a divine self-imprecation also often cite the fact that they are not comfortable with God calling "upon himself divine sanctions." Ibid., 64.

17. For a concise discussion of biblical oaths, see M. H. Pope, "Oaths," in *The Interpreter's Dictionary of the Bible,* ed. George A. Buttrick et al. (Nashville: Abingdon, 1962), 3:575–77.

18. Translation from Joseph A. Fitzmyer, *The Aramaic Inscriptions of Sefire* (Rome: Pontifical Biblical Institute, 1967), 14–15, as found in Hamilton, *The Book of Genesis, 1–17,* 432. For another example of such rituals in the vassal treaties of Esarhaddon, see Hamilton, *The Book of Genesis,* 432.

19. Elsewhere the Lord swears by himself (Genesis 22:16; 26:3) or by his life (Numbers 14:21).

20. Sarna, *Genesis,* 116.

21. Hendiadys is a Greek term that literally means "one by means of two." It is a term for a figure of speech in which two nouns are joined by

a conjunction (usually "and") to express a single idea instead of a noun with an adjective. Examples in the Bible include "[they] buried him [Samuel] in *Ramah, even in his own city*" (1 Samuel 28:3, emphasis added), meaning his own city Ramah; "thou hast prepared *the light and the sun*" (Psalm 74:16, emphasis added), meaning the sunlight.

22. The other lists mention seven, six, five, or three ethnic groups. See Sarna, *Genesis,* 117 and 359 n. 3.

Chapter 12

Joseph Smith Vindicated Again: Enoch, Moses 7:48, and Apocryphal Sources

Andrew C. Skinner

Many times in the past 170 years, Joseph Smith's prophetic calling and powers have been reconfirmed.[1] However, one of the most interesting, as well as unusual, examples of such vindication is found in Pearl of Great Price texts that center on the enigmatic figure of Enoch the seer.

References to the antediluvian patriarch in the Bible are scant indeed. Everything about Enoch in the Old Testament can be read in less than a minute (see Genesis 5:18–24). The New Testament book of Jude adds only two more verses (see Jude 1:14–15). And the book of Hebrews explains in one verse that "by faith Enoch was translated that he should not see death; and was not found, because God had translated him: for before his translation he had this testimony, that he pleased God" (Hebrews 11:5). Outside of the Bible, though, the body of Enoch material is extensive. In apocryphal sources Enoch is a popular figure and receives significant attention. The collection known as *1 Enoch* is comparable in size to the biblical book of Isaiah and is believed by scholars to have been "created, transmitted, and developed in 'pious' Jewish circles of the 4th to 1st centuries B.C.E."[2]

Latter-day Saints know that Enoch was a mighty prophet who carried out a significant antediluvian ministry and also that the Prophet Joseph Smith restored by revelation a greatly expanded corpus of Enoch material when he worked on that portion of his inspired revision of the Bible in December 1830. The Prophet related:

> It may be well to observe here, that the Lord greatly encouraged and strengthened the faith of His little flock, which had embraced the fulness of the everlasting Gospel, as revealed to them in the Book of Mormon, by giving some more extended information upon the Scriptures, a translation of which had already commenced. . . . [I]t seems the Apostolic Church had some of these writings, as Jude mentions or quotes the Prophecy of Enoch, the seventh from Adam. To the joy of the little flock . . . did the Lord reveal the following doings of olden times, from the prophecy of Enoch [Moses 7:1–69 follows here].[3]

Modern prophets typically expand what we have received in the Bible and reveal more of the ancient word of God—rarely do they shrink the corpus. Latter-day Saints accept the details of Enoch's life and ministry as found in the Pearl of Great Price (mainly Moses 6 and 7) and believe these verses are neither fictitious traditions nor late compositions originating from "'pious' Jewish circles" from the fourth to the first centuries B.C. but rather are authentic ancient descriptions of the experiences of the powerful seventh patriarch of the human family. Of course, one can understand why it may look to some readers outside the Latter-day Saint tradition as though Joseph Smith simply copied down and incorporated into his own King James Version a few pseudepigraphic passages about Enoch known from late antiquity. However, certain thought-provoking issues and characteristics of the Enoch passages in the Pearl of Great Price resist such an easy dismissal of Joseph Smith's restored canon.

One issue is the availability in 1830 America—or rather the lack thereof—of Enoch material from which to create a revised or enhanced biblical text centering on the ancient seer. Another is the "unlearned" Prophet's uncanny ability to capture the essence of Enoch's life in such a small amount of space (remember that the pseudepigraphic book of *1 Enoch* alone is the size of the book of Isaiah) while at the same time remaining faithful to the salient points found in the full range of Enoch traditions and texts, some of which did not even come to light until the twentieth century. A third issue is the clear and striking description of the Savior's atonement in the meridian of time found in Joseph Smith's Enoch texts but not in any of the apocryphal Enoch sources. And a fourth issue is the odd-sounding description of mother-earth (in Moses 7:48), whose voice cries out for redress because of her wicked inhabitants. While this motif is found in *1 Enoch* (the so-called *Ethiopic Enoch*), Moses 7:48 most resembles an Aramaic fragment of an Enoch text found among the Dead Sea Scrolls from Qumran Cave 4, which, however, was not discovered until after 1952 and not published until 1976 by J. T. Milik as 4QEnGiants[a] 8.[4]

Availability of Enoch Texts

To review the history of different interpreters' interactions with the writings and traditions associated with Enoch is to look at a story filled with many ups and downs, as well as large gaps. Scholars contend that a book of Enoch was well known to different groups of Jews during intertestamental times but not before. (Evidence of its existence and use in Old Testament times is lacking—an argument scholars use against the authenticity of the Book of Moses passages about Enoch.) The Dead Sea Scrolls community at Qumran, to which I shall return shortly, took pains to preserve its Enoch texts. The writers of various apocryphal and pseudepigraphical works seem to have drawn upon either a book of Enoch or an established corpus of Enoch traditions of the kind collected for other biblical figures (see, for example, *Testaments of the Twelve Patriarchs;* the *Assumption of Moses;* Baruch; and *4 Ezra*). However, references to a book of Enoch in Jewish texts after the second century A.D. are rarely, if ever, found.[5]

Among the early Christians, Enoch was obviously well known. According to R. H. Charles, an early twentieth-century expert on the Apocrypha and Pseudepigrapha, the book of Enoch had more influence on the New Testament "than . . . all the other apocryphal and pseudepigraphical works taken together."[6] Concepts found in *1 Enoch* are attested in various New Testament books, with Jude 1:14–15 being a quotation of *1 Enoch* 1:9. But during the Middle Ages, beginning in the fourth century, interest in Enoch generally waned, the notable exception being the Byzantine historian George Syncellus (ca. A.D. 800), who cited a passage from Enoch in his writings.[7]

As the Renaissance dawned, providing the impetus for the Reformation, excitement developed over what was reported to be an authentic book of Enoch discovered by Pico della Mirandola (1463–94), classicist and Christian Hebraist extraordinaire. For the next few hundred years, manuscripts containing Enoch traditions and quotations were lauded or discredited by verdicts that ran the gamut from "authentic" to "stinking fables."[8] Then, in 1773, the explorer James Bruce discovered three Ethiopic manuscripts in Abyssinia, including what scholars still regard as the entire, or almost the entire, *First Book of Enoch*. In 1886–87, portions of the Greek version of *1 Enoch* (1:1–32:6) were unearthed from a Christian grave site at Akhmim, Egypt.[9] However, scholarly interest in these finds was minimal for several years.

As Michael Stuart reported, "the honour of revealing to the [modern] world the [hidden] treasure" of the book of Enoch, which had remained buried, so to speak, for so long, went to an Oxford scholar named Richard Laurence.[10] In 1821, he produced not just the first English version, but really the first modern-language translation of the Ethiopic book of Enoch under the title *The book of Enoch the prophet, an apocryphal production, . . . now first translated from an Ethiopic ms. in the Bodleian Library.* He issued revised editions in 1833, 1838, and 1842. These were followed by other English, Latin, German, and French translations by various scholars, as well as a critical Ethiopic edition.[11]

The point to be made here against the backdrop of all this history is that the only edition of the book of Enoch potentially available to the Prophet Joseph Smith in 1830, when he produced that portion of his Inspired Version of the Bible containing Enoch's story, was the Laurence translation of 1821—a fact to which all scholars will attest. To believe that the Prophet obtained a rare copy of that work, which had been produced in England for scholars, and then found the time to pore over its pages and digest its nuances strains credibility beyond the breaking point, particularly when one considers the lack of formal education possessed by the Prophet.

When scholars in England obtained Laurence's edition of the book of Enoch, their wholehearted efforts seem to have gone into dismissing and suppressing it, not promoting and disseminating it. It seems that Joseph Smith could not have obtained a copy of it even if he had known about it. The Prophet himself said that a book of Enoch was among the "lost books" of the Bible and was "now nowhere to be found."[12] Furthermore, between 1821 and 1830 the Prophet was so busy with other matters of divine consequence—such as receiving the revelations recorded in the Doctrine and Covenants, translating and publishing the Book of Mormon, and organizing the church (not to mention moving around to avoid life-threatening persecution)—that one wonders when he would have found the time to internalize Laurence's book of Enoch and reproduce it in distilled form.

Essence of Enoch

Yet, in 1830, when the study of Enoch was still in its infancy, the Prophet Joseph Smith managed to come up with many crucial elements of Enoch's life and ministry that appear scattered throughout the corpus of nonbiblical texts associated with the seer. But Joseph was able to weave these elements into a seamless fabric of the antediluvian patriarch's story, as though that story had once been conveyed that way anciently (which it had). Some of the striking parallels between Joseph Smith's work and the Enoch traditions now available include the following:

- Enoch, like other prophets, journeyed forth, had the spirit of God descend upon him, and was transfigured in order to endure a heavenly environment and heavenly beings (see Moses 6:26–27; compare *1 Enoch* 71:1; also Moses 1:11).
- Enoch came to understand the nature and condition of unrepentant mortals—that the wicked bring upon themselves death and hell by their own actions (see Moses 6:29; compare *1 Enoch* 63:9).
- Enoch, seeking communion with heaven, prostrated himself on the ground, and the Lord spoke to him (see Moses 6:31–32; compare *1 Enoch* 14:24).
- Enoch referred to a book of remembrance based on a divine pattern (see Moses 6:46; compare *1 Enoch* 93:2–3).
- Enoch knew of the phrase *Son of Man* (see Moses 6:57; compare *1 Enoch* 48:2), though modern scholarship usually regards it as a reference to Enoch himself.
- Enoch understood God's ruling power over many creations (see Moses 6:61; 7:30, 36; compare *1 Enoch* 14:22; 39:11; 84:3).
- Enoch was taught that all things in the universe bear record of and glorify God (see Moses 6:63; compare *1 Enoch* 69:21–24).
- Enoch saw the heavens weep because of the wickedness of humankind (see Moses 7:28; compare *1 Enoch* 100:11–13).
- Enoch saw the tribulation and torment of the wicked (see Moses 7:38–39; compare *1 Enoch* 45:2).

- Enoch wept over the wickedness of humankind (see Moses 7:41, 44; compare *Secrets of Enoch* 41).
- Enoch saw Noah build an ark (see Moses 7:43; compare *1 Enoch* 89:1).
- Enoch saw that the Lord would gather his people and that the earth would be redeemed (see Moses 7:62, 64–65; compare *1 Enoch* 45:4–5; 51:5).
- Enoch saw that the righteous of the earth would one day dwell with the righteous who descended from heaven (see Moses 7:62–63; compare *1 Enoch* 39:1, 5).
- Enoch's Zion will return from heaven (see Moses 7:63; compare *1 Enoch* 39:1).
- God showed Enoch all things (see Moses 7:67; compare *1 Enoch* 19:3).
- God himself "took Enoch"—meaning that he was translated (into the highest heaven, according to *2 Enoch* 67; compare Moses 7:21–23, 69).

The Atonement at the Center

Despite all the striking similarities between Joseph Smith's account of Enoch and the apocryphal sources, two outstanding differences are noteworthy. First, the Enoch texts in the Book of Moses constantly, even relentlessly, put the Lord at the center of all action. He is the prime mover and source of activity affecting the ultimate destiny of this earth and its inhabitants as seen by the seer. In apocryphal literature, Enoch is shown the government of the cosmos and the progression of earth's history. Also in Joseph Smith's version of Enoch, the great patriarch is shown such scenes, but Jesus Christ is at the heart of them.

Closely related to the first, the second difference and most significant unique feature of Enoch's record in the Pearl of Great Price is the clear and unadulterated description of the atoning sacrifice of Jesus Christ and its impact on this earth as well as on the heavens. In fact, both the first and second comings of the Son of God in the flesh are prophesied and described in impressive detail. Such descriptions constitute the greatest contribution and restoration of lost information of the many verses of Joseph Smith's inspired revision of the life and ministry of Enoch. The prophetic visions of the Lord's redemptive acts reported in the Book of Moses ought to be regarded as the real essence and true significance of Enoch's multidimensional record. Consider the verses in Moses 7 that help put the atonement in its cosmic context; these begin by describing Enoch's emotional and spiritual despair brought on by his vision of the earth's future turmoil and unmitigated wickedness. He refuses to be comforted (see Moses 7:44) until he is shown the coming of Jesus Christ in the flesh.

> And the Lord said: Blessed is he through whose seed Messiah shall come; for he saith—I am Messiah, the King of Zion, the Rock of Heaven, which is broad as eternity; whoso cometh in at the gate and climbeth up by me shall never fall; wherefore, blessed are they of whom I have spoken, for they shall come forth with songs of everlasting joy.
>
> And it came to pass that Enoch cried unto the Lord, saying: When the Son of Man cometh in the flesh, shall the earth rest? I pray thee, show me these things.
>
> And the Lord said unto Enoch: Look, and he looked and beheld the Son of Man lifted up on the cross, after the manner of men;
>
> And he heard a loud voice; and the heavens were veiled; and all the creations of God mourned; and the earth groaned; and the rocks were rent; and the saints arose, and were crowned at the right hand of the Son of Man, with crowns of glory;
>
> And as many of the spirits as were in prison came forth, and stood on the right hand of God; and the remainder were reserved in chains of darkness until the judgment of the great day. (Moses 7:53–57)

The foregoing is more than the core of Enoch's vision; these verses constitute the essence of the plan of salvation. The Messiah came to this earth to be crucified so that the righteous spirits in prison could go free, while others would have to wait for the day of judgment because of their wickedness.

Though he sees the atonement of the Son of God, the record indicates that Enoch still is not completely comforted; he weeps again, asking once more when the earth will rest. He is then shown the second coming of the Lord in power and glory to fulfill all his promises to the antediluvian patriarchs.

> And Enoch beheld the Son of Man ascend up unto the Father; and he called unto the Lord, saying: Wilt thou not come again upon the earth? Forasmuch as thou art God, and I know thee, and thou hast sworn unto me, and commanded me that I should ask in the name of thine Only Begotten; thou hast made me, and given unto me a right to thy throne, and not of myself, but through thine own grace; wherefore, I ask thee if thou wilt not come again on the earth.
>
> And the Lord said unto Enoch: As I live, even so will I come in the last days, in the days of wickedness and vengeance, to fulfil the oath which I have made unto you concerning the children of Noah. (Moses 7:59–60)

Mother Earth

In Joseph Smith's version of the Enoch story, both the first and second comings of the Messiah are directly connected to times of great wickedness. In fact, this account draws attention to the Messiah's mortal mission by its linkage to the unusual and very vivid description of the personification of the earth, as reported in Moses 7:48:

> And it came to pass that Enoch looked upon the earth; and he heard a voice from the bowels thereof, saying: Wo, wo is me, the mother of men; I am pained, I am weary, because of the wickedness of my children. When shall I rest, and be cleansed from the filthiness which is gone forth out of me? When will my Creator sanctify me, that I may rest, and righteousness for a season abide upon my face?

The mother-earth motif, a category into which Moses 7:48 clearly seems to fall, is one of the earliest and most common concepts found in the ancient mythologies and religious frameworks of the Near East. It cuts across cultures and time periods.[13] Thus it is not unexpected that echoes of the earth's protests to heaven against humankind's wicked ways, as portrayed in Moses 7:48, are also found in two sections of *1 Enoch,* as well as among the Dead Sea Scrolls, specifically in some Aramaic fragments discovered in Cave 4 at Qumran.

Enoch was a figure of special interest to the people of Qumran, "doubtless due to sectarian concern about issues pertaining to revelatory authority, calendrical computation, scribal wisdom, and eschatological [end of the world] events."[14] Not surprisingly, and with the possible exception of calendrical concerns, these are matters of great interest to Latter-day Saints as well and may help us see why the Lord revealed so much about Enoch to the Prophet Joseph Smith. (In fact, it is not difficult to see why these concepts would be of special import to any community claiming to be a group of covenant-based Israelites seeking to live by revealed truth until God established his ultimate kingdom on earth.) Eleven Aramaic manuscripts, all recovered from Cave 4, constitute the oldest surviving texts of Enoch literature outside the Latter-day Saint corpus—copies of writings purported to have been authored by the seer himself. Additionally, the Dead Sea Scrolls include other writings in which the figure of Enoch plays a prominent role (see 4Q203 [4QEnGiants[a] 8] and 4Q530 [4QGiants[b] 2]). In this regard, the *Book of Giants* is an expansion of the story found in Genesis 6:1–4 about the birth of giants in the land and reflects the same pervasive wickedness mentioned in Moses 6 and 7. The standard critical edition of these Aramaic fragments is the one published by J. T. Milik in 1976 (hereafter 4QEnGiants[a] 8 or simply 4QEnGiants).[15]

A comparison of the "mother-earth" or "pleading-earth" passages from the apocryphal collections of Enoch, including the

Aramaic texts from Qumran, with Moses 7:48, cited above, is instructive.

1 Enoch 7:4–6; 8:4	*1 Enoch 9:2, 10*	4QEnGiantsª 8, lines 3–4, 6–12[16]
The giants turned against them and devoured mankind. And they began to sin against birds, and beasts, and reptiles, and fish, and to devour one another's flesh, and drink the blood. Then *the earth laid accusation* against the lawless ones. . . . And as men perished, they cried, and their cry went up to heaven.	And they said one to another: '*The earth,* made without inhabitant, *cries* the voice of their crying up to the gates of heaven. . . . And now, behold, the souls of those who have died are crying and making their suit to the gates of heaven, and their lamentations have ascended: and cannot cease because of the lawless deeds which are wrought on the earth.	The copy of the second tablet of the E[pistle . . . written] by Enoch . . . Let it be known to you that [you] n[ot . . .] and your works and those of your wives [. . .] themselves [and their] children and the wives of [their children . . .] by your prostitution on the earth. And it befell you [. . . And *the earth complains*] and accuses you, and the works of your children too, [and its voice rises right to the portals of heaven, complaining and accusing (you) of] the corruption by which you have corrupted it. [. . .] until the coming of Raphael. Lo, a destruction [. . . on men and on animals: the birds which fly on the face of heaven, and the animals which live on the earth]

Though the parallels between Moses 7, *1 Enoch,* and 4QEn-Giants are impressive, one notes certain differences between the three accounts; one significant difference is the specific identification of the earth in Moses 7:48 as the "mother of men"—a designation missing in *1 Enoch* and 4QEnGiants. Such a notion immediately recalls the earliest literate cultures of ancient Mesopotamia rather than the later religious context of postexilic Israel. As one scholar notes, "the Sumerian Earth-mother is repeatedly referred to in Sumerian and Babylonian names as the mother of mankind. . . . This mythological doctrine is thoroughly accepted in Babylonian religion. . . . In early Accadian, this mythology is already firmly established among the Semites."[17]

Thus, this ethos pervading Sumerian-Akkadian religious belief—the idea that mother-earth was regarded as the mother of men—is also reflected in Moses 7:48 and may well represent one of the early episodes upon which other conceptions of the divine earth-mother image are based, as seen in ancient cultures of the Near East. In other words, Joseph Smith's Enoch text discloses an early Semitic milieu just as legitimately as a late one, from which many non–Latter-day Saint scholars believe all the Enoch material derives. The Enoch-centered verses of Moses 7 are different from other Enoch texts because they actually bear evidence of the authentic ancient context of Enoch's day, closer chronologically to the Sumerian-Akkadian cultural complex (2400–1900 B.C.) than the time frame of the intertestamental period (400–1 B.C.), when texts associated with Enoch had already been filtered through centuries of transmission.

A second difference between Moses 7, *1 Enoch,* and 4QEn-Giants is the nature of the wickedness portrayed therein. In *1 Enoch* the wickedness described seems to be some sort of violence directed against humankind, as well as unspecified sin directed against birds, beasts, reptiles, and fish. But in 4QEnGiants the wickedness of people is defined explicitly as "prostitution" (Aramaic *znwtkwn* זנותכון). And in Moses 7:48 wickedness is equated with "filthiness" in eloquent parallel construction: "the wickedness of my children . . . the filthiness which is gone forth out of me." The texts of Moses 7 and 4QEnGiants appear intuitively closer to each other than *1 Enoch* seems to the other two, because filthiness, immorality, and idolatry are closely associated with each other in Semitic-based biblical culture. See, for example, Ezra 6:21; 9:11; Ezekiel 16:36; 24:13; Revelation 17:4.[18]

A third difference between Moses 7:48 and *1 Enoch* 7, 8, and 9 is the nature of the complaint registered by the earth. In Moses 7 the *earth* itself complains of and decries the wickedness of the people, while the *1 Enoch* texts emphasize the cries of *men* ascending to heaven. Though J. T. Milik's edition of 4QEnGiants posits several reconstructions of the text at this point, enough remains to indicate that the Qumran version of Enoch originally portrayed a scene more closely paralleling Moses 7:48, where the earth complains because of the wickedness of its inhabitants and that complaint rises to the portals of heaven. This resonance between these two texts is important given Joseph Smith's obvious unawareness of the Qumran material. It would seem to hark back to a common strand of early Enoch traditions, which Joseph Smith said originated in the ancient antediluvian patriarchal period.

A fourth and final difference between the texts of Moses 7, *1 Enoch*, and 4QEnGiants involves what one might term the ultimate motivation behind earth's cry for redress against the intense wickedness on her surface, and the result that follows. In Moses 7:48 mother earth pleads for a cleansing of and sanctification from the pervasive wickedness by means of a heavenly personage and heavenly powers. The earth importunes, "When shall I rest, and be cleansed from the filthiness which is gone forth out of me? When will my Creator sanctify me, that I may rest, and righteousness for a season abide upon my face?" This plea for redemption through a creator, and the resultant rest from wickedness as righteousness dwells on the earth, is nowhere to be found in *1 Enoch*.

However, one again notes that the 4QEnGiants text parallels Moses 7:48; here the earth complains about the corruption instigated by her inhabitants "until the coming of Raphael," and then in 4QEnGiants[a] 8, lines 11–12, we read, "Lo, a destruction," which destruction certainly must be regarded as a type of cleansing from the prevalent wickedness on the earth, just as is mentioned in other scriptural passages (see, for example, Job 21:17, 30; Proverbs 10:29). In fact, in Joseph Smith's inspired revision of the Gospel ("Testimony") of Matthew, the destruction of the wicked is equated with the end of the world in preparation for the consummate righteousness brought about by Christ's second coming and millennial reign (see Matthew 24:4 JST or Joseph Smith—Matthew 1:4; Matthew 13:39, 41). Given all we know about the theology of the Qumran covenanters, it seems probable that the destruction mentioned in 4QEnGiants would have been seen as a great cleansing episode, signaling the end of the world in preparation for the consummate righteousness that was expected to prevail on the earth after the end times.

When speaking of a cleansing and sanctification of the earth, Moses 7:48 is clearly alluding to the coming of Jesus Christ and his atonement, which would cleanse the earth from the filthiness that had overrun it. In this passage Enoch heard the earth plead to know when her Creator (who is none other than Jesus Christ according to Moses 1:29–33) would sanctify her. And several verses later (see Moses 7:53–56), Enoch was privileged to receive the answer to that question as he was shown the coming of the Messiah in the flesh and his atoning sacrifice, particularly the crucifixion. While the later Mosaic law amply testified to the fact that it was well understood that cleansing came through atonement (see Leviticus 16:30; Numbers 8:21), knowledge of the Atoning One already seems to have been lost or ignored.

Conclusion

Joseph Smith's inspired revision of the Bible is significant for many reasons, but especially for its restored knowledge that the antediluvian patriarchs knew about the coming of the Messiah in the flesh and his all-powerful atoning sacrifice. In bringing this fact to light, the Prophet Joseph helps us to see how these ancient seers possessed, in its fullest sense, the spirit of prophecy as defined by John the Revelator when he wrote that "the testimony of Jesus is the spirit of prophecy" (Revelation 19:10). Standing prominently among the antediluvian prophet-patriarchs in the inspired revision of the Bible is Enoch, about whom we now know so much owing to Joseph Smith's own revelatory experiences, and whose ministry we now understand to be centered on a revealed witness of the first and second comings of Christ.

Indeed, the Enoch story in the Book of Moses links Enoch's visions of the atonement with one of the most unusual episodes, found heretofore only in apocryphal sources. Moses 7 describes and clarifies for us the context of the mother-earth or pleading-earth episode also depicted in *1 Enoch* 7, 8, and 9 and in a fragment from the Dead Sea Scrolls, 4QEnGiants. In every way, Moses 7:48 is a superior rendition. From a doctrinal standpoint, it not only confirms that the Savior's atonement was taught from the beginning of time, but it also illustrates what the ancients believed long ago—that the earth is a living entity. President Joseph Fielding Smith offered this commentary on Moses 7:48:

> The Lord here informs us that the earth on which we dwell is a living thing, and that the time must come when it will be sanctified from all unrighteousness. In the Pearl of Great Price, when Enoch is conversing with the Lord, he hears the earth crying for deliverance from the iniquity upon her face. . . . It is not the fault of the earth that wickedness prevails upon her face, for she has been true to the law which she received and that law is the celestial law. Therefore the Lord says that the earth shall be sanctified from all unrighteousness.[19]

In addition, the parallels or similarities between the Moses 7 account and the 4QEnGiants account, and the concomitant absence of such similarities in the *1 Enoch* account, become a powerful witness of the Prophet's divine call, especially when one remembers that there was no earthly way for the Prophet to base his work on the Dead Sea Scrolls version—the earliest of all the known Enoch texts—because the scrolls were not to be discovered for another hundred years. Thus we conclude that Joseph Smith was forced to produce scripture the old-fashioned way—pure unadulterated revelation from God.

Notes

On related issues, see Daniel C. Peterson's paper, "On the Motif of the Weeping God in Moses 7," in this volume, 285–317.

1. Examples range from the fulfillment of specific prophecies given by Joseph Smith, such as the beginning of the American Civil War, to the publication of an entire volume of scripture that has been shown to fit extraordinarily well within the ancient cultural and linguistic context from which it purports to originate, to the hundreds of doctrinal clarifications essential to biblically centered Christianity.

2. George W. E. Nickelsburg, "Enoch, First Book of," in *The Anchor Bible Dictionary,* ed. David N. Freedman et al. (New York: Doubleday, 1992), 2:515.

3. Joseph Smith, *History of the Church of Jesus Christ of Latter-day Saints,* 2nd ed. (Salt Lake City: Deseret Book, 1950), 1:131–33.

4. J. T. Milik, *The Books of Enoch: Aramaic Fragments of Qumrân Cave 4* (Oxford: Clarendon, 1976), 314–16.

5. Martin Rist, "Enoch, Book of," in *The Interpreter's Dictionary of the Bible* (Nashville: Abingdon, 1962), 2:104.

6. R. H. Charles, ed. and trans., *The Book of Enoch, or 1 Enoch* (London: Oxford University Press, 1913), xcv. All quotations from *1 Enoch* in this essay come from this translation. A more recent collection is James H. Charlesworth, *The Old Testament Pseudepigrapha* (New York: Doubleday, 1983), 1:5–315.

7. See Hugh Nibley, *Enoch the Prophet* (Salt Lake City: Deseret Book and FARMS, 1986), 99.

8. It was a Prussian scholar named Job Ludolf who rendered the latter verdict. See the whole discussion in ibid., 101, as well as the scholars Nibley cites in his notes.

9. Rist, "Enoch," 103.

10. Michael Stuart, "Christology of the Book of Enoch," *The American Biblical Repository,* 2nd ser., 3 (January 1840): 88; cited in Nibley, *Enoch the Prophet,* 105.

11. Ibid. Rist, "Enoch," 103, makes the point that Laurence's work was the first modern-language edition of the book of Enoch.

12. *History of the Church,* 1:132.

13. Mircea Eliade and Lawrence E. Sullivan, "Earth," in *The Encyclopedia of Religion,* ed. Mircea Eliade (New York: Macmillan, 1987), 4:534.

14. John C. Reeves, "Enoch," in *The Encyclopedia of the Dead Sea Scrolls,* ed. Lawrence H. Schiffman and James C. VanderKam (New York: Oxford University Press, 2000), 1:249.

15. Milik, *The Books of Enoch.*

16. Ibid., 315, brackets in original.

17. Stephen H. Langdon, *Semitic,* vol. 5 in The Mythology of All Races (New York: Cooper Square, 1964), 12–13.

18. For passages that regard idolatry as "spiritual adultery," see, for example, Leviticus 17:7; Judges 2:17; and Jeremiah 3:6, 8–9.

19. Joseph Fielding Smith, *Church History and Modern Revelation* (Salt Lake City: The Council of the Twelve Apostles of the Church of Jesus Christ of Latter-day Saints, 1953), 2:131, cited in H. Donl Peterson, *The Pearl of Great Price: A History and Commentary* (Salt Lake City: Deseret Book, 1987), 212.

CHAPTER 13

THE HIGHER AND LESSER LAWS

John A. Tvedtnes

Joseph Smith provided a wealth of information—particularly in the Joseph Smith Translation of the Bible—on the events that took place at Mount Sinai in the time of Moses, including the following details: (1) God originally intended to make the higher or Melchizedek Priesthood available to all Israel but instead gave a lesser priesthood to the tribe of Levi; (2) this resulted from the unwillingness of the Israelites to accept one of the responsibilities of the higher priesthood, which was to stand in the presence of God; (3) God cursed the Israelites with a carnal law, omitting from the second set of tablets elements of the higher law (including the covenant of priesthood) that had been on the first set of tablets; and (4) the higher law was to be restored through Christ at a later time.

While the Bible gives partial support to the last of these and barely hints at the first, it says nothing about the Israelites' rejection of the higher priesthood and the fact that the two sets of tablets differed in their content. But, as we shall see, some early Jewish and Christian traditions support Joseph Smith's teachings about these matters.

The Lord's Intentions at Sinai

When the Lord spoke to Moses out of the burning bush, he instructed, "When thou hast brought forth the people out of Egypt, ye shall serve God upon this mountain" (Exodus 3:12). This passage suggests that the Lord wanted all Israel to meet him on the mount. But when they arrived at the site, only Moses, Aaron and his two eldest sons, and the seventy elders of Israel were allowed to ascend the mountain, where they ate in the presence of the Lord (Exodus 24:9–11). This change of plans is best understood by examining the biblical text.

Before revealing the Ten Commandments, the Lord told Moses to inform the Israelites: "If ye will obey my voice indeed, and keep my covenant . . . ye shall be unto me a kingdom of priests, and an holy nation" (Exodus 19:5–6). But when he uttered the Ten Commandments, "all the people saw the thunderings, and the lightnings, and the noise of the trumpet, and the mountain smoking: and when the people saw it, they removed, and stood afar off. And they said unto Moses, Speak thou with us, and we will hear: but let not God speak with us, lest we die. And Moses said unto the people, Fear not: for God is come to prove you, and that his fear may be before your faces, that ye sin not. And the people stood afar off, and Moses drew near unto the thick darkness where God was" (Exodus 20:18–21; see Deuteronomy 5:23–27).

From this, it seems that the people were unwilling to communicate directly with God and wanted Moses to be their intermediary.[1] By so doing, they rejected the responsibility of being a "kingdom of priests," rejecting the higher priesthood that holds the keys of communing directly with God (D&C 107:18–20). Joseph Smith explained that "God cursed the children of Israel because they would not receive the last law from Moses. . . . The Israelites prayed that God would speak to Moses and not to them; in consequence of which he cursed them with a carnal law."[2] The situation is also described in Doctrine and Covenants 84:19–26:

And this greater priesthood administereth the gospel and holdeth the key of the mysteries of the kingdom, even the key of the knowledge of God. Therefore, in the ordinances thereof, the power of godliness is manifest. And without the ordinances thereof, and the authority of the priesthood, the power of godliness is not manifest unto men in the flesh; For without this no man can see the face of God, even the Father, and live. Now this Moses plainly taught to the children of Israel in the wilderness, and sought diligently to sanctify his people that they might behold the face of God; But they hardened their hearts and could not endure his presence; therefore, the Lord in his wrath, for his anger was kindled against them, swore that they should not enter into his rest while in the wilderness, which rest is the fulness of his glory. Therefore, he took Moses out of their midst, and the Holy Priesthood also; And the lesser priesthood continued, which priesthood holdeth the key of the ministering of angels and the preparatory gospel.

Some elements of this revelation are also found in the medieval Jewish text known as the *Zohar*.[3] This is how *Zohar* Numbers 221a explains why Israel did not receive the great blessings of the law:

When Israel left Egypt, God desired to make them on earth like ministering angels above, and to build for them a holy house which was to be brought down from the heaven of the firmaments, and to plant Israel as a holy shoot after the pattern of the celestial prototype. . . . But as they provoked God in the wilderness they died there and God brought their children into the land, and the house was built by human hands, and therefore it did not endure. In the days of Ezra also on account of their sins they were forced to build it themselves and therefore it did not endure. All this time the first building planned by God had not yet been set up. . . . It is for this building that we are waiting, not a human structure which cannot endure. . . . This work should have been completed when Israel first went forth from Egypt, but it has been deferred to the end of days in the last deliverance.[4]

The Lord's desire to make Israel like the "ministering angels" (also noted in *Zohar* Exodus 114a, which is discussed later in this article) is significant since, in Jewish tradition, the angels serve as priests in God's heavenly temple. As such, the story supports Joseph Smith's teachings on the subject.

Israel's Disobedience Weakened Moses' Power

Rabbinic tradition holds that all Israel heard the first two of the Ten Commandments directly from God but that Moses delivered the other eight.[5] This is reflected in *Zohar* Numbers 261a–b, which declares that all Israel heard the divine voice uttering these two commandments, but that

> Israel were terrified and drew back, and therefore they said: Do thou [Moses] speak to us; we do not desire to be spoken to by the mighty Power from on high, but only from the place of the Female,[6] not higher. Said Moses to them: Of a truth ye have weakened my power, and also another power. For had not Israel drawn back and had they listened to the remaining words as to the first, the world would never have been laid waste subsequently and they would have endured for generations upon generations. For at the first moment they did die, for so it had to be on account of the tree of death, but after they revived and stood up God desired to bring them up to the Tree of Life,[7] which is above the tree of death, that they might endure for ever, but they drew back and were not willing; therefore was the power of Moses weakened and another power with him. Said the Holy One, blessed be He: I desired to stablish you in an exalted place that ye might cleave to life, but ye desired the place of the Female.[8]

The weakening of Moses' power by Israel's rejection of the privilege of communing with the Lord is also noted in *Zohar* Exodus 58a, where we read that when Moses met God on the mount, "the Holy One took hold of him and made him sit before Him and taught him the Torah, and spread over him the radiance of that 'pleasantness,' so that his countenance shone in all those firmaments and all the hosts of heaven trembled before him when he descended with the Torah. When the Israelites committed the sin of the Golden Calf below, the Holy One took away from Moses one thousand parts of that splendour."[9]

Like Doctrine and Covenants 84, the *Zohar* notes that when God removed Moses from the midst of Israel, they lost something. *Zohar* Deuteronomy 283b, speaking of the difference between the time of Moses and of Joshua, says, "One is from the higher source and the other from the lower. As long as Moses was alive the orb of the sun was in the ascendant and illumined the world, but as soon as Moses departed the orb of the sun was gathered in and the moon came forth. . . . Then the orb of the sun shone forth and Moses became like the orb of the sun to Israel; and when Moses was gathered in the orb of the sun was gathered in and the moon shone and Joshua used the light of the moon. Alas for this degradation!"[10]

We read in *Zohar* Exodus 156a–b that "on the death of Moses, the sun in his splendour was darkened and the Written Torah was locked up, that light of the luminous mirror. The Moon withdrew her light when King David died, and the Oral Torah ceased to shine. Since that time the lights of the Torah have remained hidden, and controversy has increased over the Mishnah (i.e. the traditional Law), and the wise men dispute, and all the great thinkers are in confusion, so that to succeeding generations the joy of the Torah has been lost."[11]

Israel's Disobedience Likened to the Fall of Adam

The *Zohar* frequently compares events at Mount Sinai with the fall of Adam and Eve and compares the original law revealed to Moses to the tree of life, making the tree that brought death into the world a lesser law (see the citation from *Zohar* Numbers 261a–b, above). The comparison makes sense when we consider that, at the time of the fall, our first parents were cut off from the presence of God (2 Nephi 9:6; Alma 42:7, 9, 11, 14; Helaman 14:16; D&C 29:41), while at Sinai the Israelites rejected the privilege of standing in God's presence (D&C 84:19–26). *Zohar* Genesis 36b explains that, because of the fall of Adam and Eve, "the terrestrial world was cursed and dislodged from its estate on account of the defilement of the serpent, until Israel stood before Mount Sinai."[12] In *Zohar* Genesis 63b Rabbi Jose elucidates that

> The world was not properly settled, nor was the earth purged from the defilement of the serpent, until Israel stood before Mount Sinai, where they laid fast hold of the Tree of Life [Torah], and so established the world firmly. Had not Israel backslided and sinned before the Holy One, blessed be He, they would never have died, since the scum of the serpent had been purged out of them.[13] But as soon as they sinned, the first tablets of the Law were broken—those tablets which spelt complete freedom, freedom from the serpent who is the "end of all flesh."[14]

The freedom mentioned here and in *Zohar* Exodus 113b–114a (discussed later) is expressed in the prophecy of the new covenant found in Jeremiah 31 (also discussed later). This freedom comes through the atonement of Christ, who liberates us from the death brought by Satan in the Garden of Eden. He brings us back into the presence of God (2 Nephi 2:8–10; Alma 42:23) and makes us kings and priests unto God (Revelation 1:6).

Another passage that compares the fall of Adam to the events in Sinai is found in *Zohar* Genesis 52a:

> Until he sinned, man [Adam] was gifted with the wisdom of celestial illumination, and he did not for an instant quit the Tree of Life. But when he was seduced by his desire to know what was below, he weakly followed it until he became separated from the Tree of Life, and knew evil and forsook good. . . . Before they sinned, the human pair used to hear a voice from above, and were endowed with the higher wisdom; they stood

erect with heavenly radiance, and knew no fear. When they sinned, they were not able to stand up even before an earthly voice. A similar thing happened later with the Israelites. When Israel stood before Mount Sinai, the impurity of the serpent was removed from them, so that carnal passion was suppressed among them, and in consequence they were able to attach themselves to the Tree of Life, and their thoughts were turned to higher things and not to lower. Hence they were vouchsafed heavenly illuminations and knowledge which filled them with joy and gladness. Further, God girt them with cinctures [belts or aprons] of the letters of the Holy Name, which prevented the serpent from gaining power over them or defiling them as before. When they sinned by worshipping the calf, they were degraded from their high estate and lost their illumination, they were deprived of the protective girdle of the Holy Name and became exposed to the attacks of the evil serpent as before, and so brought death into the world.[15]

In the cases of both Adam and Israel, the result of disobedience was that death was introduced into the world. "Assuredly, had Adam held fast to the tree of life, which is nothing else but the Torah [law], he would not have brought death upon himself and upon the rest of the world. . . . And had Israel not sinned and forsaken the tree of life they would not have brought death anew into the world" (*Zohar* Genesis 131b).[16] We can compare this with Nephi's statement that "the wicked are rejected from the righteous, and [rejected] from that tree of life" (1 Nephi 15:36).

Zohar Genesis 37b speaks of "Moses, through whose agency the Law was given and who thus bestowed life on men from the tree of life. And in truth had Israel not sinned, they would have been proof against death, since the tree of life had been brought down to them."[17] Here, as in other *Zohar* passages, the tree of life is said to represent the Torah or law of Moses.

The *Zohar* has some rather interesting things to say about Psalm 82:6–7, in which God declares, "Ye are gods; and all of you are children of the most High. But ye shall die like men, and fall like one of the princes." According to *Zohar* Numbers 162a, the early rabbis explained this passage in terms of the events at Mount Sinai: "'This,' they said, 'is what God said when Israel at Mount Sinai said "we will do" before "we will hear" [Exodus 24:7], but when they followed their evil imagination He said, "Verily like Adam ye shall die"; like Adam, that is, whose death drew him down to the dust in order that the evil imagination in him might be wiped out.'"[18] To this, Rabbi Ilai added that the Israelites "stood at Mount Sinai, with bodies free from all taint; but when they drew upon themselves the evil imagination, they were changed into other bodies,"[19] just as the bodies of Adam and Eve became mortal when they ate the fruit of the tree. *Zohar* Exodus 236b, referring to the worship of the golden calf, notes, "And so, whereas Israel standing at Mount Sinai were purged of the primitive venom that the evil spirit injected into the world, thereby bringing death to all mankind, now the same evil spirit defiled them anew, took hold of them and brought again death to them and to all mankind and for all their generations to follow." The passage then cites Psalm 82:6–7 regarding the fall of heavenly beings.[20]

The idea that both Adam and Israel brought death into the world through disobedience ties to the concept of their being cut off from the presence of God, mentioned above. The Book of Mormon (Alma 42:9; Helaman 14:16, 18) and Doctrine and Covenants 29:41 define spiritual death as being cut off from the presence of God. *Zohar* Exodus 113b–114a explains the situation as follows:

> As to the words "graven upon the tables" (*ḥarut ʿal ha-luḥoth*), it has already been pointed out that this phrase contains an allusion to *ḥeruth*—that is, freedom. Freedom from what? From the angel of death, from subjection to the kingdoms of this world, from all things earthly and from all things evil. And what is freedom? It is the seal of the world to come, in which is every kind of freedom."[21]

The angel of death is Satan who, as the serpent, is called the "end of all flesh" in *Zohar* Genesis 63b, cited earlier. We are reminded of the Book of Mormon teaching that Christ rescues us from "that monster, death and hell . . . the death of the body, and also the death of the spirit" (2 Nephi 9:10; see 9:19, 26). But before we discuss Christ's role in restoring the higher law that was on the first set of tablets, we must turn to a discussion of the lesser law.

The Lesser Law

The Bible confirms that the law given to Israel through Moses was a lesser law, though it does not speak of the higher law written on the first set of tablets. Referring to the time of the Egyptian exodus, the Lord told Ezekiel:

> I lifted up mine hand unto them also in the wilderness, that I would scatter them among the heathen, and disperse them through the countries;[22] because they had not executed my judgments, but had despised my statutes, and had polluted my sabbaths, and their eyes were after their fathers' idols. Wherefore I gave them also statutes that were not good, and judgments whereby they should not live. (Ezekiel 20:23–24; see Psalm 81:8–13; Acts 7:38–42)

The Lord did not say that the statutes were bad, but that they were "not good," suggesting that he could have given Israel something better. But that better or higher law, as Joseph Smith taught, was replaced by a lesser law of carnal commandments. This is also suggested in the Lord's word to Jeremiah:

> For I spake not unto your fathers, nor commanded them in the day that I brought them out of the land of Egypt, concerning burnt offerings or sacrifices: but this thing commanded I them, saying, Obey my voice, and I will be your God, and ye shall be my people: and walk ye in all the ways that I have commanded you, that it may be well unto you. But they hearkened not, nor inclined their ear, but walked in the counsels and in the imagination of their evil heart, and went backward, and not forward. (Jeremiah 7:22–24)

This passage cites Exodus 19:5, in which the Lord commanded the Israelites assembled at the foot of Mount Sinai to obey him. It was only after they disobeyed that he imposed the law of complex offerings and sacrifices.

Two Sets of Tablets, Two Sets of Laws

When Moses came down from Mount Sinai and found the people worshiping the golden calf, he cast the tablets containing the law to the ground, shattering them (Exodus 32:19–20; Deuteronomy 9:15–17). Having taken measures to punish the evildoers, he returned to the mountaintop, where the Lord instructed him to prepare a second set of tablets (Exodus 34:1; Deuteronomy 10:1–5). This much is found in the standard biblical account. But the Joseph Smith Translation adds valuable information:

> And the Lord said unto Moses, Hew thee two other tables of stone, like unto the first, and I will write upon them also, the words of the law, according as they were written at the first on the tables which thou brakest; but it shall not be according to the first, for I will take away the priesthood out of their midst; therefore my holy order, and the ordinances thereof, shall not go before them; for my presence shall not go up in their midst, lest I destroy them. But I will give unto them the law as at the first, but it shall be after the law of a carnal commandment; for I have sworn in my wrath, that they shall not enter into my presence, into my rest, in the days of their pilgrimage. Therefore do as I have commanded thee, and be ready in the morning, and come up in the morning unto mount Sinai, and present thyself there to me, in the top of the mount. (Exodus 34:1–2 JST)

According to this passage, several elements found on the first set of tablets were missing from the second set. These are "the priesthood . . . my holy order, and the ordinances thereof . . . my presence." We have also noted that the Israelites, by refusing to commune directly with God, rejected the opportunity to receive the higher priesthood, which meant that they would not be able to "endure his presence" (D&C 84:24). The story of the second set of tablets is also found in the Joseph Smith Translation of Deuteronomy 10:1–2:

> At that time the Lord said unto me, Hew thee two other tables of stone like unto the first, and come up unto me upon the mount, and make thee an ark of wood. And I will write on the tables the words that were on the first tables, which thou breakest, save the words of the everlasting covenant of the holy priesthood, and thou shalt put them in the ark.

From the writings of the apostle Paul, it is clear that salvation did not come by means of the law of Moses.[23] But neither Paul nor any of the other New Testament writers suggested, as did Joseph Smith, that the law contained on the first set of tablets was superior to or different from the law on the second set of tablets. And while New Testament writers taught that the law brought by Christ was higher than that taught by Moses, they did not suggest, as did Joseph Smith, that the higher law or covenant had already been offered to Israel but was removed when Moses destroyed the first set of tablets on which it was written. But this information is confirmed in extracanonical sources. One of these is the *Epistle of Barnabas,* which was already widely circulated and respected in the Christian community by the second century A.D.[24] Chapter 4 clearly supports Joseph Smith's understanding of the matter:

> I further beg of you . . . not to be like some, adding largely to your sins, and saying, "The covenant is both theirs [the Jews'] and ours." But they thus finally lost it, after Moses had already received it. For the Scripture saith, "And Moses was fasting in the mount forty days and forty nights, and received the covenant from the Lord, tables of stone written with the finger of the hand of the Lord," but turning away to idols, they lost it. For the Lord speaks thus to Moses: "Moses, go down quickly; for the people whom thou hast brought out of the land of Egypt have transgressed." And Moses understood [the meaning

of God], and cast the two tables out of his hands; and their covenant was broken, in order that the covenant of the beloved Jesus might be sealed upon our heart, in the hope which flows from believing in Him.[25]

This passage suggests that the first set of tablets contained a covenant that was broken and that this was the same covenant Jesus later brought back to the earth. That this is the meaning of the passage is confirmed by *Epistle of Barnabas* 14, which gives a similar account, adding that while Moses received the law, the rest of the Israelites were unworthy of it:

> But let us inquire if the Lord has really given that testament which He swore to the fathers that He would give to the people. He did give it; but they were not worthy to receive it, on account of their sins. . . . Moses . . . received from the Lord two tables, written in the spirit by the finger of the hand of the Lord. And Moses having received them, carried them down to give to the people. . . . And Moses understood that they had again made molten images; and he threw the tables out of his hands, and the tables of the testament of the Lord were broken. Moses then received it, but they [the Israelites] proved themselves unworthy. Learn now how *we* [Christians] have received it. Moses, as a servant, received it; but the Lord himself, having suffered in our behalf, hath given it to us, that we should be the people of inheritance.[26]

The *Book of the Rolls,* attributed to the first-century A.D. Christian writer, Clement of Rome, cites Noah's instructions to Shem regarding the burial of Adam, then adds, "Thus it was written in the tables which Moses received from the hand of the Lord and broke at the time of his anger against his people" (*Book of the Rolls* f.115).[27] Since the words attributed to Noah are not found in the Old Testament books attributed to Moses, this clearly implies that the first set of tablets given to Moses contained information omitted from the second set.

Another pseudepigraphic text, *4 Ezra*, thought to have been written late in the first century A.D., has God declaring, "I revealed myself in a bush and spoke to Moses when my people were in bondage in Egypt; and I sent him and led my people out of Egypt; and I led him up on Mount Sinai, where I kept him with me many days; and I told him many wondrous things, and showed him the secrets of the times and declared to him the end of the times. Then I commanded him, saying, 'These words you shall publish openly, and these you shall keep secret'" (*4 Ezra* 14:3–6).[28] The idea that Moses did not reveal to the people everything he had learned is also found in *Zohar* Exodus 174a, where we read, "All the treasures of the Supernal King are disclosed by means of one key, which reveals in secret chambers supernal tracings. Who can comprehend what is hidden in the spring of wisdom? Moses revealed it not on the day whereon he made known other deep mysteries, although all things were revealed through him."[29]

The idea of higher and lesser laws is also found in *Zohar* Exodus 200a, which speaks of the "supernal book and the lower book, [which] constitute together the Law (Torah), the one the written Law, it being undisclosed and only to be revealed in the world to come, the other the oral Law. Of the written Law the writing is made, as it were, into a Palace of the central point, wherein the Law is concealed. The lower Law, on the other hand, is not embodied in writing, and hence is not constructed into a Palace for the central point beneath as is the superior Law for the supernal point."[30] That the law on the first tablets differed from that on the second set of tablets is confirmed by the early rabbis cited in the fourth- or fifth-century A.D. *Rabbah* (Exodus 46:1; 47:7).[31] In this tradition, the second set of tablets contained information not on the first set—a point to which we shall return later.

Zohar Exodus 114a declares: "Had not the tablets been broken, the world would not have suffered as it subsequently did, and the Israelites would have been in the likeness of the supernal angels above."[32] In the second-century A.D. Jewish text *ʾAbot de Rabbi Nathan* 2, we read that the first set of tablets broken by Moses had been inscribed and hidden away since the creation.[33] When Moses saw the Israelites sinning with the golden calf, he declared, "How can I give them the tables of the commandments? I shall be obligating them to major commandments and condemning them to death at the hands of Heaven; for thus it is written in the Commandments, Thou shalt have no other gods before Me." As he started back, the seventy elders came and grabbed one end of the tablets, but Moses was able to retain them. But when he looked at the tablets, he saw that the writing thereon had disappeared;[34] since they appeared useless, he broke them. The text then quotes Rabbi Yose the Galilean as saying that the reason Moses broke the tablets before the eyes of Israel (Deuteronomy 9:17) was so they would not later ask him where the first tablets were. Several other rabbis then replied that Moses broke the tablets only because God told him to do so.[35]

The Commandments, Statutes, and Judgments

To the Galatians Paul wrote, "Wherefore then serveth the law [of Moses]? It was added because of transgressions, till the seed [Christ] should come to whom the promise was made" (Galatians 3:19; cf. Mosiah 3:14). This suggests that the carnal law with which Joseph Smith said the Israelites were cursed was superimposed atop something else they had received from God—presumably something that was part of the higher law.[36] Because the Ten Commandments are authoritatively cited as the word of God in the Old and New Testaments, as well as the Book of Mormon and the Doctrine and Covenants, they must be part of the higher law that remained even under the covenant made at Sinai. They would therefore not be part of the lesser "handwriting of ordinances" of which Paul said that Christ "took it out of the way, nailing it to his cross" (Colossians 2:14).

Christ told the Nephites, "in me is the law of Moses fulfilled" (3 Nephi 9:17; see 3 Nephi 12:18–19, 46; 15:4–5, 8). But he seems to have suggested that only the lesser portion of that law had been fulfilled when he said, "Behold, ye have the commandments before you, and the law is fulfilled" (3 Nephi 12:19). The prophet Abinadi, while noting that salvation does not come by the law of Moses, indicated that it was nonetheless important to keep the Ten Commandments that were part of that law (Mosiah 12:31–33; 13:27–30; see Alma 25:16).

In order to understand this subject, we must note that the law of Moses was comprised of three divisions, the commandments (sometimes called "law" or "testimonies"), the statutes (sometimes called "ordinances"), and the judgments.[37] These same three divisions of the law are listed in the Book of Mormon,[38] where the word *performances* sometimes is substituted for *judgments.*[39] From some of the Book of Mormon passages (Alma 30:3; 2 Nephi 25:24–25, 30; 4 Nephi 1:12), we learn that it was the statutes and judgments (or ordinances and performances) that would be done away in Christ, while the commandments would remain as part of the higher law that Christ revealed during his ministry.

The Messiah Restores the Law

The loss of the higher law is suggested by the tradition in the *Zohar* that the law (Torah) will be made fully known only when the Messiah comes. *Zohar* Leviticus 23a has Rabbi Judah saying that "God will one day reveal the hidden mysteries of the Torah, namely, at the time of the Messiah," in support of which he cites Isaiah 11:9 and Jeremiah 31:34,[40] the latter of which we shall discuss shortly. Compare the statement in *Zohar* Leviticus 22b: "as long as Moses was alive, he used to check Israel from sinning against God. And because Moses was among them, there shall not be a generation like that one till the Messiah comes, when they shall see the glory of God like him."[41]

In *Zohar* Genesis 117b–118a, Rabbi Jose and Rabbi Judah examine a book they found hidden in a cave; the book "had been given to Adam the first man, and by means of which he knew all the wisdom of the supernal holy beings." Suddenly, a wind swept the book from their hands and out of sight. When they later asked Rabbi Simeon about it, "he said to them: 'Were you, perhaps, scrutinising those letters which deal with the coming of the Messiah? . . . The Holy One, blessed be He, does not desire that so much should be revealed to the world, but when the days of the Messiah will be near at hand, even children will discover the secrets of wisdom.'"[42] *Zohar* Exodus 147a has Rabbi Simeon saying, "Blessed is this generation! There will be none other like unto it until King Messiah shall appear, when the Torah shall be restored to her ancient pride of place."[43]

Another Jewish tradition is found in the Babylonian Talmud, where we read that when the Israelites accepted the covenant at Sinai and were made a kingdom of priests, they received two crowns. But when they removed the crowns, destroying angels snatched them away. It is believed that the faithful will receive those crowns during the Messianic age (TB *Shabbat* 88a).

Midrash Alpha Beta di R. Akiba says that "In the future the Holy One, blessed be He, will sit in the Garden of Eden and expound [the Tora]. And all the pious will sit before Him, and all the Supernal Family will stand on its feet. . . . And the Holy One, blessed be He, will expound to them the meanings of a new Tora which He will give them through the Messiah."[44]

The New Covenant

The epistle to the Hebrews identifies Jesus as "the mediator of the new covenant" (Hebrews 12:24; see Galatians 3:20 JST; D&C 76:69; 107:19). The term *new covenant* was drawn from Jeremiah's prophecy.

> Behold, the days come, saith the Lord, that I will make a
> new covenant with the house of Israel, and with the house of
> Judah: Not according to the covenant that I made with their fa-
> thers in the day that I took them by the hand to bring them out
> of the land of Egypt; which my covenant they brake, although I

was an husband unto them, saith the Lord: But this shall be the covenant that I will make with the house of Israel; After those days, saith the Lord, I will put my law in their inward parts, and write it in their hearts; and will be their God, and they shall be my people. And they shall teach no more every man his neighbour, and every man his brother, saying, Know the Lord: for they shall all know me, from the least of them unto the greatest of them, saith the Lord: for I will forgive their iniquity, and I will remember their sin no more. (Jeremiah 31:31–34)

The new covenant would replace the covenant made with Israel at the time of the exodus from Egypt and would include forgiveness of sins. The law of this covenant would be written in the hearts of the people rather than on tablets of stone, meaning that it would be taught by the Spirit, so that all who sought him could come to know the Lord.

Hebrews 8:7–13; 10:16–20 cites the Jeremiah 31 passage as evidence that the covenant of Moses was to be replaced by a higher covenant under Christ. For this reason, the early Christians saw themselves as the chosen of God in the place of Israel. This led Peter to paraphrase the Lord's original promise at Sinai (Exodus 19:6), saying, "But ye are a chosen generation, a royal priesthood, an holy nation, a peculiar people; that ye should shew forth the praises of him who hath called you out of darkness into his marvellous light" (1 Peter 2:9). The writing of the law in the hearts of men, rather than on tablets of stone, is found not only in Jeremiah 31:33, but is expressed in other parts of the Bible as well (Isaiah 51:7; Proverbs 3:3; Ezekiel 11:19–20; 2 Corinthians 3:3). It evidently refers to the fact that once the higher priesthood would be made available through Christ, God would speak directly to the hearts of his people.

The Law of Moses and the Sermon on the Mount

Jesus spoke of the law of Moses in his Sermon on the Mount (Matthew 5–7), which he also delivered to the Nephites in the

New World following his resurrection (3 Nephi 12–14). He declared, "Think not that I am come to destroy the law, or the prophets: I am not come to destroy, but to fulfil" (Matthew 5:17). He emphasized that it was important to keep the commandments found in the law (Matthew 5:19), but added, "For I say unto you, That except your righteousness shall exceed the righteousness of the scribes and Pharisees, ye shall in no case enter into the kingdom of heaven" (Matthew 5:20). He then went on to illustrate what he meant.

Rather than simply prohibit murder, the Savior commanded his disciples to avoid anger (Matthew 5:21–22). He taught that the way to avoid committing sexual sins was to banish lustful thoughts from one's mind (Matthew 5:27–28). Honesty of speech, he said, was superior to having to swear oaths to establish one's truthfulness (Matthew 5:33–37). Love is superior to revenge (Matthew 5:38–48). Christ's message can be summed up by saying that in order to avoid sinful acts, we must begin by having pure thoughts. By emphasizing the internalization of God's commandments, Jesus was fulfilling the prophecy of Jeremiah 31:33 that, under the new covenant, the law would be written on the heart.

This brings us back to Joseph Smith's statement that "God cursed the children of Israel because they would not receive the last law from Moses."[45] Does the "last law" refer to the last of the Ten Commandments, which commands us not to covet? That commandment differs from all the others in that it could not be enforced under the law of Moses. This is because the law required the testimony of two or three witnesses to condemn the guilty party (Deuteronomy 17:6; 19:15; Hebrews 10:28). A witness might testify that a man was guilty of blasphemy, idolatry, breaking the sabbath, stealing, murdering, and so forth, but no one could read the heart of an individual to know if he was covetous.

Obedience to the Law

Under the law of Moses, obedience was enforced by fear of punishment, sometimes by stoning or some other method of execution, because the law of justice required punishment for sins. Under Christ, who brought the law of mercy, we are free from the punishment of sin, if we repent (Mosiah 15:7–9; 2 Nephi 2:5–10). This is what Paul meant by being "free from the law" (Romans 6:14–15, 22–23), not that one was free to commit sin, but that one could repent in Christ and avoid the penalties for sin required by the law. The law of Moses was written on tablets of stone, while the law of Christ is written in the heart, or the thoughts of his followers (Jeremiah 31:31–34; Ezekiel 11:19; 36:26–27; 2 Corinthians 3:2–3).

Our motivation for obedience to the law of God should not be fear of punishment or hope of reward. Rather, we should be motivated by a love of God and by our desire to do right (John 14:15; 1 John 5:2–3; D&C 42:29; 124:87).[46] On this issue, Latter-day Saints and modern Jews are agreed, despite the fact that the law of Moses in ancient times was often enforced by fear of punishment. This is the attitude of which Jesus spoke when he said, "Blessed are they which do hunger and thirst after righteousness" (Matthew 5:6). When we desire to do good as much as we desire to eat and drink and breathe, then and only then are we doing it for the right reason. Hence, "not every one that saith unto me, Lord, Lord, shall enter into the kingdom of heaven. . . . Lord, Lord, have we not prophesied in thy name? and in thy name have cast out devils? and in thy name done many wonderful works?" (Matthew 7:21–23).

The entire Sermon on the Mount can be summed up in Christ's commandment, "Be ye therefore perfect, even as your Father which is in heaven is perfect" (Matthew 5:48). So important is the commandment to be holy and righteous like God that it has often been repeated, before the law (Genesis 17:1), in the law itself (Exodus 22:31; Numbers 15:40; Leviticus 19:2; 20:7–8, 26; 21:8; Deuteronomy 18:13), and after the coming of Christ (2 Corinthians 13:9). In our day, God has repeated the commandment (D&C 38:42; 43:11, 16; 88:68, 74; 101:4–5; 112:28, 33; 133:4–5, 62).

If there is one thing for which Jesus found his fellow Jews at fault, it is that some of them did not keep the law of Moses (John 7:19). The Book of Mormon teaches us that salvation cannot be obtained without obedience to the Ten Commandments (Mosiah 12:31–37). Yet it also teaches that the law by itself, without the atonement of Christ, was not sufficient for salvation, lacking the principle of mercy (Mosiah 13:27–33; 16:14–15; see all of Mosiah 14–15).

The law was given by Moses, but grace and truth came through Jesus Christ (John 1:17). Christ, then, did not destroy the law but fulfilled it, in that he returned the portion that Israel had rejected in Moses' day and retained the Ten Commandments. Indeed, the law looked forward to Christ (2 Nephi 25:24–30; Jacob 4:5; Mosiah 3:14–16; Alma 13:16; 25:15–16; 30:3; 34:13–14; 3 Nephi 1:24–25; 9:17–20; 12:17–19; 15:2–10). The law and the prophets, according to Jesus, were in effect until the coming of John the Baptist, after which came the doctrines of the kingdom of God (Luke 16:16–17; see Matthew 11:12–13). As Latter-day Saints, we see in the teachings of Jesus the fulfillment of the law of Moses (D&C 22). This does not mean that the law was not valid, only that the reasons for obedience to its precepts are based on different premises. Obedience to the law of Moses was anciently ensured through a strict set of rules, the breaking of which could bring severe punishments. Jesus taught us obedience based on agency and a desire to do good. In order to assist us to follow this plan, he has given us the Holy Ghost to guide us in our decisions.

Summary

The prophecy in Jeremiah 31:31–34 promised that the new covenant would bring forgiveness of sins and the spirit of God to place the law in the hearts of men. Because these elements had been lost to Israel at Sinai, they later become highly dependent on the written law and developed a series of written rabbinic explanations of the law of Moses. Christ condemned this "tradition of the elders" (Matthew 15:1–6). The early rabbis justified its existence by saying that it constituted an "oral law" revealed to Moses atop the mountain at the same time as the "written law" and passed down from Moses to Joshua, to the elders, to the prophets, and to the rabbis (Mishnah ʾAbot 1:1). In one tradition, it was even held that the two tablets of the law contained laws, *midrash* (explanation), and *haggadot* (traditions).[47]

But other rabbinic traditions, as we have seen, support Joseph Smith's teaching that the higher law had been presented to Israel, who rejected it, making it necessary for God to give a lesser law that withheld many of the blessings he wanted to give them. Those blessings were to be restored in the time of the Messiah. While all Christians believe that Christ brought a higher law, Latter-day Saints believe that this law had been known to earlier generations as well. The early Jewish and Christian texts that tell the same story were unavailable to Joseph Smith and have only come to our attention in later years.

Notes

1. Brigham Young explained the situation thus: "If they had been sanctified and holy, the children of Israel would not have travelled one year with Moses before they would have received their endowments and the Melchizedec [*sic*] Priesthood. But they could not receive them, and never did. Moses left them, and they did not receive the fulness of that Priesthood. After they came to the land of Canaan, they never would have desired a king, had they been holy. The Lord told Moses that he would show himself to the people; but they begged Moses to plead with the Lord not to do so." *Journal of Discourses,* 6:100.

2. Joseph Smith, *History of the Church of Jesus Christ of Latter-day Saints,* 2nd ed. (Salt Lake City: Deseret Book, 1950), 5:555.

3. Though this kabbalistic text was composed in its present form in Spain in the thirteenth century A.D., the *Zohar* reflects a number of early traditions, many of them known from more ancient texts, attributing them to rabbis of the first centuries A.D.

4. *The Zohar* (New York: Bennet, 1958), 5:330–31. The version of the *Zohar* that I cite herein has various translators for the five volumes:

vol. 1, Harry Sperling and Maurice Simon; vols. 2 and 3, Harry Sperling, Maurice Simon, and Paul P. Levertoff; vol. 4, Maurice Simon and Paul P. Levertoff; and vol. 5, Maurice Simon and Harry Sperling. They were all published by Bennet in New York.

5. *Midrash Rabbah* Exodus 42:8.

6. In Kabbalah, the heaven is compared to a man and earth to a woman, as in several ancient Near Eastern cosmologies.

7. The tree of life in the *Zohar* usually refers to the Torah or law of Moses—a point that will become important for a later discussion in this essay. See *Zohar* Genesis 131b, 193a, 199a, 202b; Exodus 17b; Leviticus 53b; Numbers 148b; Deuteronomy 260a, 261a.

8. *The Zohar*, 5:345–46.

9. Ibid., 3:181.

10. Ibid., 5:369–70.

11. Ibid., 4:47–48.

12. Ibid., 1:136.

13. Ibid., 1:207. According to *Zohar* Exodus 17b, God sent serpents among the Israelites "to punish Israel should she separate herself from the Tree of Life, which is the Torah" (ibid., 3:55). Similarly, *Zohar* Exodus 184a declares that "had the Israelites not sinned, the Holy One would have resolved to remove him [the devil] altogether from the world. Therefore He led them through his very dominion and territory. But when they sinned the serpent stung them many a time" (ibid., 4:124). Compare this with the statement in *Zohar* Exodus 227a: "When the sacrifices brought by Noah were offered up, a fragrance was diffused in the world; but not so sweet as when, later on, Israel stood at Mount Sinai. Then the world was truly filled with a fragrance, and thus the Destroyer was no more to be seen. Indeed, the Holy One, blessed be He, was about to remove altogether the Destroyer from the world, when Israel, after the lapse of only a few days, committed a sin in making the Golden Calf. . . . The Destroyer thus regained power over the world, inflicting punishment over it, as before" (ibid., 4:274–75).

14. Ibid., 1:207.

15. Ibid., 1:165.

16. Ibid., 2:25.

17. Ibid., 1:140.

18. Ibid., 5:233

19. *Zohar* Numbers 162b, in ibid., 5:234.

20. *The Zohar,* 4:306.

21. Ibid., 3:339.

22. The passage evidently alludes to the wording of Deuteronomy 4:26–27.

23. Romans 7:4; 8:2–4; Galatians 2:16, 21; 3:12–13, 24–26. Hebrews 7:11 notes that perfection did not come by the Levitical Priesthood.

24. A number of early church fathers cited the *Epistle of Barnabas* in their own writings to illustrate principles of doctrine.

25. *Epistle of Barnabas* 4, in *Ante-Nicene Fathers,* ed. Alexander Roberts and James Donaldson (1885; reprint, Peabody, Mass.: Hendrickson, 1994), 1:138–39.

26. *Epistle of Barnabas* 14, in ibid., 146.

27. Margaret D. Wilson, *Apocrypha Arabica* (London: Clay, 1901), 31.

28. Bruce M. Metzger, trans., in James H. Charlesworth, ed., *The Old Testament Pseudepigrapha* (Garden City, N.Y.: Doubleday, 1983), 1:553. In *4 Ezra* 14:37–48, we read that Ezra and a group of five men rewrote the lost scriptures in ninety-four books, of which twenty-four were to be made public, while seventy were to be held back for the wise only; see ibid., 1:554–55.

29. *The Zohar,* 4:102–3.

30. Ibid., 4:178.

31. The rabbis did not always agree with one another on issues of scriptural interpretation. Consequently, one passage (*Midrash Rabbah* Exodus 47:6) says that the second set of tablets was a duplicate of the first set.

32. *The Zohar,* 3:339.

33. For a discussion, see John A. Tvedtnes, *The Book of Mormon and Other Hidden Books: "Out of Darkness unto Light"* (Provo, Utah: FARMS, 2000), 129–32.

34. That the writing on the tablets disappeared when Moses saw the golden calf is affirmed in other early rabbinic sources. For example, see *Pseudo-Philo* 12:5.

35. Judah Goldin, trans., *The Fathers According to Rabbi Nathan* (New York City: Schocken, 1974), 20–22.

36. Bruce R. McConkie appears to have been the first person to make this suggestion, in the entry "Law of Moses" in his *Mormon Doctrine* (Salt Lake City: Bookcraft, 1958).

37. Deuteronomy 4:1–2, 13–14; 5:31; 6:20; 11:32; 26:17; 28:45; 2 Kings 17:34, 37; 1 Chronicles 29:19; 2 Chronicles 19:10; 33:8; 34:31; Nehemiah 9:13–14; 10:29. There are many more passages in which just two of the three divisions are mentioned together.

38. It was Avraham Gileadi who first noted this phenomenon and shared the information with me in Jerusalem in 1972. It has since been discussed by Douglas H. Parker and Ze'ev W. Falk in their article on "Law of Moses" in *Encyclopedia of Mormonism*, 2:810–12.

39. First Nephi 17:22; 2 Nephi 5:10; 25:25, 30; Mosiah 6:6; Alma 8:17; 25:14–15; 31:9–10; 58:40; Helaman 3:20; 15:5; 4 Nephi 1:12. In several more passages two of the three divisions are mentioned together (2 Nephi 1:16; Omni 1:2; Mosiah 13:30; Alma 30:3, 23; Helaman 6:34; 3 Nephi 25:4).

40. *The Zohar,* 4:372.

41. Ibid.

42. Ibid., 1:366–67.

43. Ibid., 4:16–17.

44. The Hebrew text was published in volume 3 of Adolph Jellinek, *Bet ha-Midrasch* (1854; reprint, Jerusalem: Wahrmann, 1967). The English translation used here is from Raphael Patai, *The Messiah Texts: Jewish Legends of Three Thousand Years* (Detroit: Wayne State University, 1988), 252.

45. *History of the Church,* 5:555.

46. This is why Satan's plan to take away men's agency had to be rejected in the premortal heavenly council.

47. *Midrash Rabbah* Exodus 46:1; 47:7; this is contradicted in 47:6, which says that the second set of tables was identical to the first, containing only the Ten Commandments.

CHAPTER 14

MORMON CATECHISMS

Davis Bitton

One of the most compelling obligations felt by early members of the Church of Jesus Christ of Latter-day Saints was that of preaching the gospel to others. Above all else, the Saints were to carry the message to the world. They were also instructed to teach the gospel to their children. Both audiences could learn through the scriptures, sermons, tracts, and personal testimonies of others, but it soon became apparent that more effective results could be obtained if the message were studied systematically. To this end, various published aids began to appear. One of the most useful of such aids to teaching the gospel during much of the nineteenth century was the catechism. In the broad sense, a catechism is a prepared series of questions and answers intended for instruction in the basics of the faith.[1] Although such an approach may not have been enjoyed by everyone, it had the enormous advantage of making preparations specific and "testable." Since catechisms were used widely by the Protestant and Catholic communities in the nineteenth century, it is not surprising that their Latter-day Saint contemporaries began to develop their own.

One of the earliest examples of using the question-and-answer approach to study the restored gospel was the *Lectures on Faith,* printed in the front of the first edition of the Doctrine and Covenants in 1835 and in subsequent editions down to the early twentieth century.[2] Five of the seven lectures are divided into two parts: in the first, a series of numbered paragraphs sets forth the teachings on the topic; and in the second, the same material is reviewed, as it were, by means of a series of questions and answers. "It was found," explained the official church newspaper, "that by annexing a catechism to the lectures as they were presented, the class made greater progress than otherwise."[3]

The starting section includes the following basic questions:

Q. What is faith?

A. It is the "assurance of things hoped for, the evidence of things not seen" (JST Heb. 11:1); that is, it is the assurance we have of the existence of unseen things. And being the assurance which we have of the existence of unseen things, it must be the principle of action in all intelligent beings. "Through faith we understand that the worlds were framed by the word of God" (Heb. 11:3; Lecture 1:8–9).

Q. How do you prove that faith is the principle of action in all intelligent beings?

A. First, by duly considering the operations of your own mind; and secondly, by the direct declaration of scripture.[4]

The next section deals with God as "the object in whom the faith of all other rational and accountable beings centers for life and salvation."[5] Following a long series of questions on the generations of "begats" from Adam to Abraham, the subsequent questions deal with the existence of God:

Q. What testimony did men have, in the first instance, that there is a God?

A. Human testimony, and human testimony only (Lecture 2:56).

Q. What excited the ancient Saints to seek diligently after a knowledge of the glory of God, his perfections, and attributes?

A. The credence they gave to the testimony of their fathers (Lecture 2:56).

Q. How do men obtain a knowledge of the glory of God, his perfections, and attributes?

A. By devoting themselves to his service, through prayer and supplication incessantly, strengthening their faith in him, until, like Enoch, the brother of Jared, and Moses, they obtain a manifestation of God to themselves (Lecture 2:55).[6]

God is described in the lectures as merciful, gracious, long-suffering, unchanging, and truthful; he is no respecter of persons. Knowledge, faith or power, justice, judgment, mercy, truth—the lectures discuss all these traditional attributes. Finally, the lectures proclaim, God is love.[7]

The sixth section draws a connection between faith and sacrifice. Faith, or unshaken confidence, is necessary if the Saints are to endure the expected persecution, and this faith cannot come except on the basis of sacrifice—a willingness to give all, even one's life. "This lecture is so plain, and the facts set forth so self-evident," the section concludes, "that it is deemed unnecessary to form a catechism upon it: the student is therefore instructed to commit the whole to memory." The statement clearly implies that the previous lectures did have a "catechism" intended to be memorized. The final lecture, on the effects of faith, is also without appended catechism.

The Articles of Faith, a series of "We believes," originally written in 1842 as part of Joseph Smith's answer to editor John Wentworth, were an implicit catechism.[8] That is, they can be viewed as answers to specific questions:

Q. What kind of God do Mormons believe in?

A. We believe in God, the Eternal Father, and in His Son, Jesus Christ, and in the Holy Ghost.

Q. Do Mormons believe that men will be punished for Adam's sins?

A. We believe that men will be punished for their own sins and not for Adam's transgression. (see Articles of Faith 1–2)

The questions, of course, are not part of the original document. The eventual popularity of the Articles of Faith as simple statements worthy of memorization by Latter-day Saint children suggests that they occupied a functional position very close to that of the memorized catechism.

In 1845, in Orson Pratt's *Prophetic Almanac for 1845,* a broad range of doctrines was presented in short questions and answers.

What is man? The offspring of God.

What is God? The Father of man.

Who is Jesus Christ? He is our brother.

What is man in embryo? He is a helpless babe.

What is man in progress? He is man.

What is man perfected? He is as Christ, and Christ is as the Father, and they all are one. . . .

What is his [man's] final destiny? To be like God.

What has God been? Like man.

What is man without revelation? A vessel in a fog without a compass. . . .

What is Mormonism? It is all truth.

How old is it? Without beginning of days or end of years.

Appreciated for its succinct answers, this Orson Pratt catechism, called "The Mormon Creed," was published in the *Millennial Star* in 1848.[9]

Another early question-answer presentation was "Good Tidings" by Parley P. Pratt. Written before 1857, it may have first circulated through the newspapers he edited—the *Millennial Star* in England from 1840 to 1842 or *The Prophet* in New York City in 1845. This catechism concludes with the following:

Q.—Is it not uncharitable to consider the Christian world all wrong, except such as obey the fulness of the Gospel? and still more so to tell them of it?

A.—No. The man who tells his generation the truth, according to the "law and the testimony," is more charitable to them than ten thousand men who cry, Peace and safety, and prophesy smooth things, when sudden destruction is near at hand.

Q.—But what will become of all the people who have lived and died since the Gospel was perverted and before it was restored again?

A.—They will be judged according to their works, and according to the light which they enjoyed in their day; and, no doubt many of them will rise up in judgment against this generation, and condemn it; for, had they enjoyed the privileges which we enjoy, they would, no doubt, have gladly embraced the truth in all its fulness. They desired to see the latter-day glory, but died without the sight.[10]

Nothing is said about preaching the gospel in the spirit world or performing vicarious ordinance work for the dead. Pratt may have considered the subject too advanced to treat in an elementary question-answer format.

Not so reticent, and delightful in its unapologetic directness, was a rhymed catechism entitled "The Angel's Gospel" by Welsh convert John S. Davis:

What was witnessed in the heavens? Why, an angel earth-
ward bound.
Had he something with him bringing? Yes, the gospel, joyful sound!
It was to be preached in power On the earth, the angel said,
To all men, all tongues and nations That upon its face are
spread.

Had we not before the gospel? Yes, it came of old to men.
Then what is this latter gospel? 'Tis the first one come again.
This was preached by Paul and Peter And by Jesus Christ,
the Head.
This we latter Saints are preaching; We their footsteps wish
to tread.

Where so long has been the gospel? Did it pass from earth
away?

> Yes, 'twas taken back to heaven Till should dawn a brighter
> day.
> What became of those departed, Knowing not the gospel
> plan?
> In the spirit world they'll hear it; God is just to every man.[11]

Evan Stephens set it to music and published it in the 1889 *Latter-day Saints' Psalmody*.[12]

About the same time, in 1848, Thomas Smith published a series of questions and answers in the *Millennial Star*. "I was in hopes that some more able person would have taken this in hand," Smith wrote, "as I have seen the want of something of the kind for some time past; the question being often put—what books can I give my children? how am I to teach them?" Smith's questions and answers are brief and to the point:

> Q. What Sunday school do you attend?
> A. The Latter-day Saints.'
> Q. Why are they called Saints?
> A. It is the name by which the people of God were known
> in all ages of the world ...
> Q. You said Joseph Smith was called by present revelation?
> A. Yes.
> Q. What do you mean by revelation?
> A. It means the communication of God's will to man.

In the hostile setting of Great Britain, the Latter-day Saints expected to be challenged. To assist them, Thomas Smith sometimes included scriptural proofs, as in the following:

> Q. How are the sick healed?
> A. By the laying on of hands, and anointing of oil.
> Q. Can you prove this?
> A. Yes, Mark, c. 6, v. 13; Mark, c. 16, v. 18; James, c. 5, v. 30.[13]

One wonders whether young children readily memorized or understood such references.

David Moffat, a Scottish laborer, had also recognized a need. The following year he wrote:

> Being a father of four children and a member of the Church of Jesus Christ of Latter-day Saints, I am desirous that my children should be taught in their youth the rudiments of those principles that I now entertain. But whether I should be able to abide by the principles of the above church or not, I am willing that my children should, and continue therein. Having asked counsel from the council of the branch, I was permitted to form a Child's Ladder, whereby they may ascend to a greater height than their progenitors, in the scale of intelligence and truth. I have, therefore, furnished you with about 100 questions and answers, if you deem them worthy let them form a little book, so as a mother can teach her children when she sitteth down, and when she walketh by the way. I have endeavoured to render them as short as possible, in order that they may be attained by the weakest mind; and where a proof was long and tedious, I have shortened it without removing its sense.[14]

There followed in three pages "The Child's Ladder, or a Series of Questions and Answers Adapted for the Use of Children of the Latter-day Saints."

Much longer than the catechism of Thomas Smith, the Moffat catechism poses such questions as What is your name? Who is the father of Jesus Christ? Hath all the fowls of the air names and the cattle of the field? Did ever any man speak face to face with God? Can this Being (God) occupy two distinct places at once? Is revelation available to every man? Who was the first Apostle in this dispensation? What does the system of the Saints embrace? The last question had a short, if not modest, answer: All truth in heaven, in earth, or in the universe.[15]

It would not be surprising if some readers found the opening section, with its emphasis on the names of man, God, unclean spirits, and so forth, somewhat tedious. And there was at least one doctrinal error, according to later definitions, in the statement that the name of God Almighty, the father of Jesus Christ, was Jehovah. Nevertheless, one assumes that quite a number of young Latter-day Saints, especially in Great Britain, used the Moffat catechism during the early 1850s.

John Jaques—who later became well known for his hymn "O Say, What Is Truth?"—published a "definitive" catechism serially in the *Millennial Star* in 1853 and 1854; the Jaques "Catechism for Children" was reprinted as a separate volume in 1854.[16] Only twenty-six years old, Jaques had been a member of the church for eight years, had labored as a traveling missionary, and was working in the office of the British Mission. At the time of its writing, he was not yet a father. In fact, the first installment of his work appeared about the time he married Zilpah Loader. An introductory statement explains:

> My attention has been, for some time past, directed to the subject of a Catechism for Children, and I have given the matter serious consideration. Of the expediency, and, indeed, necessity which exists that the children of the Saints should be instructed in the doctrines of our most holy faith, I am persuaded that all Saints are well convinced. Upon the rising generation rest the hopes of those who are now industriously engaged in advancing the interests of the Redeemer's Kingdom upon the earth. . . . How necessary, then, that the children of those who are on the Lord's side should be thoroughly instructed in the things of the Kingdom of God, and become competent and ready to step into the shoes of the parents, to prosecute the work which they have begun, to war a good warfare, and to carry on the truth to a glorious victory over error.
>
> Under a deep sense of the importance of these views, I have ventured to commence preparing some questions and answers, seeing that a suitable Catechism for Children is not extant. I have not the idea of preparing them for very young children exclusively, as I think it advisable to offer questions and answers of

such a character as will render them not unworthy of the attention of children of riper years.[17]

Jaques was not hesitant in recommending his work. Having pronounced previous efforts unsuitable, he went on to say: "It is customary for persons to modestly acknowledge their unfitness for work they undertake. Instead thereof, I will simply say that, in the absence of abler hands at catechism-compiling, I will endeavour to do my best, and leave the result with the Saints and the Almighty."[18]

The Jaques catechism apparently filled a need. A year after its original publication in the *Millennial Star,* it was published as a book in Liverpool. The first edition of 1854 quickly sold out, for in 1855 a new printing, "the tenth thousand," was released. In 1870, according to the title page, seventeen thousand had been published. By 1877 the number of copies sold reached twenty-one thousand. Then the *Catechism for Children* began to be published in Salt Lake City, where it continued to sell steadily. The edition of 1888 claimed to be the thirty-fifth thousand. Translations appeared in Danish (1860, 1872), German (1872, 1882, 1892), Swedish (1871, 1873), Hawaiian (1882, 1907), Samoan (1895), and Dutch (1897). It seems likely that during the closing decades of the nineteenth century more Latter-day Saints studied this catechism than any other single work.

The opening section establishes the child's identity through a series of questions: What is your name? Who gave you that name? On what day, and in what month and year, were you born? When were you baptized? After establishing the child's position in the scheme of things in this way, the questions proceed:

Q. What duties should you perform?

A. My duty to God, and my duty to my parents and to all mankind.

Q. What is your duty to God?

A. To love him with all my heart, and to keep His commandments.

Q. Why should you love God, and keep His command-ments?

A. Because it is by His power and goodness that I exist, and am sustained day by day.

Q. What is your duty towards your parents?

A. To love and obey them.

Q. Why should you love and obey your parents?

A. Because it is a command of God, and because they were the means of bringing me into the world; they nursed and fed me when I was a little babe, and now continually love me, and provide food, clothing, and lodging for me. They watch over me in sickness, direct me in health, and teach me to be clean, neat, industrious, and orderly, so that when I have grown up I may be useful.

Q. What is the reward of obedience to parents?

A. A long life, with the constant favour and blessing of God, and eternal life and happiness in the world to come.

Q. What is the punishment of disobedience to parents?

A. A short life, with the constant displeasure and curse of God, and misery in the world to come.

Q. What is your duty to all mankind?

A. To love them, and to treat them with kindness.

Q. Why should you love all mankind, and treat them with kindness?

A. Because God commands it, and because all mankind desire to be happy, and unless they love and strive to be kind to each other, they cannot be happy. Therefore all persons should love each other, that they may live as happily as possible.[19]

In the next chapter Jaques explains that knowledge of God comes from three sources—tradition, reason, and revelation.

Q. Which is the best way of learning that there is a God?

A. By revelation. Tradition and reason give indistinct and unsatisfactory ideas of God, and of His character and attributes. By revelation alone can a definite and satisfactory knowledge be obtained.[20]

Continuing the question-answer format, the catechism takes the child over the many revelations of God to man in the Bible, the Book of Mormon, and the revelations to Joseph Smith. The plurality of Gods is established by quoting several biblical passages. But "Must we worship more than one God? No. To us there is but one God, the Father of mankind, and the Creator of the earth."[21] Summarizing the character and attributes of God, the child answers: "God is a glorious Being, in the form of man; He is everywhere present; He sees and knows all things; He is full of wisdom, power, truth, justice, righteousness, and mercy: and He is an unchangeable Being."[22]

The different churches and denominations of Christianity are acknowledged but are quickly dismissed:

Q. There are now on the earth a great number of religious societies, each professing to be the Church of Christ, which amongst them all is the true Church?

A. The Church of Jesus Christ of Latter-day Saints.

Q. Why is this called the Church of Jesus Christ of Latter-day Saints?

A. To distinguish it from the Church that existed in former days, as these are the latter days in which we live. . . .

Q. How can the Church of Christ be known from other religious societies?

A. By various characteristics, among which may be named, its Priesthood and organization; its being led by a Prophet having direct revelation from God; its enjoying the gifts and blessings of the Holy Ghost, and promising the same to all believers; its purity and consistency of doctrine; its unity and oneness of spirit; its gathering its members from amongst the wicked; its building of temples dedicated to the Lord, instead of building churches and chapels dedicated to men and women; its being persecuted and evil-spoken of by every other society and by every other people under heaven; and, lastly, men may know the Church of Christ by obeying its doctrine and obtaining a testimony for themselves by revelation from God.[23]

Such traits of the true church, common in such early Mormon pamphlets as Parley P. Pratt's *Voice of Warning*, could be expanded upon and supported by scriptural passages.

Continuing in the Jaques catechism, a section on the ten commandments precedes one on the Word of Wisdom. After several questions and answers summarizing the revelation, specific reasons are given for some of the proscriptions:

> Q. Why are not hot drinks good for man?
>
> A. Because they relax and weaken the stomach, and indeed the whole body.
>
> Q. Why is it not good to smoke or chew tobacco?
>
> A. Because those habits are very filthy, and tobacco is of a poisonous nature, and the use of it debases men.[24]

Recognizing that the revelation (D&C 89) was given "not by commandment," the catechism asks what God must think of those who ignore his word. Answer: "That they despise His counsel, or at least do not appreciate it as they should."[25]

The different offices of the Aaronic and Melchizedek Priesthoods are reviewed. And the child was expected to memorize the names of the General Authorities of the church—the different editions of the catechism updated the identifications—much as several generations of Primary children in the twentieth century have done.

The concluding chapter, "The Dispensation of the Fullness of Times," surveys the restoration of the gospel through the instrumentality of Joseph Smith. Originally published just ten years after Joseph Smith's assassination, the catechism stresses basic points about authority and succession:

> Q. After Joseph Smith's death, on whom fell the responsibility of directing the affairs of the Church?
>
> A. On the Quorum of the Twelve Apostles, with Brigham Young as their President.
>
> Q. Did Joseph Smith before his death bestow all the keys and powers of the Holy Priesthood upon the Twelve Apostles?

A. Yes, every key that was necessary to save and exalt mankind in the celestial kingdom of God.[26]

The reorganization of the First Presidency in December 1847 is noted. Concluding sections of the catechism review the forthcoming judgments of God upon the wicked, the second coming of Jesus Christ, the millennium, and the final loosing of Satan to stir up men to war against the Saints. "But he and they who will obey him will be overthrown, and will receive their final judgment," the catechism concludes. "The heavens and the earth will pass away, and a new heavens [sic] and a new earth will be created, on which the glorified immortal Saints will live and reign as Kings and Priests throughout eternity."[27]

During the great revival of 1857–58, known as the "Reformation," zealous preachers like Jedediah Grant fired questions at congregations, but soon people were interrogated individually. "Have you shed innocent blood or assented thereunto? Have you committed adultery? Have you betrayed your brother? Have you borne false witness against your neighbor? Do you get drunk? Have you stolen? Have you lied? Have you contracted debts without the prospect of paying? Have you labored faithfully for your wages? Have you coveted that which belongs to another? Have you taken the name of the Lord in vain? Do you preside in your family as a servant of God? Have you paid your tithing in all things?" The basic list was lengthened until some versions contained as many as twenty-six questions. But unlike catechisms, their purpose was not instruction in gospel principles but self-assessment leading to repentance.[28]

Another noninstructional catechism appeared in the *Deseret News* in 1862. Entitled "Catechetical Illustrations of the Faith and Teachings of the Saints," it attempts to provide answers for frequently asked questions:

It is frequently asked, "What is the reason of your being driven from place to place?"

Because we have the priesthood of the Son of God, and all the world is opposed to it.

"For what were you driven from Jackson County, Missouri?"

For preaching and trying to practice the gospel of life and salvation.

"Were not your people abolitionists?"

They were not.

"Did they not spread an influence that slavery was not right?"

They said, as they now say, that slaves are, in many instances, abused, and that masters will be punished for abusing their slaves. . . .

"Were you not driven from Illinois in consequence of believing and practicing the doctrine called 'spiritual wife doctrine,' or polygamy?"

No. . . .

"For what were you driven from the State of Illinois?"

For the same reason that we were driven from other places, viz.—because we preach and try to practice the gospel of life and salvation. . . .

"Is there no political reason why you have been driven from place to place?"

Perhaps so, for probably the world fear[s] our political, as well as religious union, knowing that "in union there is strength." We know of no other political reason.[29]

The formal organization of the Sunday School on 11 November 1867[30] created a need to provide reading materials, lesson aids, and a regular curriculum. Quite early in this development, starting in 1866 with the first volume of the *Juvenile Instructor,* a catechism was published "for our juveniles." The questions were essentially study questions; the reader was to look up the answers. Then, in the following issue, the questions were reprinted along with answers. One long series of such questions was based on a biography of Joseph Smith published serially in the *Juvenile Instructor.*[31] When and where was he born? What were his father's and mother's names? How old was he when he went to the Lord to ask which of the sects was right? The questions continued, branching out to include other important aspects of early Mormon history:

> Q. What was President [Heber] Kimball called, even by leading Elders, before leaving Kirtland, for going on the mission [to England in 1837]?
>
> A. He was ridiculed and called a fool for listening to Joseph and being willing to go on his foreign mission. . . .
>
> Q. To what place did they [the Mormon Elders] proceed from Liverpool?
>
> A. To Preston.
>
> Q. What words were on the flag which they saw as they alighted from the coach in Preston?
>
> A. "Truth will prevail."[32]

Early Church history had been traced up to 1838 when this series ceased publication in 1869.

Running simultaneously with the catechism on church history were Bible questions and answers and a series on the Book of Mormon entitled "Catechism on the History of the Indians."[33] "From whom have the American Indians descended? Lehi. Was he a good man and a Prophet? Yes."[34] And so on.

The intended age of the audience was not always clear in these early catechisms. "The catechism for children, exhibiting the prominent doctrines of the Church of Jesus Christ of Latter-day Saints, should be in every family, school and Bible class,"[35] urged George A. Smith in 1872, probably referring to the Jaques catechism. Both children and adults could benefit, of course, but sometimes a mature understanding was assumed.

In 1874, a series entitled "Sunday Lessons for Little Learners" was prepared by George Goddard, first assistant superintendent over the Sunday Schools.[36] Goddard's introduction acknowledged that the Jaques catechism and earlier issues of the *Juvenile Instructor* furnished lessons "applicable to all grades of the more advanced pupils." By contrast, the new catechism, couched in short, simple sentences, was intended for younger children of four or five years of age.

> Q. What has God made to give us light by day?
>
> A. The sun.
>
> Q. What has He made to give light by night?
>
> A. The moon and stars.
>
> Q. Who is God?
>
> A. Our Heavenly Father.[37]

Following this cadence, the questions move into the life of Jesus and then Joseph Smith, never straying far from a child's level of understanding.

> Q. What angels were sent by the Lord to give Joseph the power and authority of the Holy Priesthood?
>
> A. Peter, James and John.
>
> Q. We have spoken of these before, as men; who were they?
>
> A. Apostles of Jesus when he lived upon the earth.
>
> Q. How did they give the authority of the priesthood to Joseph?
>
> A. They laid their hands upon him and blest him.
>
> Q. After they had done so, what rested upon him?
>
> A. The Holy Ghost.
>
> Q. What is the Holy Ghost?
>
> A. The spirit of God.
>
> Q. If Joseph Smith had been a bad boy, would the Lord have sent His Holy Spirit to be with him?
>
> A. No.
>
> Q. Who, then, will the spirit of God be with?
>
> A. Good people.
>
> Q. What must people do to please God and keep His spirit with them?
>
> A. Pray often.
>
> Q. Who besides men and women should do this?
>
> A. Little children.

Q. And will the Lord bless little children who pray often to Him?

A. Yes.

Q. What will He help them to do?

A. To mind their parents and always speak the truth.[38]

The *Juvenile Instructor* also ran more advanced questions and answers based on the Bible and Book of Mormon.[39]

That catechetical material was used in Sunday School is clear from a description of the Tenth Ward Sunday School written by Benjamin Lang.[40] Four classes used the Bible and Book of Mormon, he said, while others used readers. In the higher classes the "Church Catechism"—the Jaques catechism—was used. Examinations were given on the ancient and modern history of the church, and prizes were offered. (One is reminded of Tom Sawyer squirming in front of his Sunday school.) For such a regimen, catechisms were obviously very helpful.

At the end of the century, an official history of the Sunday School acknowledged the contributions of the *Juvenile Instructor* through its "numerous helps to Sunday School workers in the way of catechisms suited to different grades of pupils." In the list of publications offered was "a large number of catechism cards" that had received "a wide circulation."[41]

Another organization that made use of catechisms was the Primary. In the early 1880s, after a vigorous project of establishing Primaries in different settlements, Eliza R. Snow published several books intended for Primary use. One of these, a work of 120 pages, was *Bible Questions and Answers for Children*.[42] The person in charge should read the questions aloud, she explained. Another "appointee" would read the answer. Then the children would "repeat the answer in concert." As soon as the children had mastered the answers, the "prompting may be dispensed with." A chapter or part of a chapter would be taken for a lesson and "repeated week after week until it is well committed."[43] From Genesis to Revelation, the catechism took the student over the essentials of the Bible story. Nine-tenths of the work would probably have been quite acceptable to most denominations of the time. But some questions had a Mormon twist, and some dealt with more recent issues.

> Q. Who made this world?
> A. The Gods. . . .
> Q. Where was the Garden of Eden?
> A. In Jackson county, Missouri. . . .
> Q. Upon whom did Joseph [Smith] confer them [the keys]?
> A. Brigham Young.
> Q. In what manner?
> A. He sealed upon the heads of the Twelve Apostles all the Priesthood, keys and powers that had been conferred upon him by the angels of God.[44]

As an indication of how this catechism was used, Eliza R. Snow attended a Primary conference in Morgan, Utah, and asked the children "all the questions contained in one of the chapters. . . . They were greatly entertained by it, and their little faces brightened up and their eyes sparkled with the pleasant pastime."[45]

We can never know how many Latter-day Saints learned the rudiments of the restored gospel by means of these catechisms. Two prominent General Authorities, both of whom became presidents of the church, acknowledged learning from a catechism: Presidents Heber J. Grant and Joseph Fielding Smith.[46] Certainly many other people did the same.

By the end of the century some Mormon leaders, like educators elsewhere, were questioning the value of rote learning. "In day schools and Sunday Schools there is too much recitation, too much machine study being done," said James E. Talmage at the Sunday School convention in 1898. "Parrots can recite, but they do not study, they do not comprehend, they do not see the relation between the parts." Talmage was emphatic: "Rote work I should discourage under all conditions."[47] Other institutional and curricular developments just before and after the turn of the century included the religion class movement, the rise of church academies, challenging courses of study prepared for the seventies quorums and the Mutual Improvement Associations, and new lesson manuals written for Sunday School and Primary, all of which may have found the old catechisms inadequate.

Nevertheless, the ideal of committing certain things to memory was not abandoned. One prominent leader of thought, William James, did not rule out all such learning. "Constant exercise in verbal memorizing must still be an indispensable feature in all sound education," wrote James. "In every branch of study there are happily turned, concise, and handy formulas which in an incomparable way sum up results."[48] For young Latter-day Saints, these included certain passages of scripture, the Articles of Faith, and the names of the General Authorities. Having committed them to memory, students were to be "passed" on these before being promoted to the next class. In addition to the Articles of Faith, educator George H. Brimhall advocated memorizing the Lord's Prayer and the Ten Commandments. "I am not one of those who believe that a child should understand everything before it commits it to memory," he explained.[49]

In the twentieth century, the term *catechism* disappeared from the Mormon lexicon.[50] Yet some memorization continued to be required. "Memory gems" were recited in Sunday School, and scriptural themes were selected each year for the Mutual Improvement Association and recited aloud by the group. Children continued to memorize the Articles of Faith and for many years the names of General Authorities. At present, in a program called "Scripture Mastery," seminary students are encouraged to memorize twenty-five scriptural passages each year. But the extensive rote learning common among young Latter-day Saints in the past century has been abandoned.

Bearing some similarity to catechisms has been an approach to studying the gospel by posing specific questions and then giving answers. As already mentioned, this was the organization of *Lectures on Faith*. As early as 1840, in England, Elder Parley P. Pratt responded to doctrinal questions in the pages of the *Millennial Star*.[51] Later in the nineteenth century, George Q. Cannon and George Reynolds answered questions in the editorial pages of the *Juvenile Instructor*, and in the twentieth century such articles were published in the *Improvement Era* by Elder John A. Widtsoe and President Joseph Fielding Smith. Less authoritative, perhaps, but also valuable were the "Q and A" articles by non–General Authorities that appeared in the *Ensign* and *New Era*, some of which are compiled in a useful book entitled *A Sure Foundation: Answers to Difficult Gospel Questions*.[52] Not intended to be memorized, these articles, which continue to appear in the church magazines, may be the closest Latter-day Saint equivalent to the movement after World War II known as the "new catechetics."[53] Similar to earlier catechisms in following a question-answer format were missionary plans. Designed to teach the rudiments of Mormonism to nonmembers, such plans proliferated after World War II.[54] During the 1950s, *A Systematic Program for Teaching the Gospel* was published for use in all the missions of the church.[55] Questions were designed to elicit the "correct" answers: "If man has flesh and bones and is in the image of God, then God has a body of flesh and what, Mr. Jones?" Although the investigator—the catechumen—did not memorize answers, the missionary did as part of his preparation, and the teaching sessions were not regarded as free-wheeling discussions in which every opinion had equal validity. Moving from premise or scriptural passage to conclusion, using questions to elicit "correct" answers, the plans were intended to "teach the gospel."

In the manuals used today in priesthood, Sunday School, Relief Society, Young Men and Young Women, Primary, family home evening, and seminary and institute classes, as well as in church magazine articles used for home teaching and visiting teaching, questions are employed to engage the listeners. Teachers are cautioned against asking only "factual" questions. Discovery learning is highly valued. On the other hand, "correct" answers are given in some manuals for the benefit of the teacher.[56] In the same tradition, songs for Primary children help them learn by rote the Articles of Faith and the books of the Bible and Book of Mormon. Another song, "Latter-day Prophets," helps children learn the names of the presidents of the church.[57] The Mormon catechetical tradition, even though not so denominated, thus continues in vestigial form.

Will there ever be another Mormon catechism? The new "catechisms" now in use elsewhere in Christendom demonstrate the value of a standard work that sets forth the basics in a systematic fashion, and the Latter-day Saint equivalent might well be the four-volume *Encyclopedia of Mormonism*, portions of which have been reprinted in handier format. *The Catechism of the Catholic Church*, a landmark work, avoids the simplified, question-answer format still used for instructional purposes by other Protestant and Catholic catechisms.[58] It seems doubtful to me that a lengthy Mormon work structured around questions and answers will ever again become widely used, as was the Jaques catechism in the past century, but I may be wrong, for catechisms have obvious advantages where rudimentary instruction is required, where speculative discussion is not encouraged, and where a trained corps of teachers is lacking.

Notes

This article is a revised and improved version of an earlier article by the same title published in 1976 in a mimeographed series entitled *Task Papers in LDS History;* the earlier version had extremely limited circulation.

1. The term *catechism* originally meant systematic instruction in Christianity for those preparing to be baptized but came to be used for

the "written or printed summaries of the principal doctrines of the Christian faith, intended for the instruction of the unlearned and the young." *The New Schaff-Herzog Encyclopedia of Religious Knowledge,* 12 vols. (New York: Funk and Wagnalls, 1908). Accepting as a working definition of *catechism* "a manual of religious instruction usually arranged in the form of questions and answers" (*Encyclopaedia Britannica,* 15th ed., s.v. "catechism"), I here examine works within the Latter-day Saint tradition that are thus arranged.

2. Now most readily available in Larry E. Dahl and Charles D. Tate Jr., eds., *The Lectures on Faith in Historical Perspective* (Provo, Utah: BYU Religious Studies Center, 1990). In addition to the text of the lectures, this volume contains an analysis and discussion of each of the lectures by (in order) Dennis F. Rasmussen, Joseph Fielding McConkie, Rodney Turner, Robert L. Millet, Robert J. Matthews, and Ardeth G. Kapp. Authorship of the lectures has also been discussed by Noel Reynolds, "The Authorship Debate Concerning *Lectures on Faith:* Exhumation and Reburial," in *The Disciple as Witness: Essays on Latter-day Saint Doctrine in Honor of Richard Lloyd Anderson,* ed. Stephen D. Ricks, Donald W. Parry, and Andrew H. Hedges (Provo, Utah: FARMS, 2000), 355–82.

3. *Messenger and Advocate* 1 (May 1835): 122.

4. Dahl and Tate, *Lectures on Faith,* 35.

5. Ibid., 52.

6. Ibid., 63–64.

7. Ibid., 85–89, and Robert L. Millet, "The Supreme Power over All Things: The Doctrine of the Godhead in the Lectures on Faith," in Dahl and Tate, *Lectures on Faith,* 221–40.

8. The classic analysis of the Articles of Faith as responses to questions of the day is T. Edgar Lyon, "Origin and Purpose of the Articles of Faith," *Instructor* 87 (August–October 1952): 230–31, 264–65, 298–99, 319. Best in placing them in historical context is David J. Whittaker, "The 'Articles of Faith' in Early Mormon Literature and Thought," in *New Views of Mormon History: A Collection of Essays in Honor of Leonard J. Arrington,* ed. Davis Bitton and Maureen U. Beecher (Salt Lake City: University of Utah Press, 1987), 63–92.

9. *Latter-day Saints Millennial Star* 10 (1 August 1848): 238 (hereafter *MS*). Orson Pratt's fondness for the question approach is also demonstrated in "Questions on the Origin of Man," "Mormon Philoso-

phy: Space, Duration, and Matter," "Questions on the Present State of Man," and "Angels" (in two parts), published in the *New York Messenger,* 6, 13, 20, and 27 September, and 18 October 1845. He publishes answers only for the second article, and of course they could scarcely have been intended for memorization. David J. Whittaker, ed., *The Essential Orson Pratt* (Salt Lake City: Signature Books, 1991), 29–47.

10. *Scrapbook of Mormon Literature* (Chicago: Etten, 1911), 1:529–32. This work is a collection of tracts and pamphlets compiled and privately published by Ben E. Rich. According to bibliographer Chad J. Flake, *Good Tidings; or the New and Everlasting Gospel* was published as a four-page flyer in the *Millennial Star* office in the 1860s and again in about 1874. Chad J. Flake, ed., *A Mormon Bibliography, 1830–1930* (Salt Lake City: University of Utah Press, 1978), 522.

11. *Hymns of the Church of Jesus Christ of Latter-day Saints* (1985), no. 11 (though it is not often sung by congregations today); the original version in *MS* 9 (15 December 1847): 380, has some minor changes in punctuation and wording and includes an additional verse: "Where so long had been the gospel? Didn't it ever 'fall away'? What became of those neglected? 'God is just'—that's all we say. Seek no crop where 'twas not planted, Nor a day where reigns the night; Now the sunshine bright is beaming, Let all creatures see aright."

12. Karen Lynn Davidson, *Our Latter-day Hymns: The Stories and the Messages* (Salt Lake City: Deseret Book, 1988), 40.

13. *MS* 10 (15 June 1848): 183–84.

14. David Moffat, "The Child's Ladder, or a Series of Questions and Answers Adapted for the Use of Children of the Latter-day Saints," *MS* 11 (1 March 1849): 73–76.

15. Ibid.; these questions all appear in the catechism.

16. John Jaques, "Catechism for Children," *MS* 15 (1853): 756–60, 795–96, 810–12, 827–31, 837–40, 851–52; 16 (1854): 27–29, 45–47, 58–59, 113–14; John Jaques, *Catechism for Children* (Liverpool: Richards, 1854). For other editions, see Flake, *A Mormon Bibliography,* 338–39. About Jaques, see Stella Jaques Bell, *Life History and Writings of John Jaques* (Rexburg, Idaho: Ricks College Press, 1978).

17. Jaques, "Catechism for Children," *MS* 15 (19 November 1853): 756.

18. Ibid.

19. Jaques, *Catechism for Children*, 6–7.

20. Ibid., 9.

21. Ibid., 13.

22. Ibid., 19.

23. Ibid., 53–54.

24. Ibid., 63.

25. Ibid.

26. Ibid., 81.

27. Ibid., 84.

28. Howard C. Searle, "The Mormon Reformation of 1856–1857" (master's thesis, Brigham Young University, 1956), 43–45. For a list of questions and a description of Brigham Young's use of them in a sermon, see John Moon Clements Journal, 4 November 1856, Family and Church History Department Archives, The Church of Jesus Christ of Latter-day Saints (hereafter Church Archives).

29. *Deseret News Weekly*, 6 August 1862.

30. Richard Ballantyne organized it informally on 9 December 1849.

31. *Juvenile Instructor* 1 (October–December 1866): 76, 80, 88, 92; 2 (January–December 1867): 8, 24, 28, 40, 44–45, 60–61, 68, 76, 92–93, 100–101, 124, 133, 148, 165, 180 (hereafter *JI*).

32. *JI* 3 (15 August 1868): 128.

33. *JI* 3 (January–April 1868): 16, 28, 40, 56, and passim.

34. Ibid., 28.

35. George A. Smith, in *Journal of Discourses*, 14:376.

36. George Goddard, "Sunday Lessons for Little Learners," *JI* 9 (February–July 1874): 59, 65, 84, 94, 102, 120, 132, 144, 149, 168, 173; 10 (January–December 1875): 12, 24, 33, 48, 57, 72, 77, 96, 132, 156, 168, 188, 204, 216, 228, 237, 252, 257, 276, 285, 300; 11 (January–December 1876): 12 and passim. George Goddard's journal, containing many references to the use of catechisms in Sunday Schools, is housed in the Church Archives. See Davis Bitton, *Guide to Mormon Diaries and Autobiographies* (Provo, Utah: Brigham Young University Press, 1977), 124–25.

37. Goddard, "Sunday Lessons for Little Learners," *JI* 9 (28 February 1874): 59.

38. Ibid., 168.

39. *JI* 9–12 (1874–1877): passim.

40. *JI* 2 (1 January 1867): 8.

41. *Jubilee History of the Latter-day Saints Sunday Schools, 1849–1899* (Salt Lake City: Deseret Sunday School Union, 1900), 42. Several examples of these catechism cards are preserved in the Church Archives: Catechism on Reward, Catechism on the First Principles of the Gospel, Catechism on Prayer.

42. E.R.S.S. [Eliza R. Snow Smith], *Bible Questions and Answers for Children* (Salt Lake City: Juvenile Instructor Office, 1881; 2nd ed., 1883).

43. Ibid., 3 (1883 ed.).

44. Ibid., 5, 6, 78 (1883 ed.).

45. *Woman's Exponent*, 1 November 1881.

46. Ronald Walker, "Young Heber J. Grant's Years of Passage," *BYU Studies* 24/2 (1984): 134; Joseph Fielding Smith, *Answers to Gospel Questions* (Salt Lake City: Deseret Book, 1993), 4:vi.

47. *Proceedings of the First Sunday School Convention of the Church of Jesus Christ of Latter-day Saints* (Salt Lake City: Deseret Sunday School Union, 1899), 29, 32.

48. William James, *Talks to Teachers on Psychology: And to Students on Some of Life's Ideals* (1899; reprint, New York: Dover, 1962), 65.

49. *Proceedings of the First Sunday School Convention*, 43.

50. *Catechism* is one of the terms said to be "conspicuously absent from LDS language, or used infrequently." Robert W. Blair, "Vocabulary, Latter-day Saint," in *Encyclopedia of Mormonism*, 4:1537.

51. *MS* 1 (September 1840): 120–23; (February 1841): 256–59.

52. *A Sure Foundation: Answers to Difficult Gospel Questions* (Salt Lake City: Deseret Book, 1988).

53. Useful surveys are found in such reference works as *The New Schaff-Herzog Encyclopedia of Religious Knowledge* and James Hastings, *Encyclopedia of Religion and Ethics* (New York: Scribners, 1913).

54. Jay E. Jensen, "Proselyting Techniques of Mormon Missionaries" (master's thesis, Brigham Young University, 1974); Lewis C. Christian, "A Study of the Development of the Missionary Plan of the Church of Jesus Christ of Latter-day Saints, 1830–1950," typescript, paper for Religion 544, Brigham Young University, copy in Church Archives; Richard O. Cowan, "Richard Lloyd Anderson and Worldwide Church Growth," in *The Disciple as Witness*, 105–15.

55. *A Systematic Program for Teaching the Gospel* (Salt Lake City: Deseret News Press, 1953), with many subsequent printings.

56. "Teaching with Questions," in *Teaching, No Greater Call: A Resource Guide for Gospel Teaching* (Salt Lake City: The Church of Jesus Christ of Latter-day Saints, 1999), 68–70.

57. *Children's Songbook* (Salt Lake City: The Church of Jesus Christ of Latter-day Saints, 1989), 114–17, 119, 134.

58. *A New Catechism: Catholic Faith for Adults* [the Dutch catechism] (New York: Herder and Herder, 1967); *Catechism of the Catholic Church*, 2nd ed. (Rome: Libreria Editrice Vaticana, 1997); Bennet Kelley, *St. Joseph First Communion Catechism* (New York: Catholic Book, 1991); John A. Hardon, *Pocket Catholic Catechism: A Concise and Contemporary Guide to the Essentials of the Faith* (New York: Doubleday, 1989); Francis D. Kelly, *The Mystery We Proclaim: Catechesis for the Third Millennium* (Huntington, Ind.: Our Sunday Visitor, 1999).

CHAPTER 15

THE THEOLOGY OF COUNCILS

Richard Lyman Bushman

Truman Madsen and I have long shared an interest in Joseph Smith. His writings and tapes on the Prophet have affected thousands of people. Time and again when I say I am writing a biography of Joseph Smith, I am asked if I have read Truman Madsen's works about Joseph. Fortunately, on this particular topic there is plenty to go around. Joseph's thoughts, his character, his work, his struggles confound our attempts to fully comprehend them. For example, although I have long been familiar with Joseph's achievements, I was surprised to find how much attention he paid to church organization. Joseph has so long been thought of as a "dreamy visionary" who needed a Brigham Young to whip a vital but inchoate movement into shape that Joseph's involvement in church structure may come as a surprise. After examining this dimension of the Prophet's work, I am now inclined to consider Joseph the "organizer" and Brigham the "administrator" rather than to give all the organizational credit to President Young. I suppose that if Truman and I keep searching Joseph's life, many more surprises await us.

We have been content, presumably, to let Joseph originate theology and leave organization to Brigham because in our hierarchy of values, we tend to rank thought and belief above governance. We think that neglect of organization does not diminish Joseph's achievement so long as his revelations are acknowledged as the source of doctrine. What people think and believe—their inner thoughts—are more important, we assume, than the system of governance. But unless translated into action, theology has little impact. Organization, we know, affects everyday practice. It regulates lives of members of the Church of Jesus Christ of Latter-day Saints day by day and not just in theory. The organizational routines of the religious life may reach as deep into our minds and hearts as doctrines transmitted by words. In Joseph's case, I have come to believe, the form of ecclesiastical government turned some of the most fundamental doctrines of the restoration into habits of living. Belief and practice converged in church governance—hence the title of this essay: "The Theology of Councils."

In addition to commenting on doctrine and practice, I wish to offer a narrative of organizational development in the early years. I propose that church governance goes from more to less autocratic—the opposite of the usual story. Scholars have claimed that a loose, democratic structure gradually gave way in the church's first years to concentrated hierarchical authority.[1] I am saying, by contrast, that prophetic authority was highly concentrated at first and was dispersed as the years went by—into councils.

The Church of Jesus Christ among the Churches

The centralized nature of governance during the first year or two of the church's history is best seen against the background of other Christian churches and their modes of organization. For two hundred years before the Church of Christ was organized in 1830, the types of church government ranged along a spectrum from episcopal to congregational. The most centralized churches, like the Roman Catholic and the Anglican, concentrated authority in bishops—the *episcopus*—who held the ultimate authority to

appoint and ordain and also exercised great influence over doctrine. The bishop ordained priests and appointed them to their par-
ishes. He had the final word in disciplinary cases and controlled
the properties of the church. Authority flowed downward from
the bishop to the people.

At the opposite extreme from centralized rule by bishops was
the congregational church order, in which people in the congregation selected their own ministers, disciplined their members,
and controlled finances. The congregation was the seat of church
government. Authority flowed upward from the congregation.
Everything else was mere superstructure, erected on the congregational base. Congregationalism in church government corresponded to democracy in the state.

In Joseph's time, the congregationalist impulse prevailed in
America, especially among the new churches. The Universalists, for
example, met first in little societies where they heard a preacher
or read scripture. They were slow to organize formal churches requiring the adoption of disciplinary rules and a profession of faith
for fear of encroaching on the free worship of individual believers
in their congregations. Eventually, the Universalists did organize
and create a modest hierarchical structure of associations to work
out common policies, but they adamantly insisted on the independent sovereignty of individual congregations.[2] Like all congregational churches, they were wary of sharing authority with
higher bodies. If Joseph had been looking for ideas on church governance, extreme congregationalism would have been the dominant model for his time and social class.

Where did the budding Church of Jesus Christ fit within this
spectrum in 1830? Did it incline toward episcopal centralism or
congregational democracy? If early church government had been
democratic, in the spirit of other denominations, the congregation would have been the seat of power. But it seems obvious to me
that authority in Joseph's time did not rest in local congregations,

the key unit in the democratic Protestant churches. In fact, congregational organization hardly figured at all in the early church. Congregations did have the authority to approve priesthood officers and to license elders, but nothing more (see D&C 20:65). Section 20, the constitution of the church, made no provision for appointing pastors to lead local churches, the starting point of organization in other denominations. The revelation said only that elders were to take the lead of meetings, and if no elder was present, then a priest or teacher took charge. The words imply informal worship without a preestablished authority. Whoever happened to have the highest authority rose to lead the meeting (see D&C 20:44, 45, 49, 56).

Following Joseph Smith to the end of his life, I find it hard to detect in him much interest in congregational organization at any time. The plat of the City of Zion in 1833 identified no meetinghouses for a population of fifteen to twenty thousand. Presumably one of the twenty-four temples at the center of the city could have served for Sunday meetings, but none of them had a title to suggest such usage. The temples were named for various offices in the priesthood, not for wards in the city.[3] The names implied they were meeting places for quorums rather than congregations. Although Joseph assembled nearly fifteen thousand people in Nauvoo before he died, he never provided for congregational meetinghouses. People met in houses, in stores, and outdoors. The church's architectural energies went into temples, which only incidentally served for regular Sunday church services. The role of the congregation in church government was not merely diminished within the organization of the Church of Jesus Christ—it was almost totally disregarded. Although the Prophet faithfully attended Sunday worship in Kirtland and Nauvoo, his revelations said virtually nothing about congregational organization.

Actual government in the Church of Jesus Christ began at the next higher level of ecclesiastical organization: the conference.

Section 20 of the Doctrine and Covenants makes provision for quarterly conferences of elders, specifying that "the several elders composing this church of Christ are to meet in conference once in three months" (D&C 20:61). This would have been a familiar form of governance to anyone who was acquainted with Methodism. Methodist conferences, like the conferences of the Church of Jesus Christ, met quarterly to license preachers and exhorters and to conduct church business. Missionaries were sent out by the Methodists' annual conferences. Knowing the Methodists, early church members would have easily accepted the practice of governing through conferences. It would have seemed perfectly natural for the second conference in September 1830 to send missionaries to the Lamanites, as well as to deal with the dispute over Hiram Page's seer stone.[4] Joseph said the conference of January 1831 conducted "the ordinary business of the Church," and it was as an item of this "ordinary business" that the decision was made to move the headquarters of the church to Ohio.[5] Later, in June 1831, high priests were ordained for the first time at the quarterly conference of elders.[6] Looking back now, it is possible to see the quarterly conference as a comfortable starting point for an organization that was to evolve into a much more elaborate structure within a few years.

While the quarterly conferences had the air of conventional church conferences like those of Universalists and Methodists, they actually differed substantially because of Joseph's presence. Although discussion did take place, decisions were not made by debate and deliberation, followed by a vote. The most significant decisions were made by revelation to the Prophet. The fate of Hiram Page's seer stone, the missionary expedition to the Lamanites, the decision to leave New York, and the bestowal of the high priest's office came as a result of revelations to Joseph Smith. So far as can be told, he presented the revelations to the conferences for their acceptance rather than accepting motions rising from the floor. In some cases, persuasion may have been required; discussion doubtless followed, and votes were taken. But authority lay in the revealed words, not in the democracy of debate and ballot. Underneath the democratic forms, the Lord's Prophet exercised authority vested in him by virtue of his revelations.

The authority of revelation also settled many day-to-day issues that arose in the intervals between the quarterly conferences. People applied to Joseph for a commandment, as they called revelations then, and the Lord gave directions. Authority did not necessarily lie solely in the hands of Joseph Smith, for he did not rule by fiat. Authority emanated from the revealed word, which his followers distinguished from his counsel or wishes. Authority lay in him as revelator or, more properly, in the revelations themselves. This form of governance has been labeled (by Max Weber) charismatic authority, or governance by divine gift—perhaps the most concentrated form of authority imaginable. Joseph probably prevailed by force of his personality too, for he dominated every circle he entered. But ultimately the revelations, not his naturally strong character, gave him authority.

The Rise of Councils

Strangely for one who so readily assumed the leader's role, Joseph began dispersing authority soon after the church settled down in Kirtland in 1831. He adopted the practice of calling interim conferences or—as he later called them—councils to deal with problems arising between the quarterly conferences. Without any prescribed membership or rules of conduct, the conferences included the most experienced priesthood holders who happened to be available when a need arose. Joseph called them together and presented the problem—often a disciplinary matter—and they worked together on a solution.

Between 6 September 1831 and 12 November 1831, Joseph held eight conferences in Kirtland, Hiram, and Orange, Ohio.

Near the end of that period, from 1 to 12 November, four conferences came in quick succession, leading Joseph to say he had sat
in conference for nearly two weeks.[7] The participants were not
the "elders," narrowly restricted to that priesthood office, but included all priesthood holders. In his report on the conference at
Orange on 25–26 October, Joseph noted the presence of twelve
high priests, seventeen elders, four priests, three teachers, and
four deacons. In addition, "a large congregation attended."[8] Although the conferences conducted church business, they seem to
have been open to the general membership. Emma attended with
Joseph sometimes, and in the middle of one disciplinary case, the
priesthood called on a woman in the audience to testify. Since regular Sabbath services do not appear in the record for these months,
the conferences may have served the purposes of worship for the
general membership.[9]

Besides disciplining errant members, forming fund-raising
committees, deciding on publications, and sending out missionaries, the conferences were the occasion of revelations. Section 67
begins with the words, "Behold and hearken, O ye elders of my
church, who have assembled yourselves together . . ." (D&C 67:1).
Other revelations seem to have been given at conferences for the
purpose of settling matters under discussion.[10] The conferences
mixed deliberations and votes on issues with directions from God
to the Prophet.

In the spring of 1832, Joseph changed the terminology for his
meetings: he began intermixing the terms *conference* and *council.*
In April he called "a general council" of the church in Independence to acknowledge him as president of the high priesthood
following a confirmation of this office at a "conference of High
Priests, Elders, and members" in Ohio the previous January.[11] From
then on, the word *council* became increasingly common.[12]

Through 1833, the form of these councils/conferences became more regular. Joseph increasingly spoke of "a council of High

Priests" meeting to ordain people or to deal with transgressions, as if the council consisted solely of holders of that office. The Word of Wisdom was given for the benefit of a council of high priests (see D&C 89:1). Besides restricting the councils to high priests, other rules developed. In June 1833, a council ordained two additional high priests "to make out the number, (twelve) that the council, or Church court, might be organized."[13] I know of no revelation before June 1833 about twelve members of a church court. The practice seems to have developed by customary use, perhaps with biblical precedents in mind.[14]

By this time, the councils had become self-sufficient. Joseph's presence was not required to make them work. Instead of councils relying on him to give the last word, they met, deliberated, and made policy decisions in his absence. In the fall of 1833, Joseph and Sidney's departure for Canada did not prevent the councils from meeting. Under Frederick G. Williams, who presided in their absence, a council decided to discontinue work on the temple for the winter and made plans to build a printing house. These were not minor matters, and the brethren acted in full confidence, without Joseph to prompt them.[15]

By the time of the formal organization of the high council in February 1834, the composition of the council and the procedural rules could be recorded not as a revelation from on high but as a set of minutes. Precedents had been worked out in the previous year, so that the members could agree on organizational procedures. Joseph Smith was appointed president, but the duties of that office were not restricted to him. A similar council was organized in Missouri, subject to the procedures outlined in the Kirtland High Council minutes. A year later, in February 1835, the Twelve were organized as a traveling high council to manage church business outside of the two stakes organized under their own presidencies and without the direct guidance of Joseph Smith.[16]

Although Joseph still held the highest offices in the church and took precedence in any situation because of his revelatory power, everyday church governance had largely been transferred to these councils. Joseph's recorded history of the church for a year after the Twelve's organization in 1835 consists almost entirely of the minutes of the various councils. He seems to have considered their work to be the business of the church. The councils were making the important decisions, disciplining members, sending out missionaries, raising funds, erecting buildings. In Joseph's absence, the councils functioned as smoothly as if he were present. In August 1835 a grand council or conference approved the new Doctrine and Covenants while Joseph was absent in Michigan.[17] Though he presided when present, church government was functionally independent of him.

The importance of these councils in forming the young church cannot be overemphasized. Think of priesthood holders sitting in council meetings day after day as transgressors were disciplined and church plans laid. They had a chance to watch the Prophet in action as he organized affairs. As questions arose, they could compare their thoughts to his and learn from his example. Brigham Young would not have been the only one who absorbed lessons from Joseph. No wonder they could work without him after a few years; they had observed him sitting in council on so many occasions before they took over.

Consider also the impact of a council's members sitting through one discipline case after another. Before the council stood the transgressor, whose errors and counterbalancing virtues were reviewed from many perspectives. Point by point, the boundary between acceptable and unacceptable behavior was laid down. As the council member judged transgressors, he also judged himself. How did he measure up to the standards laid down in the court? Observing members being chastised or exonerated, each councilor learned the limits of saintly behavior for himself. By implication the councils defined good and bad saints by common-law tradition, worked out in specific cases involving actual people.

The councils thus created a corps of men who learned through vicarious experience how to conduct themselves as saints. They not only learned the rules of conduct but helped generate them. Council decisions represented a corporate conclusion about the nature of sainthood, giving councilors the confidence to propagate the standards throughout the church.

Equally important in the formation of church culture was the provision in section 102 that if the council lacked sufficient knowledge to decide a case, "the president may inquire and obtain the mind of the Lord by revelation" (D&C 102:23). The president of the high council received the revelation whoever he happened to be. In Joseph Smith's absence, Frederick G. Williams could obtain the mind of the Lord. In the Zion High Council, President David Whitmer inquired of God. Revelation on church business was delivered not solely to Joseph Smith but to every council president. The revelations of each president stated the mind of the Lord and carried appropriate weight. After the Council of the Twelve was organized, Joseph told them that the minutes of their deliberations would be important, "for such decision[s] will forever remain upon record, and appear an item of covenant or doctrine."[18] In other words, they would carry the same authority as the commandments or revelations by which Joseph governed the church in the early years.

Joseph Smith took great satisfaction in this dispersal of authority. After the high council was organized in 1834, he told them "that if I should now be taken away, I had accomplished the great work the Lord had laid before me, . . . and done my duty in organizing the High Council, through which council the will of the Lord might be known on all important occasions, in the building up of Zion, and establishing truth in the earth."[19]

In bringing conciliar government into being, Joseph not only distributed authority to the councils, but he dispensed the divine gift of revelation as well. After the councils were organized in 1834 and 1835, the number of revelations recorded in the Doctrine and Covenants diminished. Joseph still received large doctrinal expositions on baptism for the dead and eternal marriage. He also recorded items of instruction that came to him as nuggets of divine truth. But the day-to-day revelations on how to govern the church disappeared. Their place was filled by the minutes of the councils where the governance of the church went forward. (One exception to this trend was section 124 on the Nauvoo House.)

When Joseph died and confusion arose about his rightful successor, Brigham Young, though lacking explicit instructions, knew that a council could govern the church, and the church members went along with him. Experience had taught them that government by council did not represent a downgrading of divine leadership. They had relied on councils for a long time and knew that guidance from God could come to a council.

In some ways, the formation of governing councils was Joseph's greatest organizational achievement. Working out a hierarchy and an organizational chart did not in itself distinguish him; a modern consulting firm might have recommended a structure for a new church. But investing the church councils with the divine gift of revelation was a unique and wonderful accomplishment. To instill the faith that God would speak to the council leadership upon inquiry just as he did to the prophet could not have been achieved by mere rational organization. To this day, Latter-day Saints believe that their church organization is infused with revelation—not just at the top, but in every bishopric and auxiliary presidency.

The transfer of power from Joseph to the councils aligned the practice of church government with Mormonism's most basic doctrine—the belief that revelation leads the church. Instead of revelation being a remote ideal stated in words only, revelation was incorporated into practice. In church government, everyone has a right to revelation for his or her stewardship. Deacon quorum presidents and Young Women's class leaders are taught to seek guidance in their most minute decisions. In a sense, this belief in organizational revelation is the ultimate democratization of religious authority, conferred upon the Saints by a prophet who believed his gift rightfully belonged to all the Saints.

Notes

1. For many variants of this theme, see D. Michael Quinn, *The Mormon Hierarchy: Origins of Power* (Salt Lake City: Signature Books, 1994), 38; Thomas F. O'Dea, *The Mormons* (Chicago: University of Chicago Press, 1957), 156; and Dan Vogel, *Religious Seekers and the Advent of Mormonism* (Salt Lake City: Signature Books, 1988), 53. Jason Lindquist discusses the large question of priesthood authority in "'Unlocking the Door of the Gospel': The Concept of 'Keys' in Mormonism and Early American Culture," in *Archive of Restoration Culture: Summer Fellows' Papers, 1997–1999* (Provo, Utah: Joseph Fielding Smith Institute for Latter-day Saint History, 2000), 29–42.

2. Russell E. Miller, *The Larger Hope: The First Century of the Universalist Church in America, 1770–1875* (Boston: Unitarian Universalist Association, 1979), 63–65, 70, 75, 95. For a broader explication of this theme, see Miriam Murdock, "'Stepping Stones' of Understanding: Patterns of the Priesthood in Universalism, Freemasonry, and Mormonism," in *Archive of Restoration Culture*, 51–58.

3. Joseph Smith, *History of the Church of Jesus Christ of Latter-day Saints*, 2nd ed. (Salt Lake City: Deseret Book, 1950), 1:357–59.

4. Ibid., 109–20.

5. Ibid., 140, 142.

6. Ibid., 176.

7. Ibid., 215–37. The comment on two weeks of conferences appears on p. 235.

8. Ibid., 219.

9. At a council of high priests in Clay County, 7 July 1834, priesthood holders of all ranks were there "together with a number of Mem-

bers." Donald Q. Cannon and Lyndon W. Cook, eds., *Far West Record: Minutes of the Church of Jesus Christ of Latter-day Saints, 1830–1844* (Salt Lake City: Deseret Book, 1983), 71.

10. Doctrine and Covenants 64, 66, 68, 69, 70; section 75 was given at a conference held 25 January 1832.

11. *History of the Church,* 1:267.

12. For interchangeability of council and conference, see ibid., 327.

13. Ibid., 354.

14. Elders' councils did not require this number. Ibid., 355.

15. Ibid., 418.

16. The evolution of the Quorum of the Twelve Apostles into a general governing body of the church is traced in Ronald Esplin, "The Emergence of Brigham Young and the Twelve to Mormon Leadership (1830–1841)"(Ph.D. diss., Brigham Young University, 1981).

17. *History of the Church,* 2:243–46.

18. Ibid., 199.

19. Ibid., 124.

Chapter 16

The Refractory Abner Cole

Andrew H. Hedges

One Sunday afternoon during the winter of 1829–30, E. B. Grandin's print shop in the village of Palmyra, New York, played host to a singular confrontation involving Hyrum Smith, Oliver Cowdery, and one Abner Cole.[1] That Hyrum and Oliver would even be at Grandin's on a Sunday was unusual; the "bargain" that Joseph Smith had made with Grandin to print the Book of Mormon—then at press at the print shop—expressly denied the Smiths access to the press on Sunday, and religious strictures seem to have generally kept them at home anyway on the Sabbath.[2] On this particular Sunday, however, Hyrum had experienced some "peculiar feellings" that "led him to believe that something was going wrong" at the print shop. After expressing his concern to Oliver and debating "some time" with him over the propriety of going into town on the Sabbath, Hyrum forced the issue by telling Oliver he would "not suffer such uneasiness any longer without knowing the cause" and that he, at least, was going. His insistence carried the argument, and the two young men set off for the shop.[3]

Arriving at Grandin's, Hyrum and Oliver were surprised to see "an individual by the name of Cole, an ex-justice of the peace," hard at work printing a weekly paper, the title of which, according to Lucy Mack Smith, was *Dogberry Paper on Winter Hill.* Neither Hyrum nor Oliver was aware of the paper's existence, as Cole had reportedly distributed the "six or eight numbers" he had already published "ten or twenty miles into the country" to keep them out of the Smiths' sight. After exchanging some strained pleasantries with Cole and learning that the older man rented the press from Grandin on evenings and Sundays, Hyrum noticed that in the paper's prospectus Cole had "agreed with his subscribers to publish one form of 'Joe Smith's Gold Bible' each week, and thereby furnish them with the principal portion of the book." Looking further, Hyrum and Oliver apparently found where Cole had already "thrown together a parcel of the most vulgar, disgusting prose, and the meanest, and most low-lived doggrel, in juxtaposition with a portion of the Book of Mormon, which he had pilfered." Shocked at his discovery, Hyrum asked Cole what right he had to "print the Book of Mormon in this manner" and reminded the editor that Joseph had secured a copyright for the book.[4] Cole retorted that he had "hired the press" and would "print what I please, so help yourself." Finding that nothing they said could "dissuade [Cole] from his purpose," Hyrum and Oliver "left him to issue his paper, as he had hitherto done," and returned to the Smith farmhouse. In consultation with Joseph Sr., they decided that Joseph himself, then living over 120 miles away in Harmony, Pennsylvania, should be notified of Cole's activities.[5]

Joseph Sr. made the trip, reportedly arriving back in Manchester with the Prophet the following Sunday.[6] The day on which they returned was "one of the most blustering cold and disagreeable that I ever experienced," remembered Lucy, and father and son, having "breasted the storm all day long," were "nearly stiffened with the cold" by the time they made it home. Following a short rest at the farmhouse, Joseph took advantage of his timely arrival and proceeded alone to Grandin's, where he found Cole engaged in his usual Sunday activities. After "good naturedly" saluting the printer and examining his paper, Joseph reminded Cole of the copyright and insisted that he stop "meddling" with the Book of Mormon.[7] At this, Cole reportedly "threw off his coat, rolled up his sleeves, and came towards Joseph, smacking his fists together with vengeance" and challenged the Prophet to a fight. Remaining calm and trying to defuse the situation, Joseph simply smiled at the display, refused the challenge, and suggested—given the wintry season—that the enraged man keep his coat on. Following another frenzied outburst, Joseph again reminded Cole of the copyright and the legal avenues he, as copyright holder, could pursue that would serve his purposes far better than a brawl. No doubt impressed with the weakness of his position and Joseph's relaxed demeanor, Cole finally calmed down and "concluded to submit to an arbitration." When the arbitration "decided that he should stop his proceedings forthwith," Cole abandoned his designs and, according to Lucy Smith, "made us no further trouble."[8]

Lucy's report notwithstanding, Cole continued to take a lively interest in the Prophet, his followers, and the Book of Mormon. This interest manifested itself in a variety of editorial comments and articles in his paper, ranging from "the lowest and most contemptible doggerel that ever was imposed upon any community" to well-reasoned arguments against the legitimacy of the Book of Mormon and the new religion.[9] Except for a few noticeable gaps, Cole's withering remarks and satire on Joseph and the Book of Mormon were a regular feature in his paper—a paper printed, ironically, on the same press on which the Book of Mormon was printed. Long considered little more than a sidelight to the printing of the Book of Mormon, Cole's piracy of the text and his interest in the early church have caught the attention of several historians.[10] The newspaperman's personal background and the tactics he employed to discredit Joseph and the Book of Mormon have received the most emphasis, although several questions about these two topics remain unanswered. Unresolved, too, are the timing of his purloining of the text and his motives for defaming the Prophet and his work. This paper examines these issues in an effort to shed additional light on one of Mormonism's earliest, most vocal, and most caustic critics.

Cole's Background

We have no record of Cole's date and place of birth, although later census records indicate that it must have been sometime between 2 June 1780 and 6 August 1784 and was most likely not in New York.[11] His father, Southworth Cole, first appears in the New York census in 1810, as a resident of Canandaigua.[12] Southworth's was a large family; besides his wife, six children—ranging in age from under ten to twenty-five—shared the elder Cole's home that year. By this time Abner was on his own, appearing in the same census as a resident of Geneva. No other persons were living with him, suggesting that he was not married at the time. Sometime over the next four years he left Geneva for Palmyra, and by 1815 he had married, his wife apparently bringing three children from a previous marriage with her into the union. By 1820 Cole had three sons and a daughter of his own and by 1830 had added one more of each to his quiver.[13] To support his young and growing family, Cole worked as a lawyer of sorts during the week and, beginning in the fall of 1829, as editor and publisher of the *Reflector* under the pseudonym "Obadiah Dogberry, Jun."[14]

As brash and impulsive as Cole was with Hyrum and Joseph, it would be wrong to conclude that he was little more than the village hothead. Cole served as a justice of the peace in Palmyra from April 1814 to April 1815 and as one of thirty-two overseers of highways from April 1816 to April 1817.[15] Although of limited jurisdiction, these elected positions were important in the life of any small town of the time and indicate that a fair number of Palmyra residents found Cole both competent and likeable—at least early in his career in the town. In 1818, however, shortly after being elected as a village constable, the town meeting voted to "reconsider the vote electing Abner Cole as constable" and subsequently replaced him.[16] A brief character sketch of Cole—composed, it turns out, by himself[17]—that appeared in Grandin's *Wayne Sentinel* years later as part of a versified tribute to various newspapermen in the area gives some possible clues as to why some might have objected to his serving as a lawman, at the same time suggesting that Joseph's antagonist was not a man to trifle with:

> Now last, not least, [wrote Cole of himself] my muse
>   would name
> *Old Obadiah,* and his fame.
> Eccentric quite,—and full of fun,—
> Sad stories tells of wrong that's done—
> Flogs *fop* or *fool* where'er they'r found,
> And single-handed stands his ground—
> And with his pen discourses knowledge,
> The same as tho' he'd been to *College.*[18]

Cole's willingness and ability to "stand his ground" hints at an argumentative, even combative, streak in the *Reflector*'s editor. Lucy's account of his rough treatment of Joseph bears this out, as does the "unpleasant sparring" Grandin witnessed later between Cole and another Palmyra resident at a "charity meeting" one evening. Cole badgered his opponent until the enraged man "was in his cups," recorded Grandin.[19] Unable to restore order, the chairman of the meeting resigned on the spot. The tiff would have broken up the meeting except that the chairman's hastily appointed replacement was apparently able to bring the argument to a close.[20]

Not all his differences with others ended so easily. During the summer of 1814, for example, Cole filed formal charges against at least two people in separate incidents, one of which involved damages amounting to $800.[21] In June 1818, the tables were turned when certain merchants in Palmyra sued Cole for $150 he owed them for "goods wares & merchandize" that he "hitherto wholly refused and still refuses [to pay]," while one Gershom Gillet sued Cole the following year for the $600 he owed him.[22] The list goes on and on; in the Common Pleas of the May 1821 court term alone, Cole appears as a defendant in three of the thirty-one cases.[23] Most of these and the other suits of which we have record appear to involve unpaid debts, although in July 1818 Cole brought suit against one Levi Jackson for assault and battery—after which Jackson charged Cole with defamation of character.[24]

Given Cole's public service and outspoken nature, it seems likely that he and Joseph had crossed paths long before they met in Grandin's shop. Indeed, their acquaintance probably went back over a dozen years, when both families lived on west Main Street following the Smiths' move to Palmyra about 1816.[25] Joseph would have been a boy of ten at the time and Cole, an overseer of highways, in his early to mid-thirties. Even though they were neighbors, points of contact between the two would have been limited at this time because of the difference in their ages; however, they doubtless would have known one another. Further contact would have been even more limited following the Smiths' move to their farm some two years later, but the family's regular visits to town on business or holidays over the ensuing years would have brought them into closer proximity numerous times. Lucy's account also suggests that the two of them were well acquainted; she represents Joseph and Cole—as well as Hyrum and Cole—as recognizing and saluting each other by name in Grandin's shop, without introductions.[26]

Much about Cole's background remains obscure. It is clear from what information we do have, however, that by the winter of 1829–30 he would have been a formidable foe for young Joseph. By that time Cole was well known and well established in the community—if a little odd, apparently—and he was twice as old as Joseph. He was also witty and determined, and doubtless privy to some of Joseph's less-than-stellar moments as a youth. Long before his showdown with Joseph in Grandin's shop, Cole had surely already laid claim to whatever psychological high ground might emerge in a battle between the two.

Cole's Motives

A crossed-out sentence in Lucy's 1845 manuscript suggests that Cole had started his paper to offset his personal financial reverses, which had left him destitute of money and property by the autumn of 1829.[27] No records about Cole's personal finances confirming or contradicting the charge have come to light, but it is clear that his paper selling for one dollar, "payable in advance," for a four-month subscription[28] was a financial success. Precisely how many subscriptions Cole collected over the seventeen months the paper ran is unknown, but from the correspondence Cole printed in the paper's pages we know that people in Newark, Geneva, Canandaigua, Macedon, Manchester, Rochester, and even Syracuse, sixty miles east of Palmyra, were subscribing to the *Reflector*, suggesting a circulation of no mean proportions. At the close of the first series, Cole noted that the paper had "been sought for and read with avidity" and that its success had "exceeded our most sanguine expectations."[29] Four months later Cole could again write that "the liberal encouragement our paper has heretofore received, has induced us to offer another SERIES to the public."[30] The sales continued, and by 13 September 1830 Cole was bubbling that his paper, "unaided by missionary influence, has *crept* into very general circulation; so much so, that in all cases our *whole impression* has been disposed of at or before the expiration of each series."[31] Encouraged by the "liberal patronage" of his readers,[32] Cole published a fourth and final series between October 1830 and March 1831 before moving to Rochester.

Just how crucial an item Cole's running commentary on Joseph and the Book of Mormon was to the paper's popularity is difficult to say. Probably few people, if any, subscribed to his paper solely for his coverage of these topics, but Cole's geographical proximity to the scene of events certainly would have been a selling point for those interested in following the young prophet's career. Indeed, considering the notoriety Joseph and the Gold Bible had already garnered by 1829, anything that anybody could say about the Prophet and his work—especially anything seemingly authoritative and also derogatory—was automatically good copy. Cole's location and biting wit ensured that his treatment of Joseph was both, and he piqued enough readers' interest that many actually began requesting more coverage of the Gold Bible question. Cole obliged by publishing the extracts from the Book of Mormon that so alarmed Hyrum and Oliver, placing the blame for his breach of the law on the "solicitation of many of our readers," whose "excited . . . curiosity" on the subject would not be satisfied "for some months to come" unless he gave them a sneak preview.[33] Cole's coverage of Joseph was obviously a very popular feature of his paper and would have added materially to its success. We cannot quantify this popularity or determine its effect on Cole's income, but the lengths to which the newspaperman was willing to go to satisfy his subscribers' curiosity about the Book of Mormon suggest that these factors were substantial and that pecuniary concerns were at least partially responsible for Cole's interest in the Prophet's activities.

As real and important as the bottom line must have been for a man supporting a large family, Cole was motivated in his pursuit of Joseph by other considerations as well. A skeptic and a cynic of the first order, Cole was one of dozens of newspaper editors throughout the country who had taken upon themselves the task of policing society at large. These so-called "freethought presses" were a regular feature of the American newspaper landscape between 1825 and 1850, having emerged as a reaction to the religious excesses and emotionalism of the day.[34] Grounding themselves in the rationalism of the Enlightenment, editors like Cole scorned and ridiculed any perceived manifestation of unbridled ministerial authority or mindless acquiescence to the same, especially when it threatened to influence civil or secular affairs. Such influence need not be overt or demonstrable to catch their attention and unleash a barrage of commentary; any decision made in haste or reflective of religious values was suspect. Perceived hypocrisy, bigotry, and fanaticism in both religion and politics were duly exposed and ridiculed as well. Not necessarily nonreligious themselves, freethought editors were simply ultrasensitive to the separation that should exist between church and state and were critical of anything that seemed to elevate religious mores or blind emotionalism above reason and empiricism.

Cole and the *Reflector* fit the mold perfectly. Heading each issue of his paper with Alexander Pope's well-known injunction, "Know then thyself, presume not God to scan! The proper study of Mankind is Man," Cole filled its pages with a running commentary on the events and personalities of the day. His position and purposes were clear. Finding "most of our public journals" to be little more than "engines of party" and "supple tools of faction, whereby truth is often sacrificed at the shrine of some political Idol," Cole saw himself "displaying aloft the sacred banner of all-powerful truth, nothing doubting that in the end we shall come off victorious."

> Morality and vital piety we shall always reverence [he wrote], while bigotry, hypocricy, and fanaticism will receive no quarter [a]t our hands, and we shall ever glory in lifting the veil, tearing off the mantle, and stripping the cloak from the vain pretender, and hold him up to public ridicule.[35]

Assuring his subscribers that his "labours in the cause of truth" would not be "exclusively confined to the narrow precincts of our own flourishing village," Cole "cordially invite[d] the friends of REFORM in the neighboring VILLAGES to aid us in the cause, . . . by giving us early tidings of such passing events as may require our chastening hand." Noting that "the innocent will have nothing to fear" and that "the cause of the widow and father-less will claim and receive our peculiar care and attention," Cole nevertheless warned that he would "at all times, assume the pre-rogative of taking under our fatherly care and protection, *any* po-litical demagogue, without distinction, who from turpitude, may require chastisement." While Cole's primary objective was to ferret out the "many offences against the *well-being* of the community, which, from their undefinable character, are not strictly cogniz-able in a court of justice," he also promised to reprint "bio-graphical notices and copious extracts from *rare* history" in the pages of his paper and pledged that the "arts and sciences, to-gether with all useful knowledge, shall receive our feeble aid in their support and promulgation."[36]

At a time when the flames from revivals and camp meetings were blurring the already hazy distinction between "vain pre-tenders" and "political demagogues," Joseph Smith and the Book of Mormon were just two of the era's perceived vices that the *Reflector*'s editor sought to expose. Others included the various Christian-sponsored reform movements of the time. As one who enjoyed his liquor, for example, Cole was quick to point out the "superstition and bigotry, in company of sordid avarice," that he saw attending the Temperance movement:

> The pulpit may thunder anathemas against the "hydra-headed monster" denominated Intemperance, as if it concen-trated all the evils our frail natures are subject to; while on the other hand, the gates of paradise are almost gratuitously opened to all such as shall *piously* give ther substance into the "Lord's treasury," to be drawn from thence by its agents, who, after *prudently* satisfying their own wants, appropriate the

residue to the education of "poor and pious" young men, . . .
while the *real* poor and needy of our cities and villages perish
for lack of sustenance.[37]

Similarly, the national controversy surrounding Sunday mail
delivery attracted Cole's attention. To the horror of zealous Christian reformers, postal regulations of the time required the United
States Post Office to transport and deliver mail seven days a week.
By 1828, ministers from around the country were petitioning Congress to change the regulations to a six-day week, with no mail
being moved and delivered on Sunday. Opponents of the proposed change argued that to stop the mails on Sunday would be
mixing church and state.[38] The issue smoldered for several years,
during which time Cole had plenty to say against the proposition.
The *Reflector*'s 2 January 1830 issue, for example—the same issue
in which Cole began printing extracts from the Book of Mormon—took up the controversy at several points. After calling one
of the village's rectors to repentance for "allow[ing] his name to
head a '*Sunday mail*'" petition, Cole, in a separate article, ridiculed the current rumor that England had stopped mail delivery
on Sunday. Later still, he reported on a town meeting that addressed the issue, then quoted extensively from an editorial in
Grandin's *Wayne Sentinel* that pointed out the dangers of confounding church and state on this issue. Cole concluded his attack with a satirical petition to Congress requesting that the mails
be stopped on Saturday rather than Sunday, as the "*seventh* day of
the week, most *heathenly* called Saturday (from Saturn,) is the
true Sabbath, the same that Moses made the rebellious Jews observe and keep as holy time."[39]

None was safe from Cole's attacks. Anti-Masons, outspoken
ministers of other religions, political figures of both local and national prominence, other newspapermen—Cole went after them
all with alacrity. As one might expect, some took exception to his
tactics. Grandin, for example, spent a day in January 1831 trying

to calm down one Ovid Lovell, who was upset about a certain *Reflector* article that he felt "*reflected* on his conduct in a certain matter."[40] A month later, Cole's incessant needling had so infuriated Palmyra's Presbyterians that a group of them visited Grandin and threatened to withdraw their patronage of his paper if he continued to grant Cole the use of his press. Grandin—himself a target of Cole's criticism at one point[41]—refused to be cowed by their united front and turned them away, but not without learning firsthand about the power Cole's pen wielded in the community.[42]

While Cole cast his net wide in his hunt for subjects worthy of censure, religious personalities and issues were clearly his favorite target. Cole pursued this prey beyond the pages of his paper; in February 1831, for example, we find him opening a debate in Palmyra's "Mechanic's Institute" on the question, "Is there a Religious Sect in this country, whose Clergy, by their conduct in general, give evidence that they are aiming at the control of our Governmental Institutions?"[43] Yet in spite of this unrelenting attack on religion, he himself appears to have been a sincere believer in some sort of divinity.[44] The apparent contradiction is explained through a careful reading of his editorials, which make it clear that it was not religion per se he was opposed to, but the trappings of the overtly religious culture of the times. In an article unimaginatively entitled "Things I Dislike," it was the "haughty, proud, arrogant, bigotted, and ignorant *Priest*," the "sordid, avaricious, hypocrite, in the *guise* of a meek and lowly *christian*," and the "wretch whose face represents a practical commentary on the book of *lamentations*" who took the heat.[45] After mocking his own family on Christmas Eve 1829 for "having gone to church . . . to show some new clothing just made up in the newest fashion," Cole put his criticisms to verse:

Religion—What Is It?

'Tis not to go to church to-day,
To look devout and *seem* to pray,

And ere the morning sun goes down
Be dealing scandal through the town.

'Tis not for sects and creeds to fight,
And call our zeal the rule of right,
When all we wish is at the best,
To see our church excel the rest.

Not every sanctimonious face,
Denotes the certain reign of grace;
A phiz that *seems* to scowl at sin,
Oft veils hypocricy within.

'Tis not to make our duties walk,
Or of our own good deeds to talk;
And then to practice secret crime,
By purloining our neighbors [dime].[46]

Far from trying to destroy religion, Cole was trying to rescue it from the ministers and methods he felt were corrupting the original simplicity and truth of the biblical message. He was Israel's defender rather than its assailant—in his words, the "young and humble shepherd of Israel" who would "combat most manfully, not only the champion but the whole host of the uncircumcised."[47] Cole represented the battle in which he had engaged as a desperate one, and his disingenuous references to his own "imperfections," the "many disadvantages" he labored under, and the "countless myriads" of the enemy served to strengthen the identification he wanted to make between himself and the faith's historic champions.[48]

Cole's unflattering pseudonym, Obadiah Dogberry, served to strengthen this identification as well. The Obadiah after whom Cole named himself was doubtless the ancient prophet Obadiah, author of the shortest and perhaps one of the least known books in the Old Testament. Cole's Dogberry could only have been the constable Dogberry in Shakespeare's *Much Ado about Nothing.* Given Obadiah's obscurity and the brevity of his message, one might think this prophet an unlikely mascot for someone who viewed himself as Israel's champion. Cole, however, trying to pass himself off as the "young and humble," come-from-behind hero, probably found the Prophet's obscurity gratifying and his message of woe (albeit brief) to Israel's destroyers relevant to his own cause. Cole would have appreciated Shakespeare's Dogberry for similar reasons. Arguably a relatively minor figure in the play—he does not appear until the third act and is on the stage only four times—the unflashy constable, simple-minded to the point of buffoonery, nevertheless displays a profound reverence for virtue, justice, and deity, and his apprehension of the two "false knaves," Borachio and Conrade, is an important turning point in the story.[49]

In light of Cole's religious views, the editorial slant of his paper, and his own perceived role as a social critic, it becomes obvious that Joseph Smith and the Book of Mormon would have been prime targets for his pen. A young, uneducated farmer's son claiming to have been visited by angels; a new book of scripture with allegedly miraculous origins; a community divided over the legitimacy of the supposed prophet's claims; a disconcertingly large and growing number of zealous followers—for one as jaundiced and suspicious as Cole, everything about the new movement would have smacked of the ignorance, emotionalism, and extremism he found so objectionable. Popping up under his very nose, the whole thing was too juicy a morsel for someone with his appetite to overlook.

Dating the Confrontations

Cole began laying the groundwork for a confrontation with Joseph Smith in the first edition of his paper, where he announced that "The Gold Bible, by Joseph Smith Junior, author and proprietor, is now in press and will shortly appear. Priestcraft is short lived!"[50] Cole fired several more shots of like character at Joseph over the course of September and early October, then said nothing of the young prophet or the Nephite record until 9 December. On that date, he announced to his patrons that he had "concluded to commence publishing *extracts* from [the Book of Mormon] on or before the commencement of the second series of his paper," scheduled to begin later that month.[51] For some reason Cole was unable to keep to his time line; nothing appeared in the 16 December issue, and all he could do in the first number of the second series was take another potshot at Joseph ("'Bard of Visions' *rejected*," he wrote) and promise "'Gold Bible' next week."[52] Everything came together for him eleven days later, however, and on the first page of the second number of the new series, bearing the date of 2 January 1830, Cole published 1 Nephi 1:1–2:3.[53] Cole picked up where he had left off in the next number of the series, publishing 1 Nephi 2:4–15 on 13 January—again, on the first page—and concluded his three-part piracy of Joseph's translation on 22 January, when he published Alma 43:22–40 on the third and fourth pages of the paper.

In her account of the whole affair, Lucy made no attempt to date Hyrum and Oliver's discovery of Cole's escapades or his later confrontation with Joseph. She provided some possible clues about these dates when she reported that Hyrum and Oliver came across Cole only after he "had already issued six or eight numbers," but her approximations do little good in this regard, as the eighth number of the *Reflector* rolled off Grandin's press 21 October 1829, more than two months before Cole began publishing the extracts.[54] More helpful in dating these events is the first sentence of a letter from Oliver Cowdery to Joseph Smith—living in Harmony, Pennsylvania, at the time—dated 28 December 1829. Oliver opened his letter apologetically, telling Joseph, "It may seam supefluous for me to write as Father [Joseph Sr.] is going directly to your country."[55] This imminent journey of Joseph Sr. to Harmony was almost certainly the trip he took for the express purpose of informing Joseph of Cole's illegal proceedings in the print shop.[56]

Significantly, the day Oliver wrote the letter, 28 December, was a Monday. As we know that Joseph Sr. set out for Harmony "as soon as possible" after hearing about Cole, it is quite likely that the Sunday on which Oliver and Hyrum had discovered Cole in the print shop was the day before Oliver wrote the letter mentioning Joseph Sr.'s imminent departure—that is, Sunday, 27 December.[57] At this point no extracts had been published, but Cole certainly would have been well on his way to having the type set for the first extract from 1 Nephi, which appeared in print just a few days later.

The 1853 version of Lucy's account represents Joseph Sr. returning from Harmony with Joseph Jr. "the ensuing Sunday," or, by the above calculations, 3 January 1830.[58] This would have required Joseph Sr. to make the 240-odd-mile round-trip between Manchester and the Prophet's home near Harmony in six days at most— no small feat, considering the time of year. As difficult as such a journey may sound, there is no reason to question Lucy's memory here. A later reference by Lucy to the expense incurred from making trips to Harmony this winter[59] suggests that Joseph Sr. made the journey by stage, most of which averaged about sixty miles per day at the time through regular and frequent substitutions of horses. Lucy also recorded that shortly after Joseph returned to Harmony, the family was "again compelled to send for" him to quiet fears about how printing costs for the Book of Mormon would be paid.[60] From a contract the Prophet signed with Martin Harris to this end, we know that Joseph was back in Manchester on 16 January 1830—an unlikely, if not impossible, event had his confrontation with Cole happened much later than 3 January.[61]

If Joseph confronted Cole on 3 January, one may wonder how it was, then, that Cole went on to publish two more excerpts from the Book of Mormon over the course of the next three weeks. A careful reading of Lucy's record, however, discloses the fact that Cole did not agree in the print shop to stop violating Joseph's copyright but merely to "submit to an arbitration"—that is, have a third party review the affair and determine the legality or illegality of his printing the extracts.[62] Organizing and conducting this review would have taken some time, of course, and probably accounts for Cole's publication of two more extracts before he was forced to stop.[63]

A likely timetable for the events surrounding Cole's purloining of the Book of Mormon text, based on the above analysis of available information, might be this: Oliver and Hyrum found Cole in the print shop Sunday, 27 December 1829, as Cole was preparing the first extract for publication. Joseph Sr. left Manchester within the next couple of days, shortly after Oliver penned a short letter to the Prophet on Monday, 28 December. While Joseph Sr. was away, the first extracts were published on 2 January 1830. Father and son arrived back in Manchester on Sunday, 3 January; later that evening, after a brief rest, Joseph Jr. made his way to the print shop and confronted the belligerent Cole, who was preparing the second Book of Mormon extract for publication. Cole agreed to submit the matter to a third party for review, but that did not prevent him from publishing this second extract ten days later, 13 January. Joseph, in the meantime, had returned to Harmony, only to be summoned again to the Palmyra area—he was definitely there on 16 January—to quell fears about paying for the publication of the Book of Mormon. Cole was able to get one more extract out (22 January) before the third party decided in Joseph's favor and ended the newspaperman's mad career with the Book of Mormon text.

Cole's Subsequent Activities: A Brief Overview

Cole said nothing in his paper about his failed bid to put a substantial portion of the Book of Mormon into his subscribers' hands. Nor, for more than a month, did he even mention Joseph Smith or the Nephite record. When he finally did reintroduce the subject on 27 February 1830, it was only to compare the difficulty he had encountered in deciphering one of his correspondent's handwriting with the challenge it must have been for "the inspired man who wrote the 'Gold Bible' on 'plates of brass'" to translate from "the *reformed* Egyptian' language."[64] The silence resumed until 16 March, when Cole excoriated one Luther Howard, who had requested that Cole remove his name from his list of subscribers, for "profess[ing], *ostentatiously,* to belong to a Calvinistic church—where himself and family display a fine profusion of clothing—while he *privately* advocates the 'Gold Bible.'"[65] Over the next several months, Cole continued this policy of going after Joseph's associates rather than Joseph himself, directing a barrage of withering criticism and satirical remarks between 19 April and 22 June at Hyrum Smith; an unidentified "honest Attorney" who had cast his lot in with Joseph; Oliver Cowdery; "one of *Jo's greatest* apostles" (unnamed); an unidentified Book of Mormon witness; and another "apostle."[66] Cole's purpose during these months, as he explained later, was to "expose the hypocricy and cant of [the Book of Mormon's] pretended apostles" rather than to go after Joseph or the Book of Mormon itself, the latter being so obviously a "gross and bungling imposition" that it was hardly worthy of notice.[67]

When he heard of Joseph's success in casting an evil spirit out of Newel Knight in Colesville, however, Cole was unable to refrain from leveling a vicious personal attack on the Prophet himself. Implicitly identifying the Prophet with the "thread-bare juggler and fortune-teller" of Shakespeare's *Comedy of Errors,*[68] the *Reflector's* editor devoted an entire column of his paper to "that *spindle shanked* ignoramus *Jo Smith.*"

> This fellow appears to possess the *quint essence* of impudence [wrote Cole], while his fellow laborers are not far behind him in this particular—they go from place to place disturbing in a greater or less degree, the peace of the community—denouncing dire damnation on such as may with hold their ap-

probation from one of the most ridiculous impostures, ever promulgated.

Cole closed the piece with a satirical recital of the events in Colesville, the account of which he had evidently received from Martin Harris.[69]

Shortly before his attack on Joseph, Cole had introduced another tactic for poking fun at the Prophet and the young church. This consisted of composing his own book of "scripture"—"The Book of Pukei," he called it—which parodied the obviously well-known story of Joseph's finding and translating the plates, as well as the Book of Mormon's contents themselves.[70] "Pukei" ran only two installments,[71] but the idea of scripture-styled parodies appealed to several of Cole's subscribers, some of whom generated parodies of their own about events in their particular towns and submitted them to Cole for publication. Two of these—the "Book of Daniel" from Lyons (no pun intended, apparently) and the "First Book of John" from Syracuse—made brief allusions to Joseph Smith before focusing on more immediate concerns, although at one point "Daniel's" author directed his remarks specifically to "ye of the '*precious knowledge of Mormon.*'"[72] The oblique attacks against the Book of Mormon and Joseph's supporters continued during this time as well, with Cole duly noting everything from alleged spouse abuse to alleged tax fraud among members of the church.[73]

Following the church's success in northeastern Ohio late in 1830, Cole decided it was time to take the Book of Mormon and its believers more seriously. His hand was forced somewhat in this regard by a correspondent from Farmington, who noted with some concern that while "this most clumsy of all impositions, known among us as Jo Smith's 'Gold Bible,' is beginning to excite curiosity abroad," no one close to the scene had provided the reading public with any background or explanation of the book. "To you [Abner Cole], and you alone, do we look for an expose of the principal facts, and characters, as [are] connected with this singular business," wrote the correspondent. "I say singular, because it was hardly to be expected, that a *mummery* like the one in question, should have been gotten up at so late a period, and among a people, *professing* to be enlightened."[74]

Cole rose to the occasion, promising his readers "to give, . . . so far as in us lies, . . . a plain and unvarnished statement of facts" that might have anything to do with the "origin, rise, and progress of the book in question." To place the subject in its proper context, Cole's plan was to "introduce brief notices and sketches of the superstitions of the ancients"—especially alchemy—and of "ancient impostures" like Muhammad. "Legends, or traditions respecting hidden treasures" and "tales of modern 'money diggers'" would be appealed to when appropriate, and "other impostors" like the Morristown Ghost, Jemima Wilkinson, and Joanna Southcote would be invoked for comparative purposes. "Our readers will perceive that we have an ample field before us," the obviously excited Cole concluded. "How well we shall execute our task, time will determine."[75]

Cole followed his game plan.[76] Muhammad and Joanna Southcote were taken up in turn,[77] as were the *"peep stones"* and guardian spirits associated with the *"mania* of money digging" that had swept the region in recent years.[78] When it came time to introduce Joseph Smith into this witch's brew of heresy and hearsay, Cole abandoned any effort to be either objective or civil. "We have never been able to learn," he informed his readers, "that any of the [Smith] family were ever noted for much else than ignorance and stupidity, . . . a propensity to superstition[,] and a fondness for every thing *marvelous.*" This included young Joseph, whose "mental powers appear to be extremely limited" and who had "but little expression of countenance, other than that of dulness."[79] The idea of an ancient record was not original with this thick-headed youth, charged Cole, but rather was suggested to his mind through the practices of one "vagabond fortune-teller by the name of Walters," a "conjurer" whom Joseph and his fellow money-diggers had hired to locate buried treasure for them.[80] "The better to carry on his own deception," recounted Cole, Walters read from an old copy of Cicero's *Orations,* which he would then interpret "as a record of the former inhabitants of America, . . . [containing] a particular account of the numerous situations where they had deposited their treasures previous to their final extirpation."[81] Blatantly borrowing from Walters's ploy, continued Cole, Joseph had originally intended the Book of Mormon to be an ancient treasure map, giving "an account of the Ancient inhabitants (antideluvians,) of this country, and where they had deposited their sub-[s]tance, consisting of costly furniture, &c. at the approach of the great deluge."[82] Only later did the idea of turning his find into the basis of a new religion occur to him, Cole argued, after which the young pretender wrote the Book of Mormon by "promiscuously intermingl[ing]" portions of the Old and New Testaments of the Bible.[83]

At the same time he was unveiling his assessment of the Book of Mormon's rise and progress, Cole also printed a number of notices and articles from correspondents to the West who were following the activities of Sidney Rigdon, Parley P. Pratt, and Oliver Cowdery in Ohio and the Indian Territory.[84] Not surprisingly, these reports painted a less-than-favorable picture of events in the West and the character and activities of those converting to the church. More remarkable than their unflattering observations, however, is the fact that the topic of Mormonism was clearly the single most important feature of Cole's paper during the spring of 1831. At least one article—either his own or a correspondent's—on Mormonism appeared in each of the eight issues of the *Reflector* that Cole published between 1 January and 19 March 1831; four of the issues (1 January, 6 January, 1 February, and 9 March) contained two articles apiece, while the 14 February issue carried three. Cole's ranting about anti-Masonry and Sunday mails took a second seat to this new phenomenon, which bid fair to hold a place of pre-eminence in his paper for some time to come. Indeed, following his own sixth article on the Book of Mormon—an exposé of the alleged contradictions between the Three Witnesses' descriptions of the plates—Cole indicated that he had hardly scratched the surface of the Mormon phenomenon and promised his readers much more in the future.[85]

Through all of this, however, and in spite of Cole's crowing about his paper's popularity, it appears that a substantial number of his readers had fallen behind on paying their dues. The situation had become critical by March 1831, and in the same issue in which Cole promised more on Mormonism (19 March 1831), he also announced that "the publication of this paper, will be suspended for a short period, for the purpose of enabling our friends and patrons, to send us our dues." Few, apparently, were able (or, perhaps, wanted) to clear their debt in this regard, and Cole's anticipated "short period" of suspended publication lengthened into a permanent silence. An entry in Grandin's diary suggests he was close to getting an issue out the following April but that he apparently got no closer than printing up the proofs.[86] No later issues of the *Reflector* are known to exist.

***

By February 1832, Cole had moved to Rochester. There, under the same pseudonym, he continued in the newspaper business, publishing the *Liberal Advocate* between February 1832 and November 1834. Predictably, his editorial slant remained the same. Attacking the Christian establishment took most of his time, as it had in Palmyra, although by early 1832 he had apparently left Mormonism for bigger game. As in Palmyra, Cole eventually found his paper struggling financially in Rochester, as many of his subscribers—themselves struggling to make ends meet in the recession that followed upstate New York's boom-town economy of the 1820s—failed to pay their dues. After repeated and sometimes vitriolic reminders to his delinquent patrons failed to produce the needed money, Cole was forced to shut his press down after more than two and a half years of operation.[87] Yet his subscribers' neglect, it seems, had only hastened what was already in the works; on 13 July 1835, a mere eight months after the *Liberal Advocate* closed its doors, Cole died in Rochester.[88]

Notes

1. Lucy Mack Smith is our sole source of information about the Smiths' confrontation with Cole in Grandin's print shop. Her account was first recorded about 1845 by Martha Jane Coray and is held in the Family and Church History Department Archives, The Church of Jesus Christ of Latter-day Saints (hereafter cited as Church Archives), under Lucy Mack Smith, "The History of Lucy Smith, ca. 1845." Following the completion of the original manuscript of Lucy's history in Martha's hand in 1845, church leaders asked her twenty-seven-year-old husband Howard Coray—one-time clerk for Joseph Smith in Nauvoo—to assist her in revising the manuscript for eventual publication. This revision, which included adding material from other sources as well as streamlining Lucy's original narrative, was completed by the end of 1845, at which time it received Lucy's final approval. Eight years later, Orson Pratt published this revised manuscript in England as Lucy Mack Smith, *Biographical Sketches of Joseph Smith, the Prophet, and His Progenitors for Many Generations* (Liverpool: Richards, 1853). Given Lucy's close involvement with the original 1845 manuscript and the text of the 1853 publication, historians recognize both as primary sources of Lucy's history; accordingly, all quotations from her history used in this paper come from these two sources rather than from later revised editions. For a discussion of the development of the text and these later editions, see Scot F. Proctor and Maurine J. Proctor, eds., *The Revised and Enhanced History of Joseph Smith by His Mother* (Salt Lake City: Bookcraft, 1996), xviii–xxix. Both the 1845 manuscript and the 1853 edition have recently been published in Dan Vogel, ed., *Early Mormon Documents* (Salt Lake City: Signature Books, 1996), 1:227–450. While he has made Lucy's

record more available than it otherwise would be, Vogel's work suffers from countless transcribing errors and a highly revisionist tone in his notes. The Community of Christ (formerly Reorganized Church of Jesus Christ of Latter Day Saints) has republished the 1853 version of Lucy's history several times. For a listing of these editions, see James B. Allen, Ronald W. Walker, and David J. Whittaker, *Studies in Mormon History, 1830–1997* (Urbana: University of Illinois Press, 2000), 387. Two recent editions by Latter-day Saint editors not discussed in the preceding book are Proctor and Proctor, *The Revised and Enhanced History of Joseph Smith by His Mother* (cited above) and George A. Smith and Elias Smith, eds., *History of Joseph Smith by His Mother* (American Fork, Utah: Covenant Communications, 2000). The former is a hybrid of earlier versions, with an emphasis on Lucy's 1845 manuscript history; the latter is a reprint of the 1902 edition. Most recently, Lavina F. Anderson has published a critical edition of Lucy's history entitled *Lucy's Book: A Critical Edition of Lucy Mack Smith's Family Memoir* (Salt Lake City: Signature Books, 2001).

2. Smith, "History," Church Archives.

3. Ibid. The manuscript reads: "led him to believe something going was wrong." Original spellings have been maintained throughout this essay.

4. Smith, *Biographical Sketches*, 148–49. Joseph had secured the copyright on 11 June 1829. Joseph Smith, *History of the Church of Jesus Christ of Latter-day Saints,* ed. B. H. Roberts, 2nd ed. (Salt Lake City: Deseret Book, 1976), 1:58–59.

5. Smith, *Biographical Sketches*, 148–49.

6. Ibid., 149. The 1845 manuscript indicates that the Prophet and his father returned on a Sunday but does not specify that it was the *following* Sunday.

7. Smith, "History," Church Archives.

8. Smith, *Biographical Sketches*, 149–50.

9. Smith, "History," Church Archives.

10. For discussions of this episode and Abner Cole's further involvement with the Book of Mormon, see Russell R. Rich, "The Dogberry Papers and the Book of Mormon," *BYU Studies* 10/3 (1970): 315–20; Vogel, *Early Mormon Documents,* 1:411–14, 2:223–50, 407–8; Francis W. Kirkham, *A New Witness for Christ in America: The Book of Mormon: Evi-*

dence of Divine Power in the "Coming Forth" of the Book of Mormon (Salt Lake City: Utah Printing, 1960), 269–307, 437–38, 440–42; Francis W. Kirkham, *A New Witness for Christ in America: The Book of Mormon: Attempts to Prove the Book of Mormon Man-Made Analyzed and Answered* (Salt Lake City: Utah Printing, 1959), 36–38, 50–56, 64–77; and Richard L. Bushman, *Joseph Smith and the Beginnings of Mormonism* (Urbana: University of Illinois Press, 1988), 108–10, 112, 120–24, 140, 143.

11. This range of dates for Cole's birth is derived from the census returns for 1810 and 1830. The 1810 census, conducted 6 August, lists him as a male from twenty-six to under forty-five years of age; the 1830 census, conducted 1 June, lists him as a male from forty to under fifty years of age (microfilm of Population Schedules of the Third Census of the United States, 1810, New York, Ontario County, Palmyra Township [Washington, D.C.: National Archives, 1958], and Fifth Census of the United States, 1830, Population Schedules, New York, Wayne County, Palmyra Township [Washington, D.C.: National Archives, 1955]).

12. According to Orsamus Turner, Abner's father, Southworth Cole, settled in the Canandaigua area in 1797. O. Turner, *History of the Pioneer Settlement of Phelps and Gorham's Purchase* (Rochester, N.Y.: Alling, 1852), 186.

13. In view of the incompleteness of these early censuses, my conclusions about the timing of Cole's marriage, his wife and her children, and the children they had together rest on a number of assumptions: first, that he had not been married and divorced by 1810; second, that the three children living in his household in 1820 who were listed as at least ten but under twenty-six years of age were his stepchildren rather than servants or distant relatives; third, that the four additional children living in his household in 1820 who were listed as under ten years of age were his biological children rather than servants or relatives; and fourth, that the two children living in his household in 1830 who were listed as at least five but under ten years of age were also his biological children. At one point in his paper Cole refers to "my children," suggesting that at least some of these assumptions are true; see the *Reflector*, 22 January 1830.

14. Cole spelled the pseudonym Obadiah for the first series but changed the spelling to Obediah in the later series. The first number of the *Reflector* was issued 2 September 1829. Cole had his hand in legal

matters at least as late as March 1827, when the *Wayne Sentinel* announced that following "the foreclosure of a mortgage executed by *Abner Cole*," a certain parcel of land was available for sale. *Wayne Sentinel,* 2 March 1827. Turner also identifies Cole as "an early lawyer of Palmyra." Turner, *History of the Pioneer Settlement,* 186.

15. "Old Village Records," April 1814 and April 1816, microfilm, Palmyra King's Daughters Free Library, Palmyra, New York. I am indebted to Robert L. Lowe for helping me find this and the following reference.

16. Ibid., April 1818.

17. Egbert B. Grandin, Diary, 1 January 1831, Church Archives.

18. "Address of the Carrier, to the Patrons of the *Wayne Sentinel,*" *Wayne Sentinel,* 1 January 1831. In this and all subsequent quotations, emphasized words follow the original source.

19. The phrase *in one's cups* means to be intoxicated. Cole's opponent was apparently almost senseless with anger.

20. Grandin, Diary, 12 March 1831, Church Archives.

21. Common Pleas, 1805–1819, and Common Pleas, 1814, Special Bail, Ontario County Records and Archives Center, Canandaigua, New York.

22. Common Pleas, 1818, 1819, Narratio, Ontario County Records and Archives Center, Canandaigua, New York.

23. Common Pleas, Court Calendars, May 1821, Ontario County Records and Archive Center, Canandaigua, New York.

24. Common Pleas, 1818, Recognizances, and Common Pleas, 1819, Narratio, Ontario County Records and Archives Center, Canandaigua, New York.

25. Don Enders (senior curator, Museum of Church History and Art), personal communication to the author, 10 July 1999.

26. Smith, *Biographical Sketches,* 148–49.

27. Smith, "History," Church Archives.

28. *Reflector,* 2 September 1829.

29. Ibid., 16 December 1829.

30. Ibid., 1 May 1830.

31. Ibid., 13 September 1830.

32. Ibid., 4 October 1830.

33. Ibid., 9 December 1829.

34. Albert Post, *Popular Freethought in America, 1825–1850* (New York: Columbia University Press, 1943).

35. *Reflector,* 2 September 1829.

36. Ibid.

37. Ibid.

38. Joseph W. Barnes, "Obediah Dogberry: Rochester Freethinker," *Rochester History* 36 (July 1974): 5–6.

39. *Reflector,* 2 January 1830.

40. Grandin, Diary, 28 January 1831, Church Archives.

41. Cole referred to Grandin's *Wayne Sentinel* as a "sort of *milk and water* paper" whose editor (Grandin) was afraid to take a "decided and manly stand" on issues that might jeopardize his popularity with the community; see *Reflector,* 2 January 1830.

42. Grandin, Diary, 16 February 1831, Church Archives.

43. Ibid., 14 February 1831.

44. With his Enlightenment orientation, Cole probably would have considered himself a Deist rather than a Christian.

45. *Reflector,* 22 January 1830.

46. Ibid., 2 January 1830.

47. Ibid., 2 September 1829.

48. Ibid.

49. *Much Ado about Nothing,* 4.2.22.

50. *Reflector,* 2 September 1829.

51. Ibid., 9 December 1829.

52. Ibid., 22 December 1829.

53. This and subsequent scriptural references refer to the verses as they appear in the 1981 edition of the Book of Mormon.

54. Smith, *Biographical Sketches,* 149.

55. Oliver Cowdery to Joseph Smith, 28 December 1829, Joseph Smith Collection, retained copy in Joseph Smith Letter Book 1:4–5, Church Archives.

56. The Smiths sent to Harmony for Joseph two times during the winter of 1829–30—once in connection with Abner Cole and again in connection with concerns over how Joseph would pay for the printing costs of the Book of Mormon. The latter took place toward the middle

of January 1830 (see text) rather than at the end of December. That, and the temporal proximity of the trip to Harmony mentioned in Oliver's 28 December letter and the appearance of the Book of Mormon extracts in the *Reflector* (beginning 2 January), argues for a connection between this late December trip and the problem with Cole.

57. Smith, "History," Church Archives. Vogel has arrived at this same conclusion about the dates, although he fails to address the complexity of the issue; see Vogel, *Early Mormon Documents*, 1:414 n. 238.

58. Smith, *Biographical Sketches*, 149.

59. Ibid., 151.

60. Ibid., 150–51.

61. See "Agreement between Joseph Smith and Martin Harris," in *Witness of the Second Elder: The Documentary History of Oliver Cowdery*, ed. Richard Lloyd Anderson and Scott H. Faulring, 4 vols. (Provo, Utah: Brigham Young University Press, forthcoming). I am indebted to Anderson and Faulring for directing my attention to this contract.

62. Smith, *Biographical Sketches*, 150.

63. Vogel suggests that Cole was able to continue publishing extracts for three weeks because Joseph Sr. had been delayed in his departure for Harmony, which pushed the Prophet's arrival in Palmyra back a week or more. Vogel, *Early Mormon Documents*, 2:407–8. No evidence exists for this hypothesized delay, however. A delay of a week or more would also rule out the possibility of Joseph having time to make it back to Harmony before returning again to Manchester by 16 January to enter into the contract with Martin Harris. Who or what comprised this "arbitration" is unknown.

64. *Reflector*, 27 February 1830.

65. Ibid., 16 March 1830. Howard was the binder of the Book of Mormon and the proprietor of the *Anti-Masonic Star* (Grandin, Diary, 12 and 14 July 1831, Church Archives), which no doubt angered Cole even more.

66. See *Reflector*, 19 April, 1 May, 1 June, and 22 June 1830.

67. *Reflector*, 13 September 1830.

68. *Comedy of Errors*, 5.1.240.

69. *Reflector*, 30 June 1830.

70. For a discussion of the contents and characters mentioned in

"The Book of Pukei," see Vogel, *Early Mormon Documents,* 2:231–37 nn. 20–28.

71. *Reflector,* 12 June and 7 July 1830.

72. Ibid., 27 July, 4 August, and 14 August 1830.

73. Ibid., 7 July and 6 December 1830.

74. Ibid., 6 January 1831.

75. Ibid.

76. See Bushman, *Joseph Smith and the Beginnings of Mormonism,* 121–24, for an informative review and critique of Cole's analysis.

77. *Reflector,* 18 January and 14 February 1831, respectively.

78. Ibid., 1 February 1831.

79. Ibid.

80. For a discussion of who this "Walters" might have been, see Vogel, *Early Mormon Documents,* 2:231–33 n. 21.

81. *Reflector,* 28 February 1831.

82. Ibid., 14 February 1831.

83. Ibid., 28 February 1831.

84. See issues for 1 February, 14 February, and 9 March 1831.

85. Ibid., 19 March 1831.

86. Grandin, Diary, 23 April 1831, Church Archives.

87. For Cole's career in Rochester, see Barnes, "Obediah Dogberry," 1–24.

88. *Wayne Sentinel,* 17 July 1835.

Chapter 17

The Martyrdom: Joseph and Hyrum Smith as Testators

Daniel B. McKinlay

Early in Truman Madsen's academic studies, as an undergraduate at the University of Utah, he was called to be a member of the Ensign Stake genealogical committee. He served with my father, Lynn A McKinlay, who was the chairman. Stemming from that association were countless conversations about a number of issues for which the restored gospel gives persuasive, exhilarating, and satisfying responses. Truman and my father corresponded while Truman pursued graduate studies in philosophy at the University of Southern California and at Harvard. In Truman's early years as a faculty member at Brigham Young University, he and my father codirected three church history tours, two before Truman's call as president of the New England Mission and one the year after his release. As a seventeen-year-old, I was privileged to participate in the last of the three tours, which took place in 1966. The two directors began each day with prayer and then took turns lecturing at various sites. One of Truman's assigned lecture sites was Carthage Jail. I was impressed at how moved he was as he highlighted from memory the events associated with the martyrdom. I am pleased that he has preserved in audiotape lectures a similar recounting of that heart-rending event.[1] As a representative

of the Lynn and Sann McKinlay family, I am honored to demonstrate our love and admiration for Truman by trying to contextu-
alize in this essay one of the ramifications of that tragic yet triumphant episode of 27 June 1844.

Perhaps a preliminary note on the Prophet Joseph Smith is in
order. The veneration of Joseph Smith and his mission by Latter-
day Saints is sometimes misconstrued. Some assume that we place
the Prophet above the Savior in spiritual significance. One of our
apostolic doctrinal giants, Charles W. Penrose, corrects this mis-
apprehension and clarifies the perspective of the Church of Jesus
Christ of Latter-day Saints:

> We frequently bear testimony concerning Joseph the Prophet,
> as we ought to do, for we should "praise the man who com-
> muned with Jehovah," and whom "Jesus anointed as prophet
> and seer," but when we bear testimony that Joseph Smith was a
> Prophet of God we do in effect proclaim the truth that Jesus of
> Nazareth is the Messiah, the Son of God, the Redeemer of the
> World, the Resurrection and the Life, the Way and the Truth,
> and that only by and through Him can we approach the Father.
> That is the great doctrine for which Joseph Smith stood, and
> lived, and died as a martyr.[2]

This role of the Prophet as a witness to the second member of the
Godhead should ever be kept in mind; I emphasize here that Joseph's death was a witness.

When Elder John Taylor drew up a document announcing the
martyrdom of Joseph and Hyrum, which the Church of Jesus
Christ subsequently canonized as Doctrine and Covenants 135, he
proclaimed that "the testators are now dead, and their testament
is in force" (v. 5). His words recall the following passage in the
King James Version of the Bible (KJV): "For where a testament is,
there must also of necessity be the death of the testator. For a testament is of force after men are dead: otherwise it is of no strength
at all while the testator liveth" (Hebrews 9:16–17). Taylor's propo-

sition that the martyrdom of Joseph and Hyrum validated their witness of Jesus Christ as the Savior of mankind has impressed several of our leaders.[3] It is the purpose of this paper to defend and elaborate on John Taylor's statement and to discuss several doctrinal issues relative to the martyrdom. I begin by addressing some exegetical challenges associated with Hebrews 9:16–17. At issue is the meaning of several Greek words within their contexts in this passage.

Covenant and Testament

When the Hebrew Old Testament was translated into the Greek Septuagint (LXX), the translators chose the Greek word διαθηκη (diathēkē) to represent the Hebrew word ברית (bərît), which means "treaty or covenant." In the common Greek of New Testament times, diathēkē meant "will or testament," signifying that the death of the testator was necessary to fulfill the conditions of the inheritance. "Testament" is the translation chosen to represent the Greek diathēkē in Hebrews 9:16–17 in several modern English translations of the Bible, including the KJV. But since that same word—diathēkē—is translated as "covenant" elsewhere in Hebrews (including 9:15–22, the larger pericope in which verses 16–17 appear), as well as in most other places in the New Testament, some exegetes argue that it should also be translated as "covenant" rather than "testament" in the two verses under consideration. G. D. Kilpatrick states outright, "Basically the idea of testament fits into the passage very clumsily."[4]

In alignment with those who agree that "covenant" and not "testament" is the appropriate translation, John J. Hughes, a New Testament scholar, has published a lengthy study.[5] Many of his viewpoints could likely be compatible with a Latter-day Saint perspective. He notes that the passage in Hebrews 9:15–22 elucidates the doctrine of covenants in the early church in relation to that motif in the Old Testament and later Judaism.[6] He also acknowledges that from a Hellenistic legal perspective, *diathēkē* was the ideal counterpart for *bǝrît*, or covenant.[7] Nevertheless, he challenges the textual practice of using "testament" in those verses, which practice goes back to earlier English translations. For Hughes, "to confuse the meaning of διαθηκη in the LXX with its meaning in the papyri and classical sources [i.e., "will" or "testament"] has been, in my opinion, the fundamental error in several notable studies."[8]

In examining a sampling of commentaries on Hebrews since Hughes published his imposing essay in 1979, I am astonished to find how many have ignored it. Although some of these writers are aware of studies suggesting that *diathēkē* should always be rendered "covenant" in Hebrews, none that I have seen even acknowledges Hughes's frankly ambitious piece.

Alternatively, a number of scholars argue in favor of a translation that coincides with the KJV translation of "testament," with which we are familiar. Here is a sampling from John F. MacArthur:

> A testament, by its very nature, requires **the death** of the testator. **Covenant,** or testament, is from the Greek *diathēkē*, the basic meaning of which corresponds closely to that of our present-day *will*. A will does not take effect until the one who made it dies. Until that time, its benefits and provisions are only promises, and necessarily future. The point being made in verses 16–17 is simple and obvious.
>
> Its relevance to the Old Covenant, however, was anything but obvious to the Jews being addressed here, so the writer briefly explains how it applies. Building on verse 15, he is saying that God gave a legacy, an eternal inheritance, to Israel in the form of a covenant, a will. As with any will, it was only a type of promis[s]ory note until the provider of the will died. At this point, no mention is made of who the testator is or of how Christ fills that role in life and death.[9]

Barnabas Lindars points out the rich wordplay with the word *diathēkē*. He notes that this passage "takes advantage of the range of meaning of the Greek word for covenant *(diathēkē)*, which can also be used to denote a last will and testament. [The author of Hebrews] points out that a will does not come into force until the testator has died. Therefore, he argues, a death is necessary for a covenant to come into force." Lindars ties this to the Sinai covenant as found in Exodus 24:4–8 and points out that "it was necessary for the inauguration of the new covenant too." While some scholars, Lindars continues, have rejected the possibility that the word signifies a covenant only and not a testament or will,

> this can be done only by a very strained exegesis. In fact, [the author of] Hebrews is not juggling with words so as to take advantage of double meanings to slip in an invalid argument. From his point of view 'testament' is part of the meaning of *diathēkē,* and it suggests to him a useful *comparison.* It is no more than that. Just as the death of a person brings that person's testament into effect, so the ratification of a covenant by means of a sacrifice brings the covenant into force. To put it another way, a *diathēkē,* which means both covenant and testament, normally requires a death to bring it into effect.[10]

In response to MacArthur's comment above, I would say that "the death of the testator" indicated in Hebrews 9:16–17 that brings his testament or covenant into force is the atoning death of Christ. Without that atonement, none of the promises of the inheritance could be fulfilled. I would, however, add a qualification. In my reading of the Book of Mormon, I sense in the time immediately preceding Christ's birth—when the New World prophets testified so passionately—a kind of anticipatory acceptance of salvation. The prophets and their believing audiences were influenced by a promissory gift of salvation and experienced in rich measure the sustaining influence of the Spirit, as if the atonement had already been realized. Several of the latter-day prophets have also spoken of another aspect of the execution of a spiritual testament, or witness, in that the death of a testator is particularly relevant to the testator's own generation, or dispensation, as will be seen below.

Hughes also has problems with the context of διαθεμενος
(*diathemenos*) in the traditional translation of Hebrews 9:16–17.
The KJV translates this word as "testator," which in the Hellenistic
milieu had reference to the maker of a will or testament. Hughes
sees this word in the Hebrews passage as meaning the "ratifier of a
covenant."[11] In effect, Hughes proposes that the context demands
that a covenant had to be ratified by the death of some person or
animal (the Greek does not say "when men are dead"—it just
refers to the necessity of deaths, the word being dative plural,
νεκροις [*nekrois*]). He argues that the deaths spoken of here were
substitutionary and representative of the ratifier,[12] but he rejects
the idea of the ratifier being a testator of a will. However, from
some of the comments of scholars quoted above, a case can be
made that if *diathēkē* in Hebrews 9:16–17 indeed means a testament or will, the person outlining the will—the testator—must
die in order for the inheritance to be offered without stipulation.
In other words, the deaths of Joseph and Hyrum fulfilled the conditions of being testators, thus validating the use of the word *testament* in Taylor's reference to those biblical verses.

Doctrinal Significance of the Martyrdom

Having examined exegetically the passage in Hebrews to which
John Taylor referred in Doctrine and Covenants 135:5, I now
turn to a consideration of the doctrinal meaning of what Elder
Franklin D. Richards called the Prophet's "mighty martyrdom,"[13]
a scene that President J. Reuben Clark Jr. labeled "tragic beauty."[14]

The Prophet was martyred when he was thirty-eight and a
half years old. It is well documented that he did not expect to live
to the age of forty, though he was assured that his life would not
be taken until his work was accomplished.[15] Musing over this
theme, Brigham Young offered this reflection:

> Who delivered Joseph Smith from the hands of his enemies to
> the day of his death? It was God; though he was brought to the

brink of death time and time again, and, to all human appearances, could not be delivered, and there was no probability of his being saved. . . . Though he had prophesied that he would not live to be forty years of age, yet we all cherished hopes that *that* would be a false prophecy, and we should keep him for ever with us; we thought our faith would outreach it, but we were mistaken—he at last fell a martyr to his religion.[16]

In spite of knowing his impending fate, the Prophet himself apparently entertained a hope for a reversal: "It is more and more evident that [Thomas] Carlin is determined to have me taken to Missouri, if he can. But may the Almighty Jehovah shield and defend me from all their power, and prolong my days in peace, that I may guide His people in righteousness, until my head is white with old age."[17] Referring to the Prophet's "last charge" meeting, when he informed the apostles he was going to rest from his labors, Elder Orson Hyde remembered that the group "did not consider, at the time he bore this testimony, that he was going to die or be taken from us; but we considered that as he had been borne down with excessive labors, by day and night, he was going to retire to rest and regain his health, and we should act under his direction and bear the responsibility of the work."[18]

As the end drew near, the Prophet felt a definite presentiment of his death. While visiting Nauvoo nearly forty years after the exodus of the Latter-day Saints, Richards recalled: "From this improvised platform he made his last public speech. He felt that the cup had been prepared for him, and that to fill the sacrifice unto which he had been called, he must drink it to the fatal, cruel dregs."[19]

After the martyrdom, the Saints sought to make sense of the deaths of Joseph and Hyrum. The Lord addressed this matter in a revelation to Brigham Young at Winter Quarters: "Many have marveled because of his death; but it was needful that he should seal his testimony with his blood, that he might be honored and the wicked might be condemned" (D&C 136:39).

President Wilford Woodruff acknowledged that he was one who had "marveled":

> I used to have peculiar feelings about his death and the way in which his life was taken. I felt that if, with the consent and good feelings of the brethren that waited on him after he crossed the river to leave Nauvoo, Joseph could have had his desire, he would have pioneered the way to the Rocky Mountains. But since then I have been fully reconciled to the fact that it was according to the programme, that it was required of him, as the head of this dispensation, that he should seal his testimony with his blood.[20]

Elsewhere Woodruff more explicitly said, "If I were to tell what I think about it, I would say it was ordained of God that our Prophet and head should be sacrificed in the manner that he was."[21] Decades later, President Stephen L Richards, a grandson of Willard Richards, expressed the conviction "that Joseph of his own volition gave his life for the cause entrusted to him, which is the real essence of martyrdom." But he added, "I believe the martyrdom was inevitable. By that I mean that it was foreordained and in the divine plan."[22]

President Brigham Young taught that if the Prophet had "been destined to live he would have lived."[23] If the world in general had accepted his testimony, according to Young, the Prophet's martyrdom might have been avoided. But because he was largely rejected, the Prophet *did* seal his testimony with his blood, and it is in force in the world.[24] On another occasion Young stated that the Prophet "sealed his testimony with his blood, consequently we can, with impunity, believe on him a little better than if he were living. When he was living, his testimony was not in force upon the people as it is now."[25]

The efficacy of Joseph's martyrdom as a pure witness to those living in the dispensation of the fulness of times depends partially on those of us who are not required to die as martyrs. Elder

Henry D. Moyle maintained: "We who through the inspiration of the Almighty have received his testimony and that of his faithful brother Hyrum, are charged with responsibility to accept and to perpetuate and add our solemn witness thereto, that the blood of this generation shall not be upon us."[26]

Elder Delbert L. Stapley, sidestepping mere allusion, positively identifies the Prophet's martyrdom with the language of Hebrews 9:16–17: "Where a testament is, there must of necessity be the death of a testator, and surely this was a testament unfolding and revealing again God's kingdom with all of its saving ordinances, principles, and divine powers. A testament is not of force until after men are dead. The Prophet gave his life to seal that testimony, and thus the sacrifice of his life becomes a witness to all men of the truth and power of his holy calling and ministry."[27]

As seen above, the passage in Hebrews 9 deals primarily with the legitimizing of covenants, with a supplementary reference to wills or testaments. The Christian world divides the Bible into the Old and New Testaments. Now, in addition to those witnesses, church leaders have subtitled the Book of Mormon "Another Testament of Jesus Christ." All three of those works could appropriately be known alternatively as "covenants." John Taylor explicitly says in the first verse of Doctrine and Covenants 135: "To seal the testimony of this book [that is, the Doctrine and Covenants] and the Book of Mormon, we announce the martyrdom of Joseph Smith the Prophet, and Hyrum Smith the Patriarch." On the title page of the Book of Mormon, Moroni describes one of the book's purposes: "to show unto the remnant of the House of Israel what great things the Lord hath done for their fathers; and that they may know the covenants of the Lord, that they are not cast off forever." In his 1842 letter to John Wentworth, editor of the *Chicago Democrat,* Joseph Smith quoted the angel Moroni as telling him in his initial visit that he was "sent to bring the joyful tidings, that the covenant which God made with ancient Israel was at hand to be fulfilled."[28] A perusal of the Book of Mormon reveals that covenants figure prominently. So it is clear that Joseph and Hyrum as testators have ratified the scriptural books of covenants that pertain to our own dispensation.

Although Hebrews 9:16–17 refers to a general principle, it is meant in its context to refer to Christ's consummation of a new testament or covenant through the enactment of the atonement. In his role of atoner, Jesus is absolutely peerless. But since several of the apostles who survived Joseph Smith have applied the role of testator to him, is there a subordinate sense in which that passage also pertains to him? A few church leaders have so taught. Speaking of the Prophet, Elder Erastus Snow affirmed that "the Lord suffered his enemies to destroy him in the flesh, to take away his life, and he was made an offering—what shall I say? an offering for sin. Not in the sense in which the Savior was offered, but he was made a martyr for the truth and his blood was shed to attest the testimony that he bore to the world."[29]

President Joseph F. Smith summarizes the zenith of the Prophet's mortal mission in the following statement: "Joseph Smith was true to the covenants that he made with the Lord, true to his mission, and the Lord enabled him to accomplish his work, even to the sealing of his testimony with his shed blood. His testimony is now, and has been, in force among the children of men as verily as the blood of Jesus Christ is in force and a binding testimony upon all the world, and it has been from the day it was shed until now, and will continue until the winding up scene."[30] Brigham Young testified, "God suffered him to be slain for His testimony, that it might become a law through being sealed by his blood, which was the case the moment his blood was spilled, the same as with the law of Jesus Christ when he spilled his blood. Then the testimony became in force. It must be so; God suffered it."[31]

Again, it should be emphasized that the Prophet's martyrdom is not on the same level as Christ's universal atoning sacrifice, but the law of witnesses as it relates to the shedding of consecrated blood is at work here. The violent death of the Prophet was necessary to enforce the spiritual powers of the restoration, his death thus indirectly ratifying the atonement, which is universal. It is interesting to note that a few days before his death the Prophet exclaimed that he was "going like a lamb to the slaughter" (D&C 135:4), a simile redolent of the sacrificial imagery found in Isaiah 53:7. This chapter of Isaiah is associated in Christian circles with Jesus as the "suffering servant," or the vicarious sacrifice for sin. Several of the General Authorities, as noted in this essay, have spoken of the Prophet's murder as a sacrifice. Joseph Smith was witnessing to the truth of those aspects of the everlasting gospel that pertained specifically to *his* realm or stewardship. Some prophets in past dispensations also sealed their testimonies with their blood by dying a martyr's death and thus left their generations without excuse. An example of this is Abinadi, whose death at the hands of King Noah and his priests (except Alma) bound them to his testimony, for which they were and are required to answer. Even indirectly, we are also held responsible for his witness since it has come to us through the Book of Mormon. In other words, either we accept his teachings and repent and become clean or we "assent unto his death" and share blame with those who killed him. All prophets in the history of the world who have laid down their lives as a witness have been under the auspices of the atonement; it is the atonement that makes their sacrifices binding.

The Prophet's pronouncement that he was going like a lamb to the slaughter has telling implications concerning his spiritual status. When he made that statement, he added that he had "a conscience void of offense towards God, and towards all men" (D&C 135:4). There were times in his youth when the Prophet sought forgiveness for sin—this was one of his concerns that led to the first vision, and it was a major issue in his prayer that resulted in the initial visits of Moroni—and he was rebuked and forgiven several times during his early ministry. But by the time he rode to Carthage, he had applied the atoning blood of Christ in his life to the extent that he was ready to die. BYU professor Lynn A McKinlay asserts that "in order for the testimony to be valid in heaven, the testator must be clean—the sacrifice must be without spot or blemish." He affirms "that what Joseph said [about his clear conscience] was true, and because he was a clean, pure sacrifice, like a[n unspotted] lamb, that which he did at Carthage is valid in the heavens."[32]

In gratitude and reverence, we can list individuals, in some cases family members, who have given their lives for the gospel. But the Prophet's death carries special significance. Elder Robert D. Hales, one of the Twelve, addresses this point:

> True religious martyrs are part of an eternal gospel plan and earn an eternal reward: "Whoso layeth down his life in my cause, for my name's sake [and the gospel's], shall find it again, even life eternal" (D&C 98:13; see also Mark 8:35). The pioneers who gave their lives in the westward trek are martyrs also, but not in the same way as the prophet who held the priesthood keys and willingly gave his life in testimony to seal his work in this dispensation.[33]

When Latter-day Saints call the Prophet a martyr, they are faithful to the root meaning of the Greek word μαρτυς *(martys)*, which means a witness. Several of the latter-day apostles quoted refer to that very idea—through his death the Prophet left an inevitable witness of the whole restoration. It was after the inception of the Christian era that the term *martyr* began to be associated with the laying down of one's life for a cause. The culmination of the Prophet's ministry combines the earlier and later meanings.[34]

Latter-day prophets have testified that the law of witnesses had a wider application to the events at Carthage than just the death of the Prophet. As Elder Marvin J. Ashton taught: "When Oliver Cowdery lost his standing the Lord transferred to Hyrum Smith all the power and authority that had been given to Oliver

Cowdery, and Hyrum Smith became the Associate President of the Church—holding these keys jointly with his brother Joseph and standing with him at the head of the great and last dispensation. It was because of this great honor that Hyrum Smith was called to be the companion of the Prophet Joseph in martyrdom."[35]

The presence of John Taylor and Willard Richards, both members of the Twelve, and their subsequent testimony strengthen the witness of the martyrdom. Those who have studied the martyrdom know that prior to 27 June the Prophet was in company with several devoted friends, including Stephen Markham, John S. Fullmer, and Dan Jones. But these friends left to fulfill errands, leaving only the two members of the Twelve with Joseph and Hyrum.

Some gainsayers have alleged that the Prophet's murder did not qualify him as a martyr because he used a pistol (although not a very effective one) as a defense. But I believe that Elder Thomas S. Monson catches the true spirit of that awful moment:

> You remember in Carthage Jail, where he was incarcerated with Hyrum and with John Taylor and Willard Richards, the angry mob stormed the jail, they came up the stairway, blasphemous in their cursing, heavily armed, and began to fire at will. You remember that Hyrum dropped dead, exclaiming, "I am a dead man." John Taylor took several balls of fire within his bosom. The Prophet Joseph, with his pistol in hand, was attempting to defend his life and that of his brethren [I would here emphasize "his brethren"], and yet he could hear from the pounding on the door and sense that this mob would storm that door and would take the life, if there was any life remaining in John Taylor, and would take the life of Willard Richards. Why? Because they were anxious to kill the Prophet. And so his last great act here upon the earth was to leave the door and lead Willard Richards to safety, throw the gun on the floor and go to the window that they might see him, that the attention of this ruthless mob might be focused upon him rather than others.[36]

I agree with Elder Monson that the Prophet sought to deflect attention from Willard Richards (and perhaps John Taylor) so that they could survive the scene. They each lived to record and distribute apostolic proclamations concerning the martyrdom. Thus the two apostles, who by definition are special witnesses of Christ, also observed the final witness of Joseph and Hyrum. We see manifested here, in a very comprehensive way, the law of witnesses.

Several decades after the martyrdom, Franklin D. Richards recalled that a pall of gloom pervaded Nauvoo when the news was released to the Saints.[37] The afflicted condition of the community is well documented.[38] We are now removed by several generations from that mood of mourning and can only try to experience vicariously the keenness of feeling. But perhaps this distance affords our generation an advantage, as suggested by Elder Melvin J. Ballard:

> It has taken one or two generations to elapse before men began to see the worth and the merit of those who have been the world's greatest benefactors. And so it has been with "Mormonism," and with the Prophet Joseph Smith. He was too close to the men and the women of his own time. They felt with him as they did with Jesus. Wasn't Jesus the carpenter's son? Didn't they know his father and his brothers? Just so men thought that they knew all about Joseph Smith, and that he did not have a message of any particular consequence to them! And so they chose to turn their faces away from him. But as we recede from his day, and contemplate the man and his message, we discover that he begins to rise to his own place and position, for he will stand as one of the pinnacles in the midst of the children of men; and that which he did, men shall yet come to acknowledge was given of God, for the salvation not only of a few Latter-day Saints, but of the whole world.[39]

More recently, Elder James E. Faust has forecast the place of Joseph Smith in the world:

> As the years pass since Joseph's life and death, his history will no doubt be analyzed, picked at, criticized, challenged, and

pored over. But the evidences of the truthfulness of his statements will continue to mount. The devotion and commitment
of those who accept the restored gospel will continue to be severely tested. Their faith will be sorely tried, as has been the
case with so many in the past. But like Joseph himself, millions
will live and die faithful to the gospel he restored. As time
moves on, the stature of Joseph Smith will loom ever larger. He
will stand higher and higher in the esteem of mankind.[40]

This is consonant with a seemingly grandiose claim made by John
Taylor: "Brought up a poor farmer's boy, with very limited advantages of education, he [Joseph Smith] nevertheless introduced a
system of religion that was bold, energetic, and commanding."[41]
Plainly, the Prophet's blood-sealed message is here permanently,
both to bless and to provoke.

The Prophet was transferred to another realm, but as Elder
Marriner W. Merrill testified, "Joseph Smith, the great prophet of
the last dispensation, has a watchcare over us today, just as he had
while he was on the earth; and he is not so very far off, either."[42]
Elder Ezra Taft Benson spoke in a similar vein when he proclaimed
that "the Prophet Joseph Smith was not only 'one of the noble and
great ones,' but he gave and continues to give attention to important matters here on the earth even today from the realms above.
For in the eyes of the Lord—the God of this world under the
Father—it is all one great eternal program in which the Prophet
plays an important role—all through the eternal priesthood and
authority of God."[43]

A few leaders have spoken majestically about the martyrdom.
At the funeral of fellow apostle Ezra T. Benson, President George A.
Smith averred that Joseph's "martyrdom and that of his brother
Hyrum were crowns upon their heads, to prepare them for that
exaltation which their services to the world, as servants of God
and apostles of Jesus Christ sealed upon them."[44] In an epistle to
the saints in Britain, Woodruff wrote: "You do know [that] Joseph

Smith, the prophet, left his testimony upon the earth, and sealed that testimony with his own life and blood, and that testament is in force 'upon all the world,' and that testament is filled with the revelation of God, that stand[s] upon its pages like flames of living fire, ready to be fulfilled upon all the inhabitants of the earth."[45] B. H. Roberts expressed the view that "when Joseph Smith fell by the old well-curb at Carthage jail, pierced by the bullets of assassins, he placed the cap-stone upon his mission by sealing it with his blood."[46]

I cannot think of a better finale for this essay than to quote the testimony of Truman Madsen's grandfather, President Heber J. Grant:

> I bear witness to you here today, that I know God lives, that Jesus is the Christ, that Joseph Smith was and is a prophet of the true and living God, that he was a martyr, that he gave his life for this cause, and that his blood bears witness to the integrity, the honesty and inspiration of his mission as a prophet of the living God, because he was true even unto death.[47]

Notes

1. Truman G. Madsen, *Joseph Smith the Prophet,* audiotapes of lectures (Salt Lake City: Bookcraft, 1998); and Truman G. Madsen, *The Presidents of the Church: Insights into the Life and Teachings of Each Church President,* audiotapes of lectures (Salt Lake City: Bookcraft, 1999).

2. Charles W. Penrose, Conference Report, April 1906, 87.

3. See my section on "Doctrinal Significance of the Martyrdom," pp. 482–92.

4. George D. Kilpatrick, "Διαθηκη in Hebrews," *Zeitschrift für die Neutestamentliche Wissenschaft* 68 (1977): 263.

5. John J. Hughes, "Hebrews IX 15ff. and Galatians III 15ff.: A Study in Covenant Practice and Procedure," *Novum Testamentum* 21 (1979): 27–96.

6. Ibid., 27.

7. Ibid., 30–31.

8. Ibid., 31; see also 58.

9. John F. MacArthur, *The MacArthur New Testament Commentary: Hebrews* (Chicago: Moody, 1983), 236, emphasis in original.

10. Barnabas Lindars, *The Theology of the Letter to the Hebrews* (Cambridge: Cambridge University Press, 1991), 95–96. Thomas G. Long, *Hebrews: Interpretation: A Bible Commentary for Teaching and Preaching* (Louisville, Ky.: John Knox, 1997), 98–99, sees *diathēkē* in the Hebrews passage as a "pun and an analogy." Marie E. Isaacs, *Sacred Space: An Approach to the Theology of the Epistle to the Hebrews* (Sheffield, England: JSOT, 1992), 120, agrees with Lindars about the tie of covenant with the Sinai incident in Exodus 24:4–8, and with use of *diathēkē* in Hebrews as a "double entendre" in the sense of "the necessity for the death of a testator before a will may be proved." Paul Ellingworth, *The Epistle to the Hebrews: A Commentary on the Greek Text* (Grand Rapids, Mich.: Eerdmans, 1993), 462–63, argues for a blending of the two meanings through the use of grammatical tools. He points out how Hebrews 9 juxtaposes the old and new covenants using the imagery of the shedding of blood: "The structure of the comparison brings together the old and new covenants by implicitly comparing them both with a will. . . . The value of the illustration is thus limited to the fact that it compares two institutions in which a death plays an essential role: on the one hand, God's covenants with his people, sealed respectively by animal sacrifices, and by the death of Christ; on the other hand, a will, which comes into effect on the testator's death. Who it is that dies, and the nature of that death (violent or natural, voluntary or involuntary) are for the moment excluded from consideration. All that matters is the death itself." Harold W. Attridge, *The Epistle to the Hebrews,* ed. Helmut Koester (Philadelphia: Fortress, 1989), 253–54, argues substantially the same thing. R. McL. Wilson, *New Century Bible Commentary: Hebrews* (Grand Rapids, Mich.: Eerdmans, 1987), 157–59, sees the traditional translation as valid and believes that the main point is clear, but he believes that the flow of thought is in some measure illogical and not fully cogent.

11. Hughes, "Hebrews IX 15ff.," 40.

12. Ibid., 42–43.

13. Franklin D. Richards, "Visit to Pueblo, Independence, Carthage, Nauvoo, Richmond, etc.," *Millennial Star* 47 (27 July 1885): 468. The

fuller quotation of Richards reads: "To-day it [Carthage Jail] seems a place of peace. To the casual observer it would possess not even a passing interest. But to us who held the knowledge of the mighty events which had transpired within its walls, of the dark cloud of sin which had rested upon it, and of the mighty martyrdom which had cried aloud to heaven and the ages from its bullet-torn frame—there was something so impressive in its every stone that our hearts were filled with solemnity, and our eyes with tears."

14. J. Reuben Clark Jr., "The Prophet Joseph—Equally Burdened with Moses," in *The Annual Joseph Smith Memorial Sermons* (Logan, Utah: LDS Institute of Religion, 1966), 1:73 (speech given 4 December 1949).

15. See, for example, Brigham Young, in *Journal of Discourses,* 18:361 (6 May 1877); *Teachings of the Prophet Joseph Smith,* comp. Joseph Fielding Smith (Salt Lake City: Deseret Book, 1972), 258, 274, 328, 366. For a collection of Joseph Smith's predictions concerning the completion of his mission as well as his forthcoming death, see Richard Lloyd Anderson, "Joseph Smith's Prophecies of Martyrdom," in *Sidney B. Sperry Symposium, January 26, 1980: A Sesquicentennial Look at Church History* (Provo, Utah: BYU Religious Instruction and CES, 1980), 1–14. Ronald K. Esplin, "Joseph Smith's Mission and Timetable: 'God Will Protect Me until My Work Is Done,'" in *The Prophet Joseph: Essays on the Life and Mission of Joseph Smith,* ed. Larry C. Porter and Susan Easton Black (Salt Lake City: Deseret Book, 1988), 280–319, presents a scintillating overview of the Prophet's life, with emphasis on the reassurance he received at different points in his life that he would be spared death until his mission was complete. As cited by Esplin, in ibid., 307, the Prophet's views "at the present time [31 August 1842] are that inasmuch as the Lord Almighty has preserved me until today, he will continue to preserve me by the united faith and prayers of the Saints, until I fully accomplished my mission in this life and so fully established the dispensation of the fulness of the Priesthood . . . that all the powers of Earth and Hell can never prevail against it" (taken from the minutes of the Relief Society, 31 August 1842).

16. Brigham Young, in *Journal of Discourses,* 1:364 (1 August 1852).

17. Joseph Smith, *History of the Church of Jesus Christ of Latter-day Saints,* 2nd ed. (Salt Lake City: Deseret Book, 1950), 5:168.

18. Orson Hyde, in *Journal of Discourses*, 13:180 (6 October 1869).

19. Richards, "Visit to Pueblo," 471.

20. Wilford Woodruff, in *Journal of Discourses*, 24:54 (27 January 1883).

21. Ibid., 22:232 (26 June 1881).

22. Stephen L Richards, "Joseph Smith, Prophet-Martyr," in *The Annual Joseph Smith Memorial Sermons*, 1:103 (speech given 7 December 1952).

23. Brigham Young, in *Journal of Discourses*, 13:95 (2 January 1870).

24. *Journal of Discourses*, 11:262 (12 August 1866).

25. *Journal of Discourses*, 18:242 (23 June 1874).

26. Henry D. Moyle, "The Greatest Gift," *Improvement Era* 60 (June 1957): 412.

27. Delbert L. Stapley, Conference Report, October 1954, 49; see also Delbert L. Stapley, "An Unwavering Faith," *Improvement Era* 73 (June 1970): 75–76.

28. Published in *Times and Seasons* 3 (1 March 1842): 707.

29. Erastus Snow, in *Journal of Discourses*, 25:33 (2 February 1884).

30. Joseph F. Smith, Conference Report, October 1917, 3.

31. Brigham Young, in *Journal of Discourses*, 4:352 (7 June 1857).

32. Lynn A McKinlay, "A Trumpet with a Certain Sound," in *California Know Your Religion Speeches, 1973–74* (California: BYU California Center, 1974), 117; also in Daniel B. McKinlay, ed., *The Divine Journey Home: A Lynn A McKinlay Odyssey: An Assembly of Discourses* (Provo, Utah: n.p., 2001), 213; copy located in L. Tom Perry Special Collections, Harold B. Lee Library, Brigham Young University.

33. Robert D. Hales, "A Testimony of Prophets," *BYU 1993–94 Devotional and Fireside Speeches* (Provo, Utah: BYU Press, 1994), 164.

34. Danel W. Bachman discusses the blending of the two definitions in "Joseph Smith, a True Martyr," in *Joseph Smith: The Prophet, the Man*, ed. Susan Easton Black and Charles D. Tate Jr. (Provo, Utah: BYU Religious Studies Center, 1993), 321–23.

35. Marvin J. Ashton, "He Loveth That Which Is Right," in *BYU 1988–89 Devotional and Fireside Speeches* (Provo, Utah: BYU Print Services, 1989), 108. During an address given in general conference in April 1930 during the centennial celebration of the church, Joseph Fielding Smith said substantially the same thing, and he added his opinion that

if Oliver had continued as associate president with the Prophet, he would have died at Carthage. See Conference Report, April 1930, 91–92. Robert L. Marrott, "Witnesses, Law of," in *Encyclopedia of Mormonism,* 4:1569–70, writes: "The Prophet Joseph was likewise accompanied in his martyr's death by his brother Hyrum, a second martyr or witness, making their testimony valid forever (D&C 135:3; 136:39)."

36.   Thomas S. Monson, "Joseph Smith—Teacher by Example," in *The Annual Joseph Smith Memorial Sermons* (11 December 1963), 5–6. Wilford Woodruff, in *Journal of Discourses,* 16:267 (8 October 1873), referred to the fact that the lives of Joseph and Hyrum "were taken by the hands of wicked and ungodly men. Why was his life taken? Why were not John Taylor and Willard Richards, the only two of the Twelve at that time in Nauvoo and with him, also sacrificed? Why did Willard Richards, the largest man in the prison, stand in the midst of that shower of balls and escape without a hole in his robe or garment, or clothing? Because these things were all governed and controlled by the revelations of God and the word of the Lord. The Lord took whom he would take, and he preserved whom he would preserve."

37.   Franklin D. Richards, Conference Report, October 1898, 29.

38.   Given that state of affairs from the vantage point of the Saints, it is eerie to contemplate what George A. Smith reported about the mood of those on the other side of the conflict: "Men in high places sent gifts congratulating each other on their death; thanks were returned in the pulpit that these false prophets had been destroyed. Many acknowledged that their murder was an outrage upon the laws of the country, and discreditable to the State, but then it was a good thing they were dead." George A. Smith, *Millennial Star* 31 (18 September 1869): 603 (speech given 25 July 1869).

39.   Melvin J. Ballard, Conference Report, April 1918, 138–39.

40.   James E. Faust, "The Expanding Inheritance from Joseph Smith," *Ensign* 11 (November 1981): 77.

41.   John Taylor, *Millennial Star* 13 (28 March 1857): 195 (speech given in New York, 2 November 1856).

42.   Marriner W. Merrill, Conference Report, October 1902, 65.

43.   Ezra Taft Benson, "Joseph Smith Memorial Sermon," in *The Annual Joseph Smith Memorial Sermons* (3 December 1967), 3–4.

44. George A. Smith, *Millennial Star* 31 (6 October 1869): 655 (speech given 5 September 1869).

45. Wilford Woodruff, *Millennial Star* 41 (21 April 1879): 242.

46. B. H. Roberts, in *Journal of Discourses,* 25:143 (28 January 1884).

47. Heber J. Grant, Conference Report, April 1925, 11.

CHAPTER 18

Placing the Keystone: George Q. Cannon's Mission of Translating and Printing the Book of Mormon in the Hawaiian Language

David J. Whittaker

George Q. Cannon's life was focused on the Pacific Basin from 1850 to 1857. Much of this time he spent in the Hawaiian Islands as a missionary for the Church of Jesus Christ of Latter-day Saints; there he managed to learn the language in order to preach to the native population. A trained printer, he also desired to make published works of the Church of Jesus Christ available to a wider audience. Following almost four years in Hawaii, Cannon returned home to the Salt Lake Valley but was soon sent to San Francisco, where he directed the affairs of the Church of Jesus Christ in that area for another three years. During his Hawaiian mission years he translated the Book of Mormon into the Hawaiian language; during the earliest months of his assignment in San Francisco he established a church printing office and saw the volume through the publication process. This essay examines his missionary efforts as they relate to translating and then printing the Book of Mormon in Hawaiian, a keystone of his mission and missionary message.

I also discuss the pamphlet that Cannon published in Hawaiian to introduce the Book of Mormon. This short tract was the first imprint of the Church of Jesus Christ in the Hawaiian language and is printed here for the first time in English translation as an appendix to this essay (see pp. 518–29).

Cannon's World: The Early Mormon Print Culture

George Q. Cannon moved comfortably in the world of the print shop.[1] Converted in Liverpool, England, with his family, he immigrated to America, arriving in Nauvoo, Illinois, in 1843. At sixteen years of age he found employment in the *Times and Seasons* office of his uncle John Taylor, in whose home he was living. In this world he associated with various church leaders and broadened his education by reading the varied material that came and went in a busy printing establishment. His education in the world of practical affairs was thus nurtured among people who read, valued literacy, and cherished the printed word. Print shops in early America often functioned as bookstores for recent publications and usually provided areas for a reading room. There can be little doubt that a young man of his intelligence seized the opportunity to learn all he could in this environment and that he noted especially that the press could be a tool both of education and of persuasion.

He also experienced firsthand the effects of the decision of the Nauvoo City Council on 10 June 1844 to destroy the press of the *Nauvoo Expositor,* an event he recalled in some detail on its tenth anniversary while on his Hawaiian mission.[2] His memory of the deaths of Joseph and Hyrum Smith also remained an important part of his heritage. His own father, a cabinet maker, prepared the coffins of the martyred brothers and made the plaster casts of their faces.

He began to read when he was four years old, and he became an avid reader. Mary Jane Dilworth—a friend of his sister Elizabeth and later the wife of Francis Hammond, a fellow missionary in Hawaii—recalled seeing young Cannon during the westward movement "sitting on the tongue of his wagon reading a book." She was convinced he would amount to something because he never seemed to waste his time.[3] While walking through a wilderness area on his Hawaiian mission, he made comparisons with scenes he had earlier read in a Leatherstocking novel of James Fenimore Cooper, which experience hints at the kinds of books he was reading.[4] The journals that record this event also reveal his recognition of a good library when he saw one[5] and his hunger for the printed word: when he had received several numbers of the *Deseret News,* he noted that "they were as welcome as an old friend and was gladdening in the extreme they being filled with principles and doctrine instructive to me and I have gathered many good ideas from the perusal of this invaluable paper."[6]

From the beginning of his mission, he read and shared printed literature. He particularly liked the writings of Orson and Parley Pratt, copies of which he regularly read himself and loaned to interested persons. Even before he left California he was trying to gather copies of works by Latter-day Saint writers to take to Hawaii. In Hawaii, he both read and distributed tracts printed by the Church of Jesus Christ,[7] and, when supplies ran low, helped order more from suppliers in Liverpool.[8]

He also understood the power of the press when used by critics of the Church of Jesus Christ. He monitored the non-Mormon press and responded when he could, a practice he followed the rest of his life. In November 1853 he read John Lloyd Stephens's description of Central America and suggested its applicability for strengthening the claims for the authenticity of the Book of Mormon.[9] He obtained a copy of John W. Gunnison's *The Mormons, or Latter-day Saints, in the Valley of the Great Salt Lake* (1852) soon after it was published and after a quick reading noted his criticisms in his journal.[10] Without doubt, George Q. Cannon contributed to and helped shape Mormon print culture throughout his life. But no book would have an impact on his life comparable to that of the Book of Mormon; it touched the very core of his being, particularly during his Hawaiian mission.

Cannon served in the Hawaiian Islands from December 1850 to July 1854.[11] Originally called to preach to the nonnative population, he early concluded that the missionaries would have very little success if their efforts were confined to Europeans or others who spoke only English.[12] It was while learning Hawaiian that he decided to translate the Book of Mormon into that language.

Learning the Language

Most of Cannon's mission was spent on the island of Maui, where his initial lack of language skills to communicate with the natives and his loneliness from serving most of the time without a missionary companion forced him to turn inward. He recalled years later:

> For the first year after I left home I could scarcely think about it without my feelings getting the better of me. . . . Their very food was foreign to me and unlike anything I had ever before seen or tasted. I was much of the time separated from my companions, the Elders. Until I mastered the language and commenced preaching and baptizing the people, I was indeed a stranger among them. Before I commenced holding regular meetings, I had plenty of time for meditation, and to review all the events of my short life, and to think of the beloved home from which I was so far separated. It was then that I found the value of the Book of Mormon. It was a book which I always loved. But I learned there to appreciate it as I had never done before. If I felt inclined to be lonely, to be low spirited or homesick, I had only to turn to its sacred pages to receive consolation, new strength and a rich outpouring of the Spirit. Scarcely a page that did not contain encouragement for such as I was.[13]

In addition to its power to console and strengthen, the Book of Mormon surely had another impact on his life. His love for the native people increased as he spent time in the sacred volume: twenty-five years later he noted, in the context of his Hawaiian mission, "No man can read [the Book of Mormon], partake of its spirit and obey its teachings, without being filled with a deep love for the souls of men and a burning zeal to do all in his power to save them."[14]

While love of the Hawaiian people came early, his appreciation for their lifestyle came only gradually. After a brief visit with some newly arrived missionaries and their wives in August 1851, he reflected on his return to live among the natives:

> It seemed like leaving home—after living as I had been used to and associating with sisters of my own color and habits— it made it somewhat of a trial for me to return and mix with the Natives and conform to their manner of living again—but I am laboring for a liberal master who knows that my motives are pure, and that my desire is to bring this people to a knowledge of the great and important principles of life and salvation and ex[a]lt them from their present debased state.[15]

Such reserve would broaden into deep love as he moved more deeply into the text of the Book of Mormon. The first reference in his journals to "studying the language" was on 24 December 1850. Three days later he expressed his desire to learn the language in order to teach the gospel to the native people. By 30 December he had ordered two language vocabularies; on 12 January he noted that he began "to understand some little of what is said." During February he was fasting and praying for heavenly help to assist him in this difficult work.[16]

But book study was not enough, so on 2 March he decided to undertake a tramp around Maui to become better acquainted both with the language and the island. Carrying a missionary's valise for the first time in his life, "the common appendage of a Mormon Elder traveling," he managed to discuss the gospel with a number of natives but reflected a few days later: "I find that I will require considerable improvement [in the language] before I am able to explain our doctrine to them."[17] He continued to improve week by week, taking advantage of all opportunities to broaden his skills. In January 1852 he confided in a letter to coworkers, "English is leaving me fast. I sometimes find it difficult to express my thought and ideas with the facility usual to me formerly."[18] By April 1854 he was so fluent in Hawaiian that he again noted having difficulty speaking in English.

As early as March 1851, during a conversation with local historian David Malo, Cannon expressed his agreement with Malo's opinion that the Hawaiian people were of the house of Israel.[19] He also noted that the natives among whom he lived wished to read the Book of Mormon, especially because he was teaching them that it was their book. Cannon himself increasingly felt the power of the text he had begun translating. He confided in his journal, "I never could enter into the feelings experienced by the holy men who wrote the Book of Mormon as I can at present; my soul shrinks from the thought of sin and my heart is pained to behold the sins of the world."[20] Later, when he was raising money to purchase a press on which to print the translation, he demonstrated to a native audience "from reason and the scriptures the necessity of such a work coming forth, and the great benefit it would be to them as a people, that it was indeed their book, and full of covenants and promises for them."[21]

Cannon's language abilities gradually improved, encouraged in part by several heated discussions with local missionaries of other faiths who were growing concerned with the conversions to the Church of Jesus Christ from among their own congregations.[22] His willingness to live among the people not only helped him to acquire the basic language skills but also to earn the trust of those among whom he lived. His love was genuine: "I had no idea that I ever could have loved this people to the extent I have, or that I do; they are very near indeed to me."[23] He practiced the language out loud as he walked from village to village, and his ear for the language assisted him in picking up nuances when he was with others.

On 15 June 1851 he seems to have preached his first public sermon in Hawaiian, and on 23 June he wrote his first letter in Hawaiian, suggesting that his proficiency continued to improve. Continuing to live among the natives after attending to some church business on Oahu, Cannon reflected that "my desire [was] to bring this people to a knowledge of the great and important principles of life and salvation and ex[a]lt them from their present debased state."[24] So good were his language skills by September 1851 that he confided to his journal his concern that the other Latter-day Saint missionaries were "leaning" on him too much and not learning the language and standing "on their own."[25]

Translating the Book of Mormon

Still, the step from fluent speaker to able translator was considerable. A major assistant in Cannon's work on the translation of the Book of Mormon was Jonathan Napela, to whom he taught the gospel and with whom he was able to hone his language skills.[26] Cannon baptized Napela on 5 January 1852 and ordained him a teacher six days later. On 27 January 1852 Cannon first mentioned in his journal that he was "translating the Book of Mormon." In his later account of the mission, he also suggested that the two events were closely connected:

> I was led to commence the translation of the Book of Mormon into the language of the Islands—the Hawaiian language, as it is called. My place of residence was at Brother J. H. Napela's, [at] Wailuku. He was an educated, intelligent Hawaiian, who thoroughly understood his own language, and could give me the exact meaning of words. The meaning attached to many words depended upon the context. It was important, therefore, in translating, to know that the words used conveyed the correct idea. Unless the language used carried to the Hawaiian mind the same meaning precisely which the words in our

translation gave to us, it would not be correct. Probably but few in the nation were as well qualified as Brother Napela, to help me in this respect.[27]

He continued his normal missionary duties of course,[28] but more and more of his time was devoted to translating the Book of Mormon. In January and February he translated the text of the Word of Wisdom (D&C 89) and in April 1853 the 1843 revelation on celestial marriage (D&C 132), since the August 1852 public announcement of the Latter-day Saints' practice of plural marriage was creating problems for the Hawaiian missionaries.[29]

Officially appointed by the Hawaiian mission president to translate the Book of Mormon as part of his mission, he received three special blessings as he worked on the project. The first was given to him at a conference in April 1852 and promised

> that I should be greatly blessed in regard to the translation of the Book of Mormon[;] that I should have the spirit of prophecy and know the mind of the spirit at all times; that I should have no doubt in regard to the things that I ought to write; that my mind should be clear; that I might write every word correct and that I should be enabled to write it with all plainness unto the understanding of these people and it should be of great worth unto them and they should rejoice in the same. I should be blessed from day to day while I should remain upon these lands for the Lord is well pleased with me and with the course I have taken.[30]

Cannon received another blessing on 6 October 1852 (recorded on the 9th) and still another on 12 March 1853. In addition to spiritual promises, he was no doubt receiving a greater understanding of the text itself, and from that came an increased love for the people among whom he was laboring. On a day of translating and preaching he revealed his growing love for the native people, a love clearly related to his immersion into the text: "I feel all the anxiety of a father for them; but O how I need wisdom and patience and strength and grace to instruct them and to enable me to divest myself of every thing displeasing in the sight of My Father. I never could enter in the feelings experienced by the holy men who wrote the Book of Mormon as I can at present."[31]

The chronology of the initial translation and revisions can be followed in his journals: from 27 January 1852 to 22 July 1853 Cannon and Napela (occasionally assisted by others) produced a first draft; from 8 August to 27 September 1853 they revised and recopied the translation.

> The time occupied by me in translation, were the days and hours which were not claimed by other duties. In the beginning, my method was to translate a few pages, and then, when opportunity offered, explain to Brother Napela the ideas, whether historical or doctrinal, in great fullness. By this means he would get a pretty thorough comprehension of the part I was translating. I would then read the translation to him, going carefully over every word and sentence, and learning from him the impression the language used conveyed to his mind. In this way I was able to correct any obscure expression which might be used, and secure the Hawaiian idiom. The spirit of translation rested upon me, and it soon became a very easy labor for me.[32]

Such attention to detail had very positive effects:

> I obtained great facility of expression in the language and before I got through with the book, I had a range of words at my command, superior to the great bulk of the people. This was a very natural result. Doctrines, principles and ideas were in the Book of Mormon which were outside the ordinary thoughts of the people. The translation of these, called forth the full powers of the language, and really required—that which I felt I had while engaged in this work—the assistance of the Spirit of inspiration.[33]

Then, working with William Farrer and a Brother Kauwahi, Cannon went through the whole work again from 24 December 1853 to 31 January 1854. Cannon summarized their methods on the day they finished:

We finished reading the Book of Mormon thro' this evening and I feel full of gratitude to the Lord for granting unto me
this great privilege, that of translating this precious book into
this language. I pray that the way may be opened for it to be
printed speedily that it may go forth on its mission of life. I
have read it thro' twice with the exception of a few pages; once
to Bro Wm. [Farrer] he looking at the English version to see that
there were no words or sentences dropped; and then read again
to Bro. Kauwahi, he also looking at the English, of which he had
a slight knowledge, and all inaccuracies and idiomatic expressions corrected.[34]

He reflected in his journal that, after he had read the translation a
third time, he was then desirous of sending the sacred volume
forth on its mission.[35]

Printing the Hawaiian Translation

The day before a conference scheduled for 6 October 1853 on
Maui, the missionaries met to discuss the topics and business for
the conference. A printing press was the first item considered, particularly important as the Book of Mormon translation was nearing
completion. All present openly discussed their options, "whether
we ought to have the Book of Mormon printed by hiring or
whether we should purchase a press of our own and publish it
and other works necessary for the instruction of the saints." When
concerns were raised that the acquiring of a press would force
some of the missionaries to remain in the Islands longer than
planned, Cannon strongly insisted, "I did not consider that my
mission was fully filled until I saw the Book of Mormon in press,
if there was a prospect of it being done in a reasonable time." He
would see the project through.[36] The group decided that it would
be best to buy a press, type, and related material; a committee of
three was appointed to adopt measures for procuring these items.

A vote of those at the conference the next day agreed to support these decisions. Cannon (who was assigned the chair), along

with Benjamin F. Johnson, a member, and Philip Lewis, the new mission president, were appointed as the committee and authorized to begin soliciting donations from members for the purchase of the press.[37] Church membership in the Islands, at the time these decisions were made, was placed at 3,008 people organized into fifty-three branches. The press committee decided to undertake a "circuit" among these branches to try to raise the money.[38] In July the missionaries "thought it best to commence to preach more about the Book of Mormon" to better prepare the people to assist with donations for the printing of the sacred volume.[39]

On 10 October other translating assignments were made: William Farrer was to prepare a synopsis of the scriptures; Francis Hammond was to "translate such portions of the Doctrine and Covenants as the Presidency shall see fit"; and John Woodbury was to prepare a selection of hymns adapted "to our form of worship."[40]

The committee spent the next several months raising money for the purchase of a press. The poverty of most members made their efforts slow and generated only a small amount of cash. The project was greatly assisted with a thousand-dollar interest-free loan in December from Edward Dennis, a tinsmith in Honolulu.[41] Cannon was no doubt inspired to learn from letters received on 31 December 1853 that his mentor and uncle, John Taylor, was overseeing the publication of the Book of Mormon in both French and German.[42] Cannon also received additional encouragement in a letter from Brigham Young, who cheered his project but counseled caution regarding financial matters associated with the enterprise.[43]

The committee, having doubts about the possibility of obtaining a press for such a large project locally, initially tried to purchase the press from California,[44] and by March 1854 they were considering having the translation printed there.[45] But they persisted and a press was finally ordered from New York; however, by the time the press reached Honolulu, the missionaries had journeyed to California on their way home from their mission. The press and supplies were subsequently forwarded to Parley P. Pratt in California.[46] In February 1855 Pratt wrote to President Young that the press, papers, and other materials from the Islands would probably reach San Francisco by early April, and then "there will be nothing to hinder going ahead with printing, both in English and in the Island language, provided Elder Cannon [who had gone home to Salt Lake City via San Francisco] can return here to help. I see no way to dispense with him, as he understands both languages, is a practical printer, and has the Book of Mormon in manuscript in the Island language."[47]

Printing the Book of Mormon in California

George Q. Cannon left Hawaii 29 July 1854 with the understanding that he would continue his efforts to get the Book of Mormon printed.[48] He arrived in San Francisco on 12 August 1854 and worked with Parley P. Pratt, mostly assisting with the hand copying of Pratt's autobiography.[49] Cannon then returned to the Salt Lake Valley. His visit was brief; it lasted about five and one-half months, long enough to marry Elizabeth Hoagland on 10 December 1854 and receive a mission call to return to California to complete the work begun on his first mission, as well as assist Apostle Parley Pratt in that area.[50]

Cannon later provided more details on this assignment:

Soon after my return to the Valley I received an intimation from President Young that I would be called, at the ensuing conference, to return on a mission to the Sandwich Islands. Before this conference was held, however, the news had reached the Valley that the printing press, type and papers, had been removed from the Islands to San Francisco, and, as my labors were likely to be more available at that point, now that the press was removed there, I was called, at the Spring Conference in 1855, to take a mission to California to labor in connection with, and under the direction of Elder Parley P. Pratt. Elder Pratt was to act as editor of the paper, which it was expected we would publish; President Orson Hyde, who had been appointed to establish and take charge of a settlement in Carson Valley, was requested to superintend the financial business of the undertaking; and I was to publish the Book of Mormon in the Hawaiian language and to take charge of the printing and the publication of the paper, writing for it also as I should have opportunity. Being requested by President Young to select two elders to accompany me, to assist me in my labors, I chose Elders Joseph Bull and Matthew F. Wilkie. . . . Starting from Great Salt Lake City on the 10th of May, 1855 . . . [51]

Arriving in San Francisco, they found that Parley P. Pratt had decided to return to Utah and had left the city. Cannon rushed to catch up with him, finding him at Brother John C. Naile's ranch across San Francisco Bay.

I succeeded in obtaining an interview with him, . . . and from him learned all the particulars concerning the condition of the Mission. Finding that I had been called to labor under his direction, he deemed it wise, as he was leaving, to set me apart to preside over the Pacific Mission, subject to the direction of any of the Twelve Apostles who might visit or be called to labor in that part. [52]

Brigham Young told Cannon, "I expect that you will publish the Book of Mormon in the Hawaiian language and other works as shall best promote the interest of the cause of our Lord and Master and aid in the rolling forth and building up of the Kingdom of our God upon the earth."[53] After getting settled in California, he wrote an extensive report to Brigham Young,[54] much of which focused on the press and his plans for printing the Book of Mormon and continuing the publishing projects begun under Parley Pratt.[55]

The press, type, and paper had been received from Hawaii and stored by Parley Pratt. Cannon discovered upon examination of the printing press that the ribs were badly damaged.[56] He also met with Apostle Orson Hyde, who was visiting from Carson Valley, Nevada. Hyde convinced him to procure a suitable building in San Francisco in which to establish a print shop and to concentrate his energies on the publication of the Hawaiian edition of the Book of Mormon before he began a newspaper.[57]

Cannon, Bull, and Wilkie found a brick building in which they could rent two rooms. The building, located at 118½ Montgomery Street just east of Portsmouth Square, was owned by Samuel Brannan, with whose brother they arranged the rental agreement. A fireproof brick building was essential, since a major fire had recently swept through the wooden structures in the city.[58] After moving their printing material into this building, they were ready to begin the huge printing project. Numerous problems needed to be solved; for example English fonts could be used in the typesetting, but they lacked a sufficient number of the letters *h* and *k*, which were quite common in Hawaiian.[59]

Working with Bull and Wilkie, Cannon turned all his attention to printing the Book of Mormon. A chronology of their progress shows that by 27 July 1855 the first two 8-page signatures (16 pages) were printed;[60] by 31 August they had printed 128 pages (8 signatures); by 23 September, 240 pages (15 signatures); and by 3 December, 464 pages (29 signatures),[61] with only 56 pages to go, not counting the index, title page, and introductory matter. By 20 December, only 8 pages of the body of the work remained to be typeset.[62] Elizabeth, Cannon's wife, assisted with the proofreading. They feared that an anticipated paper shortage would slow the project in its final stages, but they finished the printing in January 1856.[63]

In a letter to Brigham Young dated 26 January, Cannon's pride and relief at the end of the project were clear:

> The book is finished, and I hope to be able to send you the first bound copy this mail. I feel grateful to our Heavenly Father for his kindness unto us in enabling us to finish it, and thus

help to fulfill His words, spoken by His servants who wrote the Book, that it "should go forth unto every nation, kindred, tongue and people."[64] These were more especially my feelings when the last form went to press, in reflecting on its completion; for, when the translation was commenced, the Saints were few in number and poor, and there was no earthly prospect then in view of it ever being published; the Lord has most singularly however opened the way.[65]

On 30 January Cannon sent a bound copy of *Ka Buke a Moramona* to Brigham Young and added this postscript to his 26 January letter, which he had not yet mailed:

> I have succeeded in getting a copy of this Book bound and forward it this mail; and hope it will meet your approbation. It is a large book, but this was owing to the size of the paper sent, as you will also see the type is large and open. This was thought to be best suited to the people as it is very rare for them to use spectacles and their amphibious habits very frequently injure their eyes when comparatively young.[66]

Brigham Young's response upon receiving the volume was surely gratifying to Cannon:

> I sincerely thank you, not only for the Book, but for the persevering assiduity, privation and untiring exertion which has been necessary to accomplish this enterprise. I also feel exceedingly gratified at the manner in which it is got up. . . . The print is very plain and altogether well executed. I feel proud of the Book and trust that it will be of great benefit to the islanders, who it most particularly concerns. It will also prove very beneficial to our Elders who go there to preach the Gospel.[67]

Binding the Hawaiian Translation

The first Hawaiian translation of the Book of Mormon was printed in an edition of two thousand copies, but because of the high costs of binding most were left unbound, a practice common among nineteenth-century printers. Translating and printing the volume were challenging enough, but getting the book bound proved to be even more difficult. Cannon addressed his concerns to Brigham Young as early as October 1855:

> I have been making inquiries for the last few days in relating to binding the Book, and find that the lowest I can get it done is 75 cents per volume; some have asked me as high as $1 per volume, and say that is the lowest it can be done. This is the price for plain, strong binding, nothing extra whatever. On the islands they have only one bindery, and that is a missionary concern, and consequently they will not do anything of the kind for us, even if we wished it. In thinking the matter over I have thought that it would be well, if it met with your approbation, to get the few tools that would be necessary to do the kind of binding needed for the majority of them, which would not be expensive, and try and do them within ourselves without having to pay out so much money. . . . But to do this it would be necessary to have a young man sent out from home who would have a tolerable knowledge of binding, it would not take a very extensive knowledge to do what is wanted the chief requisite being strength.[68]

President Young thought Cannon's idea was good, but that plan for binding the books was never executed.[69] In September 1856 Cannon borrowed one hundred dollars from a Brother Meder. When he added ten dollars to this amount, he was able to pay for the binding of two hundred copies of *Ka Buke a Moramona,* a cost of fifty-five cents per volume.[70]

Cannon reported to his leader:

> They have been sent to the Islands. They were bound in full sheep[skin] and make a handsome appearance. I have put them as low as possible (one-third of the number at 1.25, they were bound in red an attractive color among the natives, and the remainder at $1.00) as from all I can learn times are so hard there that they can not pay a high price. The scarcity of money and the languishing state of some of the branches will, I fear, make their sale somewhat dull & tedious.[71]

Brigham Young had counseled that the volumes should not be given away.[72] Despite this advice, the contemporary records indicate that the missionaries in Hawaii were unable to sell very many books.[73] Cannon had planned to keep the unbound volumes in San Francisco, binding them as the demand in Hawaii required, but by August 1857 he thought otherwise.

> It has been suggested to my mind to transfer the whole edition to the S.I. [Sandwich Islands] Mission, and for the elders now going to take them down with them. Binding materials can be obtained at tolerably reasonable rates, as well as the tools necessary to put a plain binding on them; and as Bro. Wm. Wright, who is now on the Islands, has a tolerable knowledge of the binding business, they can be bound and placed within the reach of the natives at a very low figure, and by that means obtain the general circulation necessary and which is denied them by the present plan. I do not think that it would be a good idea to give them away, as it would have a tendency to render the Book valueless in the eyes of many—they would not appreciate it as they would if they had to pay for it; but the price might be much reduced. A tanner by the name of Field, who left the Valley a year or two ago, has hinted he would furnish all the skins needed for the binding and donate them to the mission. If he should do this, the expense apart from the labor, would be very trifling.[74]

As it turned out, this was a good decision. With the coming of the Utah War, Brigham Young wrote to Cannon suggesting that the printing office in San Francisco be closed, the office materials disposed of, and the people working in the office return to Salt Lake City.[75]

Cannon sent twelve cases of the unbound copies to Hawaii, which Henry Bigler reported receiving on 24 November 1857.[76] These volumes were to be bound as needed in the Islands. Exactly how many were eventually bound is not known, although the existence of a variety of bindings on surviving copies of this first edition testifies that several were. Bigler reported in October 1857 that 114 copies of the 200 originally bound copies had been sold.[77] A report at a mission conference in Hawaii on 25 April 1858 stated that eighteen hundred copies remained unbound. There is some evidence that Walter Murray Gibson was selling the Hawaiian edition of the Book of Mormon for $1.00 each in August and September 1863.[78]

In December 1855, Cannon published the first Mormon imprint in Hawaiian, an eight-page tract entitled *He Olelo Hoolaha*.[79] Printed during the lull in their work on the Book of Mormon because of a shortage of lowercase fonts, the tract was printed on the same press as the Book of Mormon. Cannon told Brigham Young in January 1856 that he had issued fifteen hundred copies of a pamphlet giving a short history of the coming forth of the Book of Mormon, which he had just sent to the missionaries in Hawaii: "I thought it would be a good idea to publish something of this kind and prepare them to comprehend and rightly estimate the Book when they obtained it."[80]

This short work presented a summary of Joseph Smith's early life, especially of the "discovery of the plates, their contents, and the applicability of the Book to them as a people."[81] Much of the early history of Joseph Smith was taken from Orson Pratt, *An Interesting Account of Several Remarkable Visions, and of the Late Discovery of Ancient American Records* (Edinburgh: Ballantyne and Hughes, 1840), which had been reprinted a number of times by 1856. Cannon regularly used this text on his mission. Brigham Young responded positively to the translation of the tract and its distribution: "I trust that the little work which you mention that you have written and sent out as a forerunner will be instrumental in drawing the attention of the Natives to the importance of this work, it was a good idea."[82]

Conclusion

George Q. Cannon remained in California for less than three years and presided over the church in that area. Using the same press on which he had printed the Hawaiian edition of the Book of Mormon, he also issued a broadside, *Prospectus of the Western Standard,* and then edited a weekly newspaper, the *Western Standard.*[83] The Hawaiian edition was the seventh language in which the Book of Mormon was published, and it remained the only Hawaiian edition of the Book of Mormon until 1904.

Cannon remained a strong advocate of the Book of Mormon in the church.[84] He was ordained an apostle in 1860; served a number of missions, including establishing a church printing office in Liverpool, England;[85] and served as a counselor to four presidents of the church, during which time he exercised a great influence in the church. He also served church interests in the nation's capital for ten years as Utah's official delegate to Congress. Bringing his publishing experience to these various callings, he served as an editor of both the *LDS Millennial Star* and the *Deseret News* and established the *Juvenile Instructor* in 1866 as a periodical for young people; he was also very active in the Deseret Sunday School Union. His own publishing house, George Q. Cannon and Sons, continued his contributions to the Mormon print culture. The first item in his Faith-Promoting Series was his own amplified account of his Hawaiian mission, and his press issued a number of works that focused on the Book of Mormon.[86] Following his death in 1901, his publishing business was acquired by the Church of Jesus Christ and was eventually (in 1919) renamed Deseret Book Company. It remains the flagship for publishing in the church.

Cannon's work on the Book of Mormon in Hawaii proved to be the foundation for both his personal and institutional life. His missionary work with this volume marked his pioneering efforts in taking the gospel to a non-Western, non-English-speaking native audience. He was a strong advocate among church leaders at the end of the century of taking the gospel throughout the world and even concerned himself with the opening of the mission in Japan in 1901.[87] The early decisions in Hawaii to establish a special gathering place for natives in their own lands surely provided a model for Cannon's later counsel for members to stay in their country of origin and to build up the church there.[88] His missionary work with the Book of Mormon increased his love for the people among whom he was called to work, broadened his own faith in the life and mission of Joseph Smith, and clearly deepened his own understanding of the life and mission of Jesus Christ. For him, the Book of Mormon was what Joseph Smith had proclaimed it to be: the keystone of Mormonism.[89] The translation and publication of the Book of Mormon was, in very fact, the keystone of George Q. Cannon's missionary work in the Hawaiian Islands and a foundation for the rest of his life.

Appendix

He Olelo Hoolaha[90]
An Announcement

To the members of the Church of Jesus Christ of Latter-day Saints in the Hawaiian Islands and to all people who love the truth, Dear Saints and Friends:

I have some matters to write to you about, and so I decided that I should have these thoughts printed and distributed to be announced among all of you so that all may hear. I had hoped that I would be able to actually come to you and meet with you so that I can tell you these things myself face to face, but so far this has not been possible as I am consumed by other matters that prohibit me from taking leave.

In the year 1850, on the 12th of December, a number of us Elders of the Church of Jesus Christ of Latter-day Saints arrived in the Hawaiian Islands from Salt Lake City to preach to the people the gospel of Jesus Christ, to tell them that the prophecies of the prophets and disciples of Jesus have begun to be fulfilled because of the marvelous things the Lord has done in the latter days, and to say that God has spoken to man once again from heaven and He has called some as He has done in the past and given them the authority, indeed, the Holy Priesthood, to go out and establish His Church properly, and to bring into it, by baptism, believers in Jesus Christ, His Son, that they may repent of all their sins.

Some of the inhabitants of Hawaii were astonished that we would travel there "because," as they said, "it was useless since there already were elders and scriptures printed in Hawaiian as well as general availability of knowledge among the people." However, this was not God's thinking because His servants were not only sent among the people of Hawaii, but He also commanded them to go out among those of all lands to preach those things that were preached among those of Hawaii. God saw that all churches were in error before Him and had left the straight path; and all have proceeded according to their own dictates, establishing churches and teaching men according to their own commandments; and as Isaiah had said in chapter xxix, "They draw near to Him with their lips, but their hearts are far from Him."

Joseph Smith was the one chosen by God to commence this work and become a prophet for Him and to become the one to once again establish His Church here on earth in these days. He was born in the United States on the 23rd of December 1805. In his fourteenth or fifteenth year, he began to greatly ponder how he could prepare himself for the next world, but it was not clear to him what he should do. He knew that it was very important, so he was not comfortable simply relying on what men would say he should do to gain eternal salvation. If he attended a particular religious sect and inquired about it, each one would prescribe what he believed, saying, "Here is the way, come this way," each way contradicting the other. He knew that God could not approve of all ways because there were many hundreds of religious sects. If any of these sects was the Church of Christ, which was it? This is how he thought. What should he do? If he went and joined himself with any particular sect simply because of the words of a man, it would be wrong. So he determined to read the Holy Scriptures so that he could gain knowledge about such things. When he read the book, he found the verse in James, "If any of you lack wisdom, let him ask of God, that giveth to all men liberally, and upbraideth not; and it shall be given him." His heart was filled with hope at these words because he knew that if he would ask God, the knowledge would be given him. So he went to a secret place in the woods, and he called upon God to show him the true way. He was tempted greatly at the onset, but after praying to God, the darkness of his heart was dispersed and he prayed to God with great intent and faith. As he prayed thus to God, desiring Him to answer him, he saw a bright and beautiful light in the heavens above. He continued in prayer and the light descended from above and fell upon him, and when it came close to him the brightness grew in intensity and size and the woods around him became illuminated; the leaves and branches were not burned, however; because of that, his heart was filled with hope that he would be able to endure the experience. When it came upon him, his whole body felt strange and he was taken in a vision and he saw two beautiful personages, both of them appearing alike. He was told that his sins were forgiven him. He was also told that all religious sects believed in false teachings that were not in accordance with the word of God and for that reason none of those sects was recognized by God as His church and kingdom. And he was commanded not to follow after those sects because at some time in the future the true teachings or, in other words, the gospel of power and truth, would be revealed to him. After hearing these things, the vision was taken away; however, his heart was filled with great joy.

He saw angels frequently afterwards; and many things were shown to him from time to time to prepare him for the great work he was to do. It was shown to him that he was called and chosen to become an instrument in the hands of God to fulfill marvelous works in this last kingdom. And it was shown to him that the native inhabitants of the Americas, the Indians, are descendants of Israel; and at the time they traveled to America, they were a learned people and they knew the true God and they had many blessings from His hand. The prophets and righteous men among them who were inspired by the Holy Ghost were commanded to keep a sacred record of great events that occurred among them, and that record was given from one generation to the next up until the time they fell into apostasy and sin. Because of sin, the greater part of them were destroyed and the records were hidden (according to the commandments of God to some of their last prophets) so that they would not fall into the hands of sinners. It was shown to him that these plates (because these records were engraved on plates like gold in appearance) were filled with holy revelations pertaining to the gospel of the kingdom as well as prophecies regarding great events that would occur in the last days and that they would be published to all men so that His covenants would be fulfilled to the people who made the records pertaining to the restoration of their descendants to the knowledge of Him.

These records were hidden in a hill which was called Cumorah by the people of old, in New York, a state of the United States. On the 22nd of September 1827, these things were given to him and he began to translate them into English because he was given the power to do so. It was printed in the United States by him in 1830 and made available among the white race. After he received it he was given the Holy Priesthood with the authority to preach the gospel of Christ and to establish His Church. On the 6th of April 1830, the Church was first organized on earth in these days; there were only six members that day. From that time until today, the Church has grown in all lands and there are many thousands of people who can testify at this time to the truth of these things because they have this knowledge by the Holy Ghost. Many have been ordained as Priests and Elders in the Church, and they have gone forth and preached these things with power.

In these great records the account of the ancient inhabitants of America has been written from the time it was settled by people who came from the tower, to the time the word was done away with, up until the year 420. We have been shown that two different nations of people existed in ancient times in America. The first nation, which came from the tower, was called the Jaredites. The second nation of people, the ancestors of the native inhabitants of America, the Indians who inhabit the land, came from the city of Jerusalem at the time of Zedekiah, king of Judah, six hundred years before Christ's coming; they were from Israel, but the greater part of them were descendants of Joseph. The first nation of people, the Jaredites, were destroyed close to the time the descendants of Israel arrived from Jerusalem—those who obtained the land after the former people. The second nation, the descendants of Israel, were divided into two different groups after arriving in this land. This division came about after half the people, because of their righteousness, were persecuted by the remaining portion of the people. Those who were persecuted found a place to live and left the sinful part of the people, separating themselves from those people. The righteous people were called Nephites since they were led by a prophet whose name was Nephi. The sinful part of the people were called Lamanites because they were led by a sinful man whose name was Laman.

In this ancient account, it is shown that the Nephites prospered in the land according to their righteousness, and they spread across to the east, the west, and to the north, building cities, synagogues and temples; they also built fortresses and watchtowers and walls around the cities to defend against their enemies. They tilled the earth and grew a great many fruits. They fed their many flocks, and they were rich because there was much gold, silver, brass, and metal, and all manner of things among them. They made all kinds of clothing and weaponry to protect themselves from their enemies. And they also were a learned and blessed people in the days of their righteousness.

It also is shown that because of the hardness of the hearts of the Lamanites, they brought upon themselves many great punishments; however, they were not completely destroyed, but the Lord God sent upon them curses and they became a filthy nation, grotesque in appearance and their skin was dark. Before the division, they were fair and delightsome in appearance like unto the Nephites, but God cursed them in appearance and they were made dark in appearance, and they became a wild and bloodthirsty people. They were enemies to the Nephites, and they sought from time to time to destroy them. And there were many terrible wars among them; and there were many thousands of people who were killed on both sides, and the dead were piled up into a great pile on the face of the earth and covered with earth. These hills probably are the hills that are often discovered in America filled with the bones of men.

The prophets prophesied among the Nephites about many things, and many things were recorded by them. They saw many things of the kingdom of God, and great power was given to them so that they could perform many miracles. They prayed to God for mercy upon their brethren, the dark-skinned people, and the Lord made covenants with them that He would bring the knowledge of Him back to them in the last days.

The gospel of Christ also is written in this Book in truth and plainness and contains the teachings of Jesus Christ because Jesus showed Himself to them after His living in the flesh in Jerusalem and after His death and resurrection from the dead and ascension to heaven. He taught them many things, expounding the holy scriptures to them and performing miracles among them. He chose twelve disciples for Himself as he did before His death in Jerusalem, and He gave them the authority to go and preach His gospel and to establish His Church among the people. He did away with the law of Moses, He broke bread and administered it with wine to them, and He commanded His disciples to keep that authority among them. All that Jesus taught was engraved on the plates; however, not all of them were published in the Book of Mormon, but they will be revealed in time to the Saints.

After Jesus served among them and ascended to heaven, the disciples went about preaching the word among men, baptizing those who repented that their sins might be forgiven. Afterward, they lay their hands upon them that they might receive the gift of the Holy Ghost. Many miracles also were performed by them. All people on the face of the earth were converted, Nephites and Lamanites alike, to the Lord, and they became a righteous nation. And thus they dwelt on the land for three hundred years, but after that time, they began to fall away from God and do all manner of wickedness, and for that reason, God allowed punishments to fall upon them. Because a great and terrible war ensued among the Nephites and Lamanites, because the Nephites fell into great sin and resisted the teachings and words of God given down through the prophets, and despite the great enlightenment they received, they all were utterly destroyed in their last battle, except for Mormon and his son, Moroni, and some other people, as well as those who left the Nephites and joined themselves with the Lamanites.

Mormon was a holy prophet, and he kept an abridged account of the record of his ancestors that was engraven on the gold and brass plates, and he called the record the "Book of Mormon." Because of the commandments of God, he hid all the records of his ancestors which he had in a hill called Cumorah. He himself was not the one to bury the abridged record he made, but before he was killed by the Lamanites, he gave the record to his son, Moroni (also a holy prophet), for him to write the remaining portion. Moroni was the last survivor of his people; all the rest who had not joined with the Lamanites were killed by the Lamanites. And he kept a record until the year 420; then he hid the records in a hill called Cumorah (according to the commandments of the Lord) at a place where an angel revealed the plates to Joseph Smith, which he translated, by the gift and power of God, into the English language.

I have joy in these days that the printing of this Book has been completed in the Hawaiian language; it will not be long until you all will receive this Book. When this Book is made available to you, I desire that each of you purchase the Book and make it known among all your friends in all places so that they too can purchase it so that they can see and hear it and so that they cannot be left with a reason to say that they did not know about it. The price of the Book is low; it was not printed to make a profit but rather to fulfill the word of God to leave His word with all of you in your own tongue so that you may have it.

From the time of the white man's coming into possession of America and the isles of the sea, learned people have wondered where the peoples of these places sprang from and the reason for the darkness of their skin. Many books have been written by intelligent men attempting to explain these things. Some believe that the Indians are descendants of the tribes of Israel which are lost because there are many customs and practices that are done by the Indians that are the same customs and practices that are done by the Israelites. Other learned people doubt such things and they suppose that the dark-skinned people of America do not originate from there but rather that they come from other races of people. The speculations continue among some until this day. But in the Book of Mormon, these mysteries are explained; the origins of the inhabitants of America are made known as well as the reason their skin color is dark. It is not actually stated in the Book that you are descendants of them, but there are many encouraging words to those of the isles of the sea; and I believe (and to such do the words of the prophet of the Lord in these days attest) that you are descendants of the Israelites. The reason the skin of the forefathers of the Indians is dark is the same reason the skin of your forefathers is dark; and ways by which the darkness of their skin will cease are the same ways by which the darkness of your skin will cease.

Therefore, you are truly blessed by this Book, because you are the first dark-skinned people to have this Book in your own language; some of the dark-skinned people among the Indians have read this Book in English, but finally it has been printed in the language of a dark-skinned people. It is a necessary book for dark-skinned people because it was written by ancient prophets with the intent that it would be received by a race of dark-skinned people, so there are many and greatly encouraging words that were written for them in the last days. It reveals that the time will come when they will be restored to the knowledge of the things of God and His gospel of power and truth and that they will become (after they repent and forsake all their sins) a delightsome and blessed people; and the curse that came upon them because of the transgressions of their forefathers, meaning the dark skin, will begin to be taken away from them.

It will be said among some of you when the Book of Mormon will be made available among you that "The Mormons have another Bible and they will want to bring this book to replace the true Bible, and these Mormons will forsake it [the Bible]"; maybe this is what our enemies will say in derision. I want to let you know so that such a misunderstanding may be alleviated because truly it is slanderous and has no truth. This is what Mormon— one of the prophets who wrote a portion of what is contained in this Book—said to the dark-skinned people who receive the Book, "Therefore repent, and be baptized in the name of Jesus, and receive the gospel of Christ, which will be shown you, not only in this record [the Book of Mormon] but also in the record which will come to the Gentiles by way of the Jews [which is the Bible], and this book [the Bible] will come by way of the Gentiles to you. Because this is written [the Book of Mormon] that you may believe that [the Bible]; and if you believe that you would believe this also; and if you believe this, you would know of your forefathers and also of the marvelous things done by God among them; and you also would know that you are a remnant of the seed of Jacob." We know by these words that the Book of Mormon was not written to deny and replace the Bible but to justify and support it, to reveal the dealings of God among the ancient people of America, and to show that Jesus is the Christ, the eternal God, revealing himself to all men.

This Book does not teach anything erroneous; rather, it strongly forbids such things, and it teaches men to believe in Jesus Christ and repent of their sins. If this is wrong, then the Bible and the Book of Mormon are equally in error since they are alike in this respect. And this is what I have to say to all, Be careful and do not resist these things supposing it to be wrong because if you misjudge these things, then you also misjudge the Bible; rather, this is what you can do: "ask God, the Eternal Father, in the name of Christ, if these things are not true; and if ye shall ask with a sincere heart, with real intent, having faith in Christ, he will reveal the truth of it unto you, by the power of the Holy Ghost. And by the power of the Holy Ghost you may know the truth of all things."

If the people of Hawaii do not repent and abandon their sinful ways, there will be many curses and trials upon them in the time to come because we shall be judged not only by the Bible, but by the Book of Mormon as well; and it is said that by the mouths of two or three witnesses shall every word be established. You now have two witnesses of Christ and His gospel, and so if you rail against Him and harden your hearts and resist His commandments, you cannot escape the punishments.

You know, brothers and sisters, the things we, the white people from Salt Lake City, have done among you while we lived with hardship in your islands to expound these things to you without compensation by man. You also know that God has justified our works by giving His Holy Spirit to the believers and those who obey, and their hearts have been filled with unspeakable joy and gladness; hearts have been widened and eyes have been opened so that they now know and understand the holy scriptures in ways that never have been known before among the people of Hawaii; and the marvelous signs pertain to them as Jesus promised because [there were many] miracles that were performed among the believers and [their] hearts were made joyous in those things and their faith was made strong in [the things] pertaining to the Lord. Some of you have the Holy Priesthood, which is the power given by God to man to serve [in his capacity] here on earth. And so, because of all these things you have received and seen, you have inherited a work and we are blameless before God should you fall again into error and return to your former sinful ways because you are no longer ignorant as to the power of these things, and you know that they are true. And when you did righteous works, God filled you with the gift of the Spirit, and you were able to have joy from the time of the rising of the sun until the sun's setting at night. Therefore, brothers and sisters, how can you escape the judgments of God should you go in opposition to these things? Oh, how I desire to see you being steadfast and flourishing in these things so that you may become a people unto the Lord—a blessed people in things temporal and spiritual. Because of this desire of mine, I have labored with all my might to make these things known unto you and to translate and print the Book of Mormon in your tongue, so that you can read the uplifting words of the Lord unto you and His dealings among another people, and so that your knowledge will increase in the things pertaining to His gospel. I feel you will be held greatly accountable in having the Book of Mormon should you turn a deaf ear toward it, and should you hearken to it, you will be blessed greatly. Therefore, read it praying to God to reveal unto you the things that are written, so that you may become a knowledgeable and enlightened people in the things pertaining to his kingdom. Furthermore, do not find fault with the things contained in the Book, but, rather, love God that he may reveal unto you the errors therein that you may be instructed to be truly enlightened.

As I have always said to you while I lived among you, so I say now unto you that I know surely that the Book of Mormon is true and that it is from God, and that Joseph Smith was raised by God to do his work here on earth, and that the gospel of Jesus Christ that has been preached unto you at this time by the Elders of the Church is true and that it has been given for us all to embrace. I know that whoso should fight against it also fights against God, and he shall be cursed; but whoso should humble himself and ask God, in the name of Jesus, to reveal unto him the truth of these things, he shall know of the truth of all these things.

This is all I have to say unto you at this time, and I pray unto God to give His Holy Spirit unto you to help you to always hearken unto His words in all things, that you may be found at the last day at His right hand.

With love to all of you,

Sincerely,

Your elder brother,

George Q. Cannon

San Francisco, Dec. 27, 1855

Notes

An earlier version of this essay was presented at the Pioneers in the Pacific Conference, Brigham Young University—Hawaii, 7–11 October 1997. This essay has benefited from several conversations with Chad Orton, who also shared some of his own research notes from his forthcoming edition of the George Q. Cannon Hawaiian mission journals.

1. In Hawaii, when Cannon first tasted poi, he was reminded that "the smell of it and the calabash in which it was contained was so much like that of a book-binder's old, sour paste-pot that when I put it to my mouth I gagged at it, and would have vomited had I swallowed it." George Q. Cannon, *My First Mission* (Salt Lake City: Juvenile Instructor Office, 1879), 25. Cannon did eventually come to love poi.

2. George Q. Cannon journal, 10 June 1854, MS 1202, Family and Church History Department Archives, The Church of Jesus Christ of Latter-day Saints. Unless otherwise noted, all citations to manuscripts and letters are from this repository, which hereafter will be cited as Church Archives. I have had access to only the first three of Cannon's forty-seven journals. Volume 1 covers October 1849 to April 1852; volume 2, April 1852 to October 1853; and volume 3, October 1853 to October 1854. The citations herein to the Cannon journals will be to dates rather than volume numbers.

3. As suggested in Joseph J. Cannon, "George Q. Cannon," *Instructor* 79 (May 1944): 210.

4. George Q. Cannon journal, 23 July 1851. Cannon specifically says he was reminded of Cooper's scenes "in his tales of the backwoods." See the allusion to this in Cannon, *My First Mission,* 37.

5. Cannon journal, 12 November 1851. Upon examining the library of the late William A. McLane, Cannon indicated "it was a very good collection of books for this country."

6. Cannon journal, 21 July 1853. Compare the entry for 5 August 1853 in which he notes staying up all night to read the newspapers he had just received in the mail.

7. In addition to the scriptures, Latter-day Saint works he referred to in Hawaii, at least those specifically mentioned in his journals, included Orson Pratt, *An Interesting Account of Several Remarkable Visions* (1840); Orson Pratt, *Divine Authority, or Was Joseph Smith Sent of God?* (1848); Orson Pratt, *The Seer,* various numbers (Washington, D.C., 1853); Parley P. Pratt, *Voice of Warning* (1837); W. W. Phelps, *Deseret Almanac* and various issues of *Zion's Watchman* (Sydney, Australia) and of the *Deseret News.* While he never specifically mentioned it, he must have had access to a Hawaiian translation of the Bible, which had been issued before the arrival of the Mormon missionaries. His journals speak of teaching Bible classes to the natives, most of whom were literate in their own language.

8. Cannon journal, 11 March 1853. For the orders, see "European Publishing Account Ledgers and Journals," CR 271 22, MSS, Church Archives, esp. 8:370, for a listing of the printed items sent to Philip B.

Lewis, the mission president. The order was dated 24 June 1853. The shipment arrived in Hawaii in October 1853.

9. Cannon journal, 24 November 1854. The work referred to is John L. Stephens, *Incidents of Travel in Central America, Chiapas, and Yucatan* (New York: Harper and Brothers, 1841).

10. Cannon journal, 15 April 1854.

11. He arrived back in Salt Lake City on 28 November 1854. The best sources for details of his mission are the Cannon journals and correspondence and the records of his coworkers in Hawaii. The published sources include R. Lanier Britsch, *Unto the Islands of the Sea: A History of the Latter-day Saints in the Pacific* (Salt Lake City: Deseret Book, 1986); Britsch, *Moramona: The Mormons in Hawaii* (Laie, Hawaii: Institute for Polynesian Studies, Brigham Young University—Hawaii, 1989); and Davis Bitton, *George Q. Cannon: A Biography* (Salt Lake City: Deseret Book, 1999), 1–32. These volumes will lead the student to the rich published and unpublished sources.

12. This is clear in his journal entries January–February 1851 when his mission companions were concluding to leave the field as they had taught all the English-speaking people they could. See also Bitton, *George Q. Cannon,* 4–5.

13. Cannon, *My First Mission,* 58.

14. Ibid., 59.

15. Cannon journal, 26 August 1851.

16. Ibid., 24 December 1850 (first reference to "studying the language"); 27 December 1850 (expresses his desire to learn the language in order to teach the gospel); 30 December 1850 (sent for two vocabularies); 12 January 1851 (begins to "understand some little of what is said"); 10 February 1851 (fasting and praying for divine help to learn the language).

17. Ibid., 2 and 6 March 1851; Cannon, *My First Mission,* 14–15.

18. George Q. Cannon, letter to Henry Bigler or William Farrer, 12 January 1852, in "Letters to and from Missionaries in the Sandwich Islands, 1851–1860," typescript, p. 48, L. Tom Perry Special Collections, Harold B. Lee Library, Brigham Young University.

19. Cannon journal, 18 March 1851; compare entry for 17 May 1854.

20. Ibid., 8 December 1852.

21. Ibid., 17 May 1854. As early as 20 March 1851 Cannon reported in his journal that the natives had expressed a desire to read the Book of Mormon.

22. See ibid., 30 March 1851, for his reaction to an anti-Mormon lecture; compare his entry for 23 May 1851.

23. Ibid., 9 June 1854.

24. Ibid., 26 August 1851.

25. Ibid., 3 September 1851.

26. Ibid., 13 April 1851, reports their first talking long into the night.

27. Cannon, *My First Mission,* 59. According to his journal, 18–19 October 1850, Cannon obtained a copy of the Book of Mormon for his mission in October 1850 from Andrew Cahoon, whose family he was staying with in California. Cannon apparently based his translation on the 1849 (second European) edition prepared by Orson Pratt and published in Liverpool, England. This edition followed the 1841 (first European) edition, which was a reprint of the 1837 Kirtland, Ohio, edition issued by Parley P. Pratt and John Goodson. Orson Pratt had made several format changes in the 1849 edition that also appear in the Hawaiian edition. The index (really a table of contents) was moved to the front of the volume as were the statements of the Witnesses of the Book of Mormon. In a letter from Cannon to Brigham Young, 3 December 1855, Cannon noted that they had typeset the twenty-ninth signature (through page 464), which corresponded to page 503 of the "English edition," leaving fifty-six pages to typeset, excluding the title page and index. This corresponds with page 503 of the 1849 edition and the Hawaiian edition, i.e., Mormon 2; whereas in the 1837 edition it is 3 Nephi 5; in the 1840 edition it is 3 Nephi 5; and in the 1841 edition it is 3 Nephi 4. No other printed edition would correspond to or explain the relationship of the 1849 edition and the Hawaiian edition. See the comments in the letter of Joseph Bull to John G. Chambers, 3 December 1855, in the *Deseret News,* 30 January 1856, 373. Both Bull and Cannon wrote their letters on the day the twenty-ninth signature was sent to press, and both noted fifty-six or sixty pages left to typeset. Since the number of pages in the 1849 edition was 563, it would seem to best match this edition as the volume from which Cannon made his translation.

28. For example, on 15 February 1852, he organized on Maui the Makawao Branch of the Church of Jesus Christ.

29. According to his journal, Cannon learned of the *public* announcement (28 August 1852) of plural marriage on 11 November 1852. He received a copy of the *Deseret News, Extra* containing the text of Orson Pratt's 28 August discourse, which offered the first Mormon public defense of plural marriage. It also contained the text of the 1843 revelation later printed as D&C 132. Cannon preached a discourse on 7 April 1853 on the doctrine of plural marriage in order to prevent any misunderstanding in the public perceptions of the Church of Jesus Christ. Cannon made it clear that the members in Hawaii were not to meddle in these things. For the larger context, see David J. Whittaker, "The Bone in the Throat: Orson Pratt and the Public Announcement of Plural Marriage," *Western Historical Quarterly* 18 (July 1987): 293–314. A missionary companion, Benjamin F. Johnson, would write a defense of the practice, much of which grew out of his Hawaiian experience as a missionary forced to defend the teaching (Cannon journal, 13 July 1854). See Whittaker, "Early Mormon Polygamy Defenses," *Journal of Mormon History* 11 (1984): 43–63, esp. pp. 50–53; and Cannon journal, 18 April 1853.

30. Cannon journal, 13 April 1852.

31. Ibid., 8 December 1852.

32. Cannon, *My First Mission*, 60.

33. Ibid. See Cannon journal, 31 January 1854.

34. Cannon journal, 31 January 1854. See Cannon, *My First Mission*, 60–62.

35. Cannon journal, 31 January 1854.

36. Ibid., 5 April 1853. For an account of their earlier discussions about the possibilities of obtaining a printing press, see the letter of Philip B. Lewis to William Farrer, 26 March 1853, in "Letters to and from Missionaries in the Sandwich Islands, 1851–1860," typescript, pp. 122–25, esp. p. 123.

37. Cannon journal, 6 and 8 October 1853.

38. The membership statistics are in the "Manuscript History of the Hawaiian Mission," Church Archives. Cannon journal, 6 October 1853, indicates 3,008 members in fifty-three branches. His journal has a chart that breaks the membership down into specific branches and identifies priesthood holders. By July 1854, when Cannon was released from his mission, the membership was placed at 4,025, organized into seventy-five branches. See Philip B. Lewis journal, MSS, Joseph F. Smith Library,

Brigham Young University—Hawaii, typescript, p. 69 (copy in L. Tom Perry Special Collections, Harold B. Lee Library, Brigham Young University). All citations to this source will be to the typescript copy by date and page number.

39. Cannon journal, 25 July 1853; compare entry for 7 September 1853.

40. "Manuscript History of the Hawaiian Mission," 10 October 1853; Cannon journal, 10 October 1853.

41. Cannon journal, 2 December 1853; see entries for 17 January and 24 July 1854. Dennis also sold his tin shop to the mission for half of its value, taking a note for five hundred dollars. According to Lewis's journal: "Concluded a bargain with Bro Dennis to purchase his stock in trade for the benefit of the mission for which we the committee agree to give him $500, payable on demand, an[d] on Wed 25 I commenced the tinning business to raise means to establish a press and other expenses of the mission, the business has been prosperous thus far and I hope by the blessings of the Lord to be able to accomplish the object for which it was began." 24–25 January 1854, typescript, p. 64. The missionaries also received five hundred dollars from Levi Haalelea. Philip Lewis reported baptizing Eduard [Edward] Dennis on 23 April 1852 and on 13 June 1852 told of the healing of Bro. Dennis's daughter after a serious fall. See Lewis journal, typescript, pp. 22, 25. The Dennis family later moved to California, and Lewis does report attempts to repay the money owed him for his tin shop. Because Cannon refers to him as Edward in his journal, this is the spelling followed herein.

42. Cannon journal, 31 December 1853, describes receiving the 29 May 1853 letter from John Taylor. The French edition was actually translated by Curtis Bolton, but Taylor's name appears on the title page ahead of Bolton as a translator. For details, see the Curtis Bolton journals, Church Archives.

43. See Brigham Young, letter to George Q. Cannon, 30 September 1853.

44. The money they had gathered was carried to John M. Horner in California by a returning missionary, William McBride. Horner then actually ordered the press from New York. See Cannon, *My First Mission*, 62. On Horner, see Doyle L. Green, "John M. Horner, . . . California's 'First'

Farmer," *Improvement Era* 54 (April 1951): 244–46, 302–3; (May 1951): 340–45.

45. Cannon journal, 20 March and 26 May 1854. In a letter from Parley P. Pratt to Brigham Young, 18 May 1855, Pratt reported, "the press and paper has arrived in San Francisco to my charge, and is duely [*sic*] stored, and awaits the action of Bro. Cannon, who I am glad to learn is coming out to use it."

46. On 6 October 1854, 190 reams of paper and the press arrived in Hawaii on the ship *Living Age.* Lewis journal, typescript, p. 73. Lewis reports receiving a letter from Parley P. Pratt on 30 December 1854 giving instructions about the press, etc. (ibid., 75). On 8 March 1855 another letter from Parley Pratt came ordering Lewis to send the press and other materials to San Francisco. Lewis indicates that on 20 March 1855 the printing materials left the Islands for California (ibid., 77–78).

47. Pratt to Young, February 1855, Brigham Young collection, Church Archives. Benjamin F. Johnson had written to George Q. Cannon on 15 October 1854 indicating that the press and seventeen large bales of printing paper had arrived in Honolulu on 8 October. Copy in "Journal History" of the Church of Jesus Christ of Latter-day Saints, a multivolume scrapbook of historical documents housed in the Church Archives.

48. The manuscript of the translation was brought to San Francisco by Joseph A. Peck, a returning Latter-day Saint missionary who left Honolulu on 17 May 1855. Lewis journal, typescript, p. 80. No doubt Cannon left the manuscript in the Islands thinking that he would return there to print it.

49. For the details of his work with Parley P. Pratt, see Cannon journal, beginning with entry for 12 August 1854. Pratt's autobiography was not published until 1874, seventeen years after Pratt's death.

50. For a summary of these hectic months, see Davis Bitton, *George Q. Cannon,* 69–70. Their marriage was reported in the *Deseret News,* 21 December 1854.

51. George Q. Cannon, *Writings from the Western Standard, Published in San Francisco, California* (Liverpool: Cannon, 1864), vi.

52. Ibid., vi–vii. Cannon gives more detail in his 27 July 1855 letter to Brigham Young.

53. Young to Cannon, 7 May 1855.

54. Cannon to Young, 27 July 1855.

55. For an account of Parley P. Pratt's prior work in California, see David J. Whittaker, "Parley P. Pratt and the Pacific Mission: Mormon Publishing in 'That Very Questionable Part of the Civilized World,'" in *Mormons, Scripture, and the Ancient World: Studies in Honor of John L. Sorenson,* ed. Davis Bitton (Provo, Utah: FARMS, 1998), 51–84. For an overview of Cannon's work in California, see Lawrence R. Flake, "George Q. Cannon's Mission to California, 1855–1857," in *Regional Studies in LDS Church History, California,* ed. David F. Boone, Robert C. Freeman, Andrew H. Hedges, and Richard N. Holzapfel (Provo, Utah: BYU Department of Church History and Doctrine, 1998), 81–105. For the larger historical and religious context of the Mormon mission in Hawaii, see Gavan Daws, *Shoal of Time: A History of the Hawaiian Islands* (Honolulu: University Press of Hawaii, 1968), and Arrell M. Gibson with John S. Whitehead, *Yankees in Paradise: The Pacific Basin Frontier* (Albuquerque: University of New Mexico Press, 1993), esp. chap. 13, "The Missionary Frontier," 263–96.

56. George Q. Cannon, letter to John Taylor, 1 August 1855: "We proceeded to examine the press and material and found everything in good order, with the exception of the ribs of the press which were broken and which I immediately undertook to have recast."

57. See Cannon to Young, 31 August 1855. It was Hyde who suggested Cannon's newspaper be called the *Western Standard,* not the *Mormon Herald,* as Pratt had planned to name it.

58. For the details regarding the location and renting of their printing shop, see letter from Cannon to Young, 27 July 1855; also Cannon to Parley P. Pratt, 21 October 1855.

59. On the problems with English fonts, see Cannon to Young, 27 July 1855; also Matthew F. Wilkie, letter to Joseph Cain, 27 July 1855, in the *Deseret News,* 19 September 1855, 222.

60. A sample of these first printed pages was sent to Young in Cannon's letter of 27 July 1855. Young received them on 20 August 1855 and responded to their initial efforts: "I am highly gratified with the energy and perseverance you have displayed, and thank the Lord for the success that has thus far attended your labors. The proof sheets of the Book of Mormon look extremely well, the type is handsome, the impression

good and the form very well proportioned and convenient, and the book when finished will redound much to your credit, for I presume the translation is as good as the mechanical execution." Young to Cannon, 29 September 1855. It should be noted that the first proof pages were in octavo form (eight pages to a sheet) due to the lack of lowercase *k*s (a letter found much more frequently in Hawaiian than in English). By August they had obtained enough extra letters to allow them to move to the sixteen-page sheet format, "which saves us half the labor of composing, wetting papers, press work &c." Cannon to Young, 31 August 1855.

61. Cannon's letter to Young, 3 December 1855, provides the detail: "The 464th page of the Hawaiian, corresponding with the 503rd of the English edition, went to press this morning; this leaves us fifty-six pages to do, exclusive of the index, title page &c. By last mail to the States I sent to New York for some type and other material for the paper, and I expect it here, if no unexpected accident occurs, by the 20th Jan. We will have to wait until this arrives before we can very well put up the index, &c., which ought to be set up in a type a little smaller than the body of the work." Thus, in spite of the 1855 date on the title page of the work, it was actually finished in January 1856.

62. Cannon to Young, 20 December 1855.

63. The chronology of the printing can be followed through these sources: *27 July 1855*—16 pages (two 8-page signatures), Matthew F. Wilkie to Joseph Cain; *31 August 1855*—128 pages (8 signatures), Cannon to Young; *23 September 1855*—240 pages (15 signatures), Cannon to William Taylor, *Deseret News,* 14 November 1855, 286; *3 December 1855*—464 pages (29 signatures), with about 60 pages remaining, Joseph Bull to John G. Chambers, *Deseret News,* 30 January 1856, 373. The printing was finished in January 1856 and the *Deseret News,* 16 April 1856, 48, printed a notice that the Hawaiian edition was available. Bull had noted in his 3 December 1855 letter: "If no unexpected accident occurs, the body of the work will be completed by about the 19th of this month. The index and title page will have to lay over till our small type (Brevier) arrives from the east, unless we can borrow a pair of Brevier cases from some [printing] office in the city.... We have not been able to publish the Book of Mormon quite so quick as we anticipated when we first commenced, but taking all things into consideration, I think we

have done tolerably well." Brigham Young received one of the first copies, as did Edward Dennis, who had loaned them the money to obtain the press. See Cannon to Brigham Young, 26 January 1856, and, for Brigham Young's positive reaction, Young to Cannon, 3 April 1856. A close examination of the first Hawaiian edition reveals the printer's signature marks.

64. Alma 37:4; compare 1 Nephi 5:18; 19:17; 2 Nephi 26:13; 30:8; Mosiah 3:20; 15:28; and 3 Nephi 28:29.

65. Cannon to Young, 26 January 1856.

66. Ibid.; the postscript to this letter was dated 30 January.

67. Young to Cannon, 3 April 1856. The *Deseret News* noted the publication with the same enthusiasm in the issue of 16 April 1856.

68. Cannon to Young, 1 October 1855.

69. Young to Cannon, 29 November 1855.

70. Cannon's letters to Young, 26 May and 27 September 1856 and 31 August 1857 provide the details on the problems of binding the volume.

71. Cannon to Young, 27 September 1856.

72. Young to Cannon, 4 November 1856.

73. See Cannon to Daniel H. Wells, 4 March 1857, and Cannon to Young, 31 August 1857. According to Henry Bigler's journal, by 4 October 1857 only 114 copies had been sold for a total of $97.75. Henry Bigler journal "G" in the Henry E. Huntington Library, San Marino, Calif.

74. Cannon to Young, 31 August 1857.

75. Young to Cannon, 4 September 1857. In this letter Young indicated that he considered sending Cannon back to Hawaii to supervise the binding and sale of the Hawaiian edition of the Book of Mormon as well as to help the missionaries begin a newspaper there.

76. Henry Bigler journal, 24 November 1857. On 30 October 1857 Cannon wrote to Young: "Since your letter arrived I have been doing all in my power to dispose of the printing materials and to arrange all the business so that we can be, as you counselled me, ready at a moment's warning. . . . The Books of Mormon I have boxed up and sent to the Islands, paying freight, etc., so that there will be but very little expense, if the work be done among themselves, in getting them into the hands of the natives."

77. Bigler journal, 4–5 October 1857. In addition to problems with customs, Bigler reported, upon opening the boxes, "m[a]ny of the sheets

damaged being eaten by mice or otherwise spoiled." Bigler journal, 25–26 November 1857. Bigler estimated to the customs official that printed sheets for about eight hundred copies were salvageable. These and the above references in the Bigler journal were called to my attention by Chad Orton of the Church Archives.

78. "Manuscript History of the Hawaiian Mission," 25 April 1858 and 25 December 1863.

79. The full title was *He Olelo Hoolaha, I na Hoahanau o ka Ekalesai o Iesu Kristo o ka poe Hoana o na La Hope nei, ma ko Hawaii pae aina; a i na kanaka a pau i aloha i ka oiaio,* or "An Announcement, To the members of the Church of Jesus Christ of Latter-day Saints in the Hawaiian Islands, and to all people who love the truth." An English translation of his tract appears as an appendix to this essay.

80. Cannon to Young, 26 January 1856, Young to Cannon, 4 November 1856. John T. Cain, letter to Brigham Young, 13 April 1856, reported that fifteen hundred copies had arrived in Hawaii. John R. Young's letter from Hawaii to his father, Lorenzo D. Young, 15 March 1856, reported that Cannon's tract was "being circulated among the Natives, and the Saints appear to be delighted with it. We are looking anxiously for the Book of Mormon, as it has been out of press some time." "Correspondence," *Deseret News,* 20 August 1856, 190.

81. Cannon to Young, 26 January 1856.

82. Young to Cannon, 3 April 1856.

83. The *Prospectus of the Western Standard* was dated 4 January 1856 (copy in Church Archives). The *Western Standard* was published weekly in San Francisco from 23 February 1856 to 18 November 1857.

84. Consider the following statements, which are typical: "If Joseph Smith's claims as a Prophet of God had no other foundation than that which this book furnishes, then there is foundation enough for him to rank as one of the greatest prophets that has ever lived upon the face of the earth," George Q. Cannon, in *Journal of Discourses,* 22:254, (8 September 1881); and "We do not believe it possible for any honest, unprejudiced soul to read the Book of Mormon in a prayerful spirit without being convinced that its words are the words of God. There is an influence which accompanies it, and which the reader feels, if he will not reject it,

that carries with it overpowering conviction and is a testimony that God is the Author, through His inspired servants, of that Book," *Juvenile Instructor* 25 (15 August 1890): 500.

85. Cannon's key role is discussed in David J. Whittaker, "Early Mormon Pamphleteering," *Journal of Mormon History* 4 (1977): 35–49.

86. A sampling of these works include George Reynolds, *The Myth of the "Manuscript Found," or the Absurdities of the "Spaulding Story"* (Salt Lake City: Juvenile Instructor Office, 1883); George Q. Cannon, *The Life of Nephi, the Son of Lehi, Who Emigrated from Jerusalem, in Judea, to the Land Which Is Known as South America, about Six Centuries before the Coming of Our Savior* (Salt Lake City: Juvenile Instructor Office, 1883); George Q. Cannon, *Book of Mormon Stories: Adapted to the Capacity of Young Children, and Designed for Use in Sabbath Schools, Primary Associations, and for Home Reading*, 2 vols. (Salt Lake City: George Q. Cannon and Sons, 1892, 1899); and B. H. Roberts, *A New Witness for God*, 2 vols. (Salt Lake City: George Q. Cannon and Sons, 1895, 1906). For a listing of articles and published addresses by George Q. Cannon on Book of Mormon topics, see Donald W. Parry, Jeanette W. Miller, and Sandra A. Thorne, *A Comprehensive Annotated Book of Mormon Bibliography* (Provo, Utah: Research Press, 1996), 76–79.

87. For a useful overview, with the references to the comments and concerns of George Q. Cannon and his son Abraham H. Cannon, see the introductory chapters in Reid L. Neilson, "The Japanese Missionary Journals of Elder Alma O. Taylor, 1901–10" (master's thesis, Brigham Young University, 2001), esp. pp. 19–27.

88. On the gathering to Lanai, see R. Lanier Britsch, "The Lanai Colony: A Hawaiian Extension of the Mormon Colonial Idea," *Hawaiian Journal of History* 12 (1978): 68–83; for Cannon's 1894 comments, see *Collected Discourses Delivered by President Wilford Woodruff, His Two Counselors, the Twelve Apostles, and Others*, comp. Brian H. Stuy (Burbank, Calif.: BHS Publishing, 1987–92), 4:145–47 (5 October 1894 discourse); for Cannon's 1897 comments, see Conference Report, 5 October 1897, 40–41. While not announced by a president of the Church of Jesus Christ until 1907, Cannon began to stress this years before.

89. Joseph Smith said on 28 November 1841: "The Book of Mormon was the most correct of any Book on Earth & the key stone of our reli-

gion & a man would get nearer to God by abiding by its precepts than any other book." Wilford Woodruff journal, 28 November 1841. See *Wilford Woodruff's Journals,* ed. Scott Kenney (Midvale, Utah: Signature, 1985), 2:139. Throughout his mission, Cannon taught people that his own testimony was not based just on what Joseph Smith taught but on personal witnesses of the Spirit. See, for example, the long sermon addressing this matter as recorded in his journal, 25 January 1853.

90. This translation, commissioned by the L. Tom Perry Special Collections, Harold B. Lee Library, Brigham Young University, was completed in May 2000 by Richard Keao Nesmith and William K. Kelly. We have made minor changes in the punctuation, capitalization, and wording of their translation.

CHAPTER 19

The Mystical Denial of Language

Joseph Dan

The language people use to communicate mundane matters commands very little interest or respect in the spiritual world of the mystic. Yet language is a central subject of discussion of many mystical works in all religions. The term *language* in the context of the mystical discourse refers to the word of God as expressed in scripture. Inevitably, the mystic's attitude toward language expresses his fundamental relationship to the religious culture that surrounds him and sustains his spiritual existence.[1]

I present here a few examples from various periods, religions, and cultural environments to illustrate my discussion of the attitude of mystics toward religion and its linguistic expression: the Shaker movement in late-eighteenth-century England; the famous medieval mystical directory, *The Cloud of Unknowing*;[2] the Jewish mystical masterpiece, the Zohar;[3] and finally, a contemporary discussion between Michel Foucault and Georges Bataille on the subject.[4]

The Shaker Movement

The Shaker movement, which originated in England in the middle of the eighteenth century, was influenced by the Quakers (most of the Shakers first belonged to the Friends before separating and constructing their independent movement), as well as by other apocalyptic trends and beliefs that flourished in England at that time. They followed Ann Lee, who in 1770 had a revelation that Christ had been resurrected within her, as within every other believer. The experience of the coming again of Christ is the essential characteristic of the movement (though it began a generation before and had already become a distinct group in 1747). The Shakers left England and established themselves in the United States (the last remnants live today in Sabbathday Lake, Maine). This movement may be regarded as the most overt, unambiguous historical manifestation of the attitude of the mystics toward communicative language. As far as I know, adherents of this movement never expressed their linguistic theories in any systematic fashion, thus remaining loyal to their most cherished concept: if language cannot express truth, it cannot even express its rejection of itself. The Shakers denied any theological linguistic formulation and did not demand adherence to any linguistic formula.

The Shakers are characterized by their belief in the resurrection of Christ in every person. They identify every member of their denomination, male or female, with the living Christ. Whether this is a mystical or a theological attitude is debatable. What is manifestly untheological in their message is the fact that they did not develop a theology to demonstrate, explain, and elaborate this revelation. They are unique in their denial of a creative attitude toward scriptures, expressed in their refusal to create their own linguistic distillation of the new, revolutionary message which they believed that they had received; indeed, they are unique in their rejection of traditional scriptures, the Old and New Testaments, as sacred revelations of the ultimate divine truth. Truth, for them, cannot be congealed into a body of words.

The Shakers are especially unique in their understanding (intuitive rather than dialectic) that the language of religion includes not only the actual words that transmit ancient divine truth, but also the nonverbal body of rituals, norms, instructions, manuals, ethics, and customs, which together constitute religious observance and way of life. Semiotic expression was denied by them in the same way that semantic messages were.[5] In order to approach divine truth, according to them, one must reject all forms of expression that shape and regulate that truth.[6]

A contemporary historian of the Shakers, who belongs to the denomination, describes the early beginnings of the movement thus:

> In the desire to be led by the Spirit, their worship began to develop directions ultimately leading away from both Quaker and contemporary English Protestant forms. The Friends had originally sought to worship without form, and so be completely open to the Spirit's inspiration. They met in silence— the very positive silence of *waiting upon the Lord*—with every expectation of being further enlightened with inner inspiration whereby the Spirit would lead the community; those so moved would give witness through spoken reflection, exhortation, and the like. However, with their new expectations and consequent experiences, the early Shakers found that, ironically, the Quaker "formless" mode of worship could be the most constraining form of all: sitting in silence unless moved to speak. For many Shakers were experiencing quite unexpected "movements of the inner Spirit," often overflowing into emotion-charged manifestations—songs without words, strange languages, prayer through bodily gesture such as kneeling, ecstatic spontaneous dancing, and disturbing bodily agitation and trembling. (It is from this last that their mocking neighbors called them "Shaking Quakers.") Many other Shakers remained outwardly calm in manner yet welcomed all these manifestations as the signs of a great inward work. They, in turn, moved away from purely silent worship through the early development of worship songs and solemn discourses.[7]

The silence of the Quakers, sometimes interrupted by spontaneous statements, was too meaningful for the early Shakers, and this caused their separation from their original religious context. They sought a way of worship that denied any meaningful structure or expression. The "mocking neighbors," as Robley Whitson calls the surrounding society, were perceptive enough to select the trembling and shaking as the identifying characteristic of this new group because this was the least expressive, the least communicative among the various gestures and modes of behavior adopted by the new denomination. This extreme denial of communication, which sprang up within the context of the general Protestant rebellion against the extremely stylized and organized verbal and ritualistic worship of the Catholic Church, expresses the wish not to exchange one mode of expression for another—the Shakers believed that even the Quakers' silence was such a substitution—but to seek a completely noncommunicative mode. This response is the ultimate denial of language as a constituent of religion.[8]

The Shakers' concept of resurrection can be identified typologically as a form of self-deification, which is a constant element found in different forms in linguistic records of the *unio mystica*. In many cases, however, the mystic believes that he has acquired, through this union, some access to the divine language and has become the master of divine wisdom. He is unable to transmit this knowledge and wisdom through the communicative language of his fellow believers, but he seeks some way to communicate the new vistas opened before him by a torrent of words. The Shakers are different in that their complete certainty in their identification with the risen Christ did not create a body of new knowledge, new wisdom, and new language. Their shaking and trembling express the complete transcendence of any form of communication, semantic or semiotic. Ritual, prayer, custom, and order become impossible in the new realm of divinity residing on earth.

The original Christ, when he first appeared, spoke, preached, and acted in a meaningful way, and his disciples wrote treatises. The resurrected Christ in the hearts of the Shakers did none of these things; he could only tremble. The Christ of the New Testament speaks the language of religion. The Christ of the Shakers un-speaks the nonlanguage of the mystics.

The Cloud of Unknowing

The Cloud of Unknowing, a fourteenth-century work, is one of the most popular and influential treatises dealing with mysticism; despite its anonymity and absence of particular background and authority of a person or an order, it had a meaningful role in shaping Catholic spirituality and mysticism. It is a rare phenomenon, particularly among popular works, that the title of a work is a thoroughly negative phrase: *cloud* in this context means that which covers and hides, so that the title is actually a double negative. Throughout the work, which is intended to lead the believer toward union with God, negative terms abound (the "cloud of forgetting" is one of the better-known examples). The treatise is written in simple, straightforward language, staying away from philosophical or theological terminology. The concept of language itself is not problematized in the treatise, and the author does not insist on a systematic adoption of negative language; the term *love,* for instance, is central, and the author uses it as a positive, meaningful word.

The role of language in the process—or its absence—is demonstrated in the detailed instructions given in several chapters concerning the ways by which one can forsake the physical and emotional earthly realms and their temptations and immerse oneself completely in the "darkness," which is the nonplace where a person is united with God. The senses and reason are denied as a source of knowledge of true things. "All rational beings, angels and men, possess two faculties, the power of knowing and the power of loving. To the first, to the intellect, God who made them is forever unknowable, but to the second, to love, he is completely knowable."[9] *Love* is a term that represents that nonsensual and nonintellectual urge that directs the believer in his quest for God. The author does not conclude—as he could—that the realm of "love" must be nonlinguistic because language must rely on shared sensual and intellectual concepts in order to be communicative. The author's attitude toward language is expressed instead in another significant way:

> Should any thought arise and obtrude itself between you and the darkness, asking what you are seeking, and what you are wanting, answer that it is God you want: "Him I covet, him I seek, and nothing but him."
>
> Should he (the thought) ask, "What is this God?" answer that it is the God who made you and redeemed you, and who has, through his grace, called you to his love. "And," tell him, "you do not even know the first thing about him." And then go on to say, "Get down," and proceed to trample on him out of love for God; yes, even when such thoughts seem to be holy, and calculated to help you find God. Quite possibly he will bring to your mind many lovely and wonderful thoughts of his kindness, and remind you of God's sweetness and love, his grace and mercy. If you will but listen to him, he asks no more. He will go on chattering increasingly, and bring you steadily down to think of Christ's Passion. There he will show you the wonderful kindness of God, and he wants nothing so much as that you should listen to him. For he will then go on to let you see your past manner of life, and as you think of its wretchedness your mind will be well away, back in its old haunts. Before you know where you are you are disintegrated beyond belief! And the reason? Simply that you freely consented to listen to that thought, and responded to it, accepted it, and gave it its head.[10]

Continuing, the author says that these thoughts are "both good and holy" and serve a necessary purpose, but if one wishes to proceed on the quest for God, one has to "put them away deep down in the cloud of forgetting if he is ever to penetrate the cloud of unknowing between him and God."[11] It is obvious, both in this discussion and in parallel ones in the treatise, that these thoughts represent the language of religious worship, of identification with Christ's passion and the struggle against worldly temptation, leading to wholesome religious life. It may be a necessary precondition for the meaningful quest, but it is not part of the same path. In order to stop the torrent of words of this communicative religious language, one has to relegate it to the "cloud of forgetting," ignore and suppress it, "trample on [it]," and adopt a new attitude toward language:

> So when you feel by the grace of God that he is calling you to this work, and you intend to respond, lift your heart to God with humble love. And really mean God himself who created you, and bought you, and graciously called you to this state of life. And think no other thought of him. It all depends on your desire. A naked intention directed to God, and himself alone, is wholly sufficient.
>
> If you want this intention summed up in a word, to retain it more easily, take a short word, preferably of one syllable, to do so. The shorter the word the better, being more like the working of the Spirit. A word like "GOD" or "LOVE." Choose which you like, or perhaps some other, so long as it is of one syllable. And fix this word fast to your heart, so that it is always there come what may. It will be your shield and spear in peace and war alike. With this word you will hammer the cloud and the darkness above you. With this word you will suppress all thought under the cloud of forgetting. So much so that if ever you are tempted to think what it is that you are seeking, this one word will be sufficient answer. And if you would go on to

think learnedly about the significance and analysis of that same word, tell yourself that you will have it whole, and not in bits and pieces.[12]

One little word, one syllable, is the substitute offered by the author to the long, verbose discourse of religion. The single word is not chosen because of its meaning; rather, when temptation to ponder its meaning presents itself, the believer should avoid and ignore it. It is nothing but a mantra, an arbitrary focus of attention that has nothing to do with the communicative and meaningful aspects of language. The author's attitude seems to be—both here and in many other sections of the work—that language is the domain of religion, while the quest of God within the darkness, the mystical process, is meta-linguistic. In this realm of darkness, language is not only unnecessary, but it presents a danger of the return to God's beauty, kindness, mercy, and passion, all the characteristics of religion that one wishes to forget in order to be able to proceed. It should be noted that there is no emphasis here on a concept of a ladder of ascension in which religion encompasses the lower rungs and mysticism the upper ones. The presentation insists on the difference between the two attitudes rather than emphasizing a link of continuation between them. Their relationship is either/or, rather than one after the other.

This focus is even more evident when the author discusses the meaning and nature of prayer. Liturgy is the strongest statement in scriptural religions of language as a constant and meaningful verbal connection between the believer and God. The insistence on a ritual of prayer several times a day indicates a belief that words are bridging the gap between earth and heaven constantly and efficiently. *The Cloud of Unknowing* includes an unambiguous statement concerning this:

> Just as the meditations of those who seek to live the contemplative life come without warning, so too, do their prayers. I am thinking of their private prayers, of course, not those laid

down by the Holy Church. For true contemplatives could not value such prayers more, and so they use them, in the form and according to the rules laid down by the holy Fathers before us. But their own personal prayers rise spontaneously to God, without bidding of premeditation, beforehand or during their prayer.

If they are in words, as they seldom are, then they are very few words; the fewer the better. If it is a little word of one syllable, I think it is better than if it is of two, and more in accordance with the work of the Spirit. For a contemplative should always live at the highest, topmost peak spiritually.

We can illustrate this by looking at nature. A man or woman, suddenly frightened by fire, or death, or what you will, is suddenly in his extremity of spirit driven hastily and by necessity to cry or pray for help. And how does he do it? Not, surely, with a spate of words; not even in a single word of two syllables! Why? He thinks it wastes too much time to declare his urgent need and his agitation. So he bursts out in his terror with one little word, and that of a single syllable: "Fire!" it may be, or "Help!"

Just as this little word stirs and pierces the ears of the hearers more quickly, so too does a little word of one syllable, when it is not merely spoken or thought, but expresses also the intention in the depth of our spirit. Which is the same as the "height" of our spirit, for in these matters height, depth, length, and breadth all mean the same. And it pierces the ears of the Almighty God more quickly than any long psalm churned out unthinkingly.[13]

It is evident that the writer is at least impatient with, if not scornful toward, the established church's use of language. Meaning, according to him, can be found in one syllable (that is, an unstructured, nongrammatical, nonsyntactic cry), when it emerges from a believer's heart and reaches heaven. This syllable need not have any semantic value (*OM* will probably do nicely); if it did, there could not be such a strict limitation on its size. The believer does not speak to God, does not engage in conversation or explanation.

The link formed between worshiper and deity is nonsemantic. The author concedes that the "contemplative" fulfills the requirements of the church concerning the ritual of prayers, but this is not a part of his contemplative, spiritual, and mystical ascension to God. Language has to be forsaken, even trampled under one's feet, if the mystical quest is to be pursued.

The Zohar

> If a man says that a story in the Torah is there simply for the sake of the story, may his spirit depart![14] For if it were so, it would not be a supernal Torah, a Torah of truth. But in very truth the Torah is holy, supernal, a Torah of truth. Come and see. A mortal king considers it below his dignity to converse with a commoner, let alone write down a commoner's words. And if you think that the supernal king, the Holy One, blessed be He, does not have sacred words of His own, from which to make a Torah, but that He needs to collect the words of commoners, such as those of Esau, Hagar, Laban's to Jacob, the words of the ass, and of Balaam, Balak and Zimri, and that He gathers them and all the other stories written in Scripture, and makes a Torah of them, why is it called "the Torah of truth" (Malachi 2:6)?[15]

There is nothing unique in the concept that scripture has a sublime, hidden meaning, extending even to the most seemingly mundane narratives included in it. What is unusual here is the attitude of denigration toward and rejection of the literal meaning of the narratives. There is no hint of a literary appreciation of these stories; they are presented as an anthology of the meaningless utterances of gentiles, sinners, and animals. The author does not have any doubt—as he states later—that human writers of fiction could do much better as far as narrative literature is concerned. This is not just a quest for the secret meaning of the Torah, but an unambiguous rejection of its narrative language.[16] In another section, the author of the Zohar states:

Rabbi Simeon said: Woe to the man who says that the Torah intended simply to relate stories and the words of commoners, for, if this were the case, we ourselves at the present time could make a Torah from the words of commoners and do even better. If the intention was to deal with the affairs of [this] world, then the [profane] books in the world contain better things. Shall we then follow them, and make a Torah out of them? But all the words of the Torah are exalted and are supernal mysteries.

Come and see. The upper world and the lower world are measured by the same measure. Israel below, and the celestial angels above. It is written of the celestial angels that "He makes His angels spirits" (Psalm 104:4). When they descend to the world below they clothe themselves with the garments of this world. And if they were not to clothe themselves with garments that are characteristic of this world, they could not exist in this world, and the world could not tolerate them. Now if this is true of angels, how much more true it is of the Torah that created them, and created all the worlds, which exist only for its sake. When it came down into the world, the world could not have tolerated it if it had not clothed itself in the garments of this world. Consequently, the narratives of the Torah are the garments of the Torah. If a man thinks that the garment is the actual Torah itself, and not something quite other, may his spirit depart, and may he have no portion in the world to come. It is for this reason that David said: "Open my eyes, that I may behold wondrous things out of Your Torah" (Psalm 119:18)— from beneath the garment of the Torah.

Come and see. There is a garment that is seen by all. And when fools see a man in a garment that appears to them to be beautiful, they look no further. [But] the value of the garment resides in the body, and the value of the body resides in the soul. Similarly, the Torah has a body. The commandments of the Torah are the bodies of the Torah. This body is clothed in garments, which are the narratives of this world. The fools in the world look only upon the clothes, which are the narratives of the Torah; they know no more, and do not see what is beneath the clothes. Those who know more do not look upon the clothes, but upon the body beneath the clothes. The wise, the servants of the supreme King, those who stood at Mt. Sinai, look only upon the soul, which is the foundation of all, the real Torah. And in the time to come they are destined to look upon the soul of the soul of the Torah.

Come and see. So also above there is a garment and a body and a soul, and a soul's soul. The heavens with their hosts are the garment; the Assembly of Israel *[shekhinah]* is the body that receives the soul, which is the glory *[Tiferet]* of Israel, and therefore is the body for the soul. The soul that we have mentioned is the *Tiferet* of Israel, the actual Torah, and the soul's soul is *Atika Kadisha,* and the whole is interdependent.

Woe to the wicked who say that the Torah is only a story, who look upon this garment and no further. Blessed are the righteous who look upon the Torah in the correct manner. Wine can exist only in a bottle. So the Torah can exist only in this garment. Consequently, one must look at what is beneath the garment. Therefore all these matters, and all these stories are garments.[17]

The Torah consists of four levels: the lowest is the narratives, historical accounts, and so on, which are described as the "garment"; the second is the physical commandments, which are designated as the "body." This level is not rejected, but its meaningfulness is dependent on its being united with the third level, the soul, or spiritual meaning—a union that is designated in the usual Zoharic erotic metaphor of the union between the female and the male elements in the divine world. The commandments are represented by the female element, the *shekhinah,* who acquires meaning only when she is united with her husband, *Tiferet,* the masculine principle in the divine pleroma. Nothing is said here directly about the value of indulging in the "body" level alone, which means studying the Torah for the sake of the law, the *halakah.* In other places in the Zohar, this approach is criticized rather harshly.[18] It should be noted that nothing is said here directly about the nature of the "soul" of the Torah, nor about the "soul of the soul," which will be revealed only in the future, in messianic times.

The concept of two languages is apparent here, even if the terminology is different. In other sections of the Zohar, the metaphors of the tree of good and evil versus the tree of life are employed to designate the difference between the two ways in which the language of the sacred text should be read. It is evident, however, that the author denies, and denigrates, the ways in which his contemporary co-religionists read and understand scriptures. He believes that he knows another way, which is described elsewhere in the Zohar.

The Zohar, like *The Cloud of Unknowing,* was written as an anonymous work. Both books were published within a historical context of strict orthodoxy, in which loyalty to religious hierarchy was demanded as an absolute. Yet both works express unhesitatingly the rejection of the normative language of religion as utilized in daily rituals, including the word of God himself as incorporated in the scriptures and understood by their traditionalistic co-religionists. The Zohar was written in the literary format of a midrash, a hermeneutical exegesis of the Torah.[19] Yet the Zohar does not hesitate to deny in radical terms the text of the divine revelation incorporated in the Torah and to reject its understanding not only by his contemporaries but by Jewish exegetical tradition as a whole. Such an attitude reflects his belief in the existence of a different, nonlinguistic avenue by which the soul of the Torah can be accessed—the mystical one.

Foucault and Bataille on Linguistic Expression

Michel Foucault dedicated an article, "A Preface to Transgression," to an analysis of Georges Bataille's concept of language. This article was described by the author as a "homage" to Bataille and was printed in *Critique,* Bataille's journal, in 1963 (Foucault often assisted in the editing of this journal). It refers mainly to Bataille's book *Eroticism*. Foucault, in this article, emphasizes Bataille's metaphor of the eye, which is used to designate introspection, or the turning of the eye to observe the interior of the brain and of a person's soul. Throughout the article Foucault repeatedly refers to Bataille's book, which includes a section dedicated to an analysis of Christian mysticism; Foucault's discussion, therefore, is oriented toward an analysis of the concept of the inward-looking eye in a mystical context. In a key passage in this article, Foucault says:

> What significance has this insistent eye which appears to encompass what Bataille successively designated *the inner experience, the extreme possibility, the cosmic process,* or simply *meditation?* It is certainly no more metaphoric than Descartes' phrasing of the "clear perception of sight" or this sharp point of the mind which he called *acies mentis.* In point of fact, the upturned eye has no meaning in Bataille's language, can have no meaning since it marks its limit. It indicates the moment when language, arriving at its confines, overleaps itself, explodes and radically challenges itself in laughter, tears, the overturned eyes of ecstasy, the mute and exorbitated horror of sacrifice, and where it remains fixed in this way at the limit of its void, speaking of itself in a second language in which the absence of a sovereign subject outlines its essential emptiness and incessantly fractures the unity of its discourse. The enucleated or upturned eye marks the zone of Bataille's philosophical language, the void into which it pours and loses itself, but in which it never stops talking—somewhat like the interior, diaphanous, and illuminated eye of mystics and spiritualists that marks the point at which the secret language of prayer is embedded and choked by a marvellous communication which silences it. Similarly, but in an inverted manner, the eye in Bataille delineates the zone shared by language and death, the place where language discovers its being in the crossing of its limits: the nondialectical form of philosophical language.

This eye, as the fundamental figure of the place from which Bataille speaks and in which his broken language finds its uninterrupted domain, establishes the connection, prior to any form of discourse, that exists between the death of God (a sun that rotates and the great eyelid that closes upon the world), the experience of finitude (springing up in death, twisting the light which is extinguished as it discovers that the interior is an empty skull, a central absence), and the turning back of language upon itself at the moment that it fails—a conjunction which undoubtedly has no other equivalent than the association, well known in other philosophies, of sight to truth or of contemplation to the absolute. Revealed to this eye, which in its pivoting conceals itself for all time, is the being of the limit: "I will never forget the violent and marvellous experience that comes from the will to open one's eyes, facing what exists, what happens."

Perhaps in the movement which carries it to a total night, the experience of transgression brings to light this relationship of finitude to being, this moment of the limit which anthropological thought, since Kant, could only designate from the distance and from the exterior through the language of dialectics.[20]

One key element in Foucault's presentation is unacceptable to the historian. Foucault treats language as an anthropomorphic entity, which begins and ends and folds upon itself as a sovereign, independent phenomenon. A historian cannot but view language as something used by people, who are motivated by different drives and needs, and in most sentences it should be the object rather than the subject. If we reread this discussion in such a manner, making the speaker-writer the subject and language the object, I believe that we have before us a penetrating, highly intuitive, and remarkably accurate description of the language of the mystics.

The language of the "upturned eye" is nondiscursive and nondialectical (in this context it may also be regarded as nonrational). It is a language of silence, in which words cease to express and are replaced by laughter, tears, sacrifice, death—silence. In contemporary terminology, with which Foucault may not have been familiar in 1963, semantic language is replaced by semiotic expression (which legitimately includes silence). But, at the same time, Foucault emphasizes, "it does not stop talking." Even though linguistic (here, semantic) expression has reached its limit and no words can reveal the new vistas opened before the eye, words still pour out. This is one of the most characteristic phenomena concerning mystical expression: even though words are delegitimized and are declared inefficient and insufficient, they still pour out, filling up library walls and heaps of manuscripts.

The relationship between the two languages is described by Foucault as that between sight and truth, where sight may be regarded as the representative of all human senses.[21] This first language is also the language of dialectical discourse and rationalistic philosophy, that of Descartes and Kant, whereas the second language, which denies the senses, is that of the mystics and spiritualists and—what seems to be most important for Foucault—that of the nondialectical philosophers, among whom, undoubtedly, he counts Bataille and himself.[22] This language is recognized by its semiotic characteristics, its inclusion of nonsemantic elements like laughter, tears, and even death—death of man and death of God—despite the fact that words still pour out. It is, therefore, a nonsemantic, nonrational, partially verbal, irrational, and nonsensual language. All these elements are found, as Foucault is well aware, in the language of the mystics.

A Second Language?

A vast difference lies between the context of literary criticism and nondialectical philosophical discourse (the genre employed by Foucault) and mysticism (in which a person speaks within the boundaries of a particular faith, to which he or she vehemently adheres). Whether he is a heretic or an orthodox (terms which denote historical judgment rather than spiritual context), a mystic believes wholeheartedly that he is a devoted, loyal servant not only of his God but also of his church. Loyalty to God and church means, in linguistic terms, loyalty to the word of God as it is conceived in the tradition to which the mystic belongs. The denial of language—the claim that a second language takes over when the first reaches its own demise—is rather easy for a novelist, a critic, and a "nondialectical philosopher." Such a denial is very difficult for an intensely religious person who wholeheartedly believes that God presented his truth in the words incorporated in scriptures. Postulating a second language in such a context means claiming that God is bilingual, a thesis that harbors considerable religious difficulties. It has been employed from time to time, but another possibility of solving this paradox seems to have worked better: scriptures can be read in two different ways. There are not two languages but two kinds of readers, the mystics and the nonmystics. The nonmystic deludes himself that he reads and understands scriptures as a sensual and rational language. The mystic knows that this is impossible because truth cannot be conveyed by such means. He perceives in the language of scriptures the nonsensual, irrational undercurrents in which God's truth is hidden.

Foucault and Bataille discuss language while analyzing its relationship to external phenomena—erotic excitement, pain, happiness, reality, death. The mystic confronts, first and foremost, language itself, because religion is mainly a linguistic phenomenon. What he writes—the words that pour despite the demise of language—are words reacting to words, linguistic revelation reacting to a previous linguistic revelation. The resulting turmoil produces the language that denies itself—the language of the mystics.

Notes

1. The negative aspect of the language of the mystics has been forcefully presented by Michael A. Sells, *Mystical Languages of Unsaying* (Chicago: University of Chicago Press, 1994); a similar approach is presented

in Denys Turner, *The Darkness of God: Negativity in Christian Mysticism* (Cambridge: Cambridge University Press, 1995). Concerning the problem of mystical language as a whole, see Joseph Dan, "In Quest of a Historical Definition of Mysticism: The Contingental Approach," *Studies in Spirituality* 3 (1993): 58–90. See also Joseph Dan, *The Heart and the Fountain: An Anthology of Jewish Mystical Experiences* (Oxford: Oxford University Press, 2002), 1–15.

2. *The Cloud of Unknowing and Other Works,* translated into modern English with an introduction by Clifton Wolters (Harmondsworth, England: Penguin, 1961, 1978).

3. Isaiah Tishby, *The Wisdom of the Zohar: An Anthology of Texts,* trans. David Goldstein (Oxford: Oxford University Press, 1989).

4. Michel Foucault, "A Preface to Transgression," first published in "Hommage à Georges Bataille," *Critique* 195–96 (1963): 751–70; translated into English by Donald F. Bouchard and Sherry Simon and published in the volume *Michel Foucault: Language, Counter-Memory, Practice: Selected Essays and Interviews,* ed. Donald F. Bouchard (Ithaca, N.Y.: Cornell University Press, 1977), 29–52, esp. 48–49.

5. There is one aspect in which the Shakers seem to have created a new theology: the inclusion of a feminine element in the Godhead and the perception of the Trinity as bisexual. Catholic theology resisted temptations to do that, as did Islam; the Jewish Kabbalah, however, adopted that concept wholeheartedly, as did the ancient gnostics. In the context of the Shakers, however, this seems to be more the result of intuition and insistence on the identity of the human and the divine; if humanity is gender oriented, so is the Godhead. The erotic element, so prominent in Gnosticism and the Kabbalah (and in Islamic and Catholic mysticism, despite the rejection of this element from the Godhead itself), is rather absent from the Shakers' thought and practice. See the discussion of the use of the term *carnal* by the Shakers in Robley E. Whitson, ed., introduction to *The Shakers: Two Centuries of Spiritual Reflection* (New York: Paulist Press, 1983), 30–31. The book is part of the series the Classics of Western Spirituality: Spiritual Reflection. The subtitle should not be taken literally. The volume contains an anthology of two centuries of Shakers' writings, which is a testimony to the fact that for two centuries the Shakers have written almost nothing and that the little they pro-

duced is hardly a record of "reflection"; the few treatises and letters included in this anthology are exceptions that prove the rule that linguistic expression was not part of the Shakers' religious experience throughout their history.

6. History is often cruel to people who attempt to deny the power of linguistic structures. One of the best-known characteristics of the Shakers is their denial of gender differences, a remarkable idea at that time or any time. They insisted that there was no difference, as far as the resurrection is concerned, between men and women, who share equally in that experience. When enacting this belief in historical terms, however, they found themselves emphasizing rather than ignoring gender differences. They sought complete disregard of gender, but in order to express it they had to insist on absolute equality, which entailed, for instance, the strict adherence to equality rules, like always having two men and two women constituting their leadership. The enactment of equality made gender an ever-present concern of their leadership structure rather than leading to its disappearance.

7. Whitson, introduction to *Shakers*, 9.

8. Their attitude toward the Gospels and the ancient body of scriptures is complex, but the key term used by them is *opening*. Language as present in the scriptures is *closed* until opened by the believer. The language of the ancient divine message becomes incidental and is denied any normative meaning. See selected passages in the chapter "Travel in the Gospel," in *Shakers*, 86–155.

9. Wolters, *Cloud of Unknowing*, 63.

10. Ibid., 68–69.

11. Ibid., 69.

12. Ibid., 69–70.

13. Ibid., 104–5.

14. The context is a discussion of the verse "And the ark rested in the seventh month ... upon the mountain of Ararat" (Genesis 8:4). The previous paragraph concluded: "What does it matter to us whether it rested here or there? It must have rested somewhere!" It seems that this verse was selected in a similar way that the Talmud selected the verse "And Timna was concubine to Elifaz, Esau's son" (Genesis 36:12), to state that there is no difference in sanctity between this verse and "I am the Lord

thy God" (Exodus 20:2), the opening words of the Ten Commandments (TB *Sanhedrin* 99b). In other words, according to the Zohar, every biblical verse comes from the same source and represents the same level of sanctity and divine wisdom.

15. *Zohar* Numbers 149a–b, cited in Tishby, *Wisdom of the Zohar,* 3:1125.

16. The Zohar reflects in this and the following statements an attitude first presented in Judaism by an eleventh-century philosopher and mystic, Rabbi Bahya ibn Paquda, the author of *The Duties of the Heart,* trans. and commentary by Yaakov Feldman (Northvale, N.J.: Aronson, 1996), one of the most influential spiritual treatises in the history of Jewish culture (the author was influenced by Sufism, and the work includes many quotations from Sufi literature). The concluding paragraphs of the author's introduction to the treatise include a denial of the notion that the stories in the Torah convey a divine message. The author maintains that these were included in the Torah only for the purpose of differentiation between the wise and the stupid; the latter would embrace the narrative and historical material, while the wise would reject it and dedicate themselves to the sections dealing with divine matters. See Joseph Dan, *The Hebrew Story in the Middle Ages* (in Hebrew) (Jerusalem: Keter, 1974), 7–8. The language of the Zohar includes phrases that are derived from Rabbi Bahya's discussion (whose work was translated from Arabic to Hebrew by Rabbi Judah ibn Tibbon in the end of the twelfth century).

17. *Zohar* Numbers 152a; Tishby, *Wisdom of the Zohar,* 3:1126–27. In this particular case there is no need to hesitate to interpret the Zoharic statement in a radical way because we have a Hebrew version of the same statement written by the author of the Zohar, Rabbi Moshe de Leon, in an independent treatise. In this version Rabbi Moshe quotes the talmudic discussion of the verses in the talmudic tract of *Sanhedrin.* The Hebrew version includes an element that is not present in the quoted paragraphs from the Zohar: that the biblical narratives are not only worthless and undistinguished, but they include an element which, when taken literally, is ethically reprehensible. He mentions the story of Jacob acquiring the position of firstborn from his hungry brother, the story of Sarah banishing Hagar from her home, and that of Rachel steal-

ing the teraphim. He concludes that the literal level of scripture is dangerous, not just neutral in its meaninglessness. Concerning the text, see Isaiah Tishby, "Response of Rabbi Moshe de Leon concerning Kabbalah" (in Hebrew), *Kovetz Al Yad* 5 (1951): 30–31.

18. See Tishby's discussion in *Wisdom of the Zohar*, 3:1089–1100.

19. Concerning the Midrash and its relationship to mystical language, see Joseph Dan, *On Sanctity: Religion, Ethics and Mysticism in Judaism and Other Religions* (in Hebrew) (Jerusalem: Magnes Press, 1997), 87–130.

20. Foucault, "Hommage à Georges Bataille," in Bouchard, *Michel Foucault*, 48–49, emphasis in original.

21. This statement is remarkably similar to that of another French writer a generation before Foucault and Bataille: Antoine de Saint-Exupéry, who in his book *The Little Prince* refers several times to a great secret that the fox knows. When the prince is dying, the fox reveals that secret: "It's quite simple," he says, "Anything essential is invisible to the eyes" (New York: Harcourt, 2000), 63. Like Foucault, Saint-Exupéry asserts that whatever the senses may reveal belongs to the realm of the first language, the limited one that does not include truth, while nonsensual knowledge, expressed in the second language, is the vehicle for the expression of truth.

22. One of the most inspired discussions of the limitations of language was presented in the beginning of the last century by the Hebrew poet Chaim Nachman Bialik in an essay entitled "Revelation and Concealment in Language," in *Kol Kitve Chaim Nachman Bialik* (Collected Works) (Tel Aviv: Dvir, 1958), 1:192. The English translation is in Robert Alter, ed., *Modern Hebrew Literature* (New York: Behrman, 1975), 130–37. In a highly eloquent discussion, Bialik insisted (like Saint-Exupéry's fox many years later) that language is adequate for the unimportant things; when dealing with great truth, language obscures rather than reveals.

CHAPTER 20

THE BOOK OF JOB AS A BIBLICAL "GUIDE OF THE PERPLEXED"

Raphael Jospe

Maimonides (Rabbi Moses ben Maimon, 1135–1204, known in Hebrew as Rambam) treats the biblical book of Job in two chapters (3:22–23) of his monumental *Guide of the Perplexed* (Arabic *Dalalat al-Ḥaʾirin;* Hebrew *Moreh ha-Nevukhim*).[1] These two chapters form a subsection of a larger literary unit dealing with the theme of divine knowledge and providence (*Guide of the Perplexed* 3:16–24).[2] Scholars have devoted much attention to two separate subjects in Maimonides' *Guide:* first, his theory of providence in general and his interpretation of Job in particular, and second, his definition in the introduction to the *Guide* of the "perplexed" person for whom the *Guide* was written. After surveying these two seemingly unrelated subjects, I shall propose that they are not, in fact, unrelated. To the contrary, a study of Maimonides' careful use of terminology will show that the biblical character Job is, in his view, essentially the kind of "perplexed" person for whom he wrote the *Guide* and that the book of Job is, therefore, a sort of biblical "Guide of the Perplexed."

Maimonides' Theory of Providence

Divine Knowledge and Providence

In *Guide of the Perplexed* 3:16, Maimonides discusses the success of the wicked and the suffering of the righteous, which lead people to question God's knowledge of affairs in this world. The "philosophers" (meaning, in Maimonides' frame of reference, Aristotle, the ancient commentators on Aristotle, and the medieval Arabic Aristotelians)[3] maintain that either God does not know of these injustices (because he is ignorant of the affairs of this world) or he does know of them. If God knows of them, then either he is responsible for these injustices, or he is impotent to do anything about them, or he has the power to do something but fails to do it. Given the absurdity of all three of these possibilities, which impute injustice or impotence to God (assuming that he actually knows what happens in this world), the philosophers conclude that God does not and cannot possess knowledge of this world. God cannot know the particulars of this world because particulars are apprehended sensibly (and God, having no body, has no bodily senses); because there is an infinity of particulars (and the infinite, by definition, cannot be known); and because particulars are produced in time, and, as they change, there would be a corresponding change in God's knowledge of them (and God is not subject to change). Instead of imputing injustice or impotence to God, the philosophers thus impute ignorance to God and thereby compound the problem they sought to resolve.[4]

In the next chapter (*Guide of the Perplexed* 3:17), Maimonides outlines five views regarding providence. The first view is that of Epicurus, who denied divine providence and believed that everything occurs by chance. The view of Epicurus was disproved, Maimonides argues, by Aristotle, who demonstrated the existence of natural order. The second view on providence is that of Aristotle, who maintained (in Maimonides' understanding) that God's governance extends to the heavenly spheres (which, accordingly, are incorruptible and exist eternally) and to the earthly sublunar sphere, but on earth only to the species (which, accordingly, are also permanent) and not to particular individuals, which exist by chance. The third view is that of the "orthodox" Ash'ariyyah school of the Kalam (Islamic theology),[5] which affirms absolute determinism. Everything is determined by God's will, governance, and omniscience. Accordingly, this school denies the existence of natural order, chance, and human free will. The fourth view is that of the more moderate Mu'tazilah school of the Kalam, which affirms limited human free will, together with divine knowledge and wisdom. People are, therefore, justly rewarded or punished in this world or in the world to come for their actions. The fifth view on providence is that of the Torah, which teaches that people and animals have free will, that freedom was established by God at the creation of the world itself, and that there is, therefore, just reward and punishment.

Maimonides then proposes what is, in effect, a synthesis of the second and fifth views, those of Aristotle and of the Torah. Providence, he affirms, applies in the sublunar realm only to species and not to individuals (as Aristotle believed), except for individual humans:

> I believe that in this lower world, i.e., the sublunar [realm], divine providence applies only to individuals of the human species. Only in this species are all the affairs of individuals, and the good and evil that befall them, in accordance with what they deserve. . . . But as for all the other animals, and all the more, plants and other things, my opinion is that of Aristotle . . . that all of them are, in my view, due to pure chance, as Aristotle thought. (*Guide of the Perplexed* 3:17)[6]

Providence attaches to individual humans and not to animals or plants because "providence follows the divine [intellectual] emanation" and is proportionate to the intellectual development of the individual. To the extent that the individual human develops his or her intellectual faculty, he or she transcends his or her individual bodily limitations and participates in universal knowledge and reason. To this extent, he or she thus benefits from divine providence. Intellectual apprehension also provides (as Maimonides postulates elsewhere) a basis for immortality: the body and the lower functions of the soul that enliven the bodily organs perish, but the intellect survives in proportion to its actualization in knowledge.[7] The individual human being, by virtue of intellectual apprehension, thus acquires aspects of universality and permanence, which make providence possible on the level of the particular individual. Providence can attach, therefore, to individual humans but not to individual animals or plants.

Maimonides thus bridges the moral requirement, imposed by the Torah, that each individual be both responsible and accountable for his or her behavior in a providential sense, and the philosophic requirement, imposed by Aristotle, that providence can apply only to things that are universal and permanent.

The Book of Job

In the *Guide of the Perplexed* 3:22–23, Maimonides analyzes the book of Job, which, in his view, is a parable (Arabic *mathal;* Hebrew *mashal*)[8] explaining diverse views on providence. The lesson of this biblical parable, as Maimonides understands it, is that Job erred not morally but intellectually.[9] In addition, the positions represented by Job and his three associates Eliphaz, Bildad, and Zophar, as well as Elihu, correspond to four of the five views on providence discussed above (in *Guide of the Perplexed* 3:17). Only the view of Epicurus, denying providence and affirming that everything happens by chance, is not represented in the book of Job because all the book's characters agree that God knows and ultimately is the direct or indirect cause of what happens to Job.

Regarding the first point—that Job erred intellectually and not morally—Maimonides points out that Job is described in the beginning of the book as being moral and righteous in his behavior but is not described as "wise," "understanding," or "intelligent"

(Hebrew *ḥakham, mevin,* or *maskil).* Had Job been wise, his situation would not have caused him to have serious doubts regarding divine justice. This is the reason Satan is permitted to "touch" Job's body, family, and possessions but not his "soul" *(nefesh)* (Job 2:6). For Maimonides, the "soul" means the intellect. Job's error was intellectual, not moral, and therefore Job had to be able, on his own at the end of the book, to arrive at a proper theoretical understanding of divine justice. We shall return later to this fundamental lesson of the book.

Regarding the second point, all five protagonists in the story (Job, Eliphaz, Bildad, Zophar, and Elihu) are in agreement about the facts: Job was innocent and righteous, God knew what was happening to Job and, despite Job's innocence, caused him to suffer. They agree about the facts but differ as to their interpretation. Therefore, the book has no place for the Epicurean view—denying providence and affirming only chance—which is inconsistent with these basic facts.

Maimonides then correlates the various philosophical positions regarding providence, which he discussed previously, with the views of the protagonists of the biblical story. For Maimonides, each philosophical position is reflected in a key verse in the speeches of each of these characters in the book of Job.

First, Job's own position is identified by Maimonides with Aristotle's affirmation of only general providence attaching to the species and denial that divine providence extends to individual humans. Job concludes that there is no difference in God's eyes between the righteous and the wicked: "It is all one; therefore, I have said: He destroys the innocent and the wicked" (Job 9:22).

Second, Maimonides identifies the position of Eliphaz with the view of the Torah, that man has free will and is, therefore, justly rewarded and punished for his actions. Job, according to Eliphaz, deserved his punishment, on account of his sins: "Is not your evil great, and your transgressions without end?" (Job 22:5).

Third, Bildad represents the view of the Muʿtazilah school of
the Kalam, which affirms that people are justly punished and that
God can compensate for people's unwarranted suffering in this
world with reward in the world to come: "If you are pure and up-
right, [God] will arise for you and reward the habitation of your
righteousness. Although your beginning was small, your end will
increase greatly" (Job 8:6–7).

The fourth position is that of Zophar, who, Maimonides proposes, represents the view of the Ashʿariyyah school of the Kalam—
that everything is determined exclusively by God's will, and we
should neither question it nor seek reasons for what he wills: "But
would that God would speak and open his lips against you; and
tell you the secrets of wisdom. . . . Can you find out the range of
God? Can you find out the purpose of the Almighty?" (Job 11:5–7).

The fifth view is that of Elihu, who reviews the points raised
by Job's three associates but adds to them the notion of an inter-
cessor angel (Job 33:23), symbolizing the prophetic understanding that Job attains at the end of the book, finally resolving his
doubts.[10] Only then does Job truly comprehend the intellectual
error that led him to question God's justice.

Job's Intellectual Error

Job's intellectual error, which he recognized only as a result of
the prophetic experience of God's addressing him "out of the storm"
(Job 38:1), was his failure to understand that just as the divine
creation of nature in no way resembles artificial human production, so there is no similarity between the divine providential governance of the cosmos and human governance over those things
that are in our power. The purpose of the book, accordingly, is to
teach us that terms like *governance* and *providence* are properly
applied to God only equivocally. The person who understands this
theoretical truth will be able to bear his material misfortunes lightly.

In Maimonides' words:

> The notion of his providence is not the same as our notion of
> providence, nor is the notion of his governance of his creatures

the same as our governance of whatever we govern. [The two notions] cannot be included in the same definition, *as every perplexed person* thinks, and they have nothing in common except their name. Similarly, our action does not resemble his action, and cannot be included in the same definition. Just as natural actions differ from artificial actions, so do the divine governance of, and the divine providence over, and the divine purpose for those natural things differ from our governance of, our providence over, and our purpose for whatever we govern, provide for, and intend.

This is the intention of the whole book of Job; I mean to establish this foundation of belief, and to alert [us] to what should be inferred from natural subjects, so that you not err and seek in your imagination that his knowledge is like our knowledge, or that his purpose and providence and governance are like our purpose and providence and governance. When a person knows this, it will be easy for him to bear all his suffering lightly, and his suffering will not cause him any more doubts about God and whether [God] does or does not know, whether he exercises providence or neglect. Rather, he will increase his love, as it says at the end of this prophecy: "Therefore I abhor and repent, on account [of my being] dust and ashes." (Job 42:6; *Guide of the Perplexed* 3:23)[11]

Job thus realizes, because of the prophetic revelation he receives in the storm, that he has erred intellectually, although he has not sinned practically. He was righteous, but not wise. On account of his suffering, he had doubted God's providence and governance of the world. This doubt resulted from his fundamental misunderstanding and fallacious belief that divine governance and providence are analogous to human governance and providence. Only now has he come to understand that governance and providence can only be attributed equivocally to God. It is only, then, at the end of the story that Job attains this theoretical realization of his intellectual error. Previously, Job suffered from the intellectual fallacy of thinking that the two notions—divine and human governance and providence—can be "included in the same definition, *as every perplexed person* thinks." Now Job comes to know God "with a certain knowledge," whereas he previously had only known God based on "tradition" (Arabic *taqlīd;* Hebrew *qabbalah*).[12] Therefore, Job now, at the end, understands that the knowledge of God constitutes ultimate human happiness and that material misfortunes should not dominate his concern, while previously, in his ignorance, Job had imagined that bodily health, wealth, and children are the ultimate goal (Arabic *ghāyah;* Hebrew *takhlit*). "Therefore [Job] *was perplexed by such perplexities* and said the things that he said."[13] Now that he finally has a proper perspective, based on his correct understanding of the equivocal nature of divine governance and providence and of the true purpose of life, Job is no longer perplexed.

Who Is the Perplexed Person?

The *Guide of the Perplexed* was written in the form of a letter from Maimonides to a favored disciple, Joseph ben Judah.[14] In his introduction to the book, Maimonides gives as his first purpose to "explain" terms in scripture that cause "great pain and perplexity." Such equivocal, metaphorical, or ambiguous terms, when taken literally, contradict reason and therefore perplex the religious person who believes in scripture but has also been exposed to philosophy. The second purpose of the book, similarly, is to explain "obscure parables" in scripture that, when read literally rather than figuratively, similarly cause "great perplexity."

Who is the person who suffers from such "great perplexity"? Maimonides describes him thus:

> The purpose of this treatise is to arouse a religious person, whose soul has become accustomed to affirming the truth of our Torah, who is perfect in his religion and moral qualities, who has studied the sciences of the philosophers and knows their subjects, whom the human intellect has attracted to dwell

in its realm. He is distressed by the literalist understanding of the Torah and [by] what he is unable to comprehend of these equivocal, metaphorical, or ambiguous terms, and so he remains perplexed and confused. If he follows his intellect and discards what he knows of these terms, he will then think that he has discarded the foundations of the Torah. Or, if he remains with what he understood of them and does not follow his intellect and turns his back on it and moves away from it, he would cause a loss to himself and damage to his religion . . . and he will not stop suffering from heartache and great perplexity.

This treatise has a second purpose, which is to explain very obscure parables appearing in the books of the prophets, but it was not made explicit that they are parables. So it would appear to an ignorant or foolish person that they have only an external meaning and have no inner meaning. When one who knows the truth looks at them and takes them literally, he also experiences a great perplexity. But when we explain that parable or call his attention to its being a parable, he will find the correct way and be saved from this perplexity. That is why I call this treatise: the *Guide of the Perplexed*. . . .

In this treatise I address a person who has philosophized, as I have mentioned, who knows the true sciences, and who [also] believes in the subjects of religion and is perplexed about their meaning, because of the ambiguous terms and parables.[15]

The Book of Job as a Biblical "Guide of the Perplexed"

When we compare Maimonides' description of his purposes in writing the book and of the characteristics of the perplexed person in the introduction to the *Guide of the Perplexed* with his description of the purposes of the book of Job and of the character of Job in *Guide of the Perplexed* 3:22–23, we find remarkable parallelisms, both terminological and substantive, between these two seemingly unrelated passages.[16]

Parallelisms	Purpose of the *Guide* and Character of the Perplexed Person (*Guide*, introduction)	Purpose of the Book of Job and Character of Job (*Guide* 3:22–23)
1. Affirmation of the truth of the Torah	A religious person, whose soul has become accustomed to affirming the truth of our Torah,	When the story of Job was postulated, or when it occurred, what was agreed among the five, that is, Job and his associates, was [the opinion of the Torah on providence, namely,] that whatever happened to Job was known to God, and that God had caused these troubles. . . . [17] [Job] knew God only on the basis of tradition (*taqlīd; qabbalah*), in the manner of the masses who [observe] the Torah.
2. Perfect in religion	who is perfect in his religion	careful to shun sin
3. Perfect in moral qualities	and moral qualities	righteous, perfect, and just in his actions . . . Moral virtue and righteousness in actions are attributed to him.
4. Does not understand equivocal nature of terms	He is distressed by the literalist understanding of the Torah and [by] what he is unable to comprehend of	Job was not described as [possessing] knowledge; it did not say that he was a wise, understanding, or

	these equivocal, metaphorical, or ambiguous terms	intelligent person.... [Job] said everything that he did because he had no knowledge, and knew God only on the basis of tradition, in the manner of the masses who [observe] the Torah.... The notion of his providence is not the same as our notion of providence nor is the notion of his governance the same as our governance of whatever we govern. [The two notions] cannot be included in the same definition, *as every perplexed person* thinks, and they have nothing in common except their name.
5. Therefore, perplexed about the Torah or God	And so he remains perplexed and confused.... who believes in the subjects of religion and is perplexed about their meaning, because of the ambiguous terms and parables.	Know and consider how the story was postulated, *which has perplexed people* and led them to [believe] the opinions we explained above, regarding God's providence over what he created. ... Therefore [Job] *was perplexed by such perplexities* and said the things that he said.

6. Purpose of the book: to remove perplexity	The first purpose of this treatise is to explain the meanings of terms appearing in the books of prophecy.... The purpose of this treatise ... is the true knowledge of the Torah.... When we explain that parable or call his attention to its being a parable, he will find the correct way and be saved from this perplexity.	[The two notions] cannot be included in the same definition, *as every perplexed person* thinks, and they have nothing in common except their name.... This is the intention of the whole book of Job; I mean to establish this foundation of belief and to alert [us] to what should be inferred from natural subjects, so that you not err and seek in your imagination that his knowledge is like our knowledge, or that his purpose and providence and governance are like our purpose and providence and governance.
7. Understanding parables correctly	to explain very obscure parables appearing in the books of the prophets, but it was not made explicit that they are parables.	The wonderful and marvelous story of Job ... is a parable explaining people's opinions on providence.... In general, "whether he existed or did not exist," in such cases, which always exist, all people who examine *have become perplexed*.

Finally, Maimonides' treatment of the book of Job as a parable (with all due credit to the talmudic interpretation of Job to that effect) is also strikingly similar to his discussion of parables in the introduction to the *Guide of the Perplexed*. In the introduction, Maimonides proposes that when he has explained the general meaning of a parable, the reader should not search for further details, which tend to divert one's attention from the parable's intention. Indeed, it should generally suffice merely to point out that the parable is a parable, at which point its inner meaning will usually become evident.

Maimonides' treatment of the book of Job accords with these guidelines. He begins his discussion (in *Guide of the Perplexed* 3:22) with the statement that the book is a parable and was thus understood by talmudic rabbis. Even those rabbis who did assume that Job was a historical figure rather than the subject of a fictional parable certainly considered the dialogues of God and Satan to be a parable, not fact. Maimonides thus fulfills his first point regarding the treatment of parables: their status as parables must be made explicit. He then fulfills his next point regarding parables: one should not go into excessive details, which merely confuse the reader and conceal the lesson of the parable. Rather, where the mere fact of the story's being a parable does not make the parable's lesson self-evident, one needs to explicate and emphasize the general lesson of the parable, bringing out its inner meaning without confusing matters by delving into irrelevant details. This Maimonides does masterfully by cutting through the lengthy drama of the book and briefly and succinctly identifying each of its five major protagonists with a different philosophical or religious stance.

In conclusion, our comparison of Maimonides' language in the introduction to the *Guide of the Perplexed* and his discussion of the book of Job in *Guide of the Perplexed* 3:22–23 brings out the striking similarity of ideas and terminology. As Maimonides explicitly stressed in the introduction, he did not write the book loosely, nor use terms haphazardly.[18] His repeated use of the term *perplexed* or *perplexity* in the discussion of Job cannot, therefore, be accidental or coincidental. Point for point, Job fits Maimonides' description of the perplexed student in the introduction. Admittedly, Job is not described by Maimonides as having studied philosophy, as was the perplexed student.[19] On the other hand, Job's own position—that providence does not extend to individuals (based on Job 9:22)—is equated by Maimonides with the Aristotelian denial of individual providence. All the other positions (of Eliphaz, Bildad, Zophar, and Elihu) are identified not with the philosophic opinion but with various religious views (the views of the Torah, the Muʿtazilah Kalam, the Ashʿariyyah Kalam, and Elihu's introduction of the angel, representing prophetic revelation). Job himself thus represents, in Maimonides' reconstruction of the biblical drama, the philosophic stance of Aristotle.

Job, like Maimonides' student, is perplexed because of his failure to understand the equivocal nature of biblical "God language," specifically the equivocal nature of God's providence, purpose, and governance. It is only when Job makes the spiritual transition from blind belief, based on tradition, to a rational knowledge of God that he can correct his intellectual error and his perplexity can be resolved.

The perplexed student of the *Guide of the Perplexed* experiences a three-stage intellectual and spiritual "pilgrim's progress." In the first stage he is a simple religious Jew, without any exposure to philosophy and science. His blind religious belief is based on tradition. He is not yet the student in whom Maimonides is interested and whom he warmly wishes to encourage. He is not (yet) perplexed but merely ignorant of philosophy and science. It is only in the second stage that the student becomes perplexed by the apparent contradictions between faith and reason because of his exposure to philosophy. It is the student at this stage for whom

Maimonides wrote the *Guide of the Perplexed*. The *Guide* is intended, as its name makes explicitly clear, to lead the perplexed student to the third stage—namely, to a more mature and sophisticated understanding of the equivocal nature of biblical terminology. This is the ultimate level of the student's development, which Maimonides calls "the true knowledge of the Torah."

These three stages are all to be found in Maimonides' Job. In the first stage, at the very beginning of the book "when the story of Job was postulated," Job was a simple, pious person whose belief was blind and based on tradition: "[Job] knew God only on the basis of tradition, in the manner of the masses who [observe] the Torah." At that early point, the position of Job was the same as the position of Eliphaz, Bildad, Zophar, and Elihu. All five affirmed the "opinion of the Torah," or in other words, "that whatever happened to Job was known to God and that God had caused these troubles." In the second stage, much later in the book, Job has progressed from this simple, blind belief in the religious position to a more sophisticated, although also ultimately erroneous, philosophical position—namely, that of Aristotle—when he concluded that there is no individual human providence: "It is all one; therefore, I have said: He destroys the innocent and the wicked" (Job 9:22). Thus, of the five stated positions, only Job's position is philosophical.[20] Some of the others may also have made some progress; Bildad and Zophar have progressed from blind traditional faith to somewhat more sophisticated Kalam positions, but those positions are (in Maimonides' negative assessment of the Kalam)[21] far from philosophical in their method and far from true in their conclusions. Only Job, then, has progressed from philosophical ignorance (the first stage) to philosophical perplexity (the second stage), whereas the other four protagonists in the story have all failed to make any true spiritual progress and remain unperplexed in their ignorant Kalam certitude or blind religious faith. At the end of the book, Job finally comes to the third stage, "the true knowledge of the Torah," when he understands the equivocal nature of God's providence, purpose, and governance, at which point, like Maimonides' student, Job can "find the correct way and be saved from this perplexity."

Taking it one step further, just as Job fits Maimonides' description of the perplexed student for whom he wrote the *Guide,* so does the purpose of the book of Job (as Maimonides understands it) thus fit his description of the purpose of the *Guide of the Perplexed.* The purpose of both books is to resolve the perplexity of one who doubts religious teaching on philosophical grounds by correcting the intellectual error of equating divine actions with human actions. The biblical book of Job, like the *Guide of the Perplexed,* leads a person to knowledge of God by emphasizing how little we actually know and how completely equivocal the terms describing God's actions are. As Maimonides thus understands the book of Job, it is, essentially, a biblical "Guide of the Perplexed."

Notes

1. The Judeo-Arabic edition of the book—the form in which the text was originally written—was published by Isaachar Joel (Jerusalem, 1931), based on the mid-nineteenth-century edition of Salomon Munk. The standard medieval Hebrew translation is that of Samuel ibn Tibbon, of which the best edition is that of Yehudah ibn Shmuel (Jerusalem: Mosad ha-Rav Kook, 1987), based on his earlier annotated editions. Two contemporary Hebrew translations exist. Yosef Kafih published a parallel Judeo-Arabic and Hebrew edition (Jerusalem: Mosad ha-Rav Kook, 1972), and Michael Schwarz an annotated Hebrew edition (Tel Aviv: Tel Aviv University, 1996). The best complete English translation is that of Shlomo Pines (Chicago: University of Chicago Press, 1963). An annotated edition of Michael Friedlander's English translation (London: Trübner, 1881) was published by Hebrew Publishing Company (New York, 1881), and a paperback edition without the notes was issued by Dover (New York, 1956). Selections were also translated by Lenn E.

Goodman in *Rambam: Readings in the Philosophy of Moses Maimonides* (New York: Viking, 1976).

2. The first to raise questions about Maimonides' theory of providence was Samuel ibn Tibbon, medieval Hebrew translator of the *Guide of the Perplexed*. Cf. Zvi Diesendruck, "Samuel and Moses ibn Tibbon on Maimonides' Theory of Providence," *Hebrew Union College Annual* 11 (1936): 341–65. Cf. Robert Eisen, "Samuel ibn Tibbon on the Book of Job," *AJS Review* 24/2 (1999): 263–300. The recent scholarly literature in English on Maimonides includes Martin D. Yaffe, "Providence in Medieval Aristotelianism: Moses Maimonides and Thomas Aquinas on the Book of Job," *Hebrew Studies* 20–21 (1979–80): 62–74; Jacob Levinger, "Maimonides' Exegesis of the Book of Job," in *Creative Biblical Exegesis: Christian and Jewish Hermeneutics through the Centuries,* ed. Benjamin Uffenheimer and Henning G. Reventlow (Sheffield, England: JSOT Press, 1988), 81–88; Idit Dobbs-Weinstein, "Medieval Biblical Commentary and Philosophical Inquiry as Exemplified in the Thought of Moses Maimonides and St. Thomas Aquinas," in *Moses Maimonides and His Time,* ed. Eric L. Ormsby (Washington, D.C.: Catholic University of America Press, 1989), 101–20.

3. See the discussion of these sources in Shlomo Pines's introduction to his English translation of the *Guide of the Perplexed,* "The Philosophic Sources of the *Guide of the Perplexed.*"

4. In *Guide of the Perplexed* 3:19–21, Maimonides refutes the philosophic arguments against God's knowledge of sensible particulars. Our doubts regarding God's knowledge arise from our own ignorance. God knows sensible particulars from the aspect of being their creator. Human knowledge is consequent on reality, but reality is consequent on God's knowledge of it as its creator. The error of the philosophers' arguments against divine knowledge of particulars arises in the fallacy that human knowledge (which follows from created reality) and divine knowledge (which establishes created reality) are in some respect synonymous. For Maimonides, the term *knowledge* is thus applied to God and to humans purely equivocally. God, in knowing himself, knows what derives from his acts—namely, existing things. Any apparent contradictions, such as those suggested by the philosophers, arise from the fallacious analogy of divine and human knowledge.

5. The most important general studies of the Kalam are those of Harry A. Wolfson, *The Philosophy of the Kalam* (Cambridge: Harvard University Press, 1976), and *Repercussions of the Kalam in Jewish Philosophy* (Cambridge: Harvard University Press, 1979).

6. My translation; cf. Kafih ed., 513–14, and Pines trans., 471.

7. Maimonides discusses intellectual immortality in his commentary to the Mishnah, *Pereq Ḥeleq* (M *Sanhedrin* 10). Arnold Wolf's English translation of this passage was published in Isadore Twersky, ed., *A Maimonides Reader* (New York: Behrman House, 1972), 401–23.

8. Maimonides cites the talmudic statement that "Job never existed, but was a parable" (TB *Bava Batra* 15a).

9. Yaffe, "Providence in Medieval Aristotelianism," 62, points out what he calls "the very symmetry of Maimonides' and Aquinas' differences of interpretation. Whereas Maimonides argues that God's answer to Job's question about divine providence implies that Job himself, though perfectly just, remains unwise, Aquinas argues, on the contrary, that Job, though perfectly wise, is unjust."

10. Levinger, "Maimonides' Exegesis of the Book of Job," 84, identifies Elihu's view with Maimonides' own "secret" (that is, esoteric) position. Yaffe, "Providence in Medieval Aristotelianism," 62, also maintains that Maimonides (and Aquinas) wrote esoterically about Job but does not make this identification. Dobbs-Weinstein, "Medieval Biblical Commentary," 116, is of the opinion that Maimonides and Aquinas "both clearly differentiate their views from Elihu's and Job's."

11. My translation, emphasis added; cf. Kafih ed., 541; Pines trans., 496.

12. On *taqlīd* and other terms for different types of tradition, see my articles "Saʿadiah Gaʾon and Moses Mendelssohn: Pioneers of Jewish Philosophy," in *Paradigms in Jewish Philosophy,* ed. Raphael Jospe (Madison, Wis.: Associated University Presses, 1997), 37–59; "Saʿadiah Gaʾon's 'Reliable Tradition': Who Are the 'Community of the Monotheists'?" (in Hebrew), *Daʿat: A Journal of Jewish Philosophy and Kabbalah* 41 (summer 1998): 5–18.

13. My translation, emphasis added; cf. Kafih ed., 537; Pines trans., 493.

14. Maimonides' disciple is usually identified as Joseph ben Judah ibn ʿAqnin (ca. 1150–1220), a Spanish philosopher and poet. That identifi-

cation is highly suspect. The disciple is more likely Joseph ben Judah ibn Shimᵓon, a Moroccan physician, poet, and philosopher.

15. *Guide of the Perplexed*, introduction, my translation; cf. Kafih ed., 3–5; Pines trans., 5–6.

16. My translations.

17. In other words, at the beginning of the story, Job and his associates affirm the position of the Torah. During the course of the story, as a result of Job's suffering, they all come to different conclusions and represent the various points of view discussed above, at which time Job adopts the Aristotelian view negating individual, personal providence.

18. See Leo Strauss, "How to Begin to Study *The Guide of the Perplexed*," introductory essay to the Shlomo Pines translation of the *Guide*, xi–lvi. For a different perspective on Maimonides' literary approach and the structure of the *Guide of the Perplexed,* see Raphael Jospe, "Gan ᶜEden Peraqav Shel ha-Moreh (On the Number and Division of Chapters in the *Guide of the Perplexed*)," in *Shlomo Pines Jubilee Volume* (Jerusalem: Hebrew University, 1988), 387–97.

19. Eisen, "Samuel ibn Tibbon," 293–94, points out "a philosophical problem in Maimonides' reading of Job. Maimonides sees Job as a figure who initially has only moral perfection, but by the end of the story achieves intellectual perfection as well. The question that seems to have been in [Samuel] ibn Tibbon's mind is how Job in fact achieved this latter perfection. Maimonides consistently depicts the process of philosophical education as a long and laborious one; and yet there is no indication on Maimonides' part as to how and when Job went through this process. In fact, if we take the story at face value, it would seem implausible that Job would have become intellectually perfect after a few— albeit lengthy—conversations with his friends. . . . Ibn Tibbon was moved by these considerations to posit a reading that is much more realistic from a philosophical standpoint: Job simply did not achieve intellectual perfection, but only an appreciation of its value as a prerequisite for immortality. He therefore did not experience prophecy."

20. Yaffe, "Providence in Medieval Aristotelianism," 65–66, recognizes that Maimonides' Job "stands in need of a quest for wisdom, i.e., . . . must become a philosopher" but does not make the explicit connection between Job and Maimonides' perplexed student.

21. Maimonides discusses and criticizes the Kalam in *Guide of the Perplexed* 1:71–76. Before Maimonides, Judah ha-Levi had also discussed the principles of the Kalam in *Kuzari* 5:15–18.

CHAPTER 21

SALVATION AND REDEMPTION IN THE JUDAIC TRADITION

David Rosen

In presenting Judaic perspectives on salvation and redemption, distinction must be made between the national dimensions on the one hand and the personal on the other, even though the latter is of course seen as related to the national whole, for better or worse (see TB *Kiddushin* 40b).

Individual Salvation

Biblical Teachings

Redemption and salvation imply the need for deliverance from a particular situation, condition, or debt. The Hebrew word for redemption, *gǝʾullāh*, implies "the prior existence of obligation." This word is used in Leviticus to describe the financial redemption of ancestral land from another to whom it has been sold (see Leviticus 25:25); the financial redemption of a member of one family bound in servitude to another family because of debt (see Leviticus 25:48–49); and the redemption of a home, field, ritually impure animal, or agricultural tithe that had been dedicated to the sanctuary by giving its financial value plus one-fifth in lieu thereof (see Leviticus 27).

In the case of a male who died childless, his brothers assumed an obligation to "redeem" the name of the deceased—that is, to save it from extinction by ensuring the continuity of his seed, lands, and filial tribute (see Deuteronomy 25:5–10; Ruth 4:1–10). In a case of murder, the *gôʾēl* was the blood avenger who sought to requite the wrong by seeking blood for blood, redeeming thereby, if not the "wandering soul" of the deceased, certainly the honor that had been desecrated (see Numbers 35:12–29; cf. Deuteronomy 4:42).

When translated into the realm of divine activity, because God is Lord of the Universe and owns all, the notion of redemption from debt or obligation is irrelevant. Rather, it is through divine involvement in the release and deliverance of the oppressed and vulnerable that God is seen as Redeemer, liberating people from their tribulations (see 2 Samuel 4:9; 1 Kings 1:29; Psalms 11:6; 119:134), and as Savior/Guardian of the orphan and widow (see Job 19:25; Psalm 68:6; Proverbs 23:10–11). However, in a deeper theological sense, every person is seen as condemned through his or her sins, not in any inherited or vicarious sense, but simply because of the consequences of sin and the fact that "there is no person who does not sin" (1 Kings 8:46; Ecclesiastes 7:20).

Just as the term *sin* is used in the Bible in terms of dereliction of duty toward others (see Judges 11:27; 1 Samuel 2:25; 2 Kings 18:14), so sin in the religious moral context is seen as the dereliction of the individual's duty toward God in terms of covenantal obligations (see Psalm 25:5–7; cf. 2 Samuel 12:13 and Jeremiah 14:20–21). It is, however, not seen as a tragic necessity but always as the fruit of will, and thus its guilt is always deserved. Because one can choose to do good, each individual is answerable for his or her wrongdoings.

As sin therefore is seen as rebellion against God, the consequences should be extremely severe. Thus the idea that punishment for sin is death (see, for example, 1 Samuel 2:25; cf. Deuteronomy 29:19) is embodied in the formula that "each man shall die for his [own] sins" (Deuteronomy 24:16; 2 Kings 14:6; cf. Numbers 27:3). The law of retaliation *(talion)* demanded that the offender should be punished according to his sin, although the possibility existed for substitution (see 2 Samuel 12:13–14), as well as for transferring the guilt to a scapegoat and expelling it (see Leviticus 16:22).

The sin offering was accordingly seen not only as purification for the individual, but above all as a means of obtaining God's forgiveness by serving as a "ransom," or *kōfer,* for the sinner, which thus granted "atonement," or *kapparah. Kōfer* was the legal term for the ransom or gift that was both to compensate and appease; in the case of manslaughter, restitution could be made by a gift to the victim's family of an ox (see Exodus 21:30), while such *kōfer nefesh,* "ransom for a life," was not permissible in the case of murder (see Numbers 35:31–32).

Every such sacrifice may be considered as a ransom, or *kōfer,* in the original sense of making a propitiatory gift for the purpose of atonement (*ləkapper;* see Leviticus 17:11). This idea of atonement is rooted in the perception of sin as causing a rift with and a distance from God and thus of the need to reconcile the soul of the sinner with God. In order to overcome this sense of estrangement from God, the sinner offers expiatory sacrifices not simply to appease God, but to place the sinner's soul in a different relation to him.

The continued spiritualization of atonement accordingly leads to the perception of sacrifice as peripheral to, symbolic of, or at least an extension of the essential internal process. Thus repentance itself is seen as having power to effect a reconciliation between the erstwhile sinner and the merciful God, who eagerly anticipates and accepts the sincere contrition of the penitent (see, for example, Isaiah 55:7; Jeremiah 4:1; Ezekiel 18:30–33; Jonah 3:10; Micah 7:18–19). In relation to this idea, as expressed in the Pentateuch, with Moses' intercession on behalf of the errant Israelites, the essential divine attributes of compassion, forgiveness, loving-kindness, and tolerance are revealed (see Exodus 34:1–9; Numbers 14:17–20). The value of an atoning sacrifice in this light is thus understood to be both an appeal to God's forgiving mercy and an inspiration to the sinner to duly repent. But it is sincere repentance and God's abundant love and compassion rather than the sacrifice that effect the reconciliation, the full "at-one-ment."

While a variety of idioms are used to describe repentance, they are all subsumed by one verb, *shûv,* meaning "return," which is prevalent in the Bible and from which flows the rabbinic concept of *təshûvāh.* The word combines within itself the two essential requisites of repentance—namely, to turn away from evil and to turn toward the good (see Isaiah 1:17; 33:15; 58:5; Jeremiah 7:3; 26:13; Amos 5:14–15; Psalms 15; 24:4; 34:15–16; 37:27). The motion of turning implies that through such effort—a power that God has given to all humankind—sinners can redirect their destiny.

That this concept was not a total prophetic innovation but goes back to Israel's ancient tradition is clear from Amos's use of it as understood, requiring no need for explanation (see Amos 4:6–11). This text, furthermore, expresses the idea of divine punishment as an incentive to repent and gain salvation, an idea that features prominently in Job (see Job 34:14–33; 36:2–21). Aside, therefore, from its independence from sacrifice, salvation from sin is thus perceived as overwhelmingly within the hands of the human person to achieve. Naturally this idea acquired substantial impetus during the exile, when the form of sacrificial atonement was not available. Accordingly, prayer assumed a growing importance as a vehicle for reconciliation with God, as is seen through the book of Psalms (see Hosea 14:3); other means included fasting and *ṣədāqāh* ("charity," or, better, "righteous response"; see, for example, Isaiah 58:1–3; Daniel 4:24; Joel 2:15–18; Zechariah 7:5).

Rabbinic Teachings

While the rabbis taught that all of Israel are allocated a portion in the world to come (see M *Sanhedrin* 10:1), it is only through obedience to the divine covenant, the Torah, that the attainment of such is guaranteed (see *Sifre* Deuteronomy 34:5; TB *Sanhedrin* 100a; TB *Avodah Zarah* 31; TB *Ta'anit* 11a–b; cf. *Leviticus Rabbah* 27).

Because the human being is created with free will and is therefore culpable for his evil deeds (see M *Avot* 3:15–16) and because there is not a righteous person on earth who does only good and sins not (see Ecclesiastes 7:20), the attribute of divine justice would condemn all (cf. *Genesis Rabbah* 8:11). However, divine justice is perceived by the rabbis as functioning in tension with the divine attribute of mercy. The latter provides from the very outset the means to ensure salvation for all in the form of repentance, *təshûvāh* (see TB *Pesahim* 54a; TY *Pe'ah* 17:1; *Genesis Rabbah* 1:4, 12; *Lamentations Rabbah* 3:5; *Midrash* on Psalm 57:90; cf. *Pesiqta Rabbati* 158b).

Perhaps an awareness of the historic development of the idea of salvation from sin is expressed in the following passage: "They asked Wisdom 'What is the sinner's punishment?' She said to them, 'Evil pursues sinners'" [Proverbs 13:21]. "They asked Prophecy 'What is the sinner's punishment?' She said to them 'The soul that sins, it shall die'" [Ezekiel 18:4]. "They asked Torah 'What is the sinner's punishment?' She said to them 'Let them bring a guilt offering and it shall atone for him.'" "They asked the Holy One Blessed Be He 'What's the sinner's punishment?' He said to them, 'Let him repent (do *təshûvāh*) and it shall atone for him'" (see TY *Makkot* 2:6). Thus in the aforementioned tension, it is the divine attribute of mercy that gains the "upper hand" as God awaits and assists the sinner to return to him (see T *Sanhedrin* 8:3; TY *Makkot* 2:6; TY *Berakhot* 4:2; TB *Rosh ha-Shanah* 17–18; TB *Pesahim* 119a; TB *Yoma* 86a, b; *Sifre* 60b; *Sifra Behukotai* 8:6; *Canticles Rabbah* 6:1; *Ecclesiastes Rabbah* 7; *Exodus Rabbah* 19:3; *Numbers Rabbah* 10).

The perceived power of repentance is expressed in the words "The sinner who repents is on a [spiritual] level that the completely righteous [who have never sinned] cannot reach" (TB *Berakhot* 34b). In consonance with biblical teaching, such repentance is seen as dependent on sincere contrition, confession, and commitment not to backslide (see *Sifra Aharei Mot* 2:4; *Sifra Behukotai* 6:34; *Sifre* 5:5; TB *Ta'anit* 16a; TB *Hagigah* 5a; TB *Yoma* 86b; TB *Berakhot* 12b; *Pesiqta Rabbati* 198b; cf. Maimonides, *Yad,* Hilchot Teshuvah 2:2), and in the case of sins against other persons, additional requirements include reparations (where necessary) and seeking appeasement (see *Sifra Aharei Mot* 8:1; M *Yoma* 8:9, and *Bava Qamma* 8:7; Maimonides, *Yad,* Hilchot Teshuvah 2:2). Accordingly, the fulness of *təshûvāh* depends on following the "right" path. "On public fast days the elders of the congregation would declare 'Brothers it is not said of the men of Nineveh' and 'God saw their sackcloth and their fasting,' but 'And God saw their deeds that they had turned from their evil ways'" (Jonah 3:10; see M *Ta'anit* 2:1).

Such is the power of repentance that not only can a sincere act of repentance for one sin in itself atone for all one's sins (see TB *Berakhot* 12b), but sincere contrition even on the deathbed of the most errant sinner has the ability to guarantee his salvation—that is, a portion in the world to come (see T *Kiddushin* 1:15; TB *Kiddushin* 40b; TB *Avodah Zarah* 17a; *Genesis Rabbah* 65:22; *Ruth Rabbah* 6:2). While repentance, like obedience, is best undertaken out of love of God, even repentance from fear is better than none at all (see TB *Yoma* 86b). The rabbis do not see the latter as ideal, but they do not deny its efficacy.[1]

As George Moore has correctly pointed out, it is this idea of repentance that "may properly be called the Jewish doctrine of salvation."[2] However, it must be reiterated that repentance is not a process by which one makes initial entry into the grace of God and enjoys the benefits of his mercy, but rather a means by which one is *restored* to that proximity. "There is no failing in man, whether collectively or as an individual, which requires special divine intervention and which cannot be remedied, with the guidance of the Torah, by man himself."[3] "To use other language, one is already 'saved'; what is needed is the maintenance of a right attitude toward God[, even though w]ithout it, the mercy of God is of no avail."[4]

In addition, as in Job, the power of suffering is recognized as an impetus to atonement and also as an atonement in and of itself (see Mekilta *Yitro* 10; *Sifre* Deuteronomy 32; TB *Berakhot* 5a), particularly for the righteous, thus ensuring their full reward in paradise (see *Genesis Rabbah* 33; *Leviticus Rabbah* 27; TB *Kiddushin* 40b). Death itself is seen as atoning for sin (see Mekilta *Yitro* 7; *Sifre* 4:7; TB *Yoma* 86a; TB *Berakhot* 60a); this understanding seemingly developed from the idea that capital punishment at the hands of the court, as any other legally sanctioned punishment, atoned for the sin, provided that the offender had repented (see M *Sanhedrin* 6:2; T *Sanhedrin* 9:5).

It might also be mentioned that we find within rabbinic thought the concept of Gehinnom (Gehenna, or purgatory) as atonement, purification, and thus salvation for the wicked, who when purified ascend to the Garden of Eden (paradise) (see *Eduyyot* 2; *Yalqut* Isaiah 26; *Numbers Rabbah* 81). The power of the atonement, with its ultimate consequence for the soul's salvation (that is, entry into paradise), is also ascribed to poverty (see *Pesiqta Rabbati* 25:165a); sharing one's table with the poor (see TB *Berakhot* 55a; *Tanhuma Vayishlach* 6); life-transforming events (see TY *Bikkurim* 3:65; *Midrash* Samuel 17); living or being buried in the land of Israel (see *Genesis Rabbah* 96; TY *Kilʾayim* 9:32; TB *Ketubbot* 111a); and the very study of Torah, which is declared to be more effective than the sacrifices of the temple when it is accompanied by good deeds (see TB *Rosh ha-Shanah* 18a; TB *Yevamot* 105a; *Leviticus Rabbah* 25).

National Salvation

Biblical Teachings

In premonarchic Israel, the concept of salvation is identified with the national well-being and security of the tribes that have settled the land and enjoyed the bounty of the earth in safety; it refers to the "victoriousness" of the people whose enemies are humbled and subservient, as described in Moses' blessings: "Happy are you O Israel, who is like you, a people saved [*nôsha‹*] by the Lord" (Deuteronomy 33:29). The idea is subsequently related to deliverance from religioethical degeneration and the consequences of disobedience to divine charge.

In early prophetic literature, the threefold formula of warning against sin, punishment for disobedience, and deliverance becomes a recurrent theme. Even when the children of Israel as a whole are threatened with divine destruction as punishment for the sin of worshiping the golden calf, this is qualified by the guarantee of continuity and destiny through Moses himself (see Deuteronomy 9:14; cf. Exodus 32:10 and Numbers 14:12). These motifs are woven through the fabric of the book of Judges, and similarly the prophetic protest that defied kings and condemned dynasties aimed its destructiveness at salvation.

The view of the covenantal relationship as conditional upon the people's obedience, with expulsion from the land as the penalty for their disobedience, apparently drew its impetus from the Aramaean wars. With the ravaging of the people and the land came the perception that incurring divine wrath could ultimately lead to Israel's exile (see Deuteronomy 4:16; cf. 28:36, 64; 29:24–27; 31:29). Such punishment seemed designed to evoke contrition leading to divine salvation. The guarantee of the latter lies both in the character of God and in the covenantal relationship between him and Israel. Because God is merciful, "He will not forsake you nor destroy you and will not forget the Covenant of your Fathers which he swore unto them" (Deuteronomy 4:31). Thus a transformation in Israelite eschatology transfers the premonarchic view of salvation to the future as a hope for Israel's national salvation (see 1 Kings 19:10, 14).

The term *yəshūʿāh* (similarly, *təshūʿāh*), originally meaning freedom and ease from restrictions and narrow straits, was understood in the sense of victorious deliverance from one's enemies (see Judges 10:12; 1 Samuel 2:1; 14:45; 2 Samuel 22:51; Isaiah 49:8). One who leads to victory is therefore the *mōshīaʿ*, that is, savior (see, for example, Judges 3:9, 15; 6:36, 37; cf. 1 Samuel 25:26; Psalm 44:4), and the prayer *hōshīʿāh-naʾ* (hosanna, for example, in Psalm 118:25) means "give victory." Probably the king was greeted thus. Accordingly, the ultimate Savior who gives victory is naturally seen as God himself and is thus described as *Elohei Yishenu*, "our victorious God" (1 Chronicles 16:35; Psalm 79:9).

With exile, this concept of "victorious salvation" came to be understood in terms of the survival of the remnant and the return of "the saved." God was accordingly seen as the Savior who preserves the remnant, ingathers the exiles, restores the people to its land and glory (see Isaiah 12:2; 43:3, 11; 45:15, 21; 49:26; 60; 62:11; Jeremiah 31:10; Zechariah 8:7), and ultimately ushers in an era of human perfection and universal harmony in a world imbued with the spirit of God (see Isaiah 11:10; 52:10; Zechariah 14:9, 16).

The terms *yəshūʿāh* ("salvation") and *gəʾullāh* ("redemption")— as applied to the messianic advent—are identical. In the same way that God is the *mōshīaʿ*, he is the *gôʾēl*, or Redeemer (see Isaiah 41:14; 44:6, 24; 47:4; 48:17, 20; 52:9; 60:16; 62:11–12; 63:9; Psalm 74:2). It was, moreover, natural for the people to perceive the God of Israel, Father of orphans, Defender of the widows (see Psalm 68:6), and Redeemer of the afflicted (see Job 19:25 and above on individual salvation) as having a special responsibility to redeem them (see Isaiah 35:10).

Both the roots *YŠ˂ and *G˒L (as with *PDH, meaning "to release") refer to a deliverance that results in the well-being of its beneficiaries. This idea was extended to apply not only to the physical deliverance of Israel but also to its spiritual redemption from sin (see Psalm 130:8) as well as its renewal (see Jeremiah 31:30–34; 32:39–40; Ezekiel 11:17–20; 36:26; 37:23–28). The role of the Messiah, therefore, is not that of the Redeemer. God alone is the Savior. While the former is established as shepherd of God's flock (see Ezekiel 34:23), the national hope for redemption was centered on God himself. Notable in this regard is the frequent absence of a messianic personality in prophetic visions of redemption, which is similarly the case in apocryphal works such as Tobit and Ben Sira.

Rabbinic Teachings

The term *gə˒ullāh* in rabbinic literature is applied almost exclusively to national redemption, which is synonymous with national freedom. In accordance with biblical prophecy, the rabbis looked forward to a regenerative messianism in which the Israelite monarchy is reestablished, the nation is delivered from foreign servitude, the exiles are ingathered, and the temple is finally rebuilt. Their aspirations were not altogether free from the utopian and apocalyptic trends cultivated in certain circles and some of these ideas were tainted with an antinomious or an anarchistic bias. Nevertheless, fundamentally the Sages retained their realistic orientation toward a religious-national-political restoration.[5]

However, in their historiosophy, the rabbis introduced a bold mystical element into the concept of redemption with the suggestion that the divine presence itself is in exile with the people of Israel. Thus, in redeeming his people, God, so to speak, redeems himself (see *Sifre* 161; TB *Megillah* 29a).

In keeping with the prophetic vision, Jewish national revival was seen as a prior condition for the realization of the universal principles that were to unite hitherto hostile nations and pave the way to a new era where goodness would reign supreme and all peoples would be gathered beneath the wings of the divine presence (see *Tanhuma* Genesis 108; *Canticles Rabbah* 1:21; cf. T *Berakhot* 7:2). One might note that in viewing Israel as a vehicle for the ultimate redemption of all mankind, even exile itself was seen as having a redemptive value; for example, "Israel was only exiled among the Gentiles in order that proselytes would join them" (TB *Pesahim* 87b; cf. *Leviticus Rabbah* 6:5).

The Initiative in National Redemption

Within biblical literature we find a tension—if not disagreement—regarding where responsibility for the redemptive initiative lies. Indeed, these differences of perception may be seen as distinguishing different trends of thinking on the subject within rabbinic thought, within medieval Jewish philosophy and mysticism, and even within the differing Jewish religious attitudes toward the modern political reestablishment of Jewish sovereignty in the land of Israel.

In the case of personal salvation, even though such is made possible by divine grace and mercy, the active initiative must be taken by the human individual—"there is no atonement without *təshûvāh* (repentance)" is the rabbinical dictum that sums up the biblical concept.

Biblical Teachings

The requirement of *təshûvāh* is also made with regard to national salvation. However, there is a difference of opinion concerning to what extent national salvation is dependent on repentance. Clearly, in the earlier scriptures it was seen as fundamental. For Amos, salvation from exile and destruction depends on repentance. "Seek good and do not do evil, in order that you shall live, and it shall be so [that] God the Lord of Hosts shall be with you as you have said. Hate evil and love good and present justice in the gate. Perhaps God the Lord of Hosts will be gracious towards the remnant of Joseph" (Amos 5:14–15; cf. 4:9–11). In this view, the consolation of redemption is only for the righteous.

The promise in the thirtieth chapter of Deuteronomy similarly places the onus on the people: "And it shall come to pass when all these things will come upon you, the blessing and the curse, and you will take it to heart amongst the nations where the Lord has cast you away there. And you will return to the Lord your God. . . . And the Lord will return your captivity" (Deuteronomy 30:1–3). In the same way, although in Hosea we encounter the covenant born out of divine promise not to destroy Ephraim and to ingather the exiles (see Hosea 11:8–11), the initiative that brings about redemption is first and foremost the repentance of Israel: "Return O Israel to the Lord your God for you have stumbled in your iniquity" (Hosea 14:1).

Isaiah also sees redemption as coming through repentance and righteousness: "Zion will be redeemed by justice and those in it who repent by righteousness" (Isaiah 1:27). However, in contradistinction, in the latter part of Isaiah in particular, the advent of redemption is brought by divine initiative alone. Such is the overwhelming nature of the punishment that it is God alone who can redeem. Even when Israel acknowledges her sins, it is not she who initiates the process of salvation, but rather God's commitment to justice that is portrayed as leading him to wondrously redeem Israel (see Isaiah 59:12–20; cf. 54:8; 60:10).

Yet the prophet Micah articulates the idea of the divine initiative in redemption with innovative force. While he asserts the overall primacy of humankind's freedom of choice, Israel's national survival is seen as an act of God's grace, and through his redemption, Israel obtains an eschatological remission of her sins: "Who is God like You, pardoning iniquity and passing over transgression of the remnant of His inheritance. He does not maintain His anger forever because He delights in lovingkindness. *He will return* and have mercy upon us, He will subdue our iniquities and

You will cast all their sins into the depths of the sea" (Micah 7:18–19, emphasis added). Similar emphasis on divine grace as the essential active ingredient in redemptive atonement is expressed in the book of Psalms (see, for example, Psalm 130:7–8).

The question of initiative is resolved by Jeremiah through seeing the people's repentance as the beginning of salvation (see Jeremiah 24:7; 29:10–15), from which comes full divine redemption that brings (in keeping with Micah) forgiveness and purification from sin (see Jeremiah 33:8; 50:20) and finally a new and everlasting covenant (see Jeremiah 32:40; 50:5; cf. 31:32). Conversely, in the book of Lamentations the process of this redemptive tension is viewed as commencing with God: "Return us to you, O Lord, and we shall return; renew our days as of old" (Lamentations 5:21).

The tension is less balanced in Ezekiel's prophecy of redemption. He does on one occasion place the initiative before the people, calling on them to transform their own hearts and spirits and thus guarantee their salvation (see Ezekiel 18:30–31). However, Ezekiel 11:17–20 portrays the initiative as divine; moreover, it is only after the ingathering by God himself that the people's conversion takes place. This is clearly the dominant view of the prophet, and it is expressed even more powerfully in Ezekiel 36 and 37. Above all, the redemption of Israel is portrayed as resulting not only from divine impetus, but from the divine "need" that God's name be sanctified among the nations (see Ezekiel 36:22–23). This rationale for redemption reflects the tradition that appears in Exodus 32:12 and in Numbers 14:13–16 (see Deuteronomy 9:28 as the argument that led God to reconsider his decision to destroy Israel). Accordingly, redemption for the sake of God himself overshadows the idea of human repentance in Ezekiel.

Rabbinic Teachings

The question of initiative in the process of redemption led to much discussion and argument among the rabbis. The major text on the subject in the Babylonian Talmud, *Sanhedrin* 97–98, highlights the differences of opinion. The earliest of the discussions and opinions that appear in the text are from Rabbi Eliezer, the son of Hyrcanus, and Rabbi Joshua. Rabbi Eliezer declared that "if Israel repents, they will be redeemed, if not they will not be saved." In other words, salvation depends first and foremost on Israel's moral initiative. Rabbi Joshua, however, adds that "if they do not repent, the Holy One, Blessed be He, sets up before them a king whose decrees are as severe as those of Haman, and Israel will repent [will do *təshûvāh*] and be rehabilitated" (TB *Sanhedrin* 97b). Repentance is indeed an essential requirement, according to Rabbi Joshua; however, God is seen here as the initiator of negative historical experience, which draws the people back toward him.

The positions became sharper in the debate that follows between Rav (also known as Abba Arikha) and Samuel, two of the greatest Babylonian sages of the third century C.E. Rav maintains that "all appointed times of redemption are over and the matter only depends upon repentance and good deeds." Regardless of past redemptions, he says, ultimate salvation depends on Israel's initiative. Samuel, on the other hand, declares that "it is enough for the mourner to remain in his mourning" (TB *Sanhedrin* 97b). In other words, Israel's task is simply to loyally survive her historic predicament, but the initiative for redemption comes from God.

Rav's position is supported by Rabbi Joshua, the son of Levi, in the story of his encounters with the prophet Elijah and the Messiah—he concludes that the Messiah will come "today, if Israel but hearkens to God's voice" (Psalm 95:7). This view is reiterated concisely by Rabbi Jonathan: "Great is [the power of] 'təshûvāh' that it brings redemption" (TB *Yoma* 86b; cf. *Pirqe de Rabbi Eliezer* 43).

Differences of opinion may be seen throughout the various comments of the rabbis concerning national redemption. However, the divine supernatural perspective proportionately outweighs the human natural approach with an abundance of descriptions concerning the social disasters, spiritual decay, and disintegration that will precede redemption (see, for example, TB *Sanhedrin* 97a; *Sotah* 40b).

This perception is behind the declaration that Israel is under oath not to go up and forcibly reconquer the Holy Land (see TB *Ketubbot* 111a), and it is arguably this approach that is further emphasized in midrashic literature, where future redemption is compared advantageously with past redemptions. The latter did not last, according to the Midrash, because they came about through human agencies. But future redemption will be accomplished by God himself and thus be everlasting (see *Midrash* on Psalm 31:2).

Also more in consonance with the supernatural approach is the perception of divine redemption as a response to the "merit of the Fathers," whether it be that of the patriarchs Moses and Aaron or the elders (see *Exodus Rabbah* 15; cf. TY *Sanhedrin* 6:2; *Leviticus Rabbah* 36).

An approach that combines these two perceptions of redemption is contained in the words of Rabbi Yohanan (TB *Sanhedrin* 98a): "The son of David will come in a generation that is either completely innocent [and thus merits salvation] or completely culpable," such that salvation will come solely through divine initiative.

However, a more integrated reconciliation of the question of initiative, in keeping with the prophetic vision of redemption as a two-way process, is alluded to by Rabbi Akiva in the Mishnah. "Happy are you, Israel. Before whom do you purify yourselves and who purifies you! Your Father in Heaven, for it is said, 'I will sprinkle pure water upon you and you shall be pure; from all your impurities will I purify you. I will also give you a new heart and I will put a new spirit within you' (Ezekiel 36:25–26): and it is said, the Lord is the *mikveh* of Israel (Jeremiah 14:8) [literally, 'the hope of Israel,' but used here in a play of words to mean 'the ritual bath of Israel']: just as the ritual bath *[mikveh]* purifies the impure, so does God purify Israel" (M *Yoma* 8:9).

Similarly, and perhaps most reflective of this tension of initiative in redemption as found within Jeremiah in particular, are the words of Rabbi Yessa (see *Canticles Rabbah* 5:3): "The Holy One, Blessed be He, said to Israel: 'My children, open for me an aperture of repentance as small as a needle's eye and I will open for you an opening through which wagons and carriages can enter.'" Salvation is thus portrayed as a joint endeavor, and while the initiative comes from Israel's initial move along the path of *təshûvāh*, it is God who takes over in facilitating full redemption.

Later Views of Salvation and Redemption

In Medieval Jewish Philosophy

These personal and national perspectives emerge also within medieval Jewish philosophy. The viewpoint that retains basic features of talmudic soteriology on the personal level tends to see national redemption in supernatural terms. This approach is espoused by Saʿadiah Gaon,[6] as well as by Judah ha-Levi,[7] Nachmanides, Hasdai Crescas,[8] and Joseph Albo.[9]

Saʿadiah declares that since man, though created finite, is the ultimate purpose of creation, God intended from the beginning that man should attain redemption from his finite condition. For this purpose God revealed his will through the Torah at Sinai. Individual salvation is thus obtained through obedience to the divine commandments (although Saʿadiah also sees salvation as the attainment of the righteous among all peoples). However, Saʿadiah sees the messianic age of national redemption and the subsequent world of final judgment as separate miraculous events of divine initiative. In this perspective, national redemption in itself is of a supernatural character.

On the other hand, the latter is viewed as integrally related to personal salvation in the naturalist philosophical school influenced by Aristotelian and Neoplatonic concepts in Maimonides,[10] as well as in Ibn Gabirol,[11] Ibn Ezra, and Gersonides.[12] Maimonides sees the universe as the result of God's goodness. However, he does not see it as created for the sake of humankind, which he views not as the direct creation of the Godhead but rather as the product of successive series of emanations in which the material world and thus human beings are created out of matter. A mortal being overcomes its finite nature as matter by raising itself through the higher intellect via metaphysical and scientific studies. Accordingly, through transcending the material dimensions of existence and thus developing the spiritual soul, one ultimately gains immortality through the latter, which continues after the death of the material body.

In the same way, redemption is wrought not only for Israel but also for the world through a commensurate collective raising of the intellect and spirit. This is Maimonides' understanding of the nature of təshûvāh (Maimonides, Yad, Hilchot Teshuvah 6:4)— it brings salvation for both the individual and the nation (Maimonides, Yad, Hilchot Teshuvah 7:5; 9:2) and will take place in a "natural" way (cf. Maimonides, Yad, Hilchot Melachim 11:3; 12); through it all humankind will be redeemed.[13]

In Kabbalah

Similar differences of perception regarding the initiative of national salvation are to be found, *mutatis mutandis*, within Kabbalah. For the kabbalists, exile reflected the impaired condition of creation. The redemption of the Jewish people and the universal recognition of the divine presence and name would bring about salvation in the sense of full reparation. Where Kabbalah went beyond the dominant traditional view of salvation was in its portrayal of the unredeemed state of humankind and the world as the result of Adam's original sin (for example, in Ra'aya Meheimna and Tikkunei HaZohar). Although not normative, this position is nevertheless based on certain rabbinic texts—for example, *Deuteronomy Rabbah* 9; TB *Avodah Zarah* 8a; TB *Shabbat* 140b.

This idea is particularly developed in Lurianic Kabbalah. While the Spanish Kabbalists saw redemption as essentially a miraculous event unrelated to human endeavor, the alternative view espoused by the followers of Lurianic Kabbalah was that redemption is no more than an external manifestation of internal *tikkūn* ("restitution" or "reconstitution"), which depends on the deeds of Israel and its way of life. Salvation is thus seen as dependent on human action, which initiates the messianic advent.

This outlook, according to Gershom Scholem, nurtured the Sabbatian debacle; thus, in reaction, the subsequent Hassidic movement sought to mute the dangers of the utopianism within the Lurianic Kabbalah that it adopted. This was done by reverting to the traditional teaching of distinguishing between national redemption and personal salvation. Salvation for the individual is thus seen as concerned with the mystical redemption of the soul and is divested of any messianic connotation. Accordingly, human initiative is limited to this realm, while God is seen as bringing ultimate national and cosmic redemption.

Modern Zionism

Emancipation and enlightenment generated new understandings of Judaism and Jewish observance in modern society. The reformers did see this process as having "redemptive" significance for Jewry. However, they viewed this not in the traditional context of the return of the exiles to the land of Israel but rather in the context of a universal implementation of the social and civil rights and the justice to which Jews would contribute and from which they would benefit, as enunciated by the ancient prophets of Israel.

The political movement for secular national redemption—Zionism—was inspired by eighteenth-century rationalism and galvanized by nineteenth-century nationalism. Though secular, the idea was naturally expressed within the framework of the traditional Jewish concept of a national redemptive return to the land. However, paralleling the differing perceptions of the redemptive initiative were the two diametrically opposed responses to Zionism from within the Jewish religious community.

Ultraorthodoxy rejected Zionism as running contrary to the exclusively divine initiative for national redemption, as well as embodying modern secularism within Jewry, which was seen as inimical to the traditional Jewish Weltanschauung and interests. Religious Zionism, on the other hand, perceived the secular movement as part and parcel of the manifestation of the obligatory human initiative in redemption to reestablish independent Jewish life in the land. For religious Zionism, the establishment of the state of Israel was a manifestation of the divine presence itself through secular agencies. Its followers refer to the state of Israel in prayer and religious celebration as "The First Flowering of Our Redemption."

Ultraorthodoxy was forced by developments in Europe (the Shoah, or Holocaust, and destruction of the European centers of Jewish life and learning) and by the subsequent establishment of the state to qualify its opposition and come to terms with the state, at the very least as an "undesirable necessity." Nevertheless, ultraorthodoxy continued to deny the state of Israel any inherent religious, let alone redemptive, character.

Both the establishment of the state itself and the incorporation of religious Zionism into the political mainstream appeared to emphatically endorse its religiopolitical approach over that of ultraorthodoxy. This success, however, was not without its price. A moderate religious nationalist activism gave way increasingly to a prophetic dispensationalist militancy, which interpreted as the overwhelming divine agenda not only the return of the people to the land, but the return of the land to the people (albeit primarily as a result of conflict) and thus the obligation to settle it. Aside from the moral consequences of making territory a primary value, this attitude placed the bulk of religious Zionism and its leadership in an increasingly extreme right-wing position on the Israeli political spectrum and undermined religious Zionism's original aspiration to serve as a bridge between modernity and tradition within the Jewish nation.

However, not all religious Zionists took this ideological route. The religious Zionist peace movements and the new religious political party, Meimad, that joined together with the Labor Party for the 1999 elections to form one Israel, vocally inveighed against such militancy—both on practical and moral grounds. Their position reflects an activism that recognizes and places limits on the extent to which human initiative in redemption may be considered legitimate. Accordingly, this ideology of the religious peace camp in Israel may be viewed as a modern articulation of scriptural and rabbinic understanding of compromise between the divine and human initiative in the national redemptive process.

Notes

1. See Solomon Schechter, "Repentance: Means of Reconciliation," in *Aspects of Rabbinic Theology* (New York: Schocken, 1961), 313–43.

2. George F. Moore, *Judaism* (Cambridge: Harvard University Press, 1966), 1:500.

3. David Flusser, "Redemption: In the Talmud," in *Encyclopedia Judaica,* 14:3.

4. E. P. Sanders, *Paul and Palestinian Judaism: A Comparison of Patterns of Religion* (Philadelphia: Fortress, 1977), 178.

5. See Ephraim E. Urbach's discussion, "On Redemption," in *The Sages: Their Concepts and Beliefs,* trans. Israel Abrahams (Cambridge: Harvard University Press, 1987), 649–95.

6. Saʿadiah Gaʾon, *The Book of Beliefs and Opinions,* trans. Samuel Rosenblatt (New Haven: Yale University Press, 1948).

7. Judah ha-Levi, *The Kuzari: An Argument for the Faith of Israel* (New York: Shocken, 1964).

8. Hasdai Crescas, *Sefer Or Adonai (Light of the Lord)* (Jerusalem: Makor, 1970).

9. Joseph Albo, *Sefer ha-ʾIkarim* (Jerusalem: Bialik Institute, 1967).

10. Moses Maimonides, *The Guide of the Perplexed*, trans. Shlomo Pines (Chicago: University of Chicago Press, 1963).

11. Ibn Gabirol, *Mekor Hayyim* (Tel Aviv: Mahbarot le-sifrut, 1950).

12. Gersonides (Levi ben Gershom), *Milhamot ha-Shem* (Riva di Trento, 1560).

13. Maimonides, *Guide of the Perplexed*, 3:11.

CHAPTER 22

A Simḥat Torah Practice and the Ephraimite Tradition

Seth Ward

I dedicate this to Truman G. Madsen, "Head of the Academy," in friendship. In the Jewish calendar, Simḥat Torah, the "Rejoicing of the Torah," is the date on which the annual cycle of reading ends with Deuteronomy and is immediately renewed with reading from the first chapter of Genesis. This day is the final day of the fall holy days. In Israel, the ending and beginning of the reading cycle is celebrated on Shemini ʿAtzeret, the "Eighth Day of Assembly," meaning the eighth day following the seven days of Sukkot, the Feast of Tabernacles.[1]

Torah scrolls read in the synagogue contain the five books of Moses written in Hebrew on parchment leaves sewn into a scroll and mounted on two wooden rollers. In the practice of most Jews whose recent ancestors came from central and eastern Europe, after each reading of the Torah a congregant is given the honor of grasping the handles of the rollers, lifting up the Torah scroll, and displaying it to the congregation. In many Jewish congregations, on Simḥat Torah the raising of the Torah is completed in a unique manner. Rather than raising the scroll in the usual way, the congregant chosen for this honor grasps the left roller with his right hand and vice versa, flipping the Torah around as it is raised so that the text of the scroll faces the congregation rather than the person lifting it.

It is unlikely that the practice itself is ancient or expresses a profound theological lesson, and it is not my purpose to explain the principles and beliefs that in fact gave rise to it. Indeed, to quote Arnold Eisen, "Practice certainly should not be seen as the mere enactment or expression of belief. Very often it is the other way around. . . . Part of the attraction of a particular practice lies precisely in the fact that one can find it meaningful for a *variety* of reasons or in the absence of any reason whatsoever."[2] Thus what is important is often not exactly how the practice arose—often this is unrecoverable—but the reasons offered by the faithful to render it meaningful. For the believer, the words of written revelation and oral tradition are thus translated into practices that tend to fill every available moment of life with references to Torah, a process I have called "inpraxation."[3] We will look at one set of reasons for reversing the handles of the Torah Scroll on Simhat Torah, associating this practice with the biblical figure of Ephraim, son of Joseph, or with his descendants, the tribe of Ephraim.

Rabbi Abraham David Wahrman (d. 1840), sometimes known as the "Holy Excellence *(ha-gaon ha-kadosh)* of Buczacz," suggests two reasons in his book *Eshel Avraham (The Grove of Abraham).*[4] First, Wahrman connects it with the well-known talmudic saying, "Turn it and turn it, for everything is in it" (*Avot* 5:22).[5] This is, of course, a play on words. In context, "turn it" is a figure of speech that does not mean to turn the scroll around but to turn the pages over in contemplation; an idiomatic translation would be "Study the Torah again and again."[6]

The other reason he gives is that "the prince of Ephraim offered his sacrifice on the eighth day."[7] This can only be a reference to the offerings of the tribal leaders at the dedication of the desert sanctuary (Numbers 7:12–83). Today, according to the sage of

Buczacz, the celebrations on the Eighth Day of Assembly affirm that the "words of the Scribes are dear to us, both those that are new and those that are old." No doubt this is a reference to the fact that the practices of Simḥat Torah are not based on biblical commandments and are not found in the writings of the earliest rabbis. Moreover, the customs of this day (including calling each congregant to the Torah) "add extra blessings," presumably both in the technical sense of adding more repetitions of the blessing formula, "Blessed art thou, O Lord," and of increasing the blessings to be invoked upon the congregation.[8] The connection with Ephraim himself is recalled—and the practice of reversing the hands when raising the Torah scroll is finally explained—by referring to Genesis 48:14. Joseph had presented his sons to his father for a blessing. Joseph placed Ephraim on his own right, to the left of his father, who nevertheless "put his right hand on Ephraim, even though he was the younger . . . he crossed his arms [sikēl et yādāv]" (Genesis 48:14).

The words of the blessing pronounced by Father Jacob on this occasion also figure in another Simḥat Torah ritual, attested since the sixteenth century, although no explicit mention of Ephraim is made in this connection.[9] All children under the age of thirteen are called to the Torah, where they are offered Jacob's blessing to Ephraim and Manasseh: "May the Angel who redeems me from all evil . . ." (Genesis 48:16).

According to the Midrash, Jacob gave an extra blessing to Ephraim at this time: "Ephraim, you are the Head of the Academy and Leader of the tribes, and in days to come my most excellent and celebrated descendants will be called by your name."[10] The Midrash then identifies two non-Ephraimites linked to the tribe because they were called *efrati*, a Hebrew term that may be translated "Ephrathite" or "Ephraimite," thus referring either to Ephrath, another name for Bethlehem, or to a person from the tribe or geographical region of Ephraim. These are David the son of Jesse (of Judah) and Elkanah the father of Samuel, who was, according to Chronicles, a Levite.[11]

Apparently the offering of the prince of Ephraim provides the rabbi of Buczacz with the connection between the crossing of Jacob's hands and the reversing of the Torah scroll on Simḥat Torah. But this is problematic: The leader of Ephraim in fact made his offerings on the seventh day of the dedication ceremonies, not the eighth (Numbers 7:48). According to rabbinic tradition, this was indeed the Sabbath day, as the individual offerings of the tribes began on the first of Nisan, which was a Sunday, and Ephraim's sacrifice was thus on the Sabbath.[12] According to the Midrash, the honor of presenting a gift on the Sabbath fell to Ephraim as a reward for Joseph's fidelity to the Sabbath.[13]

Perhaps Ephraim's offering had—at least for Rabbi Wahrman—relevance to the independent nature of the Shemini ʿAtzeret festival. In temple practice, as understood by the rabbis, the statutory public sacrifices were considered to supersede the Sabbath, but Sabbath observance precluded personal offerings. Moreover, if Ephraim's sacrifice was merely one-twelfth of a group offering by the twelve tribes, it would not have been considered an independent sacrifice and also would have been precluded by the Sabbath. Thus the fact that the prince of Ephraim could bring his sacrifice on the Sabbath indicates that this was both a community sacrifice and an independent offering.[14] This corresponds to a point made by Wahrman, who concludes his comments on Ephraim's sacrifice and blessing by declaring that Shemini ʿAtzeret, the Eighth Day of Assembly, has "its own sacrifice and its own blessing"; the independence of this holiday is a problem raised in rabbinic literature.[15] Could it be that the argument that arose from the offering of Ephraim on the Sabbath led to this conclusion about Shemini ʿAtzeret and that this association in turn was the reason the rabbi of Buczacz thought that Ephraim's offering was made on the eighth day?

Having worked together with Truman Madsen and members of the Latter-day Saint community on *Covenant and Chosenness in Mormonism and Judaism*,[16] it comes naturally to me to recall their identification with the sons of Joseph, in particular with the tribe of Ephraim. Although celebrated in different ways and, of course, with different scriptural canons, the celebration of reading and studying scripture in a never-ending cycle is shared by Latter-day Saints and Jews. So, too, is the careful attention to the proper bounds of observing the Sabbath. Perhaps most telling is the midrashic blessing of Ephraim. It connects Ephraim with David, son of Jesse the Ephrati, who unified the tribes, founded Jerusalem on Mount Zion, and was the sweet singer of the Psalms. Moreover, it associates Ephraim's reputation with the intellectual vigor of the "Head of the Academy." How well this resonates with a community which declares that "the glory of God is intelligence,"[17] and how well this resonates with the exemplary career and character of this volume's honoree.

Notes

1. See Leviticus 23:26, 39; Numbers 29:35. Outside of Israel, the "Eighth Day of Assembly" is traditionally observed for two days, the second of which is celebrated as Simḥat Torah.

2. Arnold Eisen, *Rethinking American Judaism* (Ann Arbor, Mich.: Frankel Center for Jewish Studies, 1999), 3, emphasis in original.

3. See, for example, my introduction to *ʿAvoda and ʿIbada: Liturgy and Ritual in Islamic and Judaic Societies* (Leiden: Brill, 1999), 5/1:1–6; and Seth Ward, "Religious Ethics in the University Setting: The University of Denver Student Symposium on Jewish Ethics," *Panorama: International Journal of Comparative Religious Education and Values* 12/2 (2000): 87.

4. The title of the book is a play on words, a reference both to the author's name and to Genesis 21:33. "Grove of Abraham" follows the King James Version. Wahrman was a student of the famous Hasidic rabbi Levi Yitzhak of Berdichev; his *Eshel Avraham* is one of numerous works of

commentary, clarifications, descriptions of customs, and cross-references that adorn the side and bottom margins and back pages of each volume of traditional editions of the *Shulḥan ʿArukh*. Unfortunately, two other works are also named *Eshel Avraham*, which makes locating Wahrman's book confusing even for those highly familiar with Jewish legal literature. The other works are Abraham Oppenheim's *Eshel Avraham*, "a collection of famous Geonic responsa," according to the title page, usually printed in the margins of the *Shulḥan ʿArukh* itself; and the *Eshel Avraham* published in *Pri Megadim* (Lemberg [L'viv, Ukraine]: Pessl Balaban, 1883–84), reprinted in the back of most editions of the *Shulḥan ʿArukh*. The *Eshel Avraham* of the rabbi of Buczacz is printed after the *Pri Megadim* in many (but not all) traditional editions of the *Shulḥan ʿArukh*. In all cases, references to the *Shulḥan ʿArukh* and any of the works that are printed with it are to the section (in this case, Oraḥ Ḥayyim, dealing with life cycle, Sabbath and festivals, prayer, and ritual), followed by chapter or paragraph numbers, not pages. Wahrman's *Eshel Avraham* is not particularly well known to traditional Jews today; presumably that is why this book is omitted from some traditional editions of the *Shulḥan ʿArukh*. But his views on this subject were cited in a popular work by Abraham I. Sperling, *Sefer Taʿamei ha-Minhagim (The Reasons for Customs)* (Jerusalem: Eshkol, 1960–61), paragraphs 833–34. Wahrman is Sperling's only source for these ideas. The Sperling text corresponds exactly with that of the *Eshel Avraham* printed in the *Shulḥan ʿArukh*, which I examined.

5. Sperling, *Sefer Taʿamei*, paragraph 833, corresponding to *Eshel Avraham* on Oraḥ Ḥayyim, paragraph 665. See next note about the quotation from *Avot*.

6. This is the translation of Philip Birnbaum, *Ha-Siddur ha-Shalem: The Daily Prayer Book* (New York: Hebrew Publishing, 1949). *Avot* 5:22 is the enumeration in traditional Talmud editions; Birnbaum and many Mishnah editions enumerate this as *Avot* 5:25. It may be of interest to note that a manuscript reading may suggest a link with Joshua 1:8. Manuscripts have "turn it and turn it and meditate about it, for everything is in it"; see Yosef Kafih, *Mishnah with the Commentary of Moses Maimonides* (Jerusalem: Mosad ha-Rav Kook, 1964–65), 307. (In Kafih's edition, this passage is *Avot* 5:19.) Compare Joshua 1:8: "and thou shalt

meditate therein [in the Book of Moses] day and night"; "meditate" has the same Hebrew root in both Joshua and the Mishnah.

7. Sperling, *Sefer Ta'amei,* paragraph 834, *Eshel Avraham,* no. 665. The Sperling *Eshel Avraham* texts follow the biblical text closely but not exactly. "Prince" is the King James Version's translation for the Hebrew *nasi'*; other Bible translations often use "leader."

8. It is not clear what relationship the reversing of the Torah scroll has to the pronouncement of extra blessing formulas.

9. R. Moses Isserles (d. 1572), in the *Shulḥan 'Arukh,* Oraḥ Ḥayyim 669:1.

10. *Vayikra Rabbah* 2:3; my translation of *yafeh u-me'uleh* as "most excellent and celebrated" follows Ginzburg, *Legends of the Jews* (Philadelphia: Jewish Publication Society, 1953), 2:138. Ginzburg leaves out the reference to "Leader of the Tribes" and says "will be called Ephrati after thee." This Midrash is also cited more or less in Ginzburg's wording in the *Encyclopedia Judaica* article "Ephraim." See Ginzburg, *Legends of the Jews,* 5:366, for a list of parallels, to which may be added *Pirqe de Rabbi Eliezer* 45: "every prince and great man who arose in Israel had his name called an Ephrathite," as translated by Gerald Friedlander (1916; reprint, New York: Sepher-Hermon, 1981), 353. *Pirqe de Rabbi Eliezer,* however, makes no reference to the blessing of Ephraim. See Abraham Even-Shoshan, *Ha-Milon he-Hadash (The New Dictionary)* (Jerusalem: Kiryat Sefer, 1969), s.v. "Efrati," no. 3, for medieval and modern references to *efrati* used to mean "noble" or "elite."

11. On Elkanah, see 1 Samuel 1:1 and 1 Chronicles 6:28 (this verse is numbered 1 Chronicles 6:13 in Hebrew Bibles); on David, see 1 Samuel 17:12. On *efrati* for a member of Ephraim's tribe, see 1 Kings 11:26 and Judges 12:15. In the King James Version, "Ephrathite" and "Ephraimite" are both used to translate *efrati.*

12. Compare Exodus 40:17, and, for example, Rashi on Numbers 7:1 and 12. The discussion about this date—and its falling on Sunday—is found in *Seder 'Olam Rabbah* 7 and in TB *Shabbat* 87a. Based on rabbinic traditions about the year in which the exodus occurred, many traditional Jewish sources would date Ephraim's sacrifice almost a year later, Nisan 8, in the year 2449 of the creation, corresponding to Saturday, 4 April 1312 B.C.E. I believe talmudic references to dates should be

considered as years since the creation of Adam, not strictly the "creation era" used by Jews today; in this system the traditional date for the dedication of the sanctuary corresponds to spring, 1310 B.C.E.

13. *Bamidbar Rabbah* 14:2, end.

14. Ibid.

15. TB *Sukkah* 48a, top, with parallels noted there.

16. Rafael Jospe, Truman Madsen, and Seth Ward, eds., *Covenant and Chosenness in Mormonism and Judaism* (Madison, N.J.: Fairleigh Dickenson University Press, 2001).

17. Taken from the Latter-day Saint scripture Doctrine and Covenants 93:36, this was chosen as the title of a lecture series and book by Jacob Neusner, *The Glory of God Is Intelligence: Four Lectures on the Role of Intellect in Judaism* (Salt Lake City: BYU Religious Studies Center, 1978).

CHAPTER 23

THE TEMPLE IN LUKE AND ACTS

S. Kent Brown

The Gospel of Luke and the book of Acts weave a varicolored tapestry illustrating the temple's influences in the daily lives of people in the era of Jesus and his apostles. In fact, to demonstrate that the temple gave meaning to life and faith, Luke begins his two-volume story[1] inside the temple, taking his readers within the sanctuary, one of the most sacred spots on earth.[2] Moreover, as Luke's narrative demonstrates, the temple was a place of worship and sacrifice, of healing and teaching, of beauty and begging. All life and living came together at the temple. The pervasiveness of the temple in the spiritual lives of early Christians makes their history all the more poignant when the temple door slammed shut on them.

In the First Place

The first place that Luke mentions in his Gospel is the sanctuary of the temple, which is the holy space separated from the holy of holies by the veil of the temple. It appears in the following line: "[Zacharias's] lot was to burn incense when he went into the temple of the Lord" (Luke 1:9). The term translated as "temple" here is the Greek word *naos*, which means a sanctuary (also in Luke 1:21, 22).[3]

Hence, Luke's Gospel account of divine promises and resulting miracles opens in God's house. The first promise, of course, comes from an angel to Zacharias the priest and features the birth of an unusual child, the firstborn of Zacharias and his wife Elisabeth (see Luke 1:13–17). Thus a sacred promise of birth is associated with the sanctuary. In this connection, the line "Elisabeth conceived" (Luke 1:24)—another reference to birth—records the first in a series of miracles that follow the divine promise to Zacharias. Naturally, this series of miracles includes those tied to Jesus' birth and those growing out of his ministry.

The broader story of Luke chapter 1 concerns a family, the family of Zacharias and Elisabeth. God makes this family whole by aiding in the miraculous birth of John, later known as the Baptist. Moreover, one can see the importance that God places on this family within the progression of unusual spiritual manifestations that occur in their home, including the testimony about the coming Messiah that rests upon Elisabeth when Mary first visits her (see Luke 1:41–45) and the miraculous healing of Zacharias from his deaf and dumb condition (see Luke 1:64), to say nothing of the prophecies spoken by Mary and Zacharias (see Luke 1:46–55, 67–79).

That Luke (or his source)[4] was sensitive to sacred and less sacred space—these matters attach themselves to holy temples—becomes visible in a sequence of comments about places connected and disconnected to the temple. These comments follow his initial reference to the sanctuary in Luke 1:9. First, he writes of "the people [who] were praying without [the sanctuary] at the time of incense" (Luke 1:10). These people are standing, sitting, or kneeling in an adjoining courtyard outside the temple building itself (see Luke 1:21). Hence, in spatial terms they are several steps removed from the sanctuary—on less holy ground, as it were. Second, Luke notes that "as soon as the days of [Zacharias's] ministration were accomplished, he departed to his own house" (Luke

1:23). Though we do not know where Zacharias and Elisabeth resided—Luke writes only that they lived in "the hill country" (Luke 1:39)—at such a distance they were well away from the sanctuary.

In sum, Luke opens his story in the sanctuary, one of the most holy places on earth, and shows a sensitivity to sacred space. Additionally, the story ties the concepts of birth and family firmly to the temple experience of Zacharias.

Offerings

Luke's narrative next mentions the temple as the site of offerings. This is significant in terms of both what was offered and, perhaps, what was not offered. Mary's mandatory offering for purification, which, according to the law of Moses, was to follow the birth of a child, occurred at the proper place in the temple. According to the law of Moses, a woman was obliged to offer sacrifice forty days after the birth of a male child and eighty days after that of a female in order to regain her ritual purity. Before offering such a sacrifice, a woman was not to put her hand upon any sacred thing nor enter any hallowed place. Poor people were to offer either two turtledoves or two pigeons (see Leviticus 12:2–8). It is this sacrifice that Luke specifically notes and that Joseph and Mary perform (see Luke 2:24). What is apparently missing, however, is the payment of five shekels that redeems a family's firstborn child, even though Luke mentions this required redemption offering (see Luke 2:22–24, 39; see also Numbers 3:44–51; 18:15–16). Why?

Since the days of the exodus, Israelites were under obligation to redeem the oldest child in a family. We read that "the Lord spake unto Moses, saying, Sanctify unto me all the firstborn, whatsoever openeth the womb among the children of Israel, both of man and of beast: it is mine" (Exodus 13:1–2). The only exception to this rule that is recorded in scripture concerns Hannah and her child Samuel. According to the story, Hannah promised the Lord in prayer that if he would bless her with a son she would give up that son to him (see 1 Samuel 1:11). When a male child was born to Hannah, she nurtured him at home until he was weaned and then brought him to the sanctuary at Shiloh and left him with the high priest, Eli (see 1 Samuel 1:20–28). With all her offerings to the Lord on this occasion, she did not bring the required five-shekel payment (see Leviticus 18:15–16). Why? Because she had already dedicated him to the Lord and his service. For all intents and purposes, the child Samuel belonged to the Lord, not to his parents. Likewise, the angel who appeared to Mary had effectively dedicated Jesus to his Father's work. First, his name came from heaven (see Luke 1:31). Then, as the angel intoned, "He shall be great, and shall be called the Son of the Highest: and the Lord God shall give unto him the throne of his father David: And he shall reign over the house of Jacob for ever; and of his kingdom there shall be no end" (Luke 1:32–33). Hence, there seems to be no reason for Mary and Joseph to offer the five-shekel payment to redeem Jesus because he already belonged to God. We do not know whether they did so, but there is sufficient—and significant—reason for their inaction if they did not.

This set of scenes underscores the importance of the temple as a place of sacred offerings and commitments. More than that, Luke shows that those in his story who come to the temple for such purposes are faithful to God's law—in this case, the law of Moses—a point worth emphasizing. Demonstrating such faithfulness seems to be one of Luke's intents when he narrates the events that occurred at the temple (see Luke 2:22, 24, 27, 39). In addition, there is an underlying sense that those who are truly respectful of Moses' law are in a position to receive the new law that is to be brought forward by Jesus. Thus the temple becomes more than a place of offerings. It becomes a testing ground, as it were. In this light, participation in temple services is one of the measures of righteousness. But participation alone does not confer righteousness. A quick examination of the offices of those who were involved not only in Jesus' arrest but also in the later attempts to restrain his apostles exposes temple officials as leaders of the relentless opposition against him and his followers.[5] But in the earliest passages of Luke, those events surrounding Jesus' first presentation at the temple portray the temple itself in a positive light.

Spiritual Manifestations

Into the midst of the set of circumstances surrounding the presentation of Jesus came the aged Simeon and Anna, who prophesied about and praised the infant (see Luke 2:22–38). In Luke's narrative, the events that involve this elderly pair establish that the temple is a place of inspiration and prophecy. But these are not the only such incidents in Luke and Acts. The healing of the cripple at the Beautiful gate of the temple and Paul's vision within the temple grounds substantiate the same point (see Acts 3:1–11; 22:17–21).

Luke offers little information about the lives and temple activities of Simeon and Anna except to say, in the case of Anna, that she "served God with fastings and prayers night and day" (Luke 2:37). Rather, Luke's focus rests on their inspired interaction with Jesus' parents and the infant himself. In the case of Simeon, Luke first notes the revelation that had come to him through the Holy Ghost "that he should not see death, before he had seen the Lord's Christ" (Luke 2:26). Then appears one of the most important details in the story. Luke writes that, when Jesus' parents were in the temple to offer the sacrifice for Mary's purification, Simeon "came by the Spirit into the temple" (Luke 2:27). Not only did the Spirit guide him into the temple and, evidently, to the very spot in that huge edifice where Mary and Joseph were, but when Simeon took the child "in his arms" (2:28), the Spirit loosed a flood of wide-ranging prophecy about Jesus' future. According to Simeon's inspired words, the child would brighten into "a light to lighten the

Gentiles" and, in a similar vein, would radiate "the glory of [God's] people Israel." Thus Jesus' work would bring blessings both to Gentiles and to Israelites. Moreover, he would become "a sign which shall be spoken against," probably pointing to the opposition that Jesus would face during his ministry. That is not all. Mary's suffering—caused by witnessing the ill treatment given her son—would be as "a sword" that would "pierce through [her] own soul" (Luke 2:32, 34–35).

Even though Luke records that Anna came "in that instant" when Simeon was prophesying (Luke 2:38), almost as if her arrival were coincidental, the context points to another, richer reality. Luke's description, placing Anna next to Simeon in a tight sequence, plainly implies that she too came at the behest of the Spirit. In the words of Leon Morris, "Anna came up at the critical moment."[6] But there is more. As Joel Green observes, "Herod's temple was a massive structure; how could it be that [Anna] arrived in the right place at just the right moment apart from divine direction?"[7] Thus her "thanks . . . unto the Lord" was more than a simple expression of gratitude. She had come to the right place at the right time because of divine promptings. Her thanksgiving, therefore, grew out of the miracle of seeing this child of promise through eyes illumined by heaven. Further, she carried away a testimony about this child and "spake of him to all them that looked for redemption in Jerusalem" (Luke 2:38).

These spiritual manifestations in the temple do not stand alone. In a much later scene, Peter and John healed a crippled man at the Beautiful gate, which allows entry from the Court of the Gentiles into one of the inner courts (see Acts 3:1–11).[8] The unusual force of the miracle emerges from the fact that the "man [was] lame from his mother's womb" (Acts 3:2). The miracle reversed a situation that had occurred before his birth—that is, as a natural process. The intensity of the man's joyful response appears not only in his "walking, and leaping, and praising God" but also in the fact that he "held Peter and John" fast, not letting go, perhaps putting his arms firmly around their necks or waists (Acts 3:8, 11).

One can say the same for the apostle Paul. When he stood as a prisoner of Roman soldiers in the temple and bore witness of Christ to a hostile Jewish audience, he spoke of having returned to Jerusalem after seeing the vision of Christ on the road to Damascus and then having received a vision in the temple (see Acts 22:17–21). Paul testified that "while I prayed in the temple, I was in a trance;[9] And saw [Christ] saying unto me, Make haste, and get thee quickly out of Jerusalem: . . . for I will send thee far hence unto the Gentiles" (Acts 22:17–18, 21). The subtle but vital connection between the mention of Gentiles both in this vision and in the prophetic words of Simeon (see Luke 2:32) is suggestive. In a sense, it is as if Simeon's prophecy looked forward to the vision that Paul received: both took place at the temple and had to do with Gentiles. In addition, Paul's need to flee the temple and the city anticipated the closing of the temple doors against Jesus' followers (see Acts 21:30; on this subject, see below, "Deliverance and Closing"). In sum, the experiences of Simeon and Anna, the miraculous healing of the cripple, and the vision of Paul underscore the notion that the temple was a place for receiving the highest of spiritual blessings.

Teaching and Learning

An early incident in Luke's Gospel features Jesus' visit to the temple when he was twelve years old (see Luke 2:41–51). One of the dimensions of the temple that Luke underscores in this story—and others, too—is that it was a center of teaching and learning. During the youthful Jesus' extended stay in Jerusalem, while his parents were looking for him, he was "sitting in the midst of the doctors, both hearing them, and asking them questions" (Luke 2:46). In another passage it becomes clear that, in this scene, Jesus was a teacher of "the doctors." Luke records that "all that heard [Jesus] were astonished at his understanding and answers," plainly hinting that Jesus was more than a student in this exchange with others (Luke 2:47). The Joseph Smith Translation of this section sharpens the notion of the temple as a place of teaching and learning, specifically touching on Jesus as teacher. In describing the conversation between Jesus and "the doctors" in the temple, the JST reads that "they were hearing [Jesus], and *asking him questions*" (Luke 2:46 JST, emphasis added).

This pattern of Jesus and his disciples teaching in the temple repeats itself many times in Luke and Acts. Certainly, one of the more important experiences of this sort occurs during the last days of Jesus' life.[10] More to the point, all of Jesus' teaching recorded in Luke chapter 20 was "on one of those days" when he was in Jerusalem "as he taught the people in the temple" (Luke 20:1). Out of this occasion emerge some of the most important of Jesus' teachings about his authority and about inheritance. Such teachings include his parable of the wicked husbandmen (see Luke 20:9–16), his statement about the cornerstone that "the builders rejected" (Luke 20:17–18), his declaration on paying taxes to Caesar (see Luke 20:22–25), and his response to the Sadducees' question about marriage and the resurrection (see Luke 20:27–38).

It is also important to note that the temple continued as a place of teaching and learning even after Jesus' death and resurrection.[11] In fact, the temple seems to have become the center of the apostles' regular teaching activity, as Luke's notation about the customary place of meeting indicates: Solomon's porch that runs along the east side of the temple area (see Acts 3:11; 5:12).[12]

Were the apostles authorized to teach in the temple? According to Luke, it was an angel who, after miraculously freeing Peter and "other apostles"[13] from prison, instructed them, "Go, stand and speak in the temple to the people all the words of this [i.e., Jesus'] life" (Acts 5:20). Those who obeyed the angel did not seem surprised at the angel's command that they teach in the temple.

It seems to have been a normal expectation. Additionally, the apostles' teaching activity drew crowds on a regular basis, indicating that such was commonplace (see Acts 3:12; 4:1–2; 5:26). Of course, teaching in the temple also drew the unwanted attention of authorities who opposed the message about Jesus. In no case, however, did the authorities say that there was a rule or policy against teaching in the temple. Their objections arose because of the content of the apostles' teaching, not the place (see Acts 4:2; 5:28). Likewise, we note that the circumstances of Jesus' visit as a twelve-year-old indicate that informal teaching sessions were regular occurrences.

Worship and Prayer

Luke's story about Anna sets an approving tone for temple worship.[14] He records that she "departed not from the temple, but served God with fastings and prayers night and day" (Luke 2:37).[15] Luke's positive note, if anything, holds up such temple worship habits as exemplary. So does Jesus himself.

An early clue comes in a parable that Jesus spoke "unto certain [individuals] which trusted in themselves that they were righteous, and despised others." Jesus responded, "Two men went up into the temple to pray; the one a Pharisee, and the other a publican" (Luke 18:9–10). It seems clear from the way that Jesus introduced this parable and then concluded it that he saw praying as a normal, even expected activity in the temple. For he finally observed about the one man who had prayed sincerely that "this man went down to his house justified." Jesus even drew a further lesson from the story, indicating his positive assessment of worshiping in the temple by remarking that "every one that exalteth himself shall be abased; and he that humbleth himself shall be exalted" (Luke 18:14).

A second indicator arises in Jesus' response to those who bought and sold in the temple. These he "cast out." Recalling passages from both Isaiah and Jeremiah and repeating the Hebrew term for the temple, which also translates as "house," Jesus says, "My house is the house of prayer: but ye have made it a den of thieves" (Luke 19:45–46).[16] Jesus' actions and words make the case that, in his view, the temple was properly a place of prayer.

His apostles shared a similar view, doubtless mirroring Jesus' attitudes. Luke's last note in his Gospel affirms that the apostles acted in concert with Jesus' outlook. One can explain their actions in no other way. For, after the ascension, they "returned to Jerusalem with great joy: And were continually in the temple, praising and blessing God" (Luke 24:52–53; compare Acts 2:46). The same can be said for their activities following the events of Pentecost, when they and their hearers enjoyed an abundant outpouring of the Spirit (see Acts 2:1–41).

In the first passage that speaks of activities of the Twelve after the experiences at Pentecost, Luke writes: "Peter and John went up together into the temple at the hour of prayer, being the ninth hour" (Acts 3:1). From this passage it becomes clear that the leaders of the nascent Christian church faithfully went to the temple during at least one of the two times of daily prayer.[17] To be sure, because that day Peter and John healed the man born as a cripple, the experience at the temple became one of teaching (see Acts 3:2–4:2). But the intent of the two apostles was to pray and worship by attending "the temple at the hour of prayer."

In sum, the aggregate of passages in Luke and Acts that deal with worship at the temple all paint such experiences in very positive hues. Whether it is Anna's worship habits, Jesus' parable of the two men praying, Jesus' actions and words against temple merchants, or the activities of Jesus' apostles, the resulting picture is the same. They all regarded the temple as the chief center of worship.

Ceremonies

Closely related to the concept of worship or public prayer is that of rituals or ceremonies. As Edersheim reminds readers, the morning and evening public prayers were closely tied to the sacrifices of the two daily burnt offerings and the two ceremonies of lighting incense.[18] Such an observation recalls Luke's remark that a crowd of people who "were praying" outside the temple awaited Zacharias's appearance after his ceremonial lighting of the incense (see Luke 1:10, 21).[19] Moreover, Anna's presence in the temple "night and day" (Luke 2:37) may point to the two times that people came together daily for public prayers and for the ceremonies of lighting incense and sacrificing burnt offerings. As noted above, Luke holds Anna's activities in a positive light.

Nowhere does Luke record that Jesus himself participated directly in temple rituals. But he does recount that Jesus was present when a widow brought her offering of two small coins to the temple treasury (see Luke 21:1–4). Jesus' response was highly complimentary of this woman's gift. While Jesus was critical of "the rich men" who had also brought gifts, there is no hint that he was judgmental against ceremonies conducted in the temple.

In a later scene, Paul responded to the request of James the brother of the Lord and "the elders" that he assist other church members in the temple rituals that would bring their vows to a proper end (see Acts 21:18–26). In this passage it becomes evident that church members not only participated in ceremonies linked to the temple but also continued to see them as important, even after the sacrificial death of Jesus, which, in one sense, brought many such ordinances to an end for believers, especially those tied to the law of Moses.[20] It may be that Jesus' followers saw such ceremonies as ways to memorialize the sacrifice of Jesus and therefore continued to join in temple rituals until some time before the fall of the city in A.D. 70.

Beauty and Begging

We know from other ancient sources, particularly the works of Josephus, that the temple structure of Jesus' day was an edifice of almost unparalleled beauty.[21] The refurbished temple that was standing then was the work of King Herod. In fact, construction was still going on during Jesus' ministry and would do so for more than three decades after his ascension.[22] The subject of the temple's beauty arises in Luke's Gospel in a rather unusual but memorable way. In the account, unnamed disciples spoke "of the temple, how it was adorned with goodly[23] stones and gifts" (Luke 21:5). Jesus' stunning response about the future destruction of the temple followed immediately (see Luke 21:6, 20–24), effectively searing the rather casual remark about the temple's loveliness into the memory of those who were present. As we know, Jesus' prophecy about the fall of the temple and the city was fulfilled to the last detail. Even so, the temple was an edifice whose splendor drew the admiration of all who beheld it.

That the temple was the center of all life and living is perhaps best illustrated not only by the daily presence of a crippled beggar at one of the interior gates, the gate "which is called Beautiful," but also by his healing (see Acts 3:2–8). We have already explored the meaning of the temple in light of both the healing of this man and the ceremonial purpose for which Peter and John had come to the temple that day. It should also be added that the name of the gate ties to the general sense of the beauty and spiritually seasoning influence of the temple itself. Why does this matter? The answer rests partly in two contrasts.

The Greek term translated "beautiful" in the expression *Beautiful gate* (see Acts 3:2, 10) means basically "produced at the right season." That is, it has to do with full development or maturity, ripeness or prime of life.[24] This idea of developed or matured beauty points to a touch of irony that pushes itself between the circumstance of the invalid and the name of the gate. As we know, Luke does not record the beggar's age. Hence, we do not know how old the man was. But, even if he were as young as his late teens or his twenties, we cannot think of this crippled man as "in the prime of life" or "in the high season" of his life. Thus the term translated "beautiful" in the name *Beautiful gate* (see Acts 3:2, 10), which carries this meaning, stands in marked contrast to the circumstance of the crippled beggar. It is between these points of contrast that the miracle intrudes, healing the man and making him "beautiful" in the sense of making him whole, as if he had developed naturally and completely over the course of his life.

The second contrast concerns speed. It appears between the basic meaning of the term translated "beautiful" in Acts 3:2—developed beauty—and the raw speed with which the invalid became whole. Concerning the gate, skilled artisans would have taken considerable time to plan and shape the gate and to carve precisely the stones that went into it. By the high standards of Herod's temple, the gate was a work of art whose beauty took time to create. In contrast, the lame man became whole in an instant. Indeed, he had lain helpless all of his life—"from his mother's womb," as Luke reminds his readers (see Acts 3:2). But when Peter uttered words of command and authority—"In the name of Jesus Christ of Nazareth rise up and walk"—and "took him by the right hand, and lifted him up . . . *immediately* his feet and ankle bones received strength" (Acts 3:6–7, emphasis added). There was no ripening and careful planning; there was no maturation process. The healing happened immediately and so completely that the cripple began "walking, and leaping, and praising God" (Acts 3:8).

In the end, of course, the fact that worshipers had accepted the presence of the crippled beggar at an important place in the temple grounds forms a notable statement about the people who came regularly to the temple and about their concept of what the temple represented. For them, the temple was somehow incomplete without his presence. In the minds of worshipers, he had a right to be there. Whether any of them gave alms habitually to the lame man Luke does not tell us. But we conclude with confidence that the temple was a place not only for the prosperous but also for the poor and unfortunate.[25]

Deliverance and Closing

In the last scene that Luke describes at the temple, we follow Paul inside with a group of church members who are under a vow, evidently the Nazarite vow (see Numbers 6:1–21). In light of our discussion above, it should not surprise us that early Christians still kept ceremonies required by the law of Moses, even a generation after Jesus' atonement. On this occasion, Paul had agreed to a request by James the brother of the Lord to accompany devoted church members into the temple as they completed their vows (see Acts 21:18–26). The experience started innocently enough, but Paul had already received a number of warnings that this trip to Jerusalem would lead to his imprisonment (see Acts 20:22; 21:4, 10–11, 13). Oddly, his imprisonment turned out to be a rescue from the hands of an angry mob within the temple grounds.

Decades before, when the Antonia Fortress was under construction just outside the northwest corner of the temple grounds, King Herod commissioned a double stairway to be cut into the northern wall of the temple area, a stairway that rose from the Court of the Gentiles into the Antonia Fortress. This fortress soared menacingly over the temple area. From its tallest tower, which rose to a height of 105 feet, Roman soldiers kept watch over the temple grounds. By means of the staircase, the Roman garrison in the fortress had direct access to the Court of the Gentiles.[26]

It was actually this stairway that saved Paul's life. Luke writes that "when the seven days" of the Passover festival "were almost ended, the Jews which were of Asia . . . stirred up all the people [against Paul], and laid hands on him" (Acts 21:27). Having recognized Paul, these people of Asia felt that they would finally gain revenge against him for his despised missionary efforts among them. Evidently, Paul and his Christian friends were inside either the Court of Women or the so-called inner courtyard where only Israelites were allowed. One entry to these courtyards was through the "gate of the temple which is called Beautiful" (Acts 3:2, 10). On the balustrade that ran around both the inner courtyard and the Court of Women hung signs written in Greek and Latin that warned foreigners not to enter.[27]

These Asian Jews cried out, "This is the man, that teacheth all men every where against . . . the law, and this place." Moreover, they shouted, Paul had "brought Greeks also into the temple, and . . . polluted this holy place" (Acts 21:28). The crowd erupted. In anger, "the people . . . took Paul, and drew him out of the temple." They intended to kill him for his sacrilege but to do it outside the holy place (see Acts 21:30–31). The need to drag Paul away from the temple grounds allowed the soldiers of the Roman garrison in the fortress enough time to react. Their timely response saved his life (see Acts 21:31–33). It is one of the ironies of this story that Romans saved Paul from certain death by taking him out of the temple area and into gentile territory, the fortress.

Another irony arises at the end of Luke's narration about the tumult that occurred in the temple that day. He writes that, after the worshipers had dragged Paul "out of the temple . . . forthwith the doors were shut" (Acts 21:30). In the words of Fitzmyer, "Jerusalem's holiest place is closed to Paul and his message."[28] Among Roman soldiers, Paul began his long journey to Rome. No longer was the temple a welcoming destination for worshiping Christians. In effect, it stood thereafter as an empty shell awaiting its destruction, as Jesus plainly hinted: "Behold, your house is left unto you desolate" (Luke 13:35).[29]

From Sanctuary to Destruction

The temple is the starting place for Luke's entire two-volume story that began with the angel's appearance to Zacharias and ended with Paul safely in Rome preaching the gospel message. The angel's words to Zacharias in the sanctuary spoke of birth and, by extension, of family. In the events that rolled out of this beginning, we sense the importance of the temple for teaching and healing, for ceremonies and worship, for beauty, and for accepting and blessing the unfortunate among us. In the end, however, Luke presents an unusual twist. The temple became a place hostile to Jesus' followers. Its "doors were shut" against them (Acts 21:30). Now it stood bereft of the people who came and went under the influence of God's Spirit. Now it stood awaiting its destruction at the hands of Roman legionnaires. Even so, for as long as the temple stood, it served as a spiritual beacon and haven for those who came within its walls.

Notes

1. Virtually all studies on the New Testament Gospels conclude that the Gospel accounts were written anonymously and that the names of authors were attached only later. Moreover, most scholars now conclude that each of the Gospels was produced by the efforts of more than one person—in effect, by schools. As for myself, I accept the traditional ascription of Luke's Gospel and the book of Acts to Paul's companion, Luke the Physician.

2. The Book of Mormon notes contemporaneous temples in the New World that framed sacred space: one in Zarahemla (see Mosiah 1:18; 2:1, 5–7) and one in Bountiful (see 3 Nephi 11:1). Second Nephi 5:16 mentions the temple at Nephi, which might still have been standing; Alma 10:2 talks of an unidentified temple where Aminadi saw the writing on the wall.

3. The word that refers to the temple and its grounds is the Greek *hieron.* This term occurs thirty-nine times in Luke and Acts, with occasional reference to the Court of Women or the so-called inner court (see, for example, Acts 21:26–27, 29–30) rather than to the larger Court of the Gentiles. The word *naos* ("sanctuary") appears only at the beginning and end of the Gospel (Luke 1:9, 21, 22; 23:45), and in Acts 7:48 (Stephen's speech) and 17:24 (Paul's speech). Occasionally, one sees the influence of the Hebrew term for temple, which also translates as "house" (in Luke 13:35 [?]; 19:46 [citing Isaiah 56:7]; Acts 2:2 [?]; 7:47, 49).

4. For a number of reasons, most New Testament scholars believe that Luke drew on a source for chapters 1 and 2 of his Gospel. One of the reasons has to do with the high number of Aramaic expressions that differ markedly from how Luke expresses himself elsewhere in his two-volume work. But not all agree with this assessment. For brief reviews, see, for example, Raymond E. Brown, *The Birth of the Messiah* (Garden City, N.Y.: Doubleday, 1979), 245–46; Leon Morris, *Luke: An Introduction and Commentary*, rev. ed. (Grand Rapids, Mich.: Eerdmans, 1988), 29–30; and Richard L. Anderson, "The Testimony of Luke," in *Studies in Scripture: Volume Five, the Gospels*, ed. Kent P. Jackson and Robert L. Millet (Salt Lake City: Deseret Book, 1986), 92–96.

5. See references to temple officials in Luke 22:4, 52 ("the chief priests, and captains of the temple"); Acts 4:1 ("the priests, and the captain of the temple"); also 5:24, 26. On the captain of the temple as the person who had "supreme charge of order in and around the temple," see Emil Schürer, *The History of the Jewish People in the Age of Jesus Christ*, rev. ed. by Geza Vermes, Fergus Millar, and Matthew Black (Edinburgh: Clark, 1973–87), 2:277–78.

6. Morris, *Luke: An Introduction and Commentary*, 99.

7. Joel B. Green, *The Gospel of Luke* (Grand Rapids, Mich.: Eerdmans, 1997), 151.

8. The identity of this gate has been a matter of debate. See the summary of the various suggestions in Joseph A. Fitzmyer, *The Acts of the Apostles* (New York: Doubleday, 1998), 277–78. Each of the suggested alternatives stood on the east of the sanctuary itself.

9. The Greek term *ekstasis* appears here as *trance*. It means, literally, a "change of place." On the meanings of this term in ancient written contexts, see Gerhard Kittel et al., eds., *Theological Dictionary of the New Testament* (Grand Rapids, Mich.: Eerdmans, 1964–74), 2:449–50, 456–58.

10. For references to teaching incidents connected with the last days of Jesus' life, see Luke 19:47; 21:37, 38; 22:53.

11. For accounts of Jesus' followers teaching in the temple after his resurrection, see Acts 3:11–4:2; 5:20–21, 25, 42; 24:12.

12. Helpful descriptions and illustrations of the temple grounds in the era of Jesus and his contemporaries appear both in Dan Bahat, *The Illustrated Atlas of Jerusalem* (New York: Simon and Schuster, 1990), and

in Chaim Richman, *The Holy Temple of Jerusalem* (Jerusalem: Temple Institute, 1997).

13. Luke does not specify which apostles, besides Peter, went to prison and then were freed miraculously. The phrase *other apostles* appears in Acts 5:29 KJV; see the plural word *apostles* in Acts 5:12, 18, 40.

14. In fact, only one passage in Luke and Acts takes a disapproving tone in connection with the temple, and that is the parable of the good Samaritan, where the temple officials—the priest and the Levite—come in for implied criticism (see Luke 10:25–37). However, it is not the temple but the inaction of persons who officiate there that Jesus impugns.

15. While some scholars believe that Anna may have lived within the temple area, it is possible to understand "night and day" as a reference to the ceremonies that priests performed twice a day, in the morning and in the late afternoon. See Joseph A. Fitzmyer, *The Gospel According to Luke* (New York: Doubleday, 1981), 1:431.

16. See Isaiah 56:7 and Jeremiah 7:11.

17. Acts 3:1 says that Peter and John came at "the ninth hour," that is, about 3:00 P.M. According to Mishnah *Pesahim* 5:1, the second daily whole offering was "offered up at a half after the ninth hour," thus following the time of prayer. For a description of the two daily times set for worship, morning and evening, see Alfred Edersheim, *The Temple: Its Ministry and Services* (1874; reprint, Grand Rapids, Mich.: Eerdmans, 1983), 143–46, 152–73; see also the notes in Josephus, *Antiquities of the Jews* 3.10.1, §237; 14.4.3, §65.

18. Edersheim, *The Temple*, 152–73.

19. Priests burned incense twice a day, each time in connection with burnt offerings. See Schürer, *History of the Jewish People*, 2:299–302.

20. See especially Hebrews 10:8–18; Alma 34:10–14; 3 Nephi 9:19–20; 15:2–8; 4 Nephi 1:12.

21. Generally on the temple, see Josephus, *Antiquities of the Jews* 15.11.1–7, §§380–425; *Jewish War* 5.5.1–8, §§184–247; also compare the remarks of Schürer and others, including discussion of Greek architectural features, in *History of the Jewish People*, 1:308–9, 2:57–58.

22. Herod's reconstruction began in his eighteenth year as king—that is, in 20–19 B.C. The work did not end until the time of the Roman

prefect Albinus (A.D. 62–64), less than a decade before Roman legionnaires destroyed it. See Schürer, *History of the Jewish People,* 1:292, 308.

23. The Greek term *kaloṣ,* which is translated "goodly," means "lovely" or "beautiful" when describing objects.

24. See Henry G. Liddell and Robert Scott, *A Greek-English Lexicon,* new ed. (Oxford: Oxford University Press, 1940), 2036, s.v. "hōraios."

25. See Luke 21:1–2, where both "the rich men" and "a certain poor widow" were visitors to the temple treasury.

26. See Josephus, *Jewish War* 5.5.8, §§238–46.

27. See Josephus, *Jewish War* 5.5.2, §194; 6.2.4, §125.

28. Fitzmyer, *Acts of the Apostles,* 698.

29. It is possible to understand *house* in this passage as a reference either to the temple or to a household, including children or offspring, as in Doctrine and Covenants 84:115. Either sense points to the destruction that Jesus prophesied (see Luke 21:6, 20–24). For various interpretations about the meanings of *house* in Luke 13:35, see Fitzmyer, *The Gospel According to Luke,* 2:1036–37.

CHAPTER 24

THE DOME OF THE ROCK

David Noel Freedman and Rebecca L. Frey

The purpose of this essay is to explore information about the extraordinary building now standing on one of the most sacred spots in the world. The building is called variously the Dome of the Rock (Arabic Qubbat al-Sakhra) or the House of the Holy Shrine/ Holy Place. The entire area is the Haram al-Sharif—the Noble Sanctuary. These are the Arabic terms given by those who governed and built up the complex of structures on the mount where the Dome stands. Before and since, the site has belonged to or has been controlled by other peoples, and many other buildings have occupied it. But this building and its sponsorship have been in place for a long time—a very long time when measured by the tumultuous circumstances of the Near East, ancient and modern. This temporal fortitude deserves serious attention, if only as an example of endurance and stability in a notoriously unstable environment. Not only have nations come and gone and armies trampled this sacred space, but nature itself seems determined to rearrange its own landscape repeatedly, if not regularly, by earthquakes of varying intensity—more than one of which has leveled buildings, both large and small, all over Jerusalem—but all without noticeably damaging the Dome.[1] For thirteen hundred years the

Dome has stood on this spot, extending a welcoming hand to pilgrims and visitors to join the faithful in a common act of reverence.

The "rock" is itself a prominent feature of Jerusalem and is identified with Mount Moriah (more exactly, the mountain in the land of Moriah, mentioned in 2 Chronicles 3:1 as the place where Abraham bound his son in preparation for offering him as a sacrifice to God at the latter's command, as related in Genesis 22:9).[2] While we have no means to confirm or corroborate this identification other than the Hebrew Bible, it is part of the tradition known to Jews, Christians, and Muslims alike.

This association with Abraham—the Father of the Faithful and the common ancestor, both spiritual and physical, of the three peoples—is of the highest importance. It established the primary feature of the present building—namely, that it is, or can be, called a *martyrium*[3] (or *ciborium,* so named from the Greek *kiborion,* which refers to a drinking cup shaped like the flower of the Egyptian bean). A *martyrium* is a structure designed to enshrine or memorialize an individual, an event, or an act of faith of enduring value and importance for those who are heirs to that person.[4] The rock is thus sanctified by an extraordinary and memorable act of piety on the part of the founding father and common ancestor of the two peoples most involved with that site.

The history of building sacred structures on the Holy Mount began with the work of David and Solomon—the first and last kings of a united Israel in the tenth century B.C.E.—and continued to the final and enduring effort of ʿAbd al-Malik, the fifth Umayyad caliph, who completed the Dome in 691 C.E. as an essential part of a larger project on the Haram.

The First Temple period, that of Solomon, lasted somewhat less than four hundred years (if we date its construction to about 967–960 B.C.E. and its destruction by the Babylonians to 587–586 B.C.E., the total is about 375 years). The Second Temple was longer lived, from its construction by Zerubbabel in about 521–515 B.C.E.

until it was destroyed by the Romans in 70 C.E.[5] In fact, both temples were repaired, restored, and even more extensively renovated over time. The Second Temple was completely remodeled and replaced by the temple of Herod the Great, but it was and is customary not to consider such peaceful alterations alongside the violent destructions that typically mark the end of one temple period and the start of another.[6]

The fate of the first two temples is similar. It seems clear that the Babylonian destruction of the First Temple was deliberate and intended as retribution and reprisal for the rebellion of the last regent king, Zedekiah. At the time of the Babylonian invasion eleven years earlier, the city had surrendered peacefully, and the city and its temple were spared by the same monarch. But after the rebellion of Zedekiah—an act warned against and denounced vehemently and categorically by the great prophets Jeremiah and Ezekiel[7]—the Babylonians exacted their revenge in full and ended the kingdom and its monarchy, destroying both the city and its temple.

In the case of the Second Temple, the outcome was the same although the circumstances were different. After a prolonged siege, the city wall was breached, the city itself captured, and the temple burned. According to Josephus, Titus, the Roman general and eventual heir to the emperor Vespasian, had promised to spare the temple, but his vengeful army, increasingly frustrated by the length of the siege, could not be prevented from torching both city and temple.[8] Either way, Titus bears responsibility for the Roman action, although Josephus, as a defender and apologist for the Flavian dynasty, may have adjusted the facts or changed the tone and nuances to modify the picture and make the Roman leader seem more benign than he may actually have been.

In any case, in 587–586 B.C.E. and 70 C.E. the two temples were destroyed by enemy action in violent engagements. As it happens, a third temple, though less well known, existed temporarily on the site.[9] Sixty-five years after the debacle of 70 C.E., the Roman emperor Hadrian erected a temple to Jupiter on the site in Jerusalem either before or after the revolt of Bar Kokhba. The latter doubtless had intended to build a new temple there, and work may have begun toward that end. With the defeat of Bar Kokhba and the banning of Jews from the city, Hadrian built an entirely new city (Aelia Capitolina, so called at his pleasure, perhaps to mark the complete romanization of Jerusalem, 135 C.E.)[10] and constructed either a temple or statue to each of the gods Jupiter, Minerva, and Juno. The sources vary as to exactly where this construction took place and whether this project was one temple to all three deities or whether separate temples were built for each. Jerome refers to a "statue" to Jupiter, not mentioning either Minerva or Juno: "From the time of Hadrian to the reign of Constantine— a period of about 180 years—the spot which had witnessed the resurrection was occupied by a figure of Jupiter; while on the rock where the cross had stood, a marble statue of Venus was set up by the heathen and became an object of worship. The original persecutors, indeed, supposed that by polluting our holy places they would deprive us of our faith in the passion and in the resurrection."[11] Jerome uses the term *simulacrum* ("image") when referring to the monument to Jupiter and *statua ex marmore* ("statue of marble") when referring to Venus. It is worth noting that he does not use the term *templum,* which would refer to a structure rather than a likeness, and that both Minerva and Juno are absent from his account of Hadrian's structures on the mount. Whether temples for these goddesses were built elsewhere or whether Jerome merely omitted their presence is open to speculation. Jerome wrote this letter in about 395 C.E., 250 years after Hadrian's reorganization of the city.

No clear traces of Hadrian's building projects on the Holy Mount remain. Exactly where the temple or statue to Jupiter (and

Minerva and Juno) was and what happened to it is unclear. Hadrian's structures had vanished from the scene. Once the Roman Empire was converted to Christianity by the order of Constantine in 325 C.E., interest in restoring, repairing, or even preserving such pagan monuments would have waned, although in some cases they were or could be converted into churches (and later mosques). Once again the Holy Mount was bare of buildings, though travelers enjoyed seeing the remains of Solomon's temple on the site. With a lively imagination, the Anonymous Pilgrim of Bordeaux relates in 333 C.E. that he could see "two large pools at the side of the temple, that is, one upon the right hand, and one upon the left, which were made by Solomon; and further in the city are twin pools, with five porticoes, which are called Bethsaida. There persons who have been sick for many years are cured; the pools contain water which is red when it is disturbed. There is also here a crypt, in which Solomon used to torture devils."[12] The pilgrim goes on to describe two statues of Hadrian not far from the stone where the Jews came every year to mourn.

Around the same time, Eusebius (ca. 260–340 C.E.), bishop of Caesarea, reported that he could see the remains of the sanctuary;[13] not much later, about 400 C.E., John Chrysostom, the bishop of Constantinople, said that he too could discern the foundations.[14] He recounted how the Jews tore everything down during the reign of Emperor Julian the Apostate to begin work on their third temple (work on this structure began in 363, when Jews were allowed back into the city). Plans for a new Jewish temple on the site called for a building more splendid than the Church of the Holy Sepulchre, also, and perhaps more fittingly, called the Church of the Resurrection.[15] With Julian's death, the plans and the work came to naught, but the work had been frustrated even in the months preceding the emperor's demise. Gregory Nazianzen, John Chrysostom, Ambrose, and the philosopher-soldier Ammianus Marcellinus all report that natural disasters attended the attempted construction of a third temple, including conflagrations perhaps fueled by gases trapped in blocked subterranean passages.[16]

Except for the brief reign of Julian the Apostate, from the fourth century on, the city and land were in the hands of Christians. Then in 638 the Muslims came, and Jerusalem surrendered to the caliph Othman. The terms of the capitulation were worked out between Patriarch Sophronius and Caliph Omar.[17] Full control of the city was ceded to the Muslims with the stipulation that the Christian churches and other properties would be spared destruction and despoliation. No mention was made of Jews; officially, they had been banished from Jerusalem since the end of the Bar Kokhba rebellion, and no organized Jewish community existed in the city. The Holy Mount at this time was bare of buildings, although the ruins and remnants of earlier structures were doubtless on the site. During the intervening centuries since the violent destruction of the Second Temple and the expulsion of the Jews, the Christian community had concentrated on particular sites associated with the presence of Jesus in Jerusalem, especially the place they identified as that of his crucifixion and resurrection; that site was dominated by the Church of the Holy Sepulchre. No group at that time exhibited a special interest in the Temple Mount, and nothing remained either of Hadrian's works or of the Jews' efforts to rebuild a third temple in 363 c.e.[18] It is hardly surprising, then, that the Muslims took over this hallowed ground for their own religious purposes. It is important to observe that they were steeped in biblical tradition and that they identified the landmarks of Jerusalem with the heroes of the Old and New Testaments. For example, as well as being the Holy Mount where Abraham bound his son (the mountain in the land of Moriah in Genesis 22), the area was identified explicitly with the site of Solomon's temple in 2 Chronicles 3:1 and was the place where Jesus had preached and cleansed the temple area during his mortal ministry.

Within a few years a mosque was erected on the Haram mount, the first of the al-ʾAqsa structures to stand there. By the end of the seventh century several other buildings had been constructed, all part of a comprehensive program to reclaim one of the most sacred sites in the ancient world for the true religion stemming from Abraham, including the followers of Moses on the one hand and Jesus on the other, both of whom were and are acknowledged by Muslims as prophets of the one true God.

The principal building designed to dominate the Haram and to represent and symbolize the new factor in the return of the age-old religion was the Dome of the Rock, built on the site of the temples of Solomon and Zerubbabel (and Herod the Great). As agreed by all who have studied this structure, it is unique in the Near East, having no counterparts in the religious structures of the ancient world and few imitators in its own culture.[19] Exactly what it is and what its principal purpose or function are remain in some doubt and dispute, although a moderate consensus along broad lines may be secured.

First, we should consider the building's shape and appurtenances. The Dome is a double octagon with a rotunda or dome—not the typical shape for houses of worship, whether temples, churches, synagogues, or mosques. Nevertheless, examples of similar structures exist, most notably in Byzantine architecture (compare structures in the cities of Basra, Kufa, and Wasit), and different views attempt to explain the numerical significance of the octagon. ʿAbd al-Malik, the sponsor of the Dome of the Rock, apparently used the octagonal form in building it for two reasons. These reasons are not mutually exclusive—one addresses practicality and the other spirituality. First, the octagon is the logical base structure for a huge dome, and ʿAbd al-Malik needed a huge dome to assert the supremacy of his faith over the Christian faith as architecturally articulated in the domed Church of the Holy Sepulchre and to comment on the centrality of Jerusalem as a holy city, either in addition to or superior to Mecca. The historian

Muqaddasi (tenth century c.e.) was among the first on record to suggest that the magnificent size and shape of the Dome of the Rock are a response to the Church of the Holy Sepulchre: "And in like manner the Caliph ꜥAbd al-Malik, noting the greatness of the Church of the Holy Sepulchre and its magnificence, was moved lest it should dazzle the minds of the Muslims, and hence erected above the Rock a dome which is now to be seen there."[20] Muqaddasi is two hundred years removed from the construction of the Dome, but it is an understandable and generally accepted tradition that ꜥAbd al-Malik desired to surpass the Church of the Holy Sepulchre as a symbolic victory over Christianity.[21]

With respect to the spiritual significance of the octagon, in our view it symbolizes symmetry, totality, and perhaps perfection. The number eight figures importantly in the story of creation in the Bible and prominently in other distinctive and significant places and contexts. For instance, the sequence of the books of the Hebrew Bible shows the following pattern: Torah, 5; Prophets, 8 (former = 4, later = 4); Writings, 11. The sum of the books in the Torah and Writings thus equals 16, or twice 8. The total number of books in the Hebrew Bible (5+8+11) equals 24, or thrice 8.[22] That the octagon symbolizes the totality of heaven and earth—in effect, the universe—may be reinforced by two other features or aspects: first, the four doors to the building are connected with the four rivers of paradise, and second, the exact location is identified with the *omphalos*, or umbilicus, of the world. Jerusalem has traditionally been viewed as the very center, as is known from biblical prophecy (cf. Ezekiel 47:1–12, describing the rivers that flow out of the temple of Jerusalem from the center of the earth).

The octagon is also the only shape that mediates between the geometric articulation of the terrestrial square and celestial circle—it is the only shape that nearly squares a circle. Kim Williams, describing the sacred quality of the octagon, discusses the mathematical significance of this shape: "The use of irrational values, or incommensurables, is linked philosophically to the symbolism of the circle and the square. A circle was indefinite, its circumference and area based on the irrational p, whereas the circumference and area of a square were rational values. Philosophically the use of irrational numbers such as q shows an attempt to rationalize that which is irrational, or in other words, to make sensible that which is divine or only achievable through the intellect."[23] This mathematical complexity and its symbology contribute to the unique character of the Dome, a character that draws upon the universal language of mathematics to express the divine.

If the shape is symbolic, the same may be said of the decorations and motifs of the friezes that cover the whole extent of the outer walls. The combination of geometric designs and floral motifs is intended to evoke and depict images of paradise, colorfully described in the Qurʾan and early Islamic literature. The happy destiny of the faithful is amply depicted on the walls of the Dome and fits in with the traditional view that Jerusalem would be the scene of the general resurrection of the dead, the appearance of God at the last judgment, and the settlement of all outstanding accounts. Islam shares this view with traditional Judaism and Christianity, so the symbolism of the Dome representing the gates to paradise is fitting for its particular location. It is notable that exclusive emphasis is placed on the joys and bliss of paradise as promised to the faithful of Islam and open to the rest of humanity, but especially to the Peoples of the Book, who belong to the great monotheistic tradition.

More important even than the shape and the decoration is the lengthy inscription that runs twice around the structure, once in each direction, so that the pilgrim or inquiring visitor may read it all as she or he walks around the drum, or circumference, in either direction. The legend is written in Arabic, thereby defining the primary target audience of the inscription: by Arabs for Arabs, by Muslims for Muslims. It is a public statement meant for everyone who can read the "sacred" language, large and clear even for those in a hurry (cf. Habakkuk 2:3). This Islamic statement affirms the basic tenets of the faith and pronouncements of the Prophet Muhammad and quotes freely from the Qurʾan; in fact, this inscription constitutes the earliest written documentation of the Qurʾan and may precede any extant written manuscript of the prophet's utterances. No doubt it was derived from oral tradition and the tenacious memory of those who heard and remembered. This declaration affirms the unity and uniqueness of Allah, the God of Islam (and of the Bible), using language that, if not identical with or derived from the Bible, echoes the monotheistic affirmations found in Isaiah especially, and also Deuteronomy 32:39: "See, now, that I, I am He and there is no god with me; I cause death and I cause life, I have wounded and I will heal, and there is no deliverer from my hand."

At the same time, the inscription makes explicit reference to Jesus, acknowledged as a true prophet standing in the line from Adam through Abraham and Moses and continuing to the latest and last of them, Muhammad himself. This reference to Christianity is at once irenic and polemical. It affirms the unity of the Godhead against any trinitarian notions and, while acknowledging (or at least implying) the prophethood of Jesus, nevertheless affirms his humanity against claims of his divinity. At one and the same time, it attacks normative Orthodox Christianity, especially as believed and practiced in Jerusalem at the time, but invites Christians as People of the Book to consider the (superior) merits of Islam with its positive view of Jesus and his tradition. No doubt a similar treatment of Judaism and an approach to this other and earlier People of the Book would have been made had there been any significant Jewish population in the vicinity. But as noted, at the time of the construction of the Dome, the city and environs of Jerusalem were populated mainly by Arabic-speaking Christians.

If we take all the features of the Dome together, including its placement on the Holy Mount, its shape and design, and its decorative style, along with the contemporary inscription indicating the time and the caliph who sponsored it and the team that planned and built it in the last decade of the seventh century C.E., we come up with a unique sacral structure, variously called a *ciborium* or a *martyrium,* as noted above. The Dome of the Rock, in terms of commemoration, holds significance for all three monotheistic religions—Judaism, Christianity, and Islam.

Concerning the construction of the Dome on this site, competing theories or resolutions exist, none of which may be entirely factually accurate but all of which contribute to the understanding and appreciation of the site's role in the religious history of Jerusalem and its world. The traditional view connects the site (and the structure) with the legendary night ride by the Prophet (the *isra*) or his journey to heaven *(mi'radj).* That connection, however, was not made in the earliest sources. Since the inscription fails to mention or allude to it, we may regard it as a later accretion. The second view, which derives from the earliest written sources, holds that 'Abd al-Malik, the caliph who arranged and constructed the buildings on the Holy Mount, did so in order to rival the famous shrine at Mecca with its sacred stone, the Ka'ba, so as to divert pilgrims to Jerusalem. At the time, Mecca was under the control of a rival caliph, 'Abd Allah ibn al-Zubayr, and the outcome of the struggle between the two for preeminence of location was in doubt.[24] But shortly thereafter al-Zubayr was killed and Mecca reverted to the authority of 'Abd al-Malik. In the end, Mecca remained the primary goal of all Muslim pilgrimages, while Jerusalem was built up and presented not as a substitute or alternative to Mecca, but as an added attraction, closer to the actual center of power and authority in the Muslim empire (which was growing by leaps and bounds at this time) and more closely tied to the biblical traditions and the temples of the Bible than any other site.

A third view evokes the contemporary sociopolitical and religious situation in which the Arab caliphs found themselves—the necessity to establish themselves in the complex world of Syria-Palestine and their desire to make a firm statement about the place of Islam, especially in relation to the Byzantine Empire. Here we would emphasize the special character of the Dome among other sacred buildings on the Holy Mount and the particular details of the inscription on its walls. Together they affirm the central tenet not only of Islam but of the religions of the Book—intrinsic, inherent, and explicit monotheism, in an Islamic formulation that nevertheless echoes the Hebrew Bible. Next to laudatory statements about the latest and last of the true prophets (Muhammad) is a positive affirmation about Jesus, the preceding true prophet in the story of authentic religion, one whose presence in Jerusalem is not only recorded there but affirmed, articulated, and elaborated on by the imposing sacred building standing on its own hill (or mount) across from the Dome—the Church of the Holy Sepulchre.

In this way, the Dome of the Rock with its weighty, lengthy inscription affirms the superiority of Islam against its rivals but at the same time approves its predecessors as leading and guiding along the proper way. Above all, it invites comparison and welcomes all those pilgrims and visitors to come and see for themselves—to stand where Abraham stood with his knife raised before God and to walk around that sacred stone, to consider the roots of this religion as seen through the eyes of the first ancestor in the faith for all of them, to examine architecture and art, to read its literature, and to join the faithful in a common act of reverence and obeisance to the one God of all.

While for Jews and Christians neither the legend on the wall nor the Qur'an nor Islamic theology can ever come close to rendering a true and faithful account of their religious convictions and commitments, the Dome of the Rock represents an honest and honorable attempt to make Jerusalem a dwelling place for all of them, a common ground for believers in the one true God. Has anyone since been able to do better than that? Given the thirteen-hundred-year period of the Dome's survival, it is hard not to believe that Providence has played an important role in maintaining this building above all that have stood in its place on the Holy Mount. If it is not the Third Temple of messianic tradition and hope, then it is a surrogate and substitute that deserves to hold its place until the day of the Messiah. It comes as close as any, even if it does not yet entirely fulfill the words of the prophet Isaiah:

> And I shall bring them to my holy mountain,
> And I will make them rejoice in my house of prayer . . .
> For my house will be called "House of Prayer" for all the peoples. (Isaiah 56:7)

Notes

1. Keppell Creswell writes that the Dome fell down in 1016 but was restored to its previous condition. See K. A. C. Creswell, *The Origin of the Plan of the Dome of the Rock* (London: Council of the British School of Archaeology in Jerusalem, 1924), 13–16.

2. Genesis 22:3 and especially verse 14 connect the mountain to the land of Moriah.

3. Richard Ettinghausen and Oleg Grabar, *The Art and Architecture of Islam: 650–1250* (New Haven, Conn.: Yale University Press, 1987; 1994), 32.

4. That is, the descendants of Isaac on the one hand and of Ishmael on the other—the first two sons of the patriarch. Members of these faiths who are not descendants by blood are considered to be Abraham's adoptive heirs by virtue of their adherence to the one faith or the other.

5. For information on both the First and Second Temples, see Carol Meyers, "Temple, Jerusalem," in *The Anchor Bible Dictionary*, ed. David Noel Freedman (New York: Doubleday, 1992), 6:350–68.

6. Jerry M. Landay, *Dome of the Rock* (New York: Newsweek Book Division, 1982).

7. For instance, see Jeremiah 38 and Ezekiel 17 (the allegory of the eagles).

8. Josephus, *Jewish War* 5.10.3.

9. We do not include in the account the action of Antiochus IV Epiphanes, who is reported to have erected an altar to Baʿal Shamayim, Lord of the Heavens, in the forecourt of the Second Temple around 170 B.C.E., or even to have erected a statue of this chief god in the temple precinct, but the temple itself remained standing and was restored to proper use by Judas Maccabeus and his successors.

10. Meyers, "Temple, Jerusalem," 367.

11. Jerome, *Ad Paulinum Presbuterum* 58.3.13.

12. "The Itinerary of the Anonymous Pilgrim of Bordeaux," in *Anonymous Pilgrims I-VIII (11th and 12th Centuries),* vol. 6 of Palestine Pilgrims Text Society, trans. Aubrey Steward (1894; reprint, New York: AMS Press, 1971).

13. Eusebius, *Life of Constantine* 3.26 and 3.33.

14. Chrysostom, *Homily* 6.

15. Julian, *Epistles* 29 and 30.

16. Cf. Gregory Nazianzen, *Orations* 4, and Josephus, *Antiquities of the Jews* 16.7.1. These accounts are related by Edward Gibbon, *The Decline and Fall of the Roman Empire* (London: Dent and Sons, 1920), 2:386–87 (chap. 23). Gibbon discusses the sources for these disasters and the likelihood of such conflagrations.

17. Ettinghausen and Grabar, *Art and Architecture of Islam,* 18.

18. Tuvia Sagiv argues, in *The Temples of Mount Moriah* at www .templemount.org/mtmoriah.html, as does Giovanni Rivoira in *Moslem Architecture: Its Origins and Development,* trans. G. McN. Rushforth (New York: Hacker Art Books, 1975), 69 (followed up in Creswell, "The Dome of the Rock," 17), that the octagonal structure takes its shape from the temple to Jupiter, Minerva, and Juno erected on the site by Hadrian. Evidence that Hadrian built a temple rather than a simulacrum, that it was octagonal in shape, and that any portion of that temple remained into the seventh century is open to speculation.

19. Myriam Rosen-Ayalon, *The Early Islamic Monuments of al-Ḥaram al-Sharīf: An Iconographic Study,* Qedem 28 (Jerusalem: Hebrew University, 1989), 12.

20. Alistair Duncan, *The Noble Sanctuary: Portrait of a Holy Place in Arab Jerusalem* (London: Longman, 1972), 28.

21. See also Julian Raby and Jeremy Johns, eds., *Bayt al-Maqdis: ʿAbd al-Malik's Jerusalem* (Oxford: Oxford University Press, 1992), 1:101: "The Syrian Muslims wanted to surpass the dome which covered the spot from which *Christ* had ascended to Heaven, by constructing a new one which covered the rock from which *God* had ascended to Heaven."

22. See David Noel Freedman, *Psalm 119: The Exaltation of the Torah* (Winona Lake, Ind.: Eisenbrauns, 1999), 2, 39; and David Noel Freedman, *The Unity of the Hebrew Bible* (Ann Arbor: University of Michigan Press, 1991), 5.

23. Kim Williams, "The Sacred Cut Revisited: The Pavement of the Baptistery of San Giovanni, Florence," *Mathematical Intelligencer* 16/2 (1994): 24.

24. For a discussion of this rivalry, see Josef van Ess, "ʿAbd al-Malik and the Dome of the Rock," in Raby and Johns, *Bayt al-Maqdis,* 89–103.

CHAPTER 25

FUNDAMENTALS OF TEMPLE IDEOLOGY FROM EASTERN TRADITIONS

John M. Lundquist

Truman Madsen has been a dear friend and mentor to me since the early 1980s. Before that, I knew him at a distance as one of Brigham Young University's most inspiring and charismatic teachers and writers. He gave me an extraordinary opportunity in March 1981 when he invited me to present a paper at a symposium entitled "The Temple in Antiquity." My presentation, "The Common Temple Ideology of the Ancient Near East,"[1] was published in the resulting symposium proceedings and represented a major step forward in my temple-related research and writing. This article appears after the passage of twenty years and the publication of many articles and one book; it represents a partial repayment for the inspiration and guidance Truman has given me these many years.

My purpose here is to summarize my latest thinking on the subject of temple ideology. As I have attempted to delineate in many previous articles and most recently in my book *The Temple: Meeting Place of Heaven and Earth*,[2] a common ideology is shared by all the great temple-building traditions. Even though it may not be possible to identify every feature of this ideology in every tradition, in the larger scheme of things, these traditions all share the same underlying view of the temple. In this article I summarize some fundamental features of the temple ideology that have come more to the forefront of my thinking as a result of recent travel (particularly in Tibet, India, Japan, and Indonesia), reading, and thinking on the temple. The primary impetus to write this article came from the 1995 publication of René Guénon's *Fundamental Symbols: The Universal Language of Sacred Science*,[3] which I consider to be the greatest work of its kind ever published and a vast and inexhaustible mine of insight on the central themes of religion.

I focus here on the following topics: architecture, authority/priesthood, the cave, the center, the labyrinth, the mandala, mantras, the sacred mountain/mound complex, the mysteries, ritual initiation, sacred geometry, and secrecy. Each aspect of temple ideology, although discussed separately in alphabetical order, is linked and interrelated with all the others. For example, the cave and the labyrinth both relate to or influence the conception of architecture, center, mandala, mysteries, sacred mountain, ritual initiation, sacred geometry, and secrecy.

Architecture

The architecture of the temple cannot be fully understood without also discussing it in context of the cave, mandala, sacred mountain/mound, and sacred geometry; I therefore pass over this subject at this point but will return to it continually below, incorporating its meaning into the remaining themes. Essentially, "the temple is the concrete shape . . . of the Essence; as such it is the residence and vesture of God. . . . Ritual action and architectural form express one and the same meaning. The structure of the temple accompanies . . . the rites and their rhythmic formulae."[4] Within the great temple-building traditions, the architecture and ornamentation of a temple were conceived as a unity and were reflected in, represented by, and derived from the ritual practices and the symbolism of the temple.[5]

Authority/Priesthood

The idea of authority is anathema in modern society. In traditional societies, carrying out sacred ordinances without properly constituted authority would have been unthinkable.[6] Within Tibetan Buddhism is a saying: "Without a Lama, there is no Buddha; there is no world; there is nothing." This expression simply underscores the tremendous importance of priestly authority within a temple tradition. The Lamas know the doctrine and have the authority to teach it; without them the doctrine cannot be taught or properly known.[7] Without the Lamas the secret rituals are worthless because it is improper for unauthorized persons to presume to teach or to ritually pass on the various initiations. Every Tibetan empowerment ceremony begins with a statement of the officiating guru's authority and lineage.

The Japanese scholar-priest Kūkai, the founder of Shingon, gave an elaborate description of his own initiation into the "secret treasury of *mantra*" of the Vajrayāna path. He traced his own Vajra lineage from the day, place ("the Abhiṣeka Chapel in the East Stūpa Hall of Ch'ing-lung-ssu in Ch'ang-an"),[8] and initiation master back through several generations to Nāgārjuna, thence to the Buddha Mahāvairocana (the Dharmakāya).[9]

According to Alex Wayman, "Even the most prominent authors write authoritatively only in those fields in which they can show they are the link in the chain of teachers. This accounts for the care taken to list the lineage of teachers for the various texts."[10] In the Japanese Tendai tradition and within Tibetan Tantric Buddhism, the gods are invoked in the temple ritual and called down to be present to bless and sanctify and participate in the proceedings.[11] Books do not replace the authorities because the authorities possess the knowledge and ability to perform ritual practices that are only communicated in the sacred environment of the temple. Outside this environment, even detailed accounts of the proceedings in books would be worthless because they would no longer partake of the sacred, initiatory aura of the temple itself.

The great lineage *thangkas* (paintings) of Tibet trace the authority of a given spiritual tradition, beginning with a deity such as Vajradhara, through each successive lineage holder, up to that moment contemporary with the completion of the painting.[12] The concept of authority is actually built into the architecture and decorative program of one of the greatest Tibetan temples, the fifteenth-century Kumbum in Gyantse, Tibet. This temple, built in mandala fashion, consists of seven levels, topped by a chapel corresponding to the "holy of holies." The initiate would circumambulate each level in a clockwise direction and then ascend to the next highest level until he would reach the upper, most sacred chapel. The chapels on each level are filled with wall paintings and sculptures illustrating the Buddhist doctrine.

The ritual program of the temple is based on the Secret Vajrayāna or Highest Yoga Tantra system of Tibet. The lowest two levels are based on the Kriyātantra and Caryātantra cycles, which are the spiritually lowest and most accessible of these teachings. The third-level chapels are based on Yogātantra, the next highest level of teaching and initiation. The fourth level—which is devoted entirely to chapels with sculptures and paintings of the great lineage-holders within the Tibetan tradition, including the Indian gurus who brought the teachings to Tibet, the translators of the scriptures, the early kings of Tibet, and the lineage masters who introduced each of the great temple rituals to Tibet—must be attained before one proceeds to the highest, most secret level of teachings within this system, the Anuttaratantra (from the fifth level on up to the most sacred chapel). In other words, before the initiate could advance to the highest or "inner" levels of teaching, he would have to be instructed in the line of authority on which this tradition was founded. The chapels in the Kumbum temple, particularly those of the fourth level where the sculptures and paintings of the gurus and masters are found, are designed as though they are caves, situated deep within the sacred mountain.[13]

The Cave

Logically, caves would play a large role in the architecture and ritual of the temple simply because mountains are always honeycombed with them. "When the Maya refer to mountains there is, therefore, an assumption that they are also referring to caves."[14] The sacred mountain that forms the archetype of the temple could not be transformed into the architecture of the temple without the inclusion of caves in the architectural and ritual program.

In Mesoamerica the cave is a primary "place of emergence," the connecting point between the underworld and the upper world, meeting in the middle, on earth.[15] Mesoamerican temple pyramids have been characterized as "cave and sacred mountain" structures, giving architectural expression to the vertical aspect of the layered universe.[16] It has been suggested that the cave underneath the Pyramid of the Sun at Teotihuacan may have provided the prime orientation for the entire sacred complex and, ultimately, for the grid of the city.[17]

Within shamanic traditions the cave is the place of entryway into the underworld, the place of initiation, the place of vision.[18] Caves were "gateways to the spirit world,"[19] with the various chambers serving as "staging posts on the shamanic journey through the underworld," stages on an initiatic journey.[20]

Caves in the temple of Borobudur, on the island of Java, enhance meditation: "The Buddhas in the niches on the four faces have the appearance, from a distance, of *siddhas*, or hermits, meditating deep within caves on the sides of the sacred mountain."[21] As the initiates circumambulated the square galleries at Borobudur, rising to each new level, they would constantly have these "caves" in front of their view. They would be aware of their role in the sacred journey and that they, the initiates, were engaged in a ritual journey to the pinnacle of the sacred mountain. In the wonderful phrase of Max Pulver, the initiate is "a voyager bound for heaven."[22]

What is the role of the cave? "The darkness of night and the darkness of the cave may be taken as a symbolic expression of a religious feeling bound up with the 'earth,' and indeed in all primordial cults the 'mysteries' of birth, death, and rebirth, rising from and returning to the darkness of the earth, are shrouded in darkness."[23] "And the earth was without form, and void; and darkness was upon the face of the deep" (Genesis 1:2). "And God said, Let there be light; and there was light" (Genesis 1:3). "In the beginning this Universe existed in the shape of darkness. . . . In the beginning (of creation) there was darkness hidden in darkness."[24] We can expect that temple ritual will express in dramatic form these scriptural themes. The temple ordinances of the great traditions will lead initiates into and out of darkness, usually adopting the structure of a cave. "Cave and Mountain, in the architecture of Greater India are names for the total temple, *Ku (Guhā)* in Burma, *Giri* (mountain) in Cambodia and *Meru,* in Bali."[25]

The architectural structure of north Indian temples rises, tower upon tower, to the central peak, like the great sacred Himalayan mountain ranges, such that "the complete Prāsāda has the form of an unbroken ascent from the base to the finial. . . . Within it and below the superstructure is the Garbhagṛha, the 'womb of the house,' a small chamber, square, in the majority of preserved temples, and dark as a cave in a mountain."[26] In fact, a certain Indian temple type, the Guharāja, "Great Cave," is formed from the root word *guhā,* which means "cave." This is cognate with *gupta,* "secret," and with the Greek *kruptos,* which ultimately yields the English word "crypt."[27]

Guénon approaches the etymology of this same word from a slightly different perspective:

> The word *guha* [Sanskrit] is derived from the root *guh,* meaning "to cover" or "conceal" or "hide," as does another similar root, *gup,* whence *gupta* which applies to everything of a secret character, everything that is not externally manifested. This is

the equivalent of the Greek *kruptos* that gives the word "crypt," which is synonymous with cave. These ideas are related to the centre insofar as it is considered as the most inward and consequently the most hidden point. At the same time, they refer also to the initiatic secret, either in itself or insofar as it is symbolised by the disposition of the place where the initiation is accomplished, a hidden or "covered" place, inaccessible to the profane, whether the access to it be barred by a "labyrinthine" structure or in any other way (as for example, the "temples without doors" of Far Eastern initiation), and always regarded as an image of the centre.[28]

One of the earliest preserved Hindu temples from the early fifth century, temple number 17 at the central Indian site of Sanchi, was built to replicate a cave, while a temple at Nachna from a slightly later date, had its masonry walls "rusticated" in order to make it look like a mountain "within which the sanctum's 'womb-chamber' acted as the cave."[29] This building practice was carried out within a highly sophisticated architectural setting in India at that time, indicating that the requirements of the temple ideology dictated the rustication, not inadequate or unsophisticated architectural or building potential.

According to Titus Burckhardt, within medieval Christian sacred architecture, which "re-animates customs and forms that go back to prehistoric times, and assimilates them into its own perspective,"[30] Romanesque churches, especially in the Pyrenees region of Spain, were built in such a manner that the barrel vaulting "conferred on the nave, which ended on the east with a niche-like apse, the aspect of a cave." He relates the ideology of this practice to the ancient Oriental concepts of the cave: "It is the universe turned inward, the secret world of the heart or of the soul, in which earth, Heaven, and all things are prefigured, and which is illumined by the Divine Sun of the Spirit."[31]

The ambulatory passageway in Romanesque churches took the pilgrims around the area of the apse, where they could view sacred relics in the crypts situated underground. In the later Gothic period, these underground passageways were raised to ground level, creating the choir ambulatories of Gothic cathedrals.[32]

Stella Kramrisch emphasizes the underground depth of the sacred shrine of the Hindu temple (the Garbhagṛha, or "cave"). "The finial above it shines golden, high up, straight above the omphalos, or centre of the Garbhagṛha, the womb and cave in the mountain. Or else no floor separates the lower and the upper chamber, they are one; only the sunk level is preserved. The one and only Garbhagṛha is often much lower in level than the hall, the Maṇḍapam by which it is approached; stairs lead down to it, to a depth of seven or eight feet, or less."[33] "The underground crypt is secret. . . . The Garbhagṛha, the Cave in the Mountain, lies below its highest point. Along this axis, on any level of the temple, there is, in principle, this secret centre."[34]

Initiation and meditation occur within the inner sanctuary of the temple. Pala period Buddhist art and Pala-inspired Tibetan painting both place the deity or the initiate in this place, either taking the form of the Garbhagṛha[35] or the cave,[36] or as a depiction of both together.[37]

At the Horyuji temple, just south of Nara in Japan, the octagonal Yumedomo, or Hall of Dreams, was built in the eighth century over the hallowed site of a building in which an Asuka period prince, Shotoku Taishi of the sixth century, had retired in order to read and translate the Chinese Buddhist sutras and to receive divine revelation. Studies have shown that this building, where Prince Shotoku meditated, "had the characteristics of a space for incubation that could have been found in a mountain cave."[38] This further suggests the traditional role of the cave in the holy mountain as a place of enlightenment and divine revelation: "And he arose, and ate and drank, and went in the strength of that food forty days and forty nights to Horeb the mount of God. And there he came to a cave, and lodged there; and behold, the word of the

Lord came to him, and he said to him, 'What are you doing here, Elijah?'" (1 Kings 19:8–9 Revised Standard Version).[39]

The Center

This idea is so commonplace as to have become something of a cliché. The great temples are viewed as centers in five ways: (1) they are the projection onto the earth of the celestial temple; (2) they represent the upward extension, the architectural realization, of the primordial mound and the mountain that rises up from the mound; (3) they are established on the place of the primordial revelation, that is, the place of initial creation; (4) they are a representation of the Edenic paradise; and (5) they are designated to be such by priestly or prophetic authority. The center is a place *ritually determined* to be such (by the priestly authority), not necessarily a place or point actually central in a geographic sense. According to Guénon: "The Centre is ... the point of departure of all things, ... the only image that can be given to the primordial Unity.... [B]y its radiation, all things are produced."[40] Further, "The Supreme Centre ... is a 'symbol of the Edenic state'; ... this state remains accessible to man."[41]

The center is fixed in its earthly place through its orientation to the four cardinal directions, through its central axis that connects the worlds (underworld, earth, and heaven), and through ongoing astronomical sightings, which keep the temple and its initiates in constant communication with that ultimate place, heaven. Since the center (the temple) came down from heaven, contact with its place of origin must be maintained, thus promoting the role of astronomy.[42] According to Guénon: "The centre of the ground space, ... the point situated directly beneath the summit of the dome, should be always virtually identified with the 'Centre of the World.'" Here the rites take place that "make the construction of a building a true imitation of the very formation of the world."[43]

From a somewhat different point of view, Coomaraswamy has said: "It is recognized also, of course, that the 'whole earth is divine,' i.e., potentially an altar, but that a place is necessarily selected and prepared for an actual Sacrifice, the validity of such a site depending not upon the site itself but on that of the sacerdotal art [that is, the priestly authority]; and such a site is always theoretically both on a high place and at the center or navel of the earth, with an eastward orientation, since it is 'from the east westwards that the gods come unto men.'"[44]

The center is the source of the doctrine and spiritual authority, representing the goal toward which humankind strives. In and through the temple (the center), a vision of primordial purity and perfection is manifest, pointing in two directions: toward Eden as origin (thus the presence in temple paintings, decoration, adjacent gardens, etc., of the image of what I have called the "primordial landscape"—an image of the way the world was "in the beginning") and toward heaven as goal (thus the presence of chapels in temples representing the celestial realm).[45]

The Labyrinth

The classic study on the labyrinth, still not superseded, is that of C. N. Deedes.[46] The subject of the Egyptian labyrinth has been treated in more depth by Alan B. Lloyd.[47] The extraordinary work of Carl Schuster has now been compiled and published, with one massive volume of this vast work devoted to the labyrinth.[48] Keith Critchlow and others have studied the labyrinth at the Chartres cathedral,[49] and Lima de Freitas has written a thorough and eloquent account of the subject in the *Encyclopedia of Religion*,[50] with an extensive bibliography. Finally, Guénon devotes a substantial amount of space to the labyrinth in his book.[51]

As is the case with mandala, the term *labyrinth* has an etymology and specific meaning and context within a specific tradition. From that tradition, it has moved out into more general cultural and religious studies and is used with meanings that may or may not be intrinsic in its original meaning. The word is attested in the Minoan Linear B tablets as *da-pu-ri-to-jo* and was actually applied to the building at Knossos that we now know as the labyrinth.[52] According to Pliny, the Cretan king Minos commissioned Daedalus to build him a labyrinth; Daedalus patterned his Minoan structure on an Egyptian prototype, the famed and legendary labyrinth of Ammenemes III, a Twelfth-Dynasty pharaoh, at Hawara in the Fayum. The name *labyrinth* was applied to the Egyptian structure by classical authors, based on the legendary labyrinth of King Minos.

Although Sir Arthur Evans, the excavator of Knossos, identified the main structure as a palace, other scholars, in particular Castleden, have established the labyrinth at Knossos as a temple. Thus the floor plan of the palace of Minos at Knossos is the best-preserved example of the archetypal temple as labyrinth:

> But if we were able to visit the Labyrinth in its heyday, when the walls were complete, we would have had a very different experience. Blind walls would have separated these sanctuaries from one another. In some instances, as on the boundary between the Triton Shell Sanctuary and the Late Dove Goddess Sanctuary, there was a double wall separating them. The labyrinth was a maze with an enormous number of gloomy, unlit dead ends. On the whole, they make sense only as spaces for secret, esoteric rituals, each one with its own labyrinthine entrance route. . . . Leading into or out of these shrines there are often sacristies or vestries for robing and other preparations for ritual, inner chambers for more secret rites and stone safes let into the floor for storing sacred vessels.[53]

At Knossos, the labyrinth, the sacred mountain, Mount Juktas, and cave sanctuaries connected with it are also strongly associated.[54]

As far as the Egyptian labyrinth of Ammenemes III, Lloyd has demonstrated that it was doubtless a temple complex, covering a vast area of 1,000 x 800 ft. (established by the excavations of Petrie);

he believed that it actually enclosed within it six temples, which served as a mortuary temple and as a series of temples to various deities. Because of the badly preserved remains of this temple complex, it is difficult to square the plan with the statement of Herodotus that it consisted of fifteen hundred rooms above ground and an equal number of subterranean chambers.[55]

The labyrinth as a temple feature has been studied much and yet is still not really established in its architectural and ritual temple roles. I propose a solution to this problem. Within the temple context, the labyrinth or maze is symbolic of the difficult journey to the center and, as actualized in the architecture of the temple, serves as the ritual pathway that initiates must follow on their journey to the center. Spiral movement is representative of the configuration of the path that deities use to enter this world. Thus, the labyrinth or maze is the shape of the "pathways between the worlds" and must be used by humans to approach those earthly representations of the divine world, the temple. Labyrinths provide the means of approach to the caves, where initiation takes place.[56] The initiatic secret is found in the most inward, hidden place (the cave) or the innermost shrine of the temple. The labyrinth both allows and bars access to this place.[57]

The labyrinth also has a role in modern Maya cave ritual: "The ritual specialist chose two locations in the cave to perform his ceremonies that can be related to a high-mountain and a low-water site. Access to these locations was through 'tiny and tortuous' passageways and included scaling a rock face with a rope."[58] Only the worthy and valiant can traverse this intricate, convoluted, spiral path successfully. Others will lose their way or will be devoured by the Minotaur, as occurred in the Minoan labyrinth. This path is intimately connected with the cave and with the journey into the underworld (as we see at Knossos). The labyrinth requires a guide, as Strabo reported for the Egyptian labyrinth: "Before the entrances there lie what might be called hidden chambers which are long and many in number and have paths running through one another which twist and turn, so that no one can enter or leave any court without a guide."[59] This means that temple ritual requires a guide (by which I mean priestly authority).

The Upper Paleolithic period was the time in human culture in which mountain, cave, and maze coalesced in the same ritual context, as is seen so vividly in the cave paintings of France and Spain. According to Erich Neumann, "We are dealing with the archetype of the *way,* of the mysteries, at the end of which there is a transformation which plays itself out in the holy place, the central space, the uterus of the Great Mother. This place of transformation, however, is to be reached only by way of initiation which leads through a dangerous labyrinth pregnant with death, and in which no conscious orientation is possible."[60] The manner in which Upper Paleolithic religion stands as a foundation for all that has followed was worked out brilliantly many years ago by Gertrude R. Levy.[61] The combination of mountain, cave, and maze (that is, the form or pattern of the ritual path to the cave within the depths of the mountain) was set down in that era and has ever since stood at the center of the temple ideology.

Once the sacred mountain was transformed into a temple building, the resulting architecture had to represent all the features of the mountain, the approach to the mountain, and heaven. In other words, the temple (mountain) architecture must include representations of the mountain itself, its soaring peaks, the caves deep within it, the difficult and tortuous path the initiates must take to reach it, and the heavenly temple of which it is an earthly model. It is in temples such as the Borobudur, the Kumbum, and the Cambodian Angkor Wat that we see all these features come together in such striking fashion. And the floor plan of all these temples corresponds to the mandala configuration. The mandala floor plan, as viewed at Borobudur in particular, has subsumed within itself the mazelike (labyrinth) pattern as a feature of its design and as a part of its ritual—the circumambulation of this temple incorporates the passage into and through the labyrinth. Thus, the mandala and the labyrinth are part of the same architectural and ritual process. Chronologically, the labyrinth is an architectural stylization of the ritual pathway into the Upper Paleolithic caves of France and Spain; the mandala is then a further architectural stylization, a formalization that has persisted, of the labyrinth. The mountain, the cave, the labyrinth (mandala), and heaven—these features are at the heart of the architecture and the ritual of the temple.[62]

"Finding the way through a labyrinth, conceived as a mental, spiritual, and metaphysical enigma, corresponds to the successful conclusion of an *iter mysticum*. It can be expressed visually by transformation of the labyrinth drawing into what in Indo-Tibetan terms is known as *maṇḍala*."[63] According to Guénon, the cave is the site of the initiatic trials; the labyrinth is the way that leads to it, as well as the obstacle that prevents the unworthy from approaching.[64] Furthermore, "This passage [in the sixth book of the *Aeneid* where the gates to the cave of the Cumean Sibyl are described] must have a real symbolic value, since it is based on the close relationship between the labyrinth and the cave, both of which are connected with the same idea of a subterranean journey."[65]

The concepts of cave, labyrinth, and ritual initiation come together in the context of funerary rites. The temple ordinances provide us with a pathway to the other world. This pathway follows the spiral of the labyrinth, entering the cave, exiting to mount the heights of the mountain toward heaven and renewed life.[66]

> There is only a preparation for initiation in death to the profane world, followed by the "descent into hell" which is, of course, the same thing as the journey in the subterranean world to which the cave gives access; as for initiation itself, far from being considered as a death, it is on the contrary like a "second birth," as well as a passage from darkness to light. Now the place

of this birth is still the cave, at least when it is there that the initiation is accomplished, in fact or symbolically. . . . The passage from one state to another is always considered as having to be effected in darkness. . . . The course of the labyrinth is therefore, in this respect, a representation of the initiatic trials; and it is easy to conceive that when the labyrinth actually served as a means of access to certain sanctuaries, it could be planned so as to enable the corresponding rites to be accomplished in the very course of passage.[67]

The traversal of the labyrinth laid into the pavement along the central nave in front of the altar in a number of French Gothic cathedrals was seen as a substitute for the pilgrimage to Jerusalem. The centers of these mazes were referred to as "*'ciel'* [heaven], or 'Jerusalem.'"[68] These places therefore constituted the "Holy Land" within the sanctuary, the "centre of the world."[69] Some medieval traditions tell of an image of the Cretan Minotaur that was laid into the center of the labyrinth. It is said that the image in the center of the labyrinth at Chartres cathedral could be seen up to the time of the French Revolution, when it was removed and used to make cannon balls.[70]

The Gothic cathedral labyrinths were constructed with elaborate geometric symbolism, combining the ideas of center and pilgrimage, linking the labyrinth, and thus the cathedral itself, with the heavens, constituting a reconstruction of Neoplatonic cosmology. "The implications point to the diagram being not only the structure of the universe but also in Neoplatonic terms, a diagram of the 'shells' of reality."[71]

The labyrinth establishes the fundamental pattern of all ritual: it is convoluted and serpentine since one cannot approach a shrine directly; it is fraught with barriers, difficulties, even danger, thus defining the path to the center as an ordeal, the end goal of which brings joy and completion to the initiate; it requires indirect, "labyrinthine" movement along its route, including circular dance, since in so many sacred traditions circularity is seen as the motion and pattern of the divine world, which the shrine and the pathway to the shrine must duplicate (the meeting place of heaven and earth). Furthermore, the role of sacred dance emphasizes the wholly sacral character of ritual: neither ordinary secular walking, nor ordinary clothing, nor anything associated with everyday life is appropriate in this ritual journey. "The pathways between the worlds are also trodden by his human adherents in the dances by which they assimilate themselves with his life-force."[72]

The Mandala

A mandala is a sacred, magical, auspicious design consisting of the combination of circle and square. The shape, with its focus on the circle (referring to the heavens) and the square (referring to the earth), forms the foundation of the traditional view that the cosmic ritual structure brings heaven and earth together. In this place the initiate confronts and achieves union with the divine realm.

The English use of the term *mandala* comes from a Sanskrit word that means "round," "circle," "totality," or "assembly." The Japanese pronunciation is *mandara* and uses ideographs that mean "a place where the Buddha is protected," while the Tibetan is *dkyil 'khor; dkyil* means "central" and *'khor* means "peripheral."[73] Esoteric schools of Buddhism interpreted the etymology of the word as consisting of two roots: *manda,* meaning the essence, and *la,* meaning possession or attainment. Thus mandala means possessing or attaining the essence, in other words, the essence of supreme enlightenment.[74]

Mandala-like designs can be documented to the earliest periods of human existence and appear in many religious traditions besides Hinduism and Buddhism, such as the sacred sand paintings of the Navajos. Within the Hindu and Buddhist traditions, mandalas can be painted or constructed of sand particles or can form the architectural plan of a temple. Mandalas are used for ritual initiations and for meditation. From the psychological point of view, the mandala motif is an archetype that represents the individual's movement toward wholeness or unity. The circle represents the laying down of a sacred precinct, a protective enclosure or *temenos*, within which is found the square sanctuary, or the focal point of individual movement toward the center, where unity of life and consciousness will be found.[75]

Within Vajrayāna Buddhism, the most common mandalas are sacred, numinous shapes representing the celestial palace of the deity residing at its center. The deity at the center can be either peaceful or wrathful, depending on the stage of Yoga Tantra that the initiate has achieved, as well as the needs of the initiate. These so-called "palace" mandalas have four square walls and four gates and are surrounded by several circular precincts, which represent different stages of consciousness and barriers that must be overcome before the initiate can enter the precincts of the palace itself.

Tibetan mandalas that are devoted to meditation on a wrathful deity have four such circular barriers that the initiate must symbolically pass through before reaching the heavenly palace in the center: (1) a ring of fire in five alternating colors, symbolizing the burning away of all spiritual impurities and erroneous thinking (as well as blocking access to the sacred precincts to the unqualified); (2) a ring of *vajras*, the sacred ritual implement that stands for the adamantine character of the truth; (3) the eight traditional cremation grounds arranged in a circular fashion, representing the eight forms of consciousness and reminding the devotee of the tradition of meditating in cemeteries in order to realize the transitory nature of all earthly phenomena or of esoteric rites that would be performed in the cremation grounds;[76] and finally (4) a ring of lotus petals, symbolizing the unfolding of spiritual consciousness as one approaches the center place, the palace of the deity.[77]

The mandala is a projection of the heavenly realm onto the earth, achieved by means of sacred geometry. It is thus the primary expression of sacred geometry in temple architecture, as well as the primary vehicle for meditation in esoteric (Tibetan and Japanese) Buddhism. The mandala, whether in the form of an architectural temple plan or as a painted or sand-particle structure, represents the cosmos in its totality: hell or the underworld, the world in which we live, and the divine realm. The initiate, the one meditating, traverses this structure through ritual circumambulation either in actuality, as in the case of a temple, or in the spirit and mind, as in meditation, just as one would traverse a labyrinth, walking the difficult path of initiation to reach the center or the divine realm, where one attains enlightenment.

Initiation into the mysteries of the mandala is at the heart of esoteric Buddhism: "In the first chapter . . . , Kūkai defines the 'Teaching of the Secret Maṇḍala' *(himitsu mandarakyō),* or the 'Esoteric Teaching' *(mikkyō),* as consisting of the Dharmakāya's speech and of the language of the three mysteries, which reveal the 'wisdom of his inmost enlightenment' *(naishōchi).*"[78] Kūkai's teacher told him that the teachings of "*shingon hizō* (the secret treasury of mantrayāna) [were] so subtle and abstruse that they cannot be transmitted without the help of pictures and diagrams." So the teacher authorized a court painter and other artists to paint the *gharbadhātu* (womb-world, representing the feminine aspect of heaven) and *vajradhātu* (the diamond realm, representing the masculine aspect of the universe) mandalas.[79] The mandala is thus itself the subject and object of initiation into the mysteries, as well as an aid in understanding initiatic texts.

The world's greatest mandala temple, Borobudur in Java, shows us the sequence of the initiatic drama of mandala ritual. The initiate would ascend the structure, circumambulating the lower, square galleries first, which represent the realms of hell, followed by this world with its travails. He would approach and then reach the upper, semicircular platforms, and finally the uppermost circular level, where he would gain ultimate release, enlightenment, nirvana.[80]

But beyond the architectural aspect, the mandala, particularly in Tantric Buddhism, is transferred or projected onto the human body, where all the features of the painted or architectural mandala are represented at the appropriate places in the body, the *chakras*. Furthermore, in Tantrism, the mandala is the focal point of meditation techniques. No actual or visible mandala need be present as the initiate experiences the labyrinthine journey to the center, to enlightenment. All the architectural details of the mandala are present in the visualization process. This is expressed in one text as follows: "The body becomes a palace, the hallowed basis of all the Buddhas."[81] The Navajos use their mandala-shaped sand paintings as a means of bringing a sick person back into harmony with himself and with the universe.[82]

The sacred, auspicious shape of the mandala prescribes the architectural style of the temple building as well as the process, direction, and spiritual content of the initiation ritual.

> The most general meaning of a sanctuary is the reconciliation of earth and Heaven. Therefore it is also a *sācrātum,* a place set apart from every other earthly condition, for in it the otherwise prevailing separation of Heaven and earth, the fall of man and his world from the Eternal, are symbolically and spiritually overcome. In the architectural form of the sanctuary, this can be represented outwardly in several ways; however, the linking of the two existential poles "heaven" and "earth" is expressed with particular eloquence when the sanctuary consists of a square building surmounted by a cupola: the cupola represents heaven, whereas the earth, in its inert condition, subject to the four elements, the four natural qualities, and the four seasons, is "square."[83]

When consecrated under proper authority, the mandala becomes the heavenly palace of the deity, and the initiates are to imagine themselves sitting at the eastern door of this palace. The mandala is a temple in miniature.[84] Within Tantric Buddhism, every temple is a mandala.[85] The temples and monasteries that

were built in mandala fashion were seen to be earthly manifestations of the heavenly realm, with the entire cosmos incorporated
into the earthly structure, as at the Samye monastery in Tibet or
the temple of Borobudur in Java. They were "heaven on earth," and
the rituals carried out in them instructed the initiates in the heavenly plan. In these purified spaces the divine could be revealed,
and secret instruction was passed on through the ritual that
would benefit the initiates.[86] Many natural landscapes are mandalas.[87] Burckhardt relates the mandala concept to the ritual
processes and their underlying spiritual meaning, seeing similarities between the classical Asian mandalas, their architectural realization as temples, and the picture of the Heavenly Jerusalem and
its temple that we are given in the book of Revelation:

> The symbol of a perfect city or a perfect building as epitome
> of the timeless perfection of all things derives from such a deep
> and universal vision, and corresponds so completely to the
> spiritual essence of all architecture, that it must inevitably also
> be found outside the Christian tradition; in fact, it is present in
> every theocratic culture. It appears most clearly, and in a form
> most closely related to the Christian one, in Hinduism. The
> ground plan of the Indian temple is founded on a geometrical
> scheme which transposes the cosmic orbits, both solar and lu-
> nar, into a regular and chequered square, whose peripheral
> areas (which correspond to the signs of the zodiac) are, like the
> "gates" of the Heavenly Jerusalem, ruled by angels or *devas,*
> while its centre, which is looked on as the source of all light,
> represents the "place or locus of god" *(Brahmâsthana).*[88]
>
> The same symbolism appears again in some Buddhist
> meditation pictures, on which, inside the circle that represents
> the endless cycle of becoming and unbecoming, there is a
> square resembling a palace or a city with its gates. In the centre
> of this, an image of the Enlightened One sits on a throne. This
> brings us back to a Christian view, expounded by St. Augustine

and other Church Fathers, according to which passion and sin wander around in a circular motion, while the righteous soul, formed by the cardinal virtues, is "square," like a regularly chiselled foundation stone.[89]

Neumann brings this symbolism about mandalas together within a biblical perspective: "The symbol of the circular mandala stands at the beginning as at the end. In the beginning it takes the mythological form of paradise; in the end, of the Heavenly Jerusalem. The perfect figure of the circle from whose center radiate the four arms of a cross, in which the opposites are at rest, is a very early and a very late symbol historically. It is found in the sanctuaries of the Stone Age; it is the paradise where the four streams have their source, and in Canaanite mythology it is the central point where the great god El sits, 'at the source of the streams, in the midst of the sources of the two seas.'"[90] This scene is frequently represented in the "primordial landscape" temple decoration.[91]

Mantras

Within the Hindu-Buddhist tradition, mantras are sacred syllables and phrases, preserved primarily in the Sanskrit, Tibetan, and Japanese languages. They are pronounced, often in multiples of many thousands, to invoke blessings as part of rituals and, in the Tantric visualization process of Tibetan Buddhism, to generate the meditational deity within the mind of the initiate. Mantras, which are necessary to enjoy communication with the higher powers, are the most highly visible elements of a ritual language remaining from ancient temple ritual. Within Tibetan Buddhism, "From the germinal syllables, the smallest and most highly concentrated symbols of the deities, rays of light originate that then condense into the forms and symbols of the deities until they become recognizable with the utmost clarity and brilliance." And further,

"At the beginning of the meditational creation of the yogi the germinal syllable is seen as the origin and the center of the visionary world."[92]

This is the doctrine of creation by the Word, so well known in the ancient Egyptian texts (the Theology of Memphis) and in the Bible (the Gospel of John). Mantra also refers to the necessity within temple ritual for a secret or code language, a divine language if you will, which is required in order to attain communication with higher powers. This language can take the form of phrases (mantras), single words, or syllables (Sanskrit *bīja*—the "seed syllable"). But the language would not be a contemporary, secular, spoken language. For example, Carl Kerényi refers to the ritual language of the ancient inhabitants of Samothrace, described by Herodotus.[93] It is also possible that the (still undeciphered) Minoan Linear A script will turn out to have been a sacral language used in the ritual of the labyrinth.[94]

Mantras are the gateway to the profound secret knowledge of Tantra. Kūkai, in his work *Distinguishing the Exoteric and the Esoteric,* quotes the Buddha Vairocana as saying: "O Lord of Secrecy, as I observe the wheel of my mantra, the realm of my speech, it is the gateway to a purity so vast and boundless that it envelops the entire world. It is the gate through which the intrinsic nature of all the different sorts of living beings are manifested as they really are, the gateway that brings all living beings to bliss."[95] Mantras constitute "the sacred language necessary for the maintenance of cosmic order."[96] "In the model of maintaining cosmic order [that Kūkai] envisioned, the role of the clergy is to maintain the linguistic technology of mantra, for that makes possible the unfolding of the universe as the ultimate scripture in which all names are already consummate and need no rectification, the unfolding through which order in both nature and society is maintained."[97] Furthermore, within Japanese esoteric Buddhism "the practitioners' recitation of *mantra* is their entry into *Dharmakāya's* royal palace, where they receive their new birth from the union between *samādhi* and *mantra* of the divinities in the *maṇḍala,* and where they establish themselves as heirs in the family of the *Tathāgatas.*"[98]

Guénon has described this process better than any author I am aware of: "The repetition of these formulas aims at producing a harmonisation of the different elements of the being, and at causing vibrations which, by their repercussions throughout the immense hierarchy of states, are capable of opening up a communication with the higher states, which in a general way is the essential and primordial purpose of all rites."[99]

Mantras are sacred words and formulas, preserved in the scriptural languages, which make possible communication with higher realms. They are the secret language of this communication, if you will.[100] In "Indic culture as a whole there is an underlying conviction that the spoken word, more particularly the ritually, solemnly uttered word (or even a sound sequence without meaning) is a thing of great power."[101] However, in addition to the power assumed for this form of discourse, there is a (ritually) practical application—mantras are the means by which deities are addressed.[102] When I say "deities are addressed," this of course assumes that they are addressed in ritual, ceremonially. There can be no unceremonial or casual—"secular"—approach to the divine (that is, within the temple context).

The Sacred Mountain/Mound Complex

The idea of a sacred mountain or mound complex is of course fundamental to the idea of the center. The primordial mound, which becomes the temple-mountain, defines the center. At the place where the primordial waters of creation receded, the earth that appeared there becomes the most sacred, powerful, charged spot of earth imaginable, and it is that place that is enshrined in the most holy sanctuary in the temple.[103]

The image of the mountain provides the elevation or sectional architectural view of the temple. We will see below that the heavenly model, through sacred geometry, provides the floor plan of the temple. The mountain provides the temple building with its architectural elevation (external or side view). The ascending, soaring features of temple architecture define them as the "mountain of God."

Coomaraswamy has summarized this idea in a most interesting manner:

> The altar, like the sacred hearth, is always theoretically at the center or navel of the earth, and the solar eye of the dome is always in the center of the ceiling or *coelum* immediately above it; and these two are connected in principle. . . . [or] in fact, by an axial pillar at once uniting and separating floor and roof, and supporting the latter; as it was in the beginning, when heaven and earth, that had been one, were "pillared apart" by the Creator. It is by this pillar—regarded as a bridge or ladder, or, because of its immateriality, as a bird on wings, and regarded in any case from its base, for "there is no side path here in the world"—that the "hard ascent after Agni" . . . must be made from below to the Sundoor above; an ascent that is also imitated in countless climbing rites, and notably in that of the ascent of the sacrificial post . . . by the Sacrificer who, when he reaches its summit and raises his head above its capital, says on behalf of himself and his wife: "We have reached the heaven, reached the gods; we have become immortals; become the children of Prajāpati." For them the distance that separates heaven from earth is temporarily annihilated.[104]

The mountain, or temple, is the meeting place of heaven and earth. Through its origins in the underworld, as symbolized in the primordial mound of creation, it also unites the three world regions: underworld, earth, and heaven. A central axis or pillar uniting these three zones provides a means of access to and through them by kings or prophets.[105]

> Jacob left Beer-sheba and went toward Haran. And he came to a certain place, and stayed there that night, because the sun had set. Taking one of the stones of the place, he put it under

his head and lay down in that place to sleep. And he dreamed that there was a ladder set up on the earth, and the top of it reached to heaven; and behold, the angels of God were ascending and descending on it! . . . So Jacob rose early in the morning, and he took the stone which he had put under his head and set it up for a pillar and poured oil on the top of it. He called the name of that place Bethel; . . . and this stone, which I have set up for a pillar, shall be God's house. (Genesis 28:10–12, 18–19, 22 RSV)

Thus the temple originates in the underworld, stands on the earth as a "meeting place," and yet towers (architecturally) into the heavens and gives access to the heavens through its ritual. "'The Axis of the Universe is . . . a ladder on which there is perpetual going up and down.'"[106] The ladder rises throughout the worlds—one passes from hierarchy to hierarchy via the rungs—each one a degree of universal existence.

The architecture of the temple projects the building both as a mountain and as a structure based on a heavenly model. "When the Maya built a temple or pyramid near or on a cave site or water shrine, they were creating a house that replicated the deity's home at the mythological mountain, thus duplicating a cosmological concept."[107] "The language of the texts connects the mountain and the cave while describing works of architecture."[108]

The mountain and the temple are inseparable. The sacredness of the one (the mountain) is transferred to the other. All those features that cause or create or determine the sacredness of the mountain are attached to the temple and determine its architecture, its symbolism, and its ritual.

The Mysteries

The mysteries are something quite specific. Kerényi explains the etymology of the word: "The source of the term 'Mysteria'—as also of 'mystes' and 'mystikos'—consists in a verb whose ritual significance is 'to initiate' (Greek μυεῖν), developed from the verb μύειν, 'to close the eyes or mouth.'"[109] The Romans translated *myesis,* the act of closing the eyes, with *initiatio,* from *in-itia,* "going into." Kerényi further explains: "A festival of entering into the darkness, regardless of what issue and ascent this initiation may lead to: that is what the Mysteria were, in the original sense of the word."[110] Through the initiation (the *myesis*), the initiate became one of the *mystai.*[111]

What was the context and content of the mysteries? The context was a nighttime initiation of going into the darkness, usually into an underground cave or cavity, a subterranean shrine deep within the sacred mountain or within the temple itself. Temple ritual is based on rebirth, resurrection, and life out of death.[112] Because the temple is either a natural mountain or an architectural rendering of a sacred mountain, caves associated with this mountain would serve as the locus of rebirth ritual. That ritual would precede the ritual of "coming out into the light" and of ascending to the uppermost chapels of the temple, the heights of the sacred mountain, to heaven. Rebirth takes place in the cave. Installation into the highest heavens takes place on the heights. The initiate is "dead" while blindfolded and, following an "eye opening" ritual, becomes alive and leaves the cave to begin the ascent into the light, to the heavens. The initiate has then become an *epoptēs,* "one who sees."[113]

As to the content of the mysteries, "The Mysteria took the initiate back to the very beginning of life, its natural genesis, and not to any philosophical 'principle.'"[114] Furthermore,

> By mythological images the Attic mysteries still easily led man back to the natural roots of his existence. No special miraculous instrumentality was needed to open access to the realm in which those roots lay; it was a realm whose power had not yet been exhausted, and he who was rooted in it stood firm as a god; the festival with its natural, atmospheric wonders, and man's continuity with his history back to the profoundest sources of

his life, back to the world of his ancestors; these were enough. The presence of what had gone before, which the soul harbors as its most intimate treasure, was efficacious and powerful.[115]

How were these things enacted? According to Paul Schmitt,

The degrees of insight are transmitted by δρώμενα and λεγό-μενα (ritual actions and words). *Dromena* and *legomena* are enacted and spoken by priests and mystai. (The term, ὄργια, related by its root to ἔργα "work," also occurs.) The τελετή ("completion," from τέλος) designate the final stage of 'knowledge' and consecration. The *telos* (ultimate aim) consists in the attainment of a beatific immortality, of a desirable state after death. Symbolically, man enters the underworld, he "dies" in a dromenon [i.e., ritual action], or is "wedded," and he is always symbolically reborn; then he lives no longer in "death" but in "life."[116]

And finally, "we are told that the sacred mime, the *dromena* and *legomena,* was performed by priests with the attributes and often the masks of the gods."[117]

Kerényi describes the Lesser and the Greater Mysteries of Eleusis; the Lesser were performed at Agrai in the month of Anthesterion (our February) and served as a preparation for the Greater Mysteries at Eleusis, performed in the month of Boedromion (our September).[118] Only those initiated at Agrai could proceed to the Greater Mysteries at Eleusis. Those initiated at Agrai experienced the *myesis* and bore the designation *mystai,* or "initiate."[119] The classical sources distinguished the two stages of initiation as that of *myesis* and *epopteia* ("having seen").[120] "We do know that the mysteries consisted of things that were shown and actions that were performed—*deiknymena* and *dromena*—and probably also of things that were said, *legomena.*"[121]

At the heart of the esoteric tradition of Buddhism are the "three mysteries": mantra, mudra, and mandala. "Kūkai argues that what the *Laṅkāvatāra* called *hosshin seppō,* the 'Dharmakāya's preaching of the Dharma,' and *naishō shōgyō*, 'his noble activity of inmost enlightenment,' is in fact the Dharmakāya's three mysteries—the chanting of mantra, the gestural movements of mudrā, and the visualization of maṇḍala, the ritual acts described in various Vajrayāna texts by the Dharmakāya, acts of creating his attendant divinities, producing their maṇḍalas, and communicating with these divinities of the maṇḍala to manifest and enhance their bliss in the Dharma."[122]

Ritual Initiation

The purpose—essential and primordial—of all rites is to open up communication in higher states.[123] The temple is based on a secret doctrine, or the mysteries, which form the basis of temple initiation. The temple is a great public space that is in some parts and at some seasons of the ritual year open to a broader public at the time of the great festivals. A more restricted, "secret" part, accessible only to the few,[124] is where initiation occurs. Anytime communication with the higher worlds is desired or is in process, one would be immersed within the initiatic domain, "but it can easily be appreciated that something of a quite different order takes place when there is any question of an action that has a repercussion in the higher worlds. In such a case, one is obviously in the 'initiatic' domain in the fullest sense of that epithet."[125]

The main purposes of the temple ritual are to explain and represent the primeval paradise whence humankind came and to ritually prepare the initiates to reenter that paradise following death. Through temple ritual, the initiate experiences a *drama* of origins. Part of this usually takes place at night and involves an unveiling, a viewing of sacred objects, a *reenactment* of a creation account (a foundation story), in which the creation accounts are *made present* through their ritual reenactment. "The true myth is inseparably bound up with the cult. The once-upon-a-time is also a now, what was is also a living event. Only in its twofold unity of then and now does a myth fulfill its true essence. The cult is its present form, the re-enactment of an archetypal event, situated in the past but in essence eternal. . . . On this day the whole memory of the great ancestral experience is again true and present. The gods are at hand, as they were at the beginning of time. . . . And the mystai are witnesses of this event, which in essence is not a play, but divine presence, realized myth."[126]

Walter Otto's words here provide a caution against reducing temple ritual merely to a *play* or a *drama* carried out by priests with the initiates as actors in the creation account. Kerényi, Schmitt, and Otto portray the ritual as re-created or restored relations between the heavenly powers and the initiates in a form so powerfully real and present that the experience served as a lifelong support and foundation for a happy and meaningful life.[127]

> Participation in the Mysteries offered a guarantee of life without fear of death, of confidence in the face of death. That is why the poets looked upon the initiates as so superior to other mortals. All Greeks—actually all Greek-speaking persons, the language was the criterion—could share in this gift. It conferred on Greek existence a sense of security, and because it was able to do this, it responded to a spiritual need which, it was not unreasonable to suppose, formed a bond uniting the whole human race: this was the need for a bulwark against death.[128]

A rite is an imitation, a re-creation, or *re-presentation* of a heavenly, divine act(ion), the purpose of which is to establish contact or communication between heaven and earth. Rites serve as the technology of this communication.[129] As J. McKim Malville writes: "The temple is a participatory cosmogony, a creation myth in stone by means of which one can re-experience the creation of the world and thereby be transformed," and "Every day the properly prepared individual can return to the primordial instant of creation and within the boundaries of the temple imitate the emanation and reabsorption of the cosmos."[130]

After the creation, humans and gods walked together on the earth. With the fall from paradise and subsequent separation from the gods, men and women can experience this needed and desired communication with the gods only in the appropriate ritual space—the temple. The (re)union is awesome and overpowering. For example, after his dream, Jacob "was afraid, and said, 'How awesome is this place! This is none other than the house of god, and this is the gate of heaven'" (Genesis 28:17 RSV).

The most outstanding contribution of Guénon to the concept of ritual initiation is his idea that traditional temple ordinances consist of several levels or hierarchies of initiation and that these hierarchies correspond to the levels or states of being. In general he identifies three degrees of initiation within the great primordial traditions.

> Now what can be the significance of these three precincts [in Rome, Athens, etc.]? We thought at once that it must be a question of three degrees of initiation,
>
> . . . which [relate] the three precincts to the three circles of existence recognized by the Celtic tradition. These three circles, which are to be found under another form in Christianity, are the same as the "three worlds" of Hinduism, which moreover sometimes represents the celestial circles as so many precincts around *Meru,* the sacred mountain that symbolizes the "Pole" or the World Axis. . . . [W]here genuine initiation is concerned, its degrees correspond to so many states of the being, and it is these states which in all traditions are described as so many different worlds. . . . [T]he heavens are strictly speaking "spiritual hierarchies," that is, degrees of initiation; and it goes without saying that at the same time they relate to the degrees of universal existence, . . . in virtue of the constitutive analogy of the Macrocosm and Microcosm, the initiatic process rigorously reproduces the cosmogonic process.[131]

Within the Vajrayāna Buddhist tradition, the threefold nature of initiation is most vividly represented within temples. At Borobudur and the Kumbum, the "heavenly" levels of the architecture are divided into three levels. The uppermost chapel in the Kumbum, the *harmikā,* is subdivided into three stories, with the lower story dedicated to the ritual of the "Father Tantras," the upper devoted to the ritual of the "Mother Tantras," and the uppermost (the most holy place in the temple) devoted to the statue and ritual of the highest Tantric deity, the Ādibuddha Vajradhāra.[132] The uppermost level of the Borobudur temple is taken up by three terraces—the first two elliptical and the third (the uppermost that any initiate could reach) circular.[133]

In the biblical temple tradition, initiation begins in paradise and ends in the Heavenly Jerusalem.[134] Temple initiation recapitulates the three stages of life: birth, aging, and death. These are doubtless the "stages of existence" whereof Guénon speaks, and they stand at the foundation of the thinking of Kerényi and Schmitt, quoted above in the section on Mysteries. In its most fully developed forms, temple initiation thus celebrated birth, the passage to adulthood, marriage, death, and the reunion with ancestors.[135]

The physical direction of temple ritual is always some combination of upward, around (circumambulation), and inward toward that part of the temple that represents heaven, or toward the top of the sacred mountain (Exodus 19), where communication with the deity can occur. This upward, circular motion imitates climbing the mountain as one reaches the inward recesses of the temple. The most holy place is always the innermost, most remote, and most removed place from profane life and is represented by the mountain, the architecture of the temple, and the cave. According to Puay-Peng Ho, "the centralised building of two storeys [in the Han Dynasty Ritual Hall at Chang'an] is taken to be the cosmic mountain, the axis that connects the world of man and the world of gods. What is ritually required of the Son of

Heaven is to perform an annual sacrifice to Tian, Heaven, in the Tongtianwu, the upper chamber from which access may be gained to Tian."[136]

Sacred Geometry

Many of the themes addressed above relate to sacred geometry. It cannot be emphasized enough that the temple connects and unites the worlds. Just as the mountain gives the temple architecture its external, directly visible appearance and the cave, along with the labyrinth or maze, gives the temple its ritual processes, so heaven supplies the earthly temple with its floor plan. Because the earthly temple is a projection onto the surface of the earth of the heavenly temple, continual contact and communication must be maintained between the two spheres. This occurs through the orientation of the temple—to the four cardinal directions or the four intercardinal directions—and sightings on specific stars and other celestial bodies.[137]

The temple, with its celestial decorative motifs, gives us the topography of the heavenly realms.[138] Through the motifs, the heavenly prototype is transferred to the earth.[139] The temple is the architectural and ritual medium that makes communication between the worlds possible. Bell discusses the function of portals and doors:

> The portals ["false doors"] were not meant to function in palpable space. Rather, they worked in divine dimension. They were gateways permitting direct, *magical* communication between earth, sky, and netherworld. Ordinary mortals could not cross their thresholds, but the blessed dead and the living king, as well as priests and other initiates, could pass through them to the kingdom of heaven. Nor were these stelae the temple's only portals of otherworldly transport. The wooden doors of the sanctuary shrine, which enclosed the divine image, were called the "doors of heaven." At their opening, ritual participants were projected into the realm of the divine.[140]

The projection of the heavenly model onto the earth is done by means of "stretching the cord" rituals,[141] which are remarkably widespread among the great temple cultures. Finnestad has documented this practice in Egypt:

> Even though *Seshat* has no particular role in the cosmogony, her measuring act has an unmistakable cosmic mark, as its performance is timed and directed by a special star constellation given an analogous function in the cosmogony, namely the *Mshtjw*. Before the foundation the stars are examined and the measuring is done with reference to *Mshtjw*. In the long cosmogony text the *stretching out (pd)* of the *utmost ends (ḥntj)* takes place when this star constellation is seen. There is at this point a correspondence between the laying-out of the cosmic area *(pd ḥntj)*, and the laying out of the temple site *(pd šs)*. As the utmost ends of the cosmos are stretched out (with the wings of the Ruler-of-flying) and the limits established while it is still night, so the cord is stretched over the foundation site and its sides are established while it is still night.[142]

Guénon explains it this way: The "Lodge is the image of the Cosmos," built according to the cosmic model. The chalk-line is the "terrestrial projection" of the cosmic model.[143]

According to the Maya "Book of Council," the Popol Vuh: "Great were the descriptions and the account of how all the sky and earth were formed, how it was formed and divided into four parts; how it was partitioned, and how the sky was divided; and the measuring-cord was brought, and it was stretched in the sky and over the earth, on the four angles, on the four corners, as was told by the Creator and the Maker."[144] The Late Hellenistic cult of Serapis in Egypt combined these temple surveying techniques of several traditions.

> The temple of the cult, the Serapeion, was oriented according to astrological principles. For the nocturnal rite it was oriented toward the star Regulus in Leo, belonging to Helios (for Serapis is not only Zeus, Hades, Dionysus-Osiris, but also Helios),

and for the celebration of the founding of the cult toward the sun: at a certain hour the beams of the sun fell upon the lips of the statue of Serapis. The ancient planet worship, which no doubt lay at the source of certain local cults, the sites of which were in some specific way related to the rising sun, moon, or other heavenly body, found its place in the cosmic dromenon of the eclectic cult of Serapis.[145]

Linda Schele observed about the Maya tradition: "With that discovery [finding out what the sky looked like at sunset, midnight, and dawn on the night of the winter solstice], I realized that every major image from Maya cosmic symbolism was probably a map of the sky."[146] Additionally, "The day we had that discussion, I received a paper from José Fernandez, a young Spaniard teaching archaeoastronomy at Baylor University. José has studied the role of astronomy in the alignment of Utatlan, the capital of the K'iche' at the time of the conquest, finding that all the major temples were oriented to the heliacal setting points of stars in Orion."[147] Karen Bassie-Sweet points out how, in the Early Classic temples at Uaxactun in Guatemala, if one were to stand on the platform of Pyramid E-VII, one would observe that "the sun rises over the northeast corner of Temple E-I on the summer solstice, over the center of Temple E-II on the equinox, and over the southeast corner of Temple [E-III] on the winter solstice. These buildings, an architectural model for the east side of the world, demonstrate that the eastern midpoint was aligned with the rising of the equinox sun."[148]

Within imperial Chinese tradition, just as "the Divine Being (Shangdi or Tian) dwelt in the polar regions of the heaven . . . his astral capital should be imitated by the earthly capital, the seat of the Chinese emperor."[149] The Greeks, according to Jean Richer, "wanted to make their country a living image of the heavens."[150] He describes in great detail the ancient Greek system of aligning sacred mountains, temples, and oracles with each other as "a mirror of the celestial harmony of the zodiac and the planets of the solar system."[151] "The very shape of the sanctuaries," he writes, "unites the image of the earth with the projection of the heavens."[152]

One of the most astonishing representations of the connection between heaven and earth in sacred architecture was built into Chartres cathedral. On the Royal Portico, the cathedral's west front, the three tympanums above the doors themselves represent the Savior in the three aspects of his mission: on the right-hand entrance as he first descended to earth, on the left-hand side as he ascended to heaven, and in the middle as he sits in full glory as the triumphant Savior. Thus the doors represent him as the Alpha and Omega, the only doorway to salvation.

The seven planets are symbolized on the right-hand tympanum in the guise of the Seven Liberal Arts that are sculpted around the archivolt that surrounds the Savior seated on his mother's lap as an infant. The signs of the zodiac are carved around the archivolt of the left-hand tympanum, except for Pisces and Gemini (which are found on the right-hand door). "These belong to the unchanging heaven of the fixed stars and thus represent the kingdom of the Divine Spirit, to whom this door, with its representation of the ascension of Christ, is dedicated. The seven planets, on the other hand, govern, according to the ancient viewpoint, the world of the soul."[153] Paradoxically, while the birth of Christ is represented on the south side of the cathedral's main axis (which ordinarily would indeed be the New Testament side), his ascension is found on the north side (the Old Testament side). The solution to this seeming paradox is to be found in the solar alignment of the doors. They apparently relate to the ancient idea of the "two doors of heaven," *januae coeli*—namely, the two solstices. Through the first door, the "door of winter," the newly returning sun enters into our world, and through the second, the "door of summer," this same light leaves the world. "The location of the winter solstice, which occurs during the Christmas season, is in the southern heavens, and the location of the summer solstice in the northern; it would seem that the representational order in the west door of

Chartres cathedral is a direct reference to this: through the southern door the Divine Light descends into the world; through the northern it returns into the invisible. Between the two gates of Heaven stands the immutable axis of the world; to this the central door corresponds."[154]

Secrecy

On the topic of secrecy, Guénon asserts, "Secrecy . . . implies that the traditional truth itself is no longer accessible . . . to all men equally,"[155] and the "mountain is . . . primordial," signifying the period when all had direct access; the cave is secondary, signifying the period of "obscuration."[156] This is demonstrated in the biblical tradition by the idea that in the beginning, Adam and Eve walk with God and approach him directly. With the fall, this access was broken off. The temple and its rituals are then introduced to humankind by deity in order to restore communication. The knowledge of the temple and its rituals, however, is never really "lost." It becomes unknown to the broad masses, is "occulted," but is carried on as a secret tradition, as in Kabbalah.

The "secrets" are the content of the sacred drama within the ritual setting. Ancient Babylonian ritual texts contained the formula: "The initiate may show the initiate. The uninitiated may not see. Taboo of (such and such) god."[157] If this information is used outside the context of initiation, its meaning and power are lost. It must and will therefore remain secret, since the milieu, spirit, and meaning of initiation cannot be replicated outside the place of initiation. Initiation *is* the secret doctrine, the greatest secret and the greatest mystery. Certain things in temple ritual ("secrets") simply cannot be known by noninitiates. These include contextual things, the feeling ("spirit"), and things said or explained by religious authorities that are "non-textual" or part of an oral tradition.[158] Written or published versions of temple ritual may even mislead the reader, for a variety of reasons. "This Sūtra abounds in 'esoteric' words, i.e. in terms that by their very definition require an explanation which only a qualified teacher gives only to his initiated disciples."[159] Wayman discusses secrecy in Buddhist Tantras:

> The *Hevajratantra* was edited and translated into English. In this sense they are not secret in the sense of being withheld from the reader. But they are still secret, if one can believe the commentators, in that reading these Tantras still conveys little of what the tantrists themselves are doing in the drawn-out rites, with their multitude of details, chanting, and so on. . . . In the case of a tantric text, it will always be a mistake for any reader to think that his proven intelligence (by university degrees and the like) or his proven intuition (by life experience and the like) will enable him to penetrate the meaning of a basic Buddhist Tantra text, because the meaning is in the doing of it, and there is no substitute for someone showing how to do it. That someone of course is the guru.[160]

Heinrich Zimmer further explains how secrecy is preserved through initiation:

> The instructions are present in the stream of the oral tradition, passing from teacher to disciple, to serve only as mnemonics for the essential and the characteristic; not mentioned are many other details that are simply carried along as matter too familiar to note. . . . The text transmits occult knowledge that cannot be used effectively by any uninitiate into whose hands it might accidentally fall. The more it omits as it instructs, the more secure its occult doctrines are from profanation. What distinguishes the initiates is that they understand one another anywhere by means of simple suggestion, and that they require no more than fragmentary, allusive axioms as mnemonic devices found in a particular tradition.[161]

Within Japanese ritual, initiates can only be taught orally. "The word *mikkyo* in Japanese, which bears the connotation of a 'secret' teaching, does not so much mean privileged as it does orally transmitted instructions. The hand gestures (mudra), mantric chants (mantra), and eidetic visions (mandala) must be seen and practiced in order to be understood. . . . Nothing can substitute for a trip to the sacred mountain."[162] Within the esoteric tradition of Japanese Buddhism, initiation into the three mysteries *(honnu sanmitsu)* of mantra, mudra, and mandala is what constitutes Vajrayāna practice. "By contrast, Kūkai suggests that the Shingon School bases its interpretive operation on Vajrayāna discourse, whose salient orientation toward the ritual languages of mantra, mudrā, and maṇḍala distinguishes Shingon from other schools."[163] "Although some of the secret teaching [of Shingon] has been divulged to the world in these modern days, . . . certain religious truths and practices can only be taught orally and are known by a secret communication between teacher and pupil, and are never to be given out through the printed page or in a crowded assembly. In other words, they are esoteric in the fullest sense of the term. To study 'Shingon' on its esoteric side, it is necessary to have a personal teacher who initiates his pupil into the secret practices and the deeper significance of the doctrine."[164]

Mantras are also central to the secret aspect of temple ritual. They, the mantras, the verbal formulas, constitute central "secrets" within the oral transmission process of initiation ritual. They are at the heart of what the initiated masters know and what they pass on only to chosen adepts within the confines of the initiation ritual itself. Within many temple traditions, knowledge of the mantras or of the ritual formulaic language remains unknown to the uninitiated.[165] In Tibet, the Tantric path is referred to as the Secret Mantra Vajrayāna path. "Mudrā and mantra are *arcana sacra,* only accessible to those duly initiated, and therefore only comparatively little information, especially about the mudrās and the liturgic correspondence between mudrās and mantras, is to be found in literature dealing with Buddhism."[166] Within Indian Tantrism, those mantras that are transmitted from teacher to initiate within the initiation process are sometimes referred to as "'ear to ear' transmission *(karṇāt karṇopadeśena).*"[167] Within these traditions, extensive measures are taken to ensure the secrecy of the mantras, such as transmitting them as part of a secret code, embedding the mantric syllables within a sequence of ordinary phonemes to form a cryptogram, and "writing the mantra in reverse order."[168]

Mudras, the sacred hand gestures, act to "seal" or guarantee the efficacy and the veracity of the mantras.[169] Esoteric training within Buddhism revolves around the three mysteries of mandala, mantra, and mudra, distinguished by three languages: "the phonic language of *mantra,* the gestural language of *mudrā,* and the graphic language of *maṇḍala.*"[170] As part of the coronation ceremonies for the Japanese emperor, "his Esoteric Buddhist master" transmits to him "secret *mantras* and *mudrās* for his enthronement."[171] The mudras and mantras transmitted by the master include those of "the five eyes," "the *mudrā* of the wisdom," "the *mudrās* of reigning over the four cosmic oceans," "the precepts of the ten good deeds," and "the *mudrās* and *mantras* of the four masteries."[172] This initiation ritual prepares the emperor to become a "cakravartin, the ideal virtuous ruler *and* the exemplary lay Buddhist patron of the Saṅgha."[173] Names are also secret, including names of deities[174] and the new names that initiates receive upon conversion or upon entry into the mysteries of initiation.

The mystery is the ritual itself, the setting and the process, which should not be, indeed, cannot be reproduced outside the proper setting within the temple. To attempt to do so falls under the description given by Kerényi: "We must guard against excessive talk—a sin against the sacred atmosphere, an involuntary falsification of atmosphere."[175] "No one who had not been initiated was permitted to enter the precinct [at Eleusis] where something higher than *myesis,* the first rite, was solemnized. Even for this introduction into the secret, absolute secrecy was prescribed."[176]

It will remain for another occasion for me to attempt to integrate and synthesize these and yet other features of the temple ideology into a more complete and comprehensive study, one which I will also hope to fill out with many more specific applications to the great temple traditions of humankind.

Notes

This essay is a revised and enlarged version of a paper published in Rome, Italy: John M. Lundquist, "New Light on the Temple Ideology," *East and West* 50 (2000): 9–42.

1. John M. Lundquist, "The Common Temple Ideology of the Ancient Near East," in *The Temple in Antiquity: Ancient Records and Modern Perspectives,* ed. Truman G. Madsen (Provo, Utah: BYU Religious Studies Center, 1984), 53–76.

2. John M. Lundquist, *The Temple: Meeting Place of Heaven and Earth* (New York: Thames and Hudson, 1993).

3. René Guénon, *Fundamental Symbols: The Universal Language of Sacred Science,* comp. and ed. Michel Vālsan, trans. Alvin Moore (Cambridge, England: Quinta Essentia, 1995).

4. Stella Kramrisch, *Hindu Temple* (India: University of Calcutta, 1946), 1:165. For a wide range of illustrations of architectural temple types, see Lundquist, *Temple,* 66–67.

5. See Phyllis Granoff, "Heaven on Earth: Temples and Temple Cities of Medieval India," in *India and Beyond: Aspects of Literature, Meaning, Ritual and Thought: Essays in Honor of Frits Staal,* ed. Dick van der Meij (London: Kegan Paul, 1997), 184; Ragnhild B. Finnestad, "Temples of the Ptolemaic and Roman Periods: Ancient Traditions in New Contexts," in *Temples of Ancient Egypt,* ed. Byron E. Shafer (Ithaca: Cornell University Press, 1997), 204; George L. Hersey, *The Lost Meaning of Classical Architecture: Speculations on Ornament from Vitruvius to Venturi* (Cambridge: MIT Press, 1988), 2.

6. I dwelt on this subject in my book, Lundquist, *Temple,* 20–21, drawing extensively on my own experience as an observer of Tibetan ritual.

7. Steven M. Kossak and Jane C. Singer, *Sacred Visions: Early Paintings from Central Tibet,* with an essay by Robert Bruce-Gardner (New York: Metropolitan Museum of Art, 1998), 8.

8. Ryūchi Abé, *The Weaving of Mantra: Kūkai and the Construction of Esoteric Buddhist Discourse* (New York: Columbia University Press, 1999), 198–99; see 190.

9. See ibid., 221–22.

10. Alex Wayman, *The Buddhist Tantras: Light on Indo-Tibetan Esotericism* (New York: Weiser, 1973), 233.

11. Michael R. Saso, *Tantric Art and Meditation: The Tendai Tradition* (Honolulu: Tendai Educational Foundation, 1990), 8; Mary Van Dyke, "Grids and Serpents: A Tibetan Foundation Ritual in Switzerland," in *Constructing Tibetan Culture: Contemporary Perspectives*, ed. Frank J. Korom (St-Hyacinthe, Quebec: World Heritage, 1997), 200.

12. Jane C. Singer, "Taklung Painting," in *Tibetan Art: Towards a Definition of Style*, ed. Jane C. Casey and Philip Denwood (London: King, 1997), 59.

13. Franco Ricca and Erberto Lo Bue, *The Great Stupa of Gyantse: A Complete Tibetan Pantheon of the Fifteenth Century* (London: Serindia, 1993). For my photographs of the Kumbum Temple, along with its top plan, see John M. Lundquist, "Borobudur: The Top Plan and the Upper Terraces," *East and West* 45 (1995): 297–99, 302.

14. Karen Bassie-Sweet, *At the Edge of the World: Caves and Late Classic Maya World View* (Norman: University of Oklahoma Press, 1996), 66.

15. John B. Carlson, "A Geomantic Model for the Interpretation of Mesoamerican Sites: An Essay in Cross-Cultural Comparison," in *Mesoamerican Sites and World Views: A Conference at Dumbarton Oaks October 16th and 17th, 1976*, ed. Elizabeth P. Benson (Washington, D.C.: Dumbarton Oaks Research Library and Collections, 1981), 154.

16. Ibid., 163.

17. Ibid., quoting Doris Heyden, "An Interpretation of the Cave underneath the Pyramid of the Sun in Teotihuacan, Mexico," *American Antiquity* 40 (1975): 131–47.

18. Jean Clottes and David Lewis-Williams, *The Shamans of Prehistory: Trance and Magic in the Painted Caves*, trans. Sophie Hawkes (New York: Abrams, 1998), 27.

19. Ibid., 35.

20. Ibid., 103.

21. Lundquist, *Temple*, 18–19, with photographs, including some of my own, 40–41, 82–83.

22. Max Pulver, "Jesus' Round Dance and Crucifixion According to the Acts of St. John," in *The Mysteries: Papers from the Eranos Yearbooks*, Bollingen Series 30:2 (New York: Pantheon Books, 1955), 191.

23. Paul Schmitt, "The Ancient Mysteries in the Society of Their Time: Their Transformation and Most Recent Echoes," in *Mysteries*, 99.

24. Kramrisch, *Hindu Temple*, 164.

25. Ibid., 171. For an illustration, see Lundquist, *Temple*, 46–47.

26. Kramrisch, *Hindu Temple*, 162.

27. Ibid., 171 n. 108.

28. Guénon, *Fundamental Symbols*, 145–46.

29. Michael W. Meister, "Symbology and Architectural Practice in India," in *Sacred Architecture in the Traditions of India, China, Judaism and Islam*, ed. Emily Lyle (Edinburgh: Edinburgh University Press, 1992), 9–10.

30. Titus Burckhardt, *Chartres and the Birth of the Cathedral*, trans. William Stoddart (Bloomington, Ind.: World Wisdom Books, 1996), 33.

31. Ibid., 29, with illustrations.

32. Ibid., 33, with illustrations.

33. Kramrisch, *Hindu Temple*, 172.

34. Ibid., 174.

35. Kossak and Singer, *Sacred Visions*, 10, fig. 5, and 63.

36. Ibid., 55.

37. Ibid., 131.

38. Masao Yamaguchi, "Theatrical Space in Japan, A Semiotic Approach," *Japan and America: A Journal of Cultural Studies* 1/1 (1984): 4; J. Edward Kidder Jr., *Japanese Temples: Sculpture, Paintings, Gardens, and Architecture*, photography by Yasukichi Irie (London: Thames and Hudson, 1964), 58–59.

39. For illustrations, see Lundquist, *Temple*, 70–71. I return to the topic of the cave later in this essay when I discuss the mysteries.

40. Guénon, *Fundamental Symbols*, 46.

41. Ibid., 62 n. 13.

42. See Granoff, "Heaven on Earth," 175–76, 180, 182–85; and Dieter Arnold, "Royal Cult Complexes of the Old and Middle Kingdoms," in *Temples of Ancient Egypt*, 72–73.

43. Guénon, *Fundamental Symbols*, 178.

44. Roger Lipsey, ed., *Coomaraswamy: 1: Selected Papers, Traditional Art and Symbolism*, Bollingen Series 89 (Princeton: Princeton University Press, 1977), 4.

45. John M. Lundquist, "The Legitimizing Role of the Temple in the Origin of the State," in *Society of Biblical Literature 1982 Seminar Papers*, ed. Kent H. Richards (Chico, Calif.: Scholars Press, 1982), 274.

46. C. N. Deedes, "The Labyrinth," in *The Labyrinth: Further Studies in the Relation between Myth and Ritual in the Ancient World*, ed. Samuel H. Hooke (London: Society for Promoting Christian Knowledge, 1935), 3–42.

47. Alan B. Lloyd, "The Egyptian Labyrinth," *Journal of Egyptian Archaeology* 56 (1970): 81–100.

48. Carl Schuster, *Materials for the Study of Social Symbolism in Ancient and Tribal Art: A Record of Tradition and Continuity. Volume 3, Rebirth, Book 2, The Labyrinth and Other Paths to Other Worlds*, ed. Edmund Carpenter (New York: Rock Foundation, 1988); and, in abbreviated form, Carl Schuster and Edmund Carpenter, *Patterns That Connect: Social Symbolism in Ancient and Tribal Art* (New York: Abrams, 1996), 302–13.

49. Keith Critchlow, Jane Carroll, and Llewylyn V. Lee, "Chartres Maze: A Model of the Universe?" *Architectural Association Quarterly* 5/2 (1973): 12–20.

50. Lima de Freitas, "Labyrinth," in *Encyclopedia of Religion*, ed. Mircea Eliade (New York: Macmillan, 1987), 8:411–19.

51. Guénon, *Fundamental Symbols*, 139–45.

52. Rodney Castleden, *The Knossos Labyrinth: A New View of the "Palace of Minos" at Knossos* (London: Routledge, 1990), 7, 107, 182.

53. Ibid., 162, 64; see Marina Panagiotaki, *The Central Palace Sanctuary at Knossos* (London: British School at Athens, 1999), 189, 191, 209, 218, 222, 240–42, 273.

54. Castleden, *Knossos Labyrinth*, 108–10, 123–29.

55. Lloyd, "The Egyptian Labyrinth," 96; and see Arnold, "Royal Cult Complexes," 80–82.

56. Gertrude R. Levy, *The Gate of Horn: A Study of the Religious Conceptions of the Stone Age, and Their Influence upon European Thought* (London: Faber and Faber, 1948), 36–53.

57. Granoff, "Heaven on Earth," 186.

58. Bassie-Sweet, *At the Edge of the World,* 70.

59. Lloyd, "The Egyptian Labyrinth," 85.

60. Erich Neumann, "The Psychological Meaning of Ritual," *Quadrant: Journal of the C. G. Jung Foundation* 9/2 (1976): 8, emphasis in original.

61. See Levy, *Gate of Horn.*

62. See Lundquist, "Borobudur," with photographs and plans on 284–85, 287, 292–93, 298–99.

63. Freitas, "Labyrinth," 418.

64. See Guénon, *Fundamental Symbols,* 142.

65. Ibid., 139.

66. For illustrations, see Lundquist, *Temple,* 94–95.

67. Guénon, *Fundamental Symbols,* 140–42. For illustrations, see Lundquist, *Temple,* 86–87.

68. Critchlow, Carroll, and Lee, "Chartres Maze," 12; see Guénon, *Fundamental Symbols,* 142.

69. Guénon, *Fundamental Symbols,* 270.

70. Critchlow, Carroll, and Lee, "Chartres Maze," 12.

71. Ibid.,18. For an illustration of the Chartres labyrinth, see Lundquist, *Temple,* 86.

72. Levy, *Gate of Horn,* 50.

73. Richard Kohn, "The Ritual Preparation of a Tibetan Sand Mandala," in *Mandala and Landscape,* ed. Alexander W. Macdonald (New Delhi: Printworld, 1997), 389 and n. 60.

74. Miyeko Murase, *Tales of Japan: Scrolls and Prints from the New York Public Library* (New York: Oxford University Press, 1986), 20. See also Alex Wayman, "The *Maṇḍa* and the *-la* of the Term *Maṇḍala,*" in *Tantric Buddhism: Centennial Tribute to Dr. Benoytosh Bhattacharyya,* ed. Narendra N. Bhattacharyya (New Delhi: Manohar, 1999), 23–30.

75. John M. Lundquist, "C. G. Jung and the Temple: Symbols of Wholeness," in *C. G. Jung and the Humanities: Toward a Hermeneutics of*

Culture, ed. Karin Barnaby and Pellegrino D'Acierno (Princeton: Princeton University Press, 1990), 113–23.

76. Kossak and Singer, *Sacred Visions,* 52. The cremation grounds can function as the outermost circle, as in Nepali-inspired mandalas, or as described here. See Denise P. Leidy and Robert A. F. Thurman, *Mandala: The Architecture of Enlightenment* (New York: Asia Society Galleries, 1997), 72–73, 76–77, 85–87, 92–95.

77. Giuseppe Tucci, *The Theory and Practice of the Mandala: With Special Reference to the Modern Psychology of the Subconscious,* trans. Alan H. Brodrick (London: Rider, 1969), passim.

78. Abé, *Weaving of Mantra,* 220.

79. Ibid., 190.

80. See Lundquist, "Borobudur."

81. Wayman, *Buddhist Tantras,* 83.

82. Lundquist, *Temple,* 16–19, with illustrations on 80–81, focusing extensively on the Javanese temple of Borobudur, and on the Tibetan *Kālachakra* ritual, to illustrate the meaning of this concept. And see Macdonald, ed., *Mandala and Landscape,* passim.

83. Burckhardt, *Chartres,* 17.

84. Lundquist, "Legitimizing Role of the Temple," 274; Granoff, "Heaven on Earth," 174.

85. Van Dyke, "Grids and Serpents," 183.

86. Detlef I. Lauf, *Tibetan Sacred Art, The Heritage of Tantra,* trans. Ewald Osers (Berkeley: Shambhala, 1976), 117–68. For an illustration of Samye Monastery in its cosmic layout, see Lundquist, *Temple,* 37.

87. Van Dyke, "Grids and Serpents," 193; Macdonald, *Mandala and Landscape,* passim.

88. See Lundquist, *Temple,* 14, with an illustration, 56–57; and John M. Lundquist, "What Is Reality?" in *Temples of the Ancient World: Ritual and Symbolism,* ed. Donald W. Parry (Salt Lake City: Deseret Book and FARMS, 1994), 622–35.

89. Burckhardt, *Chartres,* 27.

90. Erich Neumann, *The Origins and History of Consciousness,* trans. R. F. C. Hull (Princeton: Princeton University Press, 1995), 37.

91. Lundquist, "Legitimizing Role of the Temple," 274; Granoff, "Heaven on Earth," 175, 177, 184, 187.

92. Lauf, *Tibetan Sacred Art*, 117–18. See Kelsang G. Gyatso, *Essence of Vajrayana: The Highest Yoga Tantra Practice of Heruka Body Mandala* (London: Tarpa, 1997), 155–58.

93. Carl Kerényi, "The Mysteries of the Kabeiroi," in *Mysteries*, 44.

94. Castleden, *Knossos Labyrinth*, 72, 161.

95. Quoted in Abé, *Weaving of Mantra*, 217.

96. Ibid., 334.

97. Ibid., 343.

98. Ibid., 303.

99. Guénon, *Fundamental Symbols*, 40. For an extraordinary description of a contemporary attempt to replicate the effect of a *mantra* within an ancient Indian Buddhist ritual space, see Carmel Berkson, *The Caves at Aurangabad: Early Buddhist Tantric Art in India* (New York: Mapin, 1986), xvi. See also Erik Haarh, "Contributions to the Study of Maṇḍala and Mudrā: Analysis of Two Tibetan Manuscripts in the Royal Library in Copenhagen," *Acta Orientalia* 23/1–2 (1958): 63–64.

100. See Charles Malamoud, *Cooking the World: Ritual and Thought in Ancient India*, trans. David White (Delhi: Oxford University Press, 1996), 197–201.

101. George Thompson, "On Mantras and Frits Staal," in *India and Beyond*, 590.

102. Van Dyke, "Grids and Serpents," 198; Haarh, "Study of Maṇḍala and Mudrā," 58.

103. See Lundquist, *Temple*, 6–10, with numerous examples, and with illustrations on 60–61, 68–69. See also Lundquist, "Legitimizing Role of the Temple," 274, 286–88.

104. *Coomaraswamy*, 7–8.

105. Lundquist, "Legitimizing Role of the Temple," 286–89, 293–95; A. R. George, "'Bond of the Lands': Babylon, the Cosmic Capital," in *Die Orientalische Stadt: Kontinuität, Wandel, Bruch*, ed. Gernot Wilhelm (Saarbrucken: SDV, 1997), 128–29; D. O. Edzard, "Deep-Rooted Skyscrapers and Bricks: Ancient Mesopotamian Architecture and Its Imagery," in *Figurative Language in the Ancient Near East*, ed. M. Mindlin et al. (London: School of Oriental and African Studies, University of London, 1987), 13–24.

106. Guénon, *Fundamental Symbols,* 229, citing Coomaraswamy. For a photograph of a medieval architectural rendering of this concept, see Lundquist, *Temple,* 43.

107. Bassie-Sweet, *At the Edge of the World,* 117.

108. Kramrisch, *Hindu Temple,* 169; for illustrations see Lundquist, *Temple,* 52–53.

109. Kerényi, "The Mysteries of the Kabeiroi," 38. Greek monuments make it clear that the initiate closed the eyes—not the mouth—with a blindfold.

110. Ibid., 39.

111. Schmitt, "The Ancient Mysteries," 94.

112. Ibid., 95.

113. Kevin Clinton, *Myth and Cult: The Iconography of the Eleusinian Mysteries, The Martin P. Nilsson Lectures on Greek Religion, delivered 19–21 November 1990 at the Swedish Institute at Athens* (Stockholm: Svenska institutet i Athen, 1992), 86.

114. Kerényi, "The Mysteries of the Kabeiroi," 39.

115. Ibid., 41.

116. Schmitt, "The Ancient Mysteries," 94–95.

117. Ibid., 103.

118. Carl Kerényi, *Eleusis: Archetypal Image of Mother and Daughter,* trans. Ralph Manheim (New York: Bollingen Foundation. 1967), 48.

119. Ibid., 46–47.

120. Ibid., 47.

121. Ibid., 52.

122. Abé, *Weaving of Mantra,* 216.

123. See Guénon, *Fundamental Symbols,* 40.

124. Lanny Bell, "The New Kingdom 'Divine' Temple: The Example of Luxor," in *Temples of Ancient Egypt,* 176.

125. Guénon, *Fundamental Symbols,* 38.

126. Walter F. Otto, "The Meaning of the Eleusinian Mysteries," in *Mysteries,* 29.

127. See also Clinton, *Myth and Cult,* 94–95.

128. Kerényi, *Eleusis,* 15–16.

129. See Malamoud, *Cooking the World,* 201–4.

130. J. McKim Malville, "Cosmogonic Motifs in Indian Temples," in *Sacred Architecture*, 34, 36; see also Van Dyke, "Grids and Serpents," 210.

131. Guénon, *Fundamental Symbols*, 57.

132. Ricca and Lo Bue, *Great Stupa of Gyantse*, 50–51, 306–13.

133. Lundquist, "Borobudur," with photographs and architectural top plans.

134. Lundquist, "What Is Reality?" and John M. Lundquist, "Biblical Temple," in *The Oxford Encyclopedia of Archaeology in the Near East*, ed. Eric M. Myers (New York: Oxford University Press, 1997), 1:324–30.

135. Otto, "Meaning of the Eleusinian Mysteries," 29–31; Kerényi, "Mysteries of the Kabeiroi," 37–42; Schmitt, "The Ancient Mysteries," 94–95, 99, 103.

136. Puay-Peng Ho, "The Symbolism of the Central Pillars in Cave-Temples of Northwest China," in *Sacred Architecture*, 65, quoting Nancy S. Steinhardt, "The Han Ritual Hall," in *Chinese Traditional Architecture*, ed. Nancy S. Steinhardt (New York: China Institute in America, China House Gallery, 1984), 69–77; see also Steinhardt, "Altar to Heaven Complex," in *Chinese Traditional Architecture*, 139–49.

137. Granoff, "Heaven on Earth," 175–76, 180, 182–85.

138. Ibid., 184.

139. Van Dyke, "Grids and Serpents," 196; Lundquist, "What Is Reality?"

140. Bell, "The New Kingdom 'Divine' Temple," 133–34, emphasis in original.

141. See Lundquist, *Temple*, 12–16, with illustrations on 56–57, 72–73, and 76–77.

142. Ragnhild B. Finnestad, *Image of the World and Symbol of the Creator: On the Cosmological and Iconological Values of the Temple of Edfu* (Wiesbaden: Harrassowitz, 1985), 59. For an illustration of this ritual from the Temple of Edfu, see Lundquist, *Temple*, 56.

143. Guénon, *Fundamental Symbols*, 266. For Tibet, see Kohn, "Ritual Preparation," 380–83; and Tucci, *Theory and Practice of the Mandala*, 37–38.

144. Quoted in Carlson, "A Geomantic Model," 143; see also Bassie-Sweet, *At the Edge of the World*, 25; and David Freidel, Linda Schele, and Joy Parker, *Maya Cosmos: Three Thousand Years on the Shaman's Path* (New York: Morrow, 1993), 107–8.

145. Schmitt, "The Ancient Mysteries," 108.

146. Freidel, Schele, and Parker, *Maya Cosmos,* 87.

147. Ibid., 103. For illustrations, see Lundquist, *Temple,* 42–43, 76.

148. Bassie-Sweet, *At the Edge of the World,* 29; see 30, fig. 3 for an illustration.

149. Jeffrey F. Meyer, "Chinese Buddhist Monastic Temples as Cosmograms," in *Sacred Architecture,* 72–73.

150. Jean Richer, *Sacred Geography of the Ancient Greeks: Astrological Symbolism in Art, Architecture, and Landscape,* trans. Christine Rhone (Albany: State University of New York Press, 1994), 11.

151. Ibid., 4.

152. Ibid., 1. For illustrations, see Lundquist, *Temple,* 34–35.

153. Burckhardt, *Chartres,* 69, with photographs on 50, 68, 86–87.

154. Ibid., 70; see also Guénon, *Fundamental Symbols,* 159–62. The extensive role of the temple ideology in the building of the great Gothic cathedrals is a subject to which I want to return at a later time. For the present, in addition to other references cited in this paper, I would like to direct the interested reader to Titus Burckhardt, *Sacred Art in East and West: Its Principles and Methods,* trans. Lord Northbourne (London: Perennial, 1967); Henry Corbin, "The *Imago Templi* in Confrontation with Secular Norms," in *Temple and Contemplation,* trans. Philip Sherrard and Liadain Sherrard (London: KPI, 1986), 263–390; Painton Cowen, *Rose Windows* (San Francisco: Chronicle Books, 1979); Paul Frankl, "The Secret of the Mediaeval Masons," *Art Bulletin* 27 (1945): 46–60; John James, "Medieval Geometry: The Western Rose of Chartres Cathedral," *Architectural Association Quarterly* 5/2 (1973): 4–10; Erwin Panofsky, ed. and trans., *Abbot Suger on the Abbey Church of St.-Denis and Its Art Treasures,* 2nd ed. by Gerda Panofsky-Soergel (Princeton: Princeton University Press, 1979); Lars I. Ringbom, *Graltempel und Paradies: Beziehungen zwischen Iran und Europa im Mittelaltar* (Stockholm: Wahlström and Widstrand, 1951); and Otto G. Von Simson, *The Gothic Cathedral: Origins of Gothic Architecture and the Medieval Concept of Order,* 3rd ed. (Princeton: Princeton University Press, 1988).

155. Guénon, *Fundamental Symbols,* 146, 148.

156. Ibid., 148, 150.

157. Paul-Alain Beaulieu, "New Light on Secret Knowledge in Late Babylonian Culture," *Zeitschrift für Assyriologie* 82 (1992): 98.

158. Clinton, *Myth and Cult,* 90–91.

159. Edward Conze, trans., *Perfect Wisdom, The Short Prajñāpāramitā Texts* (Totnes, England: Buddhist Publishing Group, 1993), vi; see also Vidya Dehejia, *Yoginī, Cult and Temples: A Tantric Tradition* (New Delhi: National Museum, 1986), xi–xii, and Kossak and Singer, *Sacred Visions,* 8.

160. Wayman, *Buddhist Tantras,* 42.

161. Heinrich R. Zimmer, *Artistic Form and Yoga in the Sacred Images of India,* trans. and ed. Gerald Chapple and James B. Lawson (Princeton: Princeton University Press, 1984), 144.

162. Saso, *Tantric Art,* xiii–xiv.

163. Abé, *Weaving of Mantra,* 200; see 207, 216–17, 220.

164. Kalpakam Sankarnarayan and Yoritomi Motohiro, "Concept of Mudra in Japanese (Shingon) Esoteric Buddhism," in *Tantric Buddhism,* 165.

165. See Irit Averbuch, *The Gods Come Dancing: A Study of the Japanese Ritual Dance of Yamabushi Kagura* (Ithaca: East Asia Program, Cornell University, 1995), 67–72.

166. Haarh, "Study of Maṇḍala and Mudrā," 68.

167. David G. White, "Tantric Sects and Tantric Sex: The Flow of Secret Tantric Gnosis," in *Rending the Veil: Concealment and Secrecy in the History of Religions,* ed. Elliot R. Wolfson (New York: Seven Bridges, 1999), 261.

168. Ibid.

169. E. Dale Saunders, "Mudrā," in *Encyclopedia of Religion,* 10:134–37.

170. Abé, *Weaving of Mantra,* 195.

171. Ibid., 361.

172. Ibid., 361–62.

173. Ibid., 362.

174. Pulver, "Jesus' Round Dance," 177; Samten G. Karmay, "The Tibetan Cult of Mountain Deities and Its Political Significance," in *Reflections of the Mountain: Essays on the History and Social Meaning of the Mountain Cult in Tibet and the Himalaya,* ed. Anne-Marie Blondeau and Ernst Steinkellner (Vienna: Osterreichische Akademie der Wissenschaften, 1996), 69; see Per Kvaerne, introduction to René de Nebesky-Wojkowitz, *Oracles and Demons of Tibet: The Cult and Iconography of the*

Tibetan Protective Deities (reprint, Graz, Austria: Akademische Druck- u. Verlagsanstalt, 1975), 177–98; see Kerényi, *Eleusis,* 18.

175. Kerényi, "Mysteries of the Kabeiroi," 38.

176. Kerényi, *Eleusis,* 47.

CHAPTER 26

"HIS HAND IS STRETCHED OUT STILL": THE LORD'S ETERNAL COVENANT OF MERCY

Ann N. Madsen

Many times in the scriptures we read of the Lord's outstretched hand or arm. It serves as a metaphor both for his forbearance and for his invitation to come to him. Nephi reports the Lord's assurance that "mine arm is lengthened out all the day long" (2 Nephi 28:32). We find such references scattered throughout Isaiah's writings. "His anger is not turned away, but his hand is stretched out still" (Isaiah 9:12, 17).[1] In his prophecies that hand is sometimes extended in anger and a moment later in mercy, but always in love. There is a sense that God is reaching for us even when we are turning away. His outstretched hand offers us his continuing covenant of peace.

Isaiah first saw the Lord in the temple in a magnificent outpouring of light and sound. The ground shook beneath his feet. Holiness reverberated, surrounding him with heavenly voices, praising God. "Holy, holy, holy is the LORD Almighty; the whole earth is full of his glory" (Isaiah 6:3 New International Version [NIV]). And indeed, it was for the man Isaiah. For a moment he glimpsed heaven and in the midst of it, the Lord, "seated on a throne, high and exalted" (Isaiah 6:1 NIV).

Isaiah was utterly overcome by the chasm he saw between himself and the Holy Being before him. His first uttered cry described his feeling of being unclean in the presence of such purity. "Woe to me! . . . I am ruined! For I am a man of unclean lips, and I live among a people of unclean lips, and my eyes have seen the King, [Jehovah][2] Almighty" (Isaiah 6:5 NIV). One can only guess at the feelings of shame, fear and awe that filled his trembling heart.

Nothing had been asked of him yet. He alone had reached deep into his own soul and assessed himself unworthy of the experience. But in moments his apprehension turned to joy, for he was touched by the Lord's messenger. He heard a voice uttering the transforming words, "See, . . . your guilt is taken away and your sin atoned for" (Isaiah 6:7 NIV). One can imagine the rapture that filled his heart replacing the dread of moments before.

But this was not all. In the midst of the light and praise, he heard the voice of the Lord himself, and it pierced him to the very center of his being. The newly cleansed Isaiah glimpsed a heavenly council; the words he heard were simple and clear. "Whom shall I send? And who will go for us?" (Isaiah 6:8 NIV). These were familiar words he had witnessed long before in a similar council. In that setting the Firstborn Son of God had offered, "Here am I, send me" (Abraham 3:27). And that had made all the difference for everyone forever.

On hearing the Lord's question, Isaiah was spectator no longer. He responded with the familiar, "Here am I. Send me!" (Isaiah 6:8 NIV). Dennis Rasmussen observes:

> With a question God gives the gift of choice. He asks; man must respond. To complete his work God Omnipotent seeks for help. Will man choose to give it? . . . Will man through his choosing finish the work that God through his choosing began? Will man freely respond, freely return? God asks, then God waits. . . . "And therefore will the Lord wait, that he may be

gracious unto you, and therefore will he be exalted, that he may have *mercy* upon you." (Isaiah 30:18.)[3]

Isaiah continues: "For the LORD is a God of *judgment:* blessed are all they that wait for him" (Isaiah 30:18 King James Version [KJV], emphasis added).

The Mercy of God and Man's Choice Culminate in Covenant

In this account of the call of Isaiah we encounter the three ideas I wish to examine in detail. They are embodied in three Hebrew words: *ḥesed, hinnənî,* and *bārāʾ* or *bərît.*

Ḥesed is defined as "goodness, kindness, mercy, love to God, piety, favour."[4] Often it is translated into English as "lovingkindness." It is a word I loved at first sight. I even loved the way it sounded. We find an example of its use in Isaiah.

> I will mention the *lovingkindnesses* of the LORD, and the praises of the LORD, according to all that the LORD hath bestowed on us, and the great goodness toward the house of Israel, which he hath bestowed on them according to his *mercies,* and according to the multitude of his *lovingkindnesses.* For he said, Surely they are my people, children that will not lie; so he was their Saviour. (Isaiah 63:7–8 KJV, emphasis added)

The second word, *hinnənî,* is really a compound with a suffix. The root is *hin; hinnā* is the word, and it means "lo! behold!" When the suffix is added, the word becomes *hinnənî,* which means, "Behold me! *Here am I!*" We might add "ready to serve," or "at your service." It is the sort of response a servant would give to his master, or a son to his father, or merely someone calling attention to himself as one who is ready to listen and obey, as in the present case. *Hinnənî* is also a word I love, with a meaning that followers of God should hope to adopt in the pattern of the prophets and the Son of God himself. Other occurrences of this term are found in Genesis 22:11, when Abraham answers an angel in this way; in

Genesis 31:11, when his grandson, Jacob, also responds to an angel in this pattern; in 1 Samuel 3:4–10, where the boy Samuel is finally instructed to change his *hinnənî* to "Speak, LORD, for thy servant heareth"; then, predating other examples, we find Jesus offering himself with the words, "Here am I, send me," in Abraham 3:27.

The third word, *bārā'*, is a root that means "covenant." Its derivation, *bərît*, is the common expression used for circumcision and carries the idea of "cutting a covenant." When applied to an agreement between God and man, it means "an alliance of friendship" accompanied by "signs or pledges."[5] *Bərît* is the word used almost exclusively in the Old Testament for "covenant."

The setting for Isaiah's life-altering experience was Solomon's temple. This too is significant as we look at the *ḥesed* of the Lord who came to meet a man in the holy of holies, a place designed specifically for that purpose. We see the precedent for this in the experiences of Moses and his people.

Moses Meets the Lord in a Holy Tent While Israel Watches

In Exodus 33 we read of the tent of meeting, which is translated "tabernacle" or "tent of the congregation" in the King James Version and is the precursor of Solomon's temple (see Exodus 40:2).

> Now Moses used to take a tent and pitch it outside the camp some distance away, calling it the "tent of meeting." Anyone [who was seeking to find] the LORD[6] would go to the tent of meeting outside the camp. And whenever Moses went out to the tent, all the people rose and stood at the entrances to their tents, watching Moses until he entered the tent. As Moses went into the tent, the pillar of cloud would come down and stay at the entrance, while the LORD spoke with Moses. Whenever the people saw the pillar of cloud standing at the entrance to the tent, they all stood and worshiped, each at the entrance to his tent. The LORD would speak to Moses face to face, as a man

speaks with his friend. Then Moses would return to the camp. (Exodus 33:7–11 NIV)

Love and Trust: Integral Parts of God's Mercy

What kind of love is engendered between a father and his child who meet face to face and speak as friends? What kind of faith? What kind of mercy? Even reading of such an encounter invites the righteous to search for and find such a sacred place—a place where they may abandon their hurried prayers to wait upon the Lord with a broken heart and contrite spirit, with pleadings that can barely be uttered in the presence of such purity. In short, they must be willing to examine their own "unclean lips" in the lively hope that their guilt may be taken away and their sins atoned for, as we see described in Isaiah.

What a pattern of trust was perpetuated as the Lord came to tent among his people! They knew that even in their wanderings he would attend to their needs; he would be close by in the center of the camp.[7] The Lord began this cycle of trust and love, and humankind completes it through the affirmation of faith. Adam answered an angel's query, "I know not, save the Lord commanded me" (Moses 5:6). With similar devotion, Isaiah answered quickly, "Here am I. Send me!" It is an eternal pattern begun in heaven. Eternal questions are asked and answered in the temple. In the temple the Lord's trust of his children and their trust of him come together. The sanctuary of the temple becomes a bridge of love, uniting the whole family of God. There the Lord promises, "I will come unto you," and mortal beings reply, "I believe You will come." Then he comes, and the cycle continues. It is a perfect pattern. "There will always be a need . . . to walk to the edge of the light of [our] knowledge and testimony into the twilight of faith."[8] The assurance that others have knelt in temples and seen and heard and felt the peace of the Lord lights the way to modern temples. Isaiah also spoke of this:

In the last days the mountain of the Lᴏʀᴅ's temple will be established as chief among the mountains; it will be raised above the hills, and all nations will stream to it. Many peoples will come and say, "Come, let us go up to the mountain of the Lᴏʀᴅ, to the house of the God of Jacob. He will teach us his *ways,* so that we may walk in his *paths.*" . . . Come, O house of Jacob, let us walk in the light of the Lᴏʀᴅ. (Isaiah 2:2–3, 5 NIV, emphasis added)

In both Isaiah 2 and Isaiah 55, the word *ways* is translated from the Hebrew word *derekh,* which means "way, road, path." In Isaiah 55:8–9 we are reminded that God's thoughts are not our thoughts, for they are higher than ours; nor are his paths our paths, for they are also higher. Yet he is willing to help us find his higher way. Isaiah tells us of a unique high *way:*

And a highway will be there; it will be called the *Way* of Holiness. The unclean will not journey on it; it will be for those who walk in that *Way;*[9] the simple will not stray from it.[10] No lion will be there, nor will any ferocious beast get up on it; . . . But *only* the redeemed will walk there, and the ransomed of the Lᴏʀᴅ will return. (Isaiah 35:8–10 NIV, emphasis added)

Return where? To the presence of the Lord. This is his focus: his children moving ever toward him to become his rightful heirs. In a one-on-one encounter with Moses the Lord explains:

The heavens, they are many, and they cannot be numbered unto man; but they are numbered unto me, for they are mine. And as one earth shall pass away, and the heavens thereof even so shall another come; and there is no end to my works, neither to my words. *For behold, this is my work and my glory—to bring to pass the immortality and eternal life of man.* (Moses 1:37–39)

If we combine this with Jesus' statement, it helps us understand the Lord's plan for us.

Jesus . . . lifted up his eyes to heaven, and said, Father, the hour is come; glorify thy Son, that thy Son also may glorify thee: As thou hast given him power over all flesh, that he should give *eternal life* to as many as thou hast given him. *And this is life eternal, that they might know thee the only true God, and Jesus Christ, whom thou hast sent.* (John 17:1–3 KJV, emphasis added)

It is as if the Lord is explaining to man, "I have built you a place to learn—an earth—and I will show you while you are there the path that will bring you back into my presence."

This lifting up and drawing all people unto him (see John 12:32) that they might eventually find themselves face to face with God *is* his work and glory, and finding their path to that moment of transcendent knowing is every mortal being's work and eventual glory. Humankind was born for glory. Both the Lord's and our tasks are essential. One without the other would be incomplete. Joseph Smith taught that as a person approaches God he or she is enlightened.

> We consider that God has created man with a mind capable of instruction, and a faculty which may be enlarged in proportion to the heed and diligence given to the light communicated from heaven to the intellect; and that the nearer man approaches perfection, the clearer are his views, and the greater his enjoyments, till he has overcome the evils of his life and lost every desire for sin; and like the ancients, *arrives at that point of faith where he is wrapped in the power and glory of his Maker and is caught up to dwell with Him.*[11]

The wrenching pathos in the Lord's bidding his children to come to him is scattered throughout Isaiah's writings. Early on he speaks of a vineyard, well prepared, well planted, and well tended, which produces only bad fruit. His plaintive cry echoes across centuries and the whole earth that that vineyard might well symbolize. "What more could have been done for my vineyard than I have done for it? When I looked for good grapes, why did it yield only bad?" (Isaiah 5:4 NIV).

Man Must Choose God

After all God has done, it remains for man to authorize, by his agency, the heavenly tutoring required to save him. Persuasion is the only tool allowed.

> God's chief way of acting is by persuasion and patience and long-suffering, not by coercion and stark confrontation. He acts by gentle solicitation and by sweet enticement. He always acts with unfailing respect for the freedom and independence that we possess. He wants to help us and pleads for the chance to assist us, but he will not do so in violation of our agency. . . .
>
> To countermand and ultimately forbid our choices was Satan's way, not God's, and the Father of us all simply never will do that. He will, however, stand by us forever to help us see the right *path*, find the right choice, respond to the true voice, and feel the influence of his undeniable Spirit. His gentle, peaceful, powerful persuasion to do right and find joy will be with us "so long as time shall last, or the earth shall stand, or there shall be one man upon the face thereof to be saved" (Moroni 7:36).[12]

In other words, each of us must respond to the Lord's invitation with his or her own *hinnənî*.

Later, Isaiah tells of God's calling out with no one to answer his plaintive call. This is repeated almost like a refrain through many chapters (see, for example, Isaiah 5:25; 9:12, 17, 21; 10:4). One can only guess at his delight when Isaiah answered so promptly with what turned out to be absolute devotion. "*Hinnənî* [Here am I]!" he cried, determined to wear away his life in serving his heavenly King.

Another striking example of this pathos concerns the lack of justice. For without justice, mercy has no starting point. Justice and mercy are inseparable. C. S. Lewis offers a window on this interplay between justice and mercy. "Mercy, detached from Justice, grows unmerciful. That is the important paradox. As there are plants which will flourish only in mountain soil, so it appears that Mercy will flower only when it grows in the crannies of the rock of Justice: transplanted to the marshland . . . it becomes a man-eating weed, all the more dangerous because it is still called by the same name as the mountain variety."[13]

> The LORD looked and was displeased that there was no justice. He saw that there was no one, he was appalled that there was no one to intercede; so his own *arm* worked salvation for him, and his own righteousness sustained him. (Isaiah 59:15–16 NIV, emphasis added)

He would do it himself. He had the power and the glory and the will.

Even more tellingly, the symbol of his hand conveys a message of absolute certainty that he will never desert us. We will not be forgotten or forsaken.

> But Zion said, "The LORD has forsaken me, the LORD has forgotten me." "Can a mother forget the baby at her breast and have no compassion on the child she has borne? Though she may forget, I will not forget you! See, I have engraved you on the palms of my hands; your walls are ever before me." (Isaiah 49:14–16 NIV)

There is magnetism in such unfailing love. We are drawn to it. Just as Jesus suggested, "I, if I be lifted up from the earth, will draw all men unto me" (John 12:32 KJV). Such kindness, such goodness entices us to come closer. There is a remembered righteousness in us, carried in the spirit through a veil into mortality.

> Sometimes during solitude I hear truth spoken with clarity and freshness; uncolored and untranslated it speaks from within myself in a language original but inarticulate, heard only with the soul, and I realize I brought it with me, was never taught it nor can I effectively teach it to another.[14]

Because persuasion is the only tool available, pointing out consequences becomes an effective means to help one choose among the many options in his or her path. Describing consequences is not coercive. It must needs be that there is an opposition in all things so that black and white are never confused with gray.

> Tell the righteous it will be well with them, for they will *enjoy* the fruit of their deeds. Woe to the wicked! Disaster is upon them! They will be *paid back* for what their hands have done. (Isaiah 3:10–11 NIV, emphasis added)

Personal accountability is real. Each individual chooses his or her rewards. The Lord whispers over and over again, "There is no joy in sin, and joy is your destiny. I offer you joy!" Or he shouts, urging us to forsake pride and greed and selfishness. But the choice is always ours. Even though the wicked are given further opportunities, the unrepentant wicked do not make a good choice.

> Though grace is shown to the wicked, they do not learn righteousness; even in a land of uprightness they go on doing evil and regard not the majesty of the LORD. O LORD, your *hand* is lifted high, but they do not see it. (Isaiah 26:10–11 NIV, emphasis added)

Still he waits. He tells them where he is and trusts them to find him. He sees the sinners punished, humbled, then penitent, and he heals them. He points out the peace that only those who have forsaken sins can know. But in the same breath he reminds all of the restlessness of sin and the utter lack of any semblance of peace.

> "I live in a high and holy place, but also with him who is contrite and lowly in spirit, to revive the spirit of the lowly and to revive the heart of the contrite. I will not accuse forever, nor will I always be angry, for then the spirit of man would grow faint before me—the breath of man that I have created. I was enraged by his sinful greed; I punished him, and hid my face in anger, yet he kept on in his willful ways. I have seen his ways, but I will heal him; I will guide him and restore comfort to him, creating praise on the lips of the mourners in Israel. Peace, peace, to those far and near," says the LORD. "And I will heal

them." But the wicked are like the tossing sea, which cannot rest, whose waves cast up mire and mud. "There is no peace," says my God, "for the wicked." (Isaiah 57:15–21 NIV)

Justice Must Be Satisfied

God paints the boundaries precisely where they are. There is no way he can deny his own justice; it is inexorable. Perhaps that is his most telling message. Yet, with justice one day to be paid, he everlastingly extends his hand, stretching to reach to mortal beings. The Sistine Chapel ceiling comes to mind, where Michaelangelo painted the hand of the Creator-God reaching through the clouds to the first man. So soaringly real is the painting that in studying it over time, one is led to feel that one of them must surely move the little distance to connect those outstretched hands, touching graceful index fingers. Who will move? What will justice require? The Lord began his "reaching out" with the first man.

Isaiah repeatedly sings a refrain that haunts the reader and confirms the idea that justice must be satisfied, that the wicked and the righteous will indeed harvest the fruit of their actions. But that same Creator-God still stretches across the vaulted sky to touch the reaching hands, the fingers of his struggling sons and daughters to lead them along the path to the Light. "For all this his anger [justice] is not turned away, but *his hand is stretched*[15] *out [in mercy] still*" (Isaiah 5:25; 9:12, 17, 21; 10:4 KJV, emphasis added).

His hand is eternally extended, reaching through a veil to his children to lead them to a place apart if they will only answer his call.[16] In that sacred, silent spot he will teach them of the path to his glory (see Isaiah 2:3, 5). He will show them how it lies behind and before them. His prophets have left glimpses of the Light, records of brief encounters with glory. They witnessed majesty, the sound of rushing waters, whiteness above all earthly whiteness, light brighter than noonday sun, a voice of thunder, and a still, small voice. Yet it was only a shadow of the full reality.

For behold, the time cometh, . . . that with power, the Lord Omnipotent who reigneth, who was, and is from all eternity to all eternity, shall come down from heaven among the children of men, and shall dwell in a tabernacle of clay, and shall go forth amongst men, working mighty miracles. . . . And lo, he shall suffer temptations, and pain of body, hunger, thirst, and fatigue, even more than man can suffer, except it be unto death; . . . And he shall be called Jesus Christ, the Son of God, the Father of heaven and earth, the Creator of all things from the beginning. (Mosiah 3:5, 7–8)

The greatest of his miracles might well be his own capacity to suffer temptations, physical pain, thirst, and hunger "even more than man can suffer," which enables him to succor others with complete compassion.

Jesus Personifies Mercy

This Light (see Isaiah 2:5; 9:2) came into the world that human beings might see clearly and know exactly how to align themselves perfectly with God—not just in heaven, but while living in this world. No longer did mortals see through a glass darkly (see 1 Corinthians 13:12); they became witnesses as he walked quietly among them, marking an everlasting path by his own footsteps. From desert valleys to verdant mountaintops, how beautiful were the feet of him (see Mosiah 15:18) who brought, and also lived, sublime tidings of the greatest joy.

Isaiah had seen this day and was moved to write, "For unto us a child is born, unto us a son is given: and the government shall be upon his shoulder: . . . Of the increase of his government and peace there shall be no end" (Isaiah 9:6–7 KJV). Isaiah even described the Savior's childhood and ministry in the north: "He will honor Galilee. . . . The people walking in darkness have seen a great light" (9:1–2 NIV). The prophet spoke of the gentleness of the Lord's ministry—of his not discarding a bruised reed or putting out a sputtering lamp which only needed trimming, of his not rejecting even the grape mash left over from the vintage while there was still some good juice in it—using metaphors calculated to show how ultimate power would be used not to put people everlastingly down, but to lift them everlastingly up, reclaiming what might have seemed lost and of little worth to a less penetrating eye.

Isaiah had spoken of the Lord's calling with no one to answer. In fulfillment, Jesus asked his dearest disciples, "Whom do men say that I the Son of man am?" Though the multitudes sometimes thought him to be a prophet, Peter was able to reply with fervor, "Thou art the Christ [in Hebrew, the Messiah], the Son of the living God" (Matthew 16:13, 16 KJV).

Isaiah had said, "Your ears will hear a voice behind you, saying, 'This is the way; walk in it'" (Isaiah 30:21 NIV). In affirmation, Jesus promised, "I will not leave you comfortless: . . . But the Comforter, which is the Holy Ghost, whom the Father will send in my name, he shall teach you all things, and bring all things to your remembrance, whatsoever I have said unto you" (John 14:18, 26 KJV).

Isaiah had repeated over and over again that although God's justice would be satisfied, he would continue to stretch forth his hand in mercy and loving-kindness all the day long. In token, Jesus had beckoned with his hand to a few trusted men to follow him. He had promised that he would make them fishers of men, teaching them to teach and reach to those who needed the strength of their strong hands in order to rise. He truly gave them power to lift up hands that hung down and to lend their strength to those who could barely stand (see Isaiah 35:3).

Isaiah penned the most sublime description of this same Jesus, the living Christ, who would gather all humankind by his supreme atoning act.

> To whom has the *arm* [compare Isaiah 59:16] of the LORD been revealed? He grew up before him like a tender shoot. . . . He had no beauty or majesty to attract us to him, nothing in his appearance that we should desire him. He was despised and rejected by men, a man of sorrows, and familiar with suffering.

. . . Surely he took up our infirmities and carried our sorrows, . . . he was pierced for our transgressions, he was crushed for our iniquities; the punishment that brought us peace was upon him, and by his wounds we are healed. We all, like sheep, have gone astray, each of us has turned to his own *way*; and the LORD has laid on him the iniquity of us all. . . .

He was assigned a grave with the wicked, and with the rich in his death, though he had done no violence, nor was any deceit in his mouth. . . .

Therefore I will give him a portion among the great, and he will divide the spoils with the strong, because he poured out his [soul, KJV] unto death, and was numbered with the transgressors. For he bore the sin of many, and made intercession for the transgressors. (Isaiah 53:1–6, 9, 12 NIV, emphasis added)

Thus we see the ultimate reaches of mercy spelled out in Gethsemane and on a cross. He had indeed engraved those he sought to draw to him on the palms of his hands (see Isaiah 49:16). A poetic response, echoing the *hinnənî* of Isaiah, reflects the deep feelings such a miracle of sacrifice evokes.

> Dear Lord Jesus,
> Thou who lovest
> The people of the Mosque,
> Who would have gathered
> The people of the synogogue,
> Whose arms continue open
> To each saffron-robed monk
> And searching nun,
> Lord of the children
> And the childlike,
> Pulled by thy love,
> Seized by thy suffering,
> Drawn to thee
> By everlasting cords,
> I come![17]

Yet, whether one reaches or never looks up, the invitation remains. The Lord continues to reach and eventually there is a meeting of minds, hearts, and hands, and the "everlasting cords" are tied. Whenever an individual plants his or her feet firmly on the path, determined to grasp the iron rod and never let go, the covenant *(bərît)* is in force. Sanctification begins. The veil thins, and wisdom streams brightly through it. Although we are incomplete, we long to be whole, and all are invited to participate in the covenant. Now the relationship shifts; trust flows in both directions unimpeded. "Thy will be done" is the watchword at all times and in all places. Redemption is beginning. Having lived far beneath our spiritual privileges, we are lifted to a new level of life and light. The difference is dizzying. Like a ship floating through the locks of a canal, being lifted by water higher and higher, we emerge on a new ocean.

Covenants Differ from Laws

Covenants promise future behavior. The Hebrews in Abraham's time spoke of "cutting a covenant," and this is literally what they did, cutting animals in half in a sacrificial mode. Circumcision was a sign in the flesh that God had a people of his own and that the people had a God who would protect and exalt them. The Abrahamic covenant included property, priesthood, and progeny, all promised by God to Abraham, his proven friend. That covenant is a prototype for the covenants entered into in today's temples. The blessings of Abraham, Isaac, and Jacob are still available and in force. The Lord spoke thus of that everlasting covenant to Abraham: "And I will establish my covenant between me and thee and thy seed after thee in their generations for an *everlasting covenant,* to be a God unto thee, and to thy seed after thee" (Genesis 17:7 KJV, emphasis added). God then promised Abraham land and gave him the token of circumcision. In addition, he and Sarai were given new names. Even though past the age of childbearing, they were also promised the miracle birth of a son and heir to the covenant.

Covenants *are* the path. They define the "Way of Holiness" Isaiah described. These holy vows bring humankind closer and closer to the Lord. One speaks in today's vernacular of bonding with a child or loved one. Covenants are truly the bonding of mortal beings to the Lord. It is a bond that he will not break; this is guaranteed by one who is the same yesterday, today, and forever.

> "You, O Israel, my servant, Jacob, whom I have chosen, you descendants of Abraham my friend, I took you from the ends of the earth, from its farthest corners I called you." I said, "You are my servant"; I have chosen you and have not rejected you. So do not fear, for I am with you; do not be dismayed, for I am your God. I will strengthen you and help you; I will uphold you with my righteous right *hand.* (Isaiah 41:8–10 NIV, emphasis added)

The Lord's mercy and love are sure. He will support his children. Those that bind themselves to him are promised transcendent blessings, riches beyond anything the world can offer.

> He gives strength to the weary and increases the power of the weak. Even youths grow tired and weary, and young men stumble and fall; but those who hope in the LORD will renew their strength. They will soar on wings like eagles; they will run and not grow weary, they will walk and not be faint. (Isaiah 40:29–31 NIV)

The proof of the Lord's trust in us is the atonement. The proof of our trust in the Lord is our willingness to be taught. Once taught, we covenant our absolute obedience. These two trusts flow together in the temple. The mercy of the Lord, the willingness of humankind, and the binding of them to one another seem to me to be captured in the three Hebrew words with which this treatise began: *ḥesed,* loving-kindness and unfailing patience on the part of the Lord; *hinnənî* (Here am I), symbolizing tender submission to the Lord by mortal beings; and *barît* (covenant), the everlasting binding of humankind to God. Elder Neal A. Maxwell helps to summarize these ideas:

> The Lord's reach for us is so redemptive and constant. His *arm*, we are told in the Book of Mormon, extends "all the day long." . . . Jesus waits with open *arms* to receive us, and if we are fully faithful, . . . we can eventually know at the entrance to His kingdom that sublime moment the prophet Mormon described when we could be "clasped in the *arms* of Jesus" (Morm. 5:11).[18]

After examining these principles primarily through the words of Isaiah, I am filled with gratitude for the elegant expressions of this great prophet. Over and over he finds the precise metaphor to spell out truth for any who have eyes to see, ears to hear, and hearts to feel. He invites us on behalf of the Lord to come up to meet him in his temple. Isaiah himself met the Lord there, as did Moses in his tent temple. The temple has become my personal center for light and truth, where I have begun to understand the significance of sacred covenants.

In addition to Isaiah, I credit others on both sides of a thin veil whose hands have showed me how one stretches to reach the Lord. Some I have singled out by quoting them in these pages but the one who has taught me most I have left until last.

> For all of us there is something about the temple that can change our lives. We need to reach for it, to honor it, if need be to sacrifice for it, even our sins. Some of us have fought against that . . . because it means change, maybe some painful change. But that change is the Spirit of God working on the soul and it will come to each one of us [if] we will honor the promptings and let the Lord take over in our lives.
>
> The Lord *is* in His temples, where He ministers personally and manifests himself to the faithful therein. With the power of Christ in His sanctuary, it is intended that all of us drink deeply, receive powerfully, and then testify worthily of that glorious truth.[19]

Notes

1. See also Isaiah 53:1; 63:5; and 65:2 for a few of many.

2. My preference is to insert the word *Jehovah* wherever the KJV or NIV has the word LORD in capital and small capital letters, which indicates the translators' substitution for the name of God. See Keith H. Meservy, "LORD=Jehovah," *Ensign* (June 2002): 29.

3. Dennis Rasmussen, *The Lord's Question: Thoughts on the Life of Response* (Provo, Utah: Keter Foundation, 1985), 5, emphasis added.

4. All Hebrew definitions are taken from Francis Brown, S. R. Driver, and Charles A. Briggs, *A Hebrew and English Lexicon of the Old Testament* (Oxford: Clarendon, 1974), 338–39, s.v. *ḥesed;* 243–44, s.v. *hinnā;* and 136–37, s.v. *bārā'* and *bərît.*

5. Ibid., 136, s.v. *bərît.*

6. See ibid., 134, s.v. *mevakesh,* "seek to find."

7. See Numbers 2:1 and 17 for a description of the tent of meeting, which was later pitched in the center of the camp, encircled by the Levites and then the rest of the tribes. This was the case both while they were camped and as they were moving from place to place.

8. Richard G. Scott, "To Acquire Knowledge and the Strength to Use It Wisely," BYU devotional, 23 January 2001.

9. The NIV translator adds a capital *W* to "way" to be certain that path is understood to be the Lord's.

10. Or, in an alternate NIV reading, "wicked fools will not go about on it."

11. *Teachings of the Prophet Joseph Smith,* comp. Joseph Fielding Smith (Salt Lake City: Deseret Book, 1972), 51, emphasis added.

12. Howard W. Hunter, "The Golden Thread of Choice," *Ensign* (November 1989): 17.

13. C. S. Lewis, *God in the Dock: Essays on Theology and Ethics* (Grand Rapids, Mich.: Eerdmans, 1970), 294.

14. Hugh B. Brown, *Eternal Quest,* ed. Charles M. Brown (Salt Lake City: Bookcraft, 1956), 435, quoted in Truman G. Madsen, *Eternal Man* (Salt Lake City: Deseret Book, 1966), frontispiece.

15. The Hebrew word is *naṭah,* which means to "stretch out, spread out, extend, incline, bend." Brown, Driver, and Briggs, *Hebrew Lexicon,* 639.

16. Several years ago, as I examined the Princeton Index of Christian Art, I found in the earliest art, ca. A.D. 300–400, many instances of the hand of God extending through a veil and often even the figure of God from the waist up extending his hand through a veil.

17. Ann Madsen, "Beneath the Violet Windows—Gethsemane," unpublished poem, 17 October 1976.

18. Neal A. Maxwell, "Insights from My Life," *Ensign* (August 2000): 10, emphasis added.

19. Truman G. Madsen, *The Radiant Life* (Salt Lake City: Bookcraft, 1994), 127–28.

Chapter 27

Rationales Are Theology in the Holiness Code

Jacob Milgrom

H and P are two priestly sources. H stands for the Holiness Code (Leviticus 17–27) and P for the Priestly Code (Leviticus 1–16). H is a supplement to and the editor of P. Both P and H are also distributed in large portions of Exodus and Numbers, but this essay will focus only on the rationales of H in Leviticus 17–27.

From the Holiness Code, I shall select one example: Leviticus 20:24–25. This selection is especially important because it fuses two major theological planks in H's program—separation and holiness—and anchors their foundation in the basic themes of creation and life. Separation (*hivdîl*; Leviticus 20:24–26) is the leitmotif of the creation story (see Genesis 1:4, 7, 14, 18) as embodied in the Priestly Code. Separation of the elements and species produces order out of chaos[1] and allows for life to multiply and fill the earth (see Genesis 1:22–28). Similarly, Israel's dietary code (Leviticus 11), which declares most of the meat in the animal kingdom off limits (*sheqets*, "abomination," or *tāmēʾ*, "impure"), is based on a reverence-for-life principle, an aspect of P's life-versus-death theme[2] throughout all of its impurity laws (Leviticus 11–15).

As shown recently by Jan Baersema,[3] P does not limit this principle to forbidden flesh. It states that a carcass (of the eight impure *sherets;* Leviticus 11:29–30) falling on moist seed (but not on dry seed) renders the seed impure (Leviticus 37–38), probably because the moist seed has germinated; it has produced life, and life must not come into contact with death (the carcass). Thus the life-death antipodes are the basis of all the dietary laws. H propels it one giant step forward in declaring *tāmēʾ,* "impure," to be the incompatible antithesis of a quality of YHWH expressed by the term *qādōsh,* "holy," a quality that should be emulated by all of Israel (see Leviticus 11:44; 19:2; 20:26). Thus adherence to the dietary laws—namely, eschewing contact with the world of impurity—forms an indispensable step in Israel's ascent on the ladder of holiness.

Israel's separation from the nations is the continuation (and climax) of the cosmic creation process. Just as YHWH has separated the mineral, vegetable, and animal species to create order in the *natural* world, so Israel must separate from the nations to be a model people, thereby creating order in the *human* world. Israel is thus charged with a universal goal.

It should not be forgotten that H was well aware (at least by oral transmission) of the antediluvian legends. The creation of the first human pair ends in failure: the violence of Cain and his descendant Lamech, miscegenation (intermarriage) with celestial beings (see Genesis 6:1–4), and *hamas,* or universal "violence" (Genesis 6:13). The polluted earth is cleansed by a flood; God tries again with the righteous survivor Noah, hoping to avert failure by imposing law (see Genesis 9:1–6).[4] This experiment also fails with Noah himself (see Genesis 9:21) and with his descendants, who defy God in Babylon by building up instead of spreading out (see Genesis 11:1–9; contra 1:28). Furthermore, H (or its redactor) is fully cognizant of the patriarchal narrative of the epic tradition of the Jahwist and Elohist traditions. Thus, God decides on an individual who willingly "spreads out" from his sinful society and builds a family obedient to God (see Genesis 18:19). P's Abraham is commanded: "Walk in my ways and be blameless *(tāmîm)*" (Genesis 17:1). Just as the life of Abraham will become a standard for blessing throughout the nations (see Genesis 12:3), so too will the exemplary lives of his progeny (see Genesis 26:4).

Israel, following YHWH's commandments, will evoke admiration and emulation throughout the world, indicated by the *nifʿal* and *hitpaʿel* of *BRK followed by the preposition *b* (in Genesis 12:3; 18:18; 22:18; 26:4; 28:14; cf. Genesis 48:20; Psalm 72:17; Isaiah 65:16; Jeremiah 4:2). The *nifʿal* bears a reflexive connotation equivalent to the *hitpaʿel*, both meaning "bless themselves by."[5] Abraham, Jacob, and their progeny will be a standard for blessing chiefly because they represent *ṣədāqāh umišpāṭ*, "righteousness and justice" (Genesis 18:18–19; 22:18).

I presume that H was fully aware of the Genesis narratives if for no other reason than being heir to P's narrative strand, which by the time of H had become integrated with the Jahwist/Elohist editor (JE).[6] Even if the cosmogonic and patriarchal legends were known to H's tradents only by oral transmission, they would have recognized that the patriarchs, in spite of (or through) their faults, were credible models of behavior. Thus when H demands that Israel separate from the nations, it has in mind that Israel's *imitatio dei* will generate a universal *imitatio israeli*.

It does not happen. In the time of Hezekiah[7] and the author of Leviticus 17–27 (with few exceptions), social injustice and individual criminality are rampant. H thereupon devises a plan whereby Israel's purpose on earth can be achieved. To P's life-death principle, which governs its impurity laws, H attaches prescriptions for attaining holiness.[8] The separation from all things impure is the first rung on the ladder of holiness. H's rungs are specified in Leviticus 19.

When H prescribes separation from Egypt and Canaan (see Leviticus 18:3) because of their sexual mores (see 18:6–23), it should be borne in mind that they serve as mere illustrations of all the improper practices *(maʿaśeh)* and laws *(ḥuqqôt)* that Israel should avoid. Instead, Israel should follow the life-giving laws of YHWH (see 18:5). In truth, nowhere does H state explicitly that the purpose of Israel's separation is to create a model people for nations to emulate. But H did inherit the tradition that the moral behavior of the patriarchs, the model for their descendants, was intended to influence the behavior of their neighbors (see Genesis 12:3; 18:18; 26:4).

Separation does not mean isolation. Israel is completely integrated into its surroundings commercially and culturally. If, in H's view, non-Israelites will witness how Israel treats the *gēr*, "alien" (Leviticus 24:22),[9] and the poor (see Leviticus 19:9–10); abolishes slavery (see Leviticus 25:39–43);[10] and cancels debts and restores confiscated land (see Leviticus 25:8–17)[11]—for which God will reward Israel with prosperity and security (see Leviticus 26:3–13)—how could they (the non-Israelites) not be induced to behave similarly (see also Deuteronomy 4:8)? How far, indeed, is the incipient transnational role from the servant poems of the exilic Isaiah, which predict that Israel will be *lǝʾôr gôyim*, "a light of the nations" (Isaiah 42:6–7; 49:6; 51:4; cf. 61:1)?

After all, the divine promise to the patriarchs and H's concrete plan for achieving holiness by separation from the ways of others and obedience to YHWH's commandments—all these lie before exilic Isaiah. Is he not standing on the shoulders of the patriarchal traditions and H's legislation?

It is a special pleasure to dedicate this brief essay to my long-time friends Truman (Amittai) and Ann (Hannah) Madsen, who stand firmly and devoutly on the "shoulders" of the Hebrew language and scripture.

Notes

1. Mary Douglas, *Purity and Danger* (London: Routledge and Kegan Paul, 1996), 55–57.

2. Jacob Milgrom, *Leviticus 1–16* (New York: Doubleday, 1991), 732–35; see the correction in Jacob Milgrom, "Does H Advocate the Centralization of Worship?" *JSOT 88* (2000): 59–76.

3. Jan J. Baersema, *Thora nen stoa over nens en natur: En bijdraga aan het milieu bebat over duurzaamheid en kwalitit* (Nijkerk, Netherlands: Callenbach, 1999).

4. Tikva Frymer-Kensky, "The Atrahasis Epic and Its Significance for Our Understanding of Genesis 1–9," *Biblical Archaeologist* 40 (1977): 147–55.

5. Rashi (Rabbi Shlomo bar Yitzhaq, 1040–1105), *Torat Hayyim* (Jerusalem: Mosad ha-Rav Kook, 1986), 151 (in Hebrew); and Shadal (Samuel David Luzzato, 1800–1865), *Commentary on the Pentateuch* (in Hebrew) (Tel Aviv: Dvir, 1965), 61, on Genesis 12:3. Compare also Arnold Ehrlich, *Hamiqra Kiphshuto,* 3 vols. (Berlin: Poppelauer, 1901), 1:32; Samuel R. Driver, *The Book of Genesis,* 5th ed. (London: Methuen, 1906), 145; Benno Jacob, *Das erste Buch der Torah: Genesis* (Berlin: Schocken, 1934), 337–39; Harry M. Orlinsky, *Notes on the New Translation of the Torah* (Philadelphia: Jewish Publication Society, 1969), 85; Moshe Weinfeld, *Genesis* (in Hebrew) (Tel Aviv: Gorden, 1975), 61.

6. Jacob Milgrom, *Leviticus 17–22* (New York: Doubleday, 2000), 1439–43.

7. Ibid., 1382–93.

8. Ibid., 1397–1400; 1711–26; compare David P. Wright, "Holiness in Leviticus and Beyond," *Interpretation* 53/4 (1999): 351–64.

9. Milgrom, *Leviticus 17–22,* 1416–20.

10. Ibid., 1400–1404; Jacob Milgrom, *Leviticus 23–27* (New York: Doubleday, 2001), 2212–28.

11. Milgrom, *Leviticus 17–22,* 1407–9 n. 6.

CHAPTER 28

"WHO SHALL ASCEND INTO THE MOUNTAIN OF THE LORD?": THREE BIBLICAL TEMPLE ENTRANCE HYMNS

Donald W. Parry

A number of the psalms in the biblical Psalter[1] pertain directly to the temple[2] and its worshipers. For instance, Psalms 29, 95, and 100 pertain to worshipers who praise the Lord as he sits enthroned in his temple; Psalm 30 is a hymn that was presumably sung at the dedication of Solomon's temple; Psalms 47, 93, and 96 through 99 are kingship and enthronement psalms that celebrate God's glory as king over all his creations; Psalms 48, 76, 87, and 122 are hymns that relate to Zion and her temple; Psalm 84 is a pilgrim's song, which was perhaps sung by temple visitors as soon as they "came within sight of the Holy City";[3] Psalm 118 is a thanksgiving hymn with temple themes; Psalms 120 through 134 are ascension texts with themes pertaining to Zion and her temple, which may have been sung by pilgrims as they approached the temple; and Psalm 150, with its thirteen attestations of "praise," lists the musical instruments used by temple musicians, including the trumpet, lute, harp, strings, pipe, and cymbals. In all, perhaps a total of one-third of the biblical psalms have temple themes.

It is well known that during the days of the temple of Jerusalem temple priests were required to heed certain threshold laws, or gestures of approach, such as anointings, ablutions, vesting with sacred clothing, and sacrifices.[4] What is less known, however, is the requirement placed on temple visitors to subscribe to strict moral qualities. Such is the concern of Psalms 15 and 24, hymns that set forth the moral qualities of those who wish to enter the temple. Both psalms are attributed to David.[5]

These two psalms share the same literary structure and have similar literary elements. Each has two questions dealing with who may enter the temple, followed by a response listing the moral qualities that individuals must have in order to enter, and both conclude with a blessing that is reserved for those who enter the temple having fulfilled the moral requirements. The structure, then, is as follows: (1) two questions, (2) a response to the questions, and (3) a blessing for those who enter the temple.

I first examine these two temple entrance psalms—Psalms 15 and 24—and then a poem in Isaiah 33:14–17. All three biblical temple entrance poems share the same structure and the same goal: that of inviting temple worshipers to be worthy to enter the temple, morally and ethically.

Psalm 15

Two Questions

The two questions of Psalm 15[6] consist of synonymous inquiries directed toward temple worshipers concerning their qualifications for admission into the sanctuary.

> Lord, who shall dwell in thy tent?
> Who shall reside[7] on thy holy mountain? (Psalm 15:1)[8]

A number of parallel terms are found in this couplet. The relative pronoun *who* and the possessive pronoun *thy* are each repeated. The two verbs *dwell* and *reside* demonstrate the same idea, and the terms *tent* and *mountain* both refer to the temple. The tent refers to the sacred portable temple used by the Israelites during their sojourn in the wilderness. In the Old Testament, the tabernacle is called the "tent of meeting" 130 times and the "tent" approximately 19 times.

The mountain has symbolic reference to the temple. In many biblical passages, "holy mountain" and "temple" are analogous structures,[9] as both are imposing features on the landscape. Ezekiel 20:40 equates the expression *holy mountain* to the temple by stating that members of the house of Israel are required to worship God at the holy mountain with their "offerings," "firstfruits," "oblations," and "holy [temple] things." Isaiah also creates two similar expressions when he writes of the "house of the God of Jacob" and the "mountain of the Lord" (Isaiah 2:3). Psalm 68:16 speaks of "the hill which God desireth to dwell in; yea, the Lord will dwell in it for ever" (see also Psalms 43:3–4; 99:9). The tent also refers to the temple of Jerusalem.

Response

Who, then, may dwell in the Lord's temple?

> He who walks with integrity[10]
> and works righteousness
> and speaks truth in his heart.
> Who has not tripped upon his tongue,[11]
> Who has not done evil to his neighbor,
> and has not lifted up a reproach against his relative.
> The reprobate, in his eyes, is despicable,
> but those who fear the Lord, he will honor.
> He has sworn to do no evil,
> and he will not falter.
> His money he has not given in interest,
> nor has he taken a bribe against the innocent.
> (Psalm 15:2–5)

Note the synonymous terms used here—the poet speaks of one's moral posture in terms of walking, tripping, faltering, and being unmovable. The poet also speaks of integrity, righteousness, and truth; he mentions explicitly the heart, tongue, and eyes, and through implication refers to the feet ("walks," "tripped"), hands ("lifted up"), and mouth ("speaks," "sworn"). Such indicates that the whole person—the whole life—is involved in preparing for entrance into the temple.

Psalm 15:2 identifies three positive requirements: those who enter the temple must possess integrity, work righteousness, and speak truth. Verse 3 identifies three negative stipulations, each possessing the negation *not*. The three are similar in content, dealing with the temple participant's relationship with humankind, and are more or less antithetical to the expressions in verse 2. To speak truth (v. 2) is the same as not "tripping upon the tongue" or speaking slanderous things about someone; one who works righteousness is one who neither does evil to a neighbor nor mocks his relative. Further, verse 2 refers to "walking" with integrity, a statement diametrically opposed to the idea of "tripping" over the tongue. The concept seems apparent—the righteous walk with integrity, but evil persons trip and fall. Compare Psalm 5:5, which affirms that "the foolish shall not stand in [the Lord's] sight."

The response comprises qualifications of those who are worthy and therefore permitted to enter the sacred domain (Psalm 15:2–5). The qualifications form a ten-part structure, consisting of three positive requirements followed by three negative conditions, then two additional positive requirements, and finally two more negative conditions.[12] In the summary below, the ten-part structure appears with the five positive requirements first and the five negative conditions following. The temple visitor

1. walks with integrity,
2. works righteousness,
3. speaks truth,

4. despises reprobates,
5. and has sworn to do no evil;
6. has not slandered ("trip on his tongue"),
7. has done no evil to his neighbor,
8. has not lifted up a reproach against his relative,
9. has not charged interest for his money,
10. and has not taken a bribe against the innocent.

The negative conditions point to the omission of sinful acts and the positive requirements refer to the commission of righteous acts. By way of comparison, both negative and positive requirements served an important role in the Mosaic law,[13] and the sacrificial offerings were performed for both sins of omission and sins of commission.

The use of the number ten may be deliberate on the part of the author, for when used symbolically, ten denotes wholeness and completeness.[14] The ten conditions listed in Psalm 15 do not represent all conditions of temple worthiness but are representative of the conditions that the individual must apply in order to enter the temple. "He who walks with integrity" (v. 2), for instance, points to all commandments.

The number ten may serve an additional purpose. Biblical scholar Craigie conjectures that temple candidates were required to name off, by counting with their ten fingers, the "moral conditions prerequisite to participation in worship."[15] Sigmund Mowinckel states with regard to the number ten that "this is certainly no mere accident";[16] he sees a relationship between Psalm 15 and the Ten Commandments—both are given in covenantal temple settings, both consist of the number ten, and both correspond to one item per finger.[17]

Blessing

> He who does these things will not be moved forever.
> (Psalm 15:5)

The blessing, summarized in a single sentence, promises, "He who does these things [that is, abides by the five positive requirements and does not commit the five negative actions] will not be moved forever." The expression *be moved forever* speaks of those who are permitted to reside in the Lord's temple forever. Such was the promise outlined in Revelation 3:12, where the righteous are told that he "that overcometh will I make a pillar in the temple of my God, and he shall go no more out" (see Psalm 73:15–20).

Psalm 24

Psalm 24 has a structure similar to that of Psalm 15; it also comprises two questions, a response, and blessings to the faithful. Psalm 24 adds two parts—a prologue that refers to earth's creation (vv. 1–2) and a statement that pertains to the identification of God (vv. 7–10). The identification of God represents a separate stanza, as the term *selah* presumably marks the end of the previous stanza.

Mowinckel holds that Psalm 24 contains the *leges sacrae,* or "laws of the sanctuary," those "special rules and special demands as to the qualifications of those to be admitted" into the temple.[18]

Two Questions

> Who shall ascend into the mountain of the Lord?
> And who shall rise up in his holy place? (Psalm 24:3)

The parallel elements in this structure are as follows: the interrogative *who* appears twice; the term *ascend* of line 1 parallels the phrase *rise up* of line 2; and *mountain of the Lord* corresponds with *his holy place.*

Response

The response to these two questions is brief:

> He whose palms are innocent,
> and whose heart is pure,

> who has not lifted his soul to falsehood,
> and has not sworn what is false. (Psalm 24:4)

Following the two questions, a list of moral qualities, presented in four lines, identifies the person who may enter the sanctuary. The first two lines contain positive statements—he who has innocent palms and a pure heart; the second two lines include negatives—he who neither possesses vanity nor swears falsely.

Blessing

The blessing designed for those who enter the temple with innocent palms and a pure heart is also composed of four lines:

> He shall lift up a blessing from the Lord.
> And righteousness from the God of his salvation.
> This is the circle (or "generation") of them that inquire of
> thee,
> that seek thy face, O God of Jacob. Selah. (Psalm 24:5–6)[19]

Those who possess the moral qualities listed in verse 4 will receive a blessing from the Lord and righteousness from God. This blessing will include the privilege of beholding the face of God once the righteous individual enters God's presence in heaven.

The Setting of Psalms 15 and 24

The context or setting of these two temple entrance hymns, Psalms 15 and 24, is unknown; it seems clear that they pertain to Solomon's temple and perhaps to all of God's temples that have been built in various dispensations of the gospel. Scholars have advanced several theories regarding the two hymns. The three most prominent theories are summarized below.

1. Biblical scholar Hermann Gunkel—followed by Sigmund Mowinckel, K. Galling, J. Begrich, and others—suggests that a priest posed the questions to temple visitors at the temple gate(s).[20] Or, similar to this proposal, Hans-Joachim Kraus suggests that the worshipers stood outside the gates of the temple and asked,

"who is worthy to enter the temple?" Then, "from the inside a priestly speaker answers them with the declaration of the conditions of entrance."[21] This may have been the role of Eli, who was sitting by the temple post (1 Samuel 1:9) when he encountered Hannah. However, the temple entrance psalms themselves do not inform us as to such a dialogue between priest and temple visitor, and the other scriptures are also silent on this particular matter.

2. Moshe Weinfeld, who rejects the idea of a priest and temple visitor dialogue at the temple gates, has suggested that the temple entrance psalms correspond with similarly stated injunctions that were inscribed on the lintels and doorposts of Egyptian temples during the Hellenistic period. Such injunctions, writes Weinfeld, had their roots in the Eighteenth Dynasty or earlier,[22] and he asks, "Could it be that in Israel, too, these were inscribed at the Temple entrances? We do not have any real evidence about the inscription of such exhortations on the temple gates in Israel. But this possibility should not be excluded."[23] In connection with this interpretation, inscriptions have been found at Greek temples (such as the Temple of Zeus Kynthios) instructing temple visitors not to enter the temple if they are impure or unclean.[24]

3. Perhaps Psalms 15 and 24 were hymns sung by worshipers in their congregations, by the Levitical choir who sang in the temple courtyard, or by a choir of priests and laymen who sang the different parts of the entrance hymn. Gunkel has proposed this theory.[25] Similarly, with regard to Psalm 24, Mitchell Dahood proposes that "the dialogue structure of the poem suggests that it was sung by alternating choirs."[26]

Isaiah 33:14–17

A third scriptural passage, Isaiah 33:14–17, has the same structure as Psalms 15 and 24—two parallel questions, a response, and a blessing.[27] This passage of Isaiah can also be identified as a temple entrance poem, but its wording points to the entrance of righteous individuals into the temple of heaven, or the celestial kingdom. Psalms 15 and 24 refer chiefly to the temple on earth.

The section begins with two parallel rhetorical questions asking who can dwell with God in his fire (Isaiah 33:14); these are followed by a response to the questions, detailing the attributes of one who is able to dwell with God (Isaiah 33:15). This in turn is succeeded by a description of the blessings of those who will be privileged to dwell with God (Isaiah 33:16–17).

Two Questions

> Who among us will dwell with devouring fire?
> Who among us will dwell with everlasting burnings?
>   (Isaiah 33:14)[28]

The two questions are parallel. The first six words of line 1 are repeated in line 2: "Who among us will dwell with . . . ?" The expression *devouring fire* of line 1 corresponds with *everlasting burnings* of line 2. The two lines form a beautiful synonymous parallelism.

The phrases *devouring fire* and *everlasting burnings* refer to the dwelling place of God—the celestial kingdom. As Joseph Smith explained, "Some shall rise to the everlasting burnings of God; for God dwells in everlasting burnings."[29] He also taught, "God Almighty Himself dwells in eternal fire; flesh and blood cannot go there, for all corruption is devoured by the fire. 'Our God is a consuming fire.' . . . Immortality dwells in everlasting burnings."[30]

Response

Isaiah's two rhetorical questions ask who will be able to abide the devouring fire of the Lord's glory. He answers these questions in verse 15:

> He who walks righteously,
> and speaks what is right,

> he who despises gain by extortion,
> who shakes his hands lest they hold a bribe,
> who stops his ears from hearing of bloodshed,
> and shuts his eyes from looking upon evil. (Isaiah 33:15)

Isaiah sets forth six statements to describe the qualities of one who will inherit and receive the glories of the celestial kingdom. The phrase *he who walks righteously* refers to one who moves forward in the Lord's paths of righteousness and obedience; *speaks what is right* relates to one who speaks the truth, does not bear false witness against another, and so forth; *he who despises gain by extortion* speaks of one who refuses to gain power, wealth, or other worldly things by oppressing another; *who shakes his hands lest they hold a bribe* designates one who refuses to bribe or to be bribed, on any level of society, in any situation; and the phrases *who stops his ears from hearing of bloodshed* and *shuts his eyes from looking upon evil* apply to one who does not participate in or condone evil actions or works. Note that the entire person is involved in obtaining righteousness, as Isaiah in these verses sets forth five parts of one's body—legs ("walks"), mouth ("speaks"), hands, ears, and eyes.

Blessing

Then Isaiah sets forth six statements to describe the blessings of those who will inherit the celestial kingdom:

> He will dwell on the heights,
> his place of defense will be fortresses of rocks,
> his bread will be given,
> his water will be sure.
> Your eyes will see the king in his beauty,
> they will see a land that is far off. (Isaiah 33:16–17)

The words *he will dwell* refer back to the parallel questions: "Who among us will dwell . . . ?" *On the heights* speaks of heaven, as does the final phrase of the blessing, *a land that is far off.* The words *bread* and *water,* sacramental in nature, pertain to the atonement of Christ; they also relate to heaven, whose inhabitants will be immortal and never want for water or bread, as they "will be sure." The phrase the *king in his beauty* speaks of the Lord in his glory and eternal nature.

Conclusion

Three biblical scriptural passages—Psalm 15, Psalm 24, and Isaiah 33:14–17—share the same structure, having two parallel questions, a response, and a statement regarding the blessings promised to the faithful. The three passages also share the same goal: that of inviting temple worshipers to be morally and ethically worthy to enter the temple. The first two passages are hymnic in nature and apply primarily to temples on earth, first to Solomon's temple and subsequently to all the Lord's temples whenever they have existed upon the earth. The third passage is prophetic in nature and pertains to the heavenly temple, or to heaven itself. Those temple worshipers who enter the earthly temples while possessing moral and ethical purity are those who will be able to dwell with God in his "devouring fire" and "everlasting burnings" (Isaiah 33:14).

Further, the three temple entrance hymns belong to the genre of literature called prophecy. Individuals who abide by the moral and ritualistic requirements identified in Psalms 15 and 24 and Isaiah 33:14–17 receive the promise of eventual entry into God's heavenly temple, or the celestial kingdom. In this manner, the three texts do not speak only to the local immediate generation of temple visitors, some of whom may have received the temple hymns from David and Isaiah, but the texts look forward to all generations of temple participants who serve God in his holy temples.

Notes

1. For a discussion regarding the origins of psalmody in ancient Israel, see Peter C. Craigie, *Psalms 1–50* (Waco, Tex.: Word Books, 1983),

25–27, who lists various hymns and songs that existed in Israel before those included in the book of Psalms. These very old hymns include the Song of the Sea (Exodus 15:1–18), the Song of Moses (Deuteronomy 32), the Song of Deborah (Judges 5), and the Song of Hannah (1 Samuel 2:1–10).

2. For a careful study of psalms that deal with the temple and worship in ancient Israel, see Sigmund Mowinckel, *The Psalms in Israel's Worship*, 2 vols., trans. D. R. Ap-Thomas (Oxford: Blackwell, 1962); and Othmar Keel, *The Symbolism of the Biblical World: Ancient Near Eastern Iconography and the Book of Psalms*, trans. Timothy J. Hallett (Winona Lake, Ind.: Eisenbrauns, 1997).

3. Carroll Stuhlmueller, *Psalms 2* (Wilmington, Del.: Glazier, 1983), 46; see Mowinckel, *Psalms in Israel's Worship*, 2:107.

4. See Donald W. Parry, "Ritual Anointing with Olive Oil in Ancient Israelite Religion," in *The Allegory of the Olive Tree: The Olive, the Bible, and Jacob 5*, ed. Stephen D. Ricks and John W. Welch (Salt Lake City: Deseret Book and FARMS, 1994), 262–89.

5. A total of seventy-three psalms are attributed to David. Others were authored by Asaph or the sons of Korah. A number of psalms do not have attributions given; see Craigie, *Psalms 1–50*, 28–29.

6. Scholars are uncertain as to the date of Psalm 15; see Craigie, *Psalms 1–50*, 151. If we accept the psalm's attribution, it was authored by King David, which would indicate a date of approximately 1000–950 B.C. While the mention of the tent in verse 1 recalls the Mosaic tabernacle, this fact should not persuade the reader to date the psalm to the pre-Davidic era.

7. The verb here is the Hebrew *shākhēn*, which literally means "to tent" or "to tabernacle." According to G. Henton Davies, *Exodus* (London: SCM Press, 1967), 197, the word means "to tabernacle, dwell among," and according to Frank M. Cross, "The Tabernacle," *Biblical Archaeologist* 10/3 (September 1947): 66, "to tent" or "to encamp."

8. The translations of Psalms 15 and 24 and Isaiah 33:14–17 are my own.

9. On the subject of the mountain as a symbol for the temple, see Donald W. Parry, "Sinai as Sanctuary and Mountain of God," in *By Study and Also by Faith: Essays in Honor of Hugh W. Nibley*, ed. John M. Lund-

quist and Stephen D. Ricks (Salt Lake City: Deseret Book and FARMS, 1990), 1:483–85.

10. No English word adequately expresses the Hebrew term *ṭāmmîm.* The term signifies "wholeness," "completeness," or "integrity." The term *integrity* comes closest to the true meaning of the Hebrew term.

11. This is an idiomatic expression, the meaning of which speaks of a person who slanders a fellow being.

12. Craigie, *Psalms 1–50,* 150.

13. The rabbis count 613 commandments in the five books of Moses—365 positive commandments and 248 negative commandments.

14. The number *ten* is used symbolically on a number of occasions in the scriptures; instances include the Ten Commandments, the law of tithing, the redemption money (Exodus 30:12–16), the ten plagues, and the parable of the ten virgins. See Ethelbert W. Bullinger, *Number in Scripture: Its Supernatural Design and Spiritual Significance* (Grand Rapids, Mich.: Kregal, 1967), 243–50.

15. Craigie, *Psalms 1–50,* 151.

16. Mowinckel, *The Psalms in Israel's Worship,* 1:158.

17. Ibid., 179.

18. Ibid., 177.

19. For a discussion of the readings in these two verses, see Donald W. Parry, "Temple Worship and a Possible Reference to a Prayer Circle in Psalm 24," *BYU Studies* 32/4 (1992): 57–62. For the reading "God of Jacob," see Mitchell Dahood, *Psalms I, 1–50* (Garden City, N.Y.: Doubleday, 1979), 152.

20. Cited in Moshe Weinfeld, "Instructions for Temple Visitors in the Bible and in Ancient Egypt," in *Egyptological Studies,* ed. Sarah Israelit-Groll, Scripta Hierosolymitana 28 (Jerusalem: Magnes, 1982): 230–31.

21. Hans-Joachim Kraus, *Psalms 1–59: A Commentary,* trans. Hilton C. Oswald (Minneapolis: Augsburg, 1988), 227.

22. Weinfeld, "Instructions for Temple Visitors," 232.

23. Ibid., 237.

24. Ibid., 245 n. 13.

25. Hermann Gunkel, "Jesaia 33, eine prophetische Liturgie," *Zeitschrift für die altestamentlichen Wissenschaft* 42 (1924): 177–208.

26. Dahood, *Psalms I, 1–50,* 151 n. xxiv.

27. A verse-by-verse commentary of these passages in Isaiah is found in Donald W. Parry, Jay A. Parry, and Tina M. Peterson, *Understanding Isaiah* (Salt Lake City: Deseret Book, 1998), 302–4; and Edward J. Young, *The Book of Isaiah* (Grand Rapids, Mich.: Eerdmans, 1999), 2:349–53.

28. The translation of Isaiah 33:14–17 cited in this article is taken from Donald W. Parry, *Harmonizing Isaiah: Combining Ancient Sources* (Provo, Utah: FARMS, 2001), 139–40.

29. *Teachings of the Prophet Joseph Smith,* comp. Joseph Fielding Smith (Salt Lake City: Deseret Book, 1972), 361.

30. Ibid., 367.

Chapter 29

Temple and Temples:
Some Linguistic Reflections

R. J. Zvi Werblowsky

Throughout the world are many kinds of sacred or conse-crated sites and areas: cities, mountains and mountaintops, caves, and holy enclosures of various types, whether open spaces or con-structions. The biblical patriarchs built altars and offered sacrifice unto the Lord under the open sky, and practically everyone has seen open air masses, at least on TV. Sacred, and usually perma-nent, edifices are erected for a variety of purposes: for the offering of sacrifice, for the performance of sacred rites and diverse forms of worship, and as the dwelling of a deity, actually or symbolically present. These various purposes are often interconnected, for ex-ample, when sacred rites are performed in a shrine not just in honor of, but in the presence of, the deity enshrined there.

Terminology of Sanctuaries

Different types of sanctuaries are designated through a varied terminology, and it would be an instructive exercise to review the relevant vocabulary in different languages. By "relevant" vocabu-lary I mean words that the speakers of a language would some-how consider equivalent or analogous to or bearing a "family re-semblance" with what we have in mind when we say "temple." We should bear in mind that terminology often serves to express distinctions, for example, church, synagogue, and mosque. Japanese language and orthography distinguish between Shinto *jinja/jingu/miya*, generally translated as "shrine," and Buddhist *tera/ji* "temple." An examination of nonalphabetic scripts would be equally instructive. With what ideograms do Chinese (and therefore also Koreans and Japanese) write "temple" and its analogues?

Some Christian groups believe that the word *church* is too reminiscent of *temple* or, if applied not to a building but to the community of believers, too institutionalized, and hence they prefer to use assembly hall, chapel, or similar terms to refer to a building. Unlike Pentecostalist "Assemblies of God," the movement founded by Jim Jones in 1953 that ended with the Jonestown horror of 1978 called itself not a church but the "People's Temple."

The biblical book of Kings often refers to "high places" *(bāmôth)* as sites of sacrificial worship. These were prohibited because sacrifice to the One God should be offered on the altar in the one temple in Jerusalem only. *High places* happens to be a very appropriate synonym for *altars* since solemn sacrifices were often performed not in buildings or on the ground but on platforms, sometimes on top of magnificent structures such as the Temple of Heaven in Beijing, which was reserved for imperial sacrifices. Worship in ancient times primarily involved animal sacrifice, but an altar could be built as a symbolic act without an accompanying sacrifice. A good illustration of this is culled from the history of the Church of Jesus Christ of Latter-day Saints. On his way back to Jerusalem after having pronounced a dedicatory prayer on the Mount of Olives on 24 October 1841 at the behest of the Prophet Joseph Smith, the apostle Orson Hyde erected an altar on the Temple Mount, thus reconfirming the biblical significance of the site.[1]

Accessibility of Temples

A more or less universal feature of temples is that they are accessible, as a whole or in graded and clearly marked areas, to certain people or groups only. To others, for example laymen, the uninitiated, those who are not members, or those in a state of impurity and pollution (however defined), temples are "out of bounds." (This inaccessibility might apply also to certain sacred areas that are not temples in a strict sense.) The temple in Jerusalem had its holy of holies, which the high priest entered once a year only, and the areas accessible to priests, nonpriestly Israelites, women, and gentiles were precisely determined. Rituals of washing and purification when approaching a sacred space or within it are common. The passport that a member of the Church of Jesus Christ needs to enter one of the church's temples is called a "temple recommend." For individuals without this recommend, visitors centers built adjacent to the consecrated temple area provide instruction and edification.

No a priori reason exists why the number of temples or other such shrines should be limited. In polytheistic religions, each god has his or her temple, and the same god, represented by his effigy (in monotheistic religions also a noniconic One God), can be worshiped in any number of sanctuaries erected wherever worshipers are found. In many instances, several deities, even if not derived from the same religious tradition (for example, Taoism and Buddhism), might be worshiped jointly or severally in the same temple, with their images placed on the same altar. This juxtaposition is a fairly common practice in China and India, where several major deities could be worshiped in a common temple compound. The Shinto-Buddhist "syncretism" known as *shinbutsu* was evident in every Japanese shrine until the enforced separation of Shintoism and Buddhism by the Meiji regime.

Worship in Sanctuaries

The ideology underlying the centralization of worship of the One God in the One Temple in Jerusalem became so dominant that biblical historians judge the reign of kings not by the moral or political record of the king but by one criterion only: whether he destroyed the many "high places" of what we must assume to have been the nonofficial but actual popular practice in the First Temple period. Temples in the plural were, by definition, heathenish. In Second Temple times, high places *(bāmôth)* no longer existed, and only the Samaritan sanctuary on Mount Gerizim tried to compete with the temple in Jerusalem. But although the temple in Jerusalem had monopolized sacrifices and priestly ritual—we shall ignore here exceptional cases such as Yeb/Elephantine—Jews also gathered in "assembly places" (Greek *synagoge*) for prayer and for hearing the Torah read and expounded. Jesus and the apostle Paul preached in such synagogues.

Synagogues developed and functioned as a complement to the one temple in Jerusalem. After its destruction and the cessation of priestly ritual, synagogues became its substitute. The term *temple* remained reserved, in traditional Jewish language, for the future House of God, the speedy rebuilding of which was the subject of messianic hope and fervent prayer. Pending that consummation, the people of God would continue to congregate in synagogues. These gathering places for communal worship will continue to exist, according to orthodox belief, also in the messianic future when the restored temple will again have become the locus of God's presence and "indwelling" among his people and the only place where priestly ritual will be performed and sacrifices offered. Traditional synagogue liturgy contains expressions of both mourning for the destruction of the temple and prayerful hope for its restoration. Reform Judaism in the nineteenth century, however, innovated a terminological inversion of this perspective. Rejecting the notions of priestly ritual and of a national return to

Zion as anachronistic and incompatible with the universalist calling of Israel, Reform Judaism provocatively substituted the term *temple* for *synagogue,* thus programmatically abandoning the belief in a rebuilding of "the" temple in a geographical Jerusalem. Israel among the nations was the vanguard of a universal ethical monotheism, and hence its houses of worship everywhere were God's temples even though no special rituals were performed in them. In contemporary Jerusalem, on the other hand, some enthusiastic rabbinic students are intensively studying the rules of priestly sacrifice, which has been in abeyance for so long, in expectation of its (imminent, as they hope) resumption in the restored temple.

The term *temple* was still used by the early Christians for their assembly and gathering until supplanted by the Greek word *ekklēsia.* A Protestant church is an *ekklēsia* in the sense of *synagogue:* here the people of God assemble for worship and for hearing the word of God read and preached, though other rites such as baptism and marriage are by preference performed also. The model of a place of gathering for worship was also adopted by Islam, although the technical term for the edifice (*masjid,* mosque) has a different meaning etymologically. Islam has sanctuaries and holy sites distinct from its mosques, but even the holiest site, the Kaʿba in Mecca, is not a temple. The structure is rarely entered by the single door in the northeastern wall, and the central ritual associated with the Kaʿba is its circumambulation. In this respect the Kaʿba is similar to the (Theravada) Buddhist stupa, which cannot be entered at all but is circumambulated with the right shoulder toward the structure.

Holy Books

In religions in which a holy book plays a central role, its relation to the temple can assume various forms. Perhaps no tradition is as book-centered as Islam, yet the Qurʾan, no matter how highly venerated, is not an object of worship in the mosque. The attitude of members of the Church of Jesus Christ to the Book of Mormon, one of the books of scripture considered holy and central to their faith, can be judged by the fact that the three witnesses to its existence and to its translation by the Prophet Joseph Smith did not revoke their testimony after their expulsion from the church. On his deathbed Oliver Cowdery (who had rejoined the church) exhorted David Whitmer to remain faithful to the testimony, and Whitmer had his testimony engraved on his tombstone. When Martin Harris died on 10 July 1875 at the age of 92, his last words were "book, book, book." Yet temples of the Church of Jesus Christ are not built for the purpose of housing a book.

The interior architecture of the Jewish synagogue is focused on the wall with the "ark" in which the Torah scrolls are kept and from which they are carried in procession for reading. But they are considered an object of veneration and not of worship. The holy ark in Jewish synagogues is undoubtedly meant to suggest associations with the ark of the covenant in the holy of holies containing the tablets with the Ten Commandments. But these tablets were distinct from the Divine Presence, which gave the sanctuary one of its appellations: *mishkān* ("dwelling place"). Rabbinic Hebrew formed the noun *shekhinah,* derived from the same root *ŠKN, "dwell," to designate the "indwelling divine presence."

Dwelling Places of the Divine

Sometimes the meaning of *temple* as primarily a dwelling place of the divine is so much taken for granted that the term is also applied metaphorically to individuals. Paul the apostle exhorts the Corinthians, "Know ye not that ye are the temple of God and that the Spirit of God dwelleth in you" and that "your body is the temple of the Holy Ghost which is in you?" (1 Corinthians 3:16; 6:19). The same metaphor can also be inverted. In reference to the New Jerusalem, "I saw no temple therein, for the Lord God Almighty and the Lamb are the temple of it" (Revelation 21:22;

see 21:3). The term *temple* imparts a special significance and value, almost of "sacredness," to an establishment. We thus find expressions such as "temple of learning" or "temple of art."

Images of the deity in the temple were the rule in the ancient Near East where, in combination with notions of divine kingship, the temple was also conceived as a palace. *Hêkhāl,* in biblical Hebrew, signifies both palace and temple. The Hebrew word *miqdāsh* (from root *QDŠ, "holy"), usually rendered as "temple," literally means "sanctuary." The sanctuary that Solomon built was God's earthly palace, a permanent residence taking the place of the premonarchic, nomadic, and mobile "tent" that was constructed in the desert as "a *miqdāsh,* that I may dwell among them" (Exodus 25:8). The temple in Jerusalem was a "royal sanctuary" in every sense, and the book of Psalms never tires of exalting the God who dwelleth in Zion (that is, in his temple on Mount Zion) as the Great King: the Lord reigneth (see Zechariah 14:9, 16–17).

In some Christian traditions the doctrine of a real presence (however defined) in the Sacrament gives the eucharistic liturgy a character that confers on the church building a more templelike quality in the sense of an "indwelling." This is emphasized spatially in Byzantine and Eastern churches by the separation, by means of the "Wall of Icons" *(ikonostasis),* of the sanctuary proper *(hieration),* which is inaccessible *(adyton)* to laymen from the main nave of the church *(naos).* The Roman Catholic Church has, since the late Middle Ages, rendered the sacred building even more like a classical temple, that is, the dwelling place of a materially present deity. Crucifixes, statues, and pictures of saints, especially of the Virgin Mary, may be numerous in church buildings and are venerated but not worshiped. The Blessed Sacrament, however, in which Christ is held to be present, serves not only for the rite of communion but is kept in a "tabernacle"—here in the sense of receptacle—on the altar, and on certain occasions exposed in a transparent monstrance (also called ostensorium) for public adoration.

Temples, as has been noted, were conceived in most traditional cultures as dwelling places of a deity or its material representation and for that reason also as the privileged place for the performance of sacred rites and for sacrificial offerings. The word *church* referred originally to the building, unlike the Greek *ekklēsia* from which it is derived, which primarily means assembly and hence, as in the Epistles of Paul, the community of saints. (The Septuagint uses *ekklēsia* for Hebrew *qāhāl*, "congregation.") From "assembly" to "place of assembly" was but a small step. In Jewish usage *synagogue* became the non-Hebrew equivalent of the Hebrew term for "house of assembly." In Christian usage the word came to designate the Jewish *ekklēsia* and served as a convenient idiom for distinguishing between the community of Jews and the community of Christians (the "church"). The word *mosque* refers to the building only, while the Muslim community calls itself ʾummah. Christians, as members of the church (or of churches) in either an organizational and institutional or in a theological and even mystical sense, go to church (as buildings) for worship. The original New Testament usage of the term *church* as an "organized body of believers" of Christ is still preserved by the Church of Jesus Christ. Members of this church do not just "go to church" in the traditional sense of the word, though their meetinghouses and facilities are principally for religious activities, including Sunday worship; most of their sacred ordinances, however, are performed in temples.

Temples of the Church of Jesus Christ do not house images of the Godhead, though there is no taboo of the Jewish, Muslim, or extreme Protestant type on statues. In fact, replicas of Bertel Thorvaldsen's *Christus* statue have become popular, and gilded statues of the angel Moroni, a symbol of the restoration and preaching of the gospel, are found atop most Latter-day Saint temples. To Latter-day Saints, the temple is a sacred, consecrated edifice, inaccessible to outsiders. Its primary function is the performance of sacred rites, or ordinances, that cannot be performed elsewhere. Members of the Church of Jesus Christ have a very characteristic and complex vocabulary for these diverse rites (such as making covenants, receiving endowments, sealing couples and families), which are not our subject here.

From the point of view of this discussion, the Shinto shrine is also a temple since the *kami* (a noniconic deity though represented by a material symbol) is enshrined there. Also Mahayana Buddhist sanctuaries are "dwelling places" in the sense that the supramundane Buddha and his innumerable manifestations, not to mention the countless Bodhisattvas, are held to be present in their effigies, the abundance of which practically smothers the visitor to a temple. Not just any statue, no matter how valuable artistically, represents the Buddha—a special ritual has to be performed that turns the effigy into an actual presence. In Hindu temples the effigy represents the deity worshiped in an even more immediate and concrete sense. The total absence of images in Shinto shrines merits special emphasis since Shinto explicitly considers itself a polytheistic religion. Polytheism too can be aniconic and is, therefore, not identical with idolatry, literally the "worship of images," as is often and incorrectly thought.

Conclusion

Mention has already been made of the message of nineteenth-century Reform Judaism, which substituted *temple* for *synagogue* although these "temples" remained functionally nothing but synagogues. The Church of Jesus Christ developed in a nineteenth-century Christian linguistic environment heavily laden with biblical associations and possessed of a wide range of words waiting, as it were, to be picked up. On the one hand it coined a novel and sometimes unusual terminology of its own for many of its beliefs and rituals. At the same time, and parallel to this process, it kept many biblical keywords as designations of certain central concepts and institutions.

Most languages, as we have seen, possess a wide vocabulary with which to designate their places of worship. This vocabulary has acquired, throughout the centuries, a variety of meanings, associations, overtones, and undertones that are present, consciously or unconsciously, in the minds of their users. Their history is an important part of the history of religions.

Note

1. Letter from Orson Hyde, 22 November 1841, in Joseph Smith, *History of the Church of Jesus Christ of Latter-day Saints,* 2nd ed. (Salt Lake City: Deseret Book, 1950), 4:459.

Works by Truman G. Madsen

Compiled by Daniel B. McKinlay

Books/Booklets

Christ and the Inner Life. 2nd ed. Salt Lake City: Bookcraft, 1978. Originally paperback; included in *Five Classics by Truman G. Madsen.*

Defender of the Faith: The B. H. Roberts Story. Salt Lake City: Bookcraft, 1980.

Eternal Man. Salt Lake City: Deseret Book, 1966. Included in *Five Classics by Truman G. Madsen.*

"The Ethics of William James." Master's thesis, University of Utah, 1951.

Fables on Foibles, for This Time of Your Life. Amherst, Mass.: New England Youth Conference, The Church of Jesus Christ of Latter-day Saints, 1964. Private circulation.

Five Classics by Truman G. Madsen. Salt Lake City: Eagle Gate, 2001.

Four Essays on Love. Salt Lake City: Bookcraft, 1971. Also published in paperback versions; included in *Five Classics by Truman G. Madsen.*

The Heritage of Heber J. Grant. Utah: n.p., 1961. Presented at the Lion House in Salt Lake City, 22 November 1961. Monograph.

The Highest in Us. Salt Lake City: Bookcraft, 1978. Included in *Five Classics by Truman G. Madsen.*

How to Stop Forgetting and Start Remembering. Cambridge, Mass: n.p., 1964. Several subsequent editions.

Joseph Smith the Prophet. Salt Lake City: Bookcraft, 1989.

LDS Church History Syllabus (with Russell R. Rich and others). Provo, Utah: BYU Department of Travel Study, 1965.

Marriage and Family: Gospel Insights (with Stephen R. Covey). Salt Lake City: Bookcraft, 1983.

My Religion and Me. Salt Lake City: Deseret Sunday School Union, 1970. Sunday School student manual for 17-year-olds.

"A Philosophical Examination of Tillich's Theory of Symbolic Meaning." Ph.D. diss., Harvard University, 1958.

The Radiant Life. Salt Lake City: Bookcraft, 1994. Included in *Five Classics by Truman G. Madsen.*

Edited and Compiled Works

"B. H. Roberts' Final Decade: Statements about the Book of Mormon (1924–33)." Provo, Utah: FARMS, 1984.

Concordance of the Doctrinal Statements of Joseph Smith (with E. Glenn Kimball). Salt Lake City: IES Printing, 1985.

Covenant and Chosenness in Judaism and Mormonism (with Raphael Jospe and Seth Ward). Madison, N.J.: Fairleigh Dickinson University Press, 2001.

Encyclopedia of Mormonism (with several other editors). New York: Macmillan, 1992.

New England Baptizer/Prophet/Advocate. New England Mission monthly bulletin (1962–65).

Reflections on Mormonism: Judaeo-Christian Parallels. Provo, Utah: BYU Religious Studies Center, 1978. Papers delivered 10–11 March 1978 at the BYU Religious Studies Center Symposium.

The Search for Human Nature. Forthcoming. Proceedings of a Jerusalem Center Symposium.

Seminar on Brigham Young, 12 May 1962. Provo, Utah: BYU Extension Publications, 1962.

Seminar on the Prophet Joseph Smith, 18 February 1961. Provo, Utah: BYU Extension Publications, 1961.

Seminar on the Prophet Joseph Smith, 17 February 1962. Provo, Utah: BYU Extension Publications, 1962.

The Temple in Antiquity: Ancient Records and Modern Perspectives. Provo, Utah: BYU Religious Studies Center, 1984.

To the Glory of God: Mormon Essays on Great Issues (with Charles D. Tate Jr.). Salt Lake City: Deseret Book, 1972.

Essays and Transcribed Speeches

"All Those Gifts." *New England Prophet* 2 (September 1964).

"Are Christians Mormon?" *BYU Studies* 15/1 (1974): 73–94. BYU forum address delivered 4 June 1974.

"Attitude and Altitude." *New England Prophet* 1 (November 1963).

"The Awesome Power of Married Love." In *Radiant Life,* 85–103.

"The Better Music." *Improvement Era* 66 (June 1963): 554–55.

"B. H. Roberts after Fifty Years: Still Witnessing for the Book of Mormon." *Ensign* (December 1983): 10–19.

"B. H. Roberts and the Book of Mormon." *BYU Studies* 19/4 (1979): 427–45. Included in *Book of Mormon Authorship: New Light on Ancient Origins,* edited by Noel B. Reynolds and Charles D. Tate Jr., 7–31. Provo, Utah: BYU Religious Studies

Center, 1982; book republished with the same title, Provo, Utah: FARMS, 1996.

"B. H. Roberts: The Book of Mormon and the Atonement." In *The Book of Mormon: First Nephi, the Doctrinal Foundation: Papers from the Second Annual Book of Mormon Symposium,* edited by Monte S. Nyman and Charles D. Tate Jr., 297–314. Provo, Utah: BYU Religious Studies Center, 1988.

"Blowing on the Coals Within." *Improvement Era* 72 (November 1969): 11–13.

"Brigham H. Roberts." In Sperry Lecture Series, 21–35. Lecture delivered 11 March 1976 at BYU.

"Can a Church University Achieve Greatness?" In *The Brigham Young University Story,* 20–23. Provo, Utah: BYU Press, 1968. Brochure; interview with Allen Young.

"Can God Be Pictured?" *BYU Studies* 8/2 (1968): 113–25.

"Can God Die?" *University of Utah Chronicle,* 10 April 1969.

"The Centrality of Family across World Faiths" (with Keith Lawrence and Shawn L. Christiansen). In *Strengthening Our Families: An In-depth Look at the Proclamation on the Family,* edited by David C. Dollahite, 370–81. Provo, Utah: BYU School of Family Life, 2000.

"Chosenness: Implications and Extensions in Mormonism and Judaism." In *Covenant and Chosenness in Judaism and Mormonism,* 131–46.

"Christ and Conquering Thoughts." In *Christ and the Inner Life,* 34–38.

"Christ and Prayer." In *Christ and the Inner Life,* 15–19.

"Christ and the Sacrament." In *Christ and the Inner Life,* 39–42.

"The Church in the Eyes of Youth: Its History." *Improvement Era* 64 (November 1961): 886–91; reprinted in *The Era of Youth,* edited by Marion D. Hanks and Elaine Cannon. Salt Lake City: Deseret Book, 1962.

"Church Talk." *Church News*, 29 December 1948, 24C. Excerpts of a talk as a returned missionary in an article by Henry A. Smith.

"Clearing the Fog." *New England Prophet* 1 (July 1963).

"The Commanding Image of Christ." In *BYU Speeches of the Year*. Provo, Utah: BYU Press, [1965]. Republished in *Revontulet* (May 1966); included in *Christ and the Inner Life*, 8–14. Speech originally delivered 16 November 1965.

"Communion with Worthies Beyond." *New England Prophet* 2 (June 1964).

"Conscience and Consciousness." In Commissioner's Lecture Series. Provo, Utah: BYU Press, 1973. Church Educational lecture delivered at LDS Institutes of Religion at Weber State College, Ricks College, and the Church College of Hawaii. Republished in *The Highest in Us*, 59–76.

"The Contribution of Existentialism." Abstract in *Proceedings of Utah Academy of Arts and Sciences* (1958): 155–56. Full article in *BYU Studies* 1/1 (1959): 9–20.

"The Convert Glow." *New England Prophet* 2 (January 1964).

"Creation and Procreation." *Instructor* 99 (June 1964): 236–39, 241. Included in *Eternal Man*, 34–42.

"A Day of Rejoicing." On-line at www.meridianmagazine.com/archives/index.html.

"The Depth of Discernment." *New England Prophet* 1 (March 1963). Reprinted on-line at www.meridianmagazine.com/archives/index.html.

"Did B. H. Roberts Lose Faith in the Book of Mormon?" (with John W. Welch). FARMS Preliminary Report. Provo, Utah: FARMS, 1985.

"Distinctions in the Mormon Approach to Death and Dying." In *Deity and Death,* edited by Spencer J. Palmer, 61–76. Provo, Utah: BYU Religious Studies Center, 1978.

"The Dynamics of Testimony: A Youth Conference Brochure." N.p., 1967.

"Eleven Golden Questions for Brassy Objections." On-line at www.meridianmagazine.com/archives/index.html.

"Elijah and the Turning of Hearts." In *Radiant Life,* 105–15.

"Emma Hale Smith." In *Joseph Smith Sr. Family Reunion, Oral Presentations, 18–19 August 1972,* 23–31. Provo, Utah: Buddy Youngreen, 1972.

"Ether 12:27 suggests that God gives men weaknesses. How and why would he do this?" I Have a Question. *Ensign* (February 1985): 49–50.

"Every Member Can Do It." *New Era* (June 1973): 45–47. Adaptation of the audiotape *Every Member a Bird Dogger.*

"Evil and Suffering." *Instructor* 99 (November 1964): 450–53. Included in *Eternal Man,* 53–61; also reprinted as a separate essay.

"Existentialism as a Philosophy." *BYU Daily Universe,* 20–23 April 1964. A series on literature and art, non-being, language, freedom, and religious experience.

"Facets of Prayer." *Improvement Era* 69 (February 1966): 157–59. Reprinted as Lesson 10, "Spirituality and Prayer," in the MIA Laurel Manual, 1969, 135–37; also in the Sunday School manual under "Finding God through Prayer"; also *Revontulet* (August 1966). Republished as "Christ and Prayer." In *Christ and the Inner Life,* 15–19.

"Forgiveness." In *Radiant Life,* 45–53.

"Forgiveness—Inseparably Linked to Happiness." On-line at www.meridianmagazine.com/archives/index.html.

"Freedom and Fulfillment." *Instructor* 100 (January 1965): 32–34. Included in *Eternal Man,* 63–70; also in *Revontulet* (March 1967).

"Freedom to Become." In *The Highest in Us,* 13–21.

"A Fruitful Tree: A Century of Love, Truth, and Service." In *Brigham Young University: The First One Hundred Years,* edited by Ernest L. Wilkinson, Leonard J. Arrington, and Bruce C. Hafen, 4:335–87. Provo, Utah: BYU Press, 1976.

"The Glory of Hebrew." *Improvement Era* 73 (July 1970): 68–69.

"The Gospel and the Sabbath." In *Radiant Life,* 69–83.

"Greater Spiritual Insights." In *Lectures in Theology.* Salt Lake Institute of Religion devotional address delivered 18 February 1972.

"The Hearts of the Children." Provo, Utah: n.p., 1977. BYU twelve-stake fireside address delivered 5 June 1977. Republished in *Suggested Readings in LDS Values and Human Behavior* (with "On Forgiveness"), 34–40. Salt Lake City: The Church of Jesus Christ of Latter-day Saints, 1980.

"The Highest in Us." In *Speeches of the Year: BYU Devotional and Ten-Stake Fireside Addresses, 1974,* 355–67. Provo, Utah: BYU Press, 1975. Fireside address delivered 3 March 1974. Included in *The Highest in Us,* 1–12.

"The Highs and the Lows." *New England Prophet* 1 (June 1963). Reprinted on-line at www.meridianmagazine.com/archives/index.html.

"The Holy Land and the Mormon Restoration." In *America—Holy Land Studies.* Vol. 2, *With Eyes toward Zion,* edited by Moshe Davis, 342–45. New York: Praeger, 1986. Proceedings of the Second International Scholars Colloquium on America—Holy Land Studies held 30 August–1 September 1985 in Washington, D.C.

"House of Glory." In *The Highest in Us,* 93–107. BYU ten-stake fireside address delivered 5 March 1972. Also in *Radiant Life,* 117–28.

"House of Glory, House of Light, House of Love" (with Ann N. Madsen). In *May Christ Lift Thee Up: Talks from the 1998 Women's Conference Sponsored by Brigham Young University and the Relief Society,* 314–39. Salt Lake City: Deseret Book, 1999. Reprinted in *The Best of Women's Conference: Selected Talks from 25 Years of BYU Women's Conferences,* 339–64. Salt Lake City: Bookcraft, 2000.

"How Can I Become Closer to the Lord?" On-line at www.meridian magazine.com/archives/index.html.

"The How of Humility." *New England Prophet* 1 (May 1963). Reprinted on-line at www.meridianmagazine.com/archives/index.html.

"How to Be Loved and Beloved." Provo, Utah: BYU Press, 1965. Pamphlet. Republished in *Four Essays on Love,* 27–39.

"How to Overcome Fear." *New England Prophet* 1 (April 1963). Reprinted on-line at www.meridianmagazine.com/archives/index.html.

"How We Know What We Know." On-line at www.meridian magazine.com/archives/index.html.

"Hugh B. Brown—Youthful Veteran." *New Era* (April 1976): 14–19.

"Human Anguish and Divine Love." In *Four Essays on Love,* 55–71. Republished in *Radiant Life,* 55–68; also published in *A Believing People,* edited by Richard H. Cracroft and Neal A. Lambert, 235–42. Provo, Utah: BYU Press, 1974.

"Hvem er Jesus Kristus? Vil han komme igjen" [Norwegian]. In *Kristus—hven er han? Jesus Kristus tibake til Jorden,* edited by Per Sjeggestad, 194–98. Oslo: Sorlands Public, n.d.

"I Am the Life." In *The Highest in Us*, 23–31. An adaptation of "Sooner or Later-day Saints," a BYU Education Week devotional address delivered 21 August 1973.

"Identity or Nothing." *Instructor* 99 (March 1964): 96–99. Included in *Eternal Man*, 23–32.

"In a Place Called Gethsemane." In *Radiant Life*, 11–17. An adaptation of "The Olive Press."

"Insights: In the Present Tense." *Ensign* (April 1975): 60. From an interview with the *Los Angeles Times*, 28 July 1974.

"The Intimate Touch of Prayer." In *The Highest in Us*, 77–91; and *Radiant Life*, 31–44.

"I, the Lord, Am Bound When Ye Do What I Say." *New England Prophet* 2 (November 1964); and *Revontulet* (June 1966).

"Joseph Smith among the Prophets." Salt Lake City: Deseret Book, 1965. Pamphlet originally published in the New England Mission. Also translated into German.

"Joseph Smith and the Depth of Discipleship." In *CES Ninth Annual Religious Education Symposium*, 43–47.

"Joseph Smith and the Problems of Ethics." In *Seminar on the Prophet Joseph Smith, 17 February 1962*, 72–89. Provo, Utah: BYU Extension Publications, 1962. Also published in *Perspectives in Mormon Ethics: Personal, Social, Legal and Medical*, edited by Donald G. Hill, 29–48. Salt Lake City: Publishers Press, 1983.

"Joseph Smith and the Sources of Love." Twenty-Third Annual Joseph Smith Memorial Sermon delivered 5 December 1965 at the Logan Institute of Religion at Utah State University. Condensed in *Dialogue* 1/1 (1966): 122–34; included in *Four Essays on Love*, 9–25.

"Joseph Smith and the Ways of Knowing." In *Seminar on the Prophet Joseph Smith, 18 February 1961*, 25–63. Provo, Utah: BYU Extension Publications, 1961.

"Joseph Smith as Charismatic." Forthcoming. Presentation delivered at the Center for Advanced Studies in Religious Sciences, Piacenza, Italy, September 2001.

"Joseph Smith's Reputation—Among Theologians." *Ensign* (September 1979): 61–63.

"The Joy of Giving." In *Addresses from the Eleventh Annual Development Conference, June 26–28, 1974, Ricks College.* Provo, Utah: Developmental Office, 1974.

"The Joy of Learning." In *ASBYU Academics Presents: Outstanding Lectures 1978–79*, 89–99.

"'The Joy of the Lord Is Your Strength' (Nehemiah 8:10)." In *Brigham Young University 2000–2001 Speeches*, 139–45. Provo, Utah: BYU Publications and Graphics, 2001. Address delivered 21 November 2000.

"The Kingship of Self-Control." *New England Prophet* 2 (July 1964).

"The Kirtland Temple and Temple Worship." In *Joseph Smith Sr. Family Reunion, Kirtland, Illinois, August 2, 3, 4, and 5, 1979*, 7–12. Provo, Utah: Buddy Youngreen, 1979.

"The Language of Love at Home." In *Four Essays on Love*, 41–52.

"The Latter-day Saint Understanding of Human Nature." In *The Search for Human Nature.*

"The Leading Question." *New England Advocate* 3 (February 1965).

"Learning to Walk in a Sunlit Land: How to Gain a Radiant Testimony, Part 1." On-line at www.meridianmagazine.com/archives/index.html.

"Learning to Walk in a Sunlit Land: How to Gain a Radiant Testimony, Part 2—Obtaining Study Thirst." On-line at www.meridianmagazine.com/archives/index.html.

"Learning to Walk in a Sunlit Land: How to Gain a Radiant Testimony, Part 3—'Turning Your Whole Life in a Prayer-Reach.'" On-line at www.meridianmagazine.com/archives/index.html.

"A Life Lived in the Spirit." *New England Prophet* 1 (October 1963). About Wilford Woodruff.

"The Lord's Way with Thoughts." *New England Advocate* 3 (April 1965). Also in *Revontulet* (July 1966).

"Man against Darkness." In *Expressions of Faith: Testimonies of Latter-day Saint Scholars,* edited by Susan Easton Black, 32–44. Salt Lake City: Deseret Book and FARMS, 1996.

"Man Illumined." In *To the Glory of God,* edited by Truman G. Madsen and Charles D. Tate Jr., 121–33. Salt Lake City: Deseret Book, 1972. Also in *Radiant Life,* 19–30.

"A Man's Reach." Salt Lake City: KSL, 1970. Album notes on Rex Campbell's poetry album.

"The Meaning and Verification of Religious Language." In *BYU Leadership Lectures,* 1–13. Provo, Utah: Extension Publications, 1961. Originally part of Evening Lecture Series on Religion delivered at the University of Utah, Utah State University, Weber State College, and Brigham Young University.

"The Meaning of Christ—The Truth, the Way, the Life: An Analysis of B. H. Roberts' Unpublished Masterwork." *BYU Studies* 15/3 (1975): 259–92.

"The Memory Marvel." *New England Advocate* 3 (January 1965).

"A Message from Truman G. Madsen." *BYU Today* 33/6 (September 1979): 2.

"Mighty in the Scriptures." *New England Prophet* 2 (August 1964).

"The Mind and the Body." *Instructor* 99 (September 1964): 362–65. Included in *Eternal Man* as "The Spirit and the Body," 43–51.

Moderator of panel discussion, 22 November 1975. In *Pearl of Great Price Symposium,* 93–101. Provo, Utah: BYU Publications, 1976.

"The Mormon Attitude toward Zionism." In *A Series of Lectures on Zionism,* edited by Yaacov Goldstein. Haifa: University of Haifa, 1981. Also translated into Hebrew.

"Mormonism as Historical." In *Reflections on Mormonism,* xi–xviii.

"Notes on the Succession of Brigham Young." In *Seminar on Brigham Young, 12 May 1962,* 3–12. Provo, Utah: BYU Extension Publications, 1963.

"Of the Garden Tomb." *New Era* (April 1971): 4–6.

"The Olive Press." In *Brigham Young University 1981–82 Fireside and Devotional Speeches,* 141–44. Provo, Utah: BYU Publications, 1982. Speech delivered 9 May 1982. Condensed in the *Ensign* (December 1982): 56–62. Republished as "The Olive Press: A Symbol of Christ." In *The Allegory of the Olive Tree,* edited by Stephen D. Ricks and John W. Welch, 1–10. Salt Lake City: Deseret Book and FARMS, 1994.

"On Breaking Three Spirit Barriers—Contention, Lightmindedness, Vain Aspiration." *New England Advocate* 3 (March 1965).

"One Thing I Know." *New England Advocate* 3 (August 1965).

"The One Unfailing Motivation." *New England Advocate* 3 (July 1965).

"On Forgiveness." Lecture presented at the annual LDS Social Services Seminary, 3 August 1978, Logan, Utah. Republished in *Suggested Readings in LDS Values and Human Behavior* (with "The Hearts of the Children"), 28–33. Salt Lake City: The Church of Jesus Christ of Latter-day Saints, 1980.

"On How We Know." In *Brigham Young University 1994–95 Devotional and Fireside Speeches,* 21–26. Provo, Utah: BYU Publications and Graphics, 1995. Speech delivered 20 September 1994. Republished as "Reverberations of Truth." In *Charting a New Millennium: The Latter-day Saints in the Coming Century,* edited by Maurine Proctor and Scot Proctor, 456–65. Salt Lake City: Aspen Books, 1998.

"On Knowing God as a Person." *New England Prophet* 2 (October 1964).

"On Paul Tillich." In *Launching Conversations between Latter-day Saints and Non-Restoration Christians,* edited by David Paulsen. Forthcoming.

"On the Consciousness of Christ." *New England Advocate* 3 (May 1965).

"On the Love of Companions." *New England Prophet* 1 (August 1963).

"On Works with Faith." *New England Prophet* 1 (September 1963).

"Paul Tillich and Religion as Ultimate Concern." Lecture delivered at Utah State University for Evening Lectures on Religion at the University of Utah, Utah State University, Weber State College, and Brigham Young University, 1959. Lithograph in private circulation.

"People We'd Like to Know More About: Dr. Truman G. Madsen" (interview by Rich Boyer and Jim Jardine). *Improvement Era* 73 (July 1970): 36–38.

"Philosophy (Chs. 1–3, 26–27, 33)." In *The Truth, the Way, the Life: An Elementary Treatise on Theology,* edited by John W. Welch, 595–617. 2nd ed. Provo, Utah: BYU Studies, 1996. Comments on specified chapters in B. H. Roberts's book.

"Philosophy and Public Policy." In *Humanities and Public Policy,* a handbook of selected readings, prepared by the Utah

Endowment for the Humanities Public Policy Committee, 9–13. Salt Lake City, 1976.

"Photo Essay, B. H. Roberts." *This People,* June/July 1982, 55–58. Taken from *Defender of the Faith.*

"Portrait of a Prophet." *Improvement Era* 66 (December 1963): 1138–50. Reprinted in *Revontulet* 66 (October 1966).

"Portrait of a Team." *New England Prophet* 1 (December 1963).

"Power from Abrahamic Tests." In *BYU Speeches of the Year.* Provo, Utah: BYU Press, 1971. Speech originally given 12 October 1971. Included in *The Highest in Us,* 49–57; reprinted on-line at www.meridianmagazine.com/archives/index.html.

"The Power of Decision." *New England Prophet* 2 (April 1964).

"The Power of Patriarchal Blessings." On-line at www.meridian magazine.com/archives/index.html.

"A Prayer and an Answer." *Improvement Era* 51 (March 1948): 151.

"Prayer and the Prophet Joseph Smith." *Ensign* (January 1976): 18–25.

"The Pre-eminence of Christ." *Millennial Star* 122 (December 1960): 513–17. Included in *Christ and the Inner Life,* 1–7.

"Problems in Universalizing Mormonism: A Response (to Sterling M. McMurrin)." *Sunstone,* December 1979, 18–20.

"The Prophet Joseph Seen through the Eyes of Youth." *Improvement Era* 66 (July 1963): 629.

"'Putting on the Names': A Jewish-Christian Legacy." In *By Study and Also by Faith: Essays in Honor of Hugh W. Nibley,* edited by John M. Lundquist and Stephen D. Ricks, 1:458–81. Salt Lake City: Deseret Book and FARMS, 1990.

"The Real Measure." *New England Prophet* 1 (January 1963). Reprinted on-line at www.meridianmagazine.com/archives/index.html.

"Religious Experience." In *Encyclopedia of Mormonism,* 3:1208–10.

"The Religious vs. the Humanistic Ground of Ethical Obligation." *University of Utah Chronicle,* 27–28 October 1966. Debate with Waldemar P. Read of the University of Utah.

"Revelation and Self-Revelation." *Instructor* 100 (July 1965): 290–92. Included in *Eternal Man,* 71–77; and in *Revontulet* (October 1966).

"The Role of Religious Symbolism: East and West." In *Mormonism: A Faith for All Cultures,* edited by F. LaMond Tullis, 207–26. Provo, Utah: BYU Press, 1978.

"The Sacramental Life." In *The Highest in Us,* 33–47. A reworking of "Mormonism and the New-Making Morality."

"Sacred Treasures." *New Era* (August 1994): 46–50. Adapted from a BYU commencement address delivered 12 August 1993.

"The Savior, the Sacrament, and Self-Worth." In *The Arms of His Love: Talks from the 1999 Women's Conference Sponsored by Brigham Young University and the Relief Society,* 243–55. Salt Lake City: Deseret Book, 2000.

"Scriptures" (with W. D. Davies). In *Encyclopedia of Mormonism,* 3:1277–80.

"Seeking the Spirit (I–IV)." *New England Baptizer* 2–3 (1962–63).

"Smith, Joseph: Teachings of Joseph Smith." In *Encyclopedia of Mormonism,* 3:1339–43.

"Souls Aflame: The Prayer Heritage of the Latter-day Saints." In *Brigham Young University 1983–84 Fireside and Devotional Speeches,* 23–27. Provo, Utah: BYU Publications, 1984. Originally delivered 8 November 1983. Republished in the *New Era* (July 1984): 44–50; included in *Radiant Life,* 1–9.

"The Strength of Purity." *New England Prophet* 2 (May 1964).

"A Study of the Text of the Inspired Revision of the Bible." *Improvement Era* 73 (March 1970): 70–71.

"The Suffering Servant." In *The Redeemer: Reflections on the Life and Teachings of Jesus the Christ,* 223–48. Salt Lake City: Deseret Book, 2000.

"The Temple and the Atonement." Provo, Utah: FARMS, 1994. Paper abridged from a lecture delivered 16 October 1994 in Saratoga, California.

"The Temple and the Atonement." In *Temples of the Ancient World,* edited by Donald W. Parry, 63–79. Salt Lake City: Deseret Book and FARMS, 1994.

"Theodicy" (with John Cobb Jr.). In *Encyclopedia of Mormonism,* 4:1473–74.

"Three Strands of Testimony. And the Price." *New England Advocate* 3 (June 1965). Reprinted on-line at www.meridian magazine.com/archives/index.html.

"Three Theories of Religious Language." *BYU Studies* 2/2 (1960): 227–40.

"Time for Reflection." In *ASBYU Academics Presents Last Lecture Series 1971–1972,* 15–22. Speech delivered 22 November 1971.

"To My Dream Girl" (author is given as "a recently returned missionary"). *Improvement Era* 53 (March 1950): 188–89. Republished in *Improvement Era* 67 (November 1964): 1004–5; also in *How Glorious Is Youth,* edited by Marion D. Hanks, Doyle L. Green, and Elaine Cannon, 201–3. Salt Lake City: Deseret Book, 1968.

"Tribute to Uncle Ashby." Presented at the Grant family reunion, Lion House, Salt Lake City, 22 November 1960.

"Truman G. Madsen." In *Why I Believe,* 215–20. Salt Lake City: Bookcraft, 2002.

"Twenty Questions." In *BYU Speeches of the Year.* Provo, Utah: BYU Press, 1968. Speech delivered 20 August 1968. Republished in *Christ and the Inner Life,* 20–33.

"The Vitality of a Veteran." *New England Prophet* 2 (February 1964).

"What Did Tolstoi See in Mormonism?" *New Era* (March 1971): 46–49.

"Whence Cometh Man?" *Instructor* 98 (June 1963): 204–6, 208. Incorporated as the lead essay in *Eternal Man*, 13–22.

"Who Are We?" *New England Prophet* 1 (February 1963). Reprinted on-line at www.meridianmagazine.com/archives/index.html.

"William James: Philosopher-Educator." *BYU Studies* 4/1 (1961): 81–105.

"Ye Are My Witnesses." In *Christ and the Inner Life*, 43–54.

"Yearning Prayer." *Improvement Era* 67 (June 1964): 42–43. Re-published in *Revontulet* (August 1966); and as "Christ and Prayer" in *Christ and the Inner Life*, 15–19.

"Ye Have Desired." *New England Prophet* 2 (December 1964).

"Zionism." In *Encyclopedia of Mormonism*, 4:1626.

Afterword, Forewords, Introductions, and Preface

Afterword to *Overcoming Chronic Pain*, by Benjamin Crue. Forthcoming.

Foreword (with Leonard J. Arrington and John W. Welch) to *An Ancient American Setting for the Book of Mormon*, by John L. Sorenson, ix–xii. Salt Lake City: Deseret Book and FARMS, 1985.

Foreword to *Grafting In: A History of the Latter-day Saints in the Holy Land*, by Steven W. Baldridge and Marilyn M. Rona, i–iv. Jerusalem: Jerusalem Branch, Israel District, The Church of Jesus Christ of Latter-day Saints, 1989.

Foreword to *Nibley on the Timely and the Timeless: Classic Essays of Hugh Nibley*, by Hugh W. Nibley, ix–xvii. Provo, Utah: BYU Religious Studies Center, 1978.

Foreword to *Wisdograms by Uncle J.*, by J. Winter Smith. Provo, Utah: BYU Press, 1973.

Foreword to *The Words of Joseph Smith*, edited by Andrew F. Ehat and Lyndon W. Cook, xi–xiv. Provo, Utah: BYU Religious Studies Center, 1980. Republished, Orem, Utah: Grandin Book, 1991.

"Guest Editor's Prologue." *BYU Studies* 9/3 (1969): 235–40. On the first vision.

"Guest Editor's Prologue." *BYU Studies* 10/3 (1970): 252–54. On Book of Mormon publication.

"Guest Editor's Prologue." *BYU Studies* 11/4 (1971): 319–21. On the Ohio era.

"Guest Editor's Prologue." *BYU Studies* 12/4 (1972): 343–45. On the Ohio era.

"Guest Editor's Prologue." *BYU Studies* 13/4 (1973): 459–61. On the Missouri era.

"Guest Editor's Prologue." *BYU Studies* 14/4 (1974): 403–5. On the Missouri era.

"Guest Editor's Prologue." *BYU Studies* 15/4 (1975): 387–90. On the Nauvoo era.

Introduction to *Each Day a Bonus: Twenty-Five Courageous Years in a Wheelchair*, by Louise Lake, xii–xiii. Salt Lake City: Deseret Book, 1972.

Introduction to *A Noble Son, Spencer W. Kimball: A Curious Combination of Cousins*, 5–8. Salt Lake City: Institute of Family Research, 1979.

Preface to *Commitment to Care: An Integrated Philosophy of Science, Education and Religion*, by Dean Turner, xiii–xv. Old Greenwich, Conn.: Devin-Adair, 1978.

Book Reviews

Review of *The American Religion: The Emergence of the Post-Christian Nation,* by Harold Bloom. *BYU Studies* 35/1 (1995): 180–89.

Review of *A Christian Natural Theology,* by John B. Cobb Jr. *BYU Studies* 6/3–4 (1965): 186–88.

Review of *The Expanding Church,* by Spencer J. Palmer. *BYU Studies* 19/2 (1979): 251–53.

Review of *Irrational Man,* by William Barrett. *BYU Daily Universe,* 8–9 March 1964.

Review of *The Philosophical Foundations of Mormon Theology,* by Sterling M. McMurrin. *BYU Studies* 1/2–2/1 (1959–60): 101–5.

Review of *The Theological Foundations of the Mormon Religion,* by Sterling M. McMurrin. *BYU Studies* 9/1 (1968): 103–9.

Audio Recordings

Are Christians Mormon? Provo, Utah: Modern Media, 1978. BYU summer forum address delivered 4 June 1974.

The Awesome Power of Married Love. Salt Lake City: Bookcraft Recordings, 1991.

B. H. Roberts' Last Book. Provo, Utah: Sun Sound Books, 1978.

The B. H. Roberts Story: Triumph over Adversity. Salt Lake City: Bookcraft Recordings, 1992.

Blessings of a Righteous Woman. Rexburg, Idaho: Ricks College Recording Services, 1977. Ricks College devotional address delivered 1 February 1977.

The Commanding Image of Christ. Provo, Utah: BYU Press, 1965. BYU devotional address delivered 16 November 1965.

Cultivate Spiritual Gifts and Fruits of the Spirit and of Pure Intelligence. Rexburg, Idaho: Ricks College Recording Services,

1981. Ricks College devotional address delivered 17 November 1981.

Elijah and the Turning of Hearts. Salt Lake City: Bookcraft Recordings, 1990.

Eternal Man. Provo, Utah: BYU Media Services, 1974. Church College of Hawaii devotional address delivered 8 February 1974.

Every Member a Bird Dogger. Salt Lake City: Bookcraft Recordings, 1984. Education Week lecture, San Jose, California.

The First Vision and Its Aftermath. Provo, Utah: Gazelam Foundation, n.d.

Four Saints for Today. Salt Lake City: Bookcraft Recordings, 1994.

The Gospel and the Sabbath. Salt Lake City: Bookcraft Recordings, 1992.

The Highest in Us. Provo, Utah: Modern Media, 1974. BYU multistake fireside address delivered 3 March 1974.

House of Glory. Provo, Utah: Brigham Young University, 1972. BYU multistake fireside address delivered 5 March 1972.

House of Glory, House of Light, House of Love (with Ann N. Madsen). Salt Lake City: Deseret Book, 1998. BYU Women's Conference address delivered 26 April 1998.

A House unto the Lord. Provo, Utah: BYU Sound Services, n.d.

In a Place Called Gethsemane (elsewhere titled "The Olive Press"). Salt Lake City: Bookcraft Recordings, 1982. BYU multistake fireside address delivered 9 May 1982.

The Intimate Touch of Prayer. Salt Lake City: Bookcraft Recordings, 1984.

The Intimate Touch of Prayer. Laie, Hawaii: BYU—Hawaii Campus Learning Resources Center Media Services, 1974. Know Your Religion lecture. Set of two tapes.

Jesus of Nazareth. Salt Lake City: Bookcraft Recordings, 1990–94. Four sets of four tapes each.

Joseph Smith and Ethics. Provo, Utah: BYU Sound Services, n.d.

Joseph Smith and the Sources of Spirituality. Lecture delivered 1 December 1994 at the BYU—Hawaii Campus.

Joseph Smith Lectures. BYU Education Week lectures, n.d. Set of four tapes. Later published as *Joseph Smith the Prophet.*

Joseph Smith's Vision of the Future Church. Lecture delivered 2 December 1994 at the BYU—Hawaii campus.

Joseph Smith: The Man and the Prophet. Lecture delivered 2 December 1994 at the BYU—Hawaii campus.

Joseph Smith the Prophet. Salt Lake City: Bookcraft Recordings, 1978. Eight lectures on four tapes.

Joseph's Personality and Character. Provo, Utah: Modern Media Publishers, 1978.

"The Joy of the Lord Is Your Strength" (Nehemiah 8:10). Provo, Utah: BYU Media Services, 2000. BYU devotional address delivered 21 November 2000.

Kirtland Temple. Provo, Utah: Modern Media Publishers, 1978.

The Life and Teachings of the Prophet Joseph. Salt Lake City: Bookcraft Recordings, 1998. Eight lectures on four tapes.

Marriage and Family: Gospel Insights (with Stephen R. Covey). Salt Lake City: Bookcraft Recordings, 1984. Set of four tapes.

Mormonism and Nature of Love. Laie, Hawaii: BYU—Hawaii Campus Learning Resources Center Media Services, 1973. Know Your Religion lecture.

Mormonism and the New-Making Morality. Provo, Utah: BYU Electronic Media, 1971. Delivered 24 February 1971 as part of BYU Talmage Lecture Series.

Our Relationship with God. Delivered 22 January 1976 as part of Ricks College Last Lecture Series.

Patriarchal Blessings. Rexburg, Idaho: Ricks College Recording Service, 2000. On-line at www.byui.edu/Presentations/

Transcripts/Devotionals/2000_02_09_Madsen.htm. Ricks College devotional address delivered 29 February 2000.

The Philosopher and the Quarterback (with Steve Young). Salt Lake City: Bookcraft Recordings, 2000. BYU Women's Conference address delivered 27 April 2000. Originally titled *Let Us Run with Patience the Race That Is Set before Us.*

Power from Abrahamic Tests. Provo, Utah: BYU Electronic Media, 1971. BYU devotional address delivered 12 October 1971.

The Presidents of the Church. Salt Lake City: Bookcraft Recordings, 1999. Set of fifteen tapes.

The Problem of Evil. Provo, Utah: BYU Electronic Media, 1966. Delivered 1 October 1966 as part of BYU Religious Lecture Series.

The Revelation of Light. Provo, Utah: BYU Electronic Media, 1971. Delivered 22 November 1971 as part of BYU Last Lecture Series. Adaptation of "Man Illumined"; also known as "Time for Reflection."

Sacred Treasures. BYU commencement address delivered 22 August 1993.

Sacrifice—the Key to Power. Salt Lake City: Bookcraft Recordings, 1984. Formerly titled *Power from Abrahamic Tests.*

The Savior, the Sacrament, and Self-Worth. Salt Lake City: Deseret Book, 1999. BYU Women's Conference address delivered 29 April 1999.

Sooner or Later-day Saints. Provo, Utah: BYU Electronic Media, 1973. BYU Education Week devotional address delivered 21 August 1973.

Souls Aflame. Salt Lake City: Bookcraft Recordings, 1990. BYU multistake fireside address delivered 8 November 1983.

The Temple and the Atonement (read by Lloyd Newell). Provo, Utah: FARMS, 2001.

Timeless Questions: Gospel Insights. Salt Lake City: Bookcraft Recordings, 1998. Eight lectures on four tapes.

Twenty Questions. Provo, Utah: BYU Electronic Media, 1968. BYU summer devotional address delivered 20 August 1968.

Videotapes

Between Heaven and Earth (with Ann Madsen and others). Salt Lake City: The Church of Jesus Christ of Latter-day Saints, 2002. Interviews with Jewish and Christian scholars, including Truman and Ann Madsen, on ancient and modern temples.

Faith of an Observer: Conversations with Hugh Nibley. Provo, Utah: BYU and FARMS, [1985]. Interview with Hugh Nibley.

Lands of the Book of Mormon (with John L. Sorenson, Stephen D. Ricks, and Susan Roylance). Provo, Utah: FARMS, [1983].

LDS Perspectives on the Dead Sea Scrolls (with others). Provo, Utah: KBYU, 1999.

Sacred Stone: Temple on the Mississippi. Provo, Utah: KBYU, 2002. Documentary on the Nauvoo Temple, narrated by Hal Holbrook. Truman G. Madsen is in several interview clips.

Poetry

"Out of Zion the Perfection of Beauty." In *Simple Gifts: Photographs and Reflections from the Landscape,* edited by Edwin J. Firmage and Edwin B. Firmage. Salt Lake City: Firmageditions, 2002. Free-verse poem.

Unpublished Manuscripts

"Analogy as Argument." Marketplace lecture delivered 13 March 1974; distributed on BYU campus.

"The Bible and the Book of Mormon: A Panel Discussion" (with three Protestants ministers). Transcript of program on CHJS-TV, St. Johns, New Brunswick, Canada, 9 December 1962.

BYU Travel Study Church History Tour Lectures, 2–7 August 1961.

BYU Travel Study Church History Tour Lectures (with Lynn A McKinlay and Howard H. Barron), 2–7 August 1962.

"The Costs of Integrity." Lecture delivered 16 February 1978; sponsored by BYU Academics Office.

"Creativity and Intuition." Address delivered to the Phi Kappa Beta ceremonies, BYU, 19 February 1985. Private circulation.

"The Essence of Mormonism." Address delivered at Bates College, Lewiston, Maine, 12 February 1963.

Fireside address delivered 23 May 1998 at the Jerusalem Center for Near Eastern Studies.

"God: Personal or Impersonal?" Based on a sermon delivered 24 November 1963 at the Lorimor Chapel, Colby College, Watertown, Maine.

"How Can We Know?" Essay prepared for investigators in the New England Mission, 1962–65. Private circulation.

"The Lost Dimension of Psychology: William James Revisited." Address delivered 4 September 1976 to the American Psychological Association 84th convention, Washington, D.C., in the symposium "Overcoming Psychology's Estrangement from Religious Phenomenon." Private circulation.

"Paul Tillich and Religion as Ultimate Concern." Delivered at Evening Lectures on Religion, Fifth Annual Series. 1958–59.

"The Phenomenology of Live Theatre." In the report of the Wingspread Conference to American Theater Association Board of Directors of the ATA Planning and Development Committee, 1976.

Remarks at the Jerusalem Center for Near Eastern Studies (with Jeffrey R. Holland), in connection with a tour by the Mormon Tabernacle Choir, 28 December 1992.

"Some Fruits of Mormonism" (with Spencer J. Palmer). Prepared by BYU Religious Study Center, 1981. Private circulation.

"A Unique Mormon Aesthetics." Keynote address delivered 7 March 1972 at the Fourth Annual Mormon Festival of Arts.

"Why Modern Jews Reject Traditional Christian Views of Christ." FARMS banquet address delivered 5 November 1999.

"Why Philosophy?" Marketplace lecture delivered 18 October 1972; distributed on BYU campus.

Contributors

Davis Bitton (Ph.D., Princeton University) is Professor Emeritus of History at the University of Utah.

M. Gerald Bradford (Ph.D., University of California, Santa Barbara) is Associate Executive Director of the Institute for the Study and Preservation of Ancient Religious Texts at Brigham Young University.

S. Kent Brown (Ph.D., Brown University) is Professor of Ancient Scripture and Director of Ancient Studies at Brigham Young University.

Richard Lyman Bushman (Ph.D., Harvard University) is Gouverneur Morris Professor of History, Emeritus, at Columbia University.

James H. Charlesworth (Ph.D., Duke University) is George L. Collord Professor of New Testament Language and Literature and Editor of the Dead Sea Scrolls Project at Princeton Theological Seminary.

Joseph Dan (Ph.D., Hebrew University of Jerusalem) is Gershom Scholem Professor of Kabbalah at the Hebrew University of Jerusalem, Israel.

James E. Faulconer (Ph.D., Pennsylvania State University) is Professor of Philosophy at Brigham Young University.

Guttorm Fløistad (Ph.D., King's College, University of London) is Professor Emeritus of History of Ideas, the Institute of Cultural Studies, University of Oslo, Norway.

David Noel Freedman (Ph.D., Johns Hopkins University) is Professor of History at University of California at San Diego and holds an endowed chair in Hebrew Biblical Studies.

Rebecca L. Frey (Ph.D. cand., University of California, Irvine) is Instructor of Classics and Humanities at San Diego State University.

Gary P. Gillum (M.L.S., Brigham Young University) is Religion and Ancient Studies Librarian in the Harold B. Lee Library at Brigham Young University.

Andrew H. Hedges (Ph.D., University of Illinois) is Associate Professor of Church History and Doctrine at Brigham Young University.

Raphael Jospe (Ph.D., Brandeis University) taught Jewish Philosophy at the Open University of Israel and at Hebrew University of Jerusalem—School for Overseas Students and served as Professor of Jewish Studies at Brigham Young University's Jerusalem Center for Near Eastern Studies.

John M. Lundquist (Ph.D., University of Michigan) is the Susan and Douglas Dillon Chief Librarian of the Asian and Middle Eastern Division at the New York Public Library.

Ann N. Madsen (M.A., Brigham Young University) is Senior Lecturer in Ancient Scripture at Brigham Young University.

Daniel B. McKinlay (Master of Theological Studies, Boston University) is Manager of the Reference Service at the Foundation for Ancient Research and Mormon Studies (FARMS) at Brigham Young University.

Louis Midgley (Ph.D., Brown University) is Professor Emeritus of Political Science at Brigham Young University.

Jacob Milgrom (Doctor of Hebrew Letters, Jewish Theological Seminary) is Professor Emeritus of Biblical Studies at the University of California at Berkeley.

Blake Thomas Ostler (J.D., University of Utah) is an attorney in private practice.

Donald W. Parry (Ph.D., University of Utah) is Associate Professor of Hebrew Language and Literature at Brigham Young University.

David L. Paulsen (Ph.D., University of Michigan) is Professor of Philosophy at Brigham Young University.

Daniel C. Peterson (Ph.D., University of California, Los Angeles) is Associate Professor of Islamic Studies and Arabic at Brigham Young University and Associate Director of the Institute for the Study and Preservation of Ancient Religious Texts.

Stephen D. Ricks (Ph.D., University of California, Berkeley, and Graduate Theological Union) is Professor of Hebrew and Cognate Learning at Brigham Young University.

David Rosen (ordination, Ponivez and Mir Rabbinical Seminaries, Israel) is the International Director of Interreligious Affairs of the American Jewish Committee. He has served as Professor of Jewish Studies at Brigham Young University's Jerusalem Center for Near Eastern Studies.

David Rolph Seely (Ph.D., University of Michigan) is Professor of Ancient Scripture at Brigham Young University.

Andrew C. Skinner (Ph.D., University of Denver) is Dean of Religious Education and Professor of Ancient Scripture at Brigham Young University.

John A. Tvedtnes (M.A., University of Utah) is Associate Director of Research at the Foundation for Ancient Research and Mormon Studies (FARMS) at Brigham Young University.

Seth Ward (Ph.D., Yale University) taught at the University of Denver's Center for Judaic Studies, where he served as Director of the Institute of Islamic-Judaic Studies.

C. Terry Warner (Ph.D., Yale University) is Professor of Philosophy at Brigham Young University.

R. J. Zvi Werblowsky (DŜL, University of Geneva) is Martin Buber Professor Emeritus of Comparative Religion at the Hebrew University of Jerusalem, Israel.

David J. Whittaker (Ph.D., Brigham Young University) is Curator of Western and Mormon Manuscripts, L. Tom Perry Special Collections, Harold B. Lee Library, and Associate Professor of History at Brigham Young University.

Index

theism, 146

theodicy, 251

theologian, 140

theology, 142–43, 229

Theophilus and creation *ex nihilo,*
    328, 329–30

Third Quest, 59, 63, 71

Thorvaldsen, 195

Three Witnesses, 468, 748

Tillich, Paul, 58, 139

Tocqueville, Alexis de
    and *Democracy in America,*
        157–77
    letters of, 165
    and loss of Catholic faith, 165
    role of faith in writings of, 140
    wife of, 165

Torah and divine providence, 567,
    569

Torah scroll, reversing, 607–11

totalitarianism, 95

transcendental idealism, 19

transubstantiation, 222

treasurer, 64

tree of life as law of Moses, 386,
    387–89

Trinity, 228

trust
    in God, 245, 251, 272
    God's, in intelligences, 272
    and Joseph Smith, 277
    living with, 274
    similarity of, with faith, 93

truth, 133–34, 197, 206–7

turtledoves, offering of, 617

Tyrrell, George, 57–58

unity, 124, 125, 130, 135–36

universality, principle of, 127

Upanishads, 131

Ur
    Abraham cast into furnace
        in, 361 n. 2
    destruction of, 298–301
    as native land of Abraham,
        353

values, 130, 132, 135

Varro, Marcus Terentius, 141–48,
    151

Vatican, 60

Vedantism, 19

Vedas, 131

Vermes, Geza, 65

vertical relationship, 187–88

Virgil, 194

virgin Mother, 289

virtue, 162, 256

visions, 82

voice of earth, 304–5

Voice of Warning, 418

voices within the laments, 303–5

Wahrman, Abraham David,
    608–10

Wayne County, story of couple
    from, 89

Weaver, Walter P., 61

weeping goddess, 303

weeping person, identity of, in
    Jeremiah, 294–95

Wenham, Gordon J., 356

Wesley, John, 230

Westphal, Merold, 191, 204